The Learning of Language

The Learning of Language

edited by
CARROLL E. REED
UNIVERSITY OF MASSACHUSETTS

A Publication of the
National Council of Teachers of English

APPLETON-CENTURY-CROFTS
EDUCATIONAL DIVISION
MEREDITH CORPORATION New York

7101-1

Library of Congress Card Number: 74-135996

PRINTED IN THE UNITED STATES OF AMERICA

390-72964-7

Acknowledgments

The editor, authors, and publishers thank the following organizations and companies for permission to reprint in this book illustrative charts, excerpts, and other references:

Bell Telephone Laboratories, Murray Hill, N.J., for illustrations from D. W. Farnsworth, "High Speed Motion Pictures of the Human Vocal Cords," *Bell Laboratories Record*, 1940, 18, 206–207.
Center for Applied Linguistics, Washington, D.C., for charts from William Labov, *The Social Stratification of English in New York City*, The Center, 1966.
Harper & Row, Publishers, New York, for excerpts from West, Ansberry, and Carr, *Rehabilitation of Speech*, 3rd ed., Harper & Row, 1957.
S. Karger, AG, Basel, Switzerland, and New York, for the table from Ilse Lehiste, "An Acoustic-Phonetic Study of Internal Open Juncture," *Phonetica*, Supplementum ad Vol. 5.
Linguistic Society of America, Washington, D.C., for the chart from G. E. Peterson, "The Phonetic Value of Vowels," *Language*, 1951, 27, 541–553.
McGraw-Hill Book Company, New York, for material adapted from J. P. Guilford, *The Nature of Human Intelligence*, McGraw-Hill, 1967.
Mouton & Co., n.v., Publishers, The Hague, for X-ray photographs based on photos in G. Fant, *The Acoustic Theory of Speech Production*, Mouton, 1960.
The University of Chicago Press, for material from J. W. French, *The Description of Aptitude and Achievement Tests in Terms of Rotated Factors*, Psychometric Monograph No. 5, University of Chicago, 1951.
The University of Michigan Press, for the map from Hans Kurath, *A Word Geography of the Eastern United States*, University of Michigan, 1949.

Preface

This volume is a tribute to the memory of David H. Russell, who was Professor of Education, University of California, Berkeley. As president of the National Council of Teachers of English in 1963, he was responsible for the book's inception early in the following year, at which time he envisioned it as "a high level interdisciplinary source of knowledge about the learning of language." It was to have a "fundamental research orientation, with generous quotation and summation from empirical studies and related sources."

Through Glenn Leggett, now president of Grinnell College, I became interested in the project and, for some months, carried on a lively exchange of letters with David. This correspondence then led to the organization of a conference at Berkeley in October 1964, at which time an advisory committee was constituted and the basic plan of the book was designed. Those who contributed to the ideas contained in this original plan were: Francis Christensen, David Olmsted, Leo Postman, David Reed, David Russell, James Squire, Sol Saporta, and myself. A group of writers was selected, with alternates, and it was confidently expected that the project would be completed in another year.

David Russell died in January, 1965, much to the sorrow of all of us who had worked with him and were stimulated by his efforts on behalf of the project. In December 1966, the advisory committee met in Riverside with the purpose of evaluating the manuscripts at hand and of making final plans for publication of the book itself. (The committee now also included Harold B. Allen, John B. Carroll, W. Nelson Francis, and Robert Politzer.) By that time, however, it had become clear that the original design was too ambitious: it turned out that in some fields there were no writers available, and a number of writers who had promised us their manuscripts were forced to default. The majority of contributions received, nevertheless, were of exceptional quality. Several of these have even been revised voluntarily by their authors in the meanwhile, because of the rapid changes taking place on the frontiers of linguistic knowledge.

v

I was finally able to deliver the edited copy to Robert F. Hogan, Executive Secretary of the NCTE, and Enid M. Olson, director of NCTE publications. The final product fulfills some, if not all, of the hopes of its intellectual progenitor, David Russell. It is somewhat shorter than originally planned and more diverse in makeup, yet the scope of those manuscripts which survived, comprehensive as they are, clearly indicates the headway that has been gained in the vast reaches of this largely unexplored subject.

I am extremely grateful to the various members of the advisory committee for their help and advice; those who were especially close to me in this endeavor were David Reed, Sol Saporta, and Francis Christensen. NCTE liaison officers were, successively, David H. Russell, Glenn Leggett, and Albert H. Marckwardt. Special credit goes to James R. Squire, without whose persistent and effective efforts the project could scarcely have been completed.

Yet, I must hasten to add that final responsibility for the contents of this volume is mine alone. I can only hope that its authors, its sponsors, and its readers will be able to regard it with a satisfaction worthy of the man who conceived it, but who did not survive to see even a single page of it—David H. Russell.

C.E.R.

Contents

Figures

Tables

The Learning of Language

1

Introduction

CHARLES A. FERGUSON
Stanford University

Systematic study of human language goes back several millennia, and scientific study of the processes of human learning in general goes back at least a century, but serious study of the phenomena of language learning at a comparable level of sophistication hardly goes back more than a decade or two. Indeed, in the last few years probably more has been discovered about various aspects of language learning than in all previous history, and this volume offers a number of reviews of the present knowledge.

The various chapters present accounts from very different points of view, but in spite of the disparity in treatment and in estimates of relative importance of different aspects among the chapters, a few themes or common features recur repeatedly and deserve special emphasis as characteristic of current thinking among specialists in the study of language learning.

The first is the increasing recognition of the enormous complexity of human language behavior, and the consequent difficulty in studying how people learn to perform it. From the beginnings of man's observations about language, there have doubtless been expressions of wonderment at its intricate workings, but recent research has provided documentation of the complexities in bewildering detail. The chapters by Wang and Malkiel are good examples: one illustrates the mass of detailed information now available on human speech sounds and the kinds of underlying principles needed to understand speakers' ability to perceive and produce the sounds of a language. The other gives a picture of the magnitude and complexity of the task of compiling a simple inventory of the vocabulary items the speakers of a language use with relative freedom and ease. Similar chapters could provide equally impressive amounts of information on syntactic and semantic phenomena, and indeed, almost every chapter included in the volume highlights some of the complexities of language. In acquiring competence in his

1

language, the child develops mastery not just of a collection of words and their meanings and some basic patterns of putting them together, but he acquires the ability to handle subtle variations in sounds, delicate grammatical and semantic categories, and syntactic relationships which continue to defy adequate linguistic characterization. Also, the complexity is not merely linguistic in this traditional sense, but appears also in the use of the language. The child must learn, from the earliest months, that there are different styles of speaking appropriate for different situations and topics, and as he grows older, he must cope with wider and wider ranges of regional and social variation in the language. This notion of complexity in language use was propounded by sociolinguists like Hymes (1962), Gumperz (1961), and Labov (1966); some indication of it is given in Labov's chapter here, and Strickland alludes to it in hers.

Another feature common to most of the chapters is the view that the speech of young children is highly structured and that the child seems to move from stage to stage by making successive hypotheses about the grammar of the language he is learning (cf. the chapters of Braine and Deese). While students of child development might have agreed with this view in past decades, it has only been in the last few years that analytic and experimental work has been carried out based on it. The first clear assertion of the general orderliness of the child's acquisition of the sound system of his language was the slim volume published by Jakobson in 1941, now finally available in English translation. Apart from the important study of Shvachkin (1948), this stimulating study was hardly followed up at all until the last few years.

In 1959 Berko published her little paper studying the acquisition of noun plurals, past tense form of verbs, and several other facts of English morphology. Apart from Guillaume's long forgotten article of twenty years before in which he tried to explain the verb forms of French nursery school children (1927), no one had troubled to explain in a systematic way the development of morphology in child language acquisition. Berko showed that the children operated with grammatical "rules" of their own and could form plurals and past tenses from nonsense words in accordance with their own rules, and she supplied evidence that English-learning children all tend to learn the details of the morphology in about the same order.

The value of analyzing child language on its own structural terms rather than merely as deviation from an adult norm was next recognized in the work of several investigators who wrote "grammars" of the speech of very young children and found again regularities and "rules" which had not been noticed before. From the time of Braine's ontogeny article (1963), and the roughly simultaneous articles of several others, linguists and psychologists have continued to analyze child syntax and to experiment with children to test psycholinguistic hypotheses about the nature of English or human language in general. The Braine chapter in this volume provides an admirable review of the literature and shows the promise of this line of research.

Interestingly enough, the desire for detailed reliable data on language development sent investigators back to the despised diary-type studies of individual children which had been popular in the twenties and thirties. Two such biographical studies carried out in the forties with incredible patience and perceptiveness by linguist fathers have earned particular praise and are consulted again and again by students of child language: Leopold's four-volume study of his bilingual daughter Hildegard up to her third year and Gvozdev's extensive study of his son Zhenya learning Russian (1939–49). The strategy currently preferred for accumulating this kind of data is for a team of investigators to follow a small number of children for a period of several years, recording spontaneous verbal material from them at regular intervals, and from time to time intervening to check out particular hypotheses or to get material of particular sorts. Such studies under way in Cambridge, Berkeley, and elsewhere produce language data in the form of tape recordings or transcriptions which are then available for exploitation by other scholars as well. Loban's extensive study (1967), referred to in the Strickland chapter, follows essentially this strategy but with more children over more years and more structured kinds of elicitation.

A third feature, common to many of the chapters, is the insistence that current psychological theories of learning fail to account for the way a child acquires his language—or for that matter the way a second language is learned in the classroom or "naturally"—and speculation that innate biological factors have greater importance in language learning than the previous generation of scholarship would acknowledge. This viewpoint comes partly from the recognition of the complexity of human language and from the claim often made by linguists, that children anywhere in the world normally acquire the basic structure of their language by age four and five. Even if the linguists' claim should have to be modified, the problem remains. How does the child learn to aspirate one *p* and not another, use *-ing* differently with stative and active verbs, manipulate patterns of negative concord, and all the rest, which his parents cannot explain to him or even state explicitly for themselves and are unable to correct or reinforce in any direct way?

This "nativistic" view of human linguistic hypotheses is also associated with the Chomsky approach to language and the writing of grammars, and Chomsky's devastating review of Skinner's *Verbal Behavior* in 1959 is one of the most cogent expressions of this view. It has been articulated more recently by Lenneberg in articles and a substantial book (1967), adducing support also from outside linguistic theory. In a somewhat similar way Fodor's chapter points to phenomena which current philosophies of language and theories of semantics deal with inadequately. Proponents of various general theories of human learning, as reported in Deese's chapter and elsewhere in this volume, have been forced to a defensive position as they try to cope explicitly with the phenomena of language learning.

Another point which appears in several of the papers is that language acquisition is not a process which everyone goes through in about the same way and is completed within a certain time; rather the learning of one's native language never ends, and there are great individual differences in language competence. Educators and speech therapists, and some psychologists, have long been concerned with these aspects of language learning, but linguists have tended to ignore them, and experimentalists in verbal behavior have tended to focus on a narrow selection of topics in them. In this volume Carroll's chapter provides a very full review of the work in this field, much of which deserves the attention of linguists and psycholinguists. The related area of speech pathology reported in West's chapter has been relatively untouched by the recent trends in psycholinguistics, although there are attempts at communication across these disciplinary boundaries. People like Lenneberg use data on language behavior under pathological conditions to check their hypotheses, and some speech theorists are beginning to try psycholinguistic findings for diagnosis and measurement purposes, as in the Lee article of 1966 which suggests devices to test retardation in syntactic development.

One final point dealt with in the chapters of this volume is the teaching of language in the educational system. The chapters by Torrey and Lado on second language learning and teaching, the chapters of Deese and Strickland concerned mostly with first language learning and teaching, and some of the other chapters as well exemplify to a considerable extent a new American outlook on language teaching. In the past the "theory" and "methods and materials" work in this field have often suffered from faddism and the search for all-inclusive magico-scientific solutions, while the experimentation has too often been global testing of method A against method B with little regard for precision in the description of language behavior and the confusing or ignoring of crucial variables.

The views which seem to be gaining ground are that language teaching means many different things, that systematic study and experimentation can give useful results, and that improvements in language teaching and progress in theoretical frameworks require contributions from a variety of disciplines. Distinctions are now being drawn between improving native language skills, teaching standard language to nonstandard speakers, and teaching second or foreign languages. Classroom behavior under observation and intended "terminal behavior" are being described in much more sophisticated psycholinguistic terms. Educators and language specialists of all kinds are recognizing that fields as far apart as physiology and theoretical linguistics or as different as computer programming, and small group interaction studies can be joined in specific research projects and in teacher education.

The chapters collected in this volume are inevitably uneven in coverage and different—even contradictory—in approach, but they reflect the present ferment and growing activity in the study of language learning.

Such recurrent themes as the few identified here, and the wealth of information and opinions contained in the various chapters, make the volume an appropriate collection to be dedicated to a scholar whose career has been devoted to the study of language in education.

REFERENCES

Berko, J. The child's learning of English morphology. *Word*, 1958, **14**, 150–177. Reprinted in S. Saporta (Ed.) *Psycholinguistics; a book of readings*, 359–375.

Braine, M. D. S. The ontogeny of English phrase structure: the first phase. *Language*, 1963, **39**, 1–13.

Chomsky, N. Review of B. F. Skinner, *Verbal behavior*. *Language*, 1959, **35**, 26–58. Reprinted in J. A. Fodor and J. J. Katz (Eds.) *The structure of language*, 547–578, and in L. A. Jakobovits and M. S. Miron (Eds.) *Readings in the psychology of language*, 142–171.

Guillaume, P. Le développement des éléments formels dans le langage de l'enfant. *J. de Psychol.*, 1927, **24**, 216–229.

Gumperz, J. J. Speech variation and the study of Indian civilization. *Amer. Anthropologist*, 1961, **63**, 976–988. Reprinted in D. Hymes (Ed.) *Language in culture and society*, 416–428.

Gvozdev, A. N. *Formirovanie u rebenka grammaticheskogo stroja russkogo jazyka*. 2 vols. Moscow: Akademija Pedagogicheskikh Nauk, 1949.

Hymes, D. The ethnography of speaking. In T. Gladwin and W. C. Sturtevant (Eds.) *Anthropology and human behavior*. Washington, D.C.: Anthropological Society of Washington, 1962. Pp. 13–53.

Jakobson, R. *Child language, aphasia, and phonological universals (Kindersprache, Aphasia, und allehemeine Lautgisetze*. Uppsala, 1941). The Hague: Mouton, 1968. Reprinted in R. Jakobson, *Selected writings*, **1**, 378–401.

Labov, W. *The social stratification of English in New York City*. Washington, D.C.: Center for Applied Linguistics, 1966.

Lee, L. L. Developmental sentence types. *J. Speech & Hear. Dis.*, 1966, **31**, 311–329.

Leopold, W. F. *Speech development of a bilingual child*. 4 vols. Evanston, Ill.: Northwestern University Press, 1939–49.

Lenneberg, E. *Biological foundations of language*. New York: John Wiley & Sons, 1967.

Loban, W. *The language of elementary school children*. Champaign, Ill.: National Council of Teachers of English, 1967.

Shvachkin, N. Kh. *Razvitie fonematicheskogo vosprijatija rechi v rannem detstve*. Izvestija Akademija Pedagogicheskikh Nauk 13, 1948.

2

The Acquisition of Language in Infant and Child

MARTIN D. S. BRAINE
University of California, Santa Barbara

Language development has been widely studied for nearly a century, and there exist major literatures on the subject in four languages—English, French, German, and Russian—as well as numerous publications in a variety of other languages. If depth of coverage is not to suffer, some limitation on

This review was prepared during tenure of a Guggenheim fellowship in 1965–66 while I was on a leave of absence from Walter Reed Army Institute of Research, and I am grateful to the Department of Psychology of the Hebrew University of Jerusalem for hospitality. I also thank I. M. Schlesinger and P. A. Kolers for comments on the manuscript. Owing to the long delay in publication, the manuscript was revised in the fall of 1968. However, comprehensiveness of coverage was not sought for the years 1966–68, although several articles published during this period are covered, including all the important ones that came to my attention. The new material is usually integrated into the text. However, in one place, in order to avoid revising a section, I merely appended the added material in parenthetical paragraphs at the end of the section; in another place, where it only confirmed my original summary, I just listed the recent references in a footnote.

For ease of reference abbreviations and notational conventions are summarized here. *NP* is used for *noun phrase* throughout the text. The symbol " $\sim$ " $=$ *in free variation with*. In grammatical rules, $U=$ utterance, $S=$ sentence, $I=$ introducer, $Pred=$ predicator, $N=$ noun, $V=$ verb, $D=$ adverb, $Prep=$ preposition, $Art=$ article, and $Mod=$ modifier. Grammatical rules employ the usual notations for rewrite grammars. Thus, rules have the form $A \rightarrow \ldots$, to be read "A may be rewritten as . . .", or "A may consist of . . .", where A is a single symbol. Alternative expansions of the same symbol are either placed one above the other enclosed by large braces, or separated by commas: e.g., $A \rightarrow b$, c, DE summarizes the rules $A \rightarrow b$, $A \rightarrow c$, and $A \rightarrow DE$. Parentheses around a symbol indicate that choice of it is optional: e.g., $A \rightarrow (B)C$ is equivalent to two rules $A \rightarrow C$ and $A \rightarrow BC$. Since none of the work reviewed has used the new rule forms and notations introduced in Chomsky (1965), the notation used is consistently that of the early period of generative grammar, i.e., that of Chomsky (1957).

In discussions concerned with the form of grammars, where symbols are arbitrarily chosen (i.e., in 1.35, 2.45, and 3.31), a capital letter indicates a category (i.e., a nonterminal symbol), and a lower-case letter a morpheme (i.e., a terminal symbol): e.g., a rule $A \rightarrow bC$ is a rule in which a category is expanded into a phrase consisting of a morpheme followed by another category, whereas $A \rightarrow BC$ indicates that A is expanded into a sequence of two categories. In grammars claiming to represent children's speech, a plus sign separates constituents, e.g., $NP \rightarrow Mod + N$.

7

breadth is essential, and this review is concerned only with the acquisition of linguistic structure. Thus, work on child language where the primary concern is with social or intellectual development will not be reviewed. Even within the area defined, the subject of lexical development will be reviewed only very sketchily; a worthwhile review of this subarea would try to integrate it with the wider literature on concept formation and conceptual development, and such a review should be a separate undertaking.

The history of the study of child language can be divided into three main periods. The first period, around the turn of the century, saw a promising beginning made on study of the development of linguistic structure. In America, the behaviorist revolution brought this period to an end and ushered in a long period of data gathering, mostly quantitative and mostly by psychologists, with only a little of the data gathered being of discernible linguistic interest. The behaviorist period lasted until the early 1950s, and during it useful communication of ideas between psychology and linguistics seems to have effectively ceased. However, in the second half of this period, the distinctive-feature concept developed in linguistic work on phonology was applied by Jakobson (1941) to child language and was followed by several important studies of phonological development by linguists. The third period began with the resumption of communication between the disciplines, and the subsequent emergence of the generative-grammar school of thought in linguistics has been a powerful stimulus to the present concentration of work on grammar acquisition, which this review reflects. In western Europe, the behaviorist revolution was less violent and less successful; on the other hand, the concept of a generative grammar has not yet stimulated or influenced much work on grammar acquisition there. The Russian work is only beginning to be known here.

Language development is a much reviewed subject. Leopold (1948) provides an interesting historical overview, particularly of the early linguistic work. Together, he and McCarthy (1954) provide an excellent summary of the midcentury status of the field, and work described by them will not be mentioned here unless the specific subjects discussed require it. For subsequent reviews or considerations of the area in English, with varying degrees of overlap with the present review, see Brown (1958, 1965), Brown and Berko (1960b), Carroll (1960, 1964a), Ervin and Miller (1963), and Ervin-Tripp (1966). The Russian literature has been reviewed in English by Slobin (1965, 1966a, c); other reviews are contained in Raevskii (1958), El'konin (1958, 1960), and Zhinkin (1959). I regret that, because of its inaccessibility to me, I shall be able to cover the Russian work only through secondary sources, principally Slobin (1966a). Stern and Stern (1928) is the German classic; see Kainz (1960, 1964) for a more recent review. Unfortunately, there exists no good English source to the German literature, which is not reviewed here. Thorough midcentury bibliographies of child language are contained in Leopold (1952) and in McCarthy (1954). Several articles in

Slavic languages, not reviewed here, are contained in Weir's (1962) reference list. Other sources for foreign languages, which are not primarily reviews, are mentioned in Section 2.25.

This review contains three main sections. The first considers questions of method. In the second section the available data on phonological development and on early grammatical and semantic development for English, French, and Russian are summarized, and issues arising out of the data are reviewed. The third section is devoted to theory of language acquisition.

1. METHODOLOGICAL QUESTIONS

This section attempts to do two things: to consider in detail various questions of fact and theory which create methodological problems for the study of the structure of children's language, and to review available methods, insofar as they differ from methods used in adult linguistics. In 1.1, some phonological problems are reviewed briefly, and in 1.2, systematic eliciting techniques for studying morphology are described. Section 1.3 considers at some length the extensive methodological problems involved in deriving a grammar from text materials gathered from a child.

1.1. Phonology

In general, methods for investigating the phonological structure of adult speech (e.g., Gleason, 1961) are appropriate for child speech with ad hoc modifications to accommodate the child's special characteristics as an informant. Thus, one seeks to compile a phonetically transcribed vocabulary list, noting for each word the range of phonetic free variation and comparing the words with each other to determine contrasts in the various utterance positions. As compared with work with adults, a greater proportion of words have to be "caught on the run," and more observations of utterances of the same word are usually necessary in order to determine the range of free variation, which is typically much greater in child than in adult speech (Albright & Albright, 1958). The phonological analysis is, of course, based on speech only, not on babbling, since it is impossible to distinguish phones in free variation from phones in contrast in vocalizations that belong to babbling.

Because of the child's limited vocabulary, it is often difficult to find appropriate minimal or near-minimal pairs. Imitations are often of service here: many children imitate readily, even quasi-nonsensical sequences, and the character of the imitations is often instructive of the phonemic distinctions of which they are capable. For example, at one point in my son's development, he appeared to distinguish [b] and [d] before middle and back vowels but not before front vowels (e.g., both *bear* and *there* were [deh]). In an effort to elicit [b] before a front vowel, he was offered the sequence [bə bə bə biy] in association with a picture of the letter *B*; he dutifully imitated, [bə bə diy], neatly demonstrating his lack of /b/ before front vowels.

Another technique that is useful is to teach the child a new word (English or invented) with the required phonological structure and to observe the phonological shape which he gives to it in his speech. Thus, at a very early stage, my son's total vocabulary consisted of [di:] 'see', [da ∼ dʌ] 'that' or 'there', [du:] 'juice', [do] 'no', and [ʔai] 'hi!'. The question arose whether he was able to contrast initial [d] with its absence (or with [ʔ]), i.e., whether or not [d] was phonemically zero. To test this, an invented word [i:] was associated with the meaning 'eat' or 'food' by appropriate gestures. After a week or two the new word was taken into his speech. However, he pronounced it [di:], indicating that he was unable to drop his initial [d]. Another invented word [dai] was then offered to test the possibility of contrast with [ʔai] 'hi'. He avoided the contrast by taking it into his speech as [da ∼ dʌ]. His initial [d] was therefore without phonemic status.

Features of child speech which can create difficulties in a phonemic analysis arise in the case of emergent phonemic distinctions. Thus, as a distinction between dental and velar stops develops, one may find the following kind of situation: words with initial *d, t, ð, θ*, contain [d] always, but words with initial *k* or *g* contain [d] about 70 percent of the time and [g] about 30 percent. *Cat* may appear as [dæt] most of the time, but as [gæt] sometimes, whereas *that* is always [dæt]. If one insists that phonemes are to have nonoverlapping allophones, then one would be forced to transcribe *cat* with /d/ when it comes out as [dæt], and with /g/ when it is [gæt]. However, such a solution treats the variation between [dæt] and [gæt] as allomorphic rather than allophonic, and psychologically, it corresponds to a claim that the child is uncertain whether *cat* begins with a dental or velar consonant, which seems unlikely. Rather, one might argue that the child must know that the first consonants of *cat* and *that* are different, since the former is sometimes [g] and the latter never is. Thus, *that* always contains /d/ realized as [d] and *cat*, /g/ with freely varying allophones [d] and [g]; this solution treats the [dæt ∼ gæt] variation as allophonic, and psychologically, it corresponds to the claim that the child knows there is a difference between /d/ and /g/ but has difficulty pronouncing /g/. It is also very likely in such cases that the child hears the phonemic difference with much more consistency than he is able to render it.

In another kind of problem there is 100 percent overlap in allophones. A simple, possibly common, example is provided by Steven (age 2–2), a child I studied. At this stage, Steven distinguished between voiced and unvoiced stops both initially and intervocalically, but not terminally; in final position all stops were unvoiced, so that, for instance, *dog* came out as [dak]. However,

Steven often added [-iy] to words; adding this suffix made terminal consonants intervocalic and led to such alterations as [dak ~ dagiy] 'dog', [ʌp ~ ʌpiy] 'up', [buk ~ bukiy] 'book', [pik ~ pigiy] 'pig'. It was clear therefore that Steven knew that the last consonant of *dog* was /g/, and of *book* /k/, even though he did not make the distinction terminally. Thus, the voiced-voiceless contrast was actually relevant in all positions. Whether Steven could hear the difference between voiced and unvoiced stops terminally, even though he could not render it, is an interesting question to which I do not know the answer. This example is discussed further in 2.13-4.

1.2. Grammar: Systematic Testing Techniques

The study of productive morphological processes is the main area of child language where effective eliciting techniques are available. Berko (1958) first used such techniques for English, and essentially similar techniques were independently developed in Russian work at the same time or earlier (e.g., Zakharova, 1958; Popova, 1958). The basic method is simple. Real or pictorial materials are used to present objects, qualities, or events, and associated with each item is a short text spoken to the child and designed to elicit particular inflexions or derivations. In order to make sure that the responses reflect productive processes rather than rote learning, many of the lexical items to be inflected are nonsense words. For example, to elicit the progressive verb form *-ing*, and agentive noun-making suffix *-er*, Berko presented a picture of a man balancing a ball on his nose. The child was told: "This is a picture of a man who knows how to /zib/. What is he doing? He is ...." "What would you call a man whose job is to /zib/?" Miller and Ervin (1964) have successfully used the method with some children as young as 30 months to elicit English plurals. However, the use of the method with very young children is limited by the fact that it presupposes a sufficient command of syntax to understand the spoken instruction. Eliciting techniques can be extended beyond morphology to a variety of constructions, e.g., to English noun compounds like *bird house* (Livant, 1962) and to some transformations, such as the negative.

Children's command of grammatical constructions can also be tested through comprehension: they may be required to obey commands employing a particular construction (e.g., Sokhin, 1959; Mehan, 1968), or they may be asked to identify which of two or more pictures is described by a sentence (e.g., Fraser, Bellugi, & Brown, 1963). The stimuli in such comprehension tests are carefully designed so that correct responses cannot occur to situational stimuli alone, but must imply a grasp of the grammatical structure used. (The materials used in the studies of Sokhin and Fraser et al. are described in considerable detail in 2.41, when data on comprehension and on the relation between speech comprehension and speech production are reviewed. For a more detailed description than is possible here of the contents of available testing techniques of all kinds, see Slobin, 1967, Appendix 1.)

The main difficulties with systematic testing techniques are that they are difficult to use with very young children, that tests for command of the basic phrase structure rules of a language are difficult to design, and that they do not yield a description of the structure of a child's idiolect as a whole.

1.3. Grammar: Analysis of Text Materials

Not only do most syntactic rules appear to be beyond the reach of systematic tests of the kind described, but also much grammar is acquired before the age at which such methods become usable. It seems inevitable, therefore, that study of the development of grammatical structure will, to a considerable extent, have to be based on analysis of text material. Unfortunately, the analysis of child text materials faces serious methodological obstacles. I consider first the problems involved in the establishment of the material to be analyzed (1.31-2) and then turn to the more difficult questions associated with deriving and justifying a grammar based on a distributional analysis of child speech (1.33-7).

1.31. *Establishing the Corpus.* The term *utterance* will be used to refer to the minimum free form to be analyzed. From a grammatical point of view an utterance is therefore a string of morphs which is not a constituent of any longer string containing it, of which no part is a constituent of any string containing material outside it, and which cannot be subdivided into further strings with these properties. An utterance is a token, not a type.

There has been almost no discussion in the literature about how the investigator decides what stretches of speech are to count as utterances for the purpose of a grammatical analysis. It is clear, however, that the main basis for segmenting tape recorded texts has been common sense. Thus, Brown and Fraser (1963) write: "We had thought that division of the flow of speech into utterances might be an uncertain business. In fact, however, the usual criteria of either a long pause or a shift of speakers worked very well. There were few instances of uncertain utterance division [p. 168]." Most investigators would probably agree that the points of separation between most utterances are rather transparently marked. However, pause duration is not an entirely satisfactory criterion: if the duration were measured, it would undoubtedly be found that pauses within utterances were sometimes longer than pauses between utterances. For English the major cues are probably the phonological junctures, ♯ marking the end of an utterance with a falling intonation and ‖ ending a segment with a rising intonation. These junctures seem to be present at a very early stage of grammatical development (cf. Weir, 1962, p. 29). Treating any instance of ♯ as the end of an utterance alone defines a sufficient body of utterances for the work of analysis to begin. Since grammatical relations often straddle ‖, it cannot safely be taken as the end of an utterance. Cases of doubt whether ‖ is utterance terminal or a mid-utterance intonation break therefore have to be decided by the developing grammar; the decision is unusually transparent. There are also occasional cases of rapid speech in which speech segments which are clearly utterances have been run together without intervening ♯ or ‖.

Establishing the corpus of utterances to be analyzed is not merely a segmentation problem. In criticizing work on child language, Chomsky (1964b) points out that the grammatical description that is important is the description of the learner's competence, not of his actual performance. He goes on to say:

It is absurd to attempt to construct a grammar that describes observed linguistic behavior directly. . . . The speaker has represented in his brain a grammar that gives an ideal account of the structure of the sentences of his language, but, when actually faced with the task of speaking or "understanding," many other factors act upon his underlying linguistic competence to produce actual performance. He may be confused or have several things in mind, change his plans in midstream, etc. Since this is obviously the condition of most actual linguistic performance, a direct record—an actual corpus —is almost useless, as it stands, for linguistic analysis of any but the most superficial kind [p. 36].

Chomsky's comment assumes that investigators have treated all stretches of speech on a tape as utterances to be reconstructed by a grammar. However, it is likely that child texts have been approached with more common sense than the criticism allows for. Most tapes do include some speech segments that contain interruptions, hesitations, false starts, repeated words, etc. It would obviously defeat the purpose of a grammatical analysis to require a grammar to generate such defective segments, and there is no evidence that investigators have treated them as utterances to be reconstructed by the grammar.

While Chomsky's point, that one should expect the child to deviate sometimes from his own rules, is a reasonable one, the actual number of utterances that deviate from the predominant patterns of construction, without showing phonological evidence of anomaly, are very small in my experience.[1] Nevertheless, such utterances do constitute a minor problem, and several investigators have been unsure whether or not a grammar ought to generate them (Miller & Ervin, 1964; Brown & Fraser, 1963). However, so long as these potentially anomalous utterances are not numerous, the

[1] That is, the strange, potentially anomalous utterances are small in number. All tapes from a given period of development will contain utterances which deviate somewhat from the predominant patterns of utterance formation in the sense that they are structurally more "advanced" than the majority of utterances. Chomsky's point, however, is not concerned with these utterances.

methodological problem is not serious. A distributional analysis is possible only insofar as utterances are structurally similar to each other. If a pattern of utterance formation is sufficiently rare, there will not be enough utterances exhibiting it to support an analysis. Thus, it is inevitable that some utterances should be left unanalyzed. The best that can be done with the marginalia is to list them, or provide a partial analysis; it is therefore immaterial whether or not the marginalia contain "mistakes" (cf. Quirk, 1965, p. 206, where a similar point is made).

1.32. *Segmenting Utterances into Morphs.* The words or morphs in child texts are essentially taken as given; i.e., the child's morphological units are assumed to be adult morphs (usually) or to be combinations of adult morphs. The diagnosis of whether such combinations as *fireman* or *broke* are mono- or bimorphemic for a child is a product of the analysis based, for instance, on the child's treatment of other noun compounds or past tense forms (see also Braine [1963b] for a rough distributional criterion used in analyzing some texts from a very early stage of development).

1.33. *The Core Problem in Deriving and Justifying a Grammar.* Much published work on the development of syntax has treated the text material as a list of unrelated utterances and has demanded of a grammar only that it generate the utterances on the list and provide them with structural descriptions.[2] The investigator has then run into the central problem that he has no information about what the child could *not* say, i.e., about what strings are ungrammatical in the child's idiolect (see Brown & Fraser [1963] for a paper in which the problem is emphasized). In general, a grammar arrived at by an investigator can be wrong in two ways: (*a*) it may fail to generate some of the grammatical utterances, or (*b*) it may generate strings which are ungrammatical. There is no methodological problem in detecting errors of the first type since these can in principle be progressively diminished by increasing the quantity of text material. However, errors of the second type are not in principle detectable in the absence of information as to what strings are ungrammatical.

Investigators have tried to avoid the above difficulty by leaning on techniques of distributional analysis of the kind described by Harris (1951, Chs. 13–19). However, Harris assumes that the corpus of text materials is an "ideal" one that potentially contains all grammatical utterances; i.e., he assumes that it is possible to manipulate an informant in such a way that "ungrammatical" can be equated with "not elicited from the informant."

---

[2] Lees (1964) criticizes investigators for requiring only that a grammar generate the utterances of a corpus and not also that it provide the utterances with structural descriptions. However, it is not clear to me that his estimate of the literature is correct. In any case, the methodological problem discussed in this section arises from the inadequacy of a finite unordered list as data, not from failure to require that a grammar describe utterance structure.

A corpus of utterances from a child is, of course, enormously far from satisfying this idealizing assumption. An analysis must be indeterminate if the only information available for analysis is that contained in a list of unrelated utterances, as Lees (1964) and I (Braine, 1965d) have argued. The article by Brown and Fraser, cited above, illustrates the application of methods of distributional analysis to child-text materials; it also provides a discussion of the problems the analyst runs into in reaching conclusions.

Brown, Fraser, and Bellugi (1964) examine a procedure for testing alternative grammatical formulations against a corpus of utterances. They divide a corpus into two halves, write a grammar based on one half, and then test this grammar against the unanalyzed half, the evaluation being based on two ratios computed on the second half. The first ratio is the number of text utterances generated by the grammar, divided by the number of text utterances not generated by the grammar. When this ratio is high the grammar "predicts" the new utterances well. However, Brown et al. point out that this ratio is necessarily highest for the grammar which portrays the child as uttering words in random order, since such a grammar automatically predicts all possible utterances in all possible future texts. The second ratio measures the extent to which the grammar properly fails to predict utterances which do not occur. The authors show that this ratio is highest in the case of the trivial grammar consisting of a simple list of the utterances in the first half. Thus, each of the ratios is highest for grammars which are essentially structureless and clearly wrong. Moreover, as the authors point out, it would be arbitrary to try to optimize the values for both ratios simultaneously, and in any case, many different grammars could be written which would do so to about the same extent. Thus, the procedure of Brown et al. does not solve the methodological problem.

It might be thought that the way out of the methodological difficulty would be to obtain judgments of grammaticalness from children. This would appear to be a hopeless task. Brown et al. (1964) report having tried and failed, and it is difficult to elicit sensible judgments of grammaticalness even from adults (Hill, 1961; Maclay & Sleator, 1960). In the typical case in adult linguistics in which judgments of grammaticalness are employed in working out grammars, the linguist is a native speaker and makes the judgments himself.

Solution of the methodological difficulty clearly requires that more data be brought into the analysis. It has been suggested (Braine, 1965d) that additional data on utterance structure are already available within the texts themselves, which are far from being lists of unrelated utterances. Two kinds of data are considered in 1.34–5. In 1.36 some rough "simplicity" criteria are outlined which a child grammar should presumably satisfy, and 1.37 considers how knowledge of the structure of the adult language may be used to decide some cases where the structure of text utterances is uncertain. While it is not clear to what extent the methodological difficulty outlined above has been resolved, it is clearly possible in practice to come to conclusions about many of the rules that a child is using.

1.34. *Replacement Sequences*. In her study of the nighttime monologues of her 2-year-old son, Weir (1962) found many sets of utterances which were clearly related to each other, both structurally and thematically. Examples are *Donkey* ♯ *Fix the donkey. Thumb* ♯ *That's a thumb. Block* ♯ *Yellow block* ♯ *Look at all the yellow block. Sit down* ♯ *Sit down on the blanket* (ibid., pp. 80–82). Weir called such sets of utterances *sequences*. Rather similar sets are also common in the daytime speech of 2-year-olds.

Such sets of utterances provide information as to similarity relations between utterances of a kind which is potentially very valuable in a grammatical analysis. However, Weir's concept of a sequence is too broad to be directly used in a grammatical analysis because she includes in the same sequence utterances which are only thematically related. I (Braine, 1965d) suggested the term *replacement sequence* for sets of utterances which are such that (*a*) the utterances of the set occur during a fairly short time period during which there is no detectable change in the eliciting situation (i.e., nothing happens in the environment to indicate that the utterances are not equivalent in meaning), and (*b*) the longer utterances of the sequence contain the lexical morphemes of the shorter utterances. Thus, we find Gregory saying *Man* ♯ *Car* ♯ *Man|car* ♯ *Man | in car* ♯ *Man | in the car* ♯; Steven is trying to report that his brother Tommy gave him a gun and says *Stevie gun* ♯ *Tommy | Stevie gun* ♯ *Tommy give gun* ♯ *Gun* ♯ *Tommy | gun* ♯ *Tommy | give Stevie gun* ♯.[3] In such replacement sequences it seems intuitively obvious that the utterances are structurally related to each other, and that, as Weir (1962) notes, the child is "building up" the more complex grammatical form slowly. Further examples are shown in Table 2-1.

An important property of such sets is that the longer utterances invariably appear to be more recent acquisitions than the shorter ones; i.e., the shorter utterances, or utterances structurally like them, are found in texts before the longer forms have developed. This fact justifies calling the longer utterances "replacements" of the shorter ones, where "replacement" is understood in a sense similar to its use in historical studies (e.g., Hoenigswald, 1960). The term *replacement* can usefully be generalized to relate forms which are not found together in contemporaneous texts. One seems to find the following sort of situation: in the earliest texts in which it occurs *man car* is not further developed; shortly afterwards it has a contemporary replacement *man in the car* as in the sequence cited above; later, *man car* is rarely, if ever, found, but *man in the car* is replaced by *there man in car, there's a man in the*

---

[3] These examples, and also those in Table 2-1, are from my tapes of children about 27 months old. "|" indicates a mid-utterance intonation break. The examples, the discussion of replacement sequences, and much of Sections 1.34–6 have been reported in unpublished papers (Braine, 1963, 1965d). I am also indebted to Wick Miller for correspondence on some points.

Table 2-1. Examples of Replacement Sequences of Three Children

NP expansion

Truck | fall down ‡ Big truck | fall down ‡ This fall down ‡ (S)
Want more ‖ Some more ‖ Want some more ‡ (S)
Yellow balloon ‡ Two yellow balloon ‡ (J)
Car | on machine ‡ Big car | on machine ‡ (J)
Noise ‡ Noise car ‡ (J)

Predicate phrase expansions

Get Stevie truck ‡ Stevie truck ‡ Find Stevie truck | Mom ‡ (S)
Other coffee ‡ Daddy | other coffee ‡ Daddy have it coffee ‡ (J)
Stand up ‡ Cat stand up ‡ Cat stand up | table ‡ (J)
Open it ‡ Open | powder ‡ Open it | powder ‡ Open the powder ‡ Open powder ‡ (G)

Expansions with an object complement

Stevie | byebye car ‡ Mommy take | Stevie byebye car ‡ (S)
Stevie soldier up ‖ Mommy ‖ make Stevie soldier up | Mommy ‡ (S)
Daddyman stand up | Mommy ‡ Stevie make daddyman | stand up ‡ (S)

NOTE: S = Steven; J = Jonathan; G = Gregory.

car, and still later, no doubt, by *a man's in the car*. Thus, one may find a continuous series of temporally overlapping replacements relating an early form to one or more "terminal replacements" which are grammatical from the standpoint of adult English.

In general, replacement sequences indicate the extent and kind of grammatical free variation and thus provide information similar to that provided by same-different judgments on utterances. Such information can be used in a variety of ways. As a first example, Table 2-1 shows Steven expanding *truck* to *big truck* and then substituting *this* for the phrase. Such a sequence makes clear that the immediate constituents are (as one might expect) *truck*, *big truck*, and *this*, on the one hand, and *fall down*, on the other hand. As a second example, we find that on some occasions *man car* is expanded to *man in the car* as above, and on other occasions to *man's car*, and we also find evidence in the texts that other combinations of two nouns may be susceptible to replacement in more than one way. Such replacement sequences provide direct evidence of a constructional homonym, and there-fore, that the grammar must describe $N + N$ combinations in more than one way. As a third example, consider the last three sequences in Table 2-1. (The respective terminal replacements are, approximately, *Mommy took Stevie out in the car*, *Make Stevie's soldier stand up*, and *Stevie is making the [Daddy-]man stand up*.) In each case, the apparent combination of object followed by complement occurs first as an independent utterance susceptible to analysis as a subject-predicate form. Such sequences would obviously be consistent with a transformational view of Steven's early object-complement constructions, since it looks very much as if the child is uttering the string to be embedded immediately before he embeds it.

In addition, replacement sequences seem to provide some information about subordination relations. There appears to be sufficient consistency in what is present and absent that it may well be possible to distinguish components present in the shortest utterances and presumably essential for the child (the "head" or "center," perhaps) from apparently less essential components added in the longer utterances.

It was urged (Braine, 1963c, 1965d) that a child grammar should generate utterances so that replacing constructions come out as expansions (or sometimes, no doubt, as transformations) of the utterance forms replaced. In my recordings of children 24–30 months old, 30–40 percent of the utterances seem to be part of a replacement sequence. Bringing these sequences into a distributional analysis may place sufficient restrictions on the analysis that at least the main features of structure can be justified. This seems as much as one should ask: all grammars based on text material must become vague at some level of detail.

1.35. *Inferring Structure from Relative Frequency of Constructions.* The possibility has been suggested (though not discussed in the literature) that the relative frequency of different constructions in a corpus might be a source of information about structure. For example, suppose a fragment of a grammar with the rules $S \rightarrow AF$, $S \rightarrow FB$, $F \rightarrow P$, $F \rightarrow Q$, where A, B, F, P, Q are phrase classes. The rules imply that the choice of P or Q as the realization of F is independent of the context of F. It follows that the ratio (number of utterances of structure AP)/(number of utterances of structure AQ) should be approximately equal to the ratio (number of utterances of structure PB)/(number of utterances of structure QB). Testing whether the ratios are in fact about equal provides an indirect test of the adequacy of the set of rules.

In general, it might be required of a child grammar that it be possible to assign probabilities in some coherent way to the various expansion rules at the higher nodes of the grammar so as to predict the relative frequencies of the various construction types in the corpus. However, no work has yet been reported which explores the feasibility or usefulness of this sort of test of a grammar.

1.36. *Simplicity.* It is inevitable that simplicity serve to some extent as a criterion for a grammar. While the published literature contains no discussion of what constitutes simplicity in the case of a child's system undergoing rapid change through time, I would suggest that it reduces to the two following principles, one synchronic and the other diachronic:

a. At any stage of development, no more distinctions should be attributed to a child than there is evidence for. This principle prevents diachronic simplicity being achieved trivially by reading many adult English rules into the child at early stages and conjoining these with a set of "erase" rules which remove segments present in later sentences; such treatment of the child's utterances as "elliptical" English sentences admittedly might achieve simple diachronic statements—development would consist merely of the disappearance of "erase" rules—but it suffers from the defect that it treats the early stages as actually more complex than later stages, since the child is assumed to command not only much of English grammar but, in addition, a set of "erase" rules. Incidentally, the formulation of such erase rules would be quite complicated (see 2.41–2 for further discussion of such rules).

b. Adjacent stages of development should each be formulated so as to minimize the difference between them. It might be thought that this principle would occasionally conflict with the preceding one. In practice, this seems not to be so, perhaps because of the replacement phenomena described earlier: the fact that "old" and "new" forms occur contemporaneously and substitute for each other means that a synchronic analysis will necessarily consider some diachronic data; i.e., the direction of the later development is partly foreshadowed in a more or less synchronous corpus.

1.37. *Use of the Investigator's Knowledge of the Adult System.* Since the purpose of the analysis is to discover the child's own generative rules, the analyst clearly must treat the idiolect contained in his corpus of texts as a linguistic system sui generis. However, this requirement does not mean that the investigator sets aside his knowledge of the adult system. Knowledge of the adult system is used in several ways. First, it serves as a set of hypotheses as to the rules that may be present in the texts: children's texts usually reflect partial knowledge of the adult system; i.e., children tend to overgeneralize rules present in the adult system rather than create unrelated rules. Second, owing to the finite nature of the corpus, there are many words that cannot be assigned to classes purely on the basis of the contexts in which they occur; they do not occur in enough contexts, or not in contexts that are diagnostic. Here the investigator first establishes what part-of-speech distinctions the child does make on the basis of the corpus alone. These distinctions will usually be found to correspond to some broad distinctions made in the adult system. The indeterminate cases in the text material can then be classified according to these correspondences, unless the texts provide contrary evidence.

Knowledge of the adult system is also used to assign structure in the case of constructional homonyms. Again, the existence and the nature of the homonym are first established on the sole basis of the internal relations in the corpus. Once the homonym and its correspondences in the adult system have been established, structure can be assigned to indeterminate cases in the way that the investigator's gloss of the utterance indicates to be appropriate. Thus, if it is already established that some $N+N$ combinations are NPs of modifier-head structure and that others are primitive sentential forms, then an utterance of *Daddy coffee* will be an NP if glossed as 'Daddy's coffee', and a primitive sentence if glossed as (say) 'Daddy took mommy's coffee'.

Most texts contain many utterances which are quite opaque if taken alone; e.g., consider *Want more stand up the truck*. If one knows already that *more* can be either *NP*, noun modifier, or adjunct to predicating expressions (in the sense of 'again'), and further, that the sentence is glossed as 'I want more men to stand up in the back of the truck', then one is in a position to assign some tentative structure to the utterance (e.g., *more* is clearly *NP*). A different tentative structure would be assumed if the gloss were, say, 'I want the truck to be stood up again'. Opaque utterances of this sort are nearly useless in a distributional analysis until some preliminary structure has been assigned to them.

1.38. *Conclusion on Method.* There is no general method of analysis which can be mechanically applied to a corpus of text materials from a child in such a way as to guarantee discovery of the grammatical rules commanded by the child. Methods of distributional analysis will bring out many distributional regularities among utterances, but they stop well short of determining a unique grammar (or even a unique set of similar grammars). Beyond this, conclusions as to rules used by a child have to be justified in part by indirect arguments based on replacement phenomena, statistical considerations, simplicity arguments, and the like. And many questions of detail will always remain unresolved.

As compared with analysis of text materials, the testing techniques described earlier (1.2) have the advantage of yielding data on structure which are more secure and more objective (i.e., free of any possible component of analyst intuition); such data have the disadvantage that they cannot provide a picture of the idiolect as a whole. Ideally, of course, it would be desirable to combine the techniques and to use data from systematic tests to support a text-based grammar at crucial points. Unfortunately, this is difficult to accomplish because the language often develops faster than the texts are analyzed, so that tests designed to answer questions raised in the analysis may be obsolete before they can be administered.

2. THE DEVELOPMENT OF STRUCTURE IN CHILD LANGUAGE

Phonology is considered first, followed by grammar at some length, and then semantics. These sections (2.1–3) concentrate on description of the available facts, although interpretative discussion is not excluded. In 2.4, a number of issues arising out of the developmental data are reviewed.

2.1. Phonology

2.11. *Segmental Phonology.* Most of the useful information about phonological development comes from studies of individual children by linguists.

However, despite the frequent generalizations about "child language" in the literature, few good quality studies have actually been published. There is only one good developmental study of a monolingual English-speaking child (Velten, 1943). Leopold (1939–49, Vol. 2; 1953–54), Grégoire (1937–47), and Gvozdev (1949; 1961) are very detailed longitudinal studies, the children being English-German bilingual, French (Belgian), and Russian, respectively. However, Grégoire uses the term *phoneme* to refer to sounds used in babbling as well as speech and makes no systematic effort to distinguish free variation from contrast; Leopold is also not entirely free of criticism on this score but devotes much less space to babbling; unfortunately, no English source to Zhenya Gvozdev's phonology exists. Weir (1962) and Chao (1951) present fairly detailed contrastive analyses of data from a single stage of development, the languages acquired being English and Mandarin Chinese, respectively. However, Weir's child was already well developed phonologically at the time studied, and much of the phonological section of Chao's paper is difficult to follow unless read in conjunction with a work on the "National Romanization" used for transcription, since it is difficult to tell when a difference in letter signifies a difference in tone or a difference in a segmental phoneme. There are many other papers containing observations or discussions that are less detailed but of some interest (e.g., Albright & Albright, 1956, 1958; Bloch, 1921, 1924; Burling, 1959; Cohen, 1952; Durand, 1949).

The available information indicates that phonological development takes the form of a progressively developing system of contrasts. For example, between 11 and 16 months of age Velten's daughter, Joan, developed as follows: Her first two words, [ap] 'up' and [ba] 'bottle', 'bang', indicate a distinction between a vowel and a stop consonant. It was characteristic of Joan's early development, as of Leopold's children and my son, that consonants tended to be voiced initially and unvoiced terminally, so that the voiced and unvoiced realizations of consonant phonemes were in complementary distribution. Following Velten, the unvoiced member will be used to represent the phoneme; thus, the first distinction is between /p/ and /a/. Joan next developed a stop-continuant distinction /p/ vs. /s/: [bas] 'bus' and [za] 'that' show a contrast between terminal [s] and its absence ([bas] vs. [ba]), and a contrast between the initial voiced phones [z] and [b] ([za] vs. [ba]). A contrast between two stop consonants /p/ and /t/ then emerged, through the words [da] 'down', [at] 'out', and [bat] 'pocket'. Following this a distinction between continuants developed, /f/ distinguished from /s/, and shortly afterwards a vowel distinction, /u/ contrasted with /a/: [af > faf] 'Fuff', the name of a pet, [bus] 'push', [uf] 'dog'. Here Velten notes that both the stop distinction (/p/ vs. /t/) and the continuant distinction (/f/ vs. /s/) are based on the same distinctive feature, point of articulation; i.e., both represent a distinction between dental or alveolar-dental and labial or labiodental. Joan's next step was to introduce the nasals /m/ and /n/: the point-of-articulation distinction already present in the stops and non-nasal continuants is now replicated in the nasals.

The data on phonological development confirm the general lines of Jakobson's thinking (Jakobson, 1941; Jakobson & Halle, 1956), which has heavily influenced work on phonological development. According to Jakobson, the development of the sound system is describable, not as a gradual approximation of the adult phonemes one by one, but in terms of the acquisition of successive contrasts between distinctive features of maximum difference and generality, e.g., vowel vs. consonant, stop vs. nonstop, voiced vs. unvoiced, etc. Burling (1959), for example, noted that his son acquired the voiced-unvoiced distinction in all his consonants at once; similarly, Gvozdev (1949; 1961) found that contrastive palatalization appeared nearly simultaneously for many Russian consonants in his son's speech. In Joan Velten's development cited above, it can be seen that her six consonants at 16 months were formed from a system of features: *(stop × nasal × nonnasal continuant)* × *(labial × nonlabial)*.

While Jakobson's general point that development proceeds by the acquisition of distinctive features is clearly correct, his more specific proposals about the order of development have been only partially substantiated. He suggested that the order of development of features would be the same as the order of relative prevalence of the features among the languages of the world, proceeding generally from contrasts which represent gross differences to contrasts of greater subtlety. For example, the first distinction would be between a vowel and a consonant (a vowel of wide opening and a consonant produced by complete closure of the oral and nasal cavities), the next between stop and nonstop (nasal). While it is probably true that development does proceed from gross to subtle distinctions, the differences between children in the order of development of features is greater than these proposals allow for. On the receptive side, Shvachkin (El'konin, 1960) taught Russian children 11 to 22 months old words differing in only one phoneme at a time. He found that vowel distinctions were learned first, then the vowel-consonant distinction, then, in order, sonorants vs. articulated obstruents, plain vs. palatalized consonants, nasals vs. liquids, sonorants vs. unarticulated obstruents, labials vs. nonlabials, stops vs. fricatives, front vs. back nonlabials, voiced vs. unvoiced consonants, blade vs. groove sibilants, and liquids vs. /y/. Some vowel distinctions also appeared before a general distinction between vowels and consonants in my son's speech (see example in 1.1), although not in the speech of Joan Velten or of some other children described in the literature. Although difficulty of articulation is not easy to measure, it may well be an important factor affecting the order of development of features (Ervin & Miller, 1963), since there are regularities in the substitutions that children make of one phoneme for another, e.g., stops for fricatives, semivowels for vowels (Leopold, 1939–49; see also Templin's [1957] study of articulation in children 3 years and over).

In general, the number of published studies is too few to define the range of individual differences in the order of development of features; moreover, work has been reported on only a restricted number of languages. However, some generalizations appear possible, and I cannot improve on those suggested in Ervin and Miller's (1963) review; slightly reworded, these were as follows: (*a*) The vowel-consonant distinction is one of the earliest, even if not always the first. (*b*) A stop-continuant contrast appears early, the consonant being fricative or nasal. (*c*) Among consonants of the same type of articulation, the first contrast is labial-dental. (*d*) Many contrasts in place of articulation are established before voicing contrasts develop. (*e*) Affricates (e.g., /č/, /ǰ/) and liquids (/l/, /r/) develop relatively late (Lyamina & Gagua, 1964; see Ruke-Dravina [1965] on the development of *r*-phonemes). (*f*) Among vowels, a contrast between low and high precedes front vs. back. (*g*) Consonants tend to develop in initial position before final or medial positions.

In addition to describing the internal structure of a child's system, most studies have also described correspondences between the phonemic shapes of words in the speech of adult and child. The most usual relation is a many-one correspondence, in which several adult phonemes or clusters are represented by a single child phoneme, e.g., English words beginning with *b-*, *p-*, *br-*, *pl-*, *sp-*, etc., may all begin with /p-/ in a young child's speech. Sometimes these correspondences may be slightly unexpected, e.g., when *sp-*, *st-*, *sk-*, are rendered by unaspirated stops in contrast with the usual aspirated series (W. W. Gage, personal communication). However, departures from a regular one-one or many-one correspondence relation are rather frequent. Articulatory assimilations and anticipations are one source of more complex substitution rules (Albright & Albright, 1958; Chao, 1951; Leopold, 1939–49). Thus, a child with two stops /p/ and /t/ might be expected to reproduce *book* as /put/ (i.e., [but]), but may instead extend the labial articulation to the final consonant and render it as [bup]. An interesting type of complex substitution rule is cited of Morris Swadesh's son: "Final and medial consonants of the adult's words were dropped by the child. The initial consonant was replaced by a nasal if a noninitial nasal was found in the adult's word; a labial was replaced by the labial nasal /m/, and a non-labial was replaced by /n/: *blanket* /meʔ/, *green* /ni/, *candy* /ne/" (Ervin & Miller, 1963).

Another source of devious correspondences between child and adult words arises when adult allophones are allocated to different phonemes (Leopold, 1939–49; Velten, 1943). For example, for most English-speaking adults, monosyllables ending in voiced stops have a longer vowel than those ending in unvoiced stops ([bæt] 'bat' vs. [bæ·d] 'bad'). At one stage, Joan Velten lacked a voiced-unvoiced stop distinction and used vowel length to distinguish such pairs (e.g., *beat* became /put/ and *bead* /pu·t/; however, an alternative interpretation of this example is possible, see 2.14). Finally, specific exceptions to regular correspondence between adult and child words may result from archaisms: when an advance in phonological development takes place, a few words, often common ones in the child's vocabulary, may retain their old phonemic shape (Leopold, 1939–49; Velten, 1943).

2.12. *Prosody*. There has been virtually no systematic work on the development of distinctions of pitch, juncture, stress, and intonation. Several investigators (e.g., Weir, 1962; Miller & Ervin, 1964) have noted that children tend to be good mimics of prosodic features, so that these aspects of individual utterances may be imitated accurately, giving the casual observer a false impression of the child's command of the prosodic system. For English, it seems fairly clear that at least the rising and falling intonations, and similarly, ‖- and ♯-junctures are distinguished at the time of or very soon after the first appearance of word combinations. Both Weir (1962) and Miller and Ervin (1964) suggest a two-level stress system from a fairly early age. Although they mark utterance boundaries (Weir, 1962), the rising and falling intonations may not always correspond to the distinction between statement and question (Miller & Ervin, 1964). Most investigators would no doubt agree with Grégoire, speaking of his children around their second birthday: "Les mouvements affectifs se décèlent depuis longtemps dans les intonations; elles en expriment le motif, le but, ou la conséquence [Grégoire, 1947, p. 178]." Lieberman (1967) provides an interesting discussion of the early bases of prosody.

There have been some exaggerated claims relating to the early development of intonational structure: e.g., "It is widely accepted in the literature that the child effectively masters the intonation pattern of his language *before he has learned any words at all* [Bever, Fodor, & Weksel, 1965a, p. 479, italics theirs]." On the ground that perception of intonation entails control of grammar, Bever et al. build an argument that children grasp derived constituent structure very early indeed. Although little is known about the development of prosodic features, enough is known to remove any possible basis for this sort of argument. The English intonation system was by no means fully developed in Weir's son at age $2\frac{1}{2}$, long after he had begun to talk (Weir, 1962). Miller and Ervin (1964) comment that even the contrast between rising and falling intonations may be later than is generally recognized. They also note that two of their subjects used prosodic features with no analogue in adult English in their early word combinations. Given the evidence for lack of mastery of the prosodic system long after the onset of speech, it is hard to know what to make of claims that intonation is controlled before any speech has developed at all. Even if it were true that the linguist can identify the language of the infant's environment from his prelinguistic verbal play (Jakobson, 1941)—one would like to see confirmation of this claim in a blind study with a variety of infants whose linguistic environments were not known to the linguist—it would still be very unclear just what cues the linguist (or the child) was responding to. Nakazima (1962) found no differences in prelinguistic babbling between Japanese and American children.

2.13. *Phonotactics.* The term *phonotactics* refers to regularities in the arrangements of phones in utterances or, alternatively and more or less equivalently, to types of phone sequences that speakers find "natural" or "easily sayable." Phonotactic regularities in children's speech may usefully be divided into two kinds: (*a*) "primitive" regularities, i.e., types of phone sequences that children inherently seem to prefer, regardless of what language they are exposed to, and (*b*) "learned" regularities, i.e., regularities that represent an evolution towards the phonotactic patterns of the adult language.

Primitive preferences for certain types of phone sequences clearly exist. One frequent pattern, which has already been mentioned, is the voicing of initial consonants of monosyllables and the unvoicing of final consonants. The tendency to maintain the same place of articulation for all consonants of a word (e.g., the reduplicated syllables of the very young, and somewhat later, forms like [bup] for *book*) constitutes another such pattern, which is well attested by the large numbers of assimilatory errors regularly found in the speech of young children. Possibly a third pattern is a tendency to fail to locate certain features accurately, e.g., such features as nasality (cf. the examples cited earlier [2.11] of Morris Swadesh's son) or sibilance (suggested by such relatively advanced errors as [spədæšiyow] for *pistachio* and the converse [pəsketiy] for *spaghetti*).

Little effort has been expended on analysis and definition of the primitive phonotactic patterns of young children. One important question that needs to be clarified is whether they affect the child's hearing of words as well as his speech. For instance, in the case of the child who reproduces *book* as [bup], does he hear [bup] and merely reproduce what he hears, or does he hear the word correctly and therefore know that it ought to be [buk], but utter [bup] because of some difficulty in executing the articulatory command for /k/ when it follows quickly upon the command for an initial labial? If the latter, then the assimilatory tendencies involve only speech production and probably have little effect on the course of the child's learning of the phonological constitution of words. However, one should probably not be quick to assume that these primitive phonotactic patterns affect only speech production: failures of articulation of phonemes are often associated with parallel failures of discrimination (Prins, 1963), and it is well known that learned phonotactic patterns in adults are as much patterns of perception as habits of production. On the other hand, anecdotal evidence (see Leopold, 1939–49, Vol. 2, pp. 257–274, for a review) tends to support the notion that it is often primarily production that is affected.

The acquisition of the adult phonotactic patterns has been the subject of only one study: Messer (1967) shows that by around age $3\frac{1}{2}$ children are able to discriminate to a statistically significant degree between nonsense words with consonant clusters found in English and nonsense words containing clusters not found in English. He also found several cases in which the children misheard the un-English clusters as English clusters, indicating an effect of the pattern on perception.

2.14. *Morphophonemics.* Morphophonemes are phonological entities which may have more than one phonemic realization (e.g., the second vowel of *photograph* is realized as /ow/ in *photo*, as [ə] in *photograph*, and as /a/ in *photography*; the alternation /ow/-[ə]-/a/ is called "morphophonemic" alternation). The psychological literature is devoid of any mention of morphophonemes; they are nearly virgin territory also for the student of child language, and there are hardly any psychologically oriented discussions in the linguistic literature, although this literature seems to imply that a morphophoneme is a more abstract unit than a mere phoneme and, therefore, presumably more difficult for a child to learn. Let us consider some instances of morphophonemic alternations from a psychological standpoint.

A first example, described earlier (1.1), is provided by the speech of Steven, aged 2-2. Alternations such as [dak—dagiy] 'dog' and [pik—pigiy] 'pig' contrast with absence of alternation in [buk—bukiy] 'book'. Voiced and unvoiced stops are distinct in initial and intervocalic positions, but not terminally. The reason for the alternation seems obvious: Steven has registered that the last consonant of *dog* and *pig* is /g/, but he is still under the sway of his primitive phonotactic patterns, so the /g/ comes out as [k] terminally because he cannot voice final consonants. (More precisely, Steven has partially overcome the primitive pattern: he has overcome his earlier inability to unvoice initial consonants and now has the contrast in initial and intervocalic positions; he has not yet overcome his inability to voice terminals.) The contrast in Joan Velten's speech (2.11) between [but] 'beat' and [bu·t] 'bead', which led Velten to treat vowel length as phonemic for Joan, may well be another example of a true voicing contrast which is masked in the speech output by this same primitive phonotactic pattern.

Another example, in which the morphophonemic alternation is caused by assimilatory tendencies, is provided by Chao's granddaughter Canta (Chao, 1951, pp. 37–38). She rendered the Mandarin perfective particle *.le* as *.ie* after words ending in *-i*, as *.ue* after words ending in *-u*, and as *.ne* after nasal endings (see 2.41 for detailed discussion of this example).

These examples suggest that some morphophonemic alternations can occur very early; the morphophonemes involved are not in the least "abstract" in any psychological sense, and there is no indication that they pose any special difficulty for the child; the alternations are, rather, the direct result of the child's phonotactic limitations. The primitive phonotactic patterns discussed above may be the source of many such alternations at early stages of development.

A third example, similar in an essential respect to the preceding ones, is provided by the alternation between [r] and zero in the mature speech of many learners of *r*-less dialects. For instance, for many Southern British speakers *soar* and *saw* ('cut with a saw') are identical, [sɔː] or [sɔə], but *soaring* [sɔːrin] differs from *sawing* [sɔːin]. Presumably, experience with the form *soaring* informs the learner that the lexical item *soar* contains /r/, and the learned inability to pronounce [r] terminally prevents him from saying it when there is no immediately following vowel. Thus, this example differs from the preceding ones only in that the inability to make an [r] at the end of a word is part of a phonotactic pattern that is learned as part of learning the dialect, whereas Steven's inability to voice terminally is primitive, and likewise Canta's assimilatory tendencies.

The common alternation of full vowel with *schwa* ([fowtəgræf]– [fətagrəfiy], etc.) also resembles the above cases in that there is no need to assume any special learning of a morphophoneme as such. The learner can learn what the full vowel is from experience with the word containing the vowel under strong stress, and the reduction to *schwa* is a consequence of also learning a stress pattern (for the other word-form containing the lexical item) in which stress is removed from the vowel.[4]

In cases like the above, there is clearly no need for any special theory of the acquisition of morphophonemes. In phonological learning, children are apparently doing three things: acquiring a system of contrasts, learning the phonological constituents of words (i.e., the phonemes of which a word is made up), and learning phonotactic arrangements, stress patterns, etc. (including learning to overcome primitive phonotactic patterns). These acquisitions suffice to account for the kind of morphophonemic phenomena considered so far. In fact, if the phoneme is viewed in the narrow terms that Chomsky (1964a) has criticized under the title "taxonomic phonemics," then the phoneme strings that appear in a broad transcription of the child's speech are not directly learned at all. Rather, it is the underlying morphophoneme strings that are learned, and the "taxonomic" phonemes are simply the behavior that occurs when the child, trying (as it were) to speak morphophonemes, is defeated by his primitive or learned phonotactic patterns, or by a particular stress sequence.

A large class of morphophonemic alternations found at all stages of development are like the examples discussed, in that there is no reason to believe that the alternations are directly learned as such, and there is no need to posit any abstract phonological entity that has to be acquired (i.e., the child does not have to learn an equivalence relation between the two realizations of the morphophoneme and construct an abstract unit to carry the equivalence relation).

[4] One qualification is necessary here: some derived forms (e.g., *photography*, probably) enter the child's speech relatively late, after he has learned the writing system. Conceivably, the identity of a full vowel may sometimes be learned from the standard spelling of a reduced vowel.

However, there are some morphophonemic phenomena which must have a very different psychological basis, where an equivalence relation may be learned and where, therefore, there may well be ground for positing the acquisition of an abstract phonological entity. An obvious case in point is the alternation between /f/ and /v/ in *leaf—leaves, half—halves*, etc. (cf. also such pairs as *prove—proof, save—safe, brief—abbreviate*, etc.). The change to /v/ in the plural is not required by any phonotactic pattern, nor is it required by the normal English rules for forming plural nouns out of singulars. It just happens to be a property of English that some /f/'s on the ends of nouns change to /v/ before the plural suffix, and some do not; it looks, therefore, as if the learner has to learn that there is a special kind of /f/ that changes to /v/ in the plural and to learn which words contain this /f/ and which the regular /f/. To differentiate this kind of morphophonemic alternation from the preceding kind, I shall refer to it as "high-level" morphophonemic alternation and to the preceding kind as "low-level." The "special kind of /f/ that changes to /v/" may then be called a "high-level" morphophoneme.[5]

While the positing of high-level morphophonemes undoubtedly simplifies the linguistic description of a language, there is some question whether they have a real psychological existence. For instance, in the case of the plurals of nouns like *leaf, half*, etc., it is conceivable—there are no data one way or the other—that the plural of each noun is independently learned as an individual irregular plural. In that case, there would be no learning of a special kind of /f/ that changes to /v/.

The only data I know of on high-level morphophonemic alternation in children's speech appear in a study of Hebrew verb morphology in Israeli children by Bar-Adon (1959), who provides very many examples of children's rendering of the consonants of which the verb roots are composed. Hebrew lexical roots usually consist of three consonants; vowels intercalated between the consonants belong to formative morphemes distinct from the lexical root. Because they have more than one phonemic realization, several of these consonants have to be considered as morphophonemes, and their varying phonemic shapes are determined in a complex way by the position of the consonant in the root (i.e., whether first, second, or third consonant), the "conjugation" in which the root appears, and the tense form. Note the alternations between /p/ and /f/, /b/ and /v/, and /k/ and /x/ in the following examples (the lexical root consonants are capitalized): /hu šoFex/ 'he is spilling [it]', /al tišPox/ 'don't spill [it]'; /liFToax/ 'to open', /PTax/ 'open!'; /lixTov/ 'to write', /hu koTev/ 'he is writing'; /levaKeR/ 'to visit', /hu BiKeR/

<hr>

[5] Lamb (1966) presents linguistic arguments for the existence of two kinds of morphophonemic alternation, and these in fact suggested parts of this discussion. It is worth noting that Sapir's usage of the term *phoneme* seems to correspond with what is here called "low-level morphophoneme," and his famous article on the psychological reality of phonemes (Sapir, 1949) seems primarily concerned with the psychological reality of low-level morphophonemes and phonotactic rules.

'he visited'; /yivκe/ 'he will weep', /hu вaxa/ 'he wept'.[6] These and similar morphophonemic alterations are not found regularly in children's speech; instead, one shape of the consonant tends at first to be used in all forms of a particular verb, so that /šoрex/, /Fтax/, /xoтev/, /viκeʀ/ tend to replace /šoʀex/, /Pтax/, /κoтev/, /вiκeʀ/ in the above examples. Regularizations of this sort may be found as late as adolescence; they suggest that to a substantial degree the two realizations of a consonant are learned separately in each verb. In short, where the standard language contains a high-level morphophoneme, children's speech tends to contain a simple phoneme. These phenomena indicate that children have difficulty learning phonological entities at this level of abstraction under some conditions and point to the desirability of further study of such learning (including the contribution of the learning of standard spellings).

In summary, from a psychological point of view, there appear to be two kinds of morphophonemic alternation. The one, referred to above as "low-level" alternation, would be automatically accounted for by a theory of phonological learning which explained both the acquisition of phonemes and the acquisition of phonotactic rules. The other, "high-level" morphophonemic alternation, has quite a different psychological basis which is, however, not well understood.

2.15. *The Question of the Sources of Phonological Development.* The relation of phonological development to the phenomenon of babbling has been a continuous source of controversy for a long time. Frequency of vocalization during the period of prelinguistic use of the speech organs tends to reach a peak between 8 and 10 months of age, and during this period a great variety of sounds occur, including many not in the adult language (Tischler, 1957; see also Irwin, 1947a, b, 1948, 1951, 1957—however, one should read "phone" for Irwin's "phoneme"). Some theorists have tended to assume that speech sounds are selected out of the sounds used in babbling by a process of reinforcement, either direct reinforcement or through the reward of hearing oneself speak like the rewarding parent (Staats & Staats, 1963; Mowrer, 1952, 1960). A somewhat similar theory, which takes the articulatory feature as the main element selected by reinforcement, has recently been proposed by Olmsted (1966). Critics of this kind of theorizing have tended to be skeptical of the existence of any relation between babbling and phonological development in speech (Jakobson, 1941; Velten, 1943; Carroll, 1960). Thus, Velten claims that although babbling may continue for some time after speech has begun, there may also be a cessation of babbling before or at the time of the beginnings of speech. However, he cites no evidence beyond, presumably,

---

[6] These stops and affricates are not in complementary distribution. /p/ and /f/ are in direct contrast in a few environments and /b/ and /v/ in many. For the velars, the situation is particularly complex: here, there are three morphophonemes, one always realized as /k/, another always as /x/, and a third which alternates between /k/ and /x/.

his own daughter. One known difference between the prelinguistic vocalizations and the first speech sounds is that velars and glottals are relatively frequent in the early vocalizations, whereas labial and alveolar-dental consonants tend to predominate in the first words (Irwin, 1947a; Winitz & Irwin, 1958). On the other hand, when babbling continues after speech has begun, both babbling and speech seem to draw on much the same repertoire of phones during the months of overlap—at least, this was true of Leopold's children and of my son and is consistent with Winitz and Irwin's (1958) observations. Nakazima (1962) found no difference in the vocalizations of Japanese and American children until after speech had begun. Together, these observations suggest an interaction between early speech and babbling, but not one in which speech sounds are shaped out of the prelinguistic babbling repertoire. However, the relation between speech and babbling is an area with an excessively high ratio of speculation to research.

Two central questions to be asked about a class of learned behaviors are (a) What is learned? and (b) What is the mechanism of learning? For the acquisition of phonemes, the literature reviewed provides at least a preliminary answer to the first question: distinctive features are learned. This answer appears to be generally consistent with the Gibsonian concept (Gibson, 1959; Gibson & Gibson, 1955) that perceptual learning takes the form of a progressive differentiation of stimuli impinging on the sense organs, in this case auditory stimuli. It generally seems to be assumed that receptive control of a contrast somewhat precedes active control, i.e., progress in development is primarily a perceptual process, and that the newly learned auditory distinction guides production by providing the child with a criterion for monitoring his own motor output. No answer is known to the question of how such learning proceeds, although Simon and Newell (1962) have made some brief but interesting suggestions in a discussion of how it might be simulated. An important question concerns the role of feedback from the articulatory musculature in the perception and learning of phonemes (e.g., Liberman, 1957; Lisker, Cooper, & Liberman, 1962; Fant, 1960; Lane, 1965). A resolution of this controversy might contribute much toward defining the nature of the distinctive features that are acquired and to understanding the way in which experience with language interacts with preexisting auditory processing mechanisms to determine the acquisition of contrasts.

I know of no proposals concerning the mechanism of acquisition of phonotactic patterns or of prosody.

2.2. Grammar

The earliest word combinations are considered first, then the development of various aspects of English structure (2.22-4); other languages are considered in 2.25–7; and in 2.28–9, data for several languages on the order of development of categories and on morphological development are reviewed.

2.21. *Structure of the First Morpheme Combinations.* When he has a moderate single-word vocabulary (say, 50–150 words), usually somewhere between 18 and 24 months, the child first begins to put two words together. Several investigators (Braine, 1963b; Brown & Fraser, 1963; Miller & Ervin, 1964; Gvozdev, 1949) have noted that most of these early word combinations tend to follow a certain pattern: a few individual words are singled out and used in a particular utterance position in combination with a variety of other words. Thus, of 240 two-word utterances recorded by Miller and Ervin (1964) from Susan (21–24 months), 62 ended with either *on* or *off*, and a further 45 began with either *this*, *that*, *more*, *a*, *the*, and *other*. The words singled out have been called *pivot words* (Braine, 1963b). They tend to appear sequentially in the very early development; one or two may first be singled out and used in a variety of word combinations; a week or two later, another pivot may appear, and a third or fourth after a further short time interval. Several observers have noted that the characteristic nature of the construction and the oddness of many of the combinations make it clear that a productive pattern is involved, not mere imitations of adult phrases.

In my analysis of the construction (Braine, 1963b), it was observed that the words that are combined with the pivots also occur as single-word utterances, whereas the pivot words themselves may not occur alone. Thus, the construction consists of the three utterance forms, X, P_1X, and XP_2, where X is the class of single-word utterances, and P_1 and P_2 are the pivot words of first and second position, respectively. I proposed that the basis of the construction is the learning of the positions of the pivot words: the child begins to combine words by learning that a few words belong first and some others second; in the absence of other learning which might restrict generalization, the position complementary to that of the pivot is occupied by any single-word utterance in the child's vocabulary.

The period of time during which the pivotal construction appears to be the only productive construction is short. It lasted about four months in the three children described in Braine (1963b). It is clear from other work that the period is very variable and can be considerably shorter than four months. The transition to a more complex grammar is not sharp. From the beginning, a small proportion of utterances do not fall into the categories X, PX, and XP; these consist, apart from some stereotyped expressions, of sequences of X-words, or of longer utterances one of whose components may be a pivotal construction. As development proceeds, the proportion of these more complicated utterances increases—often there is a relatively sudden and dramatic increase at some point, and it becomes clear that a construction more powerful than the pivotal construction has developed, which will generate more complicated strings that often turn out to have a kind of subject-predicate structure (see 2.22). The increased output of word combinations is presumably a consequence of a more powerful grammar becoming productive (Braine, 1963b).[7]

There are two ways in which the formulae X, P_1X, XP_2 can be an oversimplification. The pivot words themselves can have some internal structure, as exemplified, for instance, in one of W. Miller's (1964a) subjects. Another early complication is a subdivision of the undifferentiated X-class. At some point in the early development, pivots may develop (e.g., *big*, *little*, *pretty*) which are paired only with nouns, not with any lexical item; some children single out *it* as a verb marker (*turn it*, *do it*, *push it*, *cut it*, etc.). There seems to be considerable individual variation in how early such differentiation begins. In some children, it appears to occur as part of the transition to a more complex grammar which has such categories as *NP* and *Predicate* among its structures. In other children, some such differentiation seems to occur earlier, before there are more complex structures which would give the lexical categories syntactic relevance.

Many writers on child language have commented that the early single word utterances and word combinations usually seem to carry the same meanings as sentences in the adult language. On different occasions, *chair* may appear to mean 'This is a chair', 'Sit down', 'Daddy is sitting down', 'I want the chair brought over to the table so I can join you at lunch', etc. Thus, through the period of rapid development of structure, the kind of content that the child attempts to communicate does not appear to change in a way which is parallel to the changes in structure.

2.22. *English: The First Sentence Structures.* The structures which absorb and replace the pivotal construction are sufficiently complicated that a large body of text material is required to describe them, and few analyses have yet been reported. In one of these (Braine, 1963c, 1965d), it was suggested that the first English "sentence" consists of a predicate-phrase head, with an optional subject. Two lines of evidence were adduced:

   a. Texts contain many replacement sequences in which utterances without subjects are followed by the same utterance incorporating an initial *NP*,

---

[7] Because of the existence during the early period of some utterances containing two X-words, Slobin (1966) renders the structure of the first word combinations as *PX*, *XP*, and *XX*. This suggestion has two defects. First, there is no evidence that there is ever a productive rule *XX* as such: by the time enough apparent *XX* forms have developed to permit analysis, it becomes clear that they are a set of fairly complex structures to which the formula *XX* does not begin to do justice (cf. 2.22). Second, the suggestion obscures the temporal course of events, i.e., the existence of an early period when the *PX* and *XP* formulae are clearly the dominant forms of a sparse output and of a later period when they are minor modifier-head structures within a very productive grammar generating a host of *XX* and other forms.

Early corpora of text material which include the transitional period are likely to be difficult to analyze because they tend to contain a sufficiently large number of utterances more complex than the pivotal forms to require discussion, yet not enough to support an analysis (cf. the texts on Susan and Christy discussed by Miller and Ervin [1964]).

indicating that the forms with and without subjects are in free variation and equivalent in the meaning the child intends to convey. Table 2-2 shows examples taken from three children. It can be seen that the substitution of subject and predicate for predicate alone occurred regardless of whether the predicate was a noun, verb, adjectival, or prepositional phrase in adult English. One of the children, Andrew, had a simple included-sentence construction consisting of *see* + Sentence; as might be anticipated from the above line of thought, in the included sentence in this construction the subject was sometimes present (e.g., *See car come, See blankets all dry*) and was sometimes left understood (e.g., *See bang jam* 'Look at me banging the jam jar', *See all broke* 'Look at it all broken').

b. There exists a technique which will usually elicit a missing subject: one pretends not to know what the understood subject is. For example, my son Jonathan says *In kitchen*, and it is clear that he intends to convey that his mother is in the kitchen. Deliberately misunderstanding, I say "Your car's in the kitchen? No, the car's over there, see." He corrects me: *Mommy in kitchen*, thus completing the replacement sequence.

Table 2-2. Sequences in Which a Predicate Phrase is Immediately Replaced by Subject + Predicate

Andrew (27 months)

Chair . . . Pussycat chair ('The cat is on the chair')
Plug in . . . Andrew plug in ('I want to plug it in myself')
Want that . . . Andrew want that
Change pants . . . Poppa change pants ('Poppa is to change my pants')
That off . . . Andrew that off ('I want to turn that off')
Off . . . Radio off ('The radio is off') '
All wet . . . This shoe all wet
More outside . . . Andrew more outside ('I want to go outside again')

Stevie (25–26 months)

Cinna toast . . . Betty cinna toast ('Betty is to have some cinnamon toast')
Man . . . Stevie man ('Stevie has a picture of a man on his pants')
Fall . . . Stick fall ('The stick fell')
Go nursery . . . Lucy go nursery ('Lucy went to the nursery')
Push Stevie . . . Betty push Stevie
Crawl downstairs . . . Tommy crawl downstairs
Build house . . . Cathy build house

Jonathan (26–27 months)

Other coffee . . . Daddy other coffee ('Daddy had the other coffee')
Close radio . . . Mommy close radio ('Mommy should close the radio')
Take off . . . Daddy take off . . . Mommy take off ('Somebody take it off!')
Hot . . . Meat hot
Back there . . . Wheel back there
On table . . . Wine on table
Up sky . . . Jona up sky ('Jonathan is looking up in the sky')

Given this definition of the early major sentence form, it was argued that most utterances are classifiable as belonging to it. In particular, most of the large apparently heterogeneous collection of one-word utterances, consisting of an English adjective, adverb, verb, or noun, come out as sentences consisting of a predicate phrase occurring alone. However, there is one important exception to this generalization: *NP*s occurring in isolation which are used to identify or name objects, pictures, etc., appear to belong to a somewhat different construction. When these are replaced by utterances which have something like a sentence form, they are preceded by an introducer, usually *it, that, here,* or *there.* These may be called "ostensive" sentences, whether or not the introducer is expressed. The major sentence form will be called the "predicative" sentence. Once the predicative sentence form has developed, *all* nontrivial utterances can be classified as either predicative or ostensive sentences.

The division into these two types of sentence emerges clearly from an analysis by Brown and Fraser (1963) of a corpus of about 500 different multi-morpheme utterances by a $25\frac{1}{2}$-month-old child they call Eve.[8] This was the first detailed analysis of a set of text materials from an English-speaking child. Their grammar is shown in the first half of Table 2-3.[9] The form of Brown and Fraser's formulation reflects their practice at the time of preferring noncommittal labels to such terms as *noun, verb,* etc. However, it is the current practice of Brown and his co-workers to use conventional labels for categories and to label the *NP* as a unit (Brown & Bellugi, 1964). Merely relabeling the categories (second half of Table 2-3) brings out the division into predicative and ostensive sentence types present in Brown and Fraser's analysis.

Table 2-3. Brown and Fraser's Grammer of Eve$_1$ (25$\frac{1}{2}$ months)

Brown and Fraser's analysis

$$\text{Utterance} \rightarrow \begin{Bmatrix} (C_1) + (C_3) + C_2 \\ (C_3) + (C_2) + C_4 \end{Bmatrix}$$

$C_1 \rightarrow$ *'s, see, that, there*
$C_2 \rightarrow$ *bear, bird, block, boat,* etc. (including human terms, e.g., *Daddy, Evie, man*)
$C_3 \rightarrow$ *a, the,* plus human terms
$C_4 \rightarrow$ *all gone, broken, fall down, tired, fix it, listen to tick-tock,* etc.

[8] A different child studied by the same authors, whom they also call Eve, will appear later. Where there might be a confusion, the Eve discussed now will be identified as Eve$_1$ and the other as Eve$_2$.

[9] The grammars, or fragments of grammars, summarized in this and subsequent sections should be taken only as stating the general features of structure of a child's system. As discussed earlier, a degree of approximation and uncertainty is inevitable in all work from text material. Brown and Fraser's claims for their grammar are extremely guarded.

The table contains one departure from Brown and Fraser's presentation: they assigned *two* to class C_1. However, they say, "It is quite likely that *two* should go with *the* and *a* in Class 3 (p. 178)." Given the indeterminacy, simplicity considerations would require assignment as a noun modifier rather than as introducer. Some of their own later discussion presupposes assignment to C_3.

The same grammar with categories relabeled

$$\text{Utterance} \rightarrow \begin{Bmatrix} S_{ost} \\ S_{pred} \end{Bmatrix} \quad \begin{aligned} S_{ost} &\rightarrow (I) + NP \\ S_{pred} &\rightarrow (NP) + Pred \end{aligned}$$

$I \rightarrow$ *'s, see, that, there*
$NP \rightarrow (Mod) + N$
$N \rightarrow$ *bear, bird, block, boat,* etc., plus human terms
$Mod \rightarrow$ *a, the, two,* plus human terms
$Pred \rightarrow$ *all gone, broken, fall down,* etc.

SOURCE: From R. W. Brown and C. Fraser, The acquisition of syntax. In C. N. Cofer and B. S. Musgrave (Eds.), *Verbal Behavior and Learning: Problems and Processes.* New York: McGraw-Hill, 1963, Table 11.

Table 2-4. Andrew's Predicative Sentences (25–27 months)

$U \rightarrow (see) + S_{pred} + (D_3)$
$S_{pred} \rightarrow (NP) + Pred. Phr.$
$Pred. Phr. \rightarrow Pred. + (D_{loc})$

$$Pred. \rightarrow \begin{Bmatrix} G_{intr} \\ (G_{tr}) + NP \\ NP \\ D_{loc} \end{Bmatrix}$$

$G_{intr} \rightarrow$ *off, bad, come, broken, ready, all messy,* etc.
$G_{tr} \rightarrow$ *all done,* English transitive verbs

$D_{loc} \rightarrow (D_1) + D_2$

$$D_2 \rightarrow \begin{Bmatrix} \text{-\textit{stairs} in context } D_1(-) \\ \textit{inside, outside} \\ (Prep) + \textit{there} \\ (Prep) + NP \end{Bmatrix}$$

$D_1 \rightarrow$ *up, down*
$Prep \rightarrow$ *in, out, on, under*
$D_3 \rightarrow$ *now, too*

Illustrative utterances

All done there now; Coffee pot all messy; Go in car; Eat egg too; Kittycat bad; Piece of bread down on floor; Up on bed too; Mama take a nap; Doggie wufwuf 'the dog is barking'.

Illustrative tree diagram

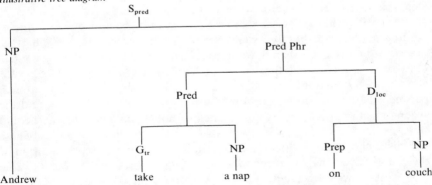

NOTE: The grammar is based on about 800 multiword utterances. It omits a very small number of predicates that appear to contain object complements, e.g., *make coffee hot.* See Table 2-6 for the *NP* structure.

At $25\frac{1}{2}$ months, Eve's predicate structure was still sufficiently undifferentiated that the predicate class was best specified by a simple listing (*broken, listen to ticktock,* etc.). A more developed predicate structure is shown by Andrew (Braine, 1963c, 1965d), summarized in Table 2-4. Andrew's predicate phrases contained two slots: a predicate head and an optional locative adverbial adjunct following the head. An interesting fact about the grammar is that it contains a distinction between transitive and intransitive, but no verb class as such. Thus, G_{intr} is an undifferentiated intransitive predicator class including English adjectival phrases, past participles, and intransitive verbs (e.g., *hot, okay, off, all wet, broken, come, sit*). The *-ing* ending has not yet developed, and intransitive verbs are not distributionally distinguishable from adjectival predicators or nondescript terms like *okay* or *ready*; even among the transitive predicators (G_{tr}) there were occasional expressions which are not transitive verbs in adult English (e.g., *all done* in *Mama all done toast* 'Mama finished her toast'). In the transitive phrases ($G_{tr} + NP$), the semantic polarity was always that usual in English: the subject *NP* was the agent of the action expressed by the predicator (e.g., *Mama fix egg, Papa wash face, Andrew take the bread*). A parallel semantic polarity also appeared for the other class of transitive terms, prepositions: the *NP* following *in, on, out, under* always indicated the location and not the located item (*on floor, under chair, in Mama room*, etc.).

Also noteworthy are the three position classes of adverbials, D_1, D_2, and D_3. When two or more of these occurred in sentences, they always appeared in the order of the subscripts. Andrew appears to be well on his way towards acquiring the five position classes of adverbials noted by Harwood (1959) in a group of Australian 5-year-olds.

From a diachronic standpoint, it was argued that the development of the main structural features of Andrew's predicate phrases can be explained by positing that he had learned a small number of rather broad distinctions. He was assumed to have begun with an undifferentiated predicate structure similar to Brown and Fraser's subject Eve (although, unlike Eve, some of Andrew's predicate phrases were *NP*s). The main features of the stage described in Table 2-4 then develop as a result of Andrew's gaining control of two distinctions. One is the distinction between transitive phrases ($G_{tr} + NP$ and *Prep + NP*) and intransitive phrases. The other distinction is positional, between the first position, occupied by the predicate phrase head, and the second position, occupied by the adjunct; although any kind of phrase could serve as head, only locative adverbials served as predicate adjuncts. These two distinctions are orthogonal and permit a 2×2 matrix representation of the phrase types that occurred as constituents of predicate phrases (Table 2-5). Thus, it was suggested, as Andrew acquires these two distinctions, the previously undifferentiated predicators are mapped into one or other of the four cells of the matrix, e.g., *Poppa book* develops to *Poppa read book*, *Marty turn* becomes *Marty turn radio*, *Pussycat chair* fills out to *Pussycat on chair*. Andrew's replacement sequences contained many expansions of this sort. After the period summarized, at around 28 months, Andrew developed the *-ing* ending, and a class distinction between verbs and other predicators emerged.

Table 2-5. Constituents of Andrew's Predicate Phrases (25–27 months) Classified on the Basis of a Pair of Orthogonal Oppositions

	Intransitive	Transitive
Occur only as First (Head) Term	go, come, sing, hot, all wet, all broken, off, ready, etc.; NPs	wash face, eat cookie, shut the door, take a nap, fix egg, etc.
Occur First or Second (Loc. Adv.)	inside, there, downstairs, etc.	on the shelf, under couch, in house, etc.

Both in the pivotal construction and in the systems of Eve and Andrew, the linguistic structures are heavily correlated with sentence position. It has been argued (Slobin, 1966a) that inflexibility of word order may be a universal of early child language. However, few children have yet been studied, and Eve and Andrew are probably not representative of the range of individual differences within English, let alone across languages. While the reliance on order may well be common, fragmentary data have been cited (Braine, 1963a, p. 338; 1963c) from a child who passed through a phase in which the order of major constituents appeared to be free. At 24–25 months of age, Gregory appeared to have no contrast between *Truck fix it* and *Fix it truck* 'fix the truck', *Gregory fix it* and *Fix it Gregory* 'I want to fix it myself', *Baby see it* and *See it baby* 'see the baby', *Fall down rabbit* and *Rabbit fall down*, etc.; similarly the orders *Inside + NP* and *NP + inside* did not express different spatial relations (e.g., *Inside Doctor Zipsa* 'Dr. Zipsa is inside his office'). The distinction between subject and object in such expressions developed gradually over a six-week period. Unlike Andrew, Gregory distinguished the verb class (marked by *it* and *-ing*) before he acquired transitive structures. Such differences between child idiolects probably reflect differences in the order of acquisition of features of structure.

[Since this section was written, two papers by Gruber have appeared which are of some importance for early stages of language development. Gruber (1967a) provides an analysis of a child, Mackie, at 26–29 months of age. An interesting property of Mackie's utterances is that they show considerable freedom of order of main sentence constituents in a manner reminiscent of the child, Gregory, cited in the preceding paragraph. Some examples are *It broken, wheels*; *Car, it broken*; *Car, he take the wheel*; *Go away wheels*; *Girl go away*; *Dumptruck all fixed*; *In there baby*; *Pony in there*; *Me catch it*; *Catch me* ('I can catch it'); *Him bad dog*. Gruber argues that the child is using a topic-comment construction, in which a topic *NP* can be appended at either end of a sentence consisting of a predicate phrase. He shows that the morphs *I, he, she, it* which appear frequently in preverbal position behave differently from the case-marked pronouns *him, me*, etc., which behave like *NP*s; he argues that *he* and *it* in *It broken wheels* and *Car, he take the wheel* are really part of the verb phrase and not to be construed as sentence subjects (cf. the use of *il* by the French child discussed in 2.271). The line of analysis is interesting and seems very reasonable for the child studied. Gruber uses his analysis to support a claim that the topic-comment construction is a linguistic universal and innate, and consequently occurs as a precursor of the subject-predicate construction in English. However, the main fact which makes the topic-comment analysis convincing is the freedom of order of major constituents in Mackie's productions, and this does not appear to be a universal stage in child language: apart from Mackie, only one of the children cited so far showed such a stage, and as noted above, constraints on constituent order are common enough for Slobin to have suggested that inflexibility of order may be universal! Conclusions about universals of child language clearly need to be based on much better knowledge of the range of individual differences that can exist.

[Gruber (1967b) is based on ten weeks from a different and younger child, Dory, and argues that her utterances can be divided into two classes, *performatives* and *reportatives*. The reportatives express attributions and seem to have a subject-predicate form (e.g., *Kathleen coming*, *Shoe on floor*, *Teddy allgone*); they are not found until the last week of the ten-week period, when many appear rather suddenly. The performatives are present throughout. Gruber defines a performative rather elusively as "a direct expression of what one is in fact doing by means of the utterance"; it "indicates something," whereas a reportative "talks about something." In Dory's utterances, the performatives comprise two semantic types: in one, the prefix *see* commonly appears, and Dory is indicating something or showing it to her mother; in the other type, Dory is demanding something, and the word *want* is often used. Essentially, Gruber's distinction seems to be one of mood, and early mood-type distinctions have not been analyzed in the work cited so far. His observations indicate that such distinctions need to be further explored (cf. the French child discussed in 2.272).

[Gruber claims that the performative-reportative distinction is a universal and innate. It seems plausible that some mood-type distinctions (e.g., as between indicating something, requesting something, and characterizing something) should be universal: it is hard to see how a social organism could dispense with them. By the same token, there seems little point in claiming them to be "innate."]

2.23. *English: Early NP Development.* Table 2-6 summarizes the *NP* structures of Eve$_1$, Andrew, and a third child, Adam, discussed at three stages of his development by Brown and Bellugi (1964). Brown and Bellugi also studied a fourth child, Eve$_2$, whose *NP* development was like Adam's, although she passed through similar stages of development when about nine months younger than Adam.

Table 2-6. Early Noun Phrase Structures

Eve_1 (25½ months)

NP → (Mod) + N
Mod → a, the, two, human terms
N → bear, bird, . . . , human terms

Andrew (25–27 months)

$$NP \rightarrow \begin{Bmatrix} N_{pro} \\ N_{name} \\ (Mod) + N \end{Bmatrix}$$

N_{pro} → more, this, more this, other (one), some (more)
N_{name} → Andrew, mama, poppa

$$Mod \rightarrow \begin{Bmatrix} a, the \\ N_{pro} \\ N_{name} + (\text{'s}) \end{Bmatrix}$$

N → car, pants, coffee (pot), piece bread, old shoes, . . .

Adam (about 27 months)

NP → (Mod) + N
Mod → a, the, big, little, poor, dirty, my, that, two, more
N → Adam, Becky, boot, coffee, tinker toy, man, . . .

Adam (about 31 months)

NP → (Art) + (Mod) + N
Art → a, the
Mod → my, your, blue, nice, . . .
N → boot, coffee, . . .

Adam (about 33 months)

Five classes of Mod; many plural forms; pronouns substitute for NPs in context.

The simplest system is Adam's first. Most *NPs* were one word long and consisted of a large undifferentiated class of nouns. A small number of modifiers could precede the nouns, and Brown and Bellugi note that the combinations were like the early pivotal constructions, except that the pivot (i.e., the modifier) occurred only before nouns. Eve_1's system was similar to Adam's, except that she had begun to differentiate human terms from ordinary nouns, using them to express the possessive (*Evie car* 'Evie's car'); the differentiation was incomplete since she was still producing *NPs* like *a daddy, two Bobby*, like Adam's early *a Becky*. Andrew's system still has only one productive modifier slot, but there was considerable differentiation within the noun class. Names were not themselves modified (he did not say *a Andrew*), but occurred as possessive modifiers, *-'s* occasionally being expressed; also, pronoun-like forms served not only as modifiers but also alone as *NPs* (*more ∼ more bread, other one ∼ other one pants*). Although isolated English adjective-noun combinations occurred, there was little indication of productive use of adjectives as noun modifiers.

Adam's development appears to have been somewhat different from Andrew's, in that he developed order classes of noun modifiers relatively sooner and differentiation of the noun class relatively later than Andrew.[10] The use of names as possessives is not mentioned by Brown and Bellugi and was presumably absent from Adam's speech in the first two periods in Table 2-6. Such deviant forms as *a your car* and *a my pencil* illustrate his second stage. No grammar was given for Adam at 33 months. Interestingly, in the

---

[10] In their description of Adam at 31 months, Brown and Bellugi include a demonstrative, *that*, as the initial component of the *NP* preceding *Art*. However, they say that sequences of *that + NP* are to be glossed as 'that is a . . .', and they make clear that when the *NP* occurs elsewhere (e.g., in predicative sentences), the demonstrative is not part of the phrase. The *that* is clearly introducer and not part of the *NP*, and I have therefore omitted it in Table 2-6.

course of learning the pronouns, *I* and *it*, at this time, instead of substituting them for the *NP* there was often a reduplication (e.g., *I Adam drive, Mommy get it my ladder*).

Although constituent structure is apparent in the material reviewed in this and the preceding subsection, the early *NP*s owe little to transformations. Since Andrew used English adjectives as predicators he had the possibility of an analogue of the *N is Adj→Adj + N* transformation; however, he did not exploit the possibility. I have also studied children (unpublished data) who, like Adam, used several adjectives productively as noun modifiers, but who did not use adjectives as predicators (or used quite a different set as predicators). It also seems likely that the possessive does not have a transformational origin early in development. It follows that the structure that is first learned for these phrases is the adult English derived phrase structure. That is, the learning of the derived phrase structure precedes the learning of the transformations.

2.24. *English: Transformations.* Investigators (e.g., W. Miller, 1964b) seem to be agreed that the early grammatical structures can be described by phrase structure rules, as exemplified in the data reviewed. Moreover, it seems logically inevitable that phrase structure development should precede the emergence of transformations, since a transformation, by definition, is a mapping of one phrase structure tree into another: a structure must first exist, in order to be mapped into another.

Menyuk (1964a) notes that the fundamentals of English phrase structure, and also many transformations, had apparently been acquired by around the third birthday in a group of bright children she studied. She has also shown that the speech of groups of children 3 to 7 years old shows a generally good fit with adult English rules, phrase structure and transformational, with considerable transformational development over the period (Menyuk, 1963a, 1964a, b, c).[11]

Two studies of transformational development are now available: Bellugi (1964) presents extensive data on the development of negative struc-

[11] However, there are problems in interpreting Menyuk's data. She always assumes that a child's sentence that is identical to an adult sentence has been generated by the same rules as the adult sentence. Clearly, this is often not so. A good example is provided by the passive. In adult speech, passive sentences without agentive phrases are assumed to be generated by deletion of the agent (*Someone broke that→That was broken by someone→That was broken*). Since agentive by-phrases are absent in most young children's speech (W. Miller, 1964b; Harwood, 1959), it follows that their sentences of the form *NP + Aux + Past participle* are not generated by the assumed adult rules; to count them as instances of the passive transformation, as Menyuk apparently does, is misleading. Young children can also generate apparently correct negations and questions by nontransformational means. Similarly, treatment of adjectival and possessive noun modifiers as transformationally derived requires justification. (See text discussion of the development of all these transformations.) It follows that Menyuk's statistics, based on counts of these "transformations," should be viewed with caution. Nevertheless, most workers would agree with Menyuk that the fundamentals of English structure, particularly the constituent structure, have been substantially acquired by the average middle-class child by around his third birthday.

tures for two children, Adam and Eve$_2$[12]; W. Miller (1964b) reports very similar data on five children for negative and interrogative structures, with some additional discussion of other transformations. Actually, the transformations that have been studied are probably not the earliest ones to develop; certainly the major singulary transformations postdate the appearance of the object complement, whose development has yet to be studied (cf. some of the replacement sequences cited in 1.34 and Table 2-1).

A primitive negative first appeared when Adam and Eve were about 30 and 21 months old, respectively. It consisted of adding *no* or *not* to a sentence, the negative usually preceding, occasionally following (e.g., *No play that, No David fun play*). There was no productive question pattern at this stage, apart from a rising intonation.

While this simple negation was still sometimes found in the next stage, about three months later, most negations were made by placing a negating item before the verb phrase. The item was *can't* or *don't* in predicative sentences (*We can't talk, I don't sit on Cromer coffee*), *don't* in imperatives (*Don't leave me*), and *no* or *not* otherwise (*There no squirrels, That no mommy*). The affirmative forms *can* and *do* were not in the children's vocabulary at this time, indicating that the usual transformation was not yet present and that *can't* and *don't* were monomorphemic. A very similar negative formed with a negated modal prefixed to the verb phrase is reported by W. Miller (1964b) for his subjects. At this stage, as in the previous one, the negative seems to be expressed through phrase structure rules. Many of the sentences formed are, of course, indistinguishable from correct English.

In the next two stages of Adam and Eve, beginning some months later, the number of modals increased and the same ones appeared in both affirmative and negative sentences, so-*n't* presumably now had separate morphemic status. Indefinite forms with *some* were at first the same in both types of sentence (*I see something, I didn't see something*); in the fourth stage, a double negative appeared (*he can't have nothing*); the correct forms with *anything* were apparently a very late development. The auxiliary system showed some advances over the second stage. A past tense morpheme appeared in both main verbs and auxiliaries, although *have* was not present as auxiliary, and there was no regular subject-verb agreement (*Cars doesn't get on tracks*); forms of *be* occurred first sporadically in copular sentences (*That not a clown, I am not a doctor*) while absent before *V-ing* (*I not crying*); *be* then became regular in copular sentences and sporadic before *V-ing*. The negatives are presumably produced transformationally during these stages.

W. Miller (1964b) believes that his five subjects began to produce negatives by transformation at an average age of 33 months, range 27 to 37 months.

---

[12] For subsequent analyses of the same data with the addition of a third child, see now Bellugi (1967) and Klima and Bellugi (1966); for a more recent discussion of these children's *wh*-questions, see Brown (1968). These later presentations do not alter the picture of transformational development presented in this section.

He found that the three transformations, negative, inversion in yes-no questions, and verb ellipsis (*It's not blue— Yes it is*), develop in close proximity to each other. At the time each developed, the number of sentences of the type increased sharply. The most frequent pattern was the negative first, then the yes-no question (an average of three months later), and the ellipsis at the same time as the question or shortly afterwards. He notes that the same structural analysis and use of the auxiliary *do* is required by all three and argues reasonably that once the analysis has been made for one, the learning of the others would follow rather rapidly. Miller describes the development of yes-no questions for the one child, Susan, who developed this transformation before the negative. Questions were first signaled only by a rising intonation. Then at 26 months, Susan formed requests by pre-fixing sentences with a modal, usually *could*, less often *can* or *will*. No trans-formation was involved since *could* was not used in affirmative sentences. At 29 months, *could* was used in both kinds of sentences, as well as other modals and some forms of *be* and *do*. At the same time as this development occurred, the unmarked question forms with a rising contour began to be outnumbered by the marked questions with a falling contour. Susan developed the negative and elliptical structures at around 31 months. For another child, mistakes suggesting a pretransformational stage of the ellipsis are cited (e.g., to *I'm Joe*, the reply is *No you don't. You're a Wick*).

Questions beginning with *wh*-words had a very similar history in Adam and in every child studied by Miller. At first, the *wh*-word was placed in front of the sentence without an inversion of subject and verb (*Where it goes?*). In Adam's second stage of negatives, there was an early form in which *why not* was prefixed to a sentence with or without a negation (*Why not he eat? Why not we can't dance?*); *why not* later gave way to *why* (*Why the kitty can't stand up? Why I didn't see something?*). Adam's affirmative *wh*-questions also appeared first without an inversion (*Why I can go?*). I observed a similar stage in my 3-year-old son, e.g., *Where mommy is? What daddy said? Why you won't let me? When mommy is coming home?* In adult English, the *wh*-word is transformationally related to the subject or object noun, or to various adverbial adjuncts of the predicate or of the sentence. The development of these relationships is not clear in the data reviewed, some of the children's forms probably containing such a relationship, and others (e.g., Adam's early forms) probably not. However, the data do indicate that a stage where the subject-auxiliary inversion is lacking is nearly universal. According to Miller, the inversion appeared increasingly after establishment of the same inversion in yes-no questions. Not surprisingly in view of the structural similarities, relative clauses appeared at about the same time as the *wh*-questions (W. Miller, 1964b).

In general for the transformations reviewed, it appears that the child first learns the positions of the auxiliary components independently in each sentence type, often with a different group of auxiliaries for each structure.

As the same auxiliaries develop in each sentence type, he presumably begins to perceive the correspondences between them (*can-can't, will-won't, don't* and the absence of auxiliary in the affirmative, etc.), and the transform relation is acquired. For the *wh*-questions, the data cited provide good evidence for the learning of an inversion rule, or for the carrying over of an inversion rule learned in the yes-no questions. It should be noted that at the time that the transformations are presumably acquired, the auxiliary system is substantially simpler than in the adult language: *have . . . -en* is lacking, forms of *be* do not occur with a modal, and the progressive forms with past participles and adjectives (*be being, be getting*) also appear to be absent. The simple set of structures and their interrelations are shown in Table 2-7. The important developmental point would appear to be that the within-column similarities (i.e., the locations of the various types of auxiliary elements in each sentence type) are learned before the row correspondences.

Table 2-7. Structure of Kernel and Transforms around the Time of Learning of the Transformations

Kernel	Negative	Question	Negative Question
Sj + V	Sj + *don't* + V	*do* + Sj + V	*don't* + Sj + V
Sj + V-*ed*	Sj + *didn't* + V	*did* + Sj + V	*didn't* + Sj + V
Sj + modal + V	Sj + modal*n't* + V	modal + Sj + V	modal*n't* + Sj + V
Sj + (*is*) + Pred	Sj + (*is*) + *not* + Pred	*is* + Si + Pred	*isn't* + Sj + Pred

NOTE: Objects and adjuncts of *V* are omitted. *Sj* = *subject*; *Pred* = *V-ing*, *NP*, or adjectival or adverbial phrase; *is* is replaceable by *was*.

Other transformations have not been directly studied, but indirect information is available for the passive. This had not developed in any of W. Miller's subjects by 42 months when the last texts were collected. Fraser et al.'s (1963) 3-year-olds were generally unable to handle passives in either comprehension or production and even had difficulty imitating them. Mehan (1968) also reports noncomprehension of passives in 3-year-olds. Harwood (1959) found that the passive transformation was extremely rare in his extensive text material on a group of working class Australian children 5 years old. However, both Miller and Harwood report sentences which contain a form of *be* or *get* with a past participle. They note that these cannot be passive transformations if the *by* + Agent phrase does not exist (see footnote 12).

As examples of such pre-passive forms, Miller provides *He said it was locked, That is broken*, and *This is torn*. Menyuk's examples, classified as passives, are *They might get locked up, Mine is painted*, and *He got tied up* (1963b, 1964a). In Harwood's material, the most common participles following *be* are *allowed, broken*, and *finished*; the participles cited by Miller and

Menyuk also occur, and *made, caught, left, killed,* and *done* occur several times each. Harwood suggests that these participles are generated as adjectives. However, according to a traditional definition, an adjective is a predicator that doubles as a noun modifier; most of these forms are not noun modifiers. It follows that, before the passive transform appears, the child already has rules—presumably phrase structure rules—which will generate passive-like predicates with nonadjectival past participle heads. The nature of these rules is suggested by the grammar described for Andrew at 27 months (Table 2-4). As Andrew gets older, the verb auxiliaries will develop, and the class of intransitive predicators (G_{intr}) will split into two parts: (*a*) intransitive verbs and (*b*) adjectives, past participles, and nondescript words like *ready*, a heterogeneous group which share the auxiliary *get*. Thus, the 3-year-old's *He got caught* or *It got left behind* is probably $NP + aux + G_{intr}$, analogous to *He got ready* or *It got hot*.

This account of the pre-passive does not, of course, explain the origin of the *by*-phrase itself. I would speculate that this begins as a general agentive-instrumental adjunct. Between 3 and 4 years of age, my daughter repeatedly used *by* to mark the agent or instrument in active sentences, e.g., *His son died by the war* (reporting the tragedy of a friend), *It already has sand on by Jonathan* (at the beach, complaining that her brother had made her shovel dirty). Adult passive sentences that she has heard seem the most plausible model for a *by*-phrase with this meaning. These observations suggest that rules generating sentences of the form $NP + aux + G_{intr} + agentive\text{-}instru\text{-}mental$ are available before the passive transform is learned. The true passive could then result from learning some sort of correspondence between sentences of the form *Subject + verb + object* and *Subject + G_{intr} + agentive-instrumental*, where G_{intr} is a past participle. After the transform is learned, the sequence *Subject + G_{intr} + agentive-instrumental* would become the derived phrase structure automatically. Thus, for the passive as for the adjective transform (cf. 2.23), the learning of the derived phrase structure probably precedes the learning of the transformation.

Looking at their developmental histories, the transformations considered appear to divide naturally into two types. For one type, exemplified by the negative and the question, what will later be the "deep" structure is at first directly expressed as surface structure; i.e., such sentences have approximately the structure $Neg + S$, and $Q + S$ from the start, the *Neg* and *Q* morphemes being at first directly realized as such in speech. For the second type, exemplified by the adjective and passive, the child appears to learn two partially independent sets of phrase structure rules: one set generates the "kernel"; the other set generates what will ultimately be the transform, and these rules define the derived phrase structure of the transforms, once the transformation is acquired. There is even some evidence (Quirk, 1965; Winter, 1965) that these rules retain some independent generative power after the transformation is learned.

2.25. *Other Languages: Main Sources.* There are good secondary sources only for Russian (Slobin, 1966a, b, c), which is reviewed briefly in 2.26. My rudimentary knowledge of German makes reading the German literature difficult and an insightful review of the problems and accomplishments of the German child impossible. The main sources are Scupin and Scupin (1907), Stern and Stern (1928), Buhler (1934), and for a recent review, Kainz (1960, 1964). Kaper (1959) contains a study of Dutch development. The development of Latvian structure in two children has been described in a monograph in German by Ruke-Dravina (1963). For French, one notes particularly Bloch (1924), Guillaume (1927a, b), Grégoire (1937, 1949, 1950), and Cohen (1952). The major source for grammatical development is Grégoire (1947), on which my review of French development (2.27) is primarily based.

For non-Indo-European languages, Chao (1951) and Burling (1959) provide some information for Mandarin and Garo, respectively. Bar-Adon (1959) is a detailed study of Hebrew verb morphology in Israeli children. The morphophonemic aspects of this work were discussed earlier (2.14). Bar-Adon attempts to treat "children's language" as a single system, a dialect of Hebrew; he deliberately neglects age differences and rarely states whether different forms are contemporaneous or replacements one of another. The result is that although the work provides a wealth of examples of children's analogical creations and structural simplifications, it unfortunately ends up being only somewhat instructive about the developmental process.

Kahane, Kahane, and Saporta (1958) compare text material for French (Grégoire, 1947) and German (Scupin & Scupin, 1907) with English material from Leopold (1939–49) and from a variety of older sources. They proceed by classifying development into two stages, an early stage where a contrast (e.g., of tense, voice, or aspect) is not formally signaled in a child's speech, and a later stage where it is. They interpret such terms as *tense* and *aspect* widely, e.g., under the title *tense* are included such contrasts as *today-yesterday* as well as *throw-throwed*. The work is singularly devoid of discussion which might eliminate potential misunderstandings of what they intend.[13] However, it provides a useful collation of source material.

Most of the work in the foreign literature antedates the concept of a generative grammar, and much of it even antedates early systematizations of the immediate constituent model (e.g., Wells, 1947). Thus, analyses of syntactic development of the kind summarized above for English are not to be found. There is undoubtedly much foreign literature which is not referenced in this section.

---

[13] There are several cases where I fail to understand the basis of their classifications; e.g., the one-word French utterances *Coco* 'Coco hears the sparrows' (p. 14) and *Costume* ([tüm]) 'I've put on my Sunday suit' (p. 16) are taken as indicating control of a transitive-intransitive distinction in which the difference between subject and object is not signaled. How can one prove a contrast with examples in which the relevant distinction is not signaled?

2.26. *Russian: Zhenya's Early Development*. Russian is a highly inflected language in which there is considerable freedom of word order. Data on the development of a Russian child come from a Soviet linguist (Gvozdev, 1949, 1961) who recorded his son's language extensively for the first nine years of his life. Zhenya began combining words at 20 months, and his first combinations appear to have been pivotal constructions. This stage was brief, and already by 22 months, the two-word utterances were outnumbered by longer ones. The first three-word utterance was a negation formed by placing *nyet* before utterances—the same early negative as that found for English by Bellugi (cf. 2.24). The short utterances rapidly filled out, e.g., from subject-object strings (*Mama niska* 'mama book') to subject-object-verb (*Mama niska tsitats* mama book read') to subject-verb-object. Subject-object-verb was apparently the dominant order for a short period, before giving way at about 23 months to subject-verb-object, which is the statistically more frequent order in Russian. Gvozdev accounts for the early order with a theory that the most recently learned forms (e.g., *tsitats* in the above example) tend to be placed at first at the end of utterances. Zhenya developed tense forms later than the infinitive, at first placing these after the infinitive, and he also acquired adjectives and possessives later than nouns, these at first following the nouns (e.g., *pyero tvayo* 'pen your'); in both cases, adult Russian prefers the reverse order. Unfortunately, no analysis of the idiolect as a whole is available for this period, at least in English.

Morphological markers entered at about 23 months. Between 23 and 24 months, nouns became marked for number; the nominative, accusative, and genitive case endings appeared as well as a diminutive suffix, and distinctions between imperative, infinitive, and past and present tenses appeared for verbs. Dative and instrumental cases emerged between 24 and 26 months, the cases developing before the prepositions that govern them (28–30 months). Gender agreement appeared shortly before the third birthday. (These ages refer to the age of first appearance of the categories; the learning of the various allomorphs for each category is a protracted process, discussed in 2.29.)

2.27. *French*. Both Grégoire's children began to combine words in the second half of the second year, the main grammatical development beginning around the second birthday. In 2.271–4, I review some general characteristics of sentence structure, verb development, the development of gender categories and agreement, and some aspects of early negatives and interrogatives.

2.271. It seems apparent from a wealth of examples that the predicative sentence with an optional subject existed from a very early age, as in the American children reviewed earlier. From its inception, this sentence-type occurred in more than one form. The most common form was the ancestor of the adult form in which the order of components is *Pronoun + Predicate +*

Subject, e.g., between 24 and 28 months, *Sale, bébé* 'Baby is dirty',[14] *Parti, un cheval* 'a horse has gone', *Est cassé aussi, bonhomme* 'the man is also broken', *Est fatigué, papa* 'Daddy is tired', *Il fait du potin, Desirée* 'Desiree is yelling', *Il est méchante, la fille* 'She's a bad girl', *Il est dans la cour, les oiseaux* 'the birds are in the yard'. Grégoire observes that the division between predicate and subject is intonationally marked (indicated by the comma in the above examples). The pronoun, *il*, when present, appears to be a kind of introducer rather than a noun substitute: *elle* is rare, and apparent errors of concord with the subject noun are numerous, although the children are acquainted with gender (note *Il est méchante, la fille*, where *la* and *méchante* concord with *fille* but not *il*). In addition to this sentence form, one finds the stylistically more elevated subject-predicate order (e.g., *Bonhomme cassé* 'the man is broken') and also the emphatic sequence *Subject + qui + Predicate* (e.g., *Petit frère qui pleure* 'little brother is crying', *Le sang qui coule* 'blood is flowing'). Grégoire remarks that in the adult colloquial, in which the latter form is common, the relative *qui* is essentially reduced to the status of an emphatic particle and appears to have the same status for the child; true relative pronouns appear only much later.

Sentences parallel to the English ostensive forms with optional introducer also appeared very early. But, unlike English, the introducer may either precede (*c'est, il y a*), or follow (*ça, là*); for several months, one of Grégoire's children used the formulae *NP + ça, NP + là*, in a way exactly equivalent to the American child's *that + NP, there + NP* ('that is a . . .', 'there is a . . .').

2.272. Grégoire's description of verb development is very incomplete from a syntactic point of view. Most of the first verb forms appear in the adult imperative or infinitive form, a fact noted also by Guillaume (1927b), and by Gvozdev (1949, 1961) for Russian, and Bar-Adon (1959) for Hebrew. Grégoire also reports tense forms from around the second birthday. However, he does not discuss the nature and sequence of the syntactic distinctions that develop among imperatives, infinitives, tense forms, and adjectival predicators. Analyzing these syntactic distinctions is crucial for an understanding of the developmental process. For what they are worth, my impressions from Grégoire's material are as follows: there was first an initial stage,

[14] For ease of identification, but with considerable misgivings, I cite the French forms in their conventional spellings, unless the child's pronunciation is of grammatical interest. Grégoire also decided to use the regular spellings much of the time, a decision which seems most unfortunate. The structure of the French written forms, particularly the verb forms, is grossly overdifferentiated with respect to the spoken forms, and their use in studying the language of French children can hardly help but prejudice the analysis. For example (p. 206), to the command [büve] 'buvez' 'drink', the child replies with a refusal [pa büve] 'not drink'. Grégoire's transcription of the child's reply as *pas buver* begs the question—not discussed—whether the child distinguishes imperative and infinitive in this context. Clearly one ought not to use a transcription which imposes such choices as that between *pas buver* and *pas buvez*.

where predicate distinctions were minimal and only one form of a verb was used (or, if more than one form was used, the forms were in free variation). The presence of such an initial stage is confirmed by Guillaume (1927b); the next development involved the imperative and infinitive and arose, probably close to 24 months, from the emergence of a distinction between "requests" and "indicatives," in the requests, the adult imperative and infinitive forms were used noncontrastively (e.g., [ped] *un livre* 'prendre . . . ' 'take a book', [met] *du lait dessus* 'mettre . . . ' 'put milk in it', *Pas* [met] *du lait dessus* 'don't put milk in it', [vəne] *près tante* 'venez . . . ' 'come near Aunty'). In the indicatives, the verb form used was an adult tense form, initially the present tense, with *va + infinitive* appearing around 27 months. Thus, after 27 months, adult infinitive forms were used both in indicatives (after *va*), and in requests (e.g., the utterance *tante va* [nir] 'tante va venir' provides a useful contrast with the request *venez près tante* at the same age, since a wealth of examples suggest that the infinitive could have substituted for *venez* in *venez près tante*, but none that the imperative could have substituted for [nir] in *tante va venir*). At a later stage of development, the requests seem to have become differentiated into true imperatives and into various forms with *devoir*, *pouvoir*, *falloir*, etc. + *infinitive*, which have the double-verb declarative structure. As the requests lose most of the infinitive forms, the primitive request-indicative distinction evolves into the mature imperative-declarative contrast.

Other major developments in predicate syntax were probably similar to those described earlier for English. A transitive-intransitive distinction was clearly present very early, orthogonal to the distinction between requests and indicatives. A distinction between verbs and other predicators presumably also occurred early; here Grégoire notes that participles like *parti* 'all gone' and *cassé* 'broken' belong in the same class as adjective predicators. Future tense forms became productive around 30 months, later than *va + infinitive*. Past tense forms became frequent shortly after the future developed, although examples of the imperfect were rare. The conditional developed late in Grégoire's children, as it did in Zhenya Gvozdev, and in the Stern's German child (Stern & Stern, 1928).

2.273. The learning of gender categories is of special interest as it represents an arbitrary classification of nouns of a kind which does not exist in English. Noun gender is signaled in French in the articles, in adjectival forms which concord with the noun, and in pronouns which substitute for it. Grégoire reports that already by the second birthday there was some sensitivity to gender, and his records contain impressively few mistakes due to ignorance of the gender category of a noun.

Despite its frequent omission in the child's speech, the major cue to gender is apparently the article. Grégoire suggests that it serves as a sort of prefix, sometimes masculine, sometimes feminine, and in fact, most of the few examples of mistakes in gender occurred in words beginning with vowels, where the gender is not marked in the definite article.[15] Gender errors in the adjective (e.g., *beau madame* [24 months], *un* [bel] *monsieur* [25 months], *petit-sotte neige* 'silly little snow') appear to have been somewhat more common than in the article, but it is difficult to know how many of them reflected ignorance of noun gender and how many were errors of other sorts (e.g., *petit-sot* may be monomorphemic and would then be correctly inflected in *petit-sotte neige*). The frequent and persistent errors apparently relating to gender occurred in the pronoun, and here the errors clearly had not to do with gender per se but were due either to a misinterpretation of the pronoun as an introducer (*Il est méchante, la fille*, and other examples above) or to a failure to analyze a complex form ([wetel], *marteau* 'ou est-elle, le marteau?' 'Where's the hammer?'—see the discussion of questions below).

Mastery of a gender distinction must include three things: (*a*) learning the existence of the category, i.e., in French, that all nouns have a gender; (*b*) learning the distribution of the gender morpheme in utterances; and (*c*) learning the various allomorphs by which gender is manifest in different circumstances. Grégoire's data bear mainly on (*b*): they indicate that the distribution of the gender morpheme is learned in stages—an initial stage where it occurs only in the article and adjective, and a later stage, following a fuller command of sentence syntax, where it occurs also in pronouns.

Just what first leads the child to the existence of the category is unclear. A natural hypothesis might be that he is first made aware of grammatical gender by the correlation of the contrasts *le-la, un-une, petit-petite*, etc., with the genuine sex distinctions in such words as *garçon, fille, homme, femme*, etc.; once having noted the existence of the contrast, he then notices that nouns in general go with one or the other set. However, although there is some indirect evidence outside Grégoire's material that genuinely sexed words do play a privileged role in the learning of gender categories,[16] there is little supporting evidence in his material. This indicates only that from

---

[15] Grégoire provides a long list of examples of the French child's difficulty in identifying the initial phoneme of these words and of his tendency to supply them with an initial consonant, usually the [l] of the article, sometimes [n] from *un* or *une*, occasionally a consonant taken from an adjective ending (e.g., [lə lo] 'the water', which contains both the agglutination and a gender error; [ləœf ~ lənœf ~ lətœf] 'the egg').

[16] The indirect evidence is of two kinds. First, gender distinctions sometimes appear first in connection with genuinely sexed objects; for example, in an Israeli child whose development I recently followed, a gender distinction in some verbs in the adult imperative form was present almost contemporaneously with the first word combinations (e.g., in *tire* and *tiri* 'see', *ten li* and *tni li* 'give me', *bo* and *boi* 'come', the first form was regularly used in addressing males and the second for females). Second—and this is very indirect evidence indeed—Ervin (1962) has shown that, in Italian, words without inherent sex nevertheless carry the sexual connotations of their gender class. She also provides a number of examples which suggest that this conclusion holds for other languages. Her observations might be expected if natural sex played a major role in the original learning of the class distinction.

a very early age, learning a noun entailed learning its gender class, and the arbitrary nature of the gender distinction was hardly a problem at all.

2.274. Negative and question transforms seem to go through pretransformational stages in French as in English. In negatives, Grégoire's children tended to use *pas* alone as the negating element. Until about 30 months, *pas* usually preceded either the sentence as a whole or the predicator, e.g., *Pas papa s'en va . . . Papa pas s'en va* 'Papa is not to go away'. Grégoire (1947) says "*pas* devance [la phrase] a la façon d'un signe algébrique qui l'annule [p. 169]." Intonation was used to signal questions from around the second birthday. Formal signals appeared first in the form of unanalyzed prefixes to sentences: locatives appeared first (e.g., [wetel] 'où est-elle' especially, but also [wiskill] 'où est-ce qu'il' and [weti] 'où est-il') with such forms as [esti] 'est-ce qu'il' and [kɛ] (a reduction of *qu'est-ce que*) occurring later. The subject-verb inversion was a late development. That the prefixing signals were single morphemes is suggested by the lack of concord with the sentence subject (e.g., [wetel] lot lom] 'où est-elle, l'autre homme?' [weti] *les . . . 'où est-il+ plural NP'*, [esti] *va venir, tante* 'is Aunty coming?').

2.28. *Order of Development of Various Grammatical Categories.* As in phonology, the predominant order of development is from broad to fine distinctions. This general trend has been noted often (e.g., Braine, 1965d; Menyuk, 1964b; Slobin, 1966a). An undifferentiated lexicon is the first stage. NPs and nouns separate off very early, whether or not they are always the first class to be distinguished. The data reviewed have shown how predicate structure develops as a series of syntactic distinctions are imposed. The successive subdivision of a generalized class of noun modifiers into articles, adjectives, possessives, etc., was described earlier for American subjects (2.23), and a similar subdivision is reported by Gvozdev for his son. Distinctions among articles and quantifiers have been discussed by Carroll (1939). The learning of noun subclass distinctions can continue into fairly late childhood. For example, in the distinction between count and mass nouns, the count noun is the original category and adult mass nouns are assimilated to it for some time; words like *water* and *toast* are used where the adult would say *glass of water* and *piece of toast*, and phrases like *a cereal* and *many toasts* (or their Russian equivalents) occur. While some grasp of the mass noun exists in 3- and 4-year-olds (Brown, 1957), Gvozdev reports that the distinction did not become stable until Zhenya was 8, and Brown and Berko's (1960a) 5- to 8-year-old American subjects assimilated nonsense words only moderately well when the words were introduced as mass nouns, although they had no difficulty when the words were introduced as count nouns. It may be that the learning of the count-mass distinction passes through an intermediate stage where there is no *class* distinction as such, but where the child does understand the semantic significance of pluralization and of the omission of the indefinite article (i.e., at this stage, *water* alone refers to the liquid, but *a water* and *waters* refer to glassfuls of it—cf. the adult contrast between *beer*, the liquid, and *a beer*, a glassful). (See 2.32 for further discussion of the count-mass distinction in nouns.)

There has been a good deal of Russian work on factors affecting the order of development of categories. The main line of thought (Gvozdev, 1949, 1961; Feofanov, 1958) appears to be that the order reflects the difficulty of the concepts typically expressed by the categories more than the variety or formal complexity of the grammatical devices signaling them. Categories of more concrete reference develop before those expressing more abstract or relational ideas and before those that are semantically arbitrary. Thus, Gvozdev notes that the conditional develops relatively late, although its structure is very simple. Feofanov finds that prepositions indicating spatial relations are not at first used figuratively and develop earlier than prepositions indicating relations of time or purpose. Bogoyavlenskii (1957) reports that among the Russian derivational noun suffixes, the diminutive and augmentative develop before the agentive. Although the phonological markers are clear, the learning of the gender distinctions is extremely pro-tracted, presumably because of their semantic arbitrariness. (However, the French data reviewed seem to indicate that semantic arbitrariness is not inevitably an obstacle to learning; and I am not sure just what the nature of the Russian child's difficulties with gender is.) Factors affecting the time of development of categories have been little discussed in the literature on English.

In discussions of the first morpheme combinations, much has been written on the question whether syntactical relations always develop earlier than morphological ones. For English, as Leopold (1939–49) noted and as is clear in the data reviewed, many syntactical relations are controlled before any inflexions develop. For Russian, which has a rich morphology, Gvozdev has also argued that syntax precedes morphology. On the other hand, from experience with Garo, Burling (1959) argues that morphology and syntax develop together in languages where inflexion is used to express major grammatical categories.

The claim that syntax always precedes morphology appears to be either false, or trivially true, depending on how it is interpreted. In one view, the claim seems to be that the morphemes in the early morpheme combinations must be words of the adult language. However, this is not always the case. In another view, what is claimed appears to be that the acquisition of categories precedes the acquisition of the inflexional and derivational morphs expressing them. This claim would appear to be necessarily true: before the child can learn, say, that the instrumental case is sometimes expressed by *-om* and sometimes by other suffixes, he must learn that the category *instru-mental case* exists. If the acquisition of the category is assigned to "syntax," then obviously syntax precedes morphology; one must learn that a distinc-tion exists before one can learn how to express it in particular circumstances.

2.29. *Learning Allomorphs of Inflexional Morphemes*. There is hardly a book or article on language development which does not contain examples of errors in which one allomorph of an inflexional or derivational morpheme is substituted for another. Such errors are extremely common, and in languages with a rich morphology, they can persist until adolescence (Gvozdev, 1949, 1961; Bar-Adon, 1959). Although relatively few studies have followed in detail the succession of changes in the same child, these few studies have been extremely revealing about the developmental process.

Based on longitudinal testing of a group of 24 children, Ervin (1964) has described the development of the English noun plural inflexion. The inflexion has two main allomorphs: /ɨz/ following nouns ending in the stridents /s/, /z/, /š/, /ž/, /č/, and /ǰ/ (*match-matches*, etc.); and /z/ following other nouns (the /z/ being automatically devoiced to /s/ following unvoiced stops, according to general English phonological rules). The /z/ allomorph developed first (see also Berko [1958]), and the devoicing following unvoiced stops was automatic from the beginning. The allomorph appeared first in familiar words, and then after an interval of a few weeks, it generalized to newly introduced nonsense words (e.g., *bik-biks*, *kie-kies*); words already ending in stridents in the singular were not inflected, although occasional backformed singulars appeared (e.g., *bok-boks* for *box*, *bun-buns* for the nonsense word introduced as *bunge*).[17] Some time after the above system was established, the /ɨz/ allomorph made its appearance. At this point the previously well-established plurals quite often underwent changes: when inflexions like *box-boxes* or *tass-tasses* first appeared, Ervin found that such plurals as *foot-footses*, *hand-handses* (or *foot-footiz*, *bik-bikiz*) temporarily replaced or completed with the preexisting *foot-foots*, *hand-hands*, *bik-biks*. This period of free variation of the allomorphs (/z/ and /ɨz/, or /z/ and /zɨz/) lasted less than two months, giving way to the adult system of conditioned variation.

The developmental sequence may be summarized as follows: first, appearance of an allomorph—not necessarily the predominant allomorph— in familiar words; second, productivity of the predominant allomorph; third, appearance of a second allomorph which replaces or varies freely with the previous one; finally, conditioned variation of the allomorphs. Wherever successive changes in an inflexion have been followed in the same child, an essentially similar developmental sequence has appeared, with minor differences reflecting the phenomena of the adult language. In the case of the English past tense morpheme, the standard language contains a host of nonproductive special forms alongside the two main allomorphs (/d/ and /ɨd/, with selection conditions analogous to the noun plural morpheme); most of the common verbs form their past tense irregularly. Here, the first stage observed in Ervin's text materials was the stage at which the /d/ allo-

[17] Ervin comments that the phonological contrasts among terminal /s/, /z/, /š/, /ž/, /č/, and /ǰ/ are often not established at this age.

morph was productive (*buyed, comed, doed*, etc.). The period of competition between the main allomorphs was attested, and after the selection conditions for these had been learned, there was a long time stretch during which the regular and irregular allomorphs for particular verbs went through a period of free variation (i.e., *did, broke*, etc., competed with *doed, breaked* prior to replacing them). The development of French inflexions has been less thoroughly studied, but the phenomena are clearly very similar to those for English and for Russian.

For Russian, the developmental sequence described has been independently reported several times in studies antedating the English work (e.g., Gvozdev, 1949, 1961; Popova, 1958; Zakharova, 1958). For example, in the learning of the instrumental case, the suffix *-om* appears first and is added to all nouns, although it is confined to masculine and neuter nouns in the adult language. When *-oi*, the feminine singular instrumental ending appears, it generalizes and may temporarily replace *-om* in masculine and neuter nouns; the endings compete before the conditions of usage of each are established. In studying the development of gender agreement between subject nouns and past tense verbs between 22 and 42 months, Popova found that the younger children overgeneralized the feminine ending *-a*; in somewhat older subjects, the masculine zero ending predominated, with a period of free variation apparently preceding the acquisition of the conditioned variation.

It seems clear to common sense that the developmental sequence described results from step-by-step learning of the allomorphs and of their conditions of usage. It is of interest that this learning sequence bears some similarity to the behavior observed in studies of the learning of "paired associates" in experimental psychology. Learning an inflexion and learning a set of paired associates both involve the acquisition of a mapping: for an inflexion, the mapping is of a set of allomorphs on a set of lexical items; in paired-associate experiments, subjects have to learn a mapping of a set of "responses" on a set of "stimuli." It is well known (Underwood & Schultz, 1960) that in learning a set of paired associates, a subject learns two things relatively independently: (*a*) what the response items are and (*b*) which responses go with which stimuli. Errors indicating knowledge of a response item but a lack of knowledge of which stimulus it belongs with are frequent and are obviously analogous to such errors as *footiz* by children. Indeed, for the experimental psychologist used to seeing simple mappings learned in a few minutes in the laboratory, the child's learning of the allomorphs of an inflexional morpheme provides an interesting slow-motion example of the acquisition of a large many-one paired-associate mapping.

2.3. Semantics and Metalinguistic Insight

2.31. *Lexicon.* Many writers on child language (e.g., Lewis, 1951) have noted that children are very often unclear about the range of reference of the first lexical items they acquire. For example, at first *Daddy* tends to refer to men in general, *door* may refer to anything that opens or closes, including a saucepan lid, *up* may include both 'up' and 'down', and *hot* both 'hot' and 'cold'. Apart from such observations, and from vocabulary counts (see McCarthy, 1954), there has been relatively little work on lexical development, and no systematic body of knowledge exists. As Carroll (1964b) remarks, it is difficult and by no means desirable to separate the acquisition of lexical items from the study of concept formation in general. Concept formation is far too large a subject for review here. Unfortunately, work on concept formation has not yet developed in such a way that it throws much light on lexical development, and only a few studies (e.g., Braun-Lamesch, 1962; Carroll & Casagrande, 1958; Ervin & Foster, 1960; Esper, 1933; Werner & Kaplan, 1950, 1952) have been more than very indirectly concerned with the subject. A view from the standpoint of a developmentally oriented school of Gestalt psychology is presented by Werner and Kaplan (1963). There has been much peda-gogically oriented Russian work on factors affecting the very early learning of vocabulary (e.g., Kol'tsova [Razran, 1961] and several studies abstracted by Slobin [1966b]; see also Slobin [1966a] for a discussion of this work). The child's developing ability to use words for purposes of self-control has been discussed by Luria (1959, 1961), but this and much related work on "verbal mediation" in children is outside the scope of this review.

2.32. *Semantic Correlates of Grammatical Categories.* Work on the develop-ment of the rules by which sentences are interpreted has been handicapped by the undeveloped state of semantics as an area of study within linguistics, so that the student of development has had little concept of the range and kind of phenomena whose development should be studied. Most of the little work on the development of semantic structure has been concerned with the seman-tic correlates of grammatical classes and has been primarily oriented towards finding an explanation for the learning of the classes. This work has suffered from lack of knowledge of how semantic and syntactic rules are integrated in natural languages. It has not been clear whether one should expect seman-tic and grammatical structure to be conceptually independent acquisitions (i.e., the grammatical structures acquired on some basis different from the basis on which the rules for interpreting them are acquired), or whether one can hope to find in the learning of their semantic correlates the basis, or a partial basis, for the learning of grammatical structures.

It is apparent that regular semantic correlates exist for many early con-structions, e.g., possessive noun modifiers in *NP*s, locative adverbials, etc. There often appears to be a close connection between the learning of a semantic correlate and the acquisition of a category. Thus, when a productive -*s* morpheme appears on nouns in text materials, it regularly indicates plurality. Gvozdev says that lexical and grammatical expressions of an idea tend to appear at the same time; e.g., Zhenya developed the Russian word for 'much, many' at the same time as the plural morpheme, and the words for 'right away' and 'soon' contemporaneously with the future tense. Where knowledge of the semantic correlate is necessary for acquisition of a category, the time of acquisition should be related to the conceptual difficulty of the correlate. This idea has been developed by Gvozdev, and his evidence was reviewed in 2.28.

The most frequently discussed semantic correlates of categories are the "thingness" of nouns and the "action" character of verbs. Brown (1957) has shown that nouns designate thinglike entities and verbs actions much more frequently in children's vocabularies than in adults'. In an experiment, he also showed that 3- and 4-year-olds are aware of semantic correlates of count nouns, mass nouns, and verbs. The subjects were presented with pictures showing an action performed on a substance in relation to an object (e.g., hands kneading a confetti-like material spilling from a container). A nonsense word introduced as a verb (*Do you know what it means to sib? In this picture you can see sibbing. Show me another picture of sibbing.*) was overwhelmingly identified as indicating the action; introduced as a count noun (*Do you know what a sib is?*), the nonsense word was identified with the object and introduced as a mass noun (*Have you ever seen any sib?*) with the substance. Similar results have been reported by Kean and Yamamoto (1965). Brown argued that, given that the semantic correlates exist and that the children know them, it is likely that they play a central role in the establishment of the classes. Similarly, Jenkins and Palermo (1964) speculate that "the 'thingness' of nouns is recognized and responded to as the implicit characteristic of the class; the 'activeness' of verbs is similarly important [p. 165]." I shall use the term *semantic-correlate theory* to refer to this kind of theory, in which a class is seen to originate from the association of the words of the class with a particular kind of entity (things, actions, etc.).

In Brown's experiment just described, two of the contexts that are used to introduce the verb (*see sibbing, . . . of sibbing*) actually introduce it as a derived noun. Thus, it could be argued that Brown was primarily concerned with the correlates of three subclasses of nouns: count nouns, mass nouns, and verbal nouns of structure *V-ing*. While Brown's data support the idea that semantic correlates of these subclasses may provide the basis for the child's learning of the subclass distinctions, his data provide no evidence that some property "thingness" is the basis on which the noun class itself is first distinguished. To the contrary, his data point up the variety of entities designated by nouns in the 4-year-old. To bear directly on the origin of the noun and verb classes, data nearer the time of acquisition are required.

Since the literature contains no data for children younger than Brown's subjects, I shall summarize some observations of my own. At 21–23 months of age, I introduced my daughter Naomi to two nonsense words, *niss* and *seb*, which I used only as isolated words in order to avoid giving her any linguistic cues to their part-of-speech status. *Niss* named an object, a kitchen utensil she was allowed to play with: I simply said the word and pointed to the object. *Seb* accompanied the action of making my fingers walk (they usually ended up tickling her). Both words were rapidly taken up into her speech. *Niss* appeared in *More niss* (asking for it), *Boomboom niss* 'the niss fell', and *This niss* 'this is a niss'. These contexts suggest that she made *niss* a noun. *Seb* appeared in two kinds of utterances. In one kind, she used it as a transitive predicator: *Seb Naomi* (she is soliciting the action), *Seb Teddy* (immediately followed by *Do Teddy*), *Seb Jonathan*, and *Daddy seb Teddy* 'Daddy should seb Teddy'. However, in two other utterances she appeared to use *seb* as a noun: *More seb* and *Bit more seb* (she is soliciting the action). This apparent double usage of action words (i.e., as nouns and as predicators) is neatly confirmed by a further observation. At 26 months, Naomi, whose knowledge of Hebrew was very slight, picked up the Hebrew word *nafal*. (In Hebrew, this word is the third person masculine singular past tense form of the verb meaning 'to fall': *hu nafal* 'he fell'.) Once, after falling down, she reported *Naomi nafal* and then continued *Nafal didn't hurt*. In the first utterance *nafal* is predicator; in the second it is clearly the subject noun.

While such observations need to be supported by much more data, they argue against the idea that "thingness" is the implicit characteristic of the noun class around the time this first develops; rather, they suggest that even at the very beginning the entities designated by nouns may be quite varied and may include actions like falling and tickling. I would suggest that the statistical finding that nouns more often designate things in young children's speech than in adults' is probably due to the child's intellectual immaturity: many of the abstractions and other nonconcrete entities to which nouns often refer in adult speech are beyond him intellectually. It is important to note in this connection that rejecting the "thingness" theory of the origin of the *NP* does not require one also to reject a semantic-correlate theory of the origin of the noun subclasses when these appear. It could very well be that *NPs* designate a variety of entities at all stages of development and that the learning of the specific differences between names, count nouns, mass nouns, etc. (e.g., in the ways these are quantified and modified) is in some sense a consequence of the child's perceiving differences in the kinds of entities designated. Such a view would be consistent with all the data reviewed. Quine (1960, Ch. 3) provides a logician's discussion of the distinctions a child has to master. However, it remains to be shown that perception of the ontological distinctions is prior to the learning of the grammatical distinctions rather than vice versa.

Conceivably, the origin of the *NP* lies in a semantic correlate other than "thingness." For example, Quine has argued that the pronoun is the natural language analogue of the variable of quantificational logic and that nouns are really pro-pronouns, as it were. This notion suggests that the origin of the *NP* is to be sought in the development of the logical functions of the quantifier and variable.

Now let us consider in more detail the development of predicate structure and the proposal that "activeness" is the original basis of the verb class. First, it should be noted that a wide variety of terms can serve as predicators when this category first develops (2.22), so that a theory that the early predicators designate a particular kind of entity would be hard to maintain. As with *NP*s, the province of this sort of semantic-correlate theory must be the development of the subdivisions. While the verb is one of the predicate subcategories, the data indicate that a good deal of predicate structure can develop before the verb becomes a well-defined class. Thus, regardless of whether or not the proposal that verbs begin as action words is correct,[18] it would not explain more important structural features of early predicate phrases, notably the head-adjunct position distinction and the transitive-intransitive distinction.

Diver (1964) provides a possible model for the semantic oppositions between subject, object, and indirect object which may be relevant to the learning of the transitive-intransitive distinction. While I am not clear how far Diver's analysis may be generalized to English, it does seem apparent in systems like Andrew's (2.22) that the transitive predicator expresses an asymmetric dyadic relation with a directional polarity, the subject *NP* being agent. Moreover, the prepositions express relations with the same logical properties (asymmetric and dyadic) but differ in content, expressing a spatial relation rather than an action with an agent-nonagent polarity. By contrast, the intransitive verbs and adjectives seem to express monadic properties without the subject *NP* being in any consistent agentive relation to the predicator (cf. Diver, 1964). A possible interpretation of the developmental data might be that at an early stage of his learning of the sense of a lexical item, the child perceives whether it expresses a monadic property or a dyadic (or triadic) relation; he learns the polarity of the relation (agent-nonagent or spatial) and the correspondence of this polarity with the subject and object positions surrounding the lexical item expressing the relation. If further work should confirm that the transitive-intransitive distinction tends to emerge simultaneously in verbal and locative phrases, this would support the idea that the child is sensitive to the formal property of asymmetry and dyadicness.

2.33. *The Child's Awareness of Structure.* What evidence there is indicates that children tend not to have insight into grammatical structure, e.g., not into diminutive and augmentative suffixes, although they use them (Bogoyavlenskii, 1957), nor into compound nouns (Berko, 1958). More surprisingly, children also apparently lack awareness of the word as a unit. Karpova

---

[18] The fact that words representing actions may serve as nouns does not disprove this proposal, since words can belong to more than one class. To disprove the proposal, one would have to show that the child will use as verbs words which do not represent actions and which he has not heard used as verbs.

(1955) first trained young children, using pictures and isolated words, to count items and report which was first, second, etc. When the children were later presented with sentences, they tended to report them as containing two parts, the subject and the predicate. If they reported more parts, concrete nouns were most often individuated, function words least often, and verbs and adjectives to an intermediate degree. American children $4\frac{1}{2}$ to 5 years old also seem to have some difficulty in segmenting short sentences into words (Huttenlocher, 1963).

2.4. Some Issues

This section reviews work bearing on several specific questions which arise from the data reviewed. More general theoretical issues are left until Section 3.

2.41. Reception vs. Production: Does the Child Use a More Complete Grammar in Comprehending Utterances Than Is Manifest in the Utterances He Constructs? While children frequently understand utterances which are more complicated than they usually produce, it has often been pointed out that such understanding tells little about the child's command of grammar. It cannot automatically be assumed that the young child who runs to get his coat when told *It's time to go out for a walk* will grasp the grammatical rules used in generating this sentence, since he might have responded the same way to the single word *walk*, or even to *Today we won't be going for a walk*. However, Chomsky (1964b) and Lees (1964) have argued that a child typically commands a much fuller grammar than is evident in his speech and that this fuller grammar is actively involved in comprehension. If valid, this claim would have important consequences. It would mean that studies based on verbal output are misleading in that they must understate real grammatical competence. It would follow that competence actually develops even faster than the data reviewed so far would indicate, perhaps much faster. Such a result would add support to the innate view of language development, since, if the rules are largely built in, one could expect extraordinary speed of development. Methodologically, the claim would indicate that grammatical development should primarily be approached from the receptive side.

At first sight, this claim appears to be at variance with the compelling arguments from adult speech that the same grammatical rules are involved in encoding and decoding sentences (Chomsky, 1957, 1961). It is made consistent by assuming that in the child some structure is eliminated after the internal computation of a sentence and before the arrival of the nerve impulses at the speech organs. One proposal is that unstressed syllables get erased, thus eliminating articles, prepositions, auxiliaries, etc. from the output. Thus, Chomsky and Lees are led to the concept of a "latent system" that is supressed in actual speech.

Before the evidence for such latent systems is considered, two preliminary points need to be made. First, elements like prepositions, articles, and auxiliaries typically pass through a stage where they are sometimes used and sometimes omitted. During this stage, a grammar based on analysis of a child's productions will have to include rules for generating these elements, even though the rules may be stated as optional; such a grammar will, of course, provide a basis for comprehension of sentences containing these elements. Thus, a demonstration that a child usually understands elements which he often omits in his speech is not evidence for a nontrivial advance of comprehension over production: a sporadically present system is manifest, not latent.

Second, the term *manifest in speech* is somewhat ambiguous: it could mean "obvious to casual inspection," or it could mean "inferrable from analysis." These are far from equivalent. For a brief illustration of the difference, consider the following example from the morphophonology of Chao's child, Canta. Chao (1951) reports, "The perfective particle *.le* . . . had been acquired for some time with the phonetic substitution *.ie*, but recently she was dissatisfied with the palatal articulation and so changed it to *.de*, which is dental enough, like *.le*, though not so good with respect to manner of articulation. But it continues to be *.ie* after words ending in *-i* [reference to Chao's vocabulary list indicates that it is still sometimes *.ie* after other endings], *.ue* after words ending in *-u*, and *.ne* after nasal endings. Thus, *yai.ie* [from] *lai.le* 'has come'; *hao.ue* [from] *hao.le* 'all right now'; *neen.ne* [from] *leeng.le* '(I'm) getting old' [pp. 37–38]."[19] To casual inspection, syllable-initial Mandarin /l/ is not manifest in Canta's speech at all. However, one has only to ask what Canta has learned about the consonant in *.le* to realize that this cannot be equated with either /d/, /n/, /w/, or /y/ and that its properties are probably those of a dental continuant with some similarity to /y/.[20] Analysis reveals that something resembling Mandarin /l/ is manifest in Canta's speech after all. The purpose of this example is to show that inferences to nonobvious structures can readily be made from the output itself and to suggest that the degree to which a structure is "manifest in

---

[19] If I understand Chao's transcription, *u*, *w*, and the *-o* of *hao* represent the same phoneme in these citations, and *y* represents the same phoneme as *i*. I shall call them /w/ and /y/.

[20] The reasoning is as follows. Let /X/ be the reflex in Canta's speech of the *l* Mandarin *.le*. Now /X/ ≠ /d/ because /X/ is sometimes realized as [y] and reference to Chao's vocabulary list indicates that Canta's reflex of Mandarin *d-* is never realized as [y]; moreover, Canta's /d/ assimilates to preceding *-n* only, not to *-i* or *-u*. Similarly, /X/ ≠ /n/, because Canta's reflex of *-n* is not realized as [d]. Similarly, /X/ ≠ /w/. Finally, /X/ ≠ /y/ because, although [y] is a frequent rendering of Mandarin *l*, her reflex of Mandarin *y-* or *i-* is never [d], but always [y] when not subject to assimilation.

The currently predominant [d] realization of /X/ suggests that /X/ is dental; the [y] realization and the assimilation to preceding *-i* or *-u* suggest that /X/ is not a stop and shares some additional feature with /y/. Thus, an underlying form with features close to those of Mandarin /l/ is required in order to account for the varied realizations of /X/ and the assimilations to which it is subject.

speech" may depend on the care with which the output has been investigated. Given the difficulty of studying the development of grammar through receptive functions, it would be unfortunate if the claim that studies of production must underestimate competence were accepted merely because of an underestimate of the information to be had from studies of production.

Chomsky presents two arguments that the child "knows" grammatical rules for which there is no evidence in his speech. The first concerns the auxiliary verb system. The argument was that there was evidence of a rather abrupt shift from speech completely free of auxiliaries to speech manifesting the full system: "Some of the data of Brown and Fraser [1963] seem to suggest that interrogatives, negatives, and other syntactically related forms appear and are distinguished from declaratives at approximately the same time, for some children. If so, this suggests that what has actually happened is that the hitherto latent system of auxiliaries is now no longer suppressed in actual speech, as previously [Chomsky, 1964b, p. 39; see also the further discussion on p. 40]." It is hard for me to see that any data in Brown and Fraser's article are pertinent.[21] The data on the development of the auxiliaries reviewed (2.24) indicate that, over a period of several months, the auxiliaries develop gradually and independently in declaratives, negatives, and questions, and only after this separate development do these constructions become a transformationally integrated system. There is no sudden transition from no auxiliaries to the full system.

Chomsky's other argument concerns a possible latent system in phonological development. He argues (1964b): "It is striking that advances are generally 'across the board.' A child who does not produce initial $s + consonant$ clusters may begin to produce them all, at approximately the same time, thus distinguishing for the first time between *cool* and *school*, etc.—but characteristically will do this in just the right words, indicating that the correct phonemic representation of these words was present to the mind even at the stage where it did not appear in speech [p. 39]." W. W. Gage drew my attention some years ago to this phenomenon which he observed in his own child; he also provided the following analysis, which I have since verified in two children. Before clusters of $/s/ + stop consonant$ developed, the children had contrasts between initial aspirated and unaspirated stops: [pʰ] [tʰ] [kʰ] in

---

[21] However, Lees (1964, p. 94) bases an argument concerning the specific auxiliary *do* on some of Brown and Fraser's data on imitations of simple sentences by six children between 2 and 3 years old. Lees notes first that in attempting to repeat *I do not want an apple*, the low-stressed auxiliary *do* was reproduced by all subjects. (This was actually a miscounting: the real figure was five out of the six subjects. Also, Lees fails to note two other sentences containing *do* as auxiliary, *Do I like to read books?* and *Where does it go?*, in each of which only two of the six children reproduced *do*.) Lees then notes that in imitating *I will not do that again*, only four subjects reproduced *do* although it was a main verb and stressed. Lees concludes, "Clearly, the child at this age may be understanding the use of auxiliaries very well, but not using them very well." Given that the data have to do with imitation (correct imitation does not guarantee comprehension), that the numbers are small, and in any case not predominantly in the direction claimed, it is hard to find any basis for the conclusion.

such words as *pit*, *pea*, *tear*, *toy*, *cup*, *cat*, contrasted with [p] [t] [k] in *spit*, *spill*, *stair*, *stand*, *school*, *sky*. (If the child controlled the voiced-unvoiced distinction, there were then three rows of stops: [b] *bit* vs. [pʰ] *pit* vs. [p] *spit*, etc.) When /s/ developed, [sp] [st] [sk] naturally replaced [p] [t] [k] in words which had previously had these as their initial consonant. Thus, a distinction between *pit* and *spit*, *cool* and *school* is already present before the advent of clusters with /s/, and therefore does not represent a distinction present in the mind but unrealized in speech. (In my subjects, it was reasonable to phonemicize initial unaspirated [p] [t] [k] as /hp/, /ht/, /hk/; the development described by Chomsky then reduces to a simple replacement /h/ > /s/ before stops.)

There have been several studies of receptive functions in recent years. Sokhin (1959) tested the understanding of Russian locative prepositions by 43 children 23 to 41 months old, by requiring them to follow the Russian equivalents of such instructions as *Put the ring on (under) the block*. Both objects were movable so the child could make a reversal error, i.e., put the block on the ring rather than the ring on the block. (Note that for a sentence like "Put the ring on the table," a reversal error is impossible since the child can't put the table on the ring, and so a correct response would be uninformative.) Eleven of the youngest children, ages 23–28 months, had difficulty in understanding the instructions at all; 18 children, ages 26–36 months, grasped that one object had to be put on (or under) another, but often made reversal errors; the remaining 14 children, ages 26–41 months, were able to follow the instructions. Feofanov (1958) has noted that the locatives are among the first prepositions to appear in Russian (as in English), and Gvozdev's son Zhenya (Gvozdev, 1949, 1961) had the use of eight different prepositions by 30 months. Simple English locatives were used without anomalies (apart from sporadic omission) by this age in the five children I have studied. Sokhin's finding of widespread errors in comprehension in many children nearly 3 years old is surprising and certainly does not indicate an advance of comprehension over production.

Fraser et al. (1963) tried to compare comprehension and production directly. They investigated the 3-year-old's command of ten grammatical distinctions (e.g., mass noun vs. count noun, tense distinctions, singular-plural, subject-object for both active and passive voice). To investigate the singular-plural distinction in the verb, the child was shown a pair of pictures: in one called *The sheep are jumping*, two sheep were jumping over a barrier; in the other called *The sheep is jumping*, one sheep was shown jumping over the barrier while the other stood to one side. Similar pairs of pictures were drawn for each of the grammatical constructions. To test comprehension, each sentence was spoken in turn and the subject was asked to point to the appropriate picture. To test production, the subject was first told the names of the pictures (but not which name went with which picture), and then each picture was indicated in turn and the subject was asked what it was called.

In addition to the tests of comprehension and production, a test of imitation was included: here no pictures were used, the child being asked only to repeat the sentences.

The results were that the children made more correct responses on the comprehension than on the production test, and imitation was superior to both. Although the comprehension scores were clearly inflated somewhat owing to the greater likelihood of guessing correctly on the comprehension than on the production test, the authors show that comprehension was somewhat superior to production even when random choices are allowed for. However, a striking feature of Fraser et al.'s results is the low overall level of the scores. For example, on the test for the distinction between subject and object in active sentences (e.g., *The train bumps the car* vs. *The car bumps the train*), only two thirds of the responses of these 3-year-olds were correct for comprehension and half for production. In my experience and in the data reviewed, this distinction is almost universally controlled in the free speech of normal middle-class children well before 3 years of age. For most of the constructions, the children seem to have been making errors several months after their age would suggest that the constructions were present in their free speech. The reason for the late errors is unclear. One possible explanation is that the technique requiring matching of sentences and pictures is too difficult for young children, and Mehan (1968) suggests that acting out sentences or obeying commands might yield fewer errors. Another possibility—a very speculative one—is that reversal errors are due to the character of the comprehension process. In understanding a sentence like *The car bumps the train*, perhaps the child is forced to consider both possibilities, the car bumping the train and the train bumping the car, before arriving at the meaning. (This is certainly true in the test situation where pictures of both actions are presented.) However, in producing such a sentence in free speech (though not in Fraser et al.'s test of production), he would presumably begin by seeing the car bump the train, and the opposite idea need never enter his mind during the sentence-construction process. Reversal errors of this kind have not been reported in the free speech of children. In any case, this study provides no evidence that grammatical competence will be underestimated if it is inferred from a child's utterances.

Although careful tests of comprehension seem difficult to conduct much below 3 years of age, an ingenious approach to grammar from the receptive side in much younger children (15 to 30 months) has recently been explored by Shipley, Smith, and Gleitman (1967). Their 96 verbal stimuli contained already familiar nouns naming toys, a noun being presented either alone or in various kinds of verbal context. Thus, the child might be presented the single word *horn*; or the "telegraphic" utterance *blow horn*; or a parallel control string with a nonsense word substituting for *blow*, e.g., *quirk horn*; or the full command *blow on the horn*; or control strings parallel to the latter with nonsense words substituting for the verb, the function words, or both, e.g., *quirk on the horn, blow slubba horn, quirk slubba horn*. The main response observed was whether the child made a relevant response, such as picking up the toy named from a group of toys. The 13 subjects were classified into three groups, mature, intermediate, and immature, on the basis of the median length of their utterances in a sample of 100 utterances of free speech. For the immature group, the data suggested that any context at all made the recognition of known words more difficult: they made a relevant response more consistently to the isolated word and to the childlike two-word tele-graph-style strings than to the full well-formed command. This result is important, since it provides evidence from the receptive side for a stage of telegraphic speech. In the intermediate and mature group, a relevant response occurred somewhat more consistently to the well-formed command than to the childlike forms. Since the utterances of these children were also telegraphic (though longer than those of the immature group), the authors take this result as tentatively confirming the Chomsky-Lees claim that children's linguistic competence will be underestimated when inferred from spontaneous speech. However, this conclusion logically requires that the children's spontaneous utterances be investigated more thoroughly than they were: the utterance samples contained only 100 utterances, and the analysis of them was apparently limited to counting words. Moreover, an appendix containing the little data available on the children's free speech indicates that at least some auxiliary verbs, pronouns, and articles were present in the mature group and in several children of the intermediate group; one can therefore infer from their output that these children's competence encompassed rules generating these items. The authors present no evidence suggesting that stronger inferences can be made from their reception data; they do not even discuss the issue.

In summary, the data reviewed seem to indicate rather conclusively that there is no large difference between sentence reception and production, inso-far as the control of grammar is concerned. The possibility of a small difference in favor of reception is still open, but it is clearly going to be difficult to demonstrate.

2.42. *The Basis of Telegraphic Speech.* Brown and his co-workers (Brown & Fraser, 1963; Brown & Bellugi, 1964) have stressed that young children's utterances tend to be similar to adult sentences, except for the omission of morphemes. The term *telegraphic speech* is presumably borrowed from the literature on agrammatism in aphasia. The morphemes that tend to be omit-ted are inflexions and other function morphemes, usually unstressed in adult speech. This reduction of adult sentences occurs in both imitations and spontaneous speech. Three main explanations have been offered for tele-graphic speech.

First, Brown and Bellugi (1964) suggest that differential stress is probably the major factor determining the omissions; other factors they suggest are morpheme position in the adult sentence (terminal morphemes tend to be retained), and the fact that the lexical items retained are often well practiced as single-word utterances. Such factors are plausible where the child is attempting to imitate an immediately preceding adult sentence (e.g., he may not have heard clearly the words with weak or tertiary stress). However, to explain omission in children's spontaneous speech along these lines leads to the idea that the child's early sentences are imperfect memorizations of adult sentences. Although this line of thought was developed by Brown and Fraser (1963), they expressed doubts about its validity, and the arguments against it seem overwhelming. Thus, texts from the earliest stage of development contain numerous examples of utterances which could hardly be incorrectly memorized adult sentences (Gvozdev, 1949, 1961; Braine, 1963b), e.g., *allgone lettuce*, *more high* 'there's more up there', *more car* 'drive around some more', etc. (Braine, 1963b). Brown and Fraser themselves note that the patterned nature of the texts would require an explanation of why the child is so selective in what he picks to memorize. Past the stage of pivotal constructions, the child clearly commands thousands (at least) of different utterances, and it is hardly conceivable that more than a fraction of these could be directly memorized, even imperfectly.

A second explanation has it that the omissions are due to *erase* rules which eliminate unstressed syllables during *print-out* (i.e., utterances are assumed to be generated much as an adult generates them, but certain components are eliminated at or prior to the arrival of the nerve impulses at the speech organs). The basis for this line of thought has been considered at length and rejected (1.36 and especially 2.41). In addition, it might be noted that stressed as well as unstressed words are quite often omitted (e.g., many of the utterances cited at various times in this review).

A third explanation (Braine, 1965d) for the omission of elements present in adult speech is that the child learns the most fundamental syntactic distinctions (e.g., between subject and predicate, between primary and adjunct predicate positions, between transitive and intransitive predicators) before he has learned some of the more detailed rules for expanding the components of the major syntactic positions. The higher nodes of the phrase structure are acquired before the intermediate and some of the lower nodes. Thus, sentences like *Pussycat chair* 'the cat is on the chair', *Momma more toast* 'Momma wants some more toast' reflect a command of the subject-predicate structure of sentences, but not of the internal structure of predicate phrases; sentences like *Pussycat on chair*, *Momma fix egg* 'Momma is fixing an egg' reflect more command over the internal structure of predicate phrases, but little command of the phrase structure nodes controlling auxiliary verbs and articles. This explanation is consistent with the data reviewed and reflects a psychologically simple and very natural view of development, namely, that development consists in the successive mastery of linguistic distinctions. As noted earlier (2.28), several writers have observed that the order of acquisition tends to be from general features to detail; however, it has not been generally realized that this fact itself provides a sufficient explanation of the phenomenon of telegraphic speech.

2.43. *Imitation, Expansion, and Practice as Stimuli to Development.* The common idea that language is learned through imitation has been shared by few serious students of language learning. As noted several times, even the earliest tests contain many utterances which are clearly not imitations of adult sentences. Actually, it is not altogether clear what goes into a child's imitation of a model sentence. Young children's imitations are often defective (e.g., Brown & Fraser, 1963). However, Menyuk (1963b) found that at around their third birthday, children who were offered a slightly defective sentence as a model often rectified the anomaly in their imitation. At least in part, such imitations must be the result of a reconstruction of the model sentence as it was understood. On the other hand, Fraser et al. (1963) found that in a controlled testing situation, imitation, at the same age, is more accurate than either comprehension or production. This result indicates that to some extent the child can imitate sentences whose structure he does not understand (or misunderstands), a fact for which Fraser et al. found direct evidence in some imitations in the testing situation. An imitation is thus not only a grammatical reconstruction.

Attempts to copy adult utterances are frequent in children's spontaneous speech. If spontaneous imitation were an important factor in grammatical development, then it would be expected that utterances which immediately echo adult models should be more advanced grammatically than those which do not. Sentence length is a crude measure of grammatical development, and it has been found (Brown & Fraser, 1963; Brown & Bellugi, 1964) that imitations and freely generated utterances are of about the same length. The authors suggest that the length (which, of course, increases with age) reflects an upper limit on some kind of immediate memory or programming span in the child's information processing system. A more delicate comparison of imitations and freely generated utterances has been reported by Ervin-Tripp (Ervin, 1964). She found that imitations were not grammatically more advanced; they could be generated by the same grammars as the freely generated utterances. She concludes that overt imitation cannot be a major factor in the development of grammar. Just what function children's many spontaneous imitations perform is unclear. Some performance models of sentence recognition assume that the recognition process consists of an internal reconstruction of a sentence matching the input sentence (e.g., Miller & Chomsky, 1963). Perhaps the child's spontaneous imitations are an externalization of his attempts to match the input signal, in order to recognize and understand it.

Not only do children imitate adult speech, but adults also imitate children's. Where the child's imitation frequently omits material, the adult's adds material; i.e., adults often respond to a child's utterance by expanding it to the nearest properly formed English sentence appropriate to the situational context (Brown & Bellugi, 1964). Thus to *Eve lunch*, the mother responds *Eve is having lunch*; to *Mommy eggnog*, *Mommy had her eggnog*; to *Throw Daddy*, *Throw it to Daddy*, etc. Brown and Bellugi report that the mothers of their two subjects responded with such expansions about 30 percent of the time. They raise the question whether such expansions are a necessary or contributing factor in the learning of grammar, pointing out that such expansions might be expected to be an effective tutorial technique since they confirm a child's utterances, and at the same time, provide him with contextually appropriate models slightly more advanced than his own utterances. Brown and Bellugi suggest experiments contrasting the effects of expansion training and of simple exposure to English on the rate of development of grammatical structure in children. An experiment of this sort has since been done in their laboratory and did *not* provide evidence for an effect of expansion training on rate of grammar acquisition (Cazden, 1965).

Slobin (1968) has taken the discussion of the role of imitation and expansion one step further. He points out that after an adult has expanded a child's utterance, the child often repeats the utterance again, presumably imitating the adult. Thus, one finds many interactions like: Child: "Pick 'mato." Adult: "Picking tomatoes up?" Child: "Pick 'mato up." Slobin shows that in these interactions the child's repetition is usually more advanced than his original utterance. Since they are grammatically progressive, Slobin suggests that these particular imitations contribute to grammatical development, although they are certainly not necessary to it. However, the role played by the adult utterances in these interchanges is uncertain; e.g., perhaps the child might have expanded *Pick 'mato* to *Pick 'mato up* even if the adult had stayed silent or had merely injected a "What?" Repetitions without an interpolated adult utterance are frequent in tapes of young children; they are the replacement sequences discussed earlier (1.34 and Tables 2-1 and 2-2), and typically in such sequences, the repetition is grammatically more advanced than the original utterance.

In general, the discussions of Slobin, Bellugi (1967), and Cazden seem to suggest that, at any given stage of development, there is probably some optimal level of richness in the verbal environment which would maximize grammatical progress. Imitations and expansions are part of a matrix of interactions in which child and adult understand each other more or less and which partially control the complexity and variety of the input to the child.

Weir's (1962) description of the pre-sleep monologues of her $2\frac{1}{2}$-year-old son contains a number of instances of apparently playful practice with grammatical structure. Anthony substituted one item for another in sentence frames, held an *NP* head constant and alternated modifiers, held the modifier constant and changed the head, changed present into past, etc. In his introduction to Weir's book, G. A. Miller notes that such play is quite common in young children and speculates that it may play a role in grammar acquisition by bringing constructions that the child already commands up to a level of complete automaticity. Regardless of whether or not it plays a direct role in grammar acquisition, this phenomenon is revealing about the child's motivation: he obviously finds linguistic structure sufficiently interesting to play with.

2.44. *Is a Motor System Necessary for Language Learning?* Lenneberg (1962) has reported a case of an 8-year-old boy with severe congenital anarthria who, although unable to speak because he cannot articulate, had little or no difficulty in language comprehension and thus obviously had acquired a substantial command of English structure. The existence of such cases would seem to invalidate all theories which assume that some form of overt motor speech activity is necessary for the learning of any aspect of language other than the motor programming of the speech organs themselves.

2.45. *Kind of Grammar: Finite State vs. More Complex Forms.* The early grammars appear to be systems of phrase structure rules. As argued above (2.24), it seems logically inevitable as well as factually true that transformations are acquired only after essential features of the phrase structure base have been learned.

A finite state grammar is a phrase structure grammar which contains only rules of the form $A \rightarrow bC$ or $A \rightarrow b$ (as opposed to rules of the form $A \rightarrow BC$, which are presupposed in immediate constituent analysis, as well as to other forms, e.g., $A \rightarrow bCd$; see footnote 1 for the convention governing the use of capital and lower-case letters in these formulae). The question has been raised whether the first grammars are not finite state systems, evolving only later into grammars manifesting an hierarchical organization of constituents.

The data reviewed indicate that children are not confined to rules of the forms $A \rightarrow bC$ and $A \rightarrow b$, even at the very beginning. To show this, it suffices to rewrite the simplest general statement of the pivotal construction (i.e., the forms X, P_1X, XP_2 as discussed in 2.21), using only rules of the form $A \rightarrow bC$ and $A \rightarrow b$. Thus, let $p_1, p_2, \ldots p_m$ be the pivot-words occurring in initial position, $p_{m+1}, p_{m+2}, \ldots p_{m+n}$ the pivot-words in final position, and $x_1, x_2, \ldots$ the members of the open class. The structures X and P_1X are reasonably generated by the rules $S \rightarrow X$, p_1X, p_2X, $\ldots p_mX$, and $X \rightarrow x_1, x_2,$ $\ldots$. A natural way to generate the XP_2 forms would be to add the rules $S \rightarrow Xp_{m+1}$, Xp_{m+2}, $\ldots$, Xp_{m+n}, which are the mirror image of the rules generating the P_1X forms. However, these rules go beyond a finite state system (because a finite state grammar cannot contain both rules of the form $A \rightarrow bC$ and $A \rightarrow Cb$, but only one of these types). To generate the XP_2 forms while staying within the bounds of a finite state system, the grammar would have to be extravagant of storage space and relist all the members of the open class a second time, e.g., $S \rightarrow x_1P_2$, x_2P_2, x_3P_2, $\ldots$, and $P_2 \rightarrow p_{m+1}, p_{m+2}, \ldots$,

p_{m+n}. It would be fantastic to imagine that the child actually does store his lexicon twice over in this way. Moreover, he clearly does not: e.g., if *see* is a first-position pivot and *there* is a final-position pivot, analyses of text materials from this stage (Braine, 1963b) imply that a new lexical item which first appears in the context *see* (____) will be available in the context (____) *there*. There would be no reason to expect such general availability if the items which follow *see* and precede *there* were listed independently. It follows that the pivotal construction is not a system of finite state rules and that children's competence is, from the first, not limited to rules of the forms $A \rightarrow bC$ and $A \rightarrow b$.[22]

Hierarchical structure is, of course, impossible so long as utterances are only two words long. It is clear from the data reviewed, however, that hierarchical organization emerges with the longer utterances. Apart from the playful exploitation of very simple recursions (*round and round and round and* . . . , or *very very very very* . . .), recursive rules appear to be absent from the early grammars. Thus, the early grammars go beyond a finite state system in the types of rules they contain, but not in the sets of sentences they generate.

3. THEORY OF CHILD LANGUAGE ACQUISITION

First, various claims are reviewed concerning the existence of special capacities for language acquisition in the human species, particularly the young of the species. Then, in 3.2 and 3.3 the problem of constructing a model of the acquisition of language is considered. The standpoint of the generative grammar school is discussed in 3.2, and in 3.3, I review work which originates within a traditional psychological frame of reference.

3.1. The Question of Innate Language Capacities

Three general claims have been made about the existence and distribution of special innate capacities for language. First, it is said that these are specific to Homo sapiens. Second, it has been argued that human language aptitudes are to a great extent independent of the processes and capacities that serve human intelligence. Third, it has been claimed that the innate language learning capacity is age-specific in humans. While all these claims have a long history, they have recently been brought back into prominence because of their congruence with generative grammar theory which posits that as part of his biological heritage, the language learner is innately endowed

---

[22] There are cases of children who do not develop second-position pivots, and their systems can therefore be expressed naturally as finite state grammars (e.g., a child discussed by W. Miller [1964a]). However, such cases do not affect the general conclusion about children's competence.

with exceedingly complex special capacities which equip him to acquire linguistic structure. In recent years, the evidence and arguments supporting the first two claims have been cogently stated in a series of publications (Lenneberg, 1961, 1962, 1964a, b, c, 1967; Lenneberg, Nichols, & Rosenberger, 1964).

3.11. *Species-Specificity.* The general notion that the species-specificity of language is rooted in some distinctive property of the human information-processing apparatus is so obviously plausible on its face that Lenneberg's many arguments on the subject will not be repeated here. An additional point is the fact that children born to deaf parents who use the sign language of the deaf apparently begin to pick up the sign language at about the same age that hearing children born to normal parents begin to talk. [23] This argues that the human language learning facility is not specific to the oral-auditory channel, and conversely, it suggests that the lack of language in higher mammals other than man may not reflect only a specific phonetic or aural lack.

Because of the total absence of a linguistic system in other mammals, comparative studies have proved vague about what is distinctive in man linguistically. For a comparative study to throw light on the species differences, it must provide some guide to which aspects of language give rise to the animal's difficulties: i.e., to be worthwhile, an attempt to teach an animal to speak must achieve some result beyond a total failure to teach anything linguistically interesting. Although past efforts (Hayes, 1951; Hayes & Hayes, 1951; cf. also Kellogg & Kellogg, 1933) indicate that this will be difficult, interesting results may be achieved in a proposed study with chimpanzees (Premack & Schwartz, 1966), in which an unusual combination of linguistic sophistication and Skinnerian animal training skills are being brought to bear on the problem. An attempt to teach the sign language of the deaf to a chimpanzee is also underway (Gardner & Gardner, 1968) and has apparently succeeded in teaching a vocabulary of a few dozen signs. This is more than any previous study has achieved, and it will be interesting to see how far the animal acquires rules for combining signs. In other recent work, macaques learned, with difficulty, to make a family of visual patterns whose combinatorial structure is describable by an exceedingly simple grammar (Hill, 1967).

3.12. *Relation to Intelligence.* The notion that human linguistic abilities are relatively independent of general intellectual capacity has considerable support. Children acquire language at an age when their intellect is quite undeveloped, and a well-developed linguistic system is consistent with rather severe mental retardation (Lenneberg, Nichols, & Rosenberger, 1964).

[23].Personal communication from staff at Gallaudet College, Washington, D.C.

Lenneberg (1964b, c, 1967) also cites the clinical condition of nanocephalic dwarfism where language develops normally, despite a brain about one third the normal size and a much reduced number of brain cells. Work with deaf children suggests that a considerable degree of conceptual development can occur despite poor language (Furth, 1964; however, Furth's position is controversial [Blank, 1965]; see also Oleron, 1957). The thesis that language and conceptual skills develop relatively independently during the early years has been argued by Vygotsky (1962) and Luria (1961). There is also an extensive literature concerned with the degree of dissociation between and among language and conceptual skills following brain injury. The extent of the independence of language and other cognitive skills and the nature of the interaction between them during development are complicated questions beyond the scope of this review.

3.13. *Age-Specificity of Human Language-Learning Capacities.* Now we consider the claim that, among human beings, it is particularly preadolescent children who are specially equipped for language learning; that the learning processes available to children become unavailable at some age, so that adolescents and adults must use other processes in acquiring new languages. This notion represents a common lay view and has been casually advanced as a self-evident truth on a number of occasions by generative grammarians (e.g., Bever, Fodor, & Weksel, 1965a; see also discussions of papers in Bellugi & Brown, 1964); however, I know of no reasoned discussion of the supporting evidence in the literature.[24] The total evidence for an age-specific ability seems to be contained in two observations:

a. Children who acquire a second language normally learn to speak it without an accent, whereas an adult normally retains an accent long after he has reached fluency. While this difference may indicate some special facility at the phonological level, it provides no evidence that the facility extends to the acquisition of syntactic or semantic structure or of vocabulary. It is not even known whether the child's phonological facility has a receptive component (e.g., an ability to identify sounds of the new language at lower signal-to-noise ratios than the fluent adult with an accent).

b. Some adults spend long periods in foreign countries without picking up the language. As evidence for special capacities in children, this particular observation seems worthless. An adult whose source of income does not depend on knowledge of the new language and who lives in a subculture where his native language is known need not be motivated to learn. Similarly, I know of cases of American children abroad who have gone to English-

[24] It is well known that the knowledge of one language may interfere with the acquisition of parts of the structure of a second language. Such interference effects occur at all ages (see Leopold [1954] for some examples in a child). Interference would be expected on the general ground that all new learning tends to be affected by past learning. Thus, interference effects of this sort have nothing to do with the theoretical issue here, which concerns the existence of a supposed *genetically* based ability which *disappears* (or diminishes).

speaking schools and played with English-speaking peers and who have lived for years without acquiring the language of the country in which they were living. The child who is sent to the local school or nursery in a foreign country is subject to what must be very effective conditions for language learning: massive exposure to the language is combined with overwhelming pressure to learn. There is no evidence that an adult receiving concentrated exposure of this sort over a long period may fail to learn.

In comparing child and adult achievements in language learning, it is important to remember that the natural standard of attainment—ability to communicate with peers—is systematically biased in favor of the child. While the native 4-year-old speaker may have mastered most of the grammar, he has mastered only a fraction of the lexicon of his language. Moreover, the part of the lexicon that he lacks is the more abstract part that is subject to unpredictable vagaries of usage and nuances of meaning. For an adult to be able to communicate with his peers without serious impoverishment of the content of his discourse, he has to command much of this huge abstract lexicon. Any adult who has mastered a second language will recall that his lasting difficulties lay much more with the lexicon than with the grammar. Thus, if one were to assume equal average facility for language learning at all ages, then the learning time required to meet the criterion of ability to communicate with peers would be expected to vary with age: the younger the learner, the less there is to learn.

Some indirect information on age as a factor in language acquisition is provided by statistics, derived from Israeli censuses, on the spread of Hebrew among different age groups in the various waves of immigrants to Israel (Bachi, 1956, especially Table 8; State of Israel, 1963, 1966). Detailed discussion of the statistics would take too much space. However, from the 1961 census figures for immigrants between 1948 and 1954, it is worth noting that among the 87,000 males in the 30–44 age group (i.e., who were young adults, age 17–37, at the time of immigration), 73 percent were using Hebrew as their main or only language in 1961, 21 percent used Hebrew as a secondary everyday language, and Hebrew was not in daily use in only 6 percent. In general, the statistics indicate that both preadolescent and young adult immigrants tend to use Hebrew as an everyday language within a few years of arriving. As compared with younger groups, Hebrew tends to be used less by middle-aged immigrants and substantially less by elderly immigrants (e.g., among the 1948–54 immigrants, it was a language in daily use for only about 35 percent of males over 65 in 1961). Whether the drop in use indicates a decrease in learning ability in advanced adulthood or decreased motivation or opportunity cannot be assessed. In any case, if there is a decline in language learning ability with age, it looks as if it is probably a slow decline associated with middle and old age, not with adolescence.

I know of only one experiment comparing children and adults. Asher and Price (1967) gave the same controlled exposure to a little Russian, to

8-, 10-, and 14-year-old children, and to college students. In three short sessions over a four-day period, the subjects heard Russian commands uttered on tape and learned the meanings of the commands just by watching an adult model obey them. Half of each age group simply watched the model act out the command; the other half copied the model's acting out of the command. There was no other teaching of Russian of any sort. In the retention tests that came later, the subjects were tested by seeing if they could act out Russian commands without the adult model. The Russian material consisted initially of one-word commands like *Sit, Walk, Squat,* then of combinations like *Run to the table, Put down the book,* and ended with instructions like *Pick up the paper and the pencil and put them on the chair.* Several of the tests used combinations of words which were not identical to those used in the training. The results were that the adults obtained nearly perfect scores on all tests; they were superior to all the children, doing about twice as well as the 8-year-olds, with the intermediate age groups in between.

It is important to distinguish the question whether children have special abilities for language learning from the question whether children and adults typically learn second languages in the same way. There are obvious reasons why adults should, in part, learn differently from children. The adult can rarely afford the time the child spends, and the educated adult has resources available, in the form of written materials and formal instruction in the language, which increase the efficiency of learning. However, illiterate adults learn new languages when they have to;[25] they presumably face essentially the same task that children do, that of discovering the structure of the language on the basis of spoken text materials. There is no evidence that they solve this task in a substantially different way than do children.

3.2. The Standpoint of Generative Grammar

3.21. *The Form of a Theory of Grammar Acquisition.* The problem of constructing an "acquisition model" for language has been considered by G. A. Miller (1964), Chomsky and Miller (1963), Katz (1966), and in somewhat more detail, by Chomsky (1965) and McNeill (1966). Most of

---

[25] A substantial fraction of the 1948–54 immigrants to Israel from Afro-Asian communities, particularly the women, were illiterate. The Israeli data cited earlier indicate that illiterates tend to use Hebrew less than other immigrant groups. Nevertheless, a great deal of language learning has occurred among the illiterate groups.

Since the illiterate tends to pick up the language only casually whereas the educated adult can pick it up both casually and through more direct study, one would have to expect illiteracy to be associated with slower acquisition. Speed of acquisition may also be adversely affected by factors connected with the status of women in communities where only the men tend to be literate.

Chomsky's papers contain at least some passing discussion of the subject. It is argued that a language learning automaton built to simulate the achievement of the child would have to have the following characteristics:

a. A specification of the possible form of a human grammar would have to be built into the automaton. That is, it is argued that tacit knowledge of the universal properties of natural languages is innate so that the child "approaches the data with the presumption that they are drawn from a language of a certain antecedently well-defined type, his problem being to determine which of the (humanly) possible languages is that of the community in which he is placed [Chomsky, 1965, p. 27]." Chomsky and Miller argue that language learning would be impossible unless advance specification of the range of possibilities was available to the learner. Moreover, human languages are not infinitely diverse, and their communalities presumably reflect the nature of the human faculties involved in language learning.

b. The automaton would have to have a procedure which would generate and test grammars of the form specified above. The procedure would treat these grammars as hypotheses about the language to be learned and test them against the input data. The child-automaton "would seek a grammar that enumerated all the sentences and none of the nonsentences and assigned structural descriptions in such a way that nonrepetitions would differ at appropriate points [Chomsky & Miller, 1963, p. 277]." The procedure would embody heuristic principles which would lead to rapid selection of promising alternative grammars to be evaluated or which would permit evaluation of certain characteristics of the grammars before others, so as to enable a rapid convergence on a set of grammars compatible with the input data. Chomsky (1965) assumes that there will always be several (probably infinitely many) "humanly possible" grammars compatible with the input data. He therefore posits that there is also built into the child a method of evaluating the various grammars compatible with the input data in such a way that the "simplest" of these is selected as the correct grammar of the language. The full sense of the term *simplest* is to be determined gradually, as work progresses (Chomsky, 1965, pp. 37–47). Thus, as Katz (1966) summarizes it, language acquisition is

. . . a process of implicit theory construction similar in character to theory construction in science but without the explicit intellectual operations of the latter. . . . The child formulates hypotheses about the rules of the linguistic description of the language whose sentences he is hearing, derives predictions from such hypotheses about the linguistic structure of sentences he will hear in the future, checks these predictions against the new sentences he encounters, eliminates those hypotheses that are contrary to the evidence, and evaluates those that are not eliminated by a simplicity principle which selects the simplest as the best hypothesis concerning the rules underlying the sentences he has heard and will hear. This process of hypothesis construction, verification, and evaluation repeats itself until the child matures past the point where the language acquisition device operates [p. 275].

c. To permit the above procedure to operate, the learner must have certain phonetic capacities for representing sentences he hears; he must also have a way of representing structural descriptions of sentences, and a method of determining what structural description a given hypothetical grammar assigns to any particular sentence received.

Chomsky and Miller also consider the input to the acquisition model. The input must obviously include a finite set of speech segments which are taken to be well-formed sentences of the language. Of course, the learner also has access to a universe of perceptual objects and events along with the sentences. According to G. A. Miller (1964), the input information includes a set of nonsentences whose ill-formedness is indicated to the learner; this negative information may be given in the form of corrections of the child's own utterances or otherwise. Saporta (1965) also argues that the input includes information about what is not grammatical. Chomsky (1965) does not appear to be completely convinced that this kind of information is available to the learner. The question whether or not the learner uses information about ill-formedness is important because, as discussed below, the answer constrains the assumptions that can be made about the structure of the learner and the nature of the learning process.

In addition to the above inputs, G. A. Miller (1964) and Chomsky and Miller (1963) assume that the learner is given indications when one item is a repetition, elaboration, or transformation of another. Chomsky (1965, pp. 31–33) also discusses the possibility that information about the situational context of sentences may provide a partial pairing of signals with structural descriptions that is, in some sense, taken as given by the learner.

3.22. *Discussion.* It is difficult to discuss the nativistic claims in detail because Chomsky and his colleagues do not make clear precisely what they mean by the term *innate*. While it seems plausible that many universals of language should reflect universal characteristics of language learners that are not learned (in any usual sense of the term *learned*), nevertheless such characteristics must have a developmental history that will need to be discovered and explained: it is not credible that they should be directly present in the genes, as the word *innate* is often taken to imply.

The aspect of the theory that most requires discussion, it seems to me, is not its nativistic character, but rather the proposal that learning proceeds by generating hypothetical grammars and testing them against the input data. Certain difficulties face a model in which learning proceeds by setting up and testing hypotheses, guesses, or predictions (Braine, 1967).[26] These difficulties apply regardless of whether the hypotheses are innately given or

---

[26] The terms *hypothesis* and *hypothesis-testing* are sometimes used much more broadly in circumstances where they do not imply a process of making and testing guesses or evaluating predictions derived from hypotheses. This is the case, for instance, in a recent proposal of Kelley (1967), discussed later.

not. The difficulties arise from the fact that, logically, the input to such a model must have certain properties, if the model is to operate efficiently. First, the input must not be misleading, i.e., it should contain very few ungrammatical strings which masquerade as grammatical: to test a prediction, what is to be predicted must be clearly identified. Second, the input must contain information about negative instances, i.e., about what kinds of strings are not sentences. Let us consider why negative instances are necessary. Grammars can be wrong in two ways: they may fail to generate some of the good sentences of the language, or they may generate strings that are not good sentences. Grammars which fail to generate some of the good sentences will presumably fail to generate some of the sentences in the learner's sample of good sentences and can thus be invalidated. However, grammars which err only because they generate strings which are not good sentences will necessarily generate all the good sentences to which the learner is exposed. How can the learner discover that such grammars are wrong unless his input data contains negative instances?

Note that, if G is the "correct" grammar of a language, then by judicious elimination of detail in G, it is possible to construct a set of grammars which generate all the sentences that G generates, but which also generate other strings classed by G as ungrammatical. For example, if G is a context-sensitive grammar, and G' is the context-free grammar obtained by suppressing the contexts in G's context-sensitive rules (i.e., each rule $\phi A\psi \rightarrow \phi\alpha\psi$ in G becomes $A \rightarrow \alpha$ in G'), then G' will typically generate all the sentences of G, will assign them the same structural descriptions that G assigns, and will also generate other sentences which are classed by G as ungrammatical. Note, moreover that G' will be simpler than G by any natural criterion of simplicity, so that a simplicity measure would presumably prefer G' over G. The most extreme grammar of this sort would be the grammar which declares that the words of the language can be strung together in random order. It is hard to see how a learner who learns by testing hypothetical grammars against his input could find out that G is the correct grammar unless he were furnished with a copious set of negative instances. As a concrete example, let G be English grammar, and let G' be the same as G. except that G' drops certain restrictions on the co-occurrence of the preposition *to* after the verbs *let* and *allow*. Thus where G has *let George do it* and *allow George to do it*, G' also permits *let George to do it* and *allow George do it*: in G', *to* and its absence are in free variation after *let* and *allow*. (Both grammars have free variation after *help*, cf. *help George do it* and *help George to do it*.) Unless he were told the nonoccurring forms, how could an hypothesis-testing learner reject G' which is confirmed by every sentence he hears; indeed, why should he ever get to consider G as a possibility?

There is little in the literature to suggest either that young children are typically given much information about what is not a sentence, or that they are able to profit from such information if they are given it. Expansions are a form of correction, and their ineffectiveness was noted earlier (2.43). Those corrections which do seem to occur with reasonable frequency have to do with rather trivial rules, e.g., special allomorphs of already acquired morphemes (*bought* for *buyed*, etc.), and presuppose a child whose grammatical development is well advanced. Moreover, the universality with which language is acquired at much the same age despite large cultural variations in child-rearing practices (Lenneberg, 1967) makes it hardly conceivable that corrections should be a necessary condition for learning, since the care with which adults correct children's speech must be assumed to vary widely, both within and among cultures.

As noted above, Chomsky and Miller assume that the child receives information indicating that one item is a repetition, elaboration, or transformation of another item and that he may in addition be provided with a partial pairing of signals with structural descriptions. Although such inputs would obviously be helpful to the learner, it is not clear that they could remove the need for information about negative instances, insofar as the learning process is one of testing hypothetical grammars. Chomsky (1965) has himself pointed out the degenerate nature of the input to the child, noting that much of the actual speech to which he is exposed consists of fragments of sentences and deviant utterances of various kinds, including ungrammatical utterances not identified as such. He has used this as an argument for an important innate component in language acquisition. It provides an equally powerful argument against an hypothesis-testing mechanism, since it is hard to see how a useful test of a hypothetical grammar could be made against this kind of input.

From laboratory work on the learning of simple artificial semantically empty systems (see 3.31 for a summary of this work), it is clear that human subjects rather readily acquire at least a limited class of grammatical structures merely as a consequence of exposure to sentences, i.e., with no other input than a sample of the sentences of the system. Moreover, a recent experiment (Braine, 1967) indicates that the learning mechanism in such experiments is robust against the inclusion in the input of some ungrammatical sentences along with the grammatical ones. In this experiment, a simple grammar defined a finite set of semantically empty sentences composed of nonsense words. A set of ungrammatical strings was also constructed; half of this was random combinations of vocabulary items, and the other half was random with the constraint that many adjacency relations in the language were conserved (specifically, they were third-order statistical approximations in the sense of Miller and Selfridge [1950]). One group of subjects listened to a tape which contained sentences drawn from a subset of the grammatical sentences. Another group listened to the same material, except that ungrammatical strings were randomly mixed in with the grammatical ones in a ratio of approximately one ungrammatical string to 13 grammatical sentences. No cues identified the ungrammatical strings as such, and both groups of subjects received the same instructions. The exposure period was followed by several tests to determine the amount of learning. These revealed that a considerable degree of learning of the grammar had taken place; for instance, in recognition tests both groups generally accepted grammatical sentences to which they had *not* been exposed and rejected ungrammatical strings to which the second group had been exposed. No significant differences between the groups were found on any of the tests, indicating that the inclusion of the ungrammatical strings in the input hardly slowed up learning at all. This and other experiments (3.31) argue that human subjects have a learning mechanism which is adequate for the discovery of at least some simple grammars and which cannot consist of generating and testing hypothetical grammars because the input information is insufficient for such a test. Moreover, to some extent this mechanism apparently provides for the forgetting of strings which contain unsystematic departures from the predominant patterns of formation of the input.

3.3. Work Rooted in Traditional Psychological Thinking about Learning

3.31. *Grammar Acquistion as Pattern Perception.* The main current line of work with its sources in traditional psychological thinking stems jointly from my position-learning proposals (Braine 1963a) and from verbal "mediation" theory (e.g., Jenkins, 1963; Jenkins & Palermo, 1964; Smith, 1963). Most of the experimental work has studied the learning of simple and artificial semantically empty linguistic systems, using the "verbal reconstructive memory" method. In such experiments, subjects are exposed to a set of strings ("sentences") in which the "morphemes" are letters or nonsense words. The strings are characterized by some regularities of construction which derive from the fact that they are a subset of the possible strings generated by a grammar. After exposure, the regularities the subjects have learned are determined by test: free recall tests, recognition tests, and a variety of special tests have been used. Since too many strings are presented to be learned by rote, a subject asked to recall strings will necessarily be driven to try to reconstruct sentences which exhibit the same regularities of construction as the strings to which he was exposed (insofar as he learned these regularities). Similarly, recognition of a string (i.e., a judgment of whether or not a given string was one of those exposed) is essentially a judgment of grammaticalness: the subject scans the string to see if it presents the pattern properties that he registered in the input. The experiment summarized in the preceding section is an instance of the technique.

The learning of a variety of structures has been investigated, and the research area is a burgeoning one. Smith (1963, 1966a) showed that subjects quickly pick up the simple regularities in the two-unit structure $S \rightarrow AB$.[27] In Smith (1965, 1966b), subjects were exposed to a more complex two-unit structure, $S \rightarrow LM$, PQ; it was found that the subjects readily learned the positions of the elements but failed to learn the subclass distinctions between L and P, and M and Q–they tended to consider LQ and PM sequences grammatical and thus learned the simpler structure $S \rightarrow AB$. A similar insensitivity to factors other than element position was found by Segal and Halwes (1965), who exposed subjects to strings of the form $S \rightarrow AB$, BC. Smith (1967) has shown that, at least in some circumstances, subjects are sensitive to an inversion rule of the form "if $a_i a_j$ is a sentence, then $a_j a_i$ is also a sentence." Learning of the pair of rules $S \rightarrow aXb$, pXq was studied in Braine (1965b), an experiment further discussed by Gough and Segal (1965) and in Braine (1965c). In Braine (1966), three utterance forms were used: fA, gPQ, fA/gPQ (where . . . /–indicates freedom of order of constituents). The child subjects readily picked up the regularities in the input. In Braine (1967, summarized in 3.22), the system used can be described by the rules $S \rightarrow A'$, B', $pA'B'$, $B'qA'r$; $A' \rightarrow Af$; $B' \rightarrow Bg$. The last three studies involved the learning of fairly complex positional relationships and contingency relations between nonneighboring elements. Rules of linear or hierarchical form were involved, and the character of the learning permitted inferences regarding the form of grammatical model the subjects tended to acquire (Braine, 1966).

On the basis of work on the learning of miniature semantically empty systems, a partial basis for the learning of phrase structure was suggested (Braine, 1963, 1965a, 1966). It was proposed (*a*) that what is learned are the temporal positions of units in verbal arrays and contingencies between morphemes, (*b*) that the position learned is the position of a unit within the next larger containing unit of a hierarchy of units, and (*c*) that position within a unit may be defined, either absolutely (e.g., first, last) or relatively to a reference point (e.g., before *f*, first after *f*, second after *f*, where *f* is some frequently occurring morpheme or "marker"). It was also argued that the learning was a case of perceptual learning. While these proposals obviously do not encompass the range of things to be learned in acquiring a natural grammar, the laboratory work so far suggests that they give a fairly good account of what tends to be learned by subjects in experimental studies of the learning of semantically empty systems.

The idea that grammar acquisition is a process of perceptual learning of pattern has been elaborated (Braine, 1967), with a suggestion as to the general nature of the learning mechanism. The model has two principal components: (*a*) a scanner which receives the input sentences and (*b*) an ordered series of intermediate memory stores, the last of which is the per-

---

[27] For brevity, the terminating rules (e.g., $A \rightarrow a_1, a_2, \ldots$; $B \rightarrow b_1, b_2, \ldots$) are omitted here and subsequently. Vocabulary size is always small. See note on page 7 for the notation used in stating structures.

manent memory store which contains the rules or pattern properties that
are finally learned. The function of the scanner is to scan each input sentence,
observe its pattern properties, and cause these to be registered in an intermediate store. Thus, if a_1f is the first input string, the scanner might register
the properties '*two words*', '*word+f*', 'a_1+word', and 'a_1+f'. At the beginning of learning, the intermediate stores are empty, and the characteristics
of the first string are listed in the first intermediate store. Once there is some
information in the intermediate stores, the properties observed in an input
string are compared with the properties then listed in the intermediate
stores. Those not already listed are recorded in the first intermediate store.
When a property noted by the scanner is the same as one listed in an intermediate store, this property moves to the next intermediate store. Thus, if
a_2f is the second input string, the properties '*two words*' and '*word+f*' will
move from the first to the second intermediate store. As properties recur in
the input, they move progressively through the series of intermediate stores
and eventually reach the permanent store.

The intermediate stores all have a built-in decay characteristic, i.e., the
information stored is lost after a period of time. This forgetting affects the
learning in important ways. First, it means that unsystematic "error" in
the input will have little or no effect on learning: random deviations from
grammaticalness may indeed be registered by the scanner, but since such
errors are by definition dissimilar one from another, they quickly disappear
without trace. Second, broad and abstract properties of the input corpus
will tend to be more readily learned than specific properties. This tendency
follows from the fact that the properties learned fastest are those that are
shared by many sentences and thus recur frequently. In general, the intermediate stores act as a kind of sieve which retains what is systematic in the
input. Specific properties will be subject to repeated forgetting and restorage,
although those that recur often enough will of course be learned—among
them, the exceptions and special cases which are so common in natural
languages.

The scanner has access to the information in the permanent store. Thus,
once some learning has taken place so that the permanent store is no longer
empty, the scanner is in a position to attempt a preliminary analysis of
incoming strings on the basis of its partial knowledge of the structure of the
input corpus. That is, the first scanning step incorporates a recognition
routine. Already learned information about the structure of the shorter strings
is used to group the elements of longer strings, so that these may be recorded
as being composed of shorter strings. Also, pattern properties registered
may be recorded as deviations from already learned properties or as special
cases of them. Thus, if the property '*word+f*' has reached the permanent
store, then the input string a_if can be recognized as a string of the form '*word
+f*', and the specific property 'a_if' is an instance of '*word+f*' can be listed in
the first intermediate store: the learner can begin to form a list of the items

in the class of words suffixed by f. Again, suppose the input sentence is $pa_i f b_j g$. Before any learning has taken place, the scanner may perhaps register only the properties 'many words' and 'p + several words'; however, if the properties '$word+f$' and '$word+g$' have reached the permanent store, then the scanner can note the property '$p+(word+f)+(word+g)$'. Thus, the sentence is assigned constituent structure.

It can be seen that the most complicated part of the model is the scanning mechanism. The properties of sentences that the scanner is sensitive to, at least initially, are taken for granted; i.e., the model does not account for their coming into existence. Moreover, since it has to be assumed that only a few properties of any particular sentence get registered at any one time, there is probably an unlearned order among the properties determining which are preferentially registered. In general, therefore, the scanner is "preset" to notice certain features of the input and ignore others. Ultimately, the general mathematical form of the grammars that the learner is capable of learning is in part determined by the range of properties that the scanner is sensitive to. Thus, this model shares one feature of the Chomsky-Miller model, in that universal properties of natural languages are for the most part built into the acquisition model. However, the model represents a different hypothesis as to how these properties are built in.

It seems very likely that a model of the kind described could, with existing knowledge, be built to simulate rather well the learning of semantically empty systems of the kind that have been employed in laboratory studies. Of course, the full nature and range of pattern properties that the scanner would have to be equipped to scan for in order for a natural language to be learned are currently unknown, and these undoubtedly include semantic attributes and relationships of and among components of sentences, inherently unrealizable in semantically empty systems. Even allowing for considerable enrichment of the scanning mechanism along these and other lines, it is foreseeable that the adequacy-in-principle of this kind of model will prove controversial. A model of this sort could be regarded as a set of "discovery procedures" for grammar acquisition, and it has been questioned whether such can exist (Chomsky, 1957). Nevertheless, the model meets two apparent requirements of an acquisition device: it can tolerate a noisy input without requiring any input information about what is not grammatical, and it predicts that the overall trend of learning should be from general to specific properties.

Another model of early stages of grammar acquisition has recently been proposed by Kelley (1967). Although it differs in many details, it shares with the model just discussed the general feature that learning is basically a process of registering properties of the input and accumulating them in memory. The general idea is that the child recognizes functional properties of familiar words in input utterances (e.g., "subject," "modifier," these being assumed to be definable in part in semantic terms) and also categorial properties ("things," "actions").[28] Recognition of these properties is accomplished by a parsing routine that is capable of skipping over unfamiliar words in input utterances. The semantic basis of the properties is such that recognizing them (together with recognition of the lexical items) is tantamount to finding a meaning for an utterance. This meaning is assessed for compatibility with the observed situational context of the input sentence and with the child's preexisting knowledge of the world. If a meaning found is absurd, the parsing routine attempts to find another analysis. When a nonabsurd meaning is found for an input utterance, an accumulator registers the positions of the functions in the sentence, the categories bearing the functions, the categorial assignments of the words, and co-occurrences of words with neighboring words and categories. Learning takes place by a process of confirmation by repetition and unlearning by forgetting.

Many aspects of the theory have been realized in a computer program able to discover a grammar generating a corpus of simple English sentences. However, as Kelley would undoubtedly agree, the simulation is seriously incomplete since crucial parts of the theory are rendered in the program in ad hoc ways. Thus, Kelley does not try to define "thing" or "action" nor the semantic aspects of his functional categories. The model thus begs important questions, e.g., whether semantic definitions that a child could use exist for "noun" and "verb" in terms of "things" and "actions" and what these definitions might be; whether there is a semantic aspect to "subjects," "modifiers," etc., of a sort which could be helpful to a learner in identifying them. The model also does not provide a non-ad hoc mechanism whereby the functional and categorial properties could change over time, either through refinement or through the acquisition of new properties. Finally, in the present state of the art, it is impossible to program knowledge of the world and recognition of situational context, so substitutes had to be devised for the simulation. On the other hand, the parsing routine is interesting, as is the general concept which implies that only sentences which are understood contribute to learning.

The role played by the perception of semantic relations is also emphasized by Schlesinger (1968), who argues that the construction of models of learning, and also of comprehension and production of utterances, would be greatly simplified if the current model of competence (Chomsky, 1965) were changed so that relations in deep structure were notional. Schlesinger suggests that grammar acquisition is primarily the learning of a mapping of the terms of semantic relations into positions in the surface structure, and he discusses some child language data in these terms.

3.32. *Mediation Theory and Word-Class Formation.* Mediation theory is a development out of stimulus-response association theory, i.e., out of

---

[28] Kelley refers to these properties as "hypotheses." However, the model is not subject to the criticisms against "hypothesis-testing" models raised in 3.22 (cf. footnote 26).

the notion that in all learning "what is learned" is reducible to associations between events, primarily between "responses" and "stimuli." In association theory, an organism's own responses can themselves serve as stimuli for further responses, leading to the formation of associative "chains": $S_1 \rightarrow R_1 (= S_2) \rightarrow R_2 (= S_3) \rightarrow R_3 \ldots$, etc. Mediation theory adds the assumption that some of the parts of an associative chain can be covert. For instance, in a chain $S_1 \rightarrow R_1 (= S_2) \rightarrow R_2$, if R_1 is covert, then the only part of the associative chain which is observable will be the response R_2 to the stimulus S_1, i.e., R_2 will appear as a response to S_1 without the learning of a direct association between R_2 and S_1. R_1 is then said to "mediate" the occurrence of R_2 to S_1. Mediation theory, then, represents one of the ways in which association theory explains the fact that organisms can respond to stimuli in ways that are not innate nor directly learned. The various ways in which associative chains, parts of which are covert, can potentially be combined to generate mediated connections between stimuli and responses are known as "mediation paradigms" (Jenkins, 1963).

Mediation theory has been invoked to explain an extremely wide variety of behaviors, including aspects of "meaning" (e.g., Mowrer, 1960) and grammar acquisition (Jenkins & Palermo, 1964). Recently, it has come under severe criticism. Fodor (1965) has argued that semantic phenomena cannot be accounted for in mediational terms. (For discussion of Fodor's paper, see Osgood [1966], Berlyne [1966], and Fodor [1966b].) In the case of grammar acquisition, no mediational explanations of the acquisition of constituent structure have been proposed, and the difficulties faced by mediation theory in explaining position learning have been indicated by Smith (1965, 1966b). Moreover, as Fodor argues for semantic phenomena, so also for grammar acquisition; it is hard to see that mediation theory can, in principle, be more powerful than the associative-chain theory from which it is derived. The most usual model for associative chains is the Markov process of finite state diagram (Osgood & Sebeok, 1954; Miller, 1951). Adding the mediation assumption, that parts of the chain need not be overt, seems formally equivalent to allowing that some of the transitions in a state diagram can be empty. Empty transitions do not increase the generative power of finite state systems (Chomsky & Miller, 1958). Hence, mediation theory as presently constituted cannot provide the answer to criticisms of associative chain and finite state models (Lashley, 1951; Chomsky, 1957).[29]

Although mediation theorists have sometimes assumed a wide grammatical scope for their viewpoint, their actual work and thinking in relation to grammar acquisition has been directed primarily to the problem of word-class formation and not to the wider aspects of syntactic structure where

[29] Actually, there is room for doubt whether the finite state model does properly reconstruct the tranditional concept of an association (Braine, 1966). However, the argument that mediation has little effect on the power of an association theory may well be restatable for other models of association.

their viewpoint is most vulnerable. It is assumed that word-class formation is a special case of the "acquired-stimulus-equivalence" paradigm. The paradigm implies two or more learning stages (which may be concurrent). In the first stage, each of a set of dissimilar stimuli, $S_{a_1}, S_{a_2}, \ldots$, are associated with a particular response, R_{a_1}; similarly, another set, $S_{b_1}, S_{b_2}, \ldots$, are associated with another response, R_{b_1}; there may or may not be other sets of stimuli $(S_{c_1}, S_{c_2}, \ldots, S_{d_1}, S_{d_2}, \ldots,$ etc.) associated with R_{c_1}, R_d, etc. In the second stage of learning, the same sets of stimuli are associated with new responses R_{a_2}, R_{b_2}, etc.; further learning stages involving R_{a_3}, R_{b_3}, etc., and then R_{a_4}, R_{b_4}, etc., may also occur. The formation of stimulus-classes is considered demonstrated when subjects show transfer from one stage to another, i.e., when the division of the stimuli learned in the first stage is not relearned in subsequent stages but carries over from one stage to another. In a possible natural language analogue, $S_{a_1}, S_{a_2}, \ldots$ might be the masculine nouns of a language, and $S_{b_1}, S_{b_2}, \ldots$ the feminine nouns (assuming a language which divides its noun lexicon into these two classes); R_{a_1} and R_{b_1} might then be the masculine and feminine definite articles, R_{a_2} and R_{b_2} the masculine and feminine indefinite articles, R_{a_3} and R_{b_3} masculine and feminine adjective inflexions, R_{a_4} and R_{b_4} third person pronouns, etc.[30]

There has been some difficulty in demonstrating transfer between the learning stages experimentally (Jenkins, 1963; Smith, 1966b). Foss and Jenkins (1966) appears to be the only relevant experiment in which transfer has been shown. This experiment suggests that a major factor determining whether or not stimulus equivalences are required is the size of the equivalence classes: they need to have many members.

According to Foss and Jenkins, transfer is mediated by the first stage responses. That is, early in the second-stage learning, an association between the first and second stage responses is learned, resulting in a chain, $S_a \rightarrow (R_{a_1}) \rightarrow R_{a_2}$; the mediator, R_{a_1}, acts, as it were, as a covert class marker. However, it is not known that this explanation is the correct one, and it seems quite likely that other explanations of the learning of such stimulus equivalences are possible. Many questions remain for further experimental analysis. The issue is an important one since a good theory of the acquisition of semantically arbitrary word classes is badly needed. The mediation theory is the only currently available theory which does not presuppose that a semantic correlate must be perceived in order for a word class to be discovered.

3.33. *Discussion.* As a set of ideas on the acquisition of linguistic structure,

---

[30] In the natural language case, the terms *stimulus* and *response* cannot, of course, be construed as inputs and outputs. The usage of these terms in the psychological literature is notoriously careless. Although association theory would appear to require that an S-R connection be a relation between an input to and an output from an information-processing system or subsystem, the actual universal practice in the literature on paired-associate learning is to use the term *responses* to refer to any set of items which is mapped on to another set and to use the term *stimuli* for the set of items onto which a mapping is made. I follow this usage here.

the psychological work reviewed is limited in scope in several obvious ways. First, no attempt has been made to provide an account of the learning of phonological structure. This deficiency is unfortunately shared with all theoretically oriented work on first-language acquisition.

Second, the work has not come to grips with the problem of explaining the acquisition of semantic structure. This seems to me the most serious defect of the work reviewed. While the linguist may choose to treat syntax as separate from semantics, it is by no means clear that the offspring of this separation—the attempt to construct a separate acquisition theory for syntax—will ultimately prove to be well motivated. It seems certain that there are grammatical structures which are inherently impossible to learn without knowledge of the semantic correlates of sentences embodying them. A clear, though perhaps trivial, example might be the rule *he* in English is substituted for *NP*s referring to males, and *she* for *NP*s referring to females. A more subtle, though perhaps more dubious, example might be the distinction between intransitive verbs and transitive verbs occurring without objects: a natural characterization of the difference between *The bell rang* and *The man rang* would bring in the fact that the subject is the agent only for *The man rang*, i.e., for the transitive verb. The kind of structure explored by Smith (1965, 1966b; see 3.31) appears to be very difficult to learn in a semantically empty system, although such structures occur in natural languages. If the set of learnable semantically empty systems is inherently less rich structurally than the set of learnable communication systems, then a theory which ignores semantic structure is bound to be incomplete as an account of grammar acquisition. In addition, the data reviewed in 2.28 and 2.32 suggest that learning the semantic correlates of classes and semantic relations between classes in a construction is often part of the process of learning the classes and the rules for generating a construction.

A third deficiency of the work reviewed is that it has so far had little to say about the learning of transformations. It has been repeatedly argued that it is impossible to develop a theory of the learning of transformations within traditional psychological frames of reference (Katz & Postal, 1964; Bever, Fodor, & Weksel, 1965a, b; Weksel, 1965). Thus, Weksel (1965) says, "What we [i.e., generative grammarians] require is not merely a modification or extension of present-day learning theory principles. Rather, we require that learning theory be abandoned as the basis for an explanation of linguistic competence and performance [pp. 694–695]." Moreover, it is clear in Weksel's review and in the critique by Bever et al. that "learning theory" is taken comprehensively to include the present writer's work and mediation theory and therefore the entire line of work summarized in 3.31–2, as well as all possible future developments out of it. The source of these negative claims is clearly the conclusion that it is impossible to develop an account of grammar acquisition which will handle "underlying" structure. This conclusion is decidedly premature.

There is at least one natural way in which the line of thought reviewed might broach the learning of transformations, namely, as the learning of changes of form. It is a commonplace that organisms are often sensitive to stimuli which are identifiable only as alterations in other already familiar stimuli. Morphology provides many examples of signals manifest primarily as alterations in already familiar items, e.g., to understand *sang* one must presumably perceive the "underlying" signal *sing*, in addition to the past tense morpheme expressed as a change in the form of *sing*. Many transformations are naturally regarded as instances of such alterations, in which one signal (e.g., 'negative' or 'question') is recognizable through the changes made in the already familiar form of another signal (the underlying sentence). Thus, if S is a sentence converted into S' by the singularly transformation T, S' can be analyzed as containing two components $S + T$. It ought not to be difficult to demonstrate the learning of changes of this sort in an artificial system in the laboratory, and laboratory studies might contribute to definition of the kinds of changes people readily learn or fail to learn.

To see a thing as a changed form of something else, the latter must be already familiar. Thus, to regard the learning of transformations as the learning of changes in form, it would have to be assumed that the learner is familiar with the kernel structure before he learns the transformation; i.e., to a substantial extent, the kernel structure must be acquired before transformations are learned. The evidence (2.22-7) indicates that this is the case, and the development of negatives and questions seems quite consistent with the notion that what is learned is an alteration in a familiar structure. For example, the negative morpheme is first realized directly as *no*, *not*, or *don't* (or their equivalents in other languages), the negating item being simply appended to the sentence or placed before the predicate phrase. No transformation is apparent until after the kernel sentence structure is fairly well developed, and the changes in form are learned in steps, the change from *some* to *any*, for instance, being learned after the changes in the auxiliary (*I want some → I don't want some > I don't want any*). Thus, the negative sentence has the structure *neg. + Sentence* from the start; the development lies in the step-by-step learning of the manifestations of the negative morpheme.

There is one kind of transformation in which learning cannot potentially be accounted for in the above manner or by any other straightforward development out of the ideas under review. These are transformations which introduce a distinction between overt and underlying structure in *kernel* sentences. The prime example in English is the affix-movement rule in the verb phrase (Chomsky, 1957, p. 39, Rule 29-ii). Since the order of elements in the underlying string is here never realized in speech, it is impossible for the learner to perceive the manifest order as a "change" in the underlying order. Moreover, as Bever et al. (1965a) point out in their critique, the underlying order itself could not be learned by a device which registers element position in overt speech. However, alternative approaches which would provide for the learning of such transformations are not available. Strong nativistic assumptions are not likely to be helpful since the order-changing rules involved are clearly not universal and therefore must be worked out from the surface structure in any model. Fodor (1966a) suggests that a special kind of inferential mechanism might be at work, but his suggestions as to the nature of the mechanism are ad hoc and, as Fodor points out, inadequate to the problem.

Another way of eliminating Bever et al.'s objection would be to change the current theory of the general form of a grammar, so as to eliminate the need for permutation transforms in the generation of kernel sentences. My reply to Bever et al. (Braine, 1965a) contended that the essentials of Chomsky's (1957) analysis of the English auxiliary verb phrase could be preserved, without the affix-movement rule being necessary in either kernel or trans-forms, by admitting simple kinds of discontinuous constituents in the phrase structure. More far-reaching changes in linguistic theory, in the direction of making the deep structure notional in nature, are currently being urged on a variety of grounds (e.g., Schlesinger, 1968; Fillmore, in press; Lakoff, 1968). Such changes would alter the general concept of a transformation, and the controversy over the learnability of permutation transformations in kernel sentences would be rendered obsolete. The whole problem of accounting for the learning of transformations will be drastically changed if such views prevail.

ENVOI

In general, this review reflects the fact that the field as a whole is in the middle of a spate of work on grammar acquisition. Knowledge of phono-logical development has hardly increased at all during the last ten years, and as yet, there is essentially no systematic knowledge of lexical and semantic development. It is hoped that the review will provide a useful presentation of current knowledge which makes clear the lacunae.

REFERENCES

Albright, R. W., & Albright, J. B. The phonology of a two-year-old child. *Word*, 1956, **12**, 382–390.

Albright, R. W., & Albright, J. B. Application of descriptive linguistics to child language. *J. Speech Res.*, 1958, **1**, 257–261.

Asher, J. J., & Price, B. S. The learning strategy of the total physical response: some age differences. *Child Develpm.*, 1967, **38**, 1219–1227.

Bachi, R. A statistical analysis of the revival of Hebrew in Israel. *Scripta Hierosolymitana*, 1956, **3**, 179–247.

Bar-Adon, A. *Lešonam hameduberet šel hayeladim beyisrael (Children's Hebrew in Israel)*. Unpublished doctoral dissertation, The Hebrew University of Jerusalem, 1959.

Bellugi, U. The emergence of inflection and negation systems in the speech of two children. Paper presented at the meeting of the New England Psychology Association, 1964. (ditto)

Bellugi, U. The acquisition of negation. Unpublished doctoral dissertation, Harvard University, 1967.

Bellugi, U., & Brown, R. W. (Eds.) The acquisition of language. *Monogr. Soc. Res. Child Develpm.*, 1964, **29**, No. 1.

Berko, J. The child's learning of English morphology. *Word*, 1958, **14**, 150–177.

Berlyne, D. E. Mediating responses: a note on Fodor's criticisms. *J. verb. Learn. verb. Behav.*, 1966, **5**, 408–411.

Bever, T. G., Fodor, J. A., & Weksel, W. On the acquisition of syntax: a critique of "contextual generalization." *Psychol. Rev.*, 1965, **72**, 467–482. (a)

Bever, T. G., Fodor, J. A., & Weksel, W. Is linguistics empirical? *Psychol. Rev.*, 1965, **72**, 493–500. (b)

Blank, M. Use of the deaf in language studies: a reply to Furth. *Psychol. Bull.*, 1965, **63**, 442–444.

Bloch, O. Les premiers stades du langage de l'enfant. *J. de Psychol.*, 1921, **18**, 693–712.

Bloch, O. La phrase dans le langage de l'enfant. *J. de Psychol.*, 1924, **21**, 18–43.

Bogoyavlenskii, D. N. *Psikhologiya usvoeniya orfografii (Psychology of learning orthography)*. Moscow: Akad. Pedag. Nauk RSFSR, 1957.

Braine, M. D. S. On learning the grammatical order of words. *Psychol. Rev.*, 1963, **70**, 323–348. (a)

Braine, M. D. S. The ontogeny of English phrase structure: the first phase. *Language*, 1963, **39**, 1–13. (b)

Braine, M. D. S. Grammatical structure in the speech of two-year-olds. *Proc. Washington Ling. Club*, 1963, **1**, 11–16. (summary of address) (c)

Braine, M. D. S. On the basis of phrase structure: a reply to Bever, Fodor, and Weksel. *Psychol. Rev.*, 1965, **72**, 483–492. (a)

Braine, M. D. S. The insufficiency of a finite state model for verbal reconstructive memory. *Psychon. Sci.*, 1965, **2**, 291–292. (b)

Braine, M. D. S. Inferring a grammar from responses: discussion of Gough and Segal's comment. *Psychon. Sci.*, 1965, **3**, 241–242. (c)

Braine, M. D. S. Three suggestions regarding grammatical analyses of children's language. Paper presented at the meeting of the Linguistic Circle of New York, Mar., 1965. In C. A. Ferguson & D. I. Slobin (in press). (d)

Braine, M. D. S. Learning the positions of words relative to a marker element. *J. exp. Psychol.*, 1966, **72**, 532–540.

Braine, M. D. S. Grammar acquisition in a heterogeneous verbal environment. 1967. (ditto)

Braun-Lamesch, M.-M. Le rôle du contexte dans la compréhension du langage chez l'enfant. *Psychol. Française*, 1962, **7**, 180–189.

Brown, R. W. Linguistic determinism and the part of speech. *J. abnorm. soc. Psychol.*, 1957, **55**, 1–5.

Brown, R. W. *Words and things*. New York: Free Press (Macmillan), 1958.

Brown, R. W. *Social psychology*. New York: Free Press (Macmillan), 1965.

Brown, R. W. The development of wh questions in child speech. *J. verb. Learn. verb. Behav.*, 1968, **7**, 279–290.

Brown, R. W., & Bellugi, U. Three processes in the child's acquisition of syntax. *Harvard educ. Rev.*, 1964, **34**, 133–151. Reprinted in E. H. Lenneberg (1964d).

Brown, R. W., & Berko, J. Word association and the acquisition of grammar. *Child Develpm.*, 1960, **31**, 1–14. (a)

Brown, R. W., & Berko, J. Psycholinguistic research methods. In P. H. Mussen (Ed.), *Handbook of research methods in child development*. New York: John Wiley & Sons, 1960. (b)

Brown, R. W., & Fraser, C. The acquisition of syntax. In C. N. Cofer & B. S. Musgrave (Eds.), *Verbal behavior and learning: problems and processes*. New York: McGraw-Hill, 1963. Reprinted in U. Bellugi & R. W. Brown (1964).

Brown, R. W., Fraser, C., & Bellugi, U. Explorations in grammar evaluation. In U. Bellugi & R. W. Brown (1964).

Bühler, K. *Sprachtheorie*. Jena: Fischer, 1934.

Burling, R. Language development of a Garo and English speaking child. *Word*. 1959, **15**, 45–68.

Carroll, J. B. Determining and numerating adjectives in children's speech. *Child Develpm.*, 1939, **10**, 215–229.

Carroll, J. B. Language development in children. In *Encyclopedia of educational research*. New York: Macmillan, 1960. Pp. 744–752.

Carroll, J. B. *Language and thought*. Englewood Cliffs: Prentice-Hall, 1964. (a)

Carroll, J. B. Words, meanings, and concept. *Harvard educ. Rev.*, 1964, **34** 178–202, (b)

Carroll, J. B., & Casagrande, J. B. The function of language classifications in behavior. In E. E. Maccoby, T. M. Newcomb, & E. L. Hartley (Eds.), *Readings in social psychology*. New York: Holt, Rinehart & Winston, 1958.

Cazden, C. B. *Environmental assistance to the child's acquisition of grammar*. Unpublished doctoral dissertation, Harvard University, 1965.

Chao, Y. R. The Cantian idiolect: an analysis of the Chinese spoken by a twenty-eight-months-old child. In W. I. Fischel (Ed.), *Semitic and oriental studies. Univ. California Publ. Semitic Philol.*, 1951, **11**, 27–44.

Chomsky, N. *Syntactic structures*. The Hague: Mouton, 1957.

Chomsky, N. On the notion "rule of grammar." In R. Jakobson (Ed.), *Structure of language and its mathematical aspects. Proc. 12th Symp. Appl. Math.* Providence: American Mathematics Society, 1961.

Chomsky, N. *Current issues in linguistic theory*. The Hague: Mouton, 1964. (a)

Chomsky, N. Discussion. In U. Bellugi & R. W. Brown (1964, 35–39). (b)

Chomsky, N. *Aspects of the theory of syntax*. Cambridge: M.I.T. Press, 1965.

Chomsky, N., & Miller, G. A. Finite state languages. *Information & Control*. 1958, **1**, 91–112.

Chomsky, N., & Miller, G. A. Introduction to the formal analysis of natural languages. In R. D. Luce, R. R. Bush, & E. Galanter (Eds.), *Handbook of mathematical psychology*. Vol. 2. New York: John Wiley & Sons, 1963.

Cohen, M. Sur l'étude du langage enfantin. *Enfance*, 1952, **5**, 181–249.

Diver, W. The system of agency in the Latin noun. *Word*, 1964, **20**, 178–190.

Durand, M. De quelques éliminations d'homonymes chez un enfant. *J. psychol. norm. path.*, 1949, **42**, 53–63.

El'konin, D. B. *Razvitie rechi v doshkol'nom vozraste* (The development of speech in preschool age). Moscow: Akad. Pedag. Nauk RSFSR, 1958.

El'konin, D. B. Nekotorye itogi izucheniya psikhicheskogo razvitiya detei doshkol'nogo vozrasta (Some results of the study of mental development of children of preschool age). In *Psikhologicheskaya nauka v SSSR*, II, 228–285. Moscow: Akad. Pedag. Nauk RSFSR, 1960. Transl. in *Psychological science in the USSR*, II, 320–407. Washington: *U.S. Joint Publ. Res. Serv. No.* 12798, 1962.

Ervin, S. M. The connotations of gender. *Word*, 1962, **18**, 248–261.

Ervin, S. M. Imitation and structural change in children's language. In E. H. Lenneberg (1964d).

Ervin-Tripp, S. M. Language development. In M. Hoffman & L. Hoffman (Eds.), *Review of child development research*. Vol. 2. Ann Arbor: Univ. of Michigan Press, 1966.

Ervin, S. M., & Foster, G. The development of meaning in children's descriptive terms. *J. abnorm. soc. Psychol.*, 1960, **61**, 271–275.

Ervin S. M., & Miller, W. R. Language development. In H. W. Stevenson (Ed.), *Child psychology. 62nd Yearb. Nat. Soc. Study Educ.*, Part I. Chicago: Univ. of Chicago Press, 1963.

Esper, E. A. Studies in linguistic behavior organization: I. Characteristics of unstable verbal reactions. *J. genet. Psychol.*, 1933, **8**, 346–379.

Fant, G. *Acoustic theory of speech production*. The Hague: Mouton, 1962.

Feofanov, M. P. Ob upotreblenii predlogov v detskoi rechi (On the use of prepositions in child speech). *Voprosy Psikhol.*, 1958, **4**, No. 3, 118–124.

Ferguson, C. A., & Slobin, D. I. (Eds.) *Readings on child language*. New York: Holt, Rinehart & Winston, forthcoming.

Fillmore, C. J. The case for case. In E. Bach & R. Harms (Eds.), *Universals in linguistic theory*. New York: Holt, Rinehart & Winston, 1968.

Fodor, J. A. Could meaning be an r_m? *J. verb. Learn. verb. Behav.*, 1965, **4**, 73–81.

Fodor, J. A. How to learn to talk: some simple ways. In F. Smith & G. A. Miller (1966). (a)

Fodor, J. A. More about mediators: a reply to Berlyne and Osgood. *J. verb. Learn. verb. Behav.*, 1966, **5**, 412–416. (b)

Foss, D. J., & Jenkins, J. J. Mediated stimulus equivalence as a function of the number of converging stimulus items. *J. exp. Psychol.*, 1966, **71**, 738–745.

Fraser, C., Bellugi, U., & Brown, R. W. Control of grammar in imitation, comprehension, and production. *J. verb. Learn. verb. Behav.*, 1963, **2**, 121–135.

Furth, H. Research with the deaf: implications for language and cognition. *Psychol. Bull.*, 1964, **62**, 145–164.

Gardner, R. A., & Gardner, B. T. Teaching sign language to a chimpanzee. 1968. (mimeo)

Gibson, J. J. Perception as a function of stimulation. In S. Koch (Ed.), *Psychology: a study of a science*. Vol. 1. New York: McGraw-Hill, 1959.

Gibson, J. J., & Gibson, E. J. Perceptual learning: differentiation or enrichment? *Psychol. Rev.*, 1955, **62**, 32–41.

Gleason, H. A. *An introduction to descriptive linguistics*. (2nd ed.) New York: Holt, Rinehart & Winston, 1961.

Gough, P. B., & Segal, E. M. Comment on "The insufficiency of a finite state model for verbal reconstructive memory." *Psychon. Sci.*, 1965, **3**, 155–156.

Grégoire, A. *L'apprentissage du langage. I. Les deux premières années. II. La troisième année et les années suivantes*. Liège: Faculté de philosophie et lettres de l'Université de Liège, 1937 (Vol. I), 1947 (Vol. II).

Grégoire, A. La renaissance scientifique de la linguistique enfantine. *Lingua*, 1950, **2**, 355–398.

Gruber, J. S. Topicalization in child language. *Foundations of Lang.*, 1967, **3**, 37–65. (a)

Gruber, J. S. Correlations between the syntactic constructions of the child and of the adult. Paper presented at a meeting of the Soc. Res. Child Develpm., 1967. (b) (ditto)

Guillaume, P. Les débuts de la phrase dans le langage de l'enfant. *J. de Psychol.*, 1927, **24**, 1–25. (a)

Guillaume, P. Le développment des élements formels dans le langage de l'enfant. *J. Psychol. norm. path.*, 1927, **24**, 203–229. (b)

Gvozdev, A. N. *Formirovanie u rebenka grammaticheskogo stroya russkogo yazyka* (Formation in the child of the grammatical structure of the Russian language). Parts I & II. Moscow: Akad. Pedag. Nauk RSFSR, 1949.

Gvozdev, A. N. *Voprosy izucheniya detskoi rechi* (Problems in the study of child language). Moscow: Akad. Pedag. Nauk RSFSR, 1961.

Harris, Z. *Methods in structural linguistics*. Chicago: Univ. of Chicago Press, 1951.

Harwood, F. W. Quantitative study of the syntax of the speech of Australia children. *Language & Speech*, 1959, **2**, 236–271.

Hayes, C. *The ape in our house*. New York: Harper & Row, 1951.

Hayes, K. J., & Hayes, C. The intellectual development of a home-raised chimpanzee. *Proc. Amer. Phil. Soc.*, 1951, **102**, 105–120.

Hill, A. A. Grammaticality. *Word*, 1961, **17**, 1–10.

Hill, C. W. Learning and retention by monkeys of concurrent conditional discrimination reversals involving stimulus manipulation. *Anim. Behav.*, 1967, **15**, 67–74.

Hoenigswald, H. M. *Language change and linguistic reconstruction*. Chicago: Univ. of Chicago Press, 1960.

Huttenlocher, J. Children's language: word-phrase relationship. *Science*, 1964, **143**, 264–265.

Irwin, O. C. Infant speech: consonantal sounds according to place of articulation. *J. Speech Dis.*, 1947, **12**, 397–401. (a)

Irwin, O. C. Infant speech: consonantal sounds according to manner of articulation. *J. Speech Dis.*, 1947, **12**, 402–404. (b)

Irwin, O. C. Development of vowel sounds. *J. Speech Hear. Dis.*, 1948, **13**, 31–34.

Irwin, O. C. Infant speech: consonantal position. *J. Speech Hear. Dis.*, 1951, **16**, 159–161.

Irwin, O. C. Phonetical description of speech development in infancy. In L. Kaiser (Ed.), *Manual of phonetics*. Amsterdam: North Holland, 1957.

Jakobson, R. *Kindersprache, Aphasie, und allgemeine Lautgesetze*. Uppsala: Almqvist & Wiksell, 1941.

Jakobson, R., & Halle, M. *Fundamentals of language*. The Hague: Mouton, 1956.

Jenkins, J. J. Mediated associations: paradigms and situations. In C. N. Cofer & B. S. Musgrave (Eds.), *Verbal behavior and learning: problems and processes*. New York: McGraw-Hill, 1963.

Jenkins, J. J., & Palermo, D. S. Mediation processes and the acquisition of linguistic structure. In U. Bellugi & R. W. Brown (1964).

Kahane, H., Kahane, R., & Saporta, S. Development of verbal categories in child language. *Internat. J. Amer. Ling.*, 1958, **24**, No. 4, Part II. *(Publ. 9 of Indiana Univ. Res. Center in Anthrop., Folklore, & Ling.)*

Kainz, F. *Psychologie der Sprache*. Vol. II. *Vergleichend-genetische Sprachpsychologie*. Stuttgart: Enke, 1960.

Kainz, F. *Sprachentwicklung im Kindes und Jugenalter*. Muenchen: Reinhardt, 1964.

Kaper, W. *Kindersprachforschung mit Hilfe des Kindes*. Groningen: Wolters, 1959.

Karpova, S. N. Osozmanie slovensnogo sostava rechi rebyonka doshkolnogo vozrasta (Awareness of the word content of speech of a preschool child). *Voprosy Psikhol.*, 1955, No. 1, 43-55.

Katz, J. J. *The philosophy of language*. New York: Harper & Row, 1966.

Katz, J. J., & Postal, P. M. *An integrated theory of linguistic descriptions*. Cambridge: M.I.T. Press, 1964.

Kean, J. M., & Yamamoto, K. Grammar signals and assignment of words to parts of speech among young children: an exploration. *J. verb. Learn. verb. Behav.*, 1965, **4**, 323-326.

Kelley, K. L. Early syntactic acquisition. Unpublished doctoral dissertation, University of California, Los Angeles, 1967. Also available as *Publication* P-3719, RAND Corporation, Santa Monica, 1967.

Kellogg, W. N., & Kellogg, L. A. *The ape and the child*. New York: Hafner, 1933.

Klima, E. S., & Bellugi, U. Syntactic regularities in the speech of children. In J. Lyons & R. J. Wales (Eds.), *Psycholinguistics papers*. Edinburgh: Edinburgh Univ. Press, 1966.

Lakoff, G. Instrumental adverbs and the concept of deep structure. *Foundations of Lang.*, 1968, **4**, 4-29.

Lamb, S. M. Prolegomena to a theory of phonology. *Language*, 1966, **42**, 536-573.

Lane, H. The motor theory of speech perception: a critical review. *Psychol. Rev.*, 1965, **72**, 275-309.

Lashley, K. S. The problem of serial order in behavior. In L. A. Jeffress (Ed.), *Cerebral mechanisms in behavior: the Hixon symposium*. New York: John Wiley & Sons, 1951.

Lees, R. B. Discussion. In U. Bellugi & R. W. Brown (1964, 92-98).

Lenneberg, E. H. Language, evolution, and purposive behavior. In S. Diamond (Ed.), *Culture in history*. New York: Columbia Univ. Press, 1961.

Lenneberg, E. H. Understanding language without ability to speak: a case report. *J. abnorm. soc. Psychol.*, 1962, **65**, 419-425.

Lenneberg, E. H. Speech as a motor skill with special reference to nonaphasic disorders. In U. Bellugi & R. W. Brown (1964). (a)

Lenneberg, E. H. A biological perspective of language. In E. H. Lenneberg (1964d). (b)

Lenneberg, E. H. The capacity for language acquisition. In J. A. Fodor & J. J. Katz (Eds.), *The structure of language: readings in the philosophy of language.* Englewood Cliffs: Prentice-Hall, 1964. (c)

Lenneberg, E. H. (Ed.), *New directions in the study of language.* Cambridge: M.I.T. Press, 1964. (d)

Lenneberg, E. H. *Biological foundations of language.* New York: John Wiley & Sons, 1967.

Lenneberg, E. H., Nichols, I. A., & Rosenberger, E. F. Primitive stages of development in mongolism. *Proc. Ass. nerv. ment. Dis.*, 1964, **42**, 119–137.

Leopold, W. F. *Speech development of a bilingual child: a linguist's record.* Vols. 1–4. Evanston: Northwestern University Studies of Humanities, 1939–1949.

Leopold, W. F. The study of child language and infant bilingualism. *Word*, 1948, **4**, 1–17.

Leopold, W. F. *Bibliography of child language.* Evanston: Northwestern Univ. Press, 1952.

Leopold, W. F. Patterning in children's language learning. *Lang. Learn.*, 1953–1954, **5**, 1–14.

Leopold, W. F. A child's learning of two languages. In H. J. Mueller (Ed.), *Report on the 5th round table conference on linguistics and language teaching. Monogr. Series in lang. and ling. No. 7.* Washington: Georgetown Univ. Press, 1954.

Lewis, M. M. *Infant speech.* New York: Humanities Press, 1951.

Liberman, A. M. Some results of research on speech perception. *J. acoust. Soc. Amer.*, 1957, **29**, 117–123.

Lieberman, P. *Intonation, perception, and language.* Cambridge: M.I.T. Press, 1967.

Lisker, L., Cooper, F. S., & Liberman, A. M. The uses of experiment in language description. *Word*, 1962, **18**, 82–106.

Livant, W. F. Productive grammatical operations: I. the noun compounding of five-year-olds. *Lang. Learn.*, 1962, **12**, 15–26.

Luria, A. R. The directive function of speech: I. its development in early childhood. *Word*, 1959, **15**, 341–352.

Luria, A. R. *The role of speech in the regulation of normal and abnormal behavior.* Oxford: Pergamon, 1961.

Lyamina, G. M., & Gagua, N. I. On the development of proper pronunciation in children from one and a half to three years of age. *Sov. Psychol. Psychiat.*, 1964, **2**, No. 4, 15–27.

Maclay, H., & Sleator, M. D. Responses to language: judgments of grammaticalness. *Internat. J. Amer. Ling.*, 1960, **26**, 275–282.

McCarthy, D. Language development in children. In L. Carmichael (Ed.), *Manual of child psychology.* (2nd ed.) New York: John Wiley & Sons, 1954.

McNeill, D. Developmental psycholinguistics. In F. Smith & G. A. Miller (1966).

Mehan, S. Linguistic comprehension in nursery and kindergarten children. Unpublished M. A. thesis, San Jose State College, 1968.

Menyuk, P. Syntactic structure in the language of children. *Child Develpm.*, 1963, **34**, 407–422. (a)

Menyuk, P. A preliminary evaluation of grammatical capacity in children. *J. verb. Learn. verb. Behav.*, 1963, **2**, 429–439. (b)

Menyuk, P. Syntactic rules used by children from preschool through first grade. *Child Develpm.*, 1964, **35**, 533–546. (a)

Menyuk, P. Alternation of rules in children's grammars. *J. verb. Learn. verb. Behav.*, 1964, **3**, 480–488. (b)

Menyuk, P. Comparison of grammar of children with functionally deviant and normal speech. *J. Speech Hear. Res.*, 1964, **17**, 109–121. (c)

Messer, S. Implicit phonology in children. *J. verb. Learn. verb. Behav.*, 1967, **6**, 609–613.

Miller, G. A. *Language and communication.* New York: McGraw-Hill, 1951.

Miller, G. A. The psycholinguists. *Encounter*, 1964, **23**, No. 1, 29–37.

Miller, G. A., & Chomsky, N. Finitary models of language users. In R. D. Luce, R. R. Bush, & E. Galanter (Eds.), *Handbook of mathematical psychology.* Vol. 2. New York: John Wiley & Sons, 1963.

Miller, G. A., & Selfridge, J. A. Verbal context and the recall of meaningful material. *Amer. J. Psychol.*, 1950, **63**, 176–185.

Miller, W. R. Patterns of grammatical development in child language. In *Proc. 9th Internat. Cong. Ling.* The Hague: Mouton, 1964. (a)

Miller, W. R. The acquisition of grammatical rules by children. Paper presented to meeting of the Linguistics Society of America, Dec., 1964. (b) (ditto)

Miller, W. R., & Ervin, S. M. The development of grammar in child language. In U. Bellugi & R. W. Brown (1964).

Mowrer, O. H. The autism theory of speech development and some clinical applications. *J. Speech Hear. Dis.*, 1952, **17**, 263–268.

Mowrer, O. H. *Learning theory and the symbolic process.* New York: John Wiley & Sons, 1960.

Nakazima, S. A comparative study of the speech developments of Japanese and American English in childhood (I)—a comparison of the developments of voices at the prelinguistic period. *Studia Phonologica*, 1962, **2**, 27–46.

Oleron, P. *Récherches sur le développement mental des sourdésmuets.* Paris: Centre National de la recherche scientifique, 1957.

Olmsted, D. L. A theory of the child's learning of phonology. *Language*, 1966, **42**, 531–535.

Osgood, C. E. Meaning cannot be r_m? *J. verb. Learn. verb. Behav.*, 1966, **5**, 402–407.

Osgood, C. E., & Sebeok, T. A. (Eds.) *Psycholinguistics: a survey of theory and research. J. abnorm. soc. Psychol.*, 1954, **49**, Part 2 (supplement).

Popova, M. I. Grammaticheskie elementy yazyka v rechi detei preddoshkol'nogo vozrasta (Grammatical elements of language in the speech of children of pre-school age). *Voprosy Psikhol.*, 1958, **4**, No. 3, 106–117.

Premack, D., & Schwartz, A. Preparations for discussing behaviorism with chimpanzee. In F. Smith & G. A. Miller (1966).

Prins, D. Relations among specific articulatory deviations and responses to a clinical measure of sound discrimination ability. *J. Speech Hear. Dis.*, 1963, **28**, 382–388.

Quine, W. V. O. *Word and object.* New York: Technology Press & John Wiley & Sons, 1960.

Quirk, R. Descriptive statements and serial relationship. *Language*, 1965, **41**, 205–217.

Raevskii, A. N. *Psikhologiya rechi v sovetskoi psikhologicheskoi nauka za 40 let* (The psychology of speech in Soviet psychological science for 40 years). Kiev: Kievskogo Gos. Univer. im. T. G. Shevchenko, 1958.

Razran, G. The observable unconscious and the inferable conscious in current Soviet psychophysiology: interoceptive conditioning, semantic conditioning, and the orienting reflex. *Psychol. Rev.*, 1961, **68**, 81–147.

Ruke-Dravina, V. *Zur Sprachentwicklung bei Kleinkindern: I. syntax.* Lund, 1963.

Ruke-Dravina, V. The process of acquisition of apical /r/ and uvular /R/ in the speech of children. *Linguistics,* 1965, No. 17, 58–68.

Sapir, E. The psychological reality of phonemes. In D. G. Mandelbaum (Ed.), *Selected writings of Edward Sapir in language, culture, and personality.* Berkeley: Univ. of California Press, 1949.

Saporta, S. Review of S. Koch (Ed.) *Psychology: a study of a science.* Vol. 6. *Investigations of man as socius: their place in psychology and the social sciences. Language,* 1965, **41,** 95–100.

Schlesinger, I. M. Production of utterances and language acquisition, 1968. (mimeo)

Scupin, E., & Scupin, G. *Bubi's erste Kindheit: ein Tagebuch über die geistige Entwicklung eines Knaben während der ersten drei Lebensjahre.* Leipzig: Grieben, 1907.

Segal, E. M., & Halwes, T. G. Learning of letter pairs as a prototype of first language learning. *Psychon. Sci.,* 1965, **3,** 451–452.

Shipley, E. F., Smith, C. S., & Gleitman, L. R. A study in the acquisition of language: free responses to commands. Technical report, 1967. (mimeo)

Simon, H. A., & Newell, A. Computer simulation of human thinking and problem solving. In W. Kessen & C. Kuhlman (Eds.), *Thought in the young child. Monogr. Soc. Res. Child Develpm.,* 1962, **27,** No. 2.

Slobin, D. I. The acquisition of Russian as a native language. In F. Smith & G. A. Miller (1966). (a)

Slobin, D. I. Abstracts of Soviet studies of child language. In F. Smith & G. A. Miller (1966). (b)

Slobin, D. I. Soviet psycholinguistics. In N. O'Connor (Ed.), *Present day Russian psychology: a symposium by seven authors.* Oxford: Pergamon, 1966. (c)

Slobin, D. I. (Ed.) A field manual for cross-cultural study of the acquisition of communicative competence. Second draft, 1967. (mimeo)

Slobin, D. I. Imitation and grammatical development in children. In N. S. Endler, L. R. Boulter, & H. Osser (Eds.), *Contemporary issues in developmental psychology.* New York: Holt, Rinehart & Winston, 1968.

Smith, F., & Miller, G. A. (Eds.), *The genesis of language.* Cambridge: M.I.T. Press, 1966.

Smith, K. H. Recall of paired verbal units under various conditions of organization. Unpublished doctoral dissertation, University of Minnesota, 1963.

Smith, K. H. Mediation and position learning in the recall of structured letter pairs. *Psychon. Sci.,* 1965, **2,** 293–294.

Smith, K. H. Grammatical intrusions in the free recall of structured letter pairs. *J. verb. Learn. verb. Behav.,* 1966, **5,** 447–454. (a)

Smith, K. H. Grammatical intrusions in the recall of structured letter pairs: mediated transfer or position learning? *J. exp. Psychol.,* 1966, **72,** 580–588. (b)

Smith, K. H. Rule-governed intrusions in the free recall of structured letter pairs. *J. exp. Psychol.,* 1967, **73,** 162–164.

Sokhin, F. A. O formirovanii yazykovykh obobshchenii v protsesse rechevogo razvitiya (On the formation of linguistic generalizations in the course of speech development). *Voprosy Psikhol.,* 1959, **5,** No. 5, 112–123.

Staats, A. W., & Staats, C. K. *Complex human behavior: a systematic extension of learning principles.* New York: Holt, Rinehart & Winston, 1963.

State of Israel. *Languages, literacy and educational attainment.* Parts I and II. Publications No. 15 (Part I) and No. 29 (Part II), 1961 Population and Housing Census. Jerusalem: Central Bureau of Statistics, 1963, Part I; 1966, Part II.

Stern, W., & Stern, C. *Die Kindersprache*. (4th ed.) Leipzig: Barth, 1928.

Templin, M. C. *Certain language skills in children: their development and interrelationships. Inst. Child Welfare Monogr. Ser.*, No. 26. Minneapolis: Univ. of Minnesota Press, 1957.

Tischler, H. Schreien, Lallen und erstes Sprechen in der Entwicklung des Sauglings. *Z. Psychol.*, 1957, **160**, 210–263.

Underwood, B. J., & Schultz, R. W. *Meaningfulness and verbal learning*. Philadelphia: Lippincott, 1960.

Velten, H. V. The growth of phonemic and lexical patterns in infant language. *Language*, 1943, **19**, 281–292.

Vygotsky, L. S. *Thought and speech*. Cambridge: M.I.T. Press, 1962.

Weir, R. H. *Language in the crib*. The Hague: Mouton, 1962.

Weksel, W. Review of Bellugi and Brown (1964). *Language*, 1965, **41**, 692–709.

Wells, R. S. Immediate constituents. *Language*, 1947, **23**, 81–117.

Werner, H., & Kaplan, B. *Symbol formation: an organismic-developmental approach to language and the expression of thought*. New York: John Wiley & Sons, 1963.

Werner, H., & Kaplan, E. Development of word meaning through verbal context. *J. Psychol.*, 1950, **29**, 251–257.

Werner, H., & Kaplan, E. *The acquisition of word meaning: a developmental study. Monogr. Soc. Res. Child Develpm.*, 1952, **15**, No. 51.

Winitz, H., & Irwin, O. C. Syllabic and phonetic structure of infants' early words. *J. Speech Dis.*, 1958, **1**, 250–256.

Winter, W. Transforms without kernels? *Language*, 1965, **41**, 484–489.

Zakharova, A. V. Usvoenie doshkol'nikami padezhnykh form (Mastery by preschoolers of the forms of grammatical case). *Doklady Akad. Pedag. Nauk RSFSR*, 1958, **2**, No. 3, 81–84.

Zhinkin, N. I. Na putyakh k izucheniyu mekhanizma rechi (Approaches to the study of the speech mechanism). In *Psikhologicheskaya nauka v SSSR*, I, 470–487. Moscow: Akad. Pedag. Nauk RSFSR, 1959. Transl. in *Psychological science in the USSR*, I, 645–668. Washington: *U.S. Joint Publ. Res. Serv. No.* 11466, 1961.

3

Development of Native Language Skills Beyond the Early Years

JOHN B. CARROLL
Educational Testing Service

INTRODUCTION

Language learning is a lifelong process. Although the foundations of language competence are laid down in early childhood, the child who enters school at the usual starting age has still far to go before his competence approaches that of adults. It will take him a few years to refine his skills with the phonology and grammar of his native language; he will continue to increase his vocabulary knowledge, certainly throughout the years of his education, and to some degree throughout the whole of his adult life. He is expected to become a fluent speaker and a good listener, and he must learn the writing system of his language, developing facility in reading, handwriting, spelling, and composition. He may perchance also acquire auxiliary skills such as typing and shorthand. The child who is to become a fully educated adult must learn a truly enormous number of separate competences and skills. Language learning is never completed.

Since language use is central to many kinds of intellectual operations, there is an intimate connection between growth in language skills and the development of intellectual processes. Nevertheless, any randomly selected sample of adults will exhibit a wide range of variation in language competence and performance. This is exhibited on many dimensions. For example, people differ in the extent of their vocabularies, in their skill in constructing sentences, in their ability to perform as public speakers, in their skills in reading and writing, and in their ability to use language in complex mental operations. This chapter is addressed to the problem of characterizing and

Preparation of this chapter was supported in part by Grant No. 5 P01 HD01762–02 to Educational Testing Service from the National Institute of Child Health and Human Development.

explaining these individual differences. Within the rather severe space limitations inherent in this type of review, it will describe typical courses of development and attempt to indicate what factors may be responsible for different rates of growth and levels of achievement.

THEORETICAL FOUNDATIONS OF THE STUDY OF INDIVIDUAL DIFFERENCES IN DEVELOPMENT

Psychologists are fairly well agreed that a complex interaction of hereditary and environmental factors underlies the development of the competences and performances with which we are concerned in this chapter, although they may disagree as to the *relative* influences of these factors. Under the heading of heredity, we must first acknowledge the existence of certain species-specific genetic factors that determine the *characteristic* course that language development takes in the child. There is a typical age at which each competence or skill appears, and in individual children, the order in which these competences appear is more or less invariant. Lenneberg (1967, pp. 128–130) gives a table of the "milestones" in vocalization and language for the normal child from 12 weeks to 4 years of age; McCarthy (1954, pp. 499–502) gives a somewhat more detailed table covering the first two years. The regularity and the sequence with which skills develop suggest that to a large extent their appearance is controlled by maturational factors that are part of the biological constitution of the child. At the same time, children differ in their rates of development. The evidence available suggests that these different rates of development are to some degree associated with genetic factors. The endowments of some children are such that they develop much faster than the average child; at the opposite extreme, there are types of mental defectives whose language development is very slow and who in fact never reach the levels attained by the normal child. Lenneberg (1967, p. 164) attributes such retardation to defects in the neural organization of the brain. Whereas the normal child has established the general basis for language at about 4 years of age, the retarded child may not attain a like facility until the age of 9 or later.

Heredity is only one of the factors determining the constitution of the individual. Conditions in prenatal life or very early childhood, diseases, accidents, etc., may cause certain deficiencies of sensory, motor, or mental capacity (blindness, deafness, brain damage, etc.) that inhibit growth of language and cognitive skills.

Under the heading of environment, we may consider all those conditions that afford children opportunities to learn the specific competences and skills that they must learn in order to use their native language effectively. Some children are reared in language-rich environments, peopled with adults and other children who have acquired, or are in the process of acquiring, high levels of language skills; if they have the necessary mental endowments, these children can reach similarly high levels of skill by modeling their performances on those of others in the environment. On the other hand, many children are brought up in "culturally disadvantaged" environments, where according to such writers as Bernstein (1960) and Deutsch (1965), they are exposed not only to nonstandard dialects but also to styles and modes of language use that are radically different from those characteristic of middle and upper social classes. (See Cazden [1966] for a review of sub-cultural differences in child language.) Environments differ not only in the quantity and kind of language which the child experiences; they differ also in many other ways—the methods of child rearing and parent teaching, the quality of schooling offered, the variety of opportunity in reading, travel, and culture learning that the child has, and specific conditions that influence the child's motivation for learning.

The interaction of all these factors makes for differentiation among individuals not only in their general rate of development but also in the particular kinds of competences and skills in which they are strong or weak. Because of the multiple causation that is undoubtedly involved, it is futile to attempt to assign values to the relative influences of heredity, environment, and specific constitutional conditions. A hereditary condition may be the most influential factor in one case, an environmental or a sensory handicap the most influential in another. Although it is possible to develop statistical predictions of development for groups of children with given characteristics, the analysis of the etiology of any particular case of retarded development, such as deficiency in vocabulary or in reading comprehension, must depend on an evaluation of the factors involved in that particular case.

The question of the constancy of rate of development must be considered from the point of view just outlined. Human characteristics have an apparent stability: the child who is gifted in language development at the age of 5 tends to be, on the average, gifted also at later ages. Likewise, the child who is retarded at age 5 will probably be retarded at later ages. Nevertheless, there is a strong suggestion in the work of Bloom (1964) that the apparent stability of human characteristics is mainly the result of a cumulative process of growth in which the stability inheres in what the individual has developed up to any given point, but in which the increments of growth are for the most part random. It would appear, for example, that by the age of about 4, the typical child has acquired half of all the mental growth he will ever acquire; the amount of mental growth he gains in any given year is almost completely independent of what he has acquired up to the start of that year. The increments of growth are, so to speak, accidents of the particular maturational and environmental influences that happen to obtain during a particular period of growth. Bloom shows that such a view is in accord with the evidence provided by longitudinal studies of correlations between mental age scores at different chronological ages: the farther apart in chronological age one takes a correlation, the lower the correlation will be. The implication is that within certain limits imposed by the individual's initial status, the consistent occurrence of favorable environmental and learning conditions over a period of years may result in an increase of the individual's status relative to others of his age; similarly, if an individual is consistently deprived of favorable environmental conditions over a period of years, his relative status will decrease to a marked extent.

DIMENSIONS OF INDIVIDUAL DIFFERENCES IN LANGUAGE DEVELOPMENT AND ATTAINMENT

All empirical research on individual differences in the growth and attainment of language skills has rested upon observations or tests of language performances. Observations vary in the degree to which they are collected systematically and with a consistent set of procedures. A test is in one sense a special variety of observation in which the performance of an individual is obtained with standard instructions and conditions in a specified situation. The degree to which this situation is actually constant for all individuals tested may vary; for example, a test with a time limit may in effect present different numbers of stimulus situations ("test items") depending upon how many of these the subject is able to attempt within the time limit. In the common usage of the term, a *standardized* test is one which has been administered to a representative sample of individuals, yielding data that have been arranged to show the range of performances that can be expected from the population of which the sample is presumably representative. For the purposes of summarization and statistical analysis, the data yielded by observations and tests are often subjected to procedures leading to quantification and the creation of *variables*. Specific behaviors observed may be counted or rated as to quality on a numerical scale; test performances lend themselves to quantification through such procedures as counting the number of correct answers given by the subject or relating the subject's responses to an age scale (e.g., on the Stanford-Binet vocabulary test, the final score is the "mental age," corresponding to the number of words correctly defined by the subject). Whether observations are quantified or not, there is the general problem of whether they are "reliable," that is, essentially replicable with minimal error. There is also the problem of whether the observations are "valid," that is, observations that truly reflect the presumed trait or characteristic that they were designed to observe or measure. Validity is therefore specific to the particular intent of the designer of the observation procedure: a procedure may be invalid for one purpose but highly valid for another purpose.

This leads immediately to the question of how an investigator decides what he wants to observe or measure, or more generally, how one conceives the structure of the underlying traits or characteristics that are of interest in a particular domain such as the development of language skills (as opposed to, say, the development of skills in mathematics). Historically, the development of our notions concerning the dimensions of individual differences in the growth of language skills has seen a continuous interplay between logical analysis, on the one hand, and inference from common experience and empirical studies, on the other. Early studies depended largely on the categories yielded by common observation and a preliminary logical analysis, i.e., they studied the development of such aspects of language ability as the articulation of sounds, sentence length, and vocabulary. More recent studies have tended to be based on a finer linguistic analysis of language competence and also on the findings of various psychological investigations of language performance, particularly performances on tests.

Elsewhere (Carroll, 1968b), I have attempted to give a logical classification of the language competences and performances that would have to be considered in order to yield a complete profile of language growth and attainment (whether in the native or a foreign language). Language competences are spelled out in Table 3-1; language performances are shown in Table 3-2. In each cell of Table 3-1, it may be presumed that there are large numbers of elements that might be tested. For example, under Spelling (a productive competence related to the lexicon of the written language), a complete examination would consist of a test of all the words in the written language. In practice, however, only a sample of words can be tested; from the results, one infers that the individual has a certain degree of "ability" or competence in spelling, for the score on the test is an indicator of the probability that the individual can spell properly any word chosen at random. As in the case of other aspects of language ability, competences in separate items tend to "go together" in the sense that in a representative sample of individuals, there tends to be a positive (though not necessarily perfect) correlation between knowing any one item and knowing any other item.

Table 3-1 refers to language *competences*, i.e., the possession of learnings that underlie and make possible a corresponding performance. The distinction between linguistic competence and linguistic performance, referred to at various points in this chapter, has been emphasized by Chomsky (1965). Linguistic competence is the inferred capacity of language users, developed in language acquisition, to generate and understand novel but grammatical sentences. For example, linguistic competence enables the speaker to generate or to understand a sentence such as *Flying planes can be dangerous* in *either* one of its possible readings; which reading he will actually produce or understand in a given situation has to do with his *performance*. Linguistic performance is affected by nonlinguistic variables, such as fatigue (sometimes leading to the production of ungrammatical sentences) or mental

Table 3-1. Chart of Linguistic Competences

Skill	Phonology and Orthography	Lexicon — Morphemes, words, idioms	Lexicon — Semantic and grammatical components of lexicon	Grammar — Morphology and syntax	Grammar — Semantic components
Spoken language: Receptive skills (listening)	Phoneme recognition and discrimination: ability to discriminate words or phrases differing in one phoneme or distinctive feature	Recognition of lexical elements as belonging to the language	Recognition of semantic and grammatical meanings (i.e., word class assignments) of lexical elements	Recognition: of morphological and syntactical features and associated phonology	Understanding:
Productive skills (speaking)	Phoneme production: ability to produce phonemes or allophonic variants in word forms or phrases, with accuracy at either phonemic or phonetic level	Ability to produce lexical elements fitting semantic and grammatical specifications		Ability to produce: morphological and syntactical features with appropriate phonology	In appropriate contexts:
Written language: Receptive skills (reading)	Recognition of the graphemic symbols of the language, with (as appropriate) ability to name them and give their sounds	Above, plus recognition of meanings and pronunciations of written forms (including special graphemic symbols, abbreviations, etc.)		Above, plus recognition of special grammar-related conventions of the written language, such as punctuation, capitalization, certain spelling changes, etc.	
Productive skills (writing)	Ability to write (by hand or other method) the graphemes of the language, state their customary ordering	Spelling		As for receptive skills, plus ability to produce written conventions in appropriate contexts	

Table 3-2. Suggested Chart of Linguistic Performance Abilities

Ability	Phonology	Lexicon	Morphology and Syntax	Integrated Language Performance
Speed of response	Articulation ability (Speed and accuracy of speech sound production)	Naming facility (Speed of responding with the names of things, actions, or ideas)	Expressional fluency (Ability to compose rapidly sentences fitting given grammatical requirements)	Oral speaking fluency
Diversity of response	"Word fluency" (Ability to recall words with given phonetic-orthographic characteristics)	Ideational fluency (Ability to call up names or ideas fitting given semantic characteristics)		Listening comprehension
Complexity of information processing	Auditory memory for speech sounds or sequences of sounds	Abstract reasoning ability (Ability to process complex linguistically coded information)		Reading comprehension (and speed)
Awareness of linguistic competence	(No pertinent evidence)	Awareness of the structure of the lexicon; facility in giving opposites, super-ordinates, etc.	Grammatical sensitivity (Ability to find analogous grammatical elements in sentences)	Writing ability

NOTE: All based on underlying competences.

indecision (sometimes leading to hesitation, rephrasing, and other pheno-mena). The distinction between competence and performance is *analogous* (but not identical) to the distinction between "underlying ability" and "observed test score," which has long been recognized in the theory of psychological measurement. Table 3-2 refers to "underlying traits" of linguistic performance, i.e., more or less stable characteristics of the indivi-dual that determine the quality of a linguistic performance. For example, a characteristic mode of linguistic performance might be one whereby the individual typically produces many incomplete or rephrased sentences, in contrast to an individual who nearly always produces completely gram-matical sentences. Thus, in the realm of linguistic performances, there is a distinction between "underlying trait" and "observed performance" (or test score). The distinction between linguistic competence and performance cross-cuts the distinction between underlying trait and observed perfor-mance:

	Underlying Trait	Observed Performance
Linguistic competence	Possession of a learned rule or habit	Correct response to a stimulus calling for manifestation of the rule or habit
Linguistic performance	Characteristic mode of linguistic response	Actual behavior on the test, revealing the characteristic mode of response

Questions of reliability and validity pertain essentially to whether a given observation or testing procedure yields replicable and useful information concerning the underlying ability or trait which it was designed to measure.

The construction of both Tables 3-1 and 3-2 has depended partly upon an examination of various empirical studies of language performances. A favorite tool of individual difference psychology is the technique known as *factor analysis*. As developed by Spearman (1927), Thurstone (1947), and others, this technique starts from a table of the intercorrelations among a large number of separate measures as applied to a sample of individuals exhibiting variations in performance and proceeds to find the smallest number of underlying dimensions or "factors" that can account for these intercorrelations. Each dimension is to some degree independent of every other dimension, and inferentially, the individuals in the sample studied exhibit independent variation with respect to each dimension. In the inter-pretation of such findings, an effort is made to "identify" or characterize each dimension by postulating the particular kinds of traits or abilities that are measured by the tests of that dimension. For example, one dimension that is often isolated in factor analytic studies of ability tests is the so-called "verbal" or "verbal knowledge" factor, represented by tests that call upon the general knowledge that the individual has of the vocabulary of his native language and also upon his ability to comprehend language with complex syntactical structure and difficult concepts. The "verbal" factor may be identified with the general *competence* that the individual has with the more advanced vocabulary and grammatical structure of his language. Still another factor often isolated in factorial studies is the so-called "word-fluency" factor. The tests represented by this factor characteristically measure the individual's ability to recall words readily with given ortho-graphic characteristics, e.g., to find anagrams inherent in a word like *generation* or to give a list of words starting with the letter *S* and ending with the letter *M*. Obviously, such tests call upon linguistic *competences* (knowledge of words with the desired characteristics), but individual differences in such competences do not appear very relevant to performance (at least in most samples that have been studied). The "word-fluency" factor therefore can be considered as representing an underlying trait of charac-teristic linguistic *performance*—a facility in producing words with given phonetic-orthographic characteristics which is largely independent of the individual's vocabulary or general verbal ability.

A compilation of the results of factor analytic studies made by French (1951) yielded the following "factors" that would seem to be at least some-what relevant to the description of language skills and their development. The fact that many of these factors have been found in numerous separate studies using different samples, different age groups, and different test ·variables lends credence to their reality.

Factor AR, Auditory Resistance: Essentially, this factor has to do with the indivi-dual's ability to perceive speech despite distortion.

Factor Ar, Articulation: ". . . clearly identified by the tests which involve speed of producing oral sounds," either in articulating particular sounds repeatedly or in oral reading of passages, particularly under instructions to read as fast as possible.

Factor D, Deduction: ". . . reasoning from the general to the specific. . . . The primarily verbal test, *Reading Comprehension*, has loadings on *Deduction* that are fairly consistent although . . . low." French suggests that the "reason for the loading of *Reading Comprehension* on *Factor D* is the deductive nature of the process of under-standing specific reading material by relating it to general principles about things and situations which have accumulated as a result of past experience."

Factor FE, Fluency of Expression: ". . . the ability to think rapidly of the wording for ideas. . . . This factor is distinguished from *Ideational Fluency* in that here the idea is given, while *Ideational Fluency* tests require the subject to supply the ideas."

Factor IF, Ideational Fluency: ". . . characterized by tests on which the task is to write down ideas about a given topic as fast as possible."

Factor M, Associative Memory: The ability to learn arbitrary associations between elements (words, nonsense syllables, digits, etc.).

Factor Na, Naming: Speed in giving names for stimuli.

Factor PS, Public Speaking: Ability to speak fluently and well in a situation calling for spontaneous speech. (French's characterization of the factor as *Public Speaking* may, however, represent an overgeneralization, since measurements of speaking ability are often taken in the absence of an audience.)

Factor SA, Speed of Association: Speed in selecting or omitting words with given semantic attributes, e.g., words that name small objects.

Factor Sp, Speed: Speed of reading tests appear among the tests defining the factor, but the factor probably has application to a wide variety of tests requiring speed of mental operations.

Factor V, Verbal Comprehension: ". . . a factor embodying the knowledge and understanding of the English language."

Factor W, Word Fluency: ". . . limited to the speed of producing any words which fit certain mechanical restrictions regarding the letters or affixes used."

Since French's summary, factor analytic studies have modified somewhat our knowledge of the dimensions of individual differences in language skills. For other discussions, the reader may be referred to writings by Vernon (1950) and Carroll (1962). Vernon, following the British tradition in factor analysis, emphasizes a *V:ed* or verbal-educational factor that appears in any test that draws upon language knowledge, whether acquired early in life or through later schooling. He shows that this factor is somewhat independent of the *g* or general-intelligence factor that is characteristically found, according to certain types of statistical procedures, in all cognitive tests. (The scope of this chapter forbids a discussion of the technical issues that differentiate forms of factor analysis.) Carroll discusses several verbal factors as factors of "verbal achievement" and stresses the idea, also advanced by Ferguson (1954), that factors represent groups of knowledges or skills that are typically developed or learned together. "It is strange, but true," Carroll states (1962), "that even now we can cite no thoroughgoing, all-inclusive factor analytic study of all the ordinary English language skills; therefore we have had to piece together our knowledge from a variety of studies. It is now pretty certain, however, that there are separate 'factors' for the traditional language modes, that is, reading, writing, speaking, and listening [p. 12]."

In the domain of speaking, factors of fluency and skill in speech performance have been established by Carroll (1941), Marge (1964), and Taylor, Smith, Ghiselin, Sheets, and Cochran (1958). Marge found, in a sample of 143 preadolescent subjects, separate speaking ability factors, one associated with ratings made by classroom teachers on the basis of general speech performance and one associated with evaluations made by speech specialists in an oral interview situation. Other factors were: Motor Skill in Speaking (apparently identical to *Factor Ar* listed by French); Speech Dominance (associated with teacher's ratings of talkativeness); Non-Distracting Speech Behavior (absence of speech mannerisms, hesitations, and distracting voice quality); Voice Quality (as rated either by teachers or by speech specialists); and Language Maturity (associated with teacher ratings of quality of grammatical usage, pronunciation, complexity of sentence structure, and vocabulary in speech). This last factor would probably be found to be closely related to the traditional verbal knowledge factor found in written tests. Taylor et al. (1958) studied a wide variety of oral, written, and situational tests of communication skills as applied to two samples of enlisted men in the Air Force and students at the University of Utah. While the complete results of these studies have not been published, it would appear that several factors of individual differences in speaking skills operated in their tests. Speaking skill in situational tests such as participation in conferences, oral reading of instructions, and giving lectures was shown to be a highly complex function of many separate factors in language skill.

In the domain of listening comprehension, Spearritt (1962) was able to isolate a factor of listening comprehension which is distinct from the verbal knowledge factor found in written tests. Although the listening comprehension and verbal knowledge factors were to some extent correlated, this was doubtless because both depend on the individual's knowledge of vocabulary and language structure. The listening factor was found to be relatively independent of certain basic abilities such as Auditory Resistance and Span Memory. The verbal comprehension factor, as measured by written tests, was probably a reflection of the individual's skill in reading. Spearritt's study utilized children in grade 6. A separate listening comprehension factor was also isolated by Taylor et al. (1958) in their study of college-age individuals.

The domain of reading is represented by the many factors, above all the verbal knowledge factor, that have have been found in analyses of written tests. Reading speed and reading comprehension have been established as distinct but rather highly correlated factors; although individuals with similar degrees of skill in comprehension may differ somewhat in speed of reading, this variation is limited. Davis (1944) attempted to show that reading comprehension could be separated into a series of separate skills such as ability to remember details, ability to make inferences, etc., but Thurstone (1946) felt that Davis's data were better interpreted as revealing one single general factor of reading skill. Through an elaborate statistical technique that they call "substrata analysis," Holmes and Singer (1966) attempted to demonstrate that individual differences in reading speed and reading comprehension can be accounted for by numerous "substrata factors," including even tonal memory, mechanical aptitude, and phonetic association, but their analysis is vitiated by fallacious statistical reasoning and must be discounted. Their factor analytic results, however, may be accepted; these reveal that both reading speed and reading comprehension, to the extent that they were adequately measured by single tests, are for the most part explained by a single factor, which they call an "audiovisual verbal symbolic-reasoning factor," which appears to be quite similar to the verbal knowledge factor found in other studies.

Abilities in reading and writing are highly correlated. Measures of general reading and of general writing ability are usually found on the verbal knowledge factor mentioned previously. From careful studies of the extent to which the essay writing examinations set by the College Entrance Examination Board correlate with objective measures of verbal aptitude and English achievement, Huddleston (1954) was forced to the conclusion that "measurable 'ability to write' is no more than verbal ability." This conclusion applies, however, only if one is thinking about a single measurement of general excellence in writing themes or essays. Different dimensions of ability can operate in essay writing. Olsen (1956) found, for example, that for a sample of preparatory school students who took a College Board General Composition Test in two successive years (thus writing two different themes), it was possible to assign ratings on four separate aspects—organization and reasoning, content, style, and mechanics—that were far from perfectly correlated among themselves in either year but that showed some consistency over the two examinations. To be sure, the test-retest correlations were low, ranging from .25 for organization and reasoning to .46 for mechanics, but this was in part due to unreliability of rating. Diederich, French, and Carlton (1961) analyzed "schools of thought" in judgments of themes and found five somewhat independent factors: Ideas (relevance, clarity, quantity, development, persuasiveness); Form (organization and analysis); Flavor (style, interest, sincerity); Mechanics (specific errors in grammar, punctuation, etc.), and Wording (choice and arrangement of words). It is not yet known, however, whether these factors represent aspects of writing ability that could be shown to be consistently displayed by a student over periods of time. It is not known, either, whether these factors would be found to be related to measurements of more general cognitive abilities. Undoubtedly, many of them would be highly related to the verbal knowledge factor; some of the results obtained by Taylor et al. (1958) suggest that writing skill is predicted by measures not only of verbal knowledge but also of associational fluency and ideational fluency. In an earlier study, Taylor (1947) had found that the number of words produced in free writing exercises was related to the Ideational Fluency factor. Maltzman (1963) reported the number of words written in themes was related to judgments of theme originality.

General language skill, particularly as measured by the verbal knowledge factor, is closely related to intelligence. Indeed, vocabulary and language comprehension tests are often important components in measures of what has been termed *verbal intelligence*. The current view of intelligence is that it is, so to speak, an average of a number of separate and to some extent independent components, including such abilities as reasoning, induction, deduction, arithmetical skill, memory, spatial visualization, and the like. A child's rating on an IQ test such as the Stanford-Binet (Terman & Merrill, 1960) is an index of his average rate of growth on these abilities. One component test in the Stanford-Binet scale that correlates very highly with composite IQ measures is the Vocabulary subtest. Vocabulary tests figure importantly in other general intelligence tests given individually such as the Wechsler Adult Intelligence Scale (Wechsler, 1955) and the Wechsler Intelligence Scale for Children (Wechsler, 1949). Tests of the verbal knowledge factor are also included in a large number of standardized group tests of intelligence, such as the California Test of Mental Maturity (Sullivan, Clark, & Tiegs, 1957), the Primary Mental Abilities Batteries (Thurstone & Thurstone, 1946–58), and the Differential Aptitude Tests (Bennett, Seashore, & Wesman, 1947–59). The Verbal score of the Scholastic Aptitude Tests administered by the College Board is a measure of a composite of verbal knowledge and general reasoning. Many of these tests are designed for populations of individuals who can be presumed to have acquired basic language skills; nevertheless, the wide ranges of scores attained on them by such populations attest to the fact that there are wide differences in the extent to which "normal" children and adults acquire language skills beyond the most elementary ones involved in primary language acquisition in the young child.

The most elaborate concept of the nature of intelligence now available is that developed by Guilford (1967). According to him, intelligence is best described as being potentially composed of more than 100 separate aspects of cognitive ability. Through a logical analysis of the results of many factor analytic studies, Guilford has constructed a sort of "periodic table" of these factors. Each factor represents a particular combination of a certain type of mental "operation," a certain type of "content," and a certain type of "product." He postulates that there are at least five types of operations (Cognition, Memory, Divergent Production, Convergent Production, and Evaluation), four types of contents (Figural, Symbolic, Semantic, and Behavioral), and six types of products (Units, Classes, Relations, Systems, Transformations, and Implications). He has attempted to fit within his system all the previously established factors of mental ability, as well as ones newly discovered. For example, what has been above termed the verbal knowledge factor is regarded by Guilford as the Cognition of Semantic Units; he states that "the most dependable and most univocal measure of this factor [coded *CMU*], is a vocabulary test of some kind, some kinds being better than others." But Guilford claims that a vocabulary test that requires the subject to supply the word that fits a given definition tends to measure not only *CMU* but also the factor *NMU* (Convergent Production of Semantic Units). Guilford thus lays stress on the attempt to identify the processes involved in the successful performance of mental tasks.

A listing of some of the factors from Guilford's compilation that may have a bearing upon the description of language skills will give an idea of the variety of separate dimensions that may exist in the verbal domain. The list presents, first, several factors concerned with what Guilford (1967) calls "symbolic" contents. By "symbol," he refers to such items as alphabetic letters, digits, and (in the auditory sphere) phonemes, that is, "signs, materials, the elements having no significance in and of themselves [p. 227]."[1]

CSU-V Cognition of Symbolic Units (Visual): This factor appears in tests that require the recognition of letter combinations, as in spelling or anagrams tests.

CSU-A Cognition of Symbolic Units (Auditory): Tests requiring recognition of words presented with some type of auditory distortion.

DSU Divergent Production of Symbolic Units: Ability to produce a variety of spelled words fitting certain orthographic requirements; probably the same as the *W* or *Word Fluency* factor mentioned earlier.

CSR Cognition of Symbolic Relations: Ability to perform tasks depending upon recognition of the alphabetical ordering of letters.

DSC Divergent Production of Symbolic Classes: Ability to perform tasks involving flexibility in recognizing different orthographic properties common to sets of words.

NSS Convergent Production of Symbolic Systems: Tasks requiring the solution of problems involving complex systems of letter-symbols.

A large variety of factors with "semantic" contents are claimed by Guildford. The term *semantic* appears to refer not only to word meanings but also to the "meanings" of sentences or of commonly experienced situations.

CMU Cognition of Semantic Units: As noted earlier, this is Guilford's characterization of what has previously been called the verbal knowledge factor, defined primarily by vocabulary tests.

DMU Divergent Production of Semantic Units: Ability to produce rapidly a variety of words or ideas fitting given semantic categories. It is probably the same as *Factor IF, Ideational Fluency*, identified by other investigators.

NMU Convergent Production of Semantic Units: Ability to supply a single word that fits a given semantic definition or to supply the name for a pictured referent.

EMU Evaluation of Semantic Units: Correctness in evaluating semantic similarities.

CMC Cognition of Semantic Classes: Facility in identifying semantic classes, as of words.

DMC Divergent Production of Semantic Classes: Flexibility in producing a variety of classifications of words or ideas. One of its best tests is "Brick Uses," which asks the subject to give a variety of unusual uses for bricks.

CMR Cognition of Semantic Relations: Correct performance on tests requiring the recognition of semantic relations, as in verbal analogies tests. This is possibly the factor that was identified by French (1951) as *D, Deduction*.

DMR Divergent Production of Semantic Relations: Fluency in producing a variety of responses having similar semantic relations with given stimuli. It is possibly the same as the factor identified by other investigators as *Associational Fluency*.

NMR Convergent Production of Semantic Relations: Accuracy in producing words with stated semantic relations to given words.

EMR Evaluation of Semantic Relations: Ability to discriminate between closely similar semantic relations of words.

[1] Adapted from *The nature of human intelligence* by J. P. Guilford. Copyright © 1967 by McGraw-Hill, Inc. Used with permission of McGraw-Hill Book Company.

CMS Cognition of Semantic Systems: Ability to structure a complex reasoning problem.

DMS Divergent Production of Semantic Systems: Ability to construct sentences in variety; similar to a factor elsewhere called *Expressional Fluency*. It is also defined by tests of theme writing scored for speed and quantity of production.

NMS Convergent Production of Semantic Systems: Principally defined by tests requiring the subject to rearrange items or ideas in temporal order.

EMS Evaluation of Semantic Systems: Ability to evaluate the validity or reasonableness of ideas or situations.

CMT Cognition of Semantic Transformations: Ability to transform or redefine concepts.

DMT Divergent Production of Semantic Transformations: An "originality" factor, involving the ability to think of unusual ways of transforming ideas.

NMT Convergent Production of Semantic Transformations: Ability to redefine concepts so as to solve problems in novel ways.

CMI Cognition of Semantic Implications: Recognition of the implications or possible consequences of hypothetical situations.

DMI Divergent Production of Semantic Implications: "Semantic elaboration," ability to produce a variety of detailed plans to meet given problem situations.

NMI Convergent Production of Semantic Implications: This factor is not yet well supported by the evidence, but it is possibly an ability to produce semantic implications that will adequately connect a series of ideas.

EMI Evaluation of Semantic Implications: Ability to evaluate the correctness of logical inferences from given evidence.

Many of these factors, it may be seen, have perhaps more to do with generalized mental operations than with specific language skills. Nevertheless, such mental operations may be presumed to constitute a substrata for language performances such as speaking, listening, reading, and writing, and for this reason, it is believed that they merit attention here. For example, it is reasonable to hypothesize that many of the "divergent production" factors underlie various forms of originality in speaking and writing, that some of the "convergent production" and "evaluation" factors underlie logicality of thought and organization in speaking and writing, and that various "cognition" factors have much to do with the comprehension of language.

Although in many respects Guilford's scheme is tentative and controversial (for a critique, see Carroll, 1968a), it represents one of the first attempts to fit the results of individual-differences research into a unified framework. The framework may have loopholes; that is to say, it may not be possible to fit all the results into the framework. Alternative conceptions of the "structure of intelligence" are possible. For example, both Carroll (1962) and Ferguson (1954) suppose that individual-difference factors can be identified in any domain of behavior where sets of responses are for any reason learned together.

I can cite at least two factors of individual differences in important basic language skills that do not seem to fit into Guilford's scheme. Both were isolated in batteries of foreign language aptitude tests (Carroll, 1958), but there is good reason to suppose that they stem from native language skills.

One is what I have called *phonetic coding ability*, the ability to store in memory, presumably by some sort of coding process, any kind of auditory phonetic material. This ability has been shown to be requisite in learning foreign languages; at the same time, it may reflect a kind of awareness or knowledge of phonetic-orthographic rules in English spelling. I have speculated that it may be a function of whether the individual received adequate "phonic" instruction in the course of learning to read his native language.

The other is a factor of *grammatical sensitivity* and *interest in language structure* that is also important in learning foreign languages but may also have some relevance to native language skills and behaviors. It is defined best by a test that requires the subject to perceive grammatical analogies, i.e., to recognize similar grammatical functions of words or phrases in different sentences; it does not, however, require the subject to know any formal grammar. There are wide individual differences among high school and college-age students on this test, even though they may all be skilled native speakers of English and thus in *unconscious* command of English grammar and even though all of them may be supposed to have had at least some exposure to training in formal grammar.

Although factor analytic investigations of cognitive abilities have usually involved high school and college-age subjects, there are sufficient studies to indicate that many of the factors are well established at early ages. For example, Bereiter (1961) has identified various fluency factors in studies of preschool children. Thurstone and Thurstone (1954) have performed factor analyses of tests given to elementary school children, finding most of the factors commonly identified at the upper age levels. It must not be concluded from these results, however, that *individuals* maintain the same relative status on these factors over a period of years; the longitudinal studies that would be required to establish individual growth curves in separate factors have not yet been done.

An interesting and instructive example of an attempt to construct a battery of language ability measures based on psycholinguistic theory is the Illinois Test of Psycholinguistic Abilities (ITPA), published by the Institute for Research on Exceptional Children at the University of Illinois. Developed in an early form by Sievers (1955; see also Sievers, McCarthy, Olson, Bateman, & Kass, 1963), this individually administered test is designed to identify psycholinguistic abilities and disabilities in children between the ages of two and one-half and nine years (McCarthy & Kirk, 1963). Its construction was based, the authors claim, on a model of psycholinguistic abilities provided by Osgood (1952, 1957), which postulated three dimensions for classifying these abilities: level of organization (integrational or automatic-sequential, grammatical, and semantic or representational); channel of communication (auditory-vocal, and perceptuomotor); and process (decoding, association, and encoding). In theory, this scheme should yield 18 different abilities, but because it was not deemed possible to measure each ability in a pure form, the subtests were designed to measure only certain combinations of abilities. The published form of the battery contains, at the Representation level, two Decoding tests (*Auditory Decoding* and *Visual Decoding*), two Association tests (*Auditory-Vocal Association* and *Visual-Motor Association*), and two Encoding tests (*Vocal Encoding* and *Motor Encoding*); at the Automatic-Sequential Level, it contains one Automatic test (*Auditory-Vocal Automatic Ability*) and two tests of Sequencing (*Auditory-Vocal Sequencing* and *Visual-Motor Sequencing*). Factor analyses of these tests are claimed by McCarthy and Kirk (1963) to indicate, generally, that each subtest measures a distinct ability, but Weener, Barritt, and Semmel (1967) have questioned this interpretation, pointing out that a general factor of linguistic ability seems to underlie most of the tests and raising the possibility that the specific variance of each subtest contains a large error-of-measurement component. Although they feel that the evidence supports the thesis that the ITPA measures several abilities, these abilities are not well differentiated by the subtest scores; further, they see little relation between the test results and the particular theoretical model that was used in constructing the battery. Empirical data, it would appear, tend to put much strain on any arbitrary theory that may be developed concerning "psycholinguistic" abilities; much more work is needed to fashion an adequate diagnostic test of these abilities.

DEVELOPMENT OF SPECIFIC LANGUAGE SKILLS

Development of Skills in Using the Sound System (Phonology)

According to Ervin and Miller (1963) in their review of language development in the child, "by the fourth year, the child's phonological system closely approximates the model, and the remaining deviations are usually corrected by the time the child enters school [p. 116]." Although this statement may be accepted as a useful generalization, it must not be interpreted as implying that the phonology of the native language is completely learned by the age of 6 or that there are no interesting individual differences among children in phonological competence or performance at this or later ages.

One aspect of phonological competence is the ability to discriminate among the basic sounds (phonemes) of the language and to make absolute identifications of those sounds. Complete understanding of spoken utterances presupposes, in principle, that the listener must be able to identify the phonemes absolutely. One can imagine a situation, for example, where either of the sentences *He had expensive plans* or *He had expansive plans* would be equally appropriate but would have quite different implications; obviously the listener must be able to identify whether *expensive* or *expansive* was uttered. Studies of the ability of children or adults to identify phonemes are relatively few in number and are beset with various methodological problems. In testing, it is difficult to rule out extraneous cues that help the individual respond in the desired way. The speech stimuli must be carefully standardized in order to rule out peculiarities of pronunciation due to dialect or to a particular occasion. Extraneous noise (whether ambient in the testing room or present in electronic speech reproduction systems) may mask the signal and make identification difficult. Finally, the testing situation may introduce an undesirable amount of artificiality. There is some question as to whether a test of discrimination between nonsense syllables, as used by Templin (1957) for 6- to 8-year-old children, allows the child to display his true capacity to discriminate among phonemes in words he knows. On a test for 3- to 5-year-old children that required selection of pictures named by words that were phonetically very similar, Templin reported mean percentages correct as 65.1 at age 3, 75.3 at age 4, and 82.4 at age 5. On the nonsense-syllable test for the older children, mean percentages correct were 83.4 at age 6, 89.4 at age 7, and 92.2 at age 8, but it is evident that some children made perfect scores. Boys were about a year behind girls, on the average, and there were differences correlated with the socioeconomic status of the children. Unfortunately, Templin did not report data as to what sounds or sound contrasts were most difficult. It would appear from her results, in any case, that not all children have perfected their ability to identify English sounds by the age of 8. There is little information available on whether these individual differences continue to hold up to adulthood in normal hearing subjects. Miller and Nicely's study (1955) shows, in any case, that adults do not discriminate phonemes perfectly in isolated syllables even with the highest signal-to-noise ratio used (+ 12db). Brown and Hildum (1956) showed that even students of linguistics perceive speech sounds partly on the basis of their expectancies.

Much more information is available on the development of speech sound production ability. Templin reports the ages at which 75 percent of her subjects "correctly" produced specific consonant sounds. The sounds *m, n, ng, p, f, h, w,* and *y* were correctly produced by 75 percent at age 3 or 3.5; *k, b, d, g, r, s, sh,* and *ch* at age 4 or 4.5; *t, th* (unvoiced), *v,* and *l* at age 6; *th* (voiced), *z, zh,* and *j* at age 7. The cluster *hw* was not "correctly" produced by 75 percent even at 8 years, but Templin ignored the fact that dialectal alternation occurs between *w* and *hw*. Correlations between total articulation scores and sounds discrimination scores were, respectively, .59, .58, .44, .67, .69, and .47 at ages 3, 4, 5, 6, 7, and 8. There does, then, seem to be a quite significant correlation between a child's ability to discriminate and to articulate English sounds. But again, information is lacking as to developmental trends in phonological competence beyond age 8. It may be assumed that different children reach an approximation to complete competence at different ages. The fact that Steer and Drexler (1960) were able to find multiple correlations in the neighborhood of .50 between articulation tests administered to a sample of kindergarten children and an articulation test administered five years later suggests that there is some developmental consistency in articulation ability. Marge (1964), in a study employing mostly fifth grade children, found a factor *Voice Quality* that was defined in part by ratings both by teachers and by speech specialists of the children's distinctness of pronunciation ("articulation") in ordinary conversation and in speech tests. "Apparently," Marge noted, "the raters and teachers perceive pleasant voices in individuals who articulate well, pronounce correctly, and speak fluently."

There are undoubtedly certain kinds of differences in articulation that persist into adulthood. Stitt and Huntington (1963) reported that judges could make reliable ratings of the articulation proficiency of adults performing oral reading of prose passages. Carroll (1941) found that normal and "fastest" oral reading speeds of adults were correlated with the speed with which particular sounds could be pronounced repeatedly; all these measures defined his *Articulation Ability* factor. Carroll was not concerned, however, with distinctness or accuracy of pronunciation but with a motoric ability that seems to control speech rate in certain situations (see also Carroll, 1967a, for normative data on speech rate in adults and comments on methods of measuring speech rates).

In learning to read, children show individual differences in their ability to take advantage of the "phonic" cues provided by orthography. Chall, Roswell, and Blumenthal (1963) describe some of these differences in terms of ability to "blend" and synthesize sounds to make words, e.g., on hearing the sounds /kə/ and /ɔhl/ to form the word *call*. In a longitudinal study of Negro children tested in grades 1 through 4, they found clear evidence of an "auditory blending ability" that was correlated with reading achievement, regardless of whether it was tested in grade 1 or grade 4. At the same time, auditory blending ability was not significantly related to measures of intelligence. These authors speculate that poor auditory blending ability is "a sign of a neurophysiological defect or of a lag in development." No information is available on the relation of this ability to sound discrimination ability or to articulation or pronunciation ability as discussed above; it is possible that it is a quite independent perceptual ability.

It is a fact, too, that children *and adults* differ considerably among themselves in the degree to which they have knowledge of the "phonic code" that underlies the relationship between orthography and pronunciation in English. Tiffin and McKinnis (1940) were among the first to demonstrate, for example, that adults differ in their ability to pronounce artificial words according to the implicit rules of English orthography (like *disbape*, which should yield /disbéyp/, but may be "mispronounced" /dáyz-bæ̀-biy/ or /dîys-báhp/.) Shannon (1959) constructed tests of "phonetic understanding" that revealed wide individual differences among prospective reading teachers. The differences appear earlier, too; Templin (1954) constructed tests of "phonic knowledge" suitable for fourth grade children and found significant correlations between these tests and measures of reading and spelling achievement. It is possible that these differences are partly due to differences in the ways individuals are taught to read; it is clear from Chall's report (1967) that there are variations in practices of teaching reading in English-speaking countries, not only in the amount of emphasis given to "phonics" (as opposed to "whole word" or "look-and-say" approaches) but also in the stage at which phonics is introduced, if at all. At the same time, it is possible that differences in phonic ability are attributable partly to more fundamental constitutional or preschool learning factors which operate to dispose the child to learn readily, or to have difficulty learning, the grapheme-phoneme correspondence rules of English regardless of the method of teaching. At present, there is little research information about sources of differences in phonic ability, except to the (relatively small) extent that differences in reading ability have been shown to be attributable to methods of teaching.

Both auditory blending ability and phonic ability, for example, may be related to the neurologically based "specific language disability" or dyslexia described by Gallagher (1950) and Vernon (1962) as afflicting a certain percentage of school-age youth, particularly males, or to what has been called Gerstmann's syndrome (Gerstmann, 1927). They may also be related to the "phonetic coding ability" described above, which Carroll and Sapon (1959, 1967) found to be important in the learning of foreign languages both at the elementary school level and at the college-adult level.

Most studies of the development of phonological competence have been concerned with individual segmental phonemes, or occasionally, phoneme clusters. There has been little study of the development of competence in other aspects of phonology, either during the phase of primary language acquisition or during later childhood or adulthood. Robinson (1967) studied the development, in grade school children and adults, of competence in pronouncing, with correct stress placement, derived words with the suffixes *-ity* (as in *polárity* < *pólar*) and *-tion* (as in *generátion* < *génerate*). She found that these competences develop very slowly; many adults appear not to have acquired rules for the pronunciation of these derived words, performing solely on the basis of separate learnings for base and derived words. (There is some question about how consistent the rules are. Dictionaries give, for example, both *révocable* and *revócable* < *revóke*.)

Development of Skills in Using the Grammatical System

It is commonly stated by linguists that by somewhere around 4, 5, or 6 years of age, the normal child has attained mastery of most of the grammatical structure of his language. Such statements seem to have been made largely on the basis of common observation or of linguistic intuition, but it is extremely difficult to know exactly what they imply. To be sure, one finds it possible to communicate with a child of this age range about most ordinary everyday experiences, and the child seems to have relatively little difficulty expressing himself. Furthermore, his speech contains most if not all of the high-frequency structures of his language, as well as many of the less frequent ones. His speech normally observes most of the rules of agreement, correct word order, etc. Yet, Zidonis (1965) observes, with respect to writing performance:

When rigorous criteria of well-formedness were applied in the analysis of writing samples, almost half of the sentences written by the ninth graders were judged to be malformed. This finding runs counter to the widespread contention of the structural linguist, who is not concerned with well-formedness as a grammatical goal, that children have acquired virtually full command of the grammar of English at an early age. The more likely contention is that the grammar of English is never fully mastered [p. 408].

Is Zidonis's observation applicable also to the *speech* of ninth graders? And if so, does this deny the validity of the common statements about grammatical mastery at an early age?

The question hinges partly upon the distinction between linguistic competence and performance (Chomsky, 1965) and partly upon the definition of what degree of linguistic competence or mastery can be considered to be satisfactory for normal communication or use of language.

If our task is to characterize the linguistic competence of the normal child on entering school, we must be concerned not with what the child says but with what he is *able* to say or understand. Comprehension ability is just as valid as speaking ability for judging linguistic competence, a conclusion that we must draw from Lenneberg's (1962) classic case of a boy who learned to understand language without being able to speak. For this reason, it is difficult to specify the linguistic competence of the first grader on the basis of the many studies of speech output that have been done. These studies are useful in telling us what grammatical structures are actually used by first graders (or children at other age or grade levels), but they will not necessarily disclose what structures are known or understood by these children. Similarly, studies of written linguistic output will not necessarily indicate the underlying competence of the writers; the conditions under which writing is done by children may inhibit the manifestation of linguistic competence in some special way.

One comes closer to ascertaining a child's degree of linguistic competence by certain testing procedures, as by asking children to repeat sentences of given structures, by asking them to exhibit performances that are critically dependent upon their understanding of certain linguistic structures, or by having them perform certain operations with linguistic material. Testing techniques initiated by Berko and Brown (1960) with young children give a fairly clear indication of what grammatical structures children can use and understand, although it must be remembered, as noted earlier, that performance on a test is still a performance and therefore may be affected by factors other than linguistic competence.

Still another aspect of linguistic competence is the individual's conscious *awareness* of that competence, i.e., his ability to dissect out the units of language and the rules by which language is generated and understood. Even an adult is not ordinarily aware of many aspects of linguistic structure, even though through education he has learned to isolate words and to observe certain rules (e.g., the avoidance of the "split infinitive") in speaking and writing. Children have trouble isolating or deliberately rearranging words (Huttenlocher, 1964) or their sounds (Bruce, 1964).

In reviewing the development of linguistic competence after the early years, therefore, we shall give first priority to studies in which linguistic competence is tested in some way. Results from studies of speech and writing outputs are reviewed in this chapter in the section on "integrated language skills" (pp. 125–145).

Menyuk (1963) attempted to make a "preliminary" evaluation of the grammatical capacities of upper middle-class children from age 2–10 to age 6–11. She had observed, in previous research, that nearly all the basic syntactic structures used by adults can be found in the grammar of children as young as 2 years 10 months, but that there was an almost steady increase in the number of children using these structures with increasing age. By a testing technique that required the children to repeat immediately spoken sentences that were either well- or ill-informed ("restricted"), she found that nearly all the well-formed transformation types used in her study could be correctly repeated even by the nursery school children; one of the significant exceptions was the *conjunction-so* transformation (*He saw him so he hit him*). Kindergarten children did even better. Further, both nursery school and kindergarten children had a strong tendency to correct ill-formed sentences. Even nursery school children tended to correct such sentences as *He wash his face, They get mad and then they pushed him, They sleeping,* and *I want to go New York*. On the other hand, in a later study (Menyuk, 1964) it was shown that even at age 7–1 significant proportions of children (again, upper middle-class children) tended to *use* "restricted" forms in their speech: 16 percent of the children used restricted forms in phrase structure, 9 percent in transformations, and 13 percent in morphology. It seems, then, that children's grammatical capacity matures faster than their performance.

Slobin (1966) noted that all the kindergarten children he studied showed comprehension of the passive construction and were able spontaneously to produce passive sentences in response to questions designed to elicit them.

Kean and Yamamoto (1965) used an extension of Brown's (1957) technique for finding out whether children in kindergarten and grades 2 and 4 could make correct inferences from syntactic cues as to the class meaning (count noun vs. transitive verb) of unfamiliar words like *bluff, blur, censor,* and *pelt,* all of which may be used either as count nouns or transitive verbs. Children's guesses in answer to questions like "Do you know what a *censor* is?" or "Do you know what it means to *censor* something?" were classified as to whether they indicated correct assignment of class meaning. The overall percentages of correct assignment were 63.3 at the kindergarten level, 72.7 at grade 2, and 75.0 at grade 4, but the count noun identifications were at about the level of 65 percent at all grades, while the transitive verb identifications showed an increase with grade. The authors felt the results suggested that "children have already acquired an adequate (usable) grammar system by the time they get to elementary school." On the other hand, one can raise questions about the lack of perfect performance even at the fourth grade level and the possibility that there are consistent individual differences in the ability to use syntactic cues.

Cooper (1967) constructed a 48-item paper-and-pencil test to investigate the receptive and productive capacities of both deaf and hearing children in using morphological rules. The items were similar in structure to some of those used by Berko and Brown with younger children. For example, in one of the productive items, a picture of a man performing an acrobatic activity was presented along with the statement, "Here is a man who knows how to *hibb*. He did it yesterday. What did he do yesterday? He (*h*)_____" to be completed by the examinee. The scores showed a negatively accelerated growth curve, from an average score of 21.3 for hearing females at age 7–8 to an average score of 44.2 (out of 48 items) for hearing females at age 17–18. Even so, performance was not perfect. Among some of the more difficult items were ones requiring the child to derive adverbs from adjective or derived adjective stems or from noun or verb stems. Furthermore, scores on the test were correlated to the extent of a coefficient of .74 with mental age and .73 with chronological age. The variability of scores decreased markedly with age in the case of hearing subjects. Graduate students got an average of 45.5 correct on the test (SD = 2.0). Ability to apply morphological rules in this type of written test thus apparently converges toward an asymptote in the teens for normal hearing subjects. Deaf subjects obtained scores averaging 29.2 (SD = 8.0) even at 19 years of age. There was a high correlation between the item difficulties for hearing subjects and those for deaf subjects, however.

There are many published tests of grammatical knowledge and usage. Most of these, however, fail to distinguish between linguistic competence in the rules of the standard language and competence in distinguishing between standard and substandard usage. Indeed, I have pointed out (Carroll, 1952) that many of the tests, such as the Language Usage Test of the Differential Aptitude Tests (Bennett, Seashore, & Wesman, 1947–59), fail to recognize that many presumably substandard usages have become standard, and they often penalize the examinee who answers on the basis of usages that are now accepted as standard. Furthermore, since most tests are pencil-and-paper written tests, they emphasize grammatical knowledge as applied in writing rather than speech. It is therefore difficult to use findings from such tests as evidence concerning the typical norms of development in linguistic competence, even with respect to the development of standard usages. Also, the performance of school children in particular linguistic knowledges could be studied only by obtaining item analysis data, which are not usually reported.

There has been little investigation of the extent to which children are aware of grammatical rules apart from specific training in these rules as given in schooling. Porter (1959) investigated whether elementary school children can learn to identify particular elements of language structure by a "guessing game" concept formation procedure. The child was (orally) given a sentence like *A cudof biced the sitev* and told that the examiner was thinking of a particular word (for example, the main verb), which the child was asked to guess. Through successive presentations of this type, it was found that the children could indeed learn grammatical concepts, i.e., to identify particular words from surrounding syntactic cues. Porter also found that children could perform these identifications even when nonsense words were used, i.e., when only morphological clues like past tense or plural morphemes were used. In one of the tests constructed by Carroll and Sapon (1967) in their foreign language aptitude battery for children in grades 3 to 6, a similar idea is implicit. From examples, the child is taught to identify subjects, transitive verbs, direct objects, and descriptive adjectives. The scores for this test show a progressive age trend such that by grade 6, a large number of children can do most of the items perfectly. Carroll and Sapon (1959) constructed a more advanced test of "grammatical sensitivity" for persons in grade 9 up through adulthood. The subject is required to identify the words or phrases in test sentences that have the same grammatical function as words or phrases in given "key" sentences. For example, given the key sentence *They made him CAPTAIN of the team*, the subject would have to recognize that in the sentence *The critics called the book the best novel of the year*, *novel* has the same function as *captain* in the key sentence. Despite the fact that in terms of underlying linguistic competence, all the subjects doubtless understand these sentences; even at the college-adult level, there are considerable individual differences in the ability to perform the task set on this test, one which presumably depends upon the ability to make a conscious analysis of grammatical structure. O'Donnell (1964) constructed a somewhat similar test for entering college freshmen, requiring students to select sentences constructed largely from nonsense words that exhibited grammatical relations similar to relations identified in key sentences. The range of scores on this test was not reported, but apparently it was sufficient to justify computing correlations with a traditional grammar test (the Iowa Grammar Information Test) and with ratings of themes written for the STEP Essay Test. The structure test correlated with the essay ratings and with grammar information test scores to about the same very moderate extent, suggesting that awareness of and ability to analyze grammatical relationships is of little importance in the ability to write good English compositions. Results with O'Donnell's test are also reported by Davis, Smith, and Bowers (1964). They found no significant increase in mean score from grade 10 to 12, but girls made better scores than boys. The fact of wide individual differences in this sort of test suggests that ability in grammatical awareness should be used as a control variable in experiments on the perception of grammaticalness (Maclay & Sleator, 1960).

The results of studies reviewed in this section throw little light on the remark from Zidonis, quoted earlier, to the effect that almost half of the sentences written by a group of ninth graders were judged to be malformed grammatically. Although there are certain aspects of grammatical competence that seem to be well mastered even at the normal school entry age, there are other aspects in which development is slow, at least for many children. We know little about the actual grammatical competence of adolescents or even adults as manifested in either speech or writing. Many of Zidonis's ninth graders were apparently unable to recognize the malformedness of the sentences they wrote. It cannot be concluded that all adults have acquired the degree of grammatical competence assumed by many linguists.

Development of Vocabulary Knowledge

It has already been noted that vocabulary knowledge is one of the best indicators of verbal intelligence and that individual differences in vocabulary are enormous. Although a considerable amount of vocabulary learning is associated with primary language acquisition in the early years, the acquisition of most of the vocabulary characteristic of an educated adult occurs during the years of schooling, and in fact one of the primary tasks of the school, as far as language learning is concerned, is to teach vocabulary. This being the case, educators have been interested in describing the normal course of vocabulary development, specifying the amount of vocabulary that must be learned at the various grade levels and developing measures of vocabulary knowledge. Here, vocabulary knowledge is usually defined in terms of *passive* or *recognition* vocabulary, i.e., the set of words in the language whose meaning or meanings the individual knows or can recognize.

There has been little concern with estimating the size of the individual's *active* or *productive* vocabulary, i.e., the number of words the individual can or is likely to use in speech or writing. Active vocabulary is primarily a matter of linguistic performance.

There has been much research on the question of vocabulary sizes at various grade levels. Some years ago, claims were made (Smith, 1941) that even at grade 1, children's recognition vocabularies are of phenomenal size, perhaps as large as 17,000, and that the basic vocabulary at grade 12 would average 47,500 words. Lorge and Chall (1963), however, have convincingly pointed out the methodological flaws that were involved in these estimates, showing that they were based on improper dictionary sampling techniques, poor test construction procedures, and fallacious reasoning. Nevertheless, the problem of estimating total recognition vocabulary size has never been satisfactorily solved. How shall vocabulary words be counted? Since many words have multiple meanings, should these multiple meanings be counted separately, and if so, how? If an individual knows the base form of a word, can it be assumed that he also can recognize the meanings of derived forms (e.g., *incorruptible* < *corrupt*)? What does it mean to "know" a word? Should one be able to define it in isolation, or is it sufficient to recognize its meaning in a given context? Since it is impracticable to test an individual's knowledge of all the words in an unabridged dictionary, much less all their separate multiple meanings, how can an adequate sample of words and word meanings be set up for testing purposes?

Most vocabulary tests, constructed according to the usual canons of test construction, present a series of words of varying "difficulty" and require the examinee to define them or to recognize their meanings among alternatives in a multiple-choice format. Occasionally, vocabulary tests are given in a completion-item format where the examinee is asked to produce a word that fits a given definition, but these tend to measure active rather than passive vocabulary. According to Guilford (1967), they measure not only vocabulary knowledge but also some other psychological function involved in producing words; it is interesting that Vandenberg (1962) found evidence for a genetic factor in individual differences in vocabulary when tested in a completion format but not when tested in a multiple-choice or recognition format. In any case, vocabulary tests ordinarily yield scores interpretable only on a relative basis; they are not scaled in such a way as to indicate the absolute size of the individual's vocabulary or even the frequency ranges of words that he is likely to know. It is therefore difficult to interpret, in any absolute way, the normative data provided in connection with the numerous existing vocabulary tests. The Seashore-Eckerson vocabulary test used by Smith (1941) was intended to provide such interpretations but was unsuccessful in doing so; for normative developmental data obtained with this test, see the study by Templin (1957).

Even when item analysis data are given in connection with vocabulary tests, it is difficult to relate these to vocabulary size because item difficulties (proportions passing the items) are only imperfectly related to word frequency in lists such as the Thorndike-Lorge word book (Thorndike & Lorge, 1944)—a relationship that has been studied by Kirkpatrick and Cureton (1949) and Wesman and Seashore (1949).

One attempt to resolve some of these problems was made by Ellegård (1960), who was able to use Thorndike-Lorge data to make estimates not only of the total range of vocabulary that would exist in unlimited samples but also of the probable sizes of English vocabularies of groups of Swedish students with various amounts of training in English; these vocabulary estimates for the students ranged from 2070 up to 17,870. By a somewhat similar technique, Oldfield (1963) estimated that the average university graduate in Britain knows the meanings of about 75,000 words. Further work needs to be done with these methods to obtain better information on vocabulary sizes. Carroll (1967b) has shown that the theoretical population of word types can be regarded as lognormally distributed with respect to frequency; it should be possible to use this theory, in combination with empirical data, in estimating both passive and active vocabularies.

A list of approximately 3000 words (and certain derived forms) known in reading by at least 80 percent of fourth grade children has been given by Dale and Chall (1948). This basic list has been supplemented by Dale and Eichholz (undated) with lists of words known (i.e., answered correctly on vocabulary tests) by at least two thirds of the children each of grades 4, 6, 8, 10, and 12. Percentage figures are given for each word (or particular meaning) in the respective grade. There are 1302 words on the fourth grade list, 6130 on the sixth grade list, 4460 on the eighth grade list, 3431 on the tenth grade list, and 2027 on the twelfth grade list, but these lists overlap considerably. While no claim was made that the lists of words known are exhaustive, Dale's aim was to "provide a list of all the words known by at least 67 percent of elementary and high school pupils." Dale's lists, then, may be regarded as giving valuable information on children's word knowledge that cannot be inferred from frequency counts. Diederich and Palmer (1956) have provided data, using a technique similar to that of Dale and Eichholz, on the difficulty levels of 4800 words from the upper rank-frequency ratings of the Thorndike (1932) list of 20,000 words (words from 6000 to 20,000 frequency rank that are not proper nouns, derived forms, technical terms, archaic or obsolete words, words common in spoken English, and certain other words "not likely to be generally useful"). There is a considerable overlap between the Diederich-Palmer list and the Dale-Eichholz lists, a fact which makes numerous comparisons possible if one assumes the equivalency of the test items used by these investigators.

Dale (1965) makes the guess that:

If we assume that children finish the first grade with an average vocabulary of 3,000 words, it is likely that they will add about 1,000 words a year from then on. The average high school senior will know about 14,000 to 15,000 words, the college senior 18,000 to 20,000.

Several investigators (Miner, 1957; Thorndike & Gallup, 1944) have conducted Gallup-poll-type national surveys of "verbal intelligence" using a wide-range 20-item vocabulary test, but from the data that have been reported, it is difficult if not impossible to estimate either the average vocabulary size of the American adult or the range of these vocabulary sizes.

Norms on standardized vocabulary tests give some idea of the progression in vocabulary development from grade to grade. Using his own specially constructed tests, Russell (1954) observed that this progression seemed to be approximately linear. This linearity, however, is partly an artifact of the score scales of the tests and cannot be interpreted as meaning that children's growth in vocabulary is linear. Until the problem of estimating vocabulary size is solved, an answer to the question of the absolute rate of growth in vocabulary will be lacking. Russell noted that in the high school grades, vocabularies tend to become specialized; some children acquire strong vocabularies in certain areas of science, others in art, others in literature, etc. Greene (1949) constructed and standardized a test, the Michigan Vocabulary Profile Test, that assesses the student's vocabulary in eight areas of knowledge: human relations, commerce, government, physical sciences, biological sciences, mathematics, fine arts, and sports. In typical college samples, correlations among scores from these areas range from near zero to .55, supporting the notion of specialization. In adulthood, vocabulary apparently tends to increase significantly up to at least the age of 40 or 50, particularly if the individual continues to expose himself to stimulating reading material (Miner, 1957). Decreasing standard deviations of test scores as age increases suggest that the adult population tends towards greater homogeneity in vocabulary knowledge (Bennett & Raskow, 1941). The declines in vocabulary test scores that are sometimes reported are due to a decline in the speed of taking the tests that occurs in older people, not to a real decline in vocabulary (Christian & Paterson, 1936). In a study of adult males in the Army, Altus (1950) concluded that vocabulary is a function of degree of literacy when the effects of general intelligence (vocabulary not included) are controlled.

As mentioned earlier, there are different ways in which a word can be "known." There have been numerous attempts (e.g., Berwick, 1959; Russell, 1954; Russell & Saadeh, 1962) to measure vocabulary in terms of the ability to discriminate different meanings of words, but it is usually found that such measures correlate strongly with measures of general vocabulary knowledge. While the individual is growing in his knowledge of a wider range of words, he is also developing in the precision and depth of his knowledge of the words he already knows.

An aspect of productive vocabulary knowledge in written language is the ability to spell. Most standardized tests of spelling get at the pupil's ability to spell certain words in the English language that present particular difficulties such as *night* and *receive*; some of these tests, unfortunately, measure not ability to spell from dictation but ability to recognize whether a word is correctly spelled—a rather different function even though correlations between recognition and recall spelling tests are usually in the range .80 to .90. Whether tested by recall or recognition, average spelling ability increases progressively throughout the school years while individual differences, if anything, increase. Test results seldom if ever control for vocabulary knowledge, and thus the scores are usually rather highly correlated with vocabulary; because of the peculiarities of English orthography, a person who does not have a word in his vocabulary has only a moderate chance of being able to spell it correctly.

Flanagan et al. (1964, pp. 3–96 to 3–105) have made an attempt to estimate the absolute spelling ability of the population of American high school students. Using a dictation spelling test composed of words drawn systematically from the 5000 most frequently used words in English, they were able to conclude that "the average student can spell correctly a very large percentage" of these words. The average ninth grader would spell about 83 percent of them correctly; the corresponding figure for the twelfth grade would be 93 percent. Despite these encouraging data, striking individual differences are revealed. Students at the 5th percentile of spelling ability would spell only 22 percent of the first 5000 words correctly at the ninth grade, and only 47 percent at the twelfth grade. Students at the 95th percentile would on the other hand spell all or nearly all correctly, even at grade 9. At all grade levels, girls are better spellers than boys on the average.

INTEGRATED LANGUAGE SKILLS: LISTENING, SPEAKING, READING, AND WRITING

We have reviewed, within space limitations, our knowledge of the development of the basic competences involved in the use of language. For many purposes, however, educators are interested in the development of what may be called *integrated language skills*, that is, skills in understanding or producing language, spoken or written.

It is obvious that superior performance in any of these integrated language skills requires not only the possession of a wide range of basic competences but also the ability to mobilize them to meet the communicative demands of a particular situation. Integrated language skills are thought of as general traits of the individual in the sense that he can be expected to perform at a certain level of effectiveness in a very wide variety of situations. For example, a person who is regarded as a superior listener is one who can understand a wide variety of spoken messages; a superior speaker is one who can speak effectively in a wide variety of situations; and so on. Actually, of course, there are limits to the generality of such traits, but for purposes of measurement and evaluation, it is convenient to assume generality.

In receptive skills, a most important variable in the performance of the individual is the overall level of difficulty inherent in the stimulus input. This sort of variable has been studied more extensively in the case of reading comprehension than in the case of listening comprehension. Ever since the 1920s, efforts have been made to develop reliable, valid, and convenient measures of what has been called *readability*, that is, the inherent difficulty of printed texts due to such variables as vocabulary load, grammatical complexity, treatment of subject matter, etc.: see reviews by Chall (1958) and Klare (1963). Typically, readability "formulas" get at vocabulary load by such indirect methods as measuring the average length of words in syllables or letters or determining the proportion of words in the text that are not found on certain lists of high-frequency words; they get at grammatical complexity by measuring average length of sentences or independent clauses. Recently, Bormuth (1966) has investigated promising measures of grammatical complexity that are based on contemporary linguistic theories. Quite different from the "readability formula" approach, however, is the "cloze procedure" developed by Taylor (1953) which attempts to measure readability of prose materials by determining the average success of panels of readers in restoring words that have been systematically deleted from the text (e.g., every fifth word): for a review of results attained by this procedure, see Hafner (1966). Measurements by "cloze" technique are often used as criterion variables in studies of readability using the formula approach. There has been only limited success in applying readability measurements to predict the "listenability" or comprehension difficulty of spoken materials (public speeches, radio broadcasts, lectures, etc.), possibly because oral presentation may introduce additional variables associated with rate of speech, clarity of pronunciation, and skilful use of intonation, stress, and pauses.

Analogously, in productive skills a critical variable is the type of task set for the speaker or writer—the topic on which he is asked to speak or write, the amount of prior preparation he is allowed to do, the kind of audience he is expected to communicate to, and the criteria on which he believes he will be judged. Braddock, Lloyd-Jones, and Schoer (1963) have reviewed research on such variables in the case of written composition. Obviously, variance due to extraneous variables must somehow be minimized if accurate measurements of basic speaking or writing competences are to be obtained.

Listening Skills

Listening to and understanding speech involves a number of basic processes, some depending upon linguistic competences, some depending upon previous knowledge that is not necessarily of a purely linguistic nature, and some depending upon psychological variables that affect the mobilization of these competences and knowledges in the particular task situation. The listener must have a continuous set to listen and understand, and as he hears the utterance, he may be helped by some kind of set to process and remember the information transmitted. His linguistic competence enables him, presumably, to recognize the formatives of the heard utterance, i.e., to dissect out of the waveform the morphemes, words, and other meaning-bearing elements of the utterance, and to construe from these elements, the grammatical description of each sentence or partial sentence in the utterance. For example, in hearing the sentence *The child that the man that helped the policeman talked to was mine* the hearer must apprehend that (in "base structure"), there are the triples *Man helped policeman, Man talked to child*, and *Child was mine* (or *I have child*), each exhibiting a grammatical relation such as subject—transitive verb—object. Fodor and Garrett (1967) have proposed that understanding a sentence requires, so to speak, a two-stage heuristic process in which the hearer consults a lexicon to find the grammatical properties of each formative and then uses these properties, along with purely grammatical signals (word order, intonation, etc.), to assign the structural description. This implies that the hearer must have a richly structured lexicon on which to draw. In addition, however, relevant previous knowledge enhances understanding when the hearer has already acquired the concepts represented by the lexical elements of the utterance and has had experiences which help him understand how these concepts are likely to be related. There must be an interaction between all these competences and knowledges that enables the hearer to interpret properly the kind of utterance that first appears to have *one* interpretation but then turns out to have another interpretation. Lashley (1951) gives the following example, to be presented orally: *Rapid righting* (likely to be heard as *writing*) *with his uninjured hand saved from loss the contents of the capsized canoe.* Here, the hearer's ability to recover the grammatical relation between *righting* and *canoe* depends in part on his knowledge that one can right a capsized canoe; otherwise, he might think that rapid writing could somehow save the canoe's contents.

"Listening comprehension" tests purport to measure the individual's global ability to understand continuous discourse of various kinds. One of the first of these was the Brown-Carlsen test (Brown & Carlsen, 1953), designed for use from grades 9 to 13. Although it consists of a series of subtasks that are supposed to be representative of listening activities, it cannot be said to be based on any analysis of the listening process such as the above; it does not help in diagnosing whether the individual's deficiency in listening is due to a lack of basic linguistic competence, a lack of background knowledge, or an inability to mobilize his competences through proper processes of attention and response. The test contains 76 items grouped into five parts: Immediate Recall, Following Directions, Recognizing Transitions, Recognizing Word Meanings, and Lecture Comprehension. The Immediate Recall and Following Directions parts strongly resemble tests often found in intelligence batteries and tend to emphasize memory for numbers and serial orderings. The very short test of Recognizing Word Meanings (10 items) is a feeble attempt to measure certain aspects of vocabulary knowledge. The section on Recognizing Transitions purports to determine whether the listener can recognize whether a spoken sentence is introductory, transitional, concluding, or none of these, and thus may depend upon some aspects of competence in using rhetorical cues. The Lecture Comprehension subtest presents about 12 minutes of continuous discourse followed by questions designed to measure "reflective" or "critical" listening, some of which are questions requiring merely memory for details and others of which probe the ability to make inferences from the material presented. The total mean scores increase with grade level, and there are wide individual differences even within a given grade. As in the case of other "standardized" listening comprehension tests, there is actually a lack of standardization of stimulus presentation because the examiner is permitted to read aloud the spoken parts himself; in view of the fact that normal oral reading rates vary considerably (Carroll, 1967b), this means that scores may be affected by the particular conditions of administration. Johnson and Frandsen (1963) found that higher reliability could be attained through a tape recorded presentation. They also found that the Lecture Comprehension subtest appeared to measure skills that are different from whatever skills are measured by the other parts.

A more ambitious attempt to develop listening comprehension tests was made by the Cooperative Test Division of Educational Testing Service (1956–1959a) in its Sequential Tests of Educational Progress (STEP) series. Two alternate forms of listening tests were made for each of four levels of educational progress: level 1 (college), level 2 (grades 10, 11, 12), level 3 (grades 7, 8, 9), and level 4 (grades 4, 5, 6). The committee designing the tests assumed that listening skills could be broken down into subabilities: Plain-sense Comprehension (identifying main ideas, remembering details and simple sequences of ideas, understanding word meanings); Interpretation (understanding implications of main ideas and significant details, interrelationships among ideas, and connotative meanings of words); and Evaluation and Application (judging validity of ideas, distinguishing fact from fancy, noting contradictions, "judging whether the speaker has created the intended mood or effect," etc.). While this analysis may represent a laudable range of educational goals, it can be seen that the test was intended to measure much more than sheer listening comprehension. Aside from the fact that the examinee has to answer the questions on the basis of spoken presentations, the test is similar to reading comprehension tests; many of the items require not only understanding of the presented spoken discourse but also a wide range of prior knowledges and reasoning abilities. From level 4 to level 1, the passages presented increase in vocabulary difficulty, grammatical complexity, and complexity of subject matter. Correspondingly, the mean "converted scores" increase from grade 4 to grade 14, but there are wide individual differences in scores within grades and great overlap between grades. For example, the 25th percentile point at grade 12 is about equal to the 75th percentile point at grade 7. Presumably, through vertical equating of the different test levels, the converted scores are on a scale with a uniform meaning throughout the levels, but it is extremely difficult to characterize what degree of "listening comprehension" ability is represented by any given converted score. Within grades, the scores are correlated with verbal intelligence test scores (the Verbal score of the School and College Ability Test) to the extent of Pearsonian coefficients within the range of .65 to .78 in grades 4 to 12. A few correlations have been reported between STEP Listening scores and reading test scores; these tend to be in the neighborhood of .65.

There is considerable question as to whether the STEP Listening Test measures any ability that is *specific* to the listening situation as opposed to general language comprehension. Kelly (1965) found that the STEP Listening Test and the Brown-Carlsen test failed to correlate significantly higher between themselves than with reading and intelligence tests. This finding may be, however, specific to the two tests compared and does not demonstrate that listening skills cannot be differentiated from other language skills such as reading comprehension. We have already noted above that Spearritt (1962), in studies of sixth grade children, was able to identify a Listening Comprehension factor that was linearly independent of his Verbal Comprehension factor. This separation could, of course, have arisen simply from differential competence in "decoding" printed discourse, such that Listening Comprehension would be the more general language comprehension factor independent of modality. Spearritt suggested that further research might disclose three linearly independent factors: "comprehension of meaningful verbal *passages* presented in *spoken* form," "comprehension of meaningful verbal *passages* presented in *printed* form," and "knowledge of word meanings." Such research has not yet been attempted; extremely careful test construction would be required in order to differentiate the competences and processes involved in these factors.

One major constraint upon the investigation of listening performance by means of tests is that the testing situation itself is likely to influence the individual to try to perform better than he ordinarily does. Kelly (1962) showed that the "actual listening behavior" of industrial supervisors bore little relation to their scores on the Brown-Carlsen test.

There have been various apparently successful attempts to "teach" certain kinds of listening behavior (Fawcett, 1966; Lundsteen, 1965, 1966), but in view of the uncertainty about what listening tests really measure, one cannot decide exactly what kinds of competences or performance capabilities are being improved in these experiments. Because basic linguistic competence (at least with respect to grammar and vocabulary) is probably relatively unsusceptible to improvement except over long periods of time and with tremendous efforts, it is probable that the teaching of "listening ability" is mostly a matter of the training of processes that lead the individual to pay closer attention to what he hears and to organize meanings for better retention, comparison, and inference.

Speaking Skills

Despite the fact that basic language competence is attained relatively early in life and despite enormous amounts of practice in speaking, adults do not always exhibit fluency and effectiveness of delivery even when speaking about relatively simple matters. To be sure, the adult who is a native speaker of his language but who speaks haltingly and confusingly is more fluent and effective in his speech than a foreigner who has not yet mastered that language, for the former is *able* to talk about anything within his experience and knowledge. The important fact is that there are large individual differences among adults in fluency of speaking performance, and there is evidence that suggests that these individual differences have their origin in early childhood and persist to a large extent throughout the pre-adult period. Until recently, however, there has been relatively little research on the assessment of speaking skills and the delineation of their development throughout the pre-adult period.

Most research on the development of speaking skills in children of school age has been based upon data obtained by placing the child in test situations specially designed to elicit speech samples from him. For example, following procedures established by McCarthy (1930), Templin (1957) had children taken into a room with an adult examiner who stimulated them with picture books and toys until 50 "remarks" could be taken down in writing. Similarly, Loban (1963) interviewed his subjects individually, and after gaining rapport through general conversation, elicited their verbal responses to a series of pictures. Strickland (1962) interviewed children in groups of two or three and obtained utterances that were apparently partly answers to the interviewer's questions and partly conversational responses of the children to each other. But when Strang and Hocker (1965) obtained speech samples from children engaged in their own daily activities, sentence lengths were shorter than those obtained from children of comparable ages by Strickland. Marge (1964) found that speech specialists' ratings of speech samples collected from sixth graders in an individual testing situation in which the children were shown pictures to talk about had little correlation with ratings of overall speaking effectiveness made by these children's teachers on the basis of classroom speech performance. The situation in which speech performance is assessed has, apparently, a great influence on the character of the speech sample attained and the standing of the child relative to other children.

In his review of methods of testing spoken English, Hitchman (1964) lists a variety of aspects for the assessment of speaking ability: public speaking, conversation, oral interpretation (the reading aloud of prose or poetry), voice and articulation, and pronunciation (i.e., deviation from a preferred dialect); but he reports few data that would allow one to conclude what the basic independent dimensions of speaking skill may be. He notes that Becker (1962) was able to find only three more or less independent dimensions underlying 11 scales on which public speaking performance could be rated: an analysis-content factor, a delivery factor, and a "language" factor. The relation of these factors to other aspects of language skills, even gross verbal intelligence, has not yet been determined. Unpublished data ensuing from an investigation conducted by Taylor et al. (1958) indicate that various kinds of speech performances (e.g., participating in a conference, reading oral instructions, delivering a speech, or giving impromptu instruction) are dependent upon, or at least correlated with, various basic factors of intellectual ability in a very complex way. General verbal intelligence, particularly as represented by tests of vocabulary knowledge, features prominently in these correlations, along with factors of ideational and expressional fluency (see above).

Many developmental studies of speech output have been reviewed by McCarthy (1954) and others; the chapter by Ruth Strickland in the present volume reviews some of the more recent ones. As has already been pointed out, these are necessarily studies of linguistic *performance* and yield only suggestive clues as to the underlying linguistic competence. The appropriate use of a given linguistic element in speech performance does, indeed, imply the existence of that element in competence, but its absence in output does not necessarily imply absence in competence. One cannot deny, however, that the study of the development of linguistic performance is at least as important as the study of the development of linguistic competence. Indeed, the former is the proper province of the psycholinguist *qua* psycholinguist. As a methodologist, too, the psycholinguist is concerned with the soundness of the techniques for sampling subjects and for collecting and analyzing data.

Probably the best example of a study of speech output conducted according to traditional methods is that of Templin (1957), who collected speech samples in Minneapolis from representative groups of children ages 3 to 8. Language development was indexed principally by mean sentence length and certain measures of grammatical complexity; there was some attention, too, to vocabulary growth. At age 8, the length of verbalizations was reported to be still on the increase, along with grammatical complexity of these verbalizations. While Templin was not particularly concerned with individual differences, it is apparent from her data that individual differences persisted even to the upper ages studied. For example, for the total subsample of age 3 children, the median and quartile deviation of the total number of words used in 50 remarks were, respectively, 206.5 and 27.4; for children at age 8, these figures were 375.0 and 42.0. She gives no data, however, on the reliability of her measures of language development. Darley and Moll (1960), studying speech samples from 150 5-year-old kindergarten children, found what they considered to be adequate reliabilities for mean length of response based on 50 responses but not for a measure of structural complexity. Their findings concerned language samples collected on only one occasion; Minifie, Darley, and Sherman (1963), however, investigated whether consistent results were yielded by each of seven language development measures when applied to 50 language responses collected on three separate occasions. Both at age 5.5 and at age 8, the reliabilities of measures obtained on a single occasion generally fell below acceptable values for characterizing the language development of an individual child. Therefore, data such as those collected by Templin and others who have used relatively small language samples must be regarded only as indicating group trends.

Other recent studies of the developmental trends in speech output using more or less traditional measures and techniques are those of Strickland (1962), a cross-sectional study of grades 1 through 6; Strang and Hocker (1965), for grade 1 only; Loban (1963, 1966, 1967), a longitudinal study of grades K through 12; Riling (1965), a cross-sectional study at grades 4 and 6; and Feenstra and Gardner (1966), a cross-sectional study at grades 3, 5, and 7. The measures of grammatical complexity and performance in sentence construction were inspired by structural linguistics of the sort developed by Fries (1952) and Francis (1958); they included measures of the degree of subordination and the number of words in "mazes" or structurally inappropriate segments. Nearly all measures in all studies show progressive age trends. At the same time, there are striking individual differences. Loban, for example, examined the speech output of two groups of children identified as "high" and "low" in "language power." Children in the high group, from kindergarten through grade 6, consistently showed fewer words in "mazes" and greater amounts of subordination in grammatical structure. The high group was superior, Loban reports, not so much in variety of grammatical patterns but rather in "dexterity" in their use to express meanings.

The most sophisticated analysis of children's speech output available thus far is that made by O'Donnell, Griffin, and Norris (1967), with a theoretical basis in transformational grammar. Children in kindergarten and in grades 1, 2, 3, 5, and 7 were asked to give spoken (and also written) responses to filmed stories. The basic index of language development was the number of words in T-units (terminable sentence segments), an index devised and validated by Hunt (1965) for written language. Numerous detailed analyses were made in terms of the incidence of "garbles" (roughly the same as Loban's "mazes"), the number of sentence-combining transformations per *T*-unit, the kinds of initial coordinating conjunctions in *T*-units, etc. Individual differences in development are clearly apparent in the data. For example, it was noted that at every grade, most of the "garbles" were attributable to a few individuals. Ability to avoid the production of "garbles" is possibly associated with the factor Non-Distracting Speech Behavior isolated by Marge (1964).

These and other studies leave little doubt that in the period from kindergarten to grade 12, there is a gradual and progressive increase in the ability of the average child to use language effectively in spontaneous speech, when effectiveness is judged by such criteria as average length of utterance, average length of communication units (such as *T*-units), relative absence of "mazes" (unintelligible or grammatically confused speech), and overall grammatical complexity. The measures used by the several investigators are somewhat different, but on the assumption that each investigator was consistent in the application of his measures over the various ages, it is interesting to note the developmental progressions indicated in Table 3-3. Unfortunately, since there are no data on adult performances using these measures, we cannot divine the point where development would level off, as it undoubtedly does. Implicit in all these studies is the occurrence of wide and persistent individual differences.

Reading Skills

Contrast reading with listening; in reading, but not normally in listening, the stimulus input can be taken in, and if necessary, rescanned at a rate that is under the control of the reader. In most writing systems, the message is already segmented into words; it is the reader's task to recognize those words and match them with representations of their spoken forms. Essentially, the reading process is one of using printed or written symbols and sequences of symbols as cues to construct some kind of representation of a spoken message. That representation may be rather full and detailed, as in the act of reading a message aloud with proper intonation, emphasis, and pauses, or it may be extremely incomplete, as it is in rapid scanning with apprehension of only certain fragments of the message. Fundamentally, however, listening and reading as receptive processes present the same problems of language comprehension, for once the printed or written message is transformed into a representation of a spoken message, it becomes an object to be comprehended just as a spoken message is an object to be comprehended. Most of the things stated above concerning listening comprehension thus apply equally to reading comprehension. The differences between reading and listening have to do with the processing of the

Table 3-3. Selected Data on Development of Speaking Skills

Study	Measure		Approx. Age: 5 / Grade: K	6 / 1	7 / 2	8 / 3	9 / 4	10 / 5	11 / 6	12 / 7	13 / 8	14 / 9	15 / 10	16 / 11	17 / 12
Templin (1957)	Words per remark		5.7	6.6	7.3	7.6									
Strickland (1962)	Mean sentence length (in Words)			11.04			13.04		13.58						
Loban (1967, Table 8)	Words per communication unit	Total Group:	5.13	6.06	6.46	6.91	7.68	7.89	8.37	9.10	9.43	9.47	9.58	10.82	11.09
		High Group:	6.01	6.89	7.17	7.65	8.52	8.72	9.39	10.45	10.85	10.84	11.09	12.16	12.94
		Low Group:	4.29	5.08	5.70	6.04	6.55	6.75	7.37	8.12	8.54	8.37	8.39	9.46	10.34
O'Donnell et al. (1967)	Words per T-unit		7.07	7.97	8.33	8.73		8.90		9.80					
Loban (1966, Table 6)	Words in mazes as % of total words	Total Group:	12.30	9.97	8.88	6.15	7.11	7.41	7.53	6.34	6.34	6.12			
		High Group:	9.17	7.57	6.65	4.98	5.43	5.17	5.17	6.11	5.51	4.34			
		Low Group:	11.92	15.51	10.49	10.62	9.74	9.27	9.49	10.95	9.83	8.85			
Loban (1967, Table 13)	Words in mazes as % of total words (with changed definition of "maze")	Total Group:	7.94	7.08	6.48	5.95	6.82	6.99	7.14	7.06	6.84	6.19	4.48	6.55	7.04
		High Group:	8.98	7.24	5.22	4.87	5.79	5.79	5.88	5.71	5.60	5.05	5.80	6.60	7.49
		Low Group:	7.76	8.07	8.04	7.50	9.41	8.32	9.29	9.83	8.97	7.99	6.79	7.97	8.42
O'Donnell et al. (1967, computed from Tables 5 and 6)	Garbles per 100 words		5.41	3.57	4.58	2.64		1.64		1.48					

input; reading involves the "decoding" or transformation of the printed input.

Whereas the young child learns to process spoken inputs as a part of native language acquisition, it is generally true that the process of decoding printed symbols must be deliberately taught to him. As Durkin (1966) has shown, a small percentage of American children learn the decoding process before reaching formal schooling, but in every case, some deliberate teaching of at least certain aspects of this process is done by a parent or an older child. In most school systems, teaching of this decoding process occupies a considerable amount of time in the first two or three grades. Chall (1967) has described the "great debate" that has raged over the past few years (indeed, for at least a century) as to how this decoding process should be taught— whether it should be taught by the early introduction of systematic instruction in letter-sound relationships ("phonics") or by first teaching whole-word recognition. She has presented evidence that an early introduction of systematic phonics is more likely to produce better readers, and she urges that teaching methods and materials be designed to feature the learning of letter-sound relationships.

How rapidly the American school system can respond to this challenge is a question, however; Shannon (1959) has shown that many teachers themselves are deficient in their knowledge of letter-sound relationships. Further, it is conceivable that even when a system of reading instruction features phonics, it can fail to produce superior readers by failing to give children sufficient practice in word recognition. The conventional system of English orthography is not a sure guide to the pronunciation of words (we may estimate that a computer algorithm for translating letters to phonemes could not be more than about 90 to 95 percent accurate unless it was also able to take account of semantic content). Even if English orthography were completely regular, superior reading skill requires a kind of instantaneous word recognition that is more than the mere ability to decode letters into phonemes. Nevertheless, it is probably true that for the past 40 or 50 years, reading instruction in English-speaking countries has tended to be deficient in teaching the decoding process, and therefore, currently accepted norms of the development of reading skills are not necessarily those which would obtain if reading instruction were optimal throughout the educational system.

In any case, it is difficult to interpret the available normative data on the development of reading skills because tests of these skills have not adequately recognized their components. The scores attained by elementary school children on the most widely used reading tests such as the Metropolitan Reading Test, the Stanford Reading Test and the Gates Reading Tests are complex functions of ability to decode words in terms of letter-sound relationships, vocabulary knowledge, reasoning ability, and general information. It is not possible to decide, on the basis of the results of these tests, when or whether a child has learned to decode words in terms of letter-sound relationships; nor is it possible, generally, to decide whether a child's low score is more a function of deficiency in vocabulary knowledge, deficiency in speedy word recognition, or deficiency in apprehending meanings of the content. Only in very recent years have test authors (e.g., Anastasiow & Hansen, 1967) attempted to develop tests for children's ability to use letter-sound relationships in recognizing words (see also diagnostic reading tests listed in Buros, 1965).

Commonly used reading tests such as those mentioned above are ordinarily calibrated or "normed" in such a way as to indicate the grade level at which the child is reading. In effect, the grade-level placements indicate the score points that are typically attained by the majority of children, selected representatively at a given grade. A child with grade-level reading placement of, say, 7.0 has attained a test score comparable to that of about 50 to 75 percent of all children tested at the beginning of the seventh grade. (There are variations in methods of norming tests, and it should also be remembered that the accuracy of normative data is dependent on the degree to which the norming samples are representative of the target population.)

In the early years of schooling, the performance of children in reading is largely determined by their success in "decoding" the printed material into a form that they can readily understand; the content they are given to read is ordinarily within their understanding once they have decoded it. By about the sixth grade, nearly all children have mastered word-recognition skills, and their performance in reading is increasingly a function of the difficulty of the material in terms of vocabulary, syntax, background information required, and conceptual complexity. As the typical child progresses through the successive years of schooling, he is able to comprehend progressively more difficult material. If difficulty of material is held constant, reading speed also increases; as difficulty increases, however, reading speeds decrease somewhat. Speed of reading and rate of comprehension are correlated in the sense that the faster readers are also the better comprehenders; this does not mean, of course, that a given child will be able to comprehend material of a given degree of difficulty better if he merely pushes himself to read faster. Training in reading may, to be sure, increase his reading speed, but if normal reading speed is improved through training, there will usually be a corresponding increase in the level of difficulty of material that he can comprehend.

Despite the availability of many standardized reading tests, there do not seem to be reliable data that would enable one to characterize the average reading performances of children at the several grade levels. Desired would be a chart that shows the typical kinds of material that the median student at each grade can read with good comprehension and also the average speed at which he would read such material if reading for the purpose of general comprehension rather than for study of detailed facts. Normative data from the STEP Reading Test (Educational Testing Service, 1957) covering grades 4 through 14 and based on a common scale depict the course of development and the wide variations in reading achievement at the different grades (see Figure 3-1). Median scores increase nearly linearly over the grades covered, although there is a suggestion of a slow tapering off at the twelfth grade. The data for the first two years of college are no doubt based on a sample that is more selective with respect to the general population, but the medians for these groups continue the linear progress exhibited by those for the precollege years. Bands have been drawn in such a way as to show the reading achieve-

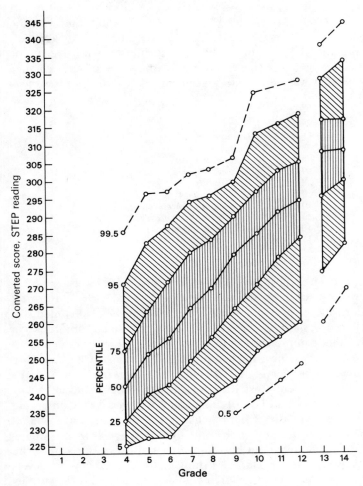

Figure 3-1. Development and Variations in Reading Achievement at Different Grades

ment scores attained by the middle 50 percent, the middle 90 percent, and the middle 99 percent of the norming samples. What is most remarkable about these data is the very wide overlap of the distributions from grade to grade. If the data are to be taken at face value, a few students (the top $\frac{1}{2}$ percent) in the fourth grade read at the levels attained by the median students at grade 10.5, and by grade 9, the top $\frac{1}{2}$ percent of the students read nearly up to the level of the college medians. On the other hand, at the twelfth grade, the bottom $\frac{1}{2}$ percent of students are reading not far above the fourth grade norm, and even at the college level, students at the 5th percentile attain scores that are characteristic of median students at grades 8 and 9.

But what do these scores mean? Numerous studies have attempted to place various kinds of literature as "appropriate" for given grade levels, but even these grade placements are based on dubious assumptions. For the elementary and high school grades, data given by Washburne and Morphett (1938) may be presented. By identifying books that children, with given grade placements on a reading test (the Stanford Reading Test), reported they enjoyed, they arrived at such grade placements of children's classics as follows:

Grade Level	Book
8.4	*Mutiny on the Bounty*
8.6	*Westward Ho*
8.9	*The Prince and the Pauper*
9.0	*Gulliver's Travels*
9.3	*Rip Van Winkle*
9.5	*The Call of the Wild*
10.0	*The Last of the Mohicans*
10.2	*Tales from Shakespeare*
10.6	*Moby Dick* (abridged)
11.0	*Captains Courageous*
11.2	*The Talisman*

Another approach to the interpretation of reading grade levels is possible through the reworking of data amassed by Flanagan et al. (1964) in Project TALENT, a nationwide project involving the testing of 440,000 students in grades 9, 10, 11, and 12 in the spring of 1960. They gave small subsamples in each grade a reading comprehension test based upon passages drawn from ten authors and ten magazines; the test was carefully constructed to ask 10 questions—graded in difficulty—on each author or magazine. Let us make the assumption that a student must attain a score of 6 or better on each set of questions to demonstrate that he can understand the passages. Comparing the scores on the special reading comprehension test with scores on a general reading comprehension test taken by the total Project TALENT sample, and extrapolating normative data both upwards and downwards from the grade 9–12 data, we can set up Table 3-4 showing the estimated grade levels at which different percentages of children would be able to read the various materials with comprehension.

Table 3-4. Grade Levels at Which Material Would Be
Comprehended by Students

Author or Magazine	Median Student	Student at 75th Percentile of Reading Ability at Grade	Student at 95th Percentile of Reading Ability at Grade
Modern Screen	7.5	about 5.0	about 2.0
Louisa May Alcott	10.3	7.6	about 3.0
Saturday Evening Post	13.0	10.6	about 5.5
Look; Sinclair Lewis	14.3	12.3	about 8.6
Time; Joseph Conrad	15.4	13.6	10.2
Saturday Review; Thomas Mann	16.2	14.6	13.3

These figures are, it must be emphasized, very approximate. The authors and magazines are mentioned only in order to give an impression of the kind of reading material that can be comprehended by the students. Obviously, there is a wide range of reading difficulty represented in any one magazine or author; the passages chosen for the special comprehension tests may have been unrepresentative; the test questions may have been harder than they might have been; and the test scores may have underestimated the actual degree of comprehension. Nevertheless, these results sound a rather pessimistic note: the average student in the American school understands much less of what he reads than one might expect at his grade level. Only in the case of the brighter students does one find reading comprehension abilities that are satisfactory.[2]

Average reading speeds also increase with grade level. According to data collected by Taylor, Frackenpohl, and Pettee (1960), word-per-minute norms for the several grades are as follows:

Grade	1	2	3	4	5	6	7	8	9	10	11	12	College
WPM	80	115	138	158	173	185	195	204	214	224	237	250	280

Presumably, these are norms for material ordinarily taught at the several grades. Reading speed decreases with increased reading difficulty of the material. For an adult population in a major city sampled and tested by

[2] My colleague Dr. Paul Diederich has suggested that I add the following note at this point:

"Grade-equivalent scores in reading that are far from the student's grade placement must be interpreted with caution. For example, if a 7th grader is two standard deviations above the mean on a 7th grade reading test, the publisher's norms may interpret this performance as 'reading at the 12th grade level.' But if one asks this student to read some typical 12th grade material, he may say that he does not understand it. He is simply very, very good at reading 7th grade material and answering 7th grade items. If another 7th grader tests at the 2nd grade level in reading, he may not respond favorably to *The Three Bears* as remedial material. We must hold fast to the notion that reading scores show where a student stands in relation to others in his grade in dealing with material and items beamed at that grade, and there is no direct way to translate this performance into the kinds of material and items of much greater difficulty that he can handle."

door-to-door interviewers, Kershner (1964) found that when adults read for general comprehension and without awareness that they would be asked questions about the material, the mean reading times (seconds) per 2000 type-spaces were 90.8, 100.6, and 113.5, respectively, for Easy, Intermediate, and Hard reading materials. However, the fastest readers had approximately the same reading rates for passages of differing difficulty. Much higher reading speeds can, of course, be attained, but except possibly after the types of special training evaluated by Spache (1962) and Taylor (1962), the amount of detailed comprehension will decrease correspondingly. Travers (1966, pp. 216–217) showed that when college-age subjects are forced to read at various WPM rates from 150 to 350, the amount of comprehension as measured by comprehension tests decreases linearly with increasing reading rate. These results suggest that an individual has a characteristic rate of processing verbally expressed information that is not affected by different rates of presenting that information. (A similar conclusion is reached in examining Travers' results for speech presented at different rates; it should be pointed out, however, that certain rates and modes of presentation yielded higher efficiency scores, i.e., allowed the individual to use his capacity to process information at maximal efficiency. Highest efficiency for both visual (reading) and simultaneous audiovisual presentations was reached at 300 WPM.)

Writing Skills

Writing ability comprises an enormous spectrum of skills. At the simplest level, it consists of the ability to write down on paper what can be formulated in speech, but even this ability requires an integration of skills in handwriting or typing, spelling, punctuation, and other mechanics of writing. And even at this level, the writer does not and cannot represent everything he hears in speech; he must observe certain rules of normalization or editing whereby repetitions, false starts, and other types of "mistakes" are eliminated; suprasegmental phonemes such as intonation and pause can be represented in the conventional writing system only indirectly. From the standpoint of the young child, writing is a matter of putting down, in order, words and punctuation marks. The dictation exercise is the prototype of a writing test at this level. Nevertheless, it is difficult to find published normative data on the growth of simple writing skills in the sense implied here.

When the child has achieved some mastery of simple mechanical skills, it is possible to ask him to write a free composition. Generally, there is some degree of control in the stimulus, which may be either a topic, as for example in the STEP Essay Test (ETS, 1957–59) or a picture or film which the child is asked to describe or to tell a story about (Loban, 1963; O'Donnell et al.,

1967). It is common knowledge among English teachers that the nature of the topic or other stimulus can have a considerable influence on the quality of the writing that results (Armstrong, 1965; Braddock et al., 1963); normative data, therefore, are preferably based on adequate samples of writings with a variety of topics or pictorial stimuli. In any case, free composition obviously requires an ability to formulate ideational content (something interesting and reasonable to say) and organize it in a logical fashion. Thus, a writing test is often partly a test of creativity and originality and may draw upon some of the factors of creative verbal production that have been mentioned earlier in this chapter (Taylor, 1947). In the testing of free composition, there is also often a time element such that this formulation and organization of content must occur fairly rapidly. At advanced levels of secondary school and college, the purely intellectual demands placed upon students by the assigned topics are often severe, with the result that a test of writing ability is likely to be a disguised form of verbal reasoning test. This is one possible reason, at least, why marks on English composition tests tend to correlate highly (to the limits permitted by their reliability) with broad measures of verbal intelligence (Huddleston, 1954).

Superior writing as produced by professional creative or technical writers involves also a number of elements that can be described only in the language of rhetoric or literacy criticism: imagination, avoidance of clichés, clear organization of thought, mastery of devices for expressing tone and flavor, development of a personal style of writing, etc. There have been a few attempts to measure such qualities in an objective manner (e.g., Carroll, 1960), but none of them can be regarded as even reasonably successful. In any case, only a small proportion of the adult population achieves great skill in these elements of superior writing.

If the range of quality in a sample of free composition is sufficiently wide, it is possible to obtain rather high agreement among judges in the evaluation of these compositions with respect to overall quality. Loban (1967, p. 93), for example, notes that there were only rare cases of disagreement between two teachers asked to assign written compositions to five categories: Superior, High Average, Low Average, Marginal, and Illiterate. These compositions, however, were elicited from a stratified random sample of children from all socioeconomic levels, and it is evident that quality varied widely. The samples, taken every year from grades 4 through 12, were judged only within grade level on a relative basis: "In the rating of the compositions, the age of the subjects was naturally taken into consideration. In other words, a twelfth grader was expected to write at a more advanced level than a fourth grader [Loban, 1967, footnote, p. 98]." The results obtained in this longitudinal study, shown in Figure 3-2, therefore give little impression of actual growth in writing ability, although Loban comments that "all subjects write at their best *relative* levels in grades seven, eight, and nine," and he speculates that the lower performance at grades 10, 11, and 12

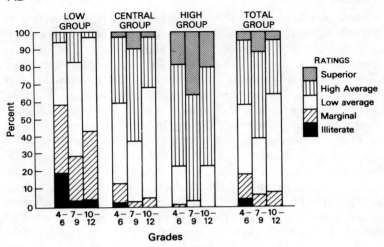

Figure 3-2. Categories of Evaluation of Writing in Free Compositions

may be due to reduced emphasis in the teaching of writing in the high school
or to a tendency to become careless about writing in the high school years.
Groups of 35 children each selected as consistently High or Low, respectively,
in verbal skills over a 13-year period show also consistently high or low
writing ability. (The Central group consists of the remainder of the group,
approximately 150 children.)

When compositions from different grade levels are pooled for ratings,
it is possible to notice progression in average quality. Diederich (1966, p.
438), for example, cites the results in Table 3-5 for compositions collected
from one senior high school and rated in a three-category scale.

Table 3-5. Progression in Quality for Compositions of
High School Students

	Academic Students (N=589)			Non-Academic Students (N=476)		
Grade:	10(238)	11(190)	12(161)	10(145)	11(167)	12(164)
High	22%	41%	53%	5%	8%	9%
Middle	65%	52%	42%	34%	53%	63%
Low	13%	7%	5%	61%	39%	28%

Among the difficulties encountered in the reliable rating of compositions
at a given grade level or for an essay writing test for college admissions is
that these compositions tend to be relatively homogeneous in overall quality.
Fostvedt (1965) found that despite careful training of teachers in the use of
various analytic rating scales, they were still not able to rate high school
English compositions with acceptable reliability. Carroll (1960), who did a

factor analysis of subjective and objective measures of the stylistic aspects of literary compositions, noted that among all the factors he obtained, lowest reliability of judgment among eight raters was found for scales measuring a factor of overall evaluation of literary merit. Godshalk, Swineford, and Coffman (1966) found that with "holistic" three-category ratings averaged over five themes and five readers per theme, reader reliability was .92 and total score reliability was .84; these data were for themes written by high school students in grades 11 and 12.

From almost time immemorial, English teachers have attempted to obtain more meaningful characterizations of compositions than are yielded by an overall quality rating. One method of doing this is to use analytic ratings of different aspects such as mechanics and organization. Generally, these ratings have been found to yield rather low intercorrelations, partly because of unreliability and partly because of the fact that these are indeed aspects of composition quality that can independently vary, as shown by studies of Olsen (1956) and Diederich et al. (1961), previously mentioned. In the latter study, a "test" factor derived from the students' performance on the Scholastic Aptitude Test and the College Board English Composition Test (an objective test of knowledge of writing skills) correlated significantly only with the ratings on Mechanics (.50) and Wording (.45), which themselves were correlated to the extent of .63. It is evident that the complete description of writing ability would have to take into account its differentiable aspects as revealed by this and other studies.

The development of writing skills can also be traced through the application of certain indices of structural complexity. Among recent studies in which this has been done are those of Sampson (1964a, 1964b), focusing on children age 10; Sam and Stine (1965) for grades 4, 5, and 6; Riling (1965) for grades 4 and 6; Armstrong (1965) for grade 5; Feenstra and Gardner (1966) for grades 3, 5, and 7; O'Donnell et al. (1967) also for grades 3, 5, and 7; and Hunt (1965) for grades 4, 8, and 12. Loban's longitudinal study (1963, 1966, 1967) obtained data from grades 3 through 12. For the purposes of this summary, we will chart results in terms of average length, in words, of "communication units" or "T-units" as studied by Loban, Hunt, and O'Donnell et al. In traditional terminology, a T-unit is roughly any sentence or part of a sentence that is an independent clause (possibly containing, however, one or more dependent clauses); average length of the T-unit is supposed to indicate "syntactic maturity."

Figure 3-3 is a plot of the average lengths of T-units found for various groups at various age levels by these investigators. Loban's High, Central, and Low groups have been described above. If we take into account the fact that Hunt's and O'Donnell's groups are predominantly middle-class children, while Loban's total group came from all socioeconomic levels, the results from the several studies are not inconsistent. The average child makes slow but consistent progress in syntactic maturity as measured by the average

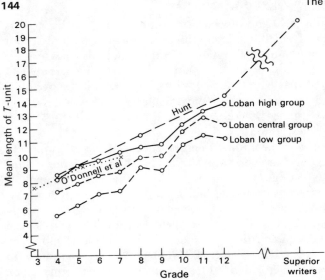

Figure 3-3. Average Lengths of *T*-units for Various Groups at Various Age Levels

length of *T*-unit. Even at grade 12, however, he is a long way from exhibiting the syntactic maturity of writers for *Harper's* or *The Atlantic*. Loban's Central group seems to reach a plateau around the eleventh or twelfth grade that can probably be taken to represent, approximately, the performance of the general population.

Unfortunately, there are no published data that would enable one to compute correlations between syntactic maturity and an overall rating of quality, but data presented by Loban (1967) suggest that even correlations within grade groups would be substantial. Nevertheless, the correlation would not be expected to be perfect, for a written composition might well have "syntactic maturity" and yet not exhibit anything like excellence in terms of organization, content, or even mechanics; conversely, excellent writing sometimes uses a simple style that would not necessarily yield a high "syntactic maturity" score.

Use of an objective measure such as the average length of *T*-units enables one to compare syntactic maturity in speech and writing. During the early years, as might be expected, the development of skill in handling language (especially syntax) is slower than the parallel development in speech, but according to O'Donnell et al. (1967, p. 95), a "crossover" occurs between grades 5 and 7 such that the control of syntax in writing advances beyond that in speech.

Relatively few studies have paid adequate attention to individual differences, or since most of them are cross-sectional in approach, to the question of how persistent these individual differences are. Sampson's

(1964a) longitudinal study, however, reported positive correlations of writing maturity at age 10 with linguistic variables measured at ages $2\frac{1}{2}$, 5, and 8. Loban's results for High and Low groups have already been cited. We can be reasonably sure, despite the lack of adequate data, that linguistic maturity in writing as in other skills is correlated with the Verbal Knowledge factor isolated in factor analytic studies, and the stability of relative linguistic maturity has much the same properties as that for Verbal Knowledge.

Because of the unavailability of sufficient research data, we have not been able to present here a clear picture of the growth of writing skills or of the individual differences in rates of growth through the school years. Also, there appear to be no reliable data on the writing skills of the adult population, as there are on vocabulary and reading skills. The writer considered presenting normative developmental data from the STEP Writing Test (Educational Testing Service, 1956–59b), but since this is a multiple-choice test of *knowledge* of certain writing skills rather than of actual free composition and has been subjected to severe criticism on a number of grounds (see the reviews in Buros, 1965, pp. 592–597), these data are of somewhat dubious relevance. Data from the STEP Essay Test (Educational Testing Service, 1957–59) could not be used because the writer questions whether the common score scale has the same meaning at all levels. However, if the reader will construct a figure from the STEP Writing Test data on the same principles as Figure 3-1, he will be struck with the enormous individual differences in whatever competences this test measures. For example, the top 5 percent of students at grade 4 are superior to the bottom 5 percent of students in the college freshman year.

VARIABLES ASSOCIATED WITH LANGUAGE DEVELOPMENT BEYOND THE EARLY YEARS

In this final section, we will briefly consider the causes of differences in rates of language development as they may be observed at ages beyond that of normal school entry. Much of the evidence has been reviewed in detail by such writers as McCarthy (1954) and May (1966).

There is clear evidence that certain speech behaviors observable as early as 1 year of age are indicative of later language development, palticularly in the case of females. In the Berkeley Growth Study data on 54 cases tested at various points throughout a span of 35 years, Bayley (1968) found a correlation of .80 for girls and one of .26 for boys between infant Vocalization Precocity scores and Wechsler-Bellevue Verbal IQ's given at 26 years of age. In a British study, Sampson (1962, 1964a) found high correlations between speech development observed at $2\frac{1}{2}$ years and measures of reading ability and written composition skill taken at 8 and 10 years respectively. If it is assumed that environment has less effect on behavior at very early ages than at later ages, these and similar findings strongly suggest that heredity has considerable influence in determining the initial rate of language development and that this influence persists, in some degree, throughout later years. On the other hand, the assumption that heredity is more important in early years can be challenged, as Anastasi (1958) does, by citing the possibility and a certain amount of evidence that different methods of child handling in early infancy may be responsible for differences among children even at 1 year of age. Nevertheless, the observation that mentally retarded children have strikingly different and consistent rates of language development— despite all efforts to accelerate them—as compared to normal children leads again to the strong suggestion of the importance of hereditary influences (Lenneberg, 1967).

Since the heredity-environment question will probably never be fully resolved until it is possible to ascertain gene composition by biochemical means, and since educators can do little about heredity, it is probably wise to direct attention to environmental factors in language development.

Almost every study of environmental influences leads one to conclude that the primary factor in language development, aside from native abilities, is the *quality* of the language exposure that the child receives. The richer this quality of language exposure, other things being equal, the faster and better the individual's language development. Whether one defines the variables under study in terms of home influences, school influences, or socioeconomic class differences, they are always associated with the amount and kind of exposure to language that the individual receives. Common observation tells us that whatever language or dialect the child learns, it is that of his immediate environment. But this is not merely a matter of a particular language or dialect; it is also a matter of the richness and appropriateness of expression that the child hears. In most cases, early language experience starts in the home. Milner (1951) showed that differences in language development of first grade Negro children were associated with the amount and variety of language experiences they had had with their parents; high-scoring children were from families that usually ate meals and had much conversation together, while low-scoring children were deprived of such stimulation. These differences were also strikingly correlated with socioeconomic status. Hess and Shipman (1965) have shown that early experiences in the home, correlated with socioeconomic status, influence not only the child's language development but also his "cognitive style," that is, his manner of attacking and analyzing problems, and we may infer that these early experiences have consequences for later development.

The major effect of low socioeconomic status, in fact, is in the area of verbal intelligence. In study after study, tests involving verbal material exhibit larger differences between social classes than most other types of tests. Havighurst and Breese (1947), for example, studying correlations of

Primary Mental Ability test scores with social class status in 13-year-olds in a midwest American city, found the highest correlation with the Verbal Knowledge factor (.42), moderate correlations for Number (.32) and Word Fluency (.30) scores, and still lower correlations for Space (.25), Reasoning (.23), and Memory (.21). Taking scores on a 20-item vocabulary test as an index of verbal intelligence, Miner (1957) obtained striking differences correlated with socioeconomic and occupational levels. Jensen (1968) claims that although lower class children are on the average little different from upper class children in basic learning capacity, they are handicapped in academic learning situations because they have been deprived of the opportunity to learn the range of concepts and verbal associations that are needed to facilitate such learning.

Early language deprivation is not necessarily correlated with low socioeconomic status; it can occur even in children of the very wealthy who have minimal contact with their parents. Children who are for any reason placed in orphanages during their early years also are likely to exhibit retarded language development, and according to Goldfarb (1943), this handicap may persist even up to adolescence.

According to Lesser, Fifer, and Clark (1965), ethnic groups in a city like New York differ markedly in the extent to which they encourage language development in their children. Jewish children were found to be significantly better in English verbal ability than all other groups studied, followed by Negroes, Chinese, and Puerto Ricans, in that order. In each group, middle-class children were superior to lower-class children, but the class difference was most marked among Negroes. On abilities other than verbal, the rankings of the groups were altered. Lesser et al. claim that these results hold even after the possible effects of bilingualism have been discounted.

The question of the effect of bilingualism on language development is a very complicated one that depends upon the relative status of the two languages involved, the type of bilingual situation, whether the child receives school instruction in his native or the foreign language (Macnamara, 1967), and many other factors. There are instances (Peal & Lambert, 1962) where bilingual children actually show greater verbal intelligence and language development than monolinguals. Available data are not inconsistent with the hypothesis that the degree to which bilingualism affects native language development is a function of the amount and kind of exposure such a condition allows the child to get to his native language, quite independently of how much exposure he receives to the other language involved.

Sex is by all accounts an important variable in language development. It has a peculiar status in that it may mediate both hereditary and environmental influences. We have already seen that constitutional differences are suggested by Bayley's finding (1968) that correlations between early vocalization and later verbal intelligence test scores are much more pronounced in girls than in boys. Many investigators have noted that girls on the average begin to talk earlier than boys, and this early talking may give girls a head start in later language development. In their early years, constitutional factors tend to make boys more active physically and less disposed to advance in language development. There is some evidence (Gallagher, 1950) that there is greater incidence of "specific language disability" in boys. On the other hand, the nearly universal finding (at least in American culture) that girls exhibit accelerated language achievements may possibly be explained as primarily due to characteristic differences between the ways boys and girls are reared and socialized. In the elementary school, girls tend to take more interest in schoolwork (which is to a large extent verbal) and are more amenable to being taught. It is not surprising, therefore, that girls consistently do better on tests of verbal intelligence and achievement, particularly tests involving written language. For example, on the STEP (Educational Testing Service, 1957) scores, girls score higher, on the average, than the boys in all grades from 4 to 12 on the Reading and Writing tests, but they are only very slightly superior, and not consistently so, on the Listening tests. Nearly all of the 10 "intellectual factors" listed by Guilford (1967, p. 404) for which there is evidence of sex differences favoring girls are factors involving language. Intellectual factors in which males tend to be superior are primarily ones involving the perception of spatial figures. The conclusion that sex differences in language development, particularly in written language, are culturally determined is reinforced by Preston's (1962) finding that whereas in the U.S. girls are superior in reading skills, boys are superior in Germany, where there are more male teachers and where cultural attitudes towards the sexes are different from those characteristic of the U.S. Nevertheless, all sex differences are of relatively small extent; the distributions of various measures of language development and skill nearly always show great overlap. Further, it is possible that current cultural and social trends in the U.S. are working towards reducing differences between boys and girls in language development. Templin (1957) found that with respect to certain indices or oral language development applied to children up to age 8, the differences favoring girls that were the rule in studies conducted in the 1930s were no longer apparent.

SUMMARY

Language development involves a large number of different competences and skills, in each of which there may be a different rate of growth dependent upon a combination of hereditary, constitutional, and environmental factors. Although a substantial degree of basic competence in the rules of the native language is attained by the normal child at school entry age, development is by no means complete at that time. Certain advanced stages of phonology are not normally mastered until about 8 years of age, and it is probably the case that complete competence in the grammatical rules of the language is not approximated until the period of adolescence, and even this statement must be qualified to apply only to the competence assumed as a basis for spoken performance, since a substantial number of adolescents do not seem to be able to manifest adequate grammatical competence in written performance. In the lexical and semantic aspects of linguistic competence, development is highly incomplete at school entry age and continues in more or less equal increments (on the average) throughout the years of schooling and to a lesser extent throughout adult life. There are individual differences in all aspects of the development of linguistic competence, particularly in vocabulary and semantic knowledge.

Different rates of growth are especially apparent in various linguistic performances—listening, speaking, reading, and writing. The evidence leads one to the conclusion that these different rates of growth are dependent upon, or manifestations of, basic individual differences in cognitive organization and personality formation, as well as wide differences in opportunities to practice and learn. Much more research, particularly from longitudinal studies employing a wide variety of measures, is needed before an adequate account of language development in the years beyond primary language acquisition can be drawn up.

REFERENCES

Altus, W. D. The relationship between vocabulary and literacy when intelligence is held constant. *J. Soc. Psychol.*, 1950, **31**, 299–301.

Anastasi, A. *Differential psychology: individual and group differences in behavior.* New York: Macmillan, 1958.

Anastasiow, N. J., & Hansen, D. Criteria for linguistic reading programs. *Element. Eng.*, 1967, **44**, 231–235.

Armstrong, D. R. *An objective measure of the quality of the written composition of fifth grade pupils.* Doctoral dissertation, University of California, 1965. In *Dissertation Abstracts*, 1966, **26**, 7174.

Bayley, N. Behavioral correlates of mental growth: birth to thirty-six years. *Am. Psychologist*, 1968, **23**, 1–17.

Becker, S. L. The ratings of speeches: scale independence. *Speech Monogr.* 1962, **29**, 38–44.

Bennett, G. K., & Raskow, S. Extension of the norms of the Columbia Vocabulary Test. *J. appl. Psychol.*, 1941, **25**, 48–51.

Bennett, G. K., Seashore, H. G., & Wesman, A. G. *Differential aptitude tests.* New York: The Psychological Corporation, 1947–1959.

Bereiter, C. Fluency abilities in preschool children. *J. genet. Psychol.*, 1961, **98**, 47–48.

Berko, J., & Brown, R. Psycholinguistic research methods. In P. H. Mussen (Ed.), *Handbook of research methods in child development*. New York: John Wiley & Sons, 1960. Pp. 517–557.

Bernstein, B. Language and social class. *Brit. J. Sociol.*, 1960, **11**, 271–276.

Berwick, M. The semantic method for testing vocabulary. *J. exp. Educ.*, 1959, **28**, 123–141.

Bloom, B. S. *Stability and change in human characteristics*. New York: John Wiley & Sons, 1964.

Bormuth, J. R. Readability: a new approach. *Read. Res. Quart.*, 1966, **1**, 79–132.

Braddock, R., Lloyd-Jones, R., & Schoer, L. *Research in written composition*. Champaign, Ill.: NCTE, 1963.

Brown, J. I., & Carlsen, G. R. *Brown-Carlsen listening comprehension test*. New York: Harcourt, Brace, & World, 1953.

Brown, R. W. Linguistic determinism and the part of speech. *J. abnorm. soc. Psychol.*, 1957, **55**, 1–5.

Brown, R. W. & Hildum, D. C. Expectancy and the perception of syllables. *Language*, 1956, **32**, 411–419.

Bruce, D. J. The analysis of word sounds by young children. *Brit. J. educ. Psychol.*, 1964, **34**, 158–170.

Buros, O. K. *The sixth mental measurements yearbook*. Highland Park: Gryphon Press, 1965.

Carroll, J. B. A factor analysis of verbal abilities. *Psychometrika*, 1941, **6**, 279–307.

Carroll, J. B. An evaluation of language tests from the standpoint of the psychology of language. *9th Yearb. nat. Council Measurmt. in Educ.*, 1952. Pp. 75–80.

Carroll, J. B. A factor analysis of two foreign language aptitude batteries. *J. gen. Psychol.*, 1958, **59**, 3–19.

Carroll, J. B. Vectors of prose style. In T. A. Sebeok (Ed.), *Style in language*. New York: Technology Press & John Wiley & Sons, 1960. Pp. 283–292.

Carroll, J. B. Factors in verbal achievement. In P. L. Dressel (Ed.), *Proc. 1961 invit. Conf. on test. Prob.* Princeton: Educational Testing Service, 1962. Pp. 11–18.

Carroll, J. B. Problems of measuring speech rate. In E. Foulke (Ed.), *Proc. Louisville Conf. on time compressed Speech*. Louisville: Univ. of Louisville, 1967. Pp. 88–94. (a)

Carroll, J. B. On sampling from a lognormal model of word-frequency distribution. In H. Kucera & W. N. Francis. *Computational analysis of present-day American English*. Providence: Brown Univ. Press, 1967. Pp. 406–424. (b)

Carroll, J. B. Review of J. P. Guilford's *Structure of intellect*. *Am. educ. Res. J.*, 1968. (a)

Carroll, J. B. The psychology of language testing. In A. Davies (Ed.), *Language testing symposium: a psycholinguistic approach*. New York & London: Oxford Univ. Press, 1968. (b)

Carroll, J. B., & Sapon, S. M. *Modern language aptitude test*. New York: The Psychological Corporation, 1959.

Carroll, J. B., & Sapon, S. M. *Modern language aptitude test—elementary form*. New York: The Psychological Corporation, 1967.

Cazden, C. B. Subcultural differences in child language: an interdisciplinary review. *Merrill-Palmer Quart. Behav. Developm.*, **12**, 185–219.

Chall, J. S. *Readability: an appraisal of research and application. Bur. Educ. Res. Monogr.* No. 34. Columbus: Ohio State Univ., 1958.

Chall, J. S. *Learning to read: the great debate. An inquiry into the old and new methods of teaching children to read 1910–1965.* New York: McGraw-Hill, 1967.

Chall, J. S., Roswell, F. G., & Blumenthal, S. H. Auditory blending ability: a factor in success in beginning reading. *Read. Teacher*, 1963, **16**, 113–118.

Chomsky, N. *Aspects of the theory of syntax.* Cambridge: M.I.T. Press, 1965.

Christian, A. M., & Paterson, D. G. Growth of vocabulary in later maturity. *J. Psychol.*, 1936, **1**, 167–169.

Cooper, R. L. The ability of deaf and hearing children to apply morphological rules. *J. Speech Hear. Res.*, 1967, **10**, 77–86.

Dale, E. Vocabulary measurement: techniques and major findings. *Element. Eng.*, 1965, **42**, 895–901, 948.

Dale, E., & Chall, J. S. A formula for predicting readability. *Educ. Res. Bull.*, 1948, **27**, 11–20; **28**, 37–54.

Dale, E., & Eichholz, G. *Children's knowledge of words.* Columbus: Bureau of Educational Research Services, undated (circa 1960). (An interim report)

Darley, F. L., & Moll, K. L. Reliability of language measures and sizes of language sample. *J. Speech Hear. Res.*, 1960, **3**, 166–173.

Davis, F. B. Fundamental factors of comprehension in reading. *Psychometrika*, 1944, **9**, 185–197.

Davis, O. L., Smith, H. G., Jr., & Bowers, N. D. High school students' awareness of structural relationships in English. *J. educ. Res.*, 1964, **58**, 69–71.

Deutsch, M. The role of social class in language development and cognition. *Am. J. Orthopsychiat.*, 1965, **25**, 78–88.

Diederich, P. B. How to measure growth in writing ability. *Eng. J.*, 1966, **55**, 435–449.

Diederich, P. B., French, J. W., & Carlton, S. T. *Factors in judgments of writing ability. Res. Bull. No. 61–15.* Princeton: Educational Testing Service, 1961.

Diederich, P. B., & Palmer, O. E. *Difficulty in grades 11 and 13 of 4,800 words from 6,000 through 20,000 in frequency. Res. Bull. No. 56–13.* Princeton: Educational Testing Service, 1956.

Durkin, D. *Children who read early: two longitudinal studies.* New York: Teachers College Press, 1966.

Educational Testing Service. *Sequential tests of educational progress: listening.* Princeton: Educational Testing Service, 1956–1959. (a)

Educational Testing Service. *Sequential tests of educational progress: writing.* Princeton: Educational Testing Service, 1956–1959. (b)

Educational Testing Service. *Sequential tests of educational progress: technical report, reading, writing, listening, social studies, science, mathematics.* Princeton: Educational Testing Service, 1957.

Educational Testing Service. *Sequential tests of educational progress: essay test.* Princeton: Educational Testing Service, 1957–1959.

Ellegård, A. Estimating vocabulary size. *Word*, 1960, **16**, 219–244.

Ervin, S. M., & Miller, W. R. Language development. In H. W. Stevenson et al. (Eds.), *Child psychology. 62nd Yearb., Nat. Soc. Study of Educ.*, 1963, Part I, 108–143.

Fawcett, Annabel E. Training in listening. *Element. Eng.*, 1966, **43**, 473–476.

Feenstra, H. J., & Gardner, R. C. *Developmental changes in oral and written language behavior in school-age children. Res. Bull. No. 34.* London, Canada: Univ. of Western Ontario, 1966.

Ferguson, G. A. On learning and human ability. *Canad. J. Psychol.*, 1954, **8**, 95–112.

Flanagan, J. C. et al. *The American high school student*. Pittsburgh: Project TALENT Office, Univ. of Pittsburgh, 1964.

Fodor, J. A., & Garrett, M. Some syntactic determinants of sentential complexity. *Percept. and Psychophysics*, 1967, **2**, 289–296.

Fostvedt, D. R. Criteria for the evaluation of high-school English composition. *J. educ. Res.*, 1965, **59**, 108–112.

Francis, W. N. *The structure of American English*. New York: Ronald Press, 1958.

French, J. W. The description of aptitude and achievement tests in terms of rotated factors. *Psychom. Monogr. No.* 5. Chicago: Univ. of Chicago Press, 1951.

Fries, C. C. *The structure of English*. New York: Harcourt, Brace & World, 1952.

Gallagher, J. Specific language disability: a cause of scholastic failure. *New England J. Med.*, 1950, **242**, 436–440.

Gerstmann, J. Fingeragnosie und isolierte Agraphie—ein neues Syndrom. *Zeitschrift für die gesamte Neurologie und Psychiatrie*, 1927, **108**, 152–177.

Godshalk, F. I., Swineford, F., & Coffman, W. E. *The measurement of writing ability*. *CEEB Res. Monogr. No.* 6. Princeton: College Entrance Examination Board, 1966.

Goldfarb, W. The effects of early institutional care on adolescent personality. *J. exp. Educ.*, 1943, **12**, 106–129.

Greene, E. B. *Michigan vocabulary profile test*. New York: Harcourt, Brace & World, 1949.

Guilford, J. P. *The nature of human intelligence*. New York: McGraw-Hill, 1967.

Hafner, L. E. Cloze procedure. *J. Read.*, 1966, **9**, 415–421.

Havighurst, R. J., & Breese, F. H. Relations between ability and social status in a midwestern community: III. Primary mental abilities. *J. educ. Psychol.*, 1947, **38**, 241–247.

Hess, R. D., & Shipman, V. Early experience and the socialization of cognitive modes in children. *Child Develpm.*, 1965, **36**, 869–886.

Hitchman, P. J. The testing of spoken English: a review of research. *Educ. Res.*, 1964, **7**, 55–72.

Holmes, J. A., & Singer, H. *Speed and power of reading in high school. Coop. Res. Monogr. No.* 14. Washington: U.S. Department of Health, Education, and Welfare, Office of Education, 1966.

Huddleston, E. M. Measurement of writing ability at the college-entrance level: objective vs. subjective testing techniques. *J. exp. Educ.*, 1954, **22**, 165–213.

Hunt, K. W. *Grammatical structures written at three grade levels. NCTE Res. Report No.* 3. Champaign, Ill: NCTE, 1965.

Huttenlocher, Janellen. Children's language: word-phrase relationship. *Science*, 1964, **143**, 264–265.

Jensen, A. R. Social class and verbal learning. In M. Deutsch et al. (Eds.), *Social-class, race, and psychological development*. New York: Holt, Rinehart & Winston, 1968.

Johnson, F. C., & Frandsen, K. Administering the Brown-Carlsen listening comprehension test. *J. Communic.*, 1963, **13**, 38–45.

Kean, J. M., & Yamamoto, K. Grammar signals and assignment of words to parts of speech among young children: an exploration. *J. verb. Learn. verb. Behav.*, 1965, **4**, 323–326.

Kelly, C. M. "Actual listening behavior" of industrial supervisors, as related to "listening ability," general mental ability, selected personality factors, and supervisory effectiveness. Doctoral dissertation, Purdue University, 1962. Pp. 215. In *Dissertation Abstracts*, 1963, **23**, 4091.

Kelly, C. M. An investigation of the construct validity of two commercially published listening tests. *Speech Monogr.*, 1965, **32**, 139–143.

Kershner, A. M. Speed of reading in an adult population under differential conditions. *J. appl. Psychol.*, 1964, **48**, 25–28.

Kirkpatrick, J. J., & Cureton, E. E. Vocabulary difficulty and word frequency. *J. appl. Psychol.*, 1949, **33**, 347–351.

Klare, G. R. *The measurement of readability*. Ames: Iowa State Univ. Press, 1963.

Lashley, K. S. The problem of serial order in behavior. In L. A. Jeffress (Ed.), *Cerebral mechanisms in behavior*. New York: John Wiley & Sons, 1951. Pp. 112–136.

Lenneberg, E. H. Understanding language without ability to speak. *J. abnorm. soc. Psychol.*, 1962, **65**, 419–425.

Lenneberg, E. H. *Biological foundations of language*. New York: John Wiley & Sons, 1967.

Lesser, G. S., Fifer, G., & Clark, D. H. Mental abilities of children in different social and cultural groups. *Monogr. Soc. Res. Child Develpm.*, 1965, **30** (4, Whole No. 102).

Loban, W. Language ability: grades seven, eight, and nine. OE–30018, *Coop. Res. Monogr. No.* 18. Washington: U.S. Office of Education, 1966.

Loban, W. Language ability: grades ten, eleven, and twelve. *Final report, USOE Coop. Program Proj. No.* 2387. Berkeley: Univ. of California, 1967.

Loban, W. The language of elementary school children. *NCTE Res. Report No.* 1. Champaign, Ill.: NCTE, 1963.

Lorge, I., & Chall, J. S. Estimating the size of vocabularies of children and adults: an analysis of methodological issues. *J. exp. Educ.*, 1963, **32**, 148–157.

Lundsteen, S. W. Critical listening—permanency and transfer of gains made during an experiment in the fifth and sixth grades. *Calif. J. educ. Res.*, 1965, **16**, 210–216.

Lundsteen, S. W. Critical listening: an experiment. *Element. School J.*, 1966, **66**, 311–315.

Maclay, H., & Sleator, M. D. Responses to language: judgments of grammaticalness. *Internat. J. Am. Ling.*, 1960, **26**, 275–282.

Macnamara, J. The effects of instruction in a weaker language. *J. soc. Issues*, 1967, **23**, 121–135.

Maltzman, I. Fluency and originality in written themes. *Percept. and motor Skills*, 1963, **16**, 281–282.

Marge, M. A factor analysis of oral communication skills in older children. *J. Speech Hear. Res.*, 1964, **7**, 31–46.

May, F. B. The effects of environment on oral language development. *Element. Eng.*, 1966, **43**, 587–595, 720–729.

McCarthy, D. *The language development of the preschool child. Inst. Child Welfare Monogr. Ser. No.* 4. Minneapolis: Univ. of Minnesota Press, 1930.

McCarthy, D. Language development in children. In L. Carmichael (Ed.), *Manual child psychology*. (2nd ed.) New York: John Wiley & Sons, 1954. Pp. 492–630.

McCarthy, J. J., & Kirk, S. A. *The construction, standardization and statistical characteristics of the Illinois test of psycholinguistic abilities*. Madison: ITPA, Inc., 1963.

Menyuk, P. A preliminary evaluation of grammatical capacity in children. *J. verb. Learn. verb. Behav.*, 1963, **2**, 429–439.

Menyuk, P. Alteration of rules in children's grammar. *J. verb. Learn. verb. Behav.*, 1964, **3**, 480–488.

Miller, G. A., & Nicely, P. E. Analysis of perceptual confusions among some English consonants. *J. acoust. Soc. Amer.*, 1955, **27**, 338–352.

Milner, E. A study of the relationships between reading readiness in grade one school children and patterns of parent-child interaction. *Child Develpm.*, 1951, **22**, 95–112.

Miner, J. B. *Intelligence in the United States.* New York: Springer, 1957.

Minifie, F. C., Darley, F. L., & Sherman, D. Temporal reliability of seven language measures. *J. Speech Hear. Res.*, 1963, **6**, 139–148.

O'Donnell, R. C. The correlation of awareness of structural relationships in English and ability in written composition. *J. educ. Res.*, 1964, **57**, 464–467.

O'Donnell, R. C., Griffin, W. J., & Norris, R. C. *Syntax of kindergarten and elementary school children: a transformational analysis. NCTE Research Report No.* 8. Champaign, Ill.: NCTE, 1967.

Oldfield, R. C. Individual vocabulary and semantic currency. *Brit. J. soc. clin. Psychol.*, 1963, **2**, 122–130.

Olsen, M. *Summary of main findings on the validity of the 1955 college board general composition test. Statistical Report* 56–9. Princeton: Educational Testing Service, 1956.

Osgood, C. E. *A psycholinguistic analysis of the language process.* Unpublished paper, University of Illinois, 1952.

Osgood, C. E. A behavioristic analysis. In *Contemporary approaches to cognition.* Cambridge: Harvard Univ. Press, 1957. Pp. 75–118.

Peal, E., & Lambert, W. E. The relation of bilingualism to intelligence. *Psychol. Monogr.*, 1962, **76** (Whole No. 546).

Porter, D. *Non-semantic identifiers of a grammatical category.* Paper presented at the meetings of the American Psychological Association, 1959.

Preston, R. C. Reading achievement of German and American children. *School & Society*, 1962, **90**, 350–354.

Riling, M. E. *Oral and written language of children in grades four and six compared with the language of their textbooks. Coop. Res. Project No.* 2410. Durant, Okla.: Southeastern State College, 1965.

Robinson, J. A. *The development of certain pronunciation skills in the case of suffixed words.* Doctoral dissertation, Harvard Graduate School of Education, 1967.

Russell, D. H. The dimensions of children's meaning vocabularies in grades four through twelve. *Univ. of Calif. Publ. in Educ.*, 1954, **11**, 315–414.

Russell, D. H., & Saadeh, I. Q. Qualitative levels in children's vocabularies. *J. educ. Psychol.*, 1962, **53**, 170–174.

Sam, N. H., & Stine, E. S. *Structural analysis of the written composition of intermediate grade children.* Report to the U.S. Office of Education, *Coop. Res. Project No.* S-057, Bethlehem, Pa., 1965.

Sampson, O. C. Reading skill at eight years in relation to speech and other factors. *Brit. J. educ. Psychol.*, 1962, **32**, 12–17.

Sampson, O. C. Written composition at ten years as an aspect of linguistic development: a longitudinal study continued. *Brit. J. educ. Psychol.*, 1964, **24**, 143–150. (a)

Sampson, O. C. A linguistic study of the written compositions of ten-year-old children. *Lang. & Speech*, 1964, **7**, 176–182. (b)

Shannon, M. R. *The measurement of phonetic understandings relevant to the teaching of reading.* Doctoral dissertation, Harvard Graduate School of Education, 1959.

Sievers, D. J. *Development and standardization of a test of psycholinguistic growth in preschool children.* Doctoral dissertation, Univ. of Illinois, 1955.

Sievers, D. J., McCarthy, J. J., Olson, J. L., Bateman, B. D., & Kass, C. E. *Selected studies on the Illinois test of psycholinguistic abilities.* Madison: ITPA, Inc., 1963.

Slobin, D. I. Grammatical transformations and sentence comprehension in childhood and adulthood. *J. verb. Learn. verb. Behav.*, 1966, **5**, 219–227.

Smith, M. K. Measurement of the size of general English vocabulary through the elementary grades and high school. *Genet. Psychol. Monogr.*, 1941, **24**, 311–345.

Spache, G. D. Is this a breakthrough in reading? *Read. Teacher*, 1962, **15**, 258–263.

Spearman, C. *The abilities of man.* New York: Macmillan, 1927.

Spearritt, D. *Listening comprehension—a factorial analysis.* Melbourne: Australian Council for Educational Research, 1962.

Steer, M. D., & Drexler, H. G. Predicting articulation ability from kindergarten tests. *J. Speech Hear. Dis.*, 1960, **25**, 391–397.

Stitt, C. L., & Huntington, D. A. Reliability of judgments of articulation proficiency. *J. Speech Hear. Res.*, 1963, **6**, 49–56.

Strang, R. G., & Hocker, M. E. First-grade children's language patterns. *Element. Eng.*, 1965, **42**, 38–41.

Strickland, R. G. The language of elementary school children: its relationship to the language of reading textbooks and the quality of reading of selected children. *Bull. School of Educ.*, Indiana Univ., 1962, **38**, No. 4.

Sullivan, E. T., Clark, W. W., & Tiegs, E. W. *California test of mental maturity, 1957 edition.* Monterey: California Test Bureau, 1957.

Taylor, C. W. A factorial study of fluency in writing. *Psychometrika*, 1947, **12**(4), 239–262.

Taylor, C. W., Smith, W. R., Ghiselin, B., Sheets, B. V., & Cochran, J. R. *Identification of communication abilities in military situations. USAF WADC tech. Report No.* 58–92, 1958.

Taylor, S. E. An evaluation of forty-one trainees who had recently completed the "Reading Dynamics" program. *Problems, programs and projects in college-adult reading.* 11th Yearb. Milwaukee: National Reading Conference, 1962. Pp. 41–56.

Taylor, S. E., Frackenpohl, H., & Pettee, J. L. *Grade level norms for the components of the fundamental reading skill. EDL Res. and Information Bull. No.* 3. Huntington: Educational Development Laboratories, 1960.

Taylor, W. L. Cloze procedure: a new tool for measuring readability. *Journalism Quart.*, 1953, **30**, 415–433.

Templin, Mildrid C. Phonic knowledge and its relation to the spelling and reading achievement of fourth grade pupils. *J. educ. Res.*, 1954, **47**, 441–454.

Templin, Mildred C. *Certain language skills in children: their development and inter-relationships.* Minneapolis: Univ. of Minnesota Press, 1957.

Terman, L. M., & Merrill, Maud A. *Stanford-Binet intelligence scale: manual for the third revision form L-M.* With revised IQ tables by Samuel R. Pinneau. Boston: Houghton Mifflin, 1960.

Thorndike, E. L. *A teacher's word book of the twenty thousand words found most frequently and widely in general reading for children and young people.* New York: Bur. of Publications, Teachers College, Columbia Univ., 1932.

Thorndike, E. L., & Lorge, I. *The teacher's word book of 30,000 words.* New York: Bur. of Publications, Teachers College, Columbia Univ., 1944.

Thorndike, R. L., & Gallup, G. H. Verbal intelligence of the American adult. *J. gen. Psychol.*, 1944, **30**, 75–85.

Thurstone, L. L. Note on a reanalysis of Davis' reading tests. *Psychometrika*, 1946, **11**, 185–188.

Thurstone, L. L. *Multiple factor analysis.* Chicago: Univ. of Chicago Press, 1947.

Thurstone, L. L., & Thurstone, T. G. *SRA primary mental abilities.* Chicago: Science Research Associates, 1946–1958.

Thurstone, L. L., & Thurstone, T. G. *SRA primary mental abilities technical supplement.* Chicago: Science Research Associates, 1954.

Tiffin, J., & McKinnis, M. Phonic ability: its measurement and relation to reading ability. *School & Society*, 1940, **51**, 190–192.

Travers, R. M. W. *Studies related to the design of audiovisual teaching materials.* Final report, Office of Education, Contract No. 3-20-003. Washington: U.S. Dept. of Health, Education, and Welfare, 1966.

Vandenberg, S. G. The hereditary abilities study: hereditary components in a psychological test battery. *Am. J. human Genet.*, 1962, **14**, 220–237.

Vernon, M. D. Specific dyslexia. *Brit. J. educ. Psychol.*, 1962, **32**, 143–150.

Vernon, P. E. *The structure of human abilities.* London: Methuen; New York: John Wiley & Sons, 1950.

Washburne, C. W., & Morphett, M. V. Grade placement of children's books. *Element. School J.*, 1938, **38**, 355–364.

Wechsler, D. *Wechsler intelligence scale for children.* New York: The Psychological Corporation, 1949.

Wechsler, D. *Wechsler adult intelligence scale.* New York: The Psychological Corporation, 1955.

Weener, P. D., Barritt, L. S., & Semmel, M. I. A critical evaluation of the Illinois test of psycholinguistic abilities. *Excep. Child.*, 1967, **33**, 373–380.

Wesman, A. G., & Seashore, H. G. Frequency vs. complexity of words in verbal measurement. *J. educ. Psychol.*, 1949, **40**, 395–404.

Zidonis, F. J. Generative grammar: a report on research. *Eng. J.*, 1965, **54**, 405–409.

4

The Psychology of Learning and the Study of English

JAMES DEESE
The Johns Hopkins University

The endless labors of an army of philosophers, linguists, psychologists, educators, teachers, and plain eccentrics have produced a mountain of literature on the psychology of language learning. There is distressingly little in that literature that should be of interest to the teacher of English. Most of it consists of exhortations to interest one's students, to reinforce, to provide for meaningful experience, and the like. Some of it consists of the laborious explication in the framework of language teaching of familiar psychological concepts, such as transfer of training. Some of it, mainly written by teachers themselves, consists of useful hints on how to teach particular points—for example, the use of prepositions. In the main, however, it is a dreadful and largely empty literature.

From time to time, however, important new ideas arise, and these do need to be brought to the attention of the classroom teacher. Sometimes these ideas are intellectually exciting, and occasionally they have important implications (if not always good ones) for the activities of the classroom. There has been, over the past twenty years, a ferment of activity in linguistics. That ferment has mainly concerned the theory of grammar, and out of the concern with that theory have come some ideas that are important to the teaching of English. They are important not only because they provide new ways of looking at the nature of language, but because they imply something about the psychology of language learning. In short, conflicting theories of grammar offer different ideas about how one should go about teaching language and teaching about language. These theories are central to my concern here.

By now, nearly all teachers of English are uncomfortably aware of the fact that there are several radically different contemporary notions of grammar. These theories of grammar are not different merely in detail. They stem from radically different ideas about the nature of language, ideas that reach into the most abstract questions of philosophy. These theories of grammar lead to different kinds of linguistic analysis and to different conceptions of the teaching of grammar and language generally. However, the theories themselves and their apparent practical implications must be separated, and it shall be one of my chief purposes to do just that.

Unfortunately, for the hapless teacher it is not simply a matter of some "new" grammar versus the grammar with which he may be familiar. There are several varieties of "new" grammars. The proponents of each have engaged in a public debate conspicuous even in this quarrelsome discipline for the polemic nature of the argument. Each of these new grammars presupposes some notions about the human mind, and they all have psychological implications. Each human being carries around in his head something that passes for a theory of grammar of his native language. One school of modern linguistics—generally called structural—seems to view that theory as arising out of ordinary human experience. Another school—generally called generative—argues that such a theory could not conceivably arise from experience, that it must reflect the innate predisposition of the human mind for languages of the human sort.

The dichotomy between structural and generative grammars is expressed by oversimplification, but it is widely accepted and provides a useful point of departure for an account of modern theories of grammar and their psychological implications. Thus, with the admission that we recognize several possible varieties of structural grammar and perhaps some different varieties of generative grammar as well, we may contrast their implications for the psychology of language learning.

Structural grammars are empirical and inductive in nature. According to structural grammarians, children discover the rules of their language. The main function of parents and teachers is to provide experience from which these rules are to be extracted. Later on, the teacher of grammar points out that these rules have names, etc., and thus makes them not merely implicit for the child but also explicit. The structural grammarian discovers the rules of the language in the way he believes children do. Generative grammars, on the other hand, tend to be rational, deductive, and genetic in nature. Generative grammarians argue that children simply impose a natively given theory of grammar upon the language they hear in some effort to understand that language.

The structural tradition grows out of an empirical point of view, largely associated with the work of the late American linguist, Leonard Bloomfield (1933). As any teacher who has been through a course in educational psychology can imagine, structural linguists have natural allies in American educational psychologists, with their strong environmentalistic views and preoccupation with the psychology of learning. The generative view is newer, though its chief proponent, Chomsky, has argued that it is largely a development of older, rationalistic ideas about language.

What about the theories of grammar themselves? In the next few pages, I shall provide an untechnical description of the two opposing traditions in the theory of grammar. It isn't easy to characterize the different points of view accurately in a brief exposition; therefore, what follows in the next few paragraphs must be regarded as an incomplete sketch.

Structural grammars are characterized by the notion that grammatical theory consists of more or less mechanical procedures for assigning elements of various languages to positions and functions within sentences of those languages. An example of a rule which results from such mechanical discovery procedures would be "nouns are elements which can occur before verbs in the environment, 'The (   )V'." The emphasis in structural theory is always upon the discovery procedures themselves. A discovery procedure is any technique which will enable a machine (or an individual totally devoid of intuitive feeling for the language) to provide a correct description of sentences in the language. As we shall note later, teachers often attempt to provide such mechanical discovery procedures for their students by providing examples the students are to follow.

C. C. Fries is the structural grammarian best known to teachers of English. He has popularized his own point of view, and that point of view is implicit in the first of Roberts' well-known textbooks for the teaching of high school grammar (Roberts' later books are heavily influenced by generative theory). Fries (1952) makes use of a *substitution-in-frame* or *slot* technique. One starts with a particular sentence. One of Fries's starting sentences is *The concert was good*. A particular element from the sentence (say the subject noun) is deleted, and other possible words are tried in its place. Thus, one discovers that *the milk was good, the play was good, the book was good*, all make acceptable sentences in English, but *the perform was good* does not. In theory, one proceeds systematically through a sample of sentences by the deletion of elements and substitution of other elements until one arrives at a reasonable classification of all of the elements of the sentences in the language.

In fact, the technique utterly fails to provide even the beginnings of a grammar. First of all, it presupposes the existence of but does not define the concept of sentence. Secondly, no sample, no matter how large, of English sentences is going to exhaust the possibilities of English sentences for the simple reason that there are an infinite number of such sentences possible. Finally, the technique totally misses the complex rules governing the relations between various constructions (e.g., the active and passive), rules that are themselves a fundamental part of the language.

In short, grammatical discovery procedures, such as those advanced by Fries, have never provided anything more than the beginning of a grammar of a particular language. The limitations are inherent, argue generative grammarians, in any simple inductive procedure for the discovery of the rules of language. In theory, the inductive discovery procedures simply sample a large number of sentences and from these, attempt to draw some inferences about the dependent relations between the various parts of the sentences. In practice, the technique cannot consist of the application of some completely mechanical rule for the discovery of structure. It must be supplemented at each step by hypotheses, by intuitions, and by assumptions. None of these is made explicit in purely structural theories.

Generative theorists have argued that structural grammars are defective in principle; in short, that such theories are beyond repair. In addition to the criticisms we have already mentioned, generative theorists point out that structural accounts of grammar ignore productivity or creativity in language. Structural descriptions are based only upon induction, and thus they can only describe a fixed set of sentences in the language. Furthermore, they accept anything that is given. Sensible constructions are mixed in with incorrect ones and ones that are merely odd. Generative theory allows that real languages consist of an infinite body of sentences, and it also allows for the fact that some sentences seem to be close to the basic structure of the language while others are derivative, novel, or agrammatical in some respect.

Generative theory makes a distinction between the surface structure and the deep structure of the language. Many rules of linguistic usage are not apparent at all on the surface but only occur in some part of the language that is never explicated by (though implicitly understood by) ordinary people. In general, surface structure arises from deep structure by application of a series of rewrite rules. These rules are capable of generating grammatical and only grammatical sentences. The rules are further developed in some essential way by certain operations (called transformations) which may be performed on linguistic sequences (called strings) at various levels (Chomsky, 1964). These operations provide for grammatical sentences, and they make possible the derivation of nongrammatical sentences from those that are grammatical. The result is a more powerful description of the grammatical structure of English than anything yet achieved by linguistics.

What are the implications of generative theory for the psychology of language learning? Among other things, generative theorists have argued that nearly all psychological analyses of language learning suffer from a fatal defect. The conception of language held by most psychologists is that of a finite-state grammar. Now a finite-state grammar isn't the kind of grammar a teacher of English is likely to have seen unless he has been reading in communication theory. Such a grammar is capable of logical and mathematical development, but it is incapable, as generative theory shows, of describing sentences in natural languages. In a finite-state grammar, the state that the language generating device is in at any moment determines the possible states to which it may go. By this kind of a grammar, the generation of a sentence is a left-to-right process in which the choice of a given element (a word or phrase) always constrains what is to follow. A succession of states generates a sentence. Certain sentences in natural languages can be developed this way, but others, such as sentences with clauses embedded in the middle, clearly cannot. Psychologists often write as if we learn all the sentences we speak by a kind of rote learning of finite-state grammars. Certain more or less limited and perhaps trivial cases of language learning may fit the finite-state model—the learning of lists of various sorts, the learning of vocabulary by flash card methods—but most of what we learn about language must be organized in a fundamentally different way. So, to the extent that psychologists are committed to finite-state conceptions of language, their commentary upon language learning is deficient.

More recently, a few psychologists have developed ideas about how we learn by substitution-in-frame or slot techniques. We have seen that generative theorists have argued that the grammars implicit in such techniques are fatally defective also. It is clear that learning by slot techniques cannot account for the ability of small children to acquire the language of their parents. However, as we shall see later, older children can and do use such techniques to aid them in arriving at hypotheses about how to characterize the language they already speak—in brief, to learn school grammar. These techniques of substitution include many familiar devices, for example, the teaching of grammatical class by identification of nonsense elements placed in real sentences. That technique has been frequently advocated in the pages of the *English Journal*. Therefore, psychological notions about learning by substitution are considerably more important to the classroom teacher than notions about rote learning. We need, however, to be absolutely clear about the deficiencies of the grammars that lie behind the teaching by substitution.

We have already seen that there are simply too many sentences of various types in any given language to permit some purely procedural rule to work in generating or learning a grammar. A more important way of saying much the same thing is to say that structural descriptions cannot in any way provide for the inherent creativity of language. It is at least a logical possibility that every sentence is different in more than one detail from every other sentence ever spoken. We do not produce sentences that we have "learned" in the past. We do not learn to put new or strange words into familiar context. Rather, we invent or create sentences. Finally, structural grammars can describe only the superficial structure of sentences. They cannot make any sense of sentences that have two or more grammatical interpretations—that is to say, ambiguous sentences. Nor can they give any satisfactory account of the relationship between various kinds of sentences, such as active, passive, queries, negative sentences, etc.

The emphasis upon creativity and the corollary deemphasis upon habit are part of the rationalistic and nativistic philosophic tradition, and generative theorists see themselves firmly in that tradition (Chomsky, 1966). It is a tradition that is antithetic to the intellectual traditions of associationism and empiricism, traditions that dominate structural grammars and most psychological theories about intellectual processes and the use of language. To the extent that generative theorists are correct (and their arguments are even more telling than this brief sketch can reveal), the standard psychological doctrines about the learning of language are often trivial, or even worse, incorrect. In fact, we cannot expect any account of the psychology of learning based chiefly on the experimental and scientific literature of psychology to give us any significant information about language learning.

Thus, generative grammar has made much psychological commentary upon language learning irrelevant. Unfortunately, while generative grammar has made great linguistic strides, it has not yet resulted in either comprehensive or particularly insightful studies in language learning as it is faced in the classroom. Generative grammarians assume that children exhibit linguistic usage based upon the interpretation placed upon the language those children hear mediated through transformational analysis. That assumption, however, has not resulted in any extensive body of information about the actual processes of learning, particularly as that process goes on in the school years. We do not at present have any general account of the processes, either superficial or deep, of the learning of language. The consequence is that something like an intellectual vacuum exists in the study of language learning. There appears to be no way of providing a completely satisfactory grammar of English (generative theory has only made a beginning at that), nor do we know anything about the most efficient ways of teaching about grammar.

The particular grammatical analyses that result from the application of transformational theory are interesting and useful; however, it is only fair to describe them as programmatic. Their most ardent champions would not say that there is anything like a completely satisfactory transformational analysis of English now in existence. Usually, generative theorists are careful to say that some long, elaborate, and abstract analysis of a point of English is not meant to produce any fundamental insight into the language itself but only to exemplify the nature of the abstract form which such an insight must take. In short, the classroom teacher must supplement transformational analysis with intuition and improvisation.

Any hope we may have that generative theory will provide us with an immediate and automatic deep understanding of language and how to teach its various aspects is doomed to disappointment. The writing, and lamentably, the reading of an essay on the psychology of learning and the teaching of English cannot be expected to be as revolutionary an activity as one might suppose, given the revolutionary accomplishments of generative theory. Though we may dismiss much of the traditional psychological apparatus as irrelevant to important problems in language learning, we cannot replace it with some detailed account out of generative theory that is judged to be more relevant.

Moreover, we are faced with one more almost ultimate disappointment. The application of generative theory to natural language requires a distinction between "well-formed" sentences and sentences described as "deviant." The distinction is not trivial, a matter of aesthetic preference, sociological description, level of usage, or anything similar. It is absolute and essential to any application of generative theory to real language. Furthermore, it is essential that there be degrees of deviation or levels of grammaticalness. The concept of levels of grammaticalness is derived from the observation that some more or less arbitrary sequences of words seem to be more like well-formed sentences than others. *The baby seems sleeping* is less agrammatical in some important intuitive sense than *Seems the baby sleeping*. Many real sentences (i.e., sentences spoken by people in ordinary situations) are probably not, by the rules of generative grammar, well-formed sentences. They must be derived from the grammar by means of an auxiliary set of principles that describes how and on what level deviations from grammaticalness take place. Generative theory pretends to be nothing more than a theory of ideal language, and in order to specify the relationship between the ideal language and language as it is used, a series of derivational steps are required which, in effect, degrade the ideal sentence into sentences of various degrees of agrammaticalness.

One of the principal arguments generative theorists make in support of the application of the notion of degrees of grammaticalness is that it is possible to form deviant or agrammatical sentences on analogy to well-formed sentences (Chomsky, 1964). The notion of analogy, certain generative theorists to the contrary, does have a role in generative theory, though its role is chiefly confined to relating grammatical structures in real sentences. Later in this essay, I shall comment in detail upon the notion of analogy, for I think it is far more central to the psychology of teaching about language than generative theorists are willing to assume.

It is possible to construct sentences of various low degrees of grammaticalness by more or less arbitrary mechanical rearrangements of words; however, most real sentences must have some element of analogy to well-formed structures in them. The aspect of the problem that troubles the classroom teacher is that well-formed sentences can only be defined by reference to theory. They must not be identified with sentences actually spoken by "fluent" or "standard" speakers of the language. They exist only as part of the theoretical structure of the theory of grammar, and they must be justified solely on the basis of the success the theory has in describing real sentences. The description of real sentences requires the interpolation between the theory and description of the notion of deviation.

Therefore, while generative theory is not characterized by the completely empirical and permissive attitude towards language typical of structural grammars, it does not provide for any automatic linguistic proscriptions either. This is an important point, because teachers have sometimes been misled into supposing that transformational grammar provides for stylistically acceptable standards. It does not. What transformational theory does is to provide an explanation for certain deviations from formally acceptable definitions. The teacher can use grammatical theory to explain, in an abstract way, why there is something linguistically strange about the (stylistically) acceptable sentence, *Misery loves company*.

In short, one of the troubles with generative theory from the standpoint of the problems of the classroom is that there are no fixed references in the theory which provide for the kind of standards the classroom teacher wants. The notion of standards in the theory evaporates into a thin abstraction that provides no guide in practice. The trouble is that generative theorists are not interested in practical problems but in the analysis of language. They approach language in the same spirit that logicians approach the analysis of propositions. A well-ordered set of rules generates well-formed sentences. That assertion is trivial. The sentences can be of a variety uninteresting to the teacher, such as *a*, *b*, *aa*, *bb*, *aaa*, *bbb*, etc. A great deal of generative theory is given over to the analysis of just such sentences (or strings). Thus, to the teacher, generative theory appears to be simply a branch (perhaps a new branch) of mathematics, with some quaint and tangential tie to natural language. There is a certain justification to that attitude. In fact, "well-formed" in generative theory does seem to refer to some more or less intuitively satisfactory body of sentences, because theorists do operate with natural languages as a basis for their intuitions (and they form their intuitions into formal theories). However, the whole enterprise, as a means of setting standards, is caught between the purely formal on the one hand and the problems of linguistic sampling on the other. In short, transformational grammar shows that there is a formal structure exhibited in natural language in much the same way that the abstract forms of logical argument may be so exhibited. Just as the study of logic has a role in rhetoric, the study of theoretical grammar has a role in the teaching of grammar and usage. But it would be grossly misleading to expect transformational analysis to provide a general guide to the formation of proscriptive rules for English. Such rules are rooted in stylistic preferences, appropriateness, and sociological levels of usage.

We may now turn to a discussion of what it is that is learned when it is asserted that language or some aspect of language is learned. Manifestly it is not, except in linguistically unusual cases, particular sentences. Underlying generalities can be apprehended by the meanest intelligence, and these generalities are the result of the operation of a special grammatical computing device located in the head. The nature of the generalities themselves is not easy to specify, however. One point of view is that they are described by the rules of generative grammar. That assertion lacks complete conviction for many reasons. For one thing, a number of specific generative rules that are linguistically satisfying are psychologically awkward. For example, generative theory would lead us to expect that, psychologically, the sentence *The boy hit the red ball* would be vastly more difficult to produce and understand than the sentence, *The boy hit the ball.* Secondly, there is a gulf between the idealized form in grammar and real sentences. Finally, generative theory makes a sharp distinction between the semantic and grammatical aspects of language, a distinction that is psychologically difficult to maintain. Traditional classroom grammar often imposes semantic interpretations upon grammatic (morphological and syntactic) forms, with some considerable psychological justification. However, we do not need to concern ourselves in detail with the adequacy of generative theory as a model for psychological processes. All we need do is accept the general point that the human brain is specialized for the interpretation and understanding of human languages. The linguistic merit of particular transformational analyses is discussed in other chapters in this book, and we may, from here on, concern ourselves with purely psychological matters.

Analogy is the root of processes in the understanding of language. An analogy occurs when some partial equivalence is perceived to exist between any two concepts. Concepts are cognitive events, and they may be linguistically represented at any level. They may be represented by words, phrases, sentences, etc. They are most characteristically represented at the various morphological levels in language (words, for the most part). When Chomsky tells us that people understand deviant sentences by reference to well-formed ones, he is telling us that there is some particular and partial equivalence between the structure of the deviant sentence and its well-formed representation at some deeper grammatical level. Concepts, however, are not solely linguistic. They may be represented by images, models, abstract relations of various sorts (such as those inherent in various branches of mathematics), and all of these representations may be used at various times in the interpretation of linguistic forms.

The partial identities between any concept and its analogous form may be represented analytically in a variety of ways. One of the most useful is through the notion of feature. A feature is any attribute of a concept that can serve to differentiate it from any other possible concept. Concepts and attributes may be invented or newly discovered, and we must regard the number of them as essentially unlimited. The notion of concepts as composed of bundles or conjunctions of features is not a new one. It is explicit in John Locke's doctrine of simple and complex ideas, and it has received a modern linguistic statement at the hands of several contemporary linguistic theorists. However, it is a purely formal device that has, at best, limited phenomenological validity in human understanding. I shall return to that important point later. For now, suffice it to say that the conditions for analogy require the intuitive apprehension of some partial equivalences between concepts, and these partial equivalences may be made explicit by an enumeration of features. For reasons to be discussed later, *single* features or attributes in common do not explain analogies. Rather, an analogy may always be represented by two or more features.

The analysis of analogy requires the description of the events which suggest the analogy together with those conditions that limit its extension. These can easily be illustrated within the context of language.

A student may model a sentence construction upon some example. In fact, he may be asked to do so when the teacher says, "Give me another sentence like that one." While grammatical theory would suggest that the analogy is usually referred to some deep grammatical structure not necessarily present in the exemplifying sentence, it need not be. I shall later show several examples in which analogous constructions invented by students are clearly based upon surface features of the exemplifying sentence. Such constructions are common in what used to be called hypercorrections (e.g., between you and I). Students often, if not always, parse or otherwise analyze constructions by analogy to those supplied in handbooks. Such an activity is familiar to any student who has solved problems in some more or less abstract subject, such as symbolic logic, algebra, or grammar. The solution is by reference to examples worked through in the textbook. The whole function of examples, of course, is to provide models for analogic solution. It is of great cognitive significance that examples, diagrams, geometric representations, and other things that mathematicians and logicians scorn are essential to untutored understanding. Cognitive crutches are important, not so much because they reveal the limits of ordinary human intelligence but because they so clearly show how human intelligence functions.

The whole approach of the analysis of ideas, as will often be conceived by the teacher of English, depends upon analogy. An English teacher may ask the didactic (and probably rhetorical) question, "How was the child Pearl in *The Scarlet Letter* like Donatello in *The Marble Faun*?" Such a question assumes that an analogy can be found, and it requests a search for the underlying features in common. In fact, the disposition to analogy is so strong that it is possible to ask for analogies between concepts chosen by some outrageous random method. One can find a perfectly sensible answer to the question, "How are philosophy and hydrogen sulphide alike?" A great deal of teaching consists in directing students to search for some features responsible for an analogy, or to explain analogies, or to invent analogies and then explain them. Depending upon whether or not such instruction is successful, the teacher may be able to direct the course of future analogies by reference to the same set of features. The teacher and the students may explore a whole series of concepts by means of the underlying features. Thus, one might imagine a search for and comparison of all the fey, childlike creatures in Hawthorne. To be successful, however, the explication of analogy cannot be a routine application of some formal calculation (for which computing machines are better adapted), but it must contain some degree of uncertainty. That uncertainty, we shall see, is guaranteed by the fact that the *analytic features that give rise to an analogy are not in the most general case the same features that appear in an explication accomplished at the same time by the same person.*

Thinking of analogies is vastly easier—vastly more human—than constructing systems which enable us to recover the analytic features or components of the relations between the concepts used to "account for" the analogy. Analogy is, in fact, inherent in our ability to perceive and judge similarity, irrespective of the formal structure of the things which are perceived as similar. The relationships which produce analogies and those which defend them are infinitely productive. The production and explication of analogies, in particular cases, overlap, but there is no compelling psychological notion why they should.

Analogies can be formally explicated by a statement of features shared between two or more concepts. The concepts themselves, then, can be regarded as a conjunction of those shared as well as the unshared features. Such conjunctive concepts I have called, in another context (Deese, 1965), nominal. The word *nominal* is meant to reflect an important aspect of the older school grammar's notion of the noun. Nominal concepts are names for ideas of a certain class. They are not the names of things, actions, etc., but of ideas which may refer to things, actions, etc. They may be defined as conjunctions of features. The features themselves define another class of concepts, and these are characterized by independence and contrast. Such features or attributes can be abstracted and isolated, so as to be independent of one another through experience. Such experience entails a series of instances of different concepts in which all attributes but one change. Consider teaching a child the meaning of "hot" and "cold." One might have him feel a number of objects, all of which were different except for being cold. Thus, a block of ice, a piece of metal, a handful of snow, and a bottle of milk fresh from the refrigerator would be examples. These would be contrasted with a glass of hot water, the radiation from a lighted match, etc. Each of the objects we exhibited to the child could be formally regarded as consisting of a bundle of features all, like hot and cold, independent of other features and in contrast with one another in some conceivable set of examples. Not all of these features will have simple names which are part of the vocabulary of the language. Those that do not must be described by circumlocutions of various sorts. Those adjectives that are named define attributes not themselves defined as conjunctions of other attributes. Consider *hot-cold, big-little, loud-soft*, etc. Their independence and contrast can easily be demonstrated by familiar usage in English.

With the important exception of color names, most of the familiar adjectives in English readily form opposites. They do so by taking an affix (usually a prefix, such as *un-, im-*, or *non-*) or by semantic pairing (*good-bad*). The values referred to by these words are universally conceived of as being in contrast with one another. Indeed, the only satisfactory way to define a particular attribute of this sort is by reference to its opposite. The fact that the attributes are independent is readily demonstrated by the ability of most speakers of English to interpret a negative element preceding an adjective of this sort as denoting the opposite, not the complement of the state named. The complement is the more general logical function of negation. To say "Your performance on the test was not good" is readily interpreted to mean, rather more gently put, that "Your performance on the test was bad." To say that a person is "not fat" implies that he is thin, and it clearly says nothing whatever about his disposition, height, nationality, or any other conceivable attribute. For such words, an overly familiar device for understatement is to add a negative element to the negative prefix, thus undoing the opposite-referring aspect of the negative prefix. For example, consider *He is not unfriendly*.

English color names (as well as those of closely related languages) are fundamentally different in structure. When I say "My car is not green," you cannot infer that it is green, blue, or any other particular hue. Color names are not names of values on independent contrasting attributes but are themselves nominal concepts. That is to say, they can be thought of as consisting of conjunctions of other features, features which themselves may not be named in the language.

There are, then, at least two varieties of semantically important concepts—nominal concepts and attributes or features. These are reflected in two primitive and universal aspects of human thought—contrast or antonymy and analogy. Analogy defines for us similarity as well as synonymy (which, we must realize, can never be complete, but only with respect to those attributes that are in common). Antonymy makes possible the independence of fundamental attributes from which nominal concepts may be formed. However, despite the readiness of people to form analogies and the availability of a device (antonymy) for specifying features, the human mind does not readily conceive of its nominal concepts as bundles of features. There are empirical psychological data that reflect this fact, and we shall discuss them shortly. Those data tend to reinforce the view that the description of nominal concepts as conjunctions of attributes is a formal and abstract representation. It is another way of saying that it is easier to form analogies than to explain them.

The general analytic problem in analogy can be characterized by the question, "How is *A* like *B*?" Such a question admits of at least four answers: (*a*) *A* is not like *B*; (*b*) *A* is like *B* in respect α; (*c*) *A* is like *B* in respect β; (*d*) *A* is like *B* in respect α and β. In no case is *A* like *B* in all respects, for some differentiating attribute can always be found (e.g., that *A* is to the left of *B*). Such a result shows us that any question about the nature of a particular analogy is necessarily ambiguous and hence (redundantly) admits of different answers. In this respect, such questions about analogy differ in principle from the much more difficult question, "How is *A* like *B* in each and every respect in which they resemble one another?" That question is analytic, and in general, it may be answered by individual human beings only in some arbitrary way or by the use of some auxiliary computing device (e.g., formal logic) applied by rote with the aid of some external memory (e.g., supplied by pencil and paper).

The fact that features or attributes are analytic and not real is revealed by the fact that concepts can be defined by a very large and often indefinite number of properties. I use the word *indefinite* in two senses. One is simply in the sense of enumeration. One can enumerate features for any concept indefinitely. I also use *indefinite* to mean that there is no exact consensus among users of a language as to what properties can be found in a particular concept. In short, human concepts are incapable of being completely described, because they can be described by an indefinite number of features, and they cannot be precisely described, because not all human users will agree as to those features that are, in some human sense, to be regarded as most essential, critical, defining, or distinctive. What is distinctive or defining depends upon the contrast desired at the moment. Thus, on one occasion it may be critical to define the concept of *dog* in such a way as to differentiate it from the concept of *cat*, while on another occasion, it may be critical to define the concept of *dog* in such a way as to differentiate it from the concept of *chief justice* (in order to show, for example, why a dog cannot be a chief justice) or perhaps from the concept of *justice* itself. Each will require a new feature. There are an indefinite number of such contrasts to be made, hence an indefinite number of defining or distinctive features.

Our linguistic concepts have a great richness of ambiguity in analogy. There will be always more than one attribute that can serve to relate concepts in analogy. Two people using precisely the same analogy may not, in fact, "mean the same thing" by the analogy. Certain speakers of the language who may be roughly characterized as teachers of English (or of linguistics, philosophy, rhetoric, or even psychology, for that matter) are often motivated to establish in their pupils some particular direction to an analogy. That is to say, they wish the analogy to be based upon some particular attribute or attributes. In such a case, the easiest resolution for the teacher is to assert that "A is like B in respect α." For a variety of reasons, including the altogether important one that the teacher himself may not be able to articulate all the respects in which he wishes his pupils to perceive A and B to be alike, indirection may be resorted to. Indirection can take many forms. Two of them are, for their pedagogical utility, of special interest. In one case, the pupil is shown that B is like A in the same way that B is like C (or that D is like E). Such a demonstration is helpful to the extent that the pupil can appreciate the comparative analogy, but as a method for explicating the analogy, it only postpones and makes more complicated the possible relations. Such activity is itself a considerable intellectual exercise, as revealed by the existence of analogy tests at the highest reaches of intelligence testing. In the other form, the student may be asked to generate instances A, B, C, etc., all of which embody some common principle. The teacher responds to each of these positively or negatively, and the pupil discovers that there is some way (from the teacher's point of view) in which *A* and *B* are alike and *A* and *C* are not. This method is familiar to teachers of English and to field linguists and anthropologists. It is the method of contrast.

The teacher of physics, mathematics, logic, and similar subjects may well have some formal criteria for guiding assent and negation in the use of contrast, but the teacher of English—whether of literature or grammar—may not. The teacher of English is more likely to be guided by his own judgment and intuition than is his fellow teacher in one of the sciences. Though grammar is in fact a set of rules, and therefore necessarily must have some logical structure, the structure is always with respect to some system of natural language that contains a large element of the arbitrary (e.g., whether adjectives precede or follow nouns). Therefore, anyone who is in the enterprise of teaching about the structure of language must resort to intuition, judgment, and invention to supplement those portions of the information which may be stated by recourse to formal rules.

These two forms of explication of analogy are of general interest because they are representative of dynamic cognitive changes that take place in the classroom. They are also well represented by a large and interesting body of research on human thinking. That research concerns what Bourne (1966) characterizes as the psychology of inference. The empirical findings that have come out of work on the psychology of inference are extensive, and they have some relevance for the intellectual problems faced by the classroom teacher.

Because these experiments in inference are abstracted examples of fairly sophisticated intellectual processes, they are more complicated than the kind of rote verbal learning study that the classroom teacher of English may be familiar with through an exposure to traditional educational psychology. A brief account of these experiments will be more rewarding than would be an account of the more traditional experimental studies of learning in the laboratory. While particular experiments differ in important detail, there are certain regularities that run through all of the experiments, and these serve to define the nature of the intellectual processes under study.

In a typical example of such an experiment, a person is put to the task of identifying all of the instances of a given concept and perhaps, in addition, of supplying some abstract rule which will correctly identify or define the concept. In most instances, the concept will be most easily defined by a simple conjunction of two or more attributes, but one of the empirical results of these studies is that people do not always choose the easiest formal rule to describe some particular concept. People will often resort to complicated combinations of conjunction and disjunction when a much simpler rule would do. There is no simple relation between the complexity of logical rules and the ability of people to use such rules in defining concepts. However, we shall ignore the interesting work on the structure of rules and deal only with the simple conjunctive rule. That situation will serve to illustrate some of the processes in analogy.

A conjunctive concept is one in which some idea—say that of *bachelor*—is described by a set of attributes—say, *unmarried, male,* etc. Such a familiar concept is unlikely to be used in an experiment. The invented or artificial concepts which are used in experiments are similar, except that they are composed of a finite (rather small, in fact) number of attributes. A person taking part in such an experiment will be asked to inspect some "stimuli." These will be small cards on which various combinations or conjunctions of attributes will be printed. A particular concept is arbitrarily defined as a conjunction of attribute values. For example, we may arbitrarily decide that all the cards consisting of large black figures (irrespective of shape) are examples of a particular concept. The subject of an experiment must then find this out. He can find it out in various ways. For example, he might point to a particular card and ask you, "Is that an instance of the concept?" Or he might try to sort all the cards that he thinks are instances of the concept together. You, as the experimenter-teacher, supply him with information as to whether he is right or wrong. The particular teaching method that is chosen will depend upon the problem.

Here are some of the general results that come out of doing such studies of concept learning or concept attainment:

1.   People can correctly label all instances of a particular concept (and include no negative instances under the assigned rubric) without being able to describe accurately the values of the attributes which define the concept. In short, people can identify a concept through its instances without being able to say how they do it. Such an ability is clearly a variety of intuition. The difficulty people have in explicating their intuitions occurs for a variety of reasons. Some of the most important have to do with limitations of memory. However, that is irrelevant to our point here. The significant fact is that there is a separation between the ability to recognize instances of a concept for what they are and the ability to provide an analytic explanation of that concept.

2.   People use varieties of strategies in solving these problems. Random, "trial and error" strategies or the absence of a systematic plan of attack is the exception. An automaton may be programmed to use a purely random strategy, but real people do not, and in fact, may not be able to use a random strategy. Human strategies are not always the most efficient ones for processing the information contained in concept instances. The particular strategies people use are dictated by limitations in memory and attention, but even when limitations in memory are eliminated (e.g., by allowing people to keep written records of their previous choices), human beings usually prefer less than perfectly efficient strategies. Strategy selection reflects something deeper than limitations of memory and attention.

Needless to say, people cannot always describe in any abstract way the strategies they use in solving problems. In fact, they may deny that their choices have been in any way dictated by a particular plan of approach. Most people try the strategy of testing hypothesis about the concept at a time rather than the strategy of testing more than one hypothesis at a time (though the latter would be more efficient).

3.   People operate by hypotheses. That is to say, people adopt definite hypotheses about the nature of the correct concept. Often the hypothesis will be incomplete. Thus, a particular person may know that it will take two or more attributes (e.g., shape and color) to define a concept, but he may only work on the hypothesis of shape. He may, for example, accept as a working hypothesis the notion that whatever else defines the concept, all round shapes are instances of the concept while all square shapes are not.

4.   People find it easier to learn from positive instances than from negative instances. That is to say, they learn better by finding out what a concept is rather than what it is not. Yet in most of the experimental studies of concept learning, there is no logical reason why this should be so. In finite conception universes, such as those used in experiments of this sort, it is perfectly possible to gain information from negative instances. In fact, negative instances can be just as rich in information as positive instances. A well-constructed automaton would learn just as efficiently from negative instances as from positive instances. However, in the more disorderly real world, it is harder (in fact, often impossible) to learn from negative instances. Real concepts may require an indefinite number of features to specify them. There are also an indefinite number of features and hence feature conjunctions that are not instances of the concept. Therefore, learning what something is not tells us very little. To tell you that the book on my desk is not by Anthony Trollope does not help you very much in finding out who actually wrote it.

In sum, people learn concepts in an orderly fashion but not as well as a well-designed computer might. One other difference between intellectual processes in people and well-designed computers is very important to teaching. It is that people do not always (in fact, most often do not) draw a sharp line between hypotheses that have been thoroughly confirmed and those that have not. People will often accept hypotheses as correct even though the confirmation has not been such as to satisfy all the logical possibilities. That is in part because people do not think of negative instances, and they do not think of the infinite number of features necessary, in real life, to specify concepts. People take for granted things that a computer could not. Thus, if you ask for a definition of a particular word, the definition will always be deficient in some respect. Someone may say that a bachelor is an *unmarried male person*. If you remind that person that approximately half of newborn babies are unmarried persons, he will indignantly tell you that he was taking it for granted that we were talking about adults. The fact is that people will nearly always miss the identification of some feature of a concept when asked for a definition, even though they are able to use that concept in ordinary thinking in such a way so as to show that they are aware of the importance of the feature for that concept. Any intellectual process that requires only action upon the relations among concepts is easier than a process that requires the specification of some particular feature important to a concept. However, we are always aware that concepts can be explicated by features, and we can nearly always produce a few, even if they are not the ones relevant to an important usage.

The structure of concepts is reflected in the morphological and semantic properties of the languages we speak. The two aspects of concepts, concept and feature, are represented by the relations of antonymy and analogy or similarity. Antonymy defines the independence of the various attributes from which nominal concepts can be formed and into which they may be decomposed. The results of the concept attainment experiments make it plain, however, that people do not think of the relations between various nominal concepts directly by way of their shared attributes. The shared attributes provide only a latent framework into which some particular relation of analogy or similarity may be decomposed. We think of the relations directly and intuitively as analogies. We may, for example, be aware that political science and psychology are both social sciences, and therefore, in some sense similar. We would find it a laborious task, however, to spell out just exactly how they are similar. We might even find the results of our labors not particularly convincing. To take another example, we may be aware that there is a certain similarity between a work of art and a burlesque of that work without being aware of what features are alike—in a word, of what is being burlesqued. We may explain the relation, but we always run the risk that someone else can quite plausibly challenge or at least amend our explanation.

All linguists know that most people are totally innocent of articulate knowledge about the features of speech sounds that are phonemic and those that are merely phonetic. But, of course, the act of speaking reveals the knowledge to exist on an intuitive level. Teachers of analytic philosophy, logic, grammar, and the like often have as their principal goal the teaching of methods to make explicit the structure of implicitly understood concepts. A theory of grammar may, for example, provide a way of accounting for relations within sentences that we intuitively feel to be there. However, the theory, for most people, always operates behind its intuitive operation. That is, in fact, why we need grammarians and why doing grammar is such a difficult business.

Generative grammar gives us a framework for carrying out particular grammatical operations. It does so by telling us what language really is and by providing some explicit operations for stating relations within particular real languages. But it does not do so automatically. We must laboriously discover and then laboriously teach these relations. The users of a language we teach may have quite a different conception, one only tangentially related to our linguistic analysis. We may explicate some linguistic concepts through analysis of a language, and our students may be brought to an awareness of the relation between their intuitions and some more rigorous and analytic system of description we teach them. But the two only intersect; they are not identical. In short, teaching students grammatical theory will not automatically enable them to discover the structure of sentences they speak. The process may be aided by the natural techniques students use to learn concepts —in a word, by analogy. Thus, we need to supplement the purely formal with quasi-empirical exercises which make use of substitution in frame techniques and similar devices. Showing students that particular constructions fit into particular frames will not enable them to discover the general grammar of their language (any more than it enables the linguist to do so), but it will serve as a way of bridging the difficult gap between the analytic formal analysis and their own intuitions. In short, the theoretical deficiences of such empirical discovery techniques as the substitution-in-frame method should not blind teachers to their utility in teaching.

We have already seen that human beings do not wait for some exhaustive empirical specification of a concept or for some logically appropriate analysis to leap to a conclusion. People test their conclusions but usually inadequately. Intuitive concepts are established on the basis of partial, incomplete, and if the concept is complicated enough, possibly contradictory analyses. The generation of hypotheses allows for the ready creation of new concepts in the heads of students as they are being taught. These new concepts may bear something less than a perfect relation to the concepts the teacher is trying to teach. But there may be enough in common so that neither the student nor the teacher is aware of the discrepancy.

The teaching of grammatical analysis, then, must suffer the fate of the teaching of formal logic and other systems of formal analysis. Students learn these, but since such systems are often alien to human understanding, they can only be consistently and completely applied with the use of external computational devices and the application of rules learned by rote. They may only incompletely transfer to ordinary intellectual activity, hence, the lamentable conclusions arrived at even by gifted and famous logicians when the issues are political or otherwise removed from the area of abstract discourse.

I hasten to add that I am not saying formal analysis should not be taught. These remarks cannot be construed to mean that the teacher, with relief, can forget about transformational grammar and linguistic theory. We must not expect too much of the formalities, however, and we must bolster and support them with intuitive devices and recognize the probable incorrectness of conclusions reached by students. A formal system will be influential to the extent that it is compatible with some natural logic (natural in the psychological sense) and the extent to which there is some motivation to apply this system in particular instances, yet the device in the head that generates language may not be capable of understanding itself in the terms of formal grammar. Furthermore, an intuitive understanding of the formal system may not conform to the formal system. That is to say, some formal system may not be understood in its own light but by reference to some intuition, perhaps formally erroneous. Many students who study modern versions of the differential calculus can follow the logic of the analysis which stems from the application of the limit theorem, but they may intuitively understand the differential calculus through the formally inadequate idea of vanishing residuals. Thus, the framing of a formal system may produce formally acceptable results but by intuitions that are not part of the system. Of course, the inevitable result is that on some occasion some formally incorrect or unacceptable outcome will occur.

The major reason for teaching something such as transformational grammar is that it does provide a formal method of analysis. It is coextensive with logical schemes and not primarily a method of describing or teaching usage in some natural language. Unlike mathematics, apparently, logic and grammar are sometimes concerned with poorly formed structures, i.e., with sequences in which their rules are exhibited in some degraded form. The study of language is partly empirical and partly concerns matters that will not appear in a well-formed grammar. In fact, linguistic inventiveness in the truly creative sense may well be beyond any purely formal grammar, such as transformational grammar.

The productivity of language is open. Rules may change, though the universals of language implied by the metatheory inherent in transformation grammar may tell us something about some of the changes. However, the very notion of agrammaticalness, so essential to the application of transformational theory to any real language, tells us that some of linguistic productivity falls through the net spread by formal theory. Given that limitation, it is hard to see how any purely formal system can describe productivity in natural language. Though, oddly enough, that productivity may well result from the application of analogy.

In short, formal grammar may be regarded with some of the same attitudes that attend upon the introduction of other formal schemes, such as logic, into any program of study designed to teach students how "to think" or "to express themselves." Just as with logic, different individuals will understand and articulate the formal scheme to their own intellectual and linguistic processes to different degrees. Methods of analysis appropriate to one individual will not be appropriate to another, nor will the method appropriate to one task necessarily serve another purpose. For many users of a language, the analytic understanding of the structure of the language will be limited and largely intuitive, just as for many people, appreciation of mathematics stops with the rote application of certain arithmetic operations (plus some awareness of the relations between those operations and events in the natural world). The skilled teacher will recognize and accept this state of affairs, though he may, in the process, offend the proprieties of formal analysis (without necessarily at the same time, offending those of social usage) in an effort to teach as much as students can grasp. Almost all handbooks, and so far as I know, almost all teachers of English grammar and usage attempt to instruct more by example than by derivation from abstract structures. "This is an example of an appositive" and "here are some prepositional phrases" are at least implied, if not said explicitly. To the extent that any student is able to identify instances of a construction he is supposed to understand, these examples will be significant and will, in fact, determine his choice of usage.

In order to create variations in constructions and forms (mainly by analogy, again), people must have some intuitively given model in mind, though they need not have an explicit representation of the model in order to produce creative variation. People need not have any clear idea of constituent structure to be able to "control the language." The excuse for teaching grammatical analysis rests not on usage but on the intrinsic value of the analysis. Even the effort to teach particular examples of socially acceptable usage may have no relation to grammatical analysis. The distinction between *shall* and *will* (even in the British form) is best taught by example rather than by any formal derivation of verbal auxiliaries or even by an attempt to provide a semantically acceptable description of what the various constructions involving *shall* and *will* express.

Both the depth and the limitations of what can be achieved by teaching some theoretically oriented version of transformational grammar can be illustrated by examples in which deep structure plays an important role. Transformational grammarians are fond of pointing to the contrast between the pair of sentences, *John is easy to please* and *John is eager to please*. Because these sentences are alike in their superficial grammatical structure but fundamentally very different, they serve to illustrate that any purely mechanical constituent analysis or parsing will not describe their grammatical structures in the fullest depth. The only analysis that will be satisfactory is one that shows them as derived from fundamentally different base structures. It is possible, for example, to show that *John* is the subject in *John is eager to please* and the object in *John is easy to please* (consider *This easily pleases John* but not *This eagerly pleases John*).

Yet the intuitions of ordinary users of the language do not agree precisely with this formal analysis in depth. When asked to generate sentences on the model of *John is easy to please*, students will produce, among other things, *Harry is willing to go* and *Jane is friendly to know*. Furthermore, when pressed to express the difference between *John is easy to please* and *John is eager to please*, students almost invariably resort to a semantic interpretation. That is, they will say that one means John is pleasant, while the other means that John is eager to do something. Students recognize a difference (though they are apt to ignore it unless pressed). The point is that a deep grammatical analysis is not simply an exposition of the intuitions of language users, as some transformational grammarians have implied. To teach a grammatical analysis that enables users to express the difference between this pair of sentences in the framework of an elegant and sophisticated theory is an accomplishment. But it does not automatically express the way in which students think about this bit of the language, and furthermore, such an analysis may be available only to gifted students, no matter how good the teaching.

It may be impossible to characterize any practical grammatical analysis as being free from some degree of arbitrariness. Particular solutions in transformational grammar often have the same taint of arbitrariness. That is because there will always be some uncertainty in applying a formal theory to the empirical facts about a language. There is no powerful way to decide in each and every case what shall be ascribed to the well-formed grammar and what to a degradation of it in some particular use. Furthermore, it is always possible that the human being, as a generator of language, does not correspond to grammatical theory. In short, there may not be as much relation between linguistic analysis and intellectual processes as we perhaps have a right to hope. I have a suspicion that the classroom teacher is well aware of particular psychological deficiencies of various grammatical analyses. In such a case, that teacher will often invent some local or particular solution designed to make the grammar more like the processes he knows to go on in the heads of his students as they think about some point of language.

Attendant upon such inadequacy is the necessary imprecision of ordinary language as a tool of communication. The extraordinary looseness and ambiguity of human language is seldom explicitly the subject of commentary, though it is often implicit in discussions of the inadequacy of particular usages or of the influence of semantic concepts upon human attitudes. The imprecision of language is much greater than these discussions imply, however. In fact, the extraordinary looseness of human communication may be the most striking and astounding feature of human language. There is a vast inferential apparatus which calls upon the unsaid and which is necessary to the interpretation of nearly everything that is actually said. Seldom do we place great demands upon our language for specificity and freedom from referential and structural ambiguity. In fact, for aesthetic and practical reasons, we may even court these ambiguities. Even when engaged in so informationally demanding a task as giving directions, the content of our verbalizations is extraordinarily deficient. If we are giving directions to someone as to how to arrive at a particular place, we rely on the orderly pattern and layout of streets as much as on the specific directions to accomplish our purpose. In fact, the general orderliness man tries to impose upon his environment makes up for some of the deficiencies in communication. Furthermore, we rely upon conventions. We rely upon relations between right-handedness and left-handedness, between mirror images and direct images, and all the various kinds of relations in the real world that are reflected in cognitive structures. Ambiguities in language are easily tolerated because nonlinguistic relations generally serve to resolve them (whenever, in fact, they require resolution). Often the reaction of a hearer or reader is so general as not to require the resolution of some ambiguity. A fairly wide choice of interpretations will do. The antecedents of indefinite pronouns may properly receive critical attention from the teacher of English whose task it is to make pupils aware of the potential for ambiguity (both for good and ill), but we need not find them intolerable in reading, say, Kenneth Rexroth. Certain languages, Japanese being the most often discussed example, contain inherent structural ambiguities of this sort. In ordinary Japanese, it is possible to eliminate completely subject phrases from sentences. The resulting linguistic structure is even more indefinite than that produced by pronouns with indefinite antecedents in Indo-European languages.

We are seldom exercised enough about the precise details of what is being said to us to be concerned to eliminate all possible ambiguity. We generally carry away only a general schematic impression of what we have read. But in formal systems, ambiguity is intolerable. It is this aspect, among others, of formal systems which make them difficult. It is scarcely possible for human beings to apply any complicated calculus without resort to pencil and paper and without certain devices committed to rote memory. We cannot think algebraically in the way in which we think in language, though in fact the case can be made that in an abstract sense most algebras are much simpler in structure than natural languages. Inborn skill in the use of language is purchased at the price of redundancy and ambiguity.

The teacher of English will be wise not to be intimidated by the proponents of any particular formal system of analysis or grammatical method, just as he will be wise not to be intimidated by any messianic zeal for some exotic teaching method, such as programmed instruction or computer assisted instruction. The study of language is partly a matter of making explicit certain formal relations, partly a matter of learning certain arbitrary conventions, partly a matter of learning to exercise one's own choice, and partly a matter of learning about history and culture. The teacher, in communicating the use of language, draws upon a variety of techniques and special systems. Grammatical theory is only one among many such systems.

Despite some sixty years of educational psychology, there is a pervasive belief in the profession of teaching to the effect that formal discipline has some extrinsic merit. All varieties of mathematics, formal logic, and such hothouse varieties of natural language as classical Latin are supposed to be good training for the intellectual powers. To these now may be added grammatical theory. There is some merit to the view that the study of these difficult disciplines is intellectually valuable, but the educational psychologists are also right in one important respect: it is that the extrinsic (as opposed to intrinsic) merit of instruction in these disciplines depends upon the extent to which they are used in ordinary intellectual activity. If they are taught simply as exercises, they are of little value. If they are taught so as to point out their relations to intellectual activity generally, to language and to the solution of problems in special fields, they are useful. Grammatical theory has intrinsic merit, of course, and deserves to be taught for that reason. If it is taught for extrinsic reasons as well, however, its application must be made explicit.

Many varieties of linguistic analysis broaden the potential for flexibility in the use and understanding of language. The study of grammatical transformations may have practical value, not only for its superior analytic power but also for its potential influence upon style. In fact, it is the impression of many teachers (an impression that seems to have a certain psychological validity) that the more or less mechanical variation imposed by certain transformational exercises can give the student a sense of power over the language. However, transformational exercises, like any purely mechanical exercises, can easily be overdone. The excuse for mechanical exercises in algebra, in fact, is greater than that for mechanical exercises in the analysis of language, for we expect manipulation of algebra to be formal and to depend upon learned skills. We expect the use of language to be intuitive and be guided at least as much by implicit cognitive activity as by explicit cognitive activity.

The choice of various methods for teaching the analysis, understanding, and use of language depends, in the last analysis, upon the different functions served by language. These functions determine the goals of instruction, and it is important, in any account of psychological processes in teaching, to remind ourselves of those goals. One of the important applications of psychological study is the alignment of goals with the various functions served by instruction.

The goal that nearly everyone thinks of first in connection with the English curriculum is improvement in level and sophistication of usage. Improvement in usage does have a place in the teaching of English, but I should not like to see it first. Rather, I should think that the teacher of English would have as his first concern the understanding of language—its history, analysis, and function. The proper place for linguistic studies in their own right is the English curriculum.

Usage always means particular usage. Some particular construction is better than another, or some particular form is to be preferred in particular contexts. How that usage is controlled is more or less independent of the grammatical analysis which may be brought to bear upon it, as we have seen. Linguists, however, sometimes seem to encourage English teachers in the belief that teaching students some more general and powerful analysis of a particular construction will enable those students to control their usage more effectively. Such is not the case. Students of language are accustomed to the notion that usage does not lead to linguistic understanding (languages of illiterate peoples are often complicated, though unrealized in an analytic way). It is equally true that understanding does not lead automatically to control of usage. I may understand something without being able to do it. I may have a fairly good understanding of the elements required for an adequate performance of a Mozart sonata, without being able to execute that performance myself. Sometimes, though not always, the discrepancy between usage and understanding is subject to change. Motivation and reinforcement, as B. F. Skinner and those who advocate programmed instruction are fond of reminding us, are important in bridging the gap between understanding and performance. But sometimes the gap exists because the analysis that leads to understanding and those steps that lead to performance are cognitively unrelated. They simply come from different underlying skills and different patterns of organization, and there may be no way of going from one to another save in a clumsy and indirect way.

Particular examples of the failure of alignment between understanding and usage abound. One of the best known of these in grammatical analysis is the so-called pseudosubjunctive. It is apparently impossible for even the best and most fastidious stylist to use the subjunctive construction in English in full agreement with the usual formal analysis (Ryan, 1961). Inspection of the various examples culled from a broad spectrum of writing strongly suggests that the elements *if then* or even *if* signal the subjunctive (of course, the subjunctive in modern English is used almost exclusively with certain forms of the verb *to be*). Furthermore, even when the subjunctive probably would have been preferred by a particular writer, he may not think to use it if the verb is too far removed in the sentence from the *if*. Thus, the pseudosubjunctive is not controlled by some deep grammatical analysis of the language but by more or less superficial habits.

The more familiar hypercorrections, of course, provide other examples. Many people who know better (people who can give a rational account of the correct form) and who are strongly motivated to follow exacting standards of usage cannot prevent an occasional *between you and I* from slipping out. These and other examples point to certain features of usage which we can only describe as habitual. Such a description is in part a confession of ignorance, and it signals a decision to retreat to the time-honored rote techniques—drill, repetition, and mechanical construction—in an effort to improve usage. These, as any experienced teacher knows, are of dubious usefulness in and of themselves, and so far as I know, we have no explicit account of the conditions which make them sometimes efficacious. I am afraid, however, that neither psychological nor linguistic theory suggests any more elegant alternative to the role of drill in the teaching of usage. Though again, we need to remind ourselves that certain psychologists make a very convincing case for the importance of motivation—the will to improve—and patterns of reinforcement in the determination of such matters. Rather than rely on the often mechanical and awkward techniques suggested by the educational psychologist for the arousal of interest and reward of good performance, the skilled teacher will rely upon his own intuition and firsthand knowledge of the social climate for learning in his own school.

Understanding and analysis are interwined. Analysis leads to new viewpoints, new analogies, and symbolization, though it is certainly possible to perform certain mechanical analyses of English without much comprehension. That is to say, understanding does not in any sense depend upon explicit analysis nor does analysis necessarily lead to understanding. Nevertheless, it is hard to see how much understanding of the structure of the language can be conveniently achieved without at least some analysis. The trick is to be sure that such analytic work does lead to understanding. No analysis should be completely mechanical, furthermore, and any exercise which is useful enough to be required of students will depend at some level upon intuition and inarticulate understanding of linguistic structures. That is to say, anything that is not, in the framework of the language as a whole, trivial will not be understandable by students except by reference to intuition. Grammatical theorists, we need to remind ourselves, do not use natural language as it comes, but instead they invent various kinds of idealized language which can exhibit formal characteristics. However, in the ordinary use of language and analysis of ordinary language we must rely on intuition.

One does not begin linguistic analysis for students at its most fundamental level. One begins at a level which will permit the student to achieve the particular insight which the teacher has in mind. It is of little concern whether or not the analysis or kind of analysis that is taught has limited utility or very great generality. Its function is to show those students who have not discovered the fact already that it is possible to characterize the structure of language in various abstract ways without resort to rote learning, particular memorization, and other devices meant to apply habit where habit does not belong. We do not, in teaching high school students about the grammar of their native tongue, begin with metagrammar or general abstract theory. We begin with some fairly realistic problems in usage. The task of the teacher is to broaden as much as possible the framework provided by these particular problems. Drill and habit are parts of the learning process, but they suffice only for the particular, not the general. It is my impression that there are still many students and an occasional teacher who need to be disabused of the notion that grammatical analysis of language can be made only by the application of ideas committed to rote memory. It is the chief fault of the old semantically oriented school grammar that it perpetuates this notion through its reliance on definitions rather than on the structural analysis of the sentence from the most general constituent structure to the most particular. Many of the notions from traditional school grammar are useful and important, but they usually do not lead to general insights. The spectrum of the goals of teaching must range from the correction of particular usage on the one hand to the appreciation of the most general aspects of language on the other. In general, the devices that are most useful in imparting one aspect of the curriculum in

English grammar are not the most useful for the other. Thus, grammatical theory provides general insight, but explication of particular constructions is best achieved through more or less mechanical exercises.

If the view of human cognitive processes implicit in this essay is correct, the easiest technique of analysis for students to understand is one that makes use of analogical thinking. Therefore, the psychologically relevant place for the teacher to begin teaching the analysis of language is with some technique, such as substitution, which uses analogy and the linguistic intuitions of students. These techniques can develop paradigms that can be generalized (to the extent of the ability of the students to grasp abstractions) later. Thus, though we recognize that local means of showing equivalence lack complete linguistic generality, students can grasp the potential of such "discovery" techniques for producing the functional regularities inherent in language. The application of any technique which relies on the process of analogy should be supplemented by analysis so far as the teacher and the students are capable of pushing it. Thus, the students must be told that their ability to fit words into a frame formed by a single sentence (or a string of nonsense items related by English syntactic markers) depends upon their implicit understanding of the constituent structure of the sentence. The next step is to make that implicit understanding explicit in the most formal and economical way at the disposal of the students and the teacher. One happy consequence of this insistence that intuitions should be made explicit is that most students are pleased to be told that they know more than they think they do.

An introduction to expansion and transformational analysis might be taught by the same technique—by, for example, showing students that there is a certain equivalence between a simple noun subject and a complete noun phrase as subject. Such equivalences can be taught without attempting to characterize the functions of the elements (e.g., nouns or sentences). In fact, if the students have been through many grades of ordinary schooling without picking up even the rudiments of grammatical analysis, it is probably wisest to forego any real explication of linguistic structure until the habit of looking for regularities based upon hunch and intuition is firmly established. Then, the teacher, to the extent that he grasps the abstract principles of formal grammatical theory and to the extent that he thinks they are relevant to his students (they will be more relevant in the Bronx High School of Science, say, than in a trade school), should present formal notions. Thus, a sentence at this stage need not be regarded simply as an intuitive mystery, or as a complete thought, but rather as an abstract symbol S, which can be rewritten as two other abstract symbols in concatenation (*subject phrase + verb phrase*) and so on until it is possible to terminate the rewrite procedures by stringing out the actual forms (words) of the language.

The teacher who is concerned more with teaching about the language than trying to correct usage will range widely. Thus, phonemics should have an important role in the English curriculum. It has been my invariable experience that certain aspects of phonemics are inherently interesting even to intelligent seventh graders. They are delighted to discover, for example, that /pin/ and /bin/ differ with respect to a single feature—turning on the vocal cords for the initial consonant in *bin* and not in *pin*. They readily appreciate morphophonemic rules for formation of the plural in English, and they find that the impermissibility of certain phonemic transitions in English provides an interesting topic for debate. Beyond these examples, of course, phonemic theory is of interest to gifted students. Etymologies and linguistic history should be an integral part of the English curriculum, and their study certainly takes some of the curse of dullness from grammatical exercises. Grammatical theory makes it possible to introduce linguistic universalism, comparative linguistics, and linguistic relativity to varying depths.

Much of this is familiar to the skilled old hand at teaching English. I worry only that skilled teachers of English may be induced, by proponents of modern grammatical theory, to abandon useful teaching techniques that are, from the point of view of linguistic theory, faulty. Transformational theorists have attacked structural linguistics and the general approach to linguistic analysis by procedural rules. These attacks have occasionally been interpreted by teachers of language to mean that all the familiar structural procedures should be jettisoned. Those teachers may breathe more easily if they realize that the polemics of the transformational theorists are not directed against use of discovery procedures for teaching purposes but against those devices as general metatheoretical procedures in linguistic theory. The transformational theorist wants to eliminate intuition from linguistic theory (or at least minimize it), but I don't think he wants to eliminate it from the classroom. So structural techniques can serve to give students a certain level of insight into their language, an insight which they might otherwise not achieve. Some students, however, will be able to grasp linguistic analysis at a much deeper level, beyond the purely procedural. In short, the teacher should not throw away his structural textbooks now that transformational grammar is in. He need only recognize the appropriate limited place of structural techniques and the large role intuition and analogy play in their use.

For any competent teacher lucky enough to be teaching bright, motivated students, there is no limit to what can be done. High school students with a bent for mathematics can grasp linguistic theory at its deepest level, and they are often fascinated by it. However, most classroom activity will have more modest goals. At the least, constituent analysis and a modern variety of parsing can be taught. I would suggest that students be shown how to break up sentences by putting brackets (or boxes, as recommended by Francis [1957]) before they are taught to place things in subsidiary or dependent relations. In so doing, the teacher should anticipate the need for dealing with discontinuous constituents. As always, the teacher should be prepared for the fact that bright and aggressive students will find some instances which violate some constituent analysis. Guided by the teacher's intuition and what has been taught before, such a construction may be characterized as anomalous and derived from some well-formed structure, or it may be accepted and derived from some other constituent or transformational analysis. The point is that the teacher should avoid a rigid commitment to the results of a particular grammatical analysis.

Certain transformational analyses recommend themselves as intermediaries between grammar and rhetoric. I have always felt that the use of teaching certain particular transformations (such as nominalizations) should not be directed so much toward an understanding of grammar as toward the teaching of rhetoric. In any event, the implications of certain transformations for the control of style are available to the teacher.

Usage should never be allowed to be the single end of the teaching of grammar. Grammatical analysis has to be its own reward, or the whole teaching enterprise becomes a dismal chore which has little validity for either the teacher or the students. Nevertheless, the implications of the grammatical analysis of usage can be discovered by students, and such a discovery makes it possible to bridge in a natural way the gap between grammar (which must always be more restricted) and rhetoric (which may be quite free).

Finally, wherever possible, traditional school grammar should be introduced. It may be compared with more abstract analyses, and it has value in itself. One function served by the introduction of traditional grammar (if the teacher doesn't take it as rigid and fixed) is that it shows the essential interdependence of meaning and grammar. There is a structure to semantics as well as to grammar, and they are inextricably intertwined. Traditional grammar recognized this. Attempts to define grammar as structure without meaning or semantics as that part of structure not described by grammar are foolish for practical purposes. The structural aspect of semantics is exemplified by any classification tree (like that in Roget's *Thesaurus*). A given noun may be said to be concrete as opposed to abstract. Concrete nouns may be animate or inanimate. A classification tree may be descended in such a way that at one point one arrives eventually at the difference between a dog and a cat. Somewhere along the line, characterization by grammatical class has been superseded by characterization according to semantic class, but exactly where would be difficult to say. I know of no arbitrary procedures that would enable one to decide the dividing line between morphology and semantics.

The dependence of grammatical analysis on meaning and its exemplification in traditional grammar is illustrated by the active-passive relation. It is all very well to point out that the passive sentence is a paraphrase of the active (which is, in an important sense, true) and that transformational rules may permit the derivation of both from a common structure, but the implication that the passive and active forms say exactly the same things needs to be challenged. The passive form is truly passive. Being acted upon implies a weakness subtly absent in the actor. Students intuitively feel these differences, and it is part of the meaningfulness associated with stylistic variations in grammatical structures. Teachers of rhetoric have long recognized the need to characterize various grammatical structures semantically, and they will label one as opposed to another construction as "vigorous," "appropriate," or "tangential."

Understanding is limited by the nature of human thought. That applies to the understanding of language as well as to the understanding of physics or geology. Physicists use "models" which they know to be not quite accurate as aids to intuitive understanding of their processes. In geological description, we resort to gross oversimplifications that may not be correct in order to comprehend the relations between geomorphic structures. Likewise, in the study of language, we fit our material to human understanding. We make the best approximation we can to the most accurate possible abstraction. For most purposes, we leave it at the limits of human understanding. We leave the complete formal characterization to an analytic system. We allow the roughness of human conceptual activity to blur formal abstractions. Potential for error is the price we pay, but flexibility and intuitive quickness, which we call insight, are the enormous gains. No formal theory of linguistics deserves the complete devotion of any classroom teacher, whose task it is to interpret language to students.

REFERENCES

Bloomfield, L. *Language*. New York: Holt, Rinehart & Winston, 1933.

Fries, C. C. *The structure of English*. New York: Harcourt, Brace & World, 1952.

Chomsky, N. *Aspects of the theory of syntax*. Cambridge: M.I.T. Press, 1964.

Chomsky, N. *Cartesian linguistics*. New York: Harper & Row, 1966.

Deese, J. *The structure of associations in language and thought*. Baltimore: Johns Hopkins Univ. Press, 1965.

Bourne, L. E., Jr. *Concept formation*. Boston: Allyn & Bacon, 1966.

Ryan, W. M. Pseudo-subjunctive *were*. *Amer. Speech,* 1961, **36**, 48–53.

Francis, W. N. *The structure of American English*. New York: Ronald Press, 1957.

5

Variation in Language

WILLIAM LABOV
University of Pennsylvania

INTRODUCTION

More discussions of language in general focus upon the use of language as a characteristic human trait, and the ability to learn language as a genetic heritage of human beings. Such a general study of language is most closely allied to psychological investigation, being concerned with those linguistic abilities that are common to all men and with the elements of language structure that are found throughout the world. One can also learn a great deal about language by viewing it as a product of social interaction—as a socially determined communicative process which is shaped to a large extent by social structure, a property of speech communities rather than of speakers. Some students of the universal properties of language consider that variations within a speech community are secondary, "low-level" phenomena that tell us no more about language structure and language learning than the ripples on the ocean tell us about the underlying currents. They believe, therefore, that the study of variation can safely be neglected.[1] This chapter will be concerned with linguistic variation as data which cannot be neglected if a coherent understanding of language structure and language change is to be attained. It is true that language, as opposed to speech, may be thought of as the pattern that we all learn as children—the system that we hold in common. It is also clear that a great deal of language learning takes place relatively late in life, especially the knowledge of the significant choices within the set of possibilities open to native speakers. Furthermore, it appears that many of the educational problems which arise today are the

---

[1] An extreme position of this type is taken by Chomsky, in the opening pages of his *Aspects of the theory of syntax* (1965).

products of unrealized differences in the structures and functions of languages used by different groups. Finally, it will appear that these differences in language convey a great deal of information: not cognitive information of the type usually considered most important—but rather a wide variety of noncognitive information on the speakers, the situations, the topics, the immediate attitudes, and underlying values which are governed by social interaction.

Two points of view are thus addressed to two different sets of constraints on language behavior: on the one hand, the limitations of genetic endowment, and on the other, social constraints on interaction. We have two modes of insight into the basic system of language: studying what is common to all speakers of a given language or of language in general and studying what differences arise between speakers as a mode of understanding the functioning of the basic machinery. There are also two kinds of language learning to be studied here: learning from parents, and learning from wider social contacts—in peer groups, in school, on the job, and from mass media. Finally, one can perceive two distinct sets of limitations on the ability to learn language: personal idiosyncrasies and defects, and defects in the process of social communication. It will be the purpose here to outline the chief dimensions of language variation in spatial, social, and temporal dimensions, to discuss certain structural principles derived from this data, and to indicate the significance of all this for the learning of language.

For the most part, the subject matter of this discussion will be speech communities of American English, so that the language differences discussed will be dialect differences that normally do not interfere with cognitive communication. But the same considerations apply to multilingual areas where the sociolinguistic differences run across unrelated languages, and some references will be given to the wider literature in these areas.

REGIONAL DIFFERENCES IN LANGUAGE

We will first consider the nature of dialect differences between neighboring geographic areas. This is the province of dialect geography, a discipline well developed in its own right (and perhaps too easily segregated from the ongoing interests of linguistics in the past). In general, we may think of three distinct sources of geographic differences such as those which prevail in the eastern United States:

a. Settlement history. The records we have on the migrations of early settlers throughout the continental United States show that dialect areas often coincide with areas settled by distinct populations. This is not so much the case with the initial settlement from southern England: so far, it has not been possible to trace the dialect peculiarities of any one colony to a particular English dialect. Once settled in America, the colonists seemed to have developed their own regional dialects[2] and carried them westward. For instance, the southern mountain area west of the Appalachians was settled largely by Pennsylvanians whose descendants still retain the Midland use of *poke* for 'paper bag,' unlike the coastal southerners who use the standard term. Farmers in Pennsylvania and in the Appalachians still call their cows in the pasture with *Sookie*, unlike northern farmers who use *Co-Boss!* or coastal southern farmers who call *Co-ee!* (Kurath, 1949).

b. Discontinuities in communication. The geography of the United States has determined certain natural barriers to the flow of people, goods, ideas, and language, and we can trace the maintenance of certain bundles of isoglosses to such natural barriers. One of these is the line which separates the northern tier of Pennsylvania counties from the rest, skirting the Susquehanna drainage area. North of this line, we find speakers who say *curtains* for 'roller shades' and *darning needle* for 'dragonfly'; while south of the line, we find *blinds* and *snake feeder* (Kurath, 1949). When we enter Ohio, Indiana, and Illinois, we find the same lines representing the original settlement patterns of Yankees in the northern portion of these states and midland people in the southern. But there are no natural bars to the even flow of communication, and the dialect boundaries are much more fluid; there are no tight bundles of isoglosses (Marckwardt, 1957).

Throughout the world, we find that isolated mountain valleys, islands, and provincial frontiers are apt to contain linguistic *relic areas*, in which older forms of the language are preserved long after they have been replaced for most speakers of the language. Martha's Vineyard, for example, separated by seven miles of open water from the mainland, preserves such archaic terms as *tempest* for 'thunderstorm' or *bannock* for 'corn meal cake' and preserves as well the original *r*-pronunciation which was overcome on the mainland by the Boston *r*-less fashion.

c. Urban dialect centers. Many of the dialect regions of the eastern United States are roughly circular in area, centered about a large city which served as a cultural center for the hinterland. The spread of the dialects of Boston, Charleston, and Richmond to a radius of about 150 miles is a clear indication of the prestige accorded to these dialects. On the other hand, the dialect of New York City seems to have had negative prestige for over a century, for it has never been imitated beyond the suburbs of the city itself. We must therefore reckon with differences in the subjective evaluation of dialects by speakers in surrounding areas, in order to understand the distribution of differences in dialect forms.

---

[2]The various British dialects were reorganized in different ways in different sections of the eastern seaboard. One of the most striking developments was in the low back vowels: in western New England, short open *o* was unrounded to [ɑ], but in eastern New England, it fell together with long open *o* to give a single phoneme /ɒ/.

What Is a Dialect?

The term *dialect* is used with a great many slightly differing meanings, in ways that often interfere with communication on the subject. When people say that someone speaks a "dialect," they may mean (*a*) that he talks with a foreign accent, or (*b*) that he talks with a quaint rural style of speech, or (*c*) that he is a poor speaker who has not mastered the norms of the standard language. Linguists generally use the term in a more neutral sense (*d*), indicating a subvariety of a language. There is no simple way to categorize the degree of language differences so that we know when we have two languages or one language with two dialects. Some writers use the extent of mutual intelligibility to define this break; others consider the number of cognate words shared by the two varieties; but perhaps the most realistic approach for complex societies is to recognize that dialects are grouped by the superordinate standard language recognized by their speakers (Ferguson & Gumperz, 1960). Thus, the local patois spoken by Frenchmen and Italians on either side of the national borders is said to show a smooth continuum of differences, but the linguistic behavior of the speakers is influenced by whether they use French or Italian in formal situations. We can best conceive the language-dialect situation as shown in Figure 5-1.

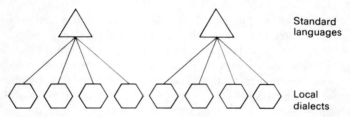

Figure 5-1. Language-Dialect Situation along National Borders

In the United States, we are not as far from these puzzling problems as one might first think. Creole dialects such as Gullah, Jamaican, or Haitian Creole are largely based on European languages as far as their lexicon is concerned, but the underlying grammar seems to be quite distinct and more closely related to the Creoles of the Caribbean or the west coast of Africa, whether they are French, Portuguese, or English-based Creoles. It is a matter of considerable importance for the study of nonstandard English used by Negro speakers generally in the United States, for if such a Creole grammar has had lasting effects upon this speech pattern, the strategy for teaching standard English should be modified (Bailey, 1964).

Similar problems arise in many situations of bilingual contact which seem at first glance to be quite straightforward. In the United States, we have many bilinguals who seem—on the face of things—to speak two different languages. But close examination of the foreign language often shows that it is heavily influenced by English in its phrase structure, its grammatical categories, its semantics, and its phonetics, as well as its vocabulary; such interpenetrating influences may be strong enough to make us wonder what it means to "speak two different languages."[3]

In the perfectly neutral sense of *dialect* suggested above, we may think of standard English as one of several dialects that a person must learn to be fully competent in the use of English. But it would be a mistake to consider standard English as merely or nothing but another dialect of English. First, because the standard is clearly superordinate in a hierarchy of prestige or appropriateness for formal speech; second, because the standard has a technical vocabulary and a literary syntax which are largely missing with other dialects; and third, because it has widespread distribution through the mass media, with less geographic differentiation than we find at the colloquial or vernacular level.

All of these characteristics of the standard reflect the vertical organization of language which is found in most present-day national states. Figure 5-2 suggests the common features of this structure which applies to the pattern of national standard, regional standard, and local dialects in such widespread areas as India, Germany, Britain, and the United States (Ferguson & Gumperz, 1960).

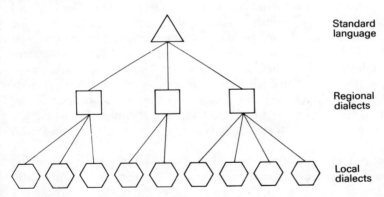

Figure 5-2. Pattern of National Standard, Regional Standard, and Local Dialects

In many countries, the middle level is even more complicated than this figure suggests; it is common to find a marketplace dialect such as Bazaar Hindustani or the Verkehrssprache of Germany as well as regional standards of cultivated speech. In the United States, we have the peculiar feature that there is no well-formed standard at one end of the scale, since we have never

---

[3]Work carried out by John Gumperz in southern India indicates that when languages of different language families are spoken by bilinguals for several centuries, they may become identical in their grammatical categories, phrase structure, and phonetics, while at the same time they may be superficially quite different in their morphologies and lexicons.

had a standardizing institution such as an academy, nor a single social class to serve as arbiters of linguistic custom. As a result, educators have difficulties in designing textbooks that seem to reflect a national standard of cultivated speech. Nevertheless, the existence of a standard can hardly be doubted when we compare the limited range of acceptable literate grammar with the nonstandard dialects of New York, Chicago, coastal Alabama, or the Ozarks.

American English Dialects

At one time, it was generally believed that American dialects could be divided into three major types: Northern, Southern, and General American (including most of the West). The work of the *Linguistic Atlas of the Eastern United States*, as directed by Hans Kurath, developed a rather different view as shown in Figure 5-3. Dialect regions were established here on the evidence of some 300 words which showed sharp regional differences (Kurath, 1949), and structural differences in sound patterns also coincide with the bundles of dialect boundaries established by this lexical evidence (Kurath & McDavid, 1961). Thus, we may note the boundaries which define a distinct *Midland* area lying between the northern and southern dialect regions. The Midland was settled originally by English dissenters, then Scotch-Irish and Palatine Germans—a collection of small farmers without a marked leisure class. Its center was Philadelphia, the one seaboard city which was most independent of British influence. From this area, pioneers and colonists moved south-westward, so that the Appalachian region and westward was settled by Midland speakers rather than by coastal southern speakers. Hence, we would tend to reject, in the light of *Atlas* findings, the one-time distinction between northern and southern dialects along a linguistic Mason-Dixon line.

Dialect boundaries defined by lexical items are especially convincing because the common use of a particular word in an entire dialect can hardly be ascribed to chance. It is possible, on the other hand, that the vowels of *cheer* and *chair* could merge independently in several regions due to a variety of causes. But only diffusion can account for the fact that roller shades are called *blinds* throughout the Midland, calves *bawl*, cows are called with *sook*, dragon flies are *snake feeders*, and people say *I want off* when they want to get off a bus. When a large continuous region shares terms that are unknown in other regions, we know that some kind of communication has taken place among the speakers which has not taken place across the dialect boundary.

At the same time, we must recognize that most of these lexical items have no serious effect on communication, and they are rapidly disappearing from the language. Some, like *sook!* are farm terms used by a diminishing number of speakers; others suffer technological obsolescence, like *singletree* or *backhouse*; some, like *pot cheese* 'cottage cheese' or *cruller* 'doughnut' are being replaced by commercial standards; and still others, like *piazza* 'porch' are giving way to the general standard. These regional markers can hardly be expected to cause difficulties for speakers from other areas (though cows raised in a *co-wench* area may have communication problems if they are purchased by a farmer from the *sook!* area). They are merely symptomatic —sometimes irritating, sometimes amusing—of communication barriers, but hardly barriers themselves and hardly carriers of social significance. Furthermore, most of these lexical items are isolated, without close structural relations to other regional markers, and so have little structural interest for linguists.[4]

On the other hand, regional differences in sound patterns do involve structural interrelations, and they carry more social significance and can interfere with communication in various ways. For example, we find speakers throughout the South who make a distinction between closed *o* and open *o* before /r/, so that *four* is distinguished from *for*, *hoarse* from *horse*, *mourning* from *morning*. The dialect boundary which separates those who make the

Figure 5-3. Major Dialect Areas of the Eastern United States (Kurath, 1949)

[4]Some portions of the regional vocabulary are highly structured and show intricate interrelationships. Words for peripheral rooms of a house such as *piazza, ell, porch, veranda* form one such set; the various terms for *pancakes, cornbread,* and other baked goods form another. As one example of a structured interrelation, it can be noted that the fish called a *scup* in New England is a *porgy* on Long Island (both from the Wampanoag *scuppaug*). The isogloss coincides with that between the *pogie* (New England) and the *menhaden*. Thus, nowhere is there any danger of confusion between [pɔgi] and [pogi] since they do not coexist.

difference from those who do not coincide with the lexical bundle which outlines the Upper and Lower South, as shown in Figure 5-3. Furthermore, there are several other important boundaries which coincide with these for most of their length: midland speakers pronounce final and preconsonantal *r*, southerners do not; the Midland does not distinguish *Mary* from *merry*, *fairy* from *ferry*, etc., while the South does; midlanders do not distinguish *which* and *witch*, *when* and *wen*, *whale* and *wail*, while southerners do. We find similar parallels of sound patterns and lexical boundaries in other areas.

One may examine American regional dialects along three relevant dimensions. The first consideration is the degree of *r*-lessness, which is maximal in the Northeast and Coastal South; the degree of consonantal constriction and the effects upon the vowel system become steadily stronger as we approach the Midwest and Far West.[5]

A second dimension of dialect differences runs along the North-South axis and is reflected by the popular term "*southern drawl.*" Slowness of speech and length of vowels is not the main consideration here but rather the weakening or loss of the diphthongal glides in /ai/, /au/, and /ɔi/, so that southern *ride* can be quite similar to northern *rod*, *proud* to northern *prod*, *oil* to northern *all*. (These pairs can coincide in the certain southern dialects as well, but not necessarily.) Along with these we find that short vowels are lengthened and followed by an ingliding schwa. The net effect of these and other associated shifts is to give southern speech an overall pattern which is readily identified by most adult Americans.

Curiously enough, if we view American dialects through these two important dimensions of the sound pattern, we return to the traditional division of northern vs. southern and eastern vs. general American or midwestern. This is no accident, since the traditional division was based on the subjective impressions of sensitive speakers, and these impressions in turn reflect those dialect differences which have the greatest social significance. Generally, speakers perceive the differences which are important to them— not necessarily in terms of cognitive information but rather in terms of "social" memory. Therefore, we might reconsider the classification of the Appalachian, Kentucky, and Tennessee speakers as "South Midland": to most Americans, they are southern, since they share the long and ingliding forms of the short vowels and the monophthongized /ai/, /au/, and /oy/ which are markers of southern speech.[6]

[5] In Philadelphia and the surrounding territory, we frequently find a weakly constricted [ə] or a humped [r]. In the Midwest, we often find a retroflex [r] which strongly influences the preceding vowel and restricts the range of distinctions: *Mary*, *merry*, and *marry* are usually homonymous. In other western areas, we have completely retroflex vowels, and it is not uncommon to find that *Murray* falls together with the other three.

[6] Completely monophthongized vowels are not as common in the careful speech of educated southerners, and frequently slight upglides are heard. In the southern mountain area, it is most common to find monophthongal [ɑ] before /r/, so that *far* and *fire* are homonymous.

The most familiar types of dialect differences are grammatical, since these come to our attention most readily and are most strongly stigmatized. Double negatives and person-number disagreements are the most persistent and well known, as in *He don't know nothing nohow*. But these are quite general in the United States; regional differences in grammar are less well marked. Atwood's study of the verb forms of the eastern United States (1953) show some nonstandard regional variants such as northern *wun't*, *hadn't ought*, *see* (preterit), and *et*; midland *boilt*, *clum*; southern *heern*, *gwine*, and double modals such as *might could*. The preterit nonstandard of *see*, for example, is chiefly *see* in the North, *seen* in the Midland, *seed* in North Carolina. When textbooks designed for national distribution incorporate lessons on such regional items, they lead to truly absurd results: for example, teaching midland and southern children not to say *hadn't ought* is simply teaching them to make mistakes they would otherwise never have heard of.

Not all grammatical differences are well marked, of course; incipient grammatical changes are well below the level of conscious attention and are difficult to locate. Occasionally, when one of these comes to the surface, the results seem bizarre and even uninterpretable to speakers from other areas. For example, in various points in New England we find *So didn't I* used to mean *So did I*; and in Ohio and adjacent areas of the Midwest, *We go there anymore* to mean the opposite of *We don't go there anymore*. On the whole, we find that grammatical differences are scattered phenomena which cause little difficulty in communication, and the most highly marked, socially significant differences are not confined to any one region. This statement does not apply to one situation which has assumed great importance in recent years: grammatical differences between northern speakers and southern speakers—Negro and white—who have migrated to northern cities. But we will return to this topic below.

How Are Regional Dialects Maintained?

It is commonplace for people to assume that regional dialects are rapidly disappearing since they hear few differences in the standard speech heard on the mass media and since there is considerable movement within modern societies. Perhaps we may expect a steady erosion of the smallest units of dialect—the patois of France, the most local dialect of Germany, the isolated rural speech of the United States. But new differences as they arise are not readily perceived, and it is not at all certain that regional differences in the United States are being wiped out by the effects of migration and mass media. Furthermore, linguistic evolution is even more rapid in the centers and suburbs of large cities so that as we begin to study the local dialects within the city we see a rich source of language differentiation.

If we look for new lexical markers, we must abandon farm words and also any terminology which is subject to standardization through mass production. But an item which is locally packaged or which is manufactured on the spot, or any type of local industry or service, will give rise to special regional terms. Thus, soda fountain confections, bottled drinks, sandwiches, haircuts, card games, and highway terminology—general names for sidewalks, street blocks, underpasses, kiosks, and the like—all of these provide a rich source for regional differentiation.

The effects of large-scale migration are not as drastic as one might suppose in leveling language differences. If children learned their language in detail from their parents, then we would expect to find in most western cities a strange mixture of heterogeneous dialects and every city gradually assuming the same mixed dialect. On the other hand, if children do not learn their dialects in detail from their parents—but rather from their peers—then we can expect to find regional dialects fairly stable despite the existence of great geographic mobility.[7] We will reconsider this problem when we turn to linguistic variation among various age levels of the population.

The other factor which may presumably be operating to reduce dialect differences is the mass media. There is no doubt that the announcers heard on network shows throughout the country—and even on local programs—have achieved a remarkable uniformity. For example, we hear strong *r*-pronunciation from announcers in Boston and New York and the South; all of these are *r*-less areas. We might ask whether the *r*-less vernacular or the *r*-pronouncing broadcast style is apt to have the greater influence on audiences. If we are to judge by the telephone conversation programs which have recently become popular in many cities, there is a linguistic gulf between the broadcaster and the average citizen who calls up to speak to him. Indeed, there is reason to think that it is natural for such differences to exist and even grow greater with time. For the social pressures which lead to uniformity and towards a single standard are much more obvious than the opposing forces which maintain differences. The nature of the standard is such that almost everyone pays lip service to it as the only "correct" mode of speech. Most speakers themselves do not know the extent to which they depart from this norm, nor why they should want to do so. The covert forces encouraging local autonomy in speech are not well delineated, but the evidence we have points to such noncognitive factors as the desire for local apartness, features of masculinity, toughness, or homespun common sense, an atmosphere of friendliness associated with local dialect, the need for novel and fashionable speech which separates one group from another, and along with these, the

---

[7] In actual field work in urban areas, we find that the rapid shifting of the population does not interefere with the formation of consistent regional dialects; it would not be possible in most cases to identify the children whose parents came from other areas in contrast to the third or fourth generation speakers.

wealth of centrifugal tendencies which motivate slang, argot, and the language of the streets. The investigation of such covert values will contribute a great deal to our understanding of language differentiation.

URBAN LANGUAGE DIFFERENCES

In the study of geographic variation, we assume a certain relative isolation of speakers or relative discontinuities in communication; in any case, the speakers of one region are seldom in face-to-face contact with speakers from another. But in urban dialects, the opposite is true: we assume contact, or the possibility of contact, as a daily occurrence in the city between speakers of radically different speech forms. In such a situation, native competence of speakers includes a wide range of style shifts, and we must adopt more subtle and sensitive means of analysis if we are to understand the underlying sociolinguistic structure. The analysis of urban language differences is not only more difficult and challenging but also more urgent in terms of the educational problems involved, the numbers of people affected, and the growing effects upon the life chances of the individual.

Types of Language Differences

In considering linguistic behavior in urban society, it is useful to consider three types of variables: *indicators, markers,* and *stereotypes.* We find first that there are some language differences which show close correlations with particular class, age, or ethnic groups, but which operate well below the level of social consciousness. For example, we find that in Phoenix, Arizona, the incomplete merger of long open *o* and short *o* is a variable: for some speakers, the pairs *cot* and *caught, stock* and *stalk* are homonyms, and for others they are not.[8] There is a strong tendency for the Anglos to show the one-phoneme, merged pattern, while Spanish and Negro groups tend to retain the two-phoneme system. But no one is aware of this fact, and very few know of the merger at all. As a rule, speakers show no shift in their use of this variable from their most casual to their most careful speech. Unlike such well-established social variables as the double negative, *dese* and *dose,* or the use of *ain't,* this systematic variation in the vowel system is quite stable from one stylistic context to another. These characteristics are typical of linguistic *indicators:* they seem to represent early stages of developing

---

[8] These data are derived from interviews carried out in 1964 in Phoenix Union High School. The author is indebted to Mr. Harry Coppinger and Mrs. Claire Downs of the English department for their assistance.

language changes which are symptomatic of group differences but have little direct effect on communication.

We often find a more complex type of linguistic variable which evidently has greater social impact in face-to-face communication. The use of a constricted [r] in final and preconsonantal position has recently become such a variable throughout most of the r-less areas of the eastern states (McDavid, 1948; Labov, 1966; Levine, 1966). There is a finely graded social stratification in which groups with more education and prestige regularly use more [r]— among younger speakers primarily. Furthermore, many speakers use almost no [r] in casual and spontaneous speech, small percentages of [r] in careful speech, and increasingly more [r] in formal styles such as that used in reading. A lecturer will begin with 30 to 40 percent [r] in final and preconsonantal position, fall off to 10 or 20 percent as he warms to his subject, and return to 25 or 30 percent in his formal peroration. An increasing number of younger speakers are aware of this variable, though as a rule they are not fully aware of their own variation. They may hear themselves as always using the prestige [r] form, and at the same time, react (unconsciously) against the use of the nonprestige form by others. We may refer to such complex variables as linguistic *markers*. There are many such markers which are general throughout the United States: the use of the historical present in narrative, variations in the objective pronouns, variant forms of adverbs, a wide range of morphological condensation,[9] and the choice of lexicon from the general vocabulary of learned, colloquial, and slang terms.

A third type of linguistic variable appears as the overt topic of comment by members of the speech community. Not only New Yorkers, but most Americans have heard of the [əɪ] sound in *work*, *shirt*, *bird*, etc., written *oi* in dialect literature and stigmatized as "Brooklynese" (Hubbell, 1940). This particular variable has been so effectively stigmatized that it is no longer used by most younger speakers; it survives only in certain lower-class groups (Labov, 1966, Ch. 9). We may refer to such variables as *stereotypes* without implying that they have no basis in linguistic reality. There are a limited number of such stereotypes, and many are quite general: dropping the *g* in *workin'*, etc.; double and triple negatives; the use of *ain't*; and the *dese* and *dose* variable mentioned earlier.

It is apparent that a young person growing up in an urban community with such complex sociolinguistic structure has a great deal to learn about language besides the core structures he learns from his parents. He must acquire a range of techniques for registering style shifts. He must learn to recognize dialect differences and to evaluate them—to interpret their

---

[9]Although morphological condensation has never been studied systematically, it is recognized and utilized by many dialect writers. *Jeat yet? No, jew?* is a well known example often cited by local people as an example of their local dialect. *Whatcha doon?* is another frequently discussed form. It is interesting to note that dialects do differ in their rules for such condensation: *Get out of the house* may appear in New York as [gɛd̥a.d̥ed̥əhaos], but in New England as [gɪtaot:haos].

significance in establishing the stylistic context and the social status of the speaker. He must also learn to produce and control the variables himself, and to the extent that he can produce the prestige forms consistently, he may gain direct advantage for himself.

Socioeconomic Stratification

The most characteristic form of "vertical" stratification in the cities is that of social class. There are many approaches to the difficult concept of social class, but no matter how we choose to define class, we will find linguistic differences which are correlated with it. To define social class, we can consider the status of speakers as they view themselves or as others see them, by their residential location, consumption of goods, or style of life. But the most manageable data concern occupation, education, and income, and these three indicators are often combined to form a single index of socioeconomic stratification. Figure 5-4 shows a typical class stratification diagram for

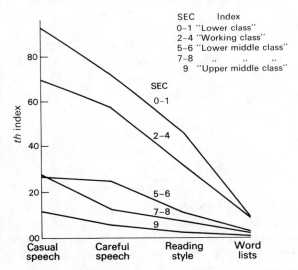

Figure 5-4. Class Stratification of *th* for Adult Native New York Speakers (Labov, 1966, Ch. 7)

New York City speakers, in which the variable first consonant of *this, then, these*, etc., is shown to depend upon stylistic context and such an index of socioeconomic class. The higher the score on the (dh) scale, the more non-standard forms are used by the speaker. This extremely regular pattern, with four-fold class and style stratification duplicated along two dimensions, can be repeated for other phonological and grammatical features (Labov, 1966). Some such complex variables are peculiar to a particular dialect;

others are quite general throughout the United States. For example, one such local marker in New York City is the height of the vowel in *bad*, *ask*, *dance*, ranging in height from [æ] to [iə]. This variable is of great interest in New York; the chief marker of formal style for most speakers—working-class and middle-class alike—is a long low vowel in these words. On the other hand, the variable unstressed word ending *-ing* has roughly the same significance throughout the United States. Forms such as *workin'* and *eatin'* are quite generally informal and used by rougher, less educated speakers in contrast to *working* and *eating* (Fischer, 1958; Labov, 1966). Figure 5-5 shows the style and class stratification for this variable in New York City.[10]

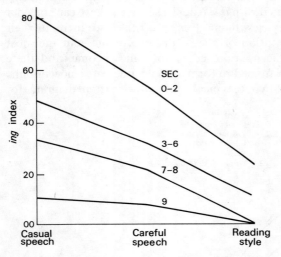

Figure 5-5. Class Stratification of *ing* for Adult White New York Speakers (Labov, 1966, Ch. 10).

Many other phonological and morphological variables show this characteristic stratification. But there are many interesting class differences in speech which lie on a more abstract plane. We find marked differences in lexical categorization—that concerning mass nouns and count nouns, for example. *Slang*, for instance, is a mass noun for most middle-class speakers, but a count noun for many working-class and lower-class speakers who say, "I don't use these slangs," or "*Boss* is a slang."

A somewhat higher level difference is responsible for the fact that

[10] Although the variable (-ing) has the same general significance throughout the country and follows the same direction of shift, it may be interpreted differently because it operates at different levels in various regions. In the South, for example, we find a much freer use of *workin'*, *huntin'*, and *fishin'* in careful speech than in the North. In the same way, we find that the level of nonstandard stops for (dh) is greater in Chicago than in New York, so that a New Yorker could not judge a Chicagoan's style or social class as accurately by his speech as he could judge a fellow New Yorker.

lower-class speakers quite generally read the passage, "It's strange how I can remember everything he did" as "It's strange how can I. . . ." Furthermore we often hear sentences such as *I don't know is he here* and *She ask him is the boy nose bleed*. These sentences share the common property that the position of tense marker, *have* and *be* relative to the subject noun phrase, is not the same as in standard English, and this general difference can be shown as a difference in the order of abstract transformational rules.[11]

The British social psychologist, Basil Bernstein, has developed a more general approach to class differences which posits two distinct codes: a restricted code characteristic of working-class speakers (but also used by the middle-class) and an elaborated code which only middle-class speakers use (Bernstein, 1964). The restricted code is described generally as providing a narrower range of syntactic alternatives than the elaborated code; it may also have a smaller lexicon, but this is not as essential a characteristic. Bernstein (1964) describes a typical restricted code in this way:

. . . an observer might be struck by the fact that the speech in these social relationships was fast, fluent, with reduced articulatory clues, the meanings might be discontinuous, dislocated, condensed and local, but the quantity of speech might not be affected, that there would be a low level of vocabulary and syntactic selection, and that the 'how' rather than the 'what' of the communication would be important. *The unique meaning of the person would tend to be implicit* [p. 62].

Bernstein's overall approach to language differences has the great merit of setting the problem firmly within the larger context of differences in social structure. He enlarges the significance of the usual distinction between language and speech—the abstract system vs. the use of that system—with the concise observation, "Between language . . . and speech is social structure." Recent work of Gumperz on code switching in several widely different communities has given empirical weight to this view by demonstrating that social groups which form closed networks have different rules for code switching than groups which participate in open networks (Gumperz, 1964). Many current studies of class differences in verbal skills are aimed at specifying the ways in which language learning is determined by social environments. It remains to be seen if the particular views on class differences set forth by Bernstein can be confirmed by hard linguistic data and if the notions of *code* and *predictability* can be specified more precisely. In one sense, a smaller vocabulary implies a limitation in the code for expressing the output of the grammar used, and therefore, an increase in predictability, but this increase in predictability would be realized only if we had a finite state grammar which produced a finite number of different sentences. Since the

[11] One way of analyzing this syntactic difference is to show that the reversal of auxiliary and subject noun phrases characteristic of yes-no questions is not re-reversed after embedding as required in the standard language. It is also possible to take the reversal shown here as the dialect equivalent of standard *if* or *wh*-word—the corresponding means of signaling questions in embedded sentences.

phrase structure grammars used by all speakers of English are recursive and produce an unlimited number of different sentences, Bernstein's conclusions do not follow from any quantitative count of vocabulary items such as rare adjectives, pronouns, and so on (e.g., an infinite number of sentence types can be produced from the 850-word vocabulary of basic English). One would have to demonstrate a limitation in the rules utilized by working-class speakers which result in a limitation on the types of structures that are in fact produced if Bernstein's point is to be validated.

The more tangible phonological and morphological variables discussed above are class markers of a fairly stable type. The use of stops and affricates for the *th-* sounds, double negatives, demonstrative locatives *this here*, irregular preterits and perfects are all variables that seem to have survived centuries of stigmatization. The nonstandard *aks* has survived beside standard *ask* since Anglo-Saxon times, although it has long been discouraged by polite society. A remarkable feature of these socioeconomic markers and stereotypes is that they are employed within the speech community with two functions: as social *and* stylistic markers. One set of factors that determines the realization of the variables is found in the social history of the speaker (his family's and his own); another set is formed by the social relations which prevail between him and the listener, the social context of the discussion, the nature of the topic, and the degree of familiarity. For the listener, the level of the linguistic variable can therefore provide information on one or several of these areas. The distinction between *cultural varieties* and *functional levels* was originally made by Kenyon (1948) as a means of isolating the value-laden cultural level from the purely functional nature of stylistic shifting. It is certainly true that some features of working-class speech—double negatives, for example—are very rare among upper middle-class speakers, even in the most casual style.[12] But by and large, the same linguistic variables are used to mark both dimensions, social distance *and* stylistic function, in a way not envisaged by Kenyon.

The complex regularities of Figures 5-4 and 5-5 demonstrate the manner in which the same linguistic variables provide the concrete manifestations of social class stratification and stylistic stratification. There is a widespread tendency for such intersection (Ferguson & Gumperz, 1960; Gumperz, 1964; Levine, 1966), although in some cases we find distinct variables utilized.[13]

What explanation can we give for this intersection of social and situa-

[12] In quantitative studies of style shifting, we frequently find that the variable in question appears to be a constant for some particular group. But we can usually find conditions when even these speakers in very familiar or jocular circumstances will demonstrate their knowledge of the use of these forms.

[13] The system of honorifics used in Japan or the linguistic levels of Javanese are cases where we do not have complete coincidence between social and stylistic variables. On the other hand, the use of the *tu* and *vous* forms in French cannot be understood without taking both factors into account, and the same can be said of the German and Russian pronominal systems.

tional significance for a single variable? It appears that one intervening variable may be recognized: the degree of audio monitoring used by the speaker to control a superposed ("learned") norm. The existence of social variation ensures the fact that speakers will differ in their familiarity with (and practice in using) the norm in question; the immediate context determines the amount of energy ("attention") available for audio monitoring. The possibility of such a simplifying intervening variable, as shown in Figure 5-6, is very attractive, but quantitative studies of attention to language (along the lines of Broadbent, 1965) are needed to confirm the notion.

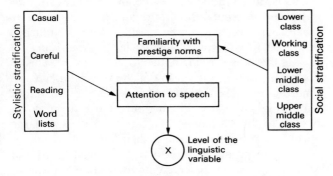

Figure 5-6. Level of the Linguistic Intervening Variable

Ethnic Differentiation

The differentiation of language patterns produced by socioeconomic gradients is only one of the many types of stratification to be found within urban societies where speakers in close contact use different linguistic forms. The highly differentiated ethnic groups found in Europe have been reformed but not dissolved in American cities; they have taken on the form of distinct interest groups and retained a certain degree of endogamy (Glazer & Moynihan, 1963). Where entire regions have been settled by single ethnic groups, we find residual effects in the English of their descendants. The *Linguistic Atlas* shows monophthongal midvowels [e:] and [o:] in *day* and *go* in two regions of the eastern Atlantic states: in the Pennsylvania German region and in coastal South Carolina where speakers are in contact with Gullah Creole (Kurath & McDavid, 1961, Maps 18, 21). These monophthongs are not characteristic of the southern British area from which the English settlers were originally drawn.

Nevertheless, many observers have been puzzled to find so few direct influences of foreign languages in American cities. Attempts to attribute characteristics of New York City and Chicago speech to a foreign substratum have been quite inconclusive, except in the area of intonation and a few scattered syntactic and lexical forms.

In several cities, we can point to the direct legacy of foreign settlement in regional words. New York City *cruller*, *stoop*, *pot cheese* are as Dutch as *Brooklyn* and *Harlem* (Kurath, 1949, Fig. 14). Yiddish-based intonation patterns (*You call that a cigarette?*, Weinreich, 1956) and syntax (*So talk already*, Feinsilver, 1962) appear in New York City English and elsewhere. It can be argued that the frequency of nonstandard stops and affricates for interdentals in Chicago English is much higher than for British dialects so far recorded, so that the substratum influence of foreign languages with no interdental fricatives is difficult to dispute. But on the whole, it is remarkable how few regional or urban characteristics can be traced to foreign influence and how many can be traced to widespread tendencies in American and British English which antedate the arrival of the foreign group. This is certainly the case with such features as the raising of the vowels of *bad* and *caught* in New York, and the centralization of *curl* and *coil*, the broad *a* in Boston, the centralization of *go* and *too* in Philadelphia and Pittsburgh. In general, urban dialects seem to show a remarkable capacity to absorb large numbers of foreign speakers without disturbing their regular evolution. Second generation speakers do not differ in most respects from third and fourth generation speakers. They seem to serve equally well as informants for linguistic surveys.

Substratum effects of ethnic origin do appear, however, if sometimes in subtle and unexpected ways. The second generation speaker does not, as a rule, imitate his foreign-speaking parent: quite the reverse—he may show a hypercorrect pattern in precisely the opposite direction from that of the substratum language. This seems to be the case, for example, in the alternating effects of Jewish and Italian groups upon the evolution of New York City English (Labov, 1966, Ch. 8).

Today, two major ethnic groups seem to provide an exception to this pattern: the Spanish-speaking and Negro groups found in many large American cities. In the Southwest, we find English dialects plainly influenced by Spanish among second and third generation speakers (Barker, 1947), and there are no immediate signs of such influence disappearing. The size of the Spanish-speaking communities may be a factor; certainly the proximity of Spanish-speaking Mexico must be taken into account; and attitudes towards American education and value systems cannot be neglected (Christian & Christian, 1966). The general analysis of factors influencing the acculturation of ethnic groups must be assumed as a prerequisite for understanding such influences upon English. Considerable descriptive work has been carried out by those primarily interested in these questions (Fishman, 1966).

The large Puerto Rican groups in eastern cities also show Spanish influence upon their English, but it is not clear at this time that the use of Spanish and its influence will be any greater or more prolonged than for

Italian, Jewish, or German communities. Among many young Puerto Rican youngsters in East Harlem, we begin to find a familiar pattern of language disloyalty: the young people abandon the parent language except for communication with their elders.

Of greatest concern to educators and social scientists are language differences characteristic of Negro speakers in the large urban ghetto areas. Some students of the situation would like to trace these differences to the effects of an underlying Creole introduced into this country from the Caribbean and West Africa (Bailey, 1964; Stewart, 1964). Whether or not this is the case, it is plain that segregation would inevitably tend to preserve and promote linguistic differentiation.

Another way of viewing the speech of northern Negroes is to consider these patterns as nothing else but transplanted southern regional dialect. It seems that almost all of the features of Negro speech can be found among some white speakers somewhere in the South; this does not of course preclude a Creole or African origin, since white speakers in the South may well have accepted the forms from a larger Negro group. This is certainly the case in the Charleston area where Gullah characteristics are found in the speech of the white community as a whole.

Whatever the ultimate origin of Negro speech patterns, it is clear that they have been carried to northern cities in the past few decades along with the large-scale migration of the rural Negro populations to Washington, New York, Boston, Philadelphia, Detroit, Cleveland, and Chicago. The migration has been so large that the northern dialects spoken by the indigenous Negro populations have largely been submerged—a process termed *dialect swamping* by McDavid (1966). The ghetto populations of these northern cities are drawn from areas of the South which differ widely in their dialect characteristics, so that one would expect considerable differences in the resulting dialect patterns in the North. Strangely enough, this does not seem to be the case. Groups of Negro adolescents in New York, Philadelphia, Detroit, Chicago, and Los Angeles are remarkably similar in their phonology, morphology, and syntax—at least in the respects in which they differ from the prevailing local standard. One finds, of course, a much larger degree of consonantal constricted [r] in final and preconsonantal position among Negro speakers in Los Angeles and Chicago than in New York or Boston. But on the whole, the deviations from standard English which cause trouble in the classroom are remarkably uniform.

We find that the most striking features common to Negro speakers, most resistant to correction, appear in an area of phonological-grammatical intersection where it is difficult to decide if rules of sound pattern or grammatical differences are the most influential (Labov, Cohen, & Robins, 1965). A higher degree of r-lessness appears in this pattern than we are accustomed to find among white speakers—intervocalic $/r/$ in *Paris* and *four o'clock* is often absent, so that *Paris* and *pass* may be homonyms. Furthermore, the presence of the copula or the auxiliary *be* may be difficult to detect or maintain when the phonetic form of this verb depends to a large extent upon /r/ as in *they're* and *you're*, and a slight difference in vowel quality is all that remains.[14] Similarly, the possessive morpheme in *their* and *your* may disappear, yielding *you book* and *they book*, without any parallel tendency in *my book* or *his book*: that is, we do not find *I book*, *me book* or *he book* in these ghetto areas.

A similar pattern of phonological-grammatical intersection concerns the vocalization of /l/: the contracted form of the future tense depends upon final /l/ for its phonetic realization. Negro speakers are not the only ones who show the absence of consonantal /l/, but the overall effects upon their grammar are significant here. *You'll find* may be homonymous with *you found*, and *they go* may be impossible to distinguish from *they'll go*.[15]

The most extensive set of homonyms which appears in this intersecting area is that involving consonant clusters ending in /t, d/ or /s, z/ (the choice of one or the other of these pairs is usually automatic in inflection). The first type of cluster may or may not signal the past tense, as in *just* or *missed*, /džəst/ or /mist/: the second type of final may be an indissoluble part of the word as in *axe* /æks/ or one of six different suffixes (plural, third person singular, possessive, contracted *is* or *has*, contracted *us*, adverbial /z/ in *besides*). When such clusters are not formed by grammatical inflections, we find that the tendency to simplify is about the same for most vernacular Negro speakers and for white speakers of comparable education or background: in fact, the pattern of distribution is remarkably similar in detail for various clusters. But when the clusters contain a morpheme boundary—that is, the final is a grammatical (meaningful) element, we find that working-class and lower-class Negro speakers behave very differently from white speakers. (We are dealing here with the basic speech patterns as shown in the excited and spontaneous conversation used within the family or in peer group interaction. In the school context or in face-to-face interviews, many Negro speakers will use patterns similar to white speakers.) The white speakers will simplify very few grammatical clusters, whereas many Negro speakers will show almost the same degree of simplification as in monomorphemic words. Such radical differences lead us to consider the existence of different underlying grammatical rules for the Negro speakers. At the same time, we find that when the next word begins with a vowel, the degree of simplification is sharply reduced for both Negro and white—a fact which demonstrates the existence of phonological rules in operation as well. Whenever we find that a following vowel does *not* tend to preserve the final /s, z/ or /t, d/ of the

[14]When consonantal /r/ gives way to a vocalic glide, the phonetic distinction between *they're* and *they* is not necessarily slight; it may be [dɛ⁻] vs. [deᴛ] and this small difference eventually gives way to homonymy.

[15]The same considerations apply to this case as with /r/ in footnote 14. The back unrounded glide which represents /l/ is usually not sufficient to maintain the contracted future morpheme.

cluster, we have firm evidence of grammatical differences from standard English in the basic vernacular. This is definitely the case with the third person singular and possessive inflections for many groups of Negro speakers. In such cases, we can confidently conclude that these inflections do not exist in the underlying grammatical system (Labov, 1966b).

It would not be difficult to fill many pages with lists of grammatical rules which differentiate Negro speech patterns from those of the surrounding white community in northern cities. No matter what the origin of such differences—an underlying Creole grammar or southern white rules ultimately derived from a British source—they are clearly associated with the Negro ethnic group for most northern whites. The evidence for such rules appears in the deletion of the present copula as in *She wild*, the general or habitual *be* in *He be workin' all the time*, the perfective *done* in *The bullet done penetrate my body*, yes-no questions of the form *You like coffee, or you like tea?*, adverbial complements such as *I learned English first one*, negative concord of the type *It ain't no cat can't get in no coop*, and inversion forms such as *I know is the boy nose bleed*. Current work in the syntax of this subsection of the speech community is devoted to the exact delineation of the rules whose effects are shown here.

Sex Differences

A general survey of the social differentiation of language shows that in a number of areas women and men have distinctly different forms in certain paradigms (Haas, 1944). It is interesting to note that in many cases the women's forms are the more archaic. In the United States, there are a few fixed differences of this type, though they are not so regular nor so apparent to native speakers. Women rarely use *her* to personify inanimate affective objects as in *Fill 'er up* or *Let 'er down*. There are certain attributives such as *adorable*, *lovely*, *darling*, which cannot be used by men without creating the impression of femininity. But the outstanding differences that we find revolve about the matter of attitudes towards nonstandard language forms.

In middle-class groups, women generally show much less familiarity with and much less tolerance for nonstandard grammar and taboo. Whereas most men can serve as excellent informants, passive or active, for nonstandard usage (double negatives, etc.), many women cannot do so. In cases where speakers show a stylistic shift from one value of a variable to another, women show much more extreme shifts than men (Labov, 1966, Ch. 8).[16] Many middle-class women are critical of their husbands' speech and find it

---

[16] For example, we find that in New York City women are much more extreme than men in shifting from *r*-less speech in casual style to *r*-pronunciation in reading style. In the same way, women correct the high vowel in *bad* [bɪ·əd] to [bæ:d] in a much more extreme fashion than men. This hypercorrect behavior is especially characteristic of lower middle-class women.

difficult to recognize the functional need for less cultivated speech patterns in daily business. This difference in the sexes does not seem to exist in rural or lower-class urban groups. Here, women can serve as well as men as informants for the nonstandard dialect and may have even less knowledge of the prestige forms if they lead an isolated life at home.

The Uniformity of Normative Patterns

Some studies of language and the learning of language concentrate upon the facts of speech alone, on the supposition that these facts of speech performance are the only "hard" and reliable data. This has been the case with many dialect geographers who work in areas where the norms of careful speech are not markedly different from the facts of casual speech—or at least not for the linguistic data being studied. Other linguists concentrate upon the normative patterns of carefully edited speech: this is the case with generative grammarians who believe that unedited texts are poor material for analysis. They concentrate upon the norms of grammaticalness which the speaker (often the theorist himself) can establish for his own speech— what may be termed *auto-prescriptive norms*. But a more sophisticated approach to the study of linguistic structure within the speech community will focus upon a higher level of abstraction: not norms alone, nor behavior alone, but rather the relation between these two. The nature of this relation often governs the process of language learning as well as the direction of linguistic change.

Some normative patterns are taught in school in response to the overt corrections applied by social institutions to certain nonstandard forms. Some of these pertain to long-standing stigmatized forms, like the metathesized form of ask /æks/; others to incoming changes in the language, like the decline of the -*ly* suffix. Usually, one expects the schools to act as a conservative force—quick to stigmatize new forms, a little behind the frontier of linguistic change, and slow to recommend a new prestige form until it is fully established in the community. This seems to be the case with *r*-pronunciation in New York City. Though speech teachers have now discarded their earlier Anglophile emphasis upon *r*-less pronunciation and teach *r*-pronunciation explicitly or implicitly, it seems clear that this change is the result rather than the cause of the change in community attitudes.

It is true that the teaching of the schools can be erratic, but on the whole, we can expect that teachers will reflect the linguistic norms of the community as they are interpreted within their own social framework. In the early stages of a linguistic change, the steady advance of a feature usually occurs well below the level of conscious awareness; but in the later stages, various sectors of the community become gradually more aware of these features and arrive at some agreement as to their social evaluation. Thus

New York City high school teachers are generally quick to stigmatize the high vowel of *here* or *where* when it appears in *bad*, *ask*, *dance*, etc., and in doing so, they reflect the uniform view of the speech community as a whole. Subjective reaction tests reveal an extraordinary uniformity in the (unconscious) reactions of New Yorkers to this variable (Labov, 1966, Ch. 11). Indeed, we find a general rule that those who show the highest degree of a stigmatized variable in their own casual speech are the most sensitive to this feature in the speech of others. In the same way, we find a remarkable uniformity on behalf of younger speakers in attributing prestige to *r*-pronunciation. This uniformity is the converse of the social stratification of actual speech noted above, in which each group follows the same pattern of stylistic shift at a different level.

The systematic investigation of subjective reactions raises the possibility that speech communities may be defined more precisely by agreement in subjective judgments rather than by agreement in speech behavior. Bloomfield (1933, Ch. 3) suggested that the speech community is in fact outlined by discontinuities in the network of communication; more recently, Gumperz (1964) has used networks of mutual obligations as the defining elements in his study of a Norwegian speech community. It may be that the speech community can best be defined by linguistic behavior at the level of subjective judgments or norms held by native speakers. Furthermore, it appears that the process of language learning is not completed until the individual has acquired the full set of norms which define his own speech community (Labov, 1964).

LANGUAGE DIFFERENCES IN AGE LEVELS

The very fact of language change has important implications for the study of language learning. The long-term evidence of language history indicates that changes in the form and function of linguistic structure are continual and frequent; it is most likely that the process of change is a normal product of the communicative process, although there is no widely accepted theoretical explanation as to why this should be so. Studies of ongoing linguistic changes within complex urban societies indicate that phonological change can be quite rapid and cover the full phonetic range in no more than half a century. It follows that children do not learn the same language that their parents learned.

Chomsky and Halle have proposed that an important part of the mechanism of linguistic change springs from the nature of the rule-forming capacity which children possess (Halle, 1962). On the one hand, it is suggested that the adult acquires certain new linguistic habits in the course of thirty or forty years—habits which most likely take the form of new rules added to the grammars formed in childhood. Some of these new rules may actually reverse the effect of the earlier rules. This is probably the case when adults learn to use constricted consonantal [r] in positions where the abstract consonant //r// has previously been converted to a vocalic segment. But the child has no knowledge of anyone else's implicit grammar when he learns to speak: he generalizes from the speech that he hears, and unless there are data to support such retrograde rules, he would inevitably produce a simpler grammar without them. At some stage in the reintroduction of constricted [r], we expect that the process will be completed rapidly by children who generalize to the simpler grammar with invariant [r]. It is also possible that such a simpler grammar, with different ordering of the rules, might have subtle but far-reaching consequences upon further developments. Although this model of linguistic change has not been given empirical support, it remains as a most plausible construct from our understanding of the child's capacity to learn language.

The model which suggests that a child generalizes from available data to produce the simplest grammatical rules to account for this data is based upon an abstraction which plainly deviates from the actual language learning situation. This model assumes a homogeneous speech community in which all of the data are presented at one time to children with uniform competence. Chomsky (1964) has himself pointed out some important consequences of the fact that children acquire vocabulary in several stages. The simplest phonological rules which we can formulate for the English vocabulary as a whole rely heavily upon certain alternations in Romance words learned relatively late in life. These rules are based on an abstract lexicon, rather remote from the sounds of the words as they are actually pronounced, but quite close to English spelling in its present form, relating the long *a* in *grave* to the short *a* in *gravity* and the long *o* in *tone* to the short *o* in *tonic*. But since children form their original phonological rules on the basis of a much more restricted lexicon, it is possible that they begin with very different rules—possibly those used in Bloomfieldian linguistics where the *a* in *grave* is a complex sound /ey/ with a simple nucleus /e/ as in *set* rather than the nucleus of /æ/ in *sat*. We may also consider the possibility that some children acquire a large Romance vocabulary fairly early, before puberty, and restructure their phonological rules to match the spelling system rather closely, while others who learn these words in their late teens or twenties may not restructure their rules and operate along much more complex (and perhaps less efficient) lines.

Some Current Changes in American English

We can derive some information on the changing patterns of English by comparing recent studies with others carried out a generation or two ago.

But we can also study the distribution of linguistic forms today across several age levels. Rather complex arguments are needed to distinguish regular age-grading from actual linguistic change (Hockett, 1950; Labov, 1966, Ch. 9).[17] But it is possible, given distribution in *apparent time* (age levels), to infer changes in *real time*.

Of the various phonological changes taking place in American English, perhaps the most widespread and substantial is the unconditioned merger of long open *o* in *caught*, *hawk*, and *dawn* with short *o* in *cot*, *hock*, and *don*. We find this merger spreading geographically and through younger age levels in northeastern New England, western Pennsylvania, scattered areas in the Midwest, and throughout the western United States with residual resistance in Los Angeles and San Francisco.[18] Various rearrangements of vowels before /r/ accompany this change. Since this merged system is not recorded in most dictionaries or teaching manuals, many teachers in the West are still instructing children to learn the distinction, word by word—not realizing that their single low back vowel is perfectly acceptable and even has great prestige for most educated speakers in the East.

Another change spreading at a considerable rate is the loss of a distinction of /i/ and /ɛ/ before nasals; *pin* and *pen*, *tin* and *ten*, *since* and *cents* are thus homonymous. This is a general southern trait which has long since passed the limits of the border states; it may be heard as far north as Gary, Indiana.

We are not entirely clear as to why these changes spread so rapidly, but we can say it is more probable that the change will be in the direction of the one-vowel system. It is easier for a speaker to lose a distinction than to separate whole word classes to learn a new distinction. Thus, many of the older regional differences in American English are rapidly disappearing in the direction of the simpler system, especially those distinctions which separated northern from midland speech. In the northern dialect region, the distinction between closed *o* and open *o* before r is rapidly disappearing, so that *hoarse–horse, four–for, mourning–morning* are homonymous for younger speakers where older speakers made the difference. Similarly, the difference between *whale* and *wail*, *which* and *witch*, *when* and *wen* is retreating at a good rate. The broad a in *pass, bath, half, dance*, etc., is suffering attrition where it was native, and it is much less often imitated in areas where it was imported.[19]

One major exception to this tendency is the advance of *r*-pronunciation

[17] *Age-grading* is a regular change in habits which speakers show from one age level to another which is a part of the general culture of the society, so that speakers in succeeding generations show the same distribution in apparent time.

[18] These observations are based on data from study of the national distribution of the /ɑ ~ ɔ/ vs. /ɑ/ isogloss carried out by the author by long-distance telephone in 1964–65.

[19] These observations are based on data from exploratory studies in urban areas carried out by the author in 1964–66 and upon a study of the cultivated regional standards used by students at Columbia University in 1966.

discussed above. In the major *r*-less areas of the East (the Northeast, New York City, and the Upper and Lower South), there has been a strong tendency since the end of World War II to adopt constricted *r* as a prestige pronunciation and a norm of careful speech. As a result, the majority of younger educated speakers will often use *r* to differentiate *card* and *cod*, *source* and *sauce*, *cord* and *cawed*, even if these words are homonymous in their native vernacular. For some younger speakers, *r*-pronunciation may become a part of their most casual speech and may even become completely consistent. Thus, in one sense, a large portion of the lexicon is becoming more differentiated. In another sense, there is a major simplification taking place, since the system of long and ingliding vowels utilized in *r*-less speech becomes weakened to the point of extinction. Along with the importation of consonantal /r/, we often find the mergers noted above and also others.

To what extent can we attribute the advance of /r/ and other phonological changes to the influence of spelling? This is part of the more general question of the influence of literacy on linguistic change as a whole. Once the change is under way, school teachers can accelerate it by teaching that *r*-pronunciation is correct: as children learn to read, the spelling *r* then helps them to separate the word classes. However, spelling has no such influence on southern British speech: British speakers do not feel that [fɔr] is a clearer guide to the word *four* than the pronunciation [fɔ:]. Furthermore, the schools are merely responding to the ongoing change, rather than initiating it. Only those teachers who are raised with the belief that [fɔr] is more correct than [fɔ:] will teach this to their students.

The mass media are undoubtedly potent factors in developments among educated speakers. Throughout the United States, we find that newscasters and announcers show comparatively few regional differences in their speech patterns.[20] Actors who play positive leading parts in soap operas and adventure stories will frequently use something close to an "educated standard," while secondary and negative characters will exploit local dialects to the full. Yet this process too has been continuing for some time, and radio announcers have long been instructed to "avoid regional peculiarities." What we need to explain is how certain features of English are gradually and implicitly defined as "regional peculiarities" while others become part of the "educated standard." Here too, the radio and television personnel are responding to larger social forces which they do not control.

We can see the process of long-term socially determined change in grammatical shifts which are rarely initiated by schools or mass media. The changing patterns in the use of *who* and *whom*, *I* and *me* are well known; Edward Sapir (1921) noted that these changes seem to be part of a long-term

---

[20] The many "conversation programs" on local radio stations in the past few years provide an excellent opportunity to observe this contrast. The broadcast interviewer in Boston, New York, or Philadelphia uses a general standard with very few regional characteristics, while his callers of various socioeconomic backgrounds are very much more local in their dialect forms.

drift in the function of oblique cases in English—a drift that we can observe and respond to but cannot explain at this time. We can note that the tag question to be added to *I'm here* is *aren't I*; this change has occurred in many areas where *ain't I* or *amn't I* were considered uncultivated and overcultivated, respectively. Here too, it is unlikely that the schoolroom is a moving force in the promotion of this irregularity in auxiliary relations. The sentence-adverbial suffix *-wise* appears to be gaining ground steadily despite the objections of authorities. In the Midwest, we find a steady increment in the use of the positive *We go there any more*, the opposite of *We don't go there any more*, without the endorsement of mass media or school books. Though there are many other examples which might be cited, it can be said in general that grammatical change is relatively slow, difficult to trace, and even more difficult to explain. Yet we cannot doubt that the process of grammatical change is as continuous and widespread as the sound changes which have been the focus of most dialect studies so far.

HOW LANGUAGE DIFFERENCES ARE LEARNED

It is commonly assumed that the complex patterns of multilingualism, style shifting, and social differentiation of language are fairly recent developments: that the basic model of the speech community is a monolingual group of single-style speakers who are only dimly aware that the dialect of the neighboring village is a little different than theirs. Recent sociolinguistic investigations in South Asia, West Africa, and the Amazon Basin show that such a simplified model is no more applicable to these areas than to western Europe. Multilingual situations are far more common than were once realized: whenever we study a community in detail, we are apt to find that competent speakers must command a complex repertory of styles. Bloomfield (1927) found to his surprise that the distinction between good and bad speakers was as strong among the Menominee as in literate American society. The extreme stratification of language in the Arabic world, termed *Diglossia* by Ferguson (1959), is not a product of literary culture; on the contrary, classical Arabic seems to stem from a formal poetic language which antedated the use of the Arabic script. Wherever we turn, we are forced to the conclusion that the child does not attain any full measure of linguistic competence in his early years: that the process of language learning is not completed until the speaker is fully adult.[21]

As the child matures, he comes under the influence of at least four

[21] "When we talk about the development of language, we are apt to think of a process, that, like learning to walk, is over and done by the time a youngster is 5 years old. All the evidence is against this attitude. Learning our language takes 15 or 20 years of full-time study and never really ceases [George Miller, *Language and Communication*, New York: McGraw-Hill, 1951, p. 154]."

successive social groups which shape his language and determine his linguistic competence and the complexity of his verbal repertoire: the family, the peer group, the school, and the job.

The Family

It is obvious that the child first learns to speak from the members of his family. Here we are concerned with the extent to which this primary influence remains as a permanent factor in the language of the adult. When parents from one dialect region move to another area and raise their children in a completely different dialect region, it is seldom that we can trace any permanent influence on their children's speech.[22] On the contrary, we find that children's speech resembles that of their peers in their own dialect area. Read's study of family words (1962) shows that certain lexical items associated with early childhood can be retained, but this contribution is hardly comparable to the massive contribution of the peer group.

The Peer Group

From a very early age, children begin to be affected by the language and habits of their friends. Studies of peer group interaction in urban areas (Labov, Cohen, & Robins, 1965) confirm a large body of anecdotal evidence that preadolescent and adolescent peer groups exert strong pressures for linguistic conformity. A great deal of the speech of such peer groups is organized into highly structured speech events, in which the speaker's performance is evaluated immediately by the group. To a very large extent, the child's family speech is remolded by the peer group; we do not know how thorough such a restructuring can be, but we do not have any principled reason to set any limits on the type of reorganization that may take place in preadolescent language.

Within the peer group, we find that there is a rich development of special vocabulary: taboo language, slang and argot, rhymes and rituals of varied sorts. Narrative skills are developed—skills in joke telling, various types of rhymes, chants and songs; all of these skills are differentially rewarded by the members of the group.

---

[22] If children's speech reflected their parents' dialects, we would not find any of the solid isoglosses which mark the regional boundaries of American speech. Whenever a family moved to a neighboring town, we would then find that the dialect of this area was diluted with the coming of the imported child, and the overall result of this mixing process would be no regional dialects at all.

The School

When a child enters school, he begins to learn a new style of careful speech to supplement the special style he may have occasionally used with visitors at home. He also learns a more formal style of pronunciation to be used in reading and a precise type of articulation to be used for reading individual words. In rapid succession, then, he develops a stylistic continuum which had been quite rudimentary in preschool years. Whether or not he manages to control the schoolroom pronunciation as well as the teacher would like, he does learn to recognize and evaluate this range of styles.

It is important to note that, in our society, this schoolroom development begins before the major influence of the peer group takes effect. Six-year-old children do not engage in spontaneous peer group activity in the way that 10-year-olds do, and the peer group does not exert the same tyrannical control over their language.

In school, the child also begins to recognize certain differences between the shapes of words as shown in spelling and the abstract representation which underlies his own vernacular. He may make certain adjustments in his own system to accommodate the spelling forms. For example, he may have an underlying form $//g\bar{o}s//$ with a plural $//g\bar{o}s+s//$ realized as [gous<del>i</del>z]; once he learns the plural *ghosts* and learns to say [gousts], he may reorganize his own grammar to provide an underlying singular $//g\bar{o}st//$, with an optional simplification of the consonant cluster to produce the vernacular plural or the full form to produce the schoolroom plural.

The school also provides the child with the Romance (Latinate, learned, literary, and scientific) vocabulary which allows him to adjust his phonological rules to fit the English corpus as a whole: whether or not this is done in any individual case is a question that we cannot answer at this time.

The school environment does more than provide speech patterns for the child: in school, he gradually becomes aware of an exterior standard of correctness—the existence of the norms of a larger speech community by which his speech will eventually be judged. Frequently, preadolescent children may be trained to shift styles regularly in careful and casual situations but without any understanding of the general social significance of this shift. Young children may know that one is supposed to say [ðɪs] and not [dɪs], *isn't* and not *ain't*, but they may have no idea of what kind of people do say [dɪs] and *ain't*. They are aware of the stylistic dimension of the variable but not of the social stratification implied. The results of subjective reaction tests indicate that children do not reach the level of adult knowledge in this respect until they are 18 or 19—though of course it should be understood that there is a considerable socioeconomic differential here in favor of the upper middle-class children (Labov, 1965).

The Job

A very regular type of social stratification of language may be found within the industrial complex, for it is by occupational rewards and penalties that society exerts the most direct control over linguistic behavior. In the Lower East Side study (Labov, 1966), it was found that the most regular stratification could be demonstrated by considering only those subjects who had worked actively on a job for some time; here the social significance of language differences is spelled out with the greatest clarity. There are, of course, other differentiating effects of specialized occupations: jargon and shop talk of various kinds. Salesmen or technicians who deal with customers of varied occupational background will show greater tolerance for non-standard English and will develop greater skill in style shifting than editorial assistants or school teachers. But our knowledge of the linguistic correlates of occupational roles must be based on meager anecdotal evidence or on lexical lists which have little social significance. This is an area where research is badly needed, since a great deal of language training in high school is based on assumptions about occupational needs which have never been demonstrated. The problem is even more acute for retraining programs such as the Job Corps: how much time should be spent in changing speech patterns of addressograph operators, IBM keypunchers, or typists? To answer this, we will have to know the unconscious subjective reactions of employers, personnel agents, and other administrators, as well as the ultimate effects upon job performance.

Superposed Varieties

The discussion of language differences in this chapter has been based upon a more complex model of linguistic structure than the discrete set of invariant units presented in introductory textbooks. To understand the task of language learning for a youth entering a complex urban society, we must introduce certain new concepts that are not usually represented in introductions to linguistic analysis.

We must deal with continuous variation and the concept of a linguistic variable as a part of the structure of a language (Labov, 1966c). We must take as our basic unit of analysis the speech community as a whole, rather than the artificially isolated idiolect of one individual speaking at one time. When we do consider the individual, we must view him in the process of acquiring a complex verbal repertoire (Gumperz, 1964), gradually gaining new linguistic competence as he enters into new social relations. While every speaker may be said to begin by learning a basic vernacular, we do not know to what extent this childhood vernacular is restructured by later experience. The sets of rules learned in the late teens and adult life, however, are in all likelihood learned in a different manner than earlier rules. It appears to be more difficult to acquire automatic motor control of linguistic forms in later life, and the role of audio monitoring becomes increasingly important.[23] Such superposed varieties are less stable, less regular in their internal structure than subsystems acquired in the preadolescent years. Language learning of later years is a process of acquiring greater control over these superposed varieties. Undoubtedly the process continues until the age when social controls are no longer as important in the life of the individual—when he can abandon the continual process of audio monitoring which is required of most working adults.

THE STRUCTURE OF LINGUISTIC VARIATION

We have presented here a broad view of systematic variation in language, in the light of recent studies of American English. Enough data are available to put together answers to the question "Why do native speakers of English differ in their use of the language?" This is an important question for teachers who must overcome the effects of this differentiation, as well as for linguists who must construct a theory to describe the English language as a whole, rather than a single variety of it. The question is most easily answered in terms of "how the difference came about":

a. A great many language differences are the results of discontinuities in communication. People from different regions who rarely speak to one another will maintain original linguistic differences and (see below) evolve new ones. Most of the dialect boundaries shown in Figure 5-3 are troughs in the flow of traffic—in a given day, fewer people travel across these lines than any other lines in the region. Discontinuities can also exist within a speech community—across ethnic lines or between the preadolescent and adult subcultures.

b. The fact of continuous language change is responsible for the maintenance and renewal of minor regional differences, as well as the gradual drift which results in the differentiation of entire languages. Language change also brings about the differentiation of age levels in a single speech community with a characteristic gradient which we can trace by quantitative means.

c. It is unusual to find systematic language differences among speakers of the same age level in the same community who are in continual contact

---

[23] By audio monitoring, we mean the feedback effect in which a person continually corrects his speech production by reference to an auditory standard. When white noise is used to mask a person's own speech, so that he cannot hear himself, there are serious disturbances in the speech production of most subjects. Some speakers show a shift in the direction of their childhood vernacular and are unable to maintain the superposed variety of articulation which they learned later in life.

with one another. (*a*) The regular patterns of stylistic and social stratification within a single community are the product of both linguistic and social factors operating on linguistic structure. (*b*) Socioeconomic stratification leads to differential familiarity and practice in the use of the overtly recognized norms for formal style. (*c*) At the same time, all speakers move toward or away from these normative patterns in various stylistic contexts, more or less according to the amount of attention given to speech. (*d*) The differentiation of prestige and nonprestige forms is reinforced by a covert set of values associated with casual and uneducated speech.

The structure of linguistic variation is governed by quantitative functions: that is, people can react to the frequency of certain forms rather than to the occurrence of a single form. They may perceive this quantitative range in categorical terms: beyond a certain frequency, a speaker is heard as "always" using a socially significant form. Such quantitative functions must take the form of a rule:

Category A is realized as Subcategory B (and not B′) in environment C with a frequency F, where F is a function of other linguistic or extralinguistic variables (sex, age, class, style, ethnic group).

In such cases, it is apparent that the realization of *A* as *B* or *B′* is not a cognitive difference: if a statement in which *B* occurs is true, the alternate form with *B′* is also true. These functions are interpreted as noncognitive affective components of meaning (Labov, 1966c). It is also apparent that variable functions of this sort must be involved in the process of linguistic change, for it is not conceivable that one set of constant categorical rules is instantly replaced with another set of such rules.

The question "why" can also be approached from the standpoint of "reason why" or "what adaptive function is served by" a given linguistic difference, but the answers to this question are much more obscure, as with most of the central problems of linguistic evolution. At the moment, we can proceed much further by concentrating upon the mechanism and structure of linguistic differentiation (Labov, 1966d). From the teacher's standpoint, we can address ourselves to the question, "Why do children insist on using language that they know is wrong?" There are several different answers which must be sharply distinguished:

1. Subcultural differences are usually older than the prestige forms, in the history of the language or of any one person. Some stigmatized forms were not stigmatized when they were learned; some of these are the most automatic patterns that a child brings to school. For example, the form *aks* as opposed to standard *ask*.

2. Other subcultural differences are developed after first contact with the standard language. They are valued and interpreted because they are different: part of their meaning lies in the stigma which the school places upon them. These differences may become stronger rather than weaker as

children reach late adolescence. Taboo words are the most obvious examples.

3. Some subcultural differences which are quite resistant to change are not endowed with any strong social value. They may be resistant because they are parts of more general rules which are not perceived or operated upon by the school system. Thus the dropping of final *t*'s may be part of a very general pattern of consonant cluster simplification or syllable final weakening. Attempts to teach the standard form will obviously be more effective when directed to the most general rule which differentiates the speakers.

This discussion of linguistic variation has outlined a number of ways in which the social process of communication controls the forms of language. The detailed study of this variation yields considerable insight into the internal structure of language, but this aspect has not been developed here. We have been concerned with the overall structure of the speech community and the ways in which differences within a single language affect the process of language learning. It is reasonable to believe that many educational problems can be attacked more successfully if teachers have a clear understanding of the types of language differences that they may encounter, the forces which maintain them, and the sources of resistance to the learning of the standard language.

REFERENCES

Atwood, E. B. *A survey of verb forms in the eastern United States. Studies in Amer. Eng. 2.* Ann Arbor: Univ. of Michigan Press, 1953.

Bailey, B. A proposal for the study of the grammar of Negro English in New York City. *Progress Literacy Reports 2.* Ithaca: Cornell Univ. Press, 1964. Pp. 19–22.

Barker, G. C. Social functions of language in a Mexican-American community. *Acta Americana*, 1947, **5**, 185–202.

Bernstein, B. Elaborated and restricted codes. In J. J. Gumperz & D. Hymes (Eds.), *The ethnography of communication. Am. Anthropologist*, 1964, **66**, No. 6, Part 2.

Bloomfield, L. Literate and illiterate speech. *Am. Speech*, 1927, **2**, 432–439.

Bloomfield, L. *Language.* New York: Holt, Rinehart & Winston, 1933.

Broadbent, D. E. Information processing in the nervous system. *Science*, 1965, **150**, 457–462.

Bronstein, A. *The phonetics of American English.* New York: Appleton-Century-Crofts, 1960.

Chomsky, N. Comments for project literacy meeting. *Project Literacy Reports 2.* Ithaca: Cornell Univ. Press, 1964. Pp. 1–9.

Chomsky, N. *Aspects of the theory of syntax.* Cambridge: M.I.T. Press, 1965.

Christian, J. M., & Christian, C. C., Jr. Spanish language and culture in the southwest. In J. A. Fishman, *Language loyalty in the United States.* The Hague: Mouton, 1966. Pp. 280–317.

Feinsilver, L. M. Yiddish idioms in American English. *Am. Speech*, 1962, **37**, 200–206.

Ferguson, C. A. Diglossia. *Word,* 1952, **15**, 325–340.

Ferguson, C. A. & Gumperz, J. J. (Eds.), *Linguistic diversity in south Asia: studies in regional, social and functional variation. Publ. 13 of Res. Center in Anthrop., Folklore, & Ling.* Bloomington: Indiana Univ. Press, 1960.

Fischer, J. L. Social influences on the choice of a linguistic variant. *Word,* 1958, **14**, 47–56.

Fishman, J. A. *Language loyalty in the United States.* The Hague: Mouton, 1966.

Glazer, N., & Moynihan, D. P. *Beyond the melting pot: the Negroes, Puerto Ricans, Jews, Italians, and Irish of New York City.* Cambridge: M.I.T. & Harvard Univ. Press, 1963.

Gumperz, J. J. Linguistic and social interaction in two communities. In J. J. Gumperz & D. Hymes (Eds.), *The ethnography of communication. Am. Anthropologist,* 1964, **66**, No. 6, Part 2.

Halle, M. Phonology in generative grammar. *Word,* 1962, **18**, 54–72.

Hockett, C. F. Age-grading and linguistic continuity. *Language,* 1950, **26**, 449–457.

Hubbell, A. F. "Curl" and "coil" in New York City. *Am. Speech,* 1940, **15**, 372–376.

Kenyon, J. Cultural levels and functional varieties of English. *Coll. Eng.,* 1948, **10**, 31–36. Reprinted in H. B. Allen (Ed.), *Readings in applied English linguistics.* (2nd ed.) New York: Appleton-Century-Crofts, 1964. Pp. 294–302.

Kurath, H. *A word geography of the eastern United States.* Ann Arbor: Univ. of Michigan Press, 1949.

Kurath, H., & McDavid, R. I., Jr. *The pronunciation of English in the Atlantic states.* Ann Arbor: Univ. of Michigan Press, 1961.

Labov, W. Stages in the acquisition of standard English. In Roger Shuy (Ed.), *Social dialects and language learning.* Champaign, Ill.: NCTE, 1964. Pp. 77–104.

Labov, W. *The social stratification of English in New York City.* Washington: Center for Applied Linguistics, 1966. (a)

Labov, W. Some sources of reading problems for Negro speakers of non-standard English. In A. Frazier (Ed.), *New directions in elementary English.* Champaign, Ill.: NCTE, 1966. Pp. 140–167. (b)

Labov, W. The linguistic variable as a structural unit. *Wash. Ling. Rev.,* 1966, **3**, 4–22. (c)

Labov, W. On the mechanism of linguistic change. *Georgetown Univ. Monogr. No. 18, Languages and Linguistics.* Washington, D.C.: Georgetown Univ., 1966. (d)

Labov, W., Cohen, P., & Robins, C. *A preliminary study of the structure of English used by Negro and Puerto Rican speakers in New York City. Final Report, Coop. Res. Project No.* 3091, Office of Education, U.S. Dept. of Health, Education, and Welfare, 1965.

Lane, H. The motor theory of speech perception: a critical review. *Psychol. Rev.,* 1965, **72**, 275–309.

Levine, L. & Crockett, H. J., Jr. Speech variation in a Piedmont community: postvocalic /r/. *Sociol. Inquiry,* 1966, **36**, 186–203.

Marckwardt, A. H. Principal and subsidiary dialect areas in the north-central states. *Publ. Amer. Dial. Soc.,* 1957, **27**, 3–15.

McDavid, R. I., Jr. Postvocalic /r/ in South Carolina: a social analysis. *Am. Speech,* 1948, **23**, 194–203.

McDavid, R. I., Jr., & Austin, W. M. Communication carriers to the culturally deprived. *Coop. Res. Project No.* 2107, 1966.

Read, A. W. Family words in English. *Am. Speech*, 1962, **37**, 5–12.

Sapir, E. *Language. An introduction to the study of speech.* New York: Harcourt, Brace & World, 1921. (Harvest Paperback, 1949).

Stewart, W. *Non-standard speech and the teaching of English.* Washington: Center for Applied Linguistics, 1964.

Weinreich, U. Notes on the Yiddish rise-fall intonation contour. In *For Roman Jakobson.* The Hague: Mouton, 1956. Pp. 633–643.

6

Second-Language Learning

JANE W. TORREY
Connecticut College

INTRODUCTION

The human being acquires his first language in a way that is fundamentally different from the way he learns reading, writing, and arithmetic. The latter skills are learned only by design and under conditions of special instruction. Without a teacher, lessons, and purposeful study, they are rarely acquired. By contrast, the ability to speak and understand a language might almost be called instinctive rather than learned behavior. All members of the species who are not grossly abnormal begin to talk at about the same early age. Although their environment must include other speaking people, there seems to be little else necessary in the way of special circumstances or instruction. All children follow a certain similar pattern of progress toward language, a pattern which is not fully known, much less imposed, by adults. On the other hand, there is no denying that language is "learned" in the sense that it is acquired by interaction with the environment. Children learn only the particular language or languages they hear and need to use. Furthermore, it is also possible for a child or adult to learn a language by way of special study, much as reading and writing are learned. Normally, this kind of learning occurs only in the case of additional languages learned after the first one has been acquired through "natural" means. The second language may be learned as well as, or even in some ways, better than the first. The purpose of this chapter is to describe what we know of the language learning process, particularly as it occurs in the very special case of learning a second language.

Many people in the world are forced to learn more than one language just in order to carry out the normal business of life in their own country, their own community, or even their own family. For others, the second language is foreign to their everday lives, but they want to be able, if necessary, to understand or communicate with people who speak it. For some, everyday life provides not only the need but also the means of learning additional languages. Some children seem to "pick up" a second language in the same way they learned their first. For others, only school or other special lessons can provide the means. The circumstances of special instruction include schools where all teaching is in the new language, elementary schools where the language is taught as a special subject, courses that are part of a high school or college curriculum, and courses that take full time for a period of weeks, as well as various forms of self-instruction. These circumstances of second-language learning are so different from one another and from first-language learning that we expect to find large differences in the learning processes.

On the other hand, the language being learned is much the same regardless of whether, for a given learner, it is his first or his second language and regardless of his method of learning. The goals of all language learning include the ability to produce original sentences that conform to the rules of the language, to express one's own meanings in those sentences, and by the same rules to understand other people's utterances in the language. This ability is what Chomsky (1965) has called linguistic "competence," to contrast it with the sheer behavior of uttering sentences. Such behavior could also be acquired by rote memorization of someone else's sentences and would not imply the competence to generate new ones, but the purpose of learning a language, whether it is the first language or the fifth, is to create sentences, not to repeat them.

The learner, too, while he changes over the years between learning his first and learning his second language, remains the same organism. At least, some of the capacities that go into learning one language are still present and govern the learning of a later one. Although maturation and previous knowledge have important effects on learning, it seems reasonable to suppose that the processes of learning the first and second languages will also be similar in important ways.

I have derived from the contemporary literature in psychology and linguistics ten basic propositions which have direct bearing on all language learning, second as well as first. The first three are psychological propositions, while the other seven deal directly with language. I will first state these propositions and then discuss the ways they apply to second-language learning.

Proposition I: Some aspects of learning capacity change with age. Age makes important differences in learners. The intellectual powers of the adolescent or adult are superior in many ways to those of a child of three. Children's memory span is limited to a few words or syllables at first, but it increases rapidly during the school years (Munn, 1964). Brown and Bellugi (1964) attribute several aspects of the grammar of a child's first sentences to the constraints on the length of an utterance imposed by the child's inability to plan ahead more than a very few words. An adult can hear and imitate a much longer series of items such as numbers or syllables. Ability to memorize verbal material, including nonsense syllables as well as connected discourse, also improves with age (Hovland, 1951).

Piaget (1923) has traced the development of thinking during the years immediately following the learning of the first language. The changes include a shift from dependence on vague intuitive analogy to more explicit analysis in terms that can be communicated to other people. Ausubel (1963) describes the trend in intellectual development as moving away from dependence upon concrete experience toward an ability to make use of abstractions. This means that the adult has a larger store of abstract concepts that can be used in classifying and understanding new experiences and a greater capacity to form new concepts to comprehend new meanings. It also means the adult can learn much more through the medium of words. He is able to learn by hearing and reading about things as well as by doing and seeing them.

On the other hand, it is obvious that adult techniques and capacities are not necessary to learn a language. A child learns one and learns it well between 18 months and 4 years of age. In fact, there is evidence that the brain of a child has capacities for language learning that do not exist in that of an adult. Lenneberg (1967) examines in detail our present information on language development in normal and retarded children and finds consistent relations between it and the anatomical and physiological development of the brain from birth through maturity. In addition, he reviews the capacities of persons of various ages to recover from aphasia due to brain injury and the typical course of that recovery. He concludes that there is a period of primary language acquisition beginning at about 15 months and continuing until puberty. During that period between the time when the brain has developed sufficiently for language learning to begin and the time it reaches its adult level of organization, the individual is able to learn the basic elements of a first language. He can also relearn to some extent language capacities he has lost through injury. After puberty, when by most biological criteria brain maturation is complete and laterality established, it is as though some essential kind of plasticity has been lost. The regaining of language abilities lost through injury does not resemble relearning but is more like a recovery from temporary inhibitions imposed by the injury upon a previously learned set of skills. Abilities not recovered in five months are permanently lost, and simple retraining is no longer useful.

Proposition II: The learning of one thing may influence the later learning of, something else. Interactions between the effects of old and new learning can be both facilitating and interfering, and it is difficult to state in any general way under what conditions transfer of training will be positive or negative or zero. Two dimensions that apply to language learning have shown some consistent effects: these are degrees of learning and the similarity of the two bodies of material learned.

The degree of interaction between materials learned at different times depends partly upon how well each is learned. If the first learning is carried to a high degree of perfection, it will interfere much less with later similar material being learned, perhaps because well-learned material is better discriminated by the subject (Gibson, 1942). It is also true almost by definition that as later learning is more complete, it will show less and less effect of earlier interfering habits.

When two sets of material to be learned are quite different or are easily discriminated by the learner, there is relatively little interaction, that is, learning one has little effect upon learning the other. If they are similar in such a way that the learning of one serves as partial learning of the other, there may be facilitation, or positive transfer. If, however, the similarities either of stimuli or responses are such that responses interfere with one another, then there will be greater interference as similarity increases (Osgood, 1953).

Proposition III: All behavior, including learning behavior, is guided by the purposes of the learner and evaluated by him in relation to his own goals. Any learning that requires effort will be strongly influenced by the learner's particular motives or purposes. These will determine not only how much energy he puts in but also on what specific exercises or material he works hardest. If he has no clear purpose in the learning, his effort will not last long. If the particular kind of study does not seem to him to be directed toward the kinds of knowledge or skills he wants to acquire, he will lose interest or devote most of his time and effort to certain selected aspects of the material.

Purposes also define success and therefore determine whether the learner will get satisfaction or reward from a given accomplishment. People set their own levels of aspiration according to what they desire and also according to what they judge to be possible. Appropriate effort does not continue unless this subjective goal is met. For effective learning to occur, the aspiration must be high enough for progress but low enough for success. The learner must have a realistic idea of what needs to be accomplished and some expectation that he can do it. He must also perceive himself as making adequate progress toward his particular goals, or his morale and effort will drop. This may occur even if, from someone else's point of view, he is learning a great deal. At the other extreme, the student sometimes sets himself too modest goals and thus feels satisfied while the teacher thinks he is failing.

Proposition IV: Language behavior is highly systematic, not a set of loosely related responses, associations, or concepts. It is important to understand that languages, all languages, are systems. Psychologically, they depend on highly integrated systems of skill and knowledge. Even the simplest sentences are the joint products of many parts of the system. Although a language course may be broken up into lessons, and lessons into vocabulary, grammar, drill, etc., none of the separate kinds of elements and no single rule is useful in and of itself outside its role in the system. An example of the interrelation of rules is the subsystem of gender in many languages. In one language, Russian, all nouns and adjectives and some verb forms manifest the gender system. A high proportion of grammatical summary material in any Russian textbook is related directly to gender. The system of case endings through which Russian sentences are structured is interwoven with the gender distinction in such a way that case could not be learned without reference to gender. At the same time, knowledge of the gender system is worthless for practical purposes without the case system, which in turn is unusable without knowledge of its place in sentence structure, particularly in relation to prepositions and verbs. In fact, it is difficult to select any grammatical rules that can be applied even in limited situations without a wealth of others. Many rules given separately in a text, for example, rules for agreement of adjective forms with nouns, are only elaborations of more general rules regarding gender.

In saying that a language is a system, I am not referring to all sets of "rules" that show up in any grammar book, but rather to those basic generative rules that Chomsky (1965) says underlie language competence. In his words:

A grammar of a language purports to be a description of the ideal speaker-hearer's intrinsic competence. If the grammar is, furthermore, perfectly explicit—in other words, if it does not rely on the intelligence of the understanding reader but rather provides an explicit analysis of his contribution—we may. . . call it a generative grammar [p. 4].

Chomsky goes on to say more explicitly how the total body of these rules is interrelated:

. . . a generative grammar must be a system of rules that can iterate to generate an indefinitely large number of structures. This system of rules can be analyzed into three major components of a generative grammar: the syntactic, phonological, and semantic components.

The syntactic component specifies an infinite set of abstract formal objects, each of which incorporates all information relevant to a single interpretation of a particular sentence.

The phonological component of a grammar determines the phonetic form of a sentence generated by the syntactic component to a phonetically represented signal. The semantic component determines the semantic interpretation of a sentence. That is, it relates a structure generated by the syntactic component to a certain semantic representation . . . [p. 15].

If we are to understand the process of language learning, we have no choice but to recognize the systematic nature of linguistic competence and to design a psychology of learning in which it is possible to explain the learning of such a system.

Corollary to Proposition IV: The single system that is a language may have many overt manifestations in performance, including producing speech, understanding spoken and written material, writing, translating, and other skills. Although the acquisition of various language skills is necessary to the learning of language, it would be a mistake to try to identify language competence as the sum of these behavioral skills. Mastery of the system of structural rules of language is a necessary condition to all linguistic skills, and the rules to be learned are much the same for spoken and written language. Everything a linguist has to say about the structure and rules of a language applies as much to listening as to speaking and much applies also to reading and writing. Carroll (1966) points out that " . . . there is such a large common element, in audio-lingual and traditional methods, . . . that one could not expect major differences in the results. The common element, of course, is the *language system being taught*, which is in most respects the same whether it is taught in its spoken or in its written aspects (pp. 14–15)."

On the other hand, we should not exaggerate the similarities, say, between reading and speaking. The rules of language connect with various kinds of behavior through subsystems in the rules themselves. Morphophonemic rules spell out the manifestations of the underlying structure in speech, other rules spell out the graphic representation of the same system, and so forth. Transfer between skills occurs because these subsets of rules operate on a common underlying system, but no transfer can occur if the individual has not had training in the other necessary subsets of rules. Thus, learning to speak will provide the greater part of the underlying structure necessary for writing skill, but if the learner has no knowledge of the writing system itself, obviously he cannot write.

Proposition V: Language learning is the acquisition of a set of rules that may generate any of an indefinite variety of specific linguistic performances. A language cannot be identified with any particular set of these performances. This statement recognizes Chomsky's distinction between competence and performance in a language. The set of rules we speak about is the generative grammar that describes competence. Chomsky (1959) speaks of grammar in this way:

. . . the construction of a grammar . . . merely characterizes abstractly the ability of one who has mastered the language to distinguish sentences from nonsentences, to understand new sentences . . . , to note certain ambiguities, etc. . . . We constantly read and hear new sequences of words, recognize them as sentences, and understand them. It is easy to show that the new events that we accept and understand as sentences are not related to those with which we are familiar by any simple notion of formal (or semantic or statistical) similarity or identity of grammatical frame. . . . It appears that we recognize a new item as a sentence not because it matches some familiar item in any simple way, but because it is generated by the grammar that each individual has somehow and in some form internalized. And we understand a new sentence, in part, because we are somehow capable of determining the process by which this sentence is derived in this grammar [p. 56].

If we could devise a grammar in which all the determiners of a given event (e.g., a word) preceded it in time, then we might be able to say that language behavior as such is learned, and that a procedure in which particular sentences or stimulus-response sequences are learned is a case of "language learning." Chomsky asserts that it is clearly not possible to devise such a grammar to account for sentences. A speaker must possess a set of linguistic rules such that the earlier parts of an utterance can be determined by plans for the parts that are to follow. A simple example in English is the sentence *Who are they?* where *are* takes the form it does because of the word *they* which follows it in the sentence. Therefore, *they* cannot be regarded as a stimulus which elicits *are* as a response. *Are* must occur because of some underlying plan for the sentence already existing in the speaker before *they* is said. Some nonsequential kind of underlying learned structure is also required to account for language that conforms to intended meanings other than stimulus objects present in the environment. In short, because language *behavior* is a sequence of events, whereas the rules and conditions that generate it are hierarchical, we must distinguish between behavior and the underlying competence.

This proposition is clearly inconsistent with a conditioning or stimulus-response model or any other purely behavioral model of learning language: language learning must be a matter of acquiring rules, not reflexes. We learn what the choices are, but not what particular responses to make. Such a concept of learning is not foreign to psychology. Tolman (1949) made a distinction between learning and performance in his theories about maze-running behavior of rats. He characterized what a rat learns as a set of dispositions, an ordered field of alternative responses, each with its expected consequences. He included in these dispositions not only potential responses but also dispositions to see and attend to certain kinds of stimulus patterns as well as expectations about them. It was necessary to conceive of learning some such hierarchy of potential responses as opposed to learning to perform any particular set of them, in order to account for the observed ability of a rat to generate any of a variety of responses according to the situation and needs of the moment. If chains of stimulus-response connections could not account for the flexibility and freedom even of a rat, it is not surprising to find them inadequate for language competence and intellectual activity in the human.

Proposition VI: The rules employed by the user of a language are not necessarily conscious. We have said that language learning is learning to behave according to rules. Yet, we are faced with the paradox that native speakers of a language usually do not consciously know these rules. Educated adults may know something about grammar, but their speech conforms to a different and much more elaborate system than any they can put into words. Children, of course, can rarely state any of the rules that describe their speech. On the other hand, second-language learners frequently know a lot of rules, yet they violate them in their actual speech (Delattre, 1947).

The question of what is meant by "consciousness" of rules is worth examining a little further, since so many people seem to think it has a bearing on the language learning process. There are several general conditions under which we are likely to expect or to speak of consciousness. First, things are commonly called "conscious" when they have been put into words. Verbalization is sometimes used as a criterion of consciousness. Second, the word *conscious* is also used in quite a different way to imply an integration or understanding of different experiences in the light of one another or in terms of some higher level abstraction. *I understand* implies *I see a relation.* Understanding, in the sense of integration, is more clearly described as the perception of a relation between things than as a verbal response. Even when no verbalization is possible, as when Köhler's (1925) apes appeared to reach "intelligent" solutions to problems, the intelligence usually was manifested when the animal suddenly brought one object into contact with another as though he had just *seen a relation between them.*

Still another psychological property of matters we call conscious is that they attract attention or interest. We attend especially to things which are novel, unexpected, or baffling. However, we do not long remain attentive to things that are completely baffling, or meaningless, but only to those for which understanding seems possible or necessary. Interest or attention is continued until some understanding is achieved. We consciously attend to things we understand partially and are motivated to understand better. Thus, people tend to be interested in things about which they know *something* but not everything, or which for some extrinsic reason, they need to understand. *Interest* is another term for a felt need to comprehend. A corollary to the last point is that conscious attention is a characteristic of adaption to a new situation or of an attempt to solve a problem. The early stages of any learning process are apt to demand attention and concentration.

These comments on the psychology of consciousness treat it not only as a natural phenomenon likely to arise in certain characteristic situations, but also as an adaptive tool, a means to the end of understanding the system. These two aspects are linked through the assumption of a motive to understand, or a natural disposition to look for a system in what is learned. Our Proposition VII states this semimotive more explicitly for the case of language.

Proposition VII: The learner of a language, regardless of his age, brings with him to the task certain predispositions which direct the process of his learning. If language is a system, then learning a language is partly a problem-solving task, a task of figuring out the system. It is plausible that at least some of what the learner is doing is testing various hypotheses (sometimes with the help of lessons) about how the system works in practice. This means that to understand the learning of a language we must know what kind of strategy the learner is likely to employ in figuring it out. How does he use the corpus of material presented to form hypotheses? What kinds of hypotheses is he likely to try? What kinds of evidence will he or can he use to test them?

In fact, we know very little about the strategy and expectations of the language learner. Chomsky (1965) argues that they must be much more specific to language systems than any present learning theory implies, but he does not attempt to describe them.

A consideration of the character of the grammar that is acquired, the degenerate quality and narrowly limited extent of the available data, the striking uniformity of the resulting grammars, and their independence of intelligence, motivation, and emotional state, over wide ranges of variation, leaves little hope that much of the structure of the language can be learned by an organism initially uniformed as to its general character.

. It is, for the present, impossible to formulate an assumption about initial, innate structure rich enough to account for the fact that grammatical knowledge is attained on the basis of evidence available to the learner. . . . The real problem is that of developing a hypothesis about initial structure that is sufficiently rich to account for acquisition of language, yet not so rich as to be inconsistent with the known diversity of language [p. 58].

Evidence we do have from children indicates that they come into the language learning situation predisposed to find some system and that they proceed to discover its particular manifestations in a given language step by step according to a predictable plan whose features are only beginning to emerge from research (Lenneberg, 1964; McNeill, 1966; Braine, 1963; Brown & Bellugi, 1964). Lest the word *predisposed* seem to imply magical predestination on the part of Mother Nature, we should remember that language is a human product, created by generations of organisms closely related biologically to today's children. If the system itself is readily solved by human beings following their own natural tendencies, no one should be surprised.

Proposition VIII: Learning a language is learning to understand and to be understood by other speakers of that language. It is much more than a commonplace for the language teacher that language is communication. This fact is central in understanding the learning process, not mere background in a process directed primarily at the learning of structure. Although linguistic analysis can proceed very far on a purely descriptive basis without reference to meanings, it is probably not possible psychologically to learn a language first and then, after the learning is complete, go out and make use of it to speak and understand.

When we speak, we select, slightly in advance, the words and grammatical constructions we are going to use. The selection is made on the basis of what we want to express or communicate. Although the structure of the system itself is a necessary part of the equipment for communication, it is hardly something that can be learned apart from the meanings it will convey. The intimate relation between the elements of structure and the meanings they represent is as much a part of what must be learned as the structure itself.

It is important also to recognize that "meaning," as we are loosely speaking of it here, is a complex and various concept. It covers such things as associative connections and internal emotional responses, which together make up much of what we usually call *connotation*. It also covers referential meaning, most obvious in the case of naming objects present in the perceptual field. However, meaning also includes linguistic representation in words, morphemes, or grammatical structures of a great many very abstract concepts and relations which cannot be associated with or conveyed by any particular stimulus pattern or by any pattern of peripheral response, visceral or otherwise. Among these are cause (because), contingency (if, then), time sequence (before, after), moral judgments (evil, ought), and many others.

Proposition IX: Learning a language is accepting a culture and therefore, in some degree, a personal identity. Culture is used here in the broad sense, as it is used in the social sciences. It includes culture with a capital *C*, the literature and thought of a nation, but it also includes all of the attitudes, mores, religion, and folk arts, whether of high or low status, that are characteristic of speakers of a language. Although it might be possible theoretically to learn a language outside its cultural context, it would require a considerable tour de force since all of the native speakers are members of the cultural group, most of the available written or spoken material in a language bears the stamp of the culture associated with it, and furthermore, most people learn a language because they want to have contact with people who belong to a culture.

The significance of the cultural aspect of language for the learning process comes partly through the fact that a learner's attitudes strongly influence his learning. Not only does a positive or negative attitude toward something being learned increase or decrease effort given to the subject as a whole, but also the pattern of specific conflicts between the learner's attitudes and those he is exposed to creates some distortion in the content of what is learned. Levine and Murphy (1943) showed that in learning controversial material, the effect of attitudes was specifically related to the detailed content, producing predictable selection and change in recall.

The relation of language to a particular culture means that an individual's strongest and most intimate attitudes are involved in its study. This involvement is more intimate than in other subject matter learning because the ego is so directly involved in language behavior. Haugen (1965b) points out that "Language is not just something we know and make use of. It is something we do. In doing it, we are performing, playing a role which is part of ourselves. It gives expression to our identity (p. 86)." It is difficult, therefore, to stand apart from one's own speech and take an objective view of it. To adopt a language pattern is to adopt a particular kind of personality associated with its culture. Thompson (1966) expresses the connection between language, culture, and personal identity as follows:

Culture largely determines how an individual views his world. It influences the way he thinks and how he expresses this thought. Language is the expression of culture; thus one cannot acquire fluency in language without acquiring some understanding of the culture which that language expresses.

Language is both the property of the group and the property of the individual. Language as group property sets the group apart from other groups and provides the medium for transmission of group beliefs, traditions, and values. Language becomes the personal property of the individual when he has learned it and can use it to communicate his thoughts and feelings to other individuals.

There is nothing more personal than one's language, or his culture. Any attempt from the outside to destroy either his language or his culture strikes deep at the inner core of personality [p. 27].

Proposition X: Language is a tool of thought. The relation between language and thought is so close that some, including early behaviorists, have even tried to maintain that they are identical. However, most psychologists today would agree that the two cannot be considered the same, but that they influence one another directly. Vygotsky and Whorf are two thinkers who have tried to spell out this relationship.

Vygotsky (1962) was convinced that the learning of words played an important role in a child's development of concepts.

Our investigation has shown that a concept is formed, not through the interplay of associations, but through an intellectual operation in which all the elementary mental functions participate in a specific combination. This operation is guided by the use of words as the means of actively centering attention, of abstracting certain traits, synthesizing them, and symbolizing them by a sign [p. 81].

Besides Vygotsky's own studies of concept formation, examples of research tending to support his view include studies of the influence of language on children's ability to follow instructions and on adults' ability to recall shapes. Lyublinskaya (Luria, 1960, p. 11) showed that children under 2 years old could learn to select a red rather than a green object much faster if the colors were named. Carmichael, Hogan, and Walter (1932) showed that names given to abstract drawings influence a subject's reproduction of the drawing at a later time.

Whorf's hypothesis (1940), that thought is molded by the structure of the thinker's language, has found limited support. One study by Brown and Lenneberg (1958) showed people better able to recognize colors for which they were able to give commonly accepted names. Lenneberg (1967) concludes that although nonlanguage factors in discrimination of physical stimuli are frequently more important, there is evidence for effects of language in organizing the more complex and less stimulus-dependent cognitive functions. In other words, as thinking becomes more abstract, it becomes more intimately dependent upon words.

IMPLICATIONS FOR LANGUAGE LEARNING AND TEACHING

The foregoing propositions were designed to be relevant to language learning in general. Their implications for second-language learning require separate discussion to point out the difference between the second and the first language and the possible implications for methods of teaching. Out of the variety of ages, purposes, and circumstances for learning a second language, I have selected two which I think are important in themselves and at the same time representative of most of the issues. First, there is the case of the adult or adolescent learning a foreign language, a language not widely spoken in his country and belonging to a culture of which he is not primarily a member. The second case is the child who must learn a second language when he enters school because he needs it in order to get an education or to function in his own society at home. Both these cases are different from the first language process but also from each other.

In discussing the relevance of the propositions to these situations of second-language learning, I would like to begin with two cautions. First, it is a long way from an abstract principle of learning to its application in any particular situation, especially to its use in teaching or designing lessons. A principle, while true in general, may not apply to every situation in the way that first seems obvious. Also, two valid principles may conflict in their implications for any given teaching policy. For example, the principle of biological readiness suggests that a child should start a new language as young as possible, but the relation of language to self-identity implies that too early and abrupt imposition of a foreign language may threaten development of self-confidence. Also, a drill that advances one skill may rigidify another. The question of how and to what extent a principle should be used is one for applied research in realistic situations. Principles are needed to guide the useful exploration of methods, but we cannot expect to derive the ideal teaching method directly from even the best set of learning principles.

My second caution is that nothing in what follows should be taken as endorsement or condemnation in toto of any of the numerous approaches that have been suggested to language teaching. Fashions change rapidly in theories of how languages should be taught, and the history of them repeats itself. Direct methods, pattern drills, audiolingual techniques, linguistic techniques of various other kinds, and even grammar-translation methods are all in use, and all have their partisans. It is possible to use one or another learning principle to support any of them, and people have learned languages well through all of them. This is not to say, of course, that they are all equally good for all purposes. The role of learning principles is not to decide between techniques but to show what effects each one may be expected to have either in advancing or in retarding progress toward mastery of a particular language skill. It is the language teacher's role to decide which are best in the circumstances.

The Adult Learner of a Foreign Language

I will first discuss the implications of the propositions for the adult learner of a foreign language. The reader should keep in mind that this discussion is for the present *exclusively* about the adult (or adolescent) learning the language of a different country or a different culture from his own through more or less formal lessons. Afterwards, I will take up separately those propositions that have special implications for the case of the child who has a different language background from that of his school.

Proposition I: Some aspects of learning capacity change with age. The fact that young children learn one or more languages without elaborate training or obvious studying has led many to the plausible conclusion that children learn languages much more easily than adults. However, in trying to summarize the psychological knowledge of the relation between age and learning capacity, we found that some of the facts imply that adults should have an advantage. Insofar as imitating a native speaker is concerned, the adult, with a markedly longer memory span, can recall and repeat longer sequences of sounds, syllables, and words. A child is forced by his own limited memory span to omit part of what he imitates and thus perhaps distort the sentence pattern. The adult also has the better long-term memorizing ability, an advantage in memorizing patterns, dialogues, or other lesson material.

Since words usually represent abstract concepts rather than concrete objects, a child, with fewer concepts already formed and greater dependence on concrete experience to form them, has fewer intellectual tools with which to grasp word meanings or the implications of grammatical structures. The adult frequently already understands many of the necessary concepts. Thus, he has a framework in which to classify the new material, an aid both in remembering and in understanding. Ausubel (1964) points out that because of his more sophisticated concept of language structure, the adult also more readily seeks and finds explicit formulations of grammatical rules. The child relies mostly upon intuition and analogy, a simple and direct but not necessarily more effective way to master sentence structure (McKinnon, 1965).

As for the biological superiority of the child's brain for learning languages, we have little information about the specific abilities it includes. It is widely agreed that children imitate speech sounds more accurately than adults and are more likely to learn to speak like a native in the second language. They seem to lose this flexibility, and at the same time develop a peculiar embarrassment about imitating foreigners some time around the age of 12. The coincidence of this change with the time of physical maturation of the brain suggests that acquiring the sound system of a language belongs among the primary language abilities which Lenneberg (1967) concludes are possible only during the extended "critical period" for language learning from 15 months to puberty. It is obvious, however, from the fact that people continue to be able to learn new languages and learn them effectively (except for the accent) long after puberty, that many essential language learning capacities are still present. The physiological evidence alone, then, does not justify any sweeping conclusion that any given age is too late to learn a language.

Proposition II: The learning of one thing may influence the later learning of something else. Psychologists have studied interference primarily in the realm of specific learned responses to stimuli, verbal or otherwise. Many aspects of language learning, on the other hand, are very difficult if not impossible to analyze into specific responses, and even where it is possible, the responses are various and on many different levels. There are, for example, the skills of recognizing and making sounds, of morphological composition of words, of syntax, and of matching words with concepts. Degrees of learning and degrees of similarity would have to be examined in terms of specific comparisons within all of these fields, and predictions of facilitation or interference would differ with the specific instances rather than with the general category of responses. For this reason, I will merely try to cite observed patterns of interference between languages and indicate some possible implications for learning techniques.

Vildomec (1963) has surveyed at length the experiences of many multilingual Europeans and summarized the kinds of interference they find. Interferences with the well-learned native language from foreign languages learned later are very few and mostly confined to more or less conscious use of separate foreign words. Effects of the native tongue on other languages, presumably less well learned, are more common. These effects are not randomly spread over all skills, however, but tend to be in what Vildomec calls the "inner form of speech" including mainly syntax, intonation patterns, and pronunciation. Interferences also occur when the concepts referred to in the different languages are overlapping but not identical. Thus, when content words in different languages are confused, it is usually attributable to confusion of their meanings. Confusions of the less meaningful elements of language such as sounds and empty function words are much more frequent than word confusions. Vildomec suggests two quite different interpretations of this selective pattern of interference. One is that of parsimony of effort. There is a tendency to use familiar sounds, intonations, and grammatical structures, and in the case of content words, to use familiar meanings whenever possible. His other interpretation is that content words are perceived as a kind of "figure" on the "ground" of sounds, function words, and syntax. The figure elements dominate while the ground elements are more readily confused, presumably because the speaker gives them less conscious attention as he uses them. Possibly this figure-ground notion would also explain why there is little interference between the bound morphemes of two languages. Morphology, being part of the structure of the figure words themselves, resists being broken by elements from another morphological system.

Vildomec also observes that reported confusions between languages are almost all on the expressive (or "response") side. People rarely report intrusion of elements of their native language in their understanding of foreign language material. He points out that this failure to observe intrusions may be partly due to the difficulty of detecting them. He also cautions against interpreting as interference, errors that stem either from the intrinsic difficulty of some material, e.g., sounds that are genuinely difficult to make, or from the fact that the speaker simply does not know the necessary elements of the new language and is forced to fall back upon his native patterns.

Vildomec's findings illustrate some of the same factors as those found by psychologists. Interferences depend partly on the degree of learning in that native languages suffer less than those learned later, and errors are greater in incompletely learned material. Similarity of languages is also a factor, being an aid, he reports, in the early stages, and a source of confusion as learning becomes more complete.

Turning to implications for teaching, the question of the amount and kind of translation that is desirable in language lessons is largely one of potential facilitation or interference, because translation between the native language and the foreign language being learned brings the corresponding meaningful elements of the two languages into close association. Translation is, of course, a versatile tool for conveying meanings. To the extent that words and phrases in the two languages refer to similar ideas, the adult learner has a valuable shortcut to abstract meanings which may be difficult or impossible to express in any other way. If there are many cognate morphemes, the learner may have a large headstart on vocabulary. On the other hand, where cognates have different meanings or where words in the new language have meanings that cut across those of the native language, the transfer from one to the other may be negative. The merit of the particular use of translation depends upon each specific instance, whether for a particular structure there is more to be gained or lost by translation. Slobin (1961) generally opposes translation in the interests of developing coordinate bilingualism, where meanings expressed in one language are kept separate and not confused by associations with the other, but he points out that it may not be harmful where the material really is translatable. He believes sentence structure and function words, however, must be taught by the direct method. (In considering translation, of course, there are other questions beside those of facilitation and interference. A habit of translation may be developed so that the learner always has to think of a native expression to understand or say anything. This can be a crippling handicap in the use of language. On the other hand, skill in translating may be one of the learner's goals in study.)

Negative transfer in syntax is a major problem. Pattern drills of all kinds are aimed at overcoming interference from the syntactical habits of the native language. Contrastive analysis of the two languages is a means of selecting the structures most subject to interference and suggesting relevant drills and perhaps explicit rules. It may also help save effort by pointing out where native structures can facilitate new learning when correspondence is close. It is worthwhile to point out, however, that the points of contrast between a native and foreign language are probably never enough in themselves to serve as a basis of a set of lessons. The proposition that a language is a self-contained system implies that the contrastive analysis is an auxiliary help but not a basis for a framework of language lessons.

Proposition III: All behavior, including learning behavior, is guided by the purposes of the learner and evaluated by him in relation to his own goals. The purposes and motives of an adult in learning a new language are sharply different from those of a child learning his first language, both in degree and kind. The child, learning his first and only language, has much greater need to learn. He has no adequate alternative means of communicating his needs, his wishes, and his love to those around him. And he is able, as he does learn, to get tremendously greater satisfaction from each step of the process because it brings him closer to those very individuals who are supremely important in his young life. In contrast, the motivation of the foreign language learner is usually pale indeed. He has a better means of communicating already available for most of his purposes, and the people to whom he can talk in his new language are usually of small importance in his life compared with that of a mother to her 3-year-old. Furthermore, the topics about which he talks in the new language are much less important to him; in fact, they sometimes have hardly any personal importance at all.

The motivation of the foreign language learner is frequently "instrumental" rather than "integrative" (Lambert, 1967); that is, he has an immediate and quite well-defined use for the language skills he aims at, and in many cases, he has no particular desire to integrate a new cultural orientation into his personality. He may wish only to be able to read or decipher limited written material. If he wants a speaking knowledge, he may need only to make himself understood on simple matters, a goal which would not necessarily include complete command of all grammatical forms or a very large vocabulary. Even an easy speaking knowledge is still far short of speaking like a native. Subtle scientific or artistic writing is only rarely intended by a learner of a foreign language. Even a serious student of a foreign culture whose goals include some degree of integration with its ways and thought commonly does not intend to mold his entire self-identity in its image, as a young child will do. Thus, the foreign language learner usually aims lower than would be expected of the native speaker with the same degree of education.

An important implication of the variety of purposes for learning languages is that the teacher must give the student a realistic understanding of what may be accomplished in a reasonable period of time and reach agreement with him about the specific goals of the course. For example, if the student regards reading as the main criterion of mastery, he feels frustrated if he does not make enough progress toward understanding novels or scientific articles and gets no compensating sense of accomplishment even if he does improve his understanding of speech. On the other hand, if he wants and expects to be able to converse in the language, reading will not satisfy him no matter how well he succeeds in it. Success is always evaluated in terms of an individual's aspiration for his particular goals, and failure means not going far enough in the direction he wants to go. Motivation for each step in a language learning sequence depends upon a person's own estimate of his success at the last step. The initial orientation to a beginning course can help give students a realistic idea of the time needed and prevent the disillusionment that comes with finding out only after two or three years of study that fluent speech is not after all so easy to acquire. Orientation may also help to raise the aspiration of some students who would otherwise not aim high enough. Rivers (1964) reports that students in language courses sometimes are quite satisfied merely to be in the course and get a passing grade. If they could be persuaded to want some specific skills, their motivation would be higher and better directed.

Proposition IV: Language behavior is highly systematic, not a set of loosely related responses, associations, or concepts. The proposition that language is a system suggests the possibility that if the system were thoroughly and explicitly known, more effective lessons could be designed that would take it into account, either by teaching it directly or by ordering experiences so as to allow its ready induction. For practical purposes at the present time, of course, we do not have a complete or nearly complete generative grammar of any language, so the question of using it as an overall design is academic. Furthermore, it would be only an indirect step from a logically complete system to the ideal pedagogical sequence. The steps in making a sound mathematical proof are not always the best steps for teaching it. Transformational grammars, for example, seem to suggest quite promising ways for formulating lessons, but applied research is necessary to determine exactly what orders of lessons or methods of drill are useful.

Some applications of the ideas of generative grammar in pedagogy have been proposed or tried in the case of native language instruction. Thomas (1965) suggests that beginning readers should be written in grammatical structures that conform to realistic contemporary speech, so that children would be able to perceive more readily the structure of their own language. He reflects here the belief of many transformationalists that grammar is basically learned by inference, within a predetermined framework of hypotheses. Bateman and Zidonis (1966) report some success in the use of actual instruction in transformational grammar as a basis for instruction in writing the native language.

As for instruction in a new language, it is to be expected that the insights of generative grammar will be applied, but it is important to keep in mind that one of these insights is that systematic grammars may not be useful bases for lesson plans. A child's "corpus" of linguistic experience, from which he puts together his first language competence, is quite unsystematic with respect to grammatical system. Not only does he hear many fragments and "sentences" constructed in apparent violation of the rules, he also gets a nearly random hodgepodge of well-formed sentences from the spoken language. Fodor (1966) suggests that the normal way a child acquires competence may be by putting together a large variety of grammatical material and drawing appropriate inferences. After identifying certain surface patterns by substitution and classification, he perceives through them some abstract base structures that conform to a small number of possible rules. Each tentative rule must be tested against further experience with surface patterns and against other such rules to extract out the total system of maximum simplicity. Fodor argues that this process of perceiving abstract base structures could occur only if a child were intrinsically disposed to organize his perceptual world in certain ways and not others. It would follow that the organization of the learning process is determined primarily from within by these predispositions. In this situation, a random exposure to well-formed sentences of the language would be the most appropriate input or lesson. Any attempt at systematic selection might distort the results of selection and revision of the rules.

It is not impossible that an adult learns a foreign language by a similar largely inductive method and that what he therefore needs is a various and fairly random experience with the structures of the language. However, it would be premature at this time to conclude that language lessons either should or should not be based upon transformational grammars. As Chomsky (1966) has pointed out, this is a question for language teachers, not for linguists or psychologists.

Corollary to Proposition IV: The single system that is a language may have many overt manifestations in performance, including producing speech, understanding spoken and written material, writing, translating, and other skills. Although language itself is an element common to the skills of pronouncing, reading, translating, and so forth, it is not identical with them. The component skills each require separate training. Printed materials cannot replace spoken samples entirely, and writing cannot entirely replace speaking for practice. What an individual can do with writing he is not necessarily able to do with the spoken word and vice versa. The transfer from one to the other is not complete either way. It has been a belief of many who have promoted audiolingual methods that speaking is more basic than the other skills in the sense that it produces greater transfer. Scherer and Wertheimer (1964) cast this particular proposition in serious doubt when they showed that training in any one skill was more beneficial for that skill than for others. People who had emphasized reading in their early training read better than those who had emphasized speaking, and those more exposed to speech training spoke better.

One reason why transfer from speaking to reading is not quite automatic after the intial sound-symbol connections have been learned is that a skilled reader does not read one letter at a time but looks at a whole word or phrase. Especially when a largely new alphabet is being learned, there is, for some at least, a considerable time between development of the ability to recognize each letter and pronounce the sound it represents and the time when a long word or a phrase can be read at a glance. Although reading is undoubtedly advanced as vocabulary and grammatical competence develop, purely visual recognition skills remain to be practiced as such.

It almost goes without saying that speaking skills require special practice. Sheer motor practice in pronunciation is necessary, and apparently phoneme discrimination training is also an aid in speech production. Similarly, more specialized skills such as writing and translating have their special demands not necessarily learned while practicing something else.

The development of each particular skill of language use includes more than simple acquisition of the necessary responses and associations. It is well known to the learning psychologist (Woodworth & Schlosberg, 1955) that after a response has been reliably learned, its latency, or the time it takes, can still be considerably reduced. Since all language skills require considerable speed or fluency to be useful, prolonged practice is always necessary. Short latency is especially important in understanding the spoken word, where much greater speed is required than in reading, writing, or speaking. The listener must not only recognize sounds, words, and syntactic structures but must do so at a very fast rate over which the speaker, not he, has control. He must also usually fill in mumbled or omitted sounds and reconstruct sentences stopped in the middle or begun half way through. It is not clear whether practice at high speeds is a necessary feature of training for fluency.

It may well be that what is needed to reduce latency or processing time is simply more and more practice to gain a thorough command of rules and wider vocabulary. It is not speed as such that primarily needs practice, but the rule mastery that makes it possible.

The variety of language skills provides a basis for some negative transfer, already mentioned under Proposition II. These skills not only compete for the learner's time and effort, but also introduce substitute responses that may inhibit the appropriate ones for a given purpose. Learning to write a foreign language in a familiar alphabet, for example, introduces a special set of interferences from previous learning of the sound-symbol relationships in the native language. Similarly, the overuse of translation inhibits direct understanding and production. The audiolingual and direct methods in language teaching have been motivated partly by the desire to avoid the interferences of written material and of translation.

On the other hand, the separate skills reinforce one another in various ways also. Although it is possible to develop considerable useful skill in reading a foreign language without being able to speak and understand speech, given a certain minimum of audiolingual skill, reading can contribute materially to speaking ability by development of vocabulary and grammatical knowledge. The use of written material expands the possibilities of practice as well as content. Rivers (1964) mentions other advantages of written presentation, such as aiding in understanding and differentiating the new sound system, especially for students with poor auditory discrimination. For some learners, writing may be a great aid to memory not only because it provides a means of keeping records readily available, but also because some people seem to learn better through visual means. In short, the same abstract competence underlies all the separate skills of language use and accounts for the positive transfer between them, but at the same time, the subsystems of rules relating to each are different enough to require considerable special practice and some attention to avoid interference.

Proposition V: Language learning is the acquisition of a set of rules that may generate any of an indefinite variety of special linguistic performances. A language cannot be identified with any particular set of these performances. The implication of this assertion for the learning process is that the learner must in some sense discern the system in order to be able to use it. Although he may memorize actual sentences or drill on patterns which are sequences of particular form classes, he does not do this in order to be able to say just those things again or even to produce sentences in exactly those patterns. The ability he aims to acquire is that of saying what he wants to say regardless of whether he has heard it or said it before.

In this sense, a language is never identical with the content of any particular course or individual experience. It is not the sum of words or sentences or patterns practiced, no matter how complete the training. The function of the sentences read, heard, and produced by the learner is not to be learned as such but somehow to create in him the ability to compose his own sentences according to the same linguistic system. The relation of language lesson material to language learning is much like the relation between examples of a principle and understanding the principle as described by Katona (1940): "We do not learn the examples; we learn by examples. The material of learning is not necessarily the object of learning: it may serve as a clue to the general principle or an integrated knowledge [p. 125]."

Although language learning is a kind of habit formation, the habits are not primarily habits of behavior in the sense of particular verbal or sound sequences. They are not habits of saying any particular sentences or sentences that resemble those learned along any directly observable stimulus or response dimensions. The rules to be learned cannot be described in terms of easily observable characteristics (Chomsky, 1965). What is to be acquired is a highly abstract system somehow derived from the lesson material. It is only through acquisition of this system that the necessary "generalization" from the learned material can take place. When these rules are adopted, they may happen to generate these same sentences again now and then. Primarily, however, they generate new and different sentences, whose particulars are determined partly by the needs of the situation in which they are used.

In fact, it should also be pointed out that too much overlearning of rote materials may actually interfere with effective language use. Rivers (1964) quotes Tolman to the effect that "continued practice after a response has been learned tends to fixate this particular response, making it harder for the individual to vary it on future occasions [p. 66]." She goes on to conclude that "whereas repetition is useful in establishing a response, 'overlearning' can fixate stereotyped responses and reduce the student's ability to select among possible alternatives [p. 67]." If drills are based upon the assumption that learning language is the learning of a particular set of sentences of linguistic performances, they might teach him to say a great deal in the language without effectively teaching him the system. This is the situation of the learner who has memorized many dialogues but is unable to carry on a conversation. Without commanding the system of rules, he is not able to use the language for his own expression and understanding.

For the language teacher, the present proposition is more a caution than an instruction. It says that mimicry and memorization are means to an end, not an end in themselves. It does not say how the rules shall be taught. To the student, it is a challenge that he must do more than learn his lesson materials; he must also figure out how to use them.

Proposition VI: The rules employed by the user of a language are not necessarily conscious. Since consciousness is a condition related to verbalization, understanding, attention, and adaptation, we would expect to find at least some degree of consciousness of rules developing in the second-language learner. The student sometimes has language rules stated for him in his lessons, and other times he explicitly formulates them for himself. In this sense, he is conscious of them. However, as Politzer (1960), Brooks (1964), Delattre (1947), and others have pointed out, knowing a rule in this sense is not the same as being able to speak rapidly and understand in accordance with the rule. The question is whether such explicit grammatical knowledge is helpful in developing the ability to use the language. Even if conscious knowledge cannot substitute for the skill, it seems reasonable to suppose that verbal formulation may help to organize the linguistic system in the mind of the learner. Although it is possible for him to infer the rule for himself, this may be a laborious process, and for some would-be learners it might never take place. Katona (1940) has shown that explicit instruction in a system promotes easy learning and long recall of organized material. Although his tasks were not automatic skills like a well-learned language, they resembled the very initial stages of learning to speak and understand patterns. In the field of language proper, McKinnon (1965) also found that explicit statement of rules facilitated the construction of grammatical sentences to conform to pictured situations.

On the other hand, the explicit stating of grammatical rules has its dangers. Most important is the danger that the learner will mistake his ability to repeat the rules for the ability to use them in producing and understanding, or that he will think that because he repeatedly applies a rule after some conscious thought in written exercise, he is necessarily making progress toward automatic practical use of the rule. Delattre's (1947) belief that explicit rules are a hindrance is based upon the fact that some learners never seem to progress from the intellectual use of the rule to the habitual unconscious use. Yet, in McKinnon's (1965) case, and also in an experiment of mine (Torrey, 1966), it has been shown possible to move from intellectual knowledge to faster automatic production through appropriate drills. Carroll (1966) concludes that "learning of grammar in foreign languages occurs through some sort of internalized process that at least at some stage is guided consciously [p. 36]."

The conflict between our assertion that conscious knowledge of rules ought to help in language learning and the empirical impression that they are frequently worse than useless deserves more attention. A possible solution to this difficulty lies in the fact that native speakers, including teachers, hold beliefs and make statements about their grammar that are incomplete, misleading, or simply wrong. At least some of the explicitly stated rules to which students have been exposed are themselves inadequate. They are not the rules we have been speaking of as the substance of language. A few examples from a fairly typical grammar textbook of its time (Turgeon, 1947) will serve to make the point. Turgeon states the following grammatical rule: "There are two forms for the singular indefinite article in French, *un* used before masculine nouns, and *une* used before feminine nouns [p. 17]."

Although the rule seems to be stating the conditions under which each form of the article is to be used, it is in fact not useful for this purpose because it gives no rule for determining the gender of the nouns. In fact, there is no rule known that will in every case correctly specify gender, i.e., choice of article. It should surprise no one, therefore, that learning this rule does not produce correct usage on the part of students.

Another reason why an explicit rule may be inadequate is that it may be misstated or badly explained. An illustration from the same text: "The definite article is used before a noun indicating a general class of things, where in English it is omitted. . . . *J'aime les gants, les chapeaux, et les mouchoirs* [pp. 52–53]." This rule is intended to compare the French use of *les* with the *zero* article used in English. However, since no translation of the illustration is provided, the student is likely to see the French as representing *I like the gloves, the hats, and the handkerchiefs,* a perfectly grammatical sentence and a perfectly correct translation of the French. The abstract reference to "a general class of things" is not an adequate statement of the conditions when in English the article is omitted. Again, the trouble with trying to learn French by this rule does not lie in the uselessness of explicit rules generally but in the ambiguity of this particular statement.

Another reason why an explicit grammatical rule, even an adequate and correct one, may not be useful to the student is that it may be too abstract. Words in the rule covering whole classes of constructions in the language are not sufficiently closely associated in the student's mind with specific instances of those constructions. This is another way of saying he does not fully know the meaning of the term used in the rule or that he does not always recognize an instance when he sees one. An example from the Turgeon text again: "The subjunctive is used . . . after expressions of approval or disapproval, necessity, and the like . . . *J'approuve qu'il soit là. Il faut que vous le trouviez* [p. 229]." In applying this rule, the speaker must be able to mobilize the rule immediately whenever he uses "an expression of approval or disapproval, necessity, (or) the like." For this purpose, the expressions must form a distinct category in his mind. He must also have complete command of that set of forms that are subjunctives, so that for any verb, he can immediately call into use the appropriate form. Examples usually given with a rule are helpful in forming such conceptual groups, but they are usually quite few in number and seldom cover even the whole range of regular forms, let alone irregular. The effectiveness of pattern drills is probably that they greatly extend the concrete representations in the learner's mind. In a pattern drill, a great many expressions of approval, etc., will be shown and a wider and representative range of subjunctive forms. The learner comes away from a pattern drill with a much more useful concept of the subjunctive, not perhaps more defined in the abstract, but more concretely elaborated in his own mind in terms of specific forms and therefore more useful.

In some cases, the rule itself is stated quite concretely. For example, Turgeon gives this one: "Many nouns and adjectives ending in *-eur* in the masculine have a feminine *-euse* (p. 53)." There is no problem of making the concept concrete in this case. *-eur* is as concrete as is needed. It seems likely that this explicit rule could be easily adopted by the learner and that it would influence his usages with relatively little drilling.

Since drills provide a corpus of many examples, they may not only help to make an abstractly defined concept more concrete, they may also correct or further specify a concept not adequately stated in the explicit rule. This kind of demonstrative definition is not only more useful to the learner than an abstraction, it also has a better chance of being correct since the corpus will be made up exclusively of constructions acceptable to the native speaker.

Explicit abstract statements of grammatical rules have at most an organizing or guiding function in the learning process. They may be helpful whenever the learner is able to recognize and remember the appropriate concrete instances of the categories referred to in the rule. He may be able to do this because the rule is stated in terms of the visible shapes of the words referred to, as in the case of the *-eur* rule, or because drill or experience have made him fully acquainted with the common range of the forms covered by an abstract term.

The purpose of stating these examples is to distinguish some of these rules from the kind of rule we are talking about in Propositions V and VI and to suggest that part of the reason that verbalized grammar rules have not always produced good results is that they have been linguistically inadequate rules.

Turning to another condition of consciousness, it was pointed out earlier that attention is attracted not just to the novel but also to things the individual feels a need to understand. New things as such attract interest, but primarily because their newness somehow poses a challenge. If learning a language is a search for a system, it would not be surprising if attention and interest were frequently directed toward the material to be learned, in other words, if the rules became conscious. In practice, language learners are likely to form explicit rules for themselves whether lessons provide them or not, since consciousness is a tool in problem solving. Students sometimes make statements like this: "I want to know not only *how* it should be said; I also want to understand *why* it is said that way." In this case, a statement of a rule is what they seek or a statement of the relation between this usage and some other. This search for understanding is part of the normal strategy of language learning, the search for the system. In this sense, consciousness functions to bring together the elements of the new language so that the system can be mastered as a whole. For example, the student may find a phrase that appears inconsistent with others he has learned, and his attention may be directed toward it in order to resolve the conflict. This kind of understanding, however, need not always involve an explicitly stated rule. It may be accomplished by an implicit analogy. This analogy may not remain very conscious, but it seems likely that the learner of a new language, with new analogies to be observed, will be for a time at least vaguely aware of them.

In relation to language learning as problem solving, what is the function of exercises and pattern drills? We have already suggested that they may have various uses. One of these is that the material, whether heard, read, or memorized, serves as a basis for inference of rules. Some language teachers believe that inference or analogy is the only good way to arrive at grammatical rules (Brooks, 1964). Children learning their first language have to get most of their rules this way since they are unable to use explicit rules at the age when they are learning. Weir's child (1962) practiced saying patterns to himself as though he were attending to and interested in language structures themselves. In this sense, he was quite conscious of the forms of language, probably more conscious than he would be later in life when he would be using the structures automatically. Recognition of a pattern or a relation between patterns is also for an adult a kind of conscious awareness of grammatical structure, even when not put into abstract words.

The corpus presented in drills not only suggests what the rules are but also provides a means of testing rules already tentatively formed. Both formation and confirmation of a hypothetical rule are important to the learner in ultimate mastery, that is, in coming to a correct and consistent use of it. Belasco (1965) described this testing process by comparing the formation of the hypothetical rule with nucleation in the formation of crystals. Something has to "click," he says, before learned material can be put together. The process he described is not unlike that suggested by Fodor (1966) for a young child.

The desire for organization is also likely to arise in second-language learning because of the need to remember. Structures remain unconscious in the native language because they are familiar and present no problems. Organization of grammatical principles into some explicit pattern or set of related rules may be sought by the student as an aid in the otherwise overwhelming memory problem. Rivers (1964) suggests that lesson materials such as pattern drills can be "a useful procedure for automatizing the details of language structure at the manipulative level (p. 129)." In other words, even after a pattern is understood in the sense that the learner sees its relation to a larger system of grammatical relationships, he may still need to drill that pattern so as to reduce its latency in his response system and make it available for use in rapid speech and understanding. A store of well-learned, easily recalled patterns may also be necessary before the individual can manage to put two and two together to solve the larger system to which they belong. Since problem solving is a mental process, the materials for it must be available "in mind," not just on paper. Memorizing well-selected sentences can help make them available for quick recall and comparison.

Consciousness may also be seen as a means of adaption. When practiced patterns have proved inadequate to get along in the world, this is when intelligence comes into play. The second-language learner is forcing himself into a situation where many of his practiced patterns will be inadequate. As long as they work, he is unconscious of them, but when he is forced to adapt to a new situation, he is likely to start thinking. Not only the task of understanding strange material but also that of remembering a complicated set of new rules of communication will challenge him to solve the problems by thinking them out and understanding the new system.

The discussion of the degree to which grammatical rules are or should be conscious has been interwoven with comment about pattern drill methods for good reason. Pattern drills have been proposed both as a substitute for explicit grammatical rules in learning a new language and as a means of making the language behavior more automatic than is possible when explicit rules are consciously applied (Fries, 1945). The implications of our discussion of the psychology of consciousness are that it may not be possible to avoid conscious formulation of rules even if the teacher deems it desirable. Some psychological findings, furthermore, suggest that conscious rules have a useful place in the earlier stages. However, pattern drills have an important function even if they are not mere substitutes for rules in that they provide a means by which rules can be found, tested, and practiced.

Proposition VII: The learner of a language, regardless of his age, brings with him to the task certain predispositions which direct the process of his learning. That even a young child is pursuing some system rather than imitating specific material is shown by the fact that children extend the normal rules to instances they could never have heard: they say "two foots" and "he goed." Second-language learners, of course, do exactly the same thing as they stumble over irregular verbs. Even when children try to imitate sentences said by adults (Ervin, 1964), they usually produce sentences that conform to their own limited system rather than "accept" the adult model. This shows that they can and do have systems, invented by themselves. Only gradually do they come to conform to the adult grammar.

Second-language learners also impose their own systems on the new language. These are frequently systems taken over partly from the native language, but at other times, they are probably guesses derived from experiences with the new language. Like children, they form new hypotheses to be tested against the output and understanding of the teacher or informant in the new language. Subjects in my experiment on learning Russian word order sometimes adopted a consistent word order different from either Russian or English (Torrey, 1966).

The proposition that language learners are predisposed to seek certain kinds of abstract systems in language implies that the designer of language lessons is not free to determine the course of acquisition arbitrarily according to his own notion of what should be learned first. It would be interesting to know in this connection whether the young child learning his first language typically follows a sequence of development that can be understood in terms of the complete system he eventually develops. McNeill (1966) suggests, for example, that a child begins by speaking in forms close to base structures without some of the transformations necessary in adult language. Thus, his initial sentences are "semigrammatical"; that is, they conform to some but not all of the adult rules. This is consistent with Fodor's (1966) suggestions about a child's approach to language learning. Most language lessons for adults start with sentences which, although simple, are fully elaborated with such things as tense and number inflections. Thus, the adult is always required to deal with several levels of grammar at once. It might be more efficient, then, to start an adult also with a kind of scientifically devised baby talk, so that he could acquire the different levels of grammar in a naturally ordered sequence. However, only a good deal of applied research based on a thorough knowledge of a child's normal progress would answer the question whether a child's procedure is a useful way to systematize lessons for adults.

Proposition VIII: Learning a language is learning to understand and be understood by other speakers of that language. For a child learning his first language, the communicating function of language is built into almost all his learning situations. He practices almost exclusively the everyday uses of language. His purposes for listening and speaking are to understand and to be understood. However, in the design of lessons for adults, communication may be forgotten in concern for structure. The adult is willing to sit in a laboratory or class, emitting responses, for example, to substitution or transformation drills, which are not necessarily being used to communicate meaning. The implication of the present proposition for learning and teaching techniques is that insofar as the drills or exercises are purely structural in the sense of being divorced in the learner's mind from their uses, they will be less than complete as learning exercises. There are several ways in which linguistic material in the drill may become divorced from its meaning. One is that the meanings may not be conveyed to the learner in the first place. Some drills purposely omit meaning in order to concentrate attention on something else. In the case of pronunciation or sound discrimination, the drill may be useful anyway, but it would be much harder to defend meaningless drilling of grammatical material. Another way meaning may be lost is through what is called "semantic satiation" (Osgood, 1963). If the same word is repeatedly said or heard by a person many times in a short period, it seems to change its perceptual characteristics. Among other things, it becomes to him more like a meaningless sound. Likewise, if a grammatical structure is repeated enough times even with different words, the learner's attention wanders from its meaning. Anomalous sentences are said in drill without being noticed. Finally, perhaps the most common reason for loss of meaning is sheer boredom. The mind wanders, and material is repeated mechanically without thought. Although the conception of language as habits of behavior suggests that the drills should go on being effective even when their meaning is ignored, it is obvious that, even if "empty" structures could be learned as such (a questionable proposition), still some practice with attention to meaning will be necessary before structures can be used to communicate or understand.

In a sense, whatever is practiced will be the thing learned. It follows that good linguistic practice must include the function of communication in the drill itself. This would not necessarily exclude structural drills in a laboratory, provided they are so designed as not to become boring and mechanical, in other words, provided the learner is kept constantly aware of what he is saying. Many otherwise desirable drills and laboratory exercises are probably vitiated by their failure to keep attention on meaning. A clear implication for the language lab is that entertainment value should not be regarded as a frill. Good pedagogy requires interesting material.

There are many different ways in which language exercises can be made or kept meaningful. Translation to or from the native tongue, especially of whole phrases and sentences in context rather than of individual words, is one simple and direct way of communicating meaning, especially the subtle conceptual or grammatical meanings that are not easily conveyed in pictures or gestures. Twaddell (1966) points out also that just verbal context alone, the structure and meaning of partially understood target language structures surrounding a new word, is more important than the dictionary as a means of understanding connected discourse. Many of the more elementary exercises incorporate the factor of communication. Dykstra and his associates are developing drill material always especially designed to have the function of communication. Johnson (1966) describes, for example, one of their drills in which one student must give instructions in the target language while another understands and carries them out. By "communication," Dykstra (1965) means a situation in which the speaker has "multiple choices of linguistic content (and) . . . a purpose superordinate to that of language practice." Garvey and her associates (1967) have also prepared a self-instructional course in elementary French, where the lack of a teacher made it particularly necessary to give explicit attention to the need for meaningful responses in drill. Some of the ways in which they made the student's responses contingent upon meaning were to have him select pictures to match phrases, obey instructions, select or produce translations, or transform French material according to instructions. Rivers (1964) cites a method of "dialogue adaptation" used in the Audio-Lingual Materials where students modify memorized dialogues to suit their own choices of meaning.

This proposition about communication, like several of the others, deals with a question of motivation as well as of intellectual content. The second-language learner can learn more effectively if he can be motivated to communicate in the particular context of learning. Interesting exercises that are fun and games that entertain through their use of the target language for communication are also ideal methods for effective learning.

Proposition IX: Learning a language is accepting a culture, and therefore, in some degree, a personal identity. The cultural implications of language introduce a large difference between first-language learning and the learning of a foreign language by an older person. With the 2-year-old, there is no question about his desire for total adaptation and rapport with the culture that is expressed through his language. His destiny is to be a member of it, and he is finding his only identity through it. For the adult, however, learning a new language always means allying himself with an alien pattern of thought, value, and self-expression. He already identifies himself with one nation and culture, and he knows something about the people whose language he is trying to learn. He has attitudes, sometimes fairly strong ones, about the other culture and about his relation to it. If the learner attributes prestige to that nation or has some other reason for wishing to identify himself with it, these attitudes are quite positive; however, there is usually also some element of negative affect or emotion simply because the culture is not his own. Usually, there are elements in it that conflict with his value system. Sometimes there is intergroup and international hostility that makes him not want to associate himself wholeheartedly with the people whose language he is learning. Since a language is a means of communication and self-expression, a person speaking a language must associate with members of that community where it is spoken and must, to some extent, even try to act like them in order to express himself in their way. Not only must the semantic content of material and conversation be understood and tolerated, but the very mannerisms of speech, the sounds, the strange intonation patterns and rhythms, and perhaps even the nonvocal gestures must be adopted and imitated. Many of these details seem ridiculous to the learner while others arouse his outright hostility. It is small wonder that adolescents and adults, who have already allied themselves with one culture, feel embarrassed or reluctant to throw themselves into the part of a foreigner or a member of a lower status minority.

The effect of perceived self-identification on language learning has been confirmed in psychological research. Anisfeld (1961) found that the attitude of Jewish children toward their religion was a definite factor in their learning of the Hebrew language. Lambert (1967) has shown that English-speaking Canadians who were sympathetic to French culture did better in the French language, especially in communication skills such as pronouncing and understanding speech. Scherer and Wertheimer (1964) showed that the attitudes of American college students studying German influenced their performance in the language. Positive attitudes toward Germans and also toward themselves speaking German were correlated with proficiency in German.

Vildomec (1963) reports that the attitude of the public is a major factor in the success of teaching Russian in Eastern Europe. Thus, an "integrative" motivation to learn, where the student wants to identify with the culture, is considered more helpful than an "instrumental" motivation, where the language skill is desired for some specific and narrower purpose, while the culture as a whole may even be resisted or rejected emotionally.

A further outcome of the connection between the language one speaks and one's own perceived identity is that as a person approaches perfection in his mastery of another language, he reaches a personality crisis. Lambert (1967), for example, has found that American students taking an intensive course in French developed along with their skill in French a kind of anomie or alienation from their own culture. This took the form of an anxiety that seemed to direct them back toward speaking English despite their agreement to speak only French and their obvious high motivation to learn French. Vildomec (1963) also reports that bilinguals suffer various kinds of crises of anxiety in trying to switch languages or deal with more than one at a time. Haugen (1965b) puts it as follows:

Coordinate bilingualism can be established only at the cost of a self-suppression and identification that may involve deep humiliation. In attempting to establish it in our students we may be attacking the very core of their personalities. . . . To lose one's accent is to identify completely with another society and another way of life. . . . A foreign accent is the foreigner's best passport and the last bastion of his original identity [p. 88].

Proposition X: Language is a tool of thought. The adult learner of a foreign language is old enough already to have adult forms of conceptualization. Unlike the 2-year-old, his language learning process is not participating in the fundamental organization and development of his ability to think abstractly. In this sense, the implications of this proposition for him are much less important. However, to the extent that languages differ in the kinds of specific concepts they represent both in words and in grammatical form, learning a second or a third one may enrich and diversify a person's thought directly through the form of the language, as well as through the access it provides to other cultural enrichment.

Elementary Education in a Second Language

The following discussion is exclusively about children in preschools or elementary schools where the language used is different from the language of their homes, where before the children can learn any subject matter, they must first learn the language forms in which it will be taught. I will make use here only of those propositions which have different implications for these school children than for adults learning foreign languages.

Actually, there are many different situations in which children meet a new language when they enter school. I will be speaking primarily of American children of non-English-speaking families. For them, the school language is the dominant language of their country, and they will use it in many aspects of life during the school years and later, even though it is not the language of their homes. I will refer from time to time also to other situations. One is that of a child whose home language is a nonstandard dialect of the language he meets in school. His language and his teacher's may be mutually fairly comprehensible, but they are still systematically different, and the difference demands special knowledge and sensitivity on the part of the teacher. Another situation is that of children in many countries where the language of the school is also that of business and government, but where it is not the native language of most of the people. This is true, for example, in some developing countries which are former colonies.

Proposition I: Some aspects of learning capacity change with age. Two kinds of practical questions may be settled by reference to our knowledge of learning capacities at different ages. One is the question of timing, the age at which the second-language training should be started. The other is that of methods by which language should be taught at different ages.

The known advantage of a younger child in learning the sound system and possibly other aspects of a language would suggest that the practice of starting first grade instruction entirely in a new language is a sound one. In some ways, the children will never be better equipped to learn language, so that massive efforts in the first grade seem justified. However, as we shall see later (Proposition IX), this is one of the cases where different psychological principles have quite opposite implications for pedagogical policy. For example, overemphasis on English at the expense of Spanish may so threaten and alienate a Spanish-speaking child that he cannot learn anything from his school. In a case like this, the advantages of early instruction must be weighed against other considerations.

As for age changes in other mental abilities, such as memory span, memorizing ability, and conceptual development, the main implications are that teaching methods should be designed to fit the age of the learner. Young children will need shorter sentences to imitate, shorter dialogues to memorize, and material that is conceptually simpler. They will need less abstract explanation and more concrete experience with objects and people. As they get older, they will be better able to learn from verbal presentations and to understand statements about language as such. The teacher's sensitivity to her pupils' particular level of conceptual development will avoid many errors and frustrations.

Proposition II: The learning of one thing may influence the later learning of something else. The basic principles of response interference operate in children as in adults. The special application to a school child lies in the fact that many aspects of his language and conceptualization are still not thoroughly learned. Interference effects are greater for partially learned than for well-earned material. The interference in this case, therefore, may work both ways. The native language may suffer as well as the second language, and neither has the chance of full development in vocabulary and syntax that occurs in children schooled in their native language. This is the so-called "balance effect" in bilingual children, the fact that for children the learning of a second language is always somewhat at the expense of the first. Macnamara (1966) has reviewed the literature in detail as well as contributed significantly to it with his own study of the effects of instruction in Irish in an English-speaking society. He concludes that such children are usually somewhat retarded in both languages. The delay in language development through the school years when instruction is largely in a second language is not only the direct result of confusion between the languages but also of simple competition of the two languages for the time and effort available to be devoted to learning. Either way, the implication for bilingual education is the same, that there are costs to be considered along with the gains in the attempted early mastery of a second language.

(It should also be recognized that the disadvantage of bilingual children is often largely of a social and economic nature. Children of immigrants or children of a poorer national group within a country are commonly the bilingual ones, and it is therefore seldom realistic to treat all their educational retardation as due to the bilingualism as such. Fishman [1967] points out that the effects of bilingualism never can be entirely separated from their socioeconomic concomitants.)

The possibility of competition and interference between languages has another implication for educators who must teach the language of instruction in addition to the subject matter. It is that, with children especially, a command of the target language is not sufficient qualification to teach it as a second language. Special linguistic training is usually needed to teach language effectively. A teacher should have a *technical* knowledge of the school language as well as of the contrast between it and the children's language in order to organize lessons and evaluate results.

It is less often recognized that teachers of children who speak a substandard dialect also need special training. Because of the similarity between dialects, the children are even less clearly aware that a difference in language exists and certainly not of the detailed nature of the difference (Haugen, 1965a). Much has been said in recent years of applying the methods of foreign-language instruction to teaching these children the standard dialect, and one of these methods must be a detailed contrastive analysis of both dialects (Stewart, 1965).

Proposition III: All behavior, including learning behavior, is guided by the purposes of the learner and evaluated by him in relation to his own goals. Motivation is more than effort; it is energy with direction. Directed effort requires both knowledge of the goal of an activity and belief in its usefulness to reach that goal. Much of the task of teaching can be seen as communicating to the pupil the knowledge of what he is to get out of each lesson. A teacher must also be able to persuade the children that the school activities are worthy of their effort. In fact, the use of intrinsic reward to reinforce correct responses is entirely dependent upon the child's understanding and acceptance of certain goals. Intrinsic reward is simply the satisfaction of having succeeded. It is the commonest and most effective type of reward. However, the subjective experience of success is not possible without knowledge of what success means, that is, knowledge of the goals of instruction. The child must not only know these goals but also accept them as his own in order to get any feeling of success or personal satisfaction out of learning.

To illustrate one of the problems of failure to understand goals, let me describe a teacher I once observed trying to help children learn to use complete sentences in writing. She set the task of saying something about the weather in February by asking, "What is it like outdoors in February?" A child raised his hand and answered, "Cold." This response was rejected with the instruction, "Make a complete sentence." The child had nothing to say because he did not know the difference between what he had said and a sentence. Perhaps he would eventually somehow catch on to the distinction, but until he did, approval or disapproval of his responses could not contribute to his learning. The only result of this lesson for him was a sense of failure.

This proposition states one of several reasons why a teacher must be in accurate and friendly communication with the child. Neither detailed exchange of information nor positive mutual feeling is enough by itself, since a child must both understand and accept the goals of each task in order to be able to profit from it. A language barrier, a culture barrier, a class barrier, or all three are very difficult and very necessary to overcome.

Proposition IV: Language behavior is highly systematic, not a set of loosely related responses, associations, or concepts. Corollary: The single system that is a language may have many overt manifestations in performance, including producing speech, understanding spoken and written material, writing, translating, and other skills. This proposition has a peculiar importance for the child who enters first grade and tries to learn reading in a language he has never heard before. Since reading is the key to all other learning, a child who does not grasp the principle early is crippled for life. To be introduced to it under difficult circumstances imposes an unnecessary burden where it is least tolerable. King (1967), writing about the role of English in the war on poverty, put it as follows:

It is important to note that in the case of the environmentally handicapped and foreign background pupils, the teaching and re-teaching of the so-called reading skills per se, before or apart from mastery of the four basic steps in the communication process (listening, speaking, thinking, writing), will in most cases produce only reading failure, with concomitant negative and deleterious effects. To try to teach a child to read a . . . language which he neither understands nor speaks is wasteful of the best efforts of, and inevitably harmful to, both the learner and the teacher . . . [p. 56].

It is being seriously proposed by many today (e.g., Andersson, 1965; Gaarder, 1965; Boyer, 1965) that school instruction should always be begun in the mother tongue with the second language introduced only gradually and with instruction by means of it waiting upon mastery of the specific words and structures needed. An important part of the rationale for these suggestions is that reading is only one manifestation of basic linguistic competence and not normally a primary one. Much effective reading training builds upon previous knowledge of language structures. It is argued, therefore, that the beginning instruction in reading should be in a native language. This does not necessarily mean that reading the second language need be postponed until spoken forms are fully mastered, but only that the particular material to be read at any time be within the linguistic competence of the child (Bell, 1965). King (1967) summarizes such a policy for non-English-speaking children as follows:

It is wasteful . . . not to reinforce what the child already knows about listening, speaking, writing, and reading in his native language. I believe, therefore, that this child . . . should receive instruction simultaneously in his native language and culture, as well as in English, and that we should capitalize on the many opportunities for transfer of training where there are so many obvious elements of identity in listening, speaking, writing, and reading skills in the language known and the language to be learned [p. 56].

Instruction in the native tongue is not always possible, however. For many languages on earth, there is little or no printed material available for teaching reading or using the skill of reading if it were learned. This is true of countries such as Kenya (Prator, 1967), where many languages are spoken but few have any very widespread use or extensive literature. In Kenya, as in many other places, there is also the fact that the best teaching materials available are in English. A similar situation exists in the case of nonstandard dialects of English and some American Indian languages in the United States. Neither materials in print nor even an established writing system exists for many children's native speech. Speakers of such a language may also not feel any need to be able to read it.

When instruction must be in a foreign language from the beginning, the problem may still be lessened by preparation of initial reading materials that take into account the particular problems of the learners. For example, many good reading materials are based upon the assumption of a good command of basic oral English. These may be completely inadequate for the non-English-speaking child. Kreidler (1966) points out, for example, that for speakers of other languages, initial reading materials should be carefully selected in terms of sentence structures, so that these basic patterns may be learned. The native speaker can learn to read from much more complex and various grammatical material since these patterns are already well known. Many lessons in phonics are based upon the assumption that the child already hears and can make certain sound distinctions. A Spanish-speaking child who cannot yet distinguish *meet* from *mit* would only be baffled by such lessons. Specialized materials are necessary to meet his particular reading problems.

Proposition V: The rules employed by the user of a language are not necessarily conscious.

Proposition VI: Learning a language is learning to understand and be under-stood by other speakers of that language. The proposition concerning explicit rules does not have the same implications for a child in the concrete intuitive stage of conceptualization (Ausubel, 1964) as it has for an older person. Explicit grammatical rules are necessarily highly abstract, and few teachers need a warning not to try to use them with young children. As Vygotsky (1962) points out, words represent concepts rather than particular objects, so that a verbalized rule must be one which is formulated in a fairly abstract way. Abstract ideas (such as parts of speech), the distinction between words and the things they refer to, and the notion of language as such (especially of the possibility of different languages or different ways of saying the same thing) are too sophisticated for most first graders. It is reported, for example, that bilingual children in nursery schools are sometimes unable to serve as interpreters for other children because they do not understand the meaning of any instruction to translate. A similar problem may arise in trying to "correct" nonstandard grammar in that the child does not distin-guish between the thing said and the words he used to say it. I once asked an 8-year-old to say something in a different way and found she thought I was accusing her of lying in the original statement. Language for her was identical with what she wanted to communicate. To say it in a different way meant to say something different. Gaarder (1967) warns against attempting to focus young children's attention on language as such even by means such as pattern drills. He quotes Penfield to the effect that language for them is not a subject to be talked about only a means to an end. For a child, apparently, language has only the function of communication; it has no perceivable structure or existence of its own.

Proposition VII: Learning a language is accepting a culture and therefore, in some degree, a personal identity. For a child entering a school whose language is not his own, the cultural implications of the second language are more serious than for a person learning a foreign language. Although the new language is different from the child's own and brings with it an alien culture, it is nevertheless usually the dominant or official language of his own country. In this sense, it cannot be considered a "foreign" language. It will assume a more important function in his life than any language of another country could. Mastery of it may mean the only possibility of success in life. It is important also that the school child learn to accept the new language and culture as part of himself, so that he can also feel a member of the larger community.

The task of intergrating newcomers into the culture has been an accepted function of the American school system for some time. Teaching English and using it as the medium of instruction, usually to the deliberate exclusion of other languages, has been a traditional method. This technique of acculturation, however, can interfere with another important adjustment that a child must make in order to succeed in school or elsewhere, that is, the development of self-respect and confidence. Coming to school as he does with an already learned language and an already formed identification of himself as a member of a different culture, his respect for himself is severely threatened if the school rejects all his skills and everything he has yet learned about himself (Hakes, 1965). The school must do more than just teach him the dominant language and inform him about its culture; it must also teach him to identify himself as a worthy member of that culture.

Those who have done research in recent years on the problems of teaching children standard English as a new language (e.g., Horn, 1966) generally agree that self-evaluation problems are the main obstacle to the success of these children in school. Because for most of them their language represents not only a different culture but one with lower status in the society, they learn to approach all aspects of school and the larger culture it represents with an attitude of hopelessness, humiliation, and low self-regard. Few of the other problems of learning can be dealt with until a child learns to expect some success from himself within the dominant culture.

The importance of making a child feel that he personally can belong to the society represented by the school is actually a powerful argument for avoiding excessive early pressure to learn its language. For example, a child cannot feel accepted by a teacher who does not speak his own language or by a school that forbids him to use it. His whole present identity is tied up in his language and culture. Rejection of it is rejection of him. Under such conditions, he cannot perceive himself as "belonging" in school. A first grader is still a very dependent creature. The teacher's personal acceptance is for him his passport to citizenship, and his motivation in school depends heavily on his desire to please her. All this is lost if the teacher makes him an alien.

It is paradoxical, then, that many of those whose original goal was to find out how to teach a new language have concluded with a recommendation that the native language of children be brought into the school and given status as a medium of instruction (Officer, 1965; Andersson, 1965; Corbin & Crosby, 1965). Gaarder (1967), describing an experimental bilingual school in Miami, gives as one of the main reasons for using the mother tongue in school "to avoid the alienation from family and linguistic community that is commonly the price of rejection of one's mother tongue [p. 110]." He argues that the deficits associated with bilingualism are probably mainly the result of this alienation rather than of the sheer fact of knowing two languages. In bilingual approach, all children start primarily in their own language, and the new one is gradually introduced, first as a foreign language and only later, as it is well enough learned, as a medium of instruction. English-speaking and Spanish-speaking children must start out in separate classes, sharing only the instruction in subjects that require little language. As each group becomes able to handle the necessary language forms, they are gradually brought together for subject matter instruction in both languages. Since English and Spanish have equal status in the school as a whole, no child is made to feel alien because of his background. Not only are the Spanish speakers given a better chance to feel themselves members of the community, but the community itself is able to "cultivate and guard [its] legitimate cultural diversity (Boyer, 1965, p. 290)."

The child who speaks a nonstandard dialect has many of the same problems with school as the one who speaks another language. He also belongs to a low status group in the society, and he also finds his language and many of his ways rejected by the teacher and the school. Although he usually understands the teacher better than does the foreign-speaking child, he has some trouble making his teacher understand and accept him. If the teacher condemns nearly everything he says as "wrong," he can but feel worthless, especially if he has no idea how to be "right." If Bernstein is right in saying (Gumperz, 1965) that language among other functions symbolizes social intimacy and distance, a child whose teacher's language is different from his own cannot accept or be accepted by the teacher. Everything conspires to prevent him from either learning or wanting to learn the standard dialect.

These facts help us to understand why it is not uncommon for children who speak other languages or dialects to refuse to learn the school language (Lin, 1965; Creswell, 1965). This occurs despite the fact that they have great future need for it and are massively exposed to it at an age when presumably they are best able to learn it. Labov (1965) believes that this is due largely to the mutual rejection of each other's language and culture that occurs between these school children and their teachers. The differences in language or dialect, the conflicts of manners and values inevitably lead to strain in which the child, the weaker party, is more likely to suffer. In most of the United States, even the stories and pictures in the schoolbooks usually portray exclusively a kind of suburban, middle-class, white child of native American parents. Their very consistency is perfectly calculated to make any other child feel himself an outsider. His problem is not one of intellectual understanding. Creswell (1965) quotes Ralph Ellison to the effect that the children's tenacious loyalty to their own way is a defense against the threat of a hostile environment, a retreat into the only world where they can feel at home.

Proposition VIII: Language is a tool of thought. The effect of language on thinking has implications for both timing and method of teaching a second language. The problem of timing arises because a child in the early grades is still in the process of moving from concrete intuitive thinking to abstract conceptual thinking (Ausubel, 1963; Vygotsky, 1962). Language development is an important factor in organizing this process and in forming the more abstract concepts. If a child is not allowed to build upon the language skill he already has but is forced instead to start again from scratch, he is at a serious disadvantage in the intellectual development appropriate to his age. Another factor, already mentioned in the discussion of earlier propositions, is the sheer competition for time and effort spent in learning the new language as against further development in the medium of the old one. Vital as the new language may be for later instruction, it is not the only building block for the future. If a child's conceptual development is severely retarded, the price for early acquisition of the new language may be too great. It follows that the introduction to science and mathematics as well as other abstract subjects should not be exclusively through the medium of a language not thoroughly known to the child. It does not necessarily follow that children can never learn these subjects through a second language or that bilingualism will permanently stunt their thinking processes. This proposition only suggests that a firm linguistic foundation should be laid for each step of conceptual learning.

The consideration that thought depends upon language also suggests some useful ways to begin the study of a new language. Horn and his associates (Ott, 1966) developed a program of reading readiness instruction based upon linguistic forms needed in scientific understanding. In this way, they not only gave Spanish-speaking children needed lessons in observing and conceptualizing the world about them, but at the same time, taught them English in a context of concrete experiences suitable to their intellectual level.

The dependence of thought upon language exists also at a higher level of sophistication. It has already been mentioned that in some developing countries, English or another European language may be selected as the medium of instruction because teaching materials are more easily available in that language. It is not only a question of elementary teaching materials, however, but also of more advanced literature and scientific work. There is little printed material in many of the world's languages, and many of them also do not yet possess the forms to express the concepts and relationships needed in much of present higher learning. Rather than adapt all the world's languages quickly to science, it may be simpler for a time to teach all the potential scientists one or more of those languages in which scientific reports are now available.

The nonstandard forms of languages deserve special mention for a similar reason. Crosby (1965) mentions the need to study the implications of nonstandard dialects for the quality of thought that is possible in them. Bernstein (1961) believes that the "public" language of the lower working classes lacks entirely many of the forms and words necessary to express school learning. As a result, says Bernstein:

In the learning of this (restricted) linguistic form, the child is progressively oriented to a relatively low level of conceptualization. It induces a lack of interest in processes, a preference to be aroused by, and to respond to, that which is immediately given, rather than responding to the implications of a matrix of relationships [p. 98].

The study of cultural disadvantage has shown that many children enter school with underdeveloped language skills. In addition to the various problems of nonstandard forms, many children also lack skill in verbalizing experiences and understanding verbal descriptions (Ott, 1967). This is true of some speakers of other languages as well as speakers of nonstandard dialects. They need special instruction in using even the language they presumably know before they can profit from some school lessons.

This proposition, like several others, implies that despite the formidable problems of instructing children in a language other than their own, the goal of bilingualism (including bidialectalism) through school instruction remains an essential one for many schools in the modern world. The most important practical implications of these propositions, then, are not those that raise doubts about whether second languages should be taught, but rather those that guide us in deciding when and how it may best be done.

REFERENCES

Andersson, T. A new focus on the bilingual child. *Mod. lang. J.*, 1965, **49**, 156–160.

Anisfeld, M., & Lambert, W. E. Social and psychological variables in learning Hebrew. *J. abnorm. soc. Psychol.*, 1961, **63**, 524–529.

Ausubel, D. P. *The psychology of meaningful verbal learning.* New York: Grune & Stratton, 1963.

Ausubel, D. P. Adults versus children in second-language learning: psychological considerations. *Mod. lang. J.*, 1964, **48**, 420–424.

Bateman, D. R., & Zidonis, F. J. *The effect of a knowledge of generative grammar upon the growth of language complexity.* NCTE Research Report No. 6. Champaign, Ill.: NCTE, 1966.

Belasco, S. Nucleation and the audio-lingual approach. *Mod. lang. J.*, 1965, **49**, 482–491.

Bell, P. W. An instructional program for Spanish-speaking elementary school pupils. In V. F. Allen (Ed.), *On teaching English to speakers of other languages: thought, and instruction.* New York: Holt, Rinehart & Winston, 1967.

Bernstein, B. Social structure, language, and learning. *Educ. Res.,* 1961, **3**, 163–176. Reprinted in J. P. DeCecco (Ed.), *The psychology of language, thought, and instruction.* New York: Holt, Rinehart & Winston, 1967.

Boyer, M. V. Poverty and the mother tongue. *Educ. Forum,* 1965, **29**, 290–296.

Braine, M. D. S. The ontogeny of English phrase structure: the first phase. *Language,* 1963, **39**, 1–13.

Brooks, N. *Language and language learning.* New York: Harcourt, Brace & World, 1964.

Brown, R. W., & Bellugi, U. Three processes in the child's acquisition of syntax. *Harvard educ. Rev.,* 1964, **34**, 133–151.

Brown, R. W., & Lenneberg, E. H. Studies in linguistic relativity. In E. E. Maccoby, T. M. Newcomb, & E. L. Hartley (Eds.), *Readings in social psychology.* New York: Holt, Rinehart & Winston, 1958.

Carmichael, L., Hogan, H. P., & Walter, A. A. An experimental study of the effect of language on the reproduction of visually perceived form. *J. exp. Psychol.,* 1932, **15**, 73–86.

Carroll, J. B. Research in foreign language teaching: the last five years. In R. G. Mead (Ed.), *Language Teaching: Broader Contexts* (Reports of the Northeast Conference on the Teaching of Foreign Languages), 1966, 12–42.

Chomsky, N. A review of *Verbal behavior* by B. F. Skinner. *Language,* 1959, **35**, 26–59.

Chomsky, N. *Aspects of a theory of syntax.* Cambridge: M.I.T. Press, 1965.

Chomsky, N. Linguistic theory. In R. G. Mead (Ed.), *Language Teaching: Broader Contexts* (Reports of the Northeast Conference on the Teaching of Foreign Languages), 1966, 43–58.

Corbin, R., & Crosby, M. *Language programs for the disadvantaged*: Report of the NCTE Task Force on Teaching English to the Disadvantaged. Champaign, Ill.: NCTE, 1965.

Creswell, T. J. The twenty billion dollar misunderstanding. In R. W. Shuy (Ed.), *Social dialects and language learning.* Champaign, Ill.: NCTE, 1965.

Crosby, M. Future research: implications growing out of the Wilmington study. In R. W. Shuy (Ed.), *Social dialects and language learning.* Champaign, Ill.: NCTE, 1965.

Delattre, P. A technique of aural-oral approach: report on a University of Oklahoma experiment in teaching French. *French Rev.,* 1947, **20**, 238–250.

Dykstra, G. Towards a design for materials development. Unpublished paper, 1965.

Ervin, S. M. Imitation and structural change in children's language. In E. H. Lenneberg (Ed.), *New directions in the study of language.* Cambridge: M.I.T. Press, 1964.

Fishman, J. Bilingualism with and without diglossia; diglossia with and without bilingualism. *J. soc. Issues,* 1967, **23**, 29–38.

Fodor, J. A. How to learn to talk: some simple ways. In F. Smith & G. A. Miller (Eds.), *The genesis of language.* Cambridge: M.I.T. Press, 1966.

Fries, C. C. *Teaching and learning English as a foreign language.* Ann Arbor: Univ. of Michigan Press, 1945.

Gaarder, A. B. Teaching the bilingual child: research, development, and policy. *Mod. lang. J.,* 1965, **49**, 165–175.

Gaarder, A. B. Organization of the bilingual school. *J. soc. Issues*, 1967, **23**, 110–120.

Garvey, C. et al. *Description of level 1 of the self-instructional French program*. Final report to the defense language institute on phase B.L.A. of contract number DA 44-196-AMC-00361(E). Washington, D.C.: Center for Applied Linguistics, 1967.

Gibson, E. J. Intra-list generalization as a factor in verbal learning. *J. exp. Psychol.*, 1942, **30**, 185–200.

Gumperz, J. J. The social group as a primary unit of analysis in dialect study. In R. W. Shuy (Ed.), *Social dialects and language learning*. Champaign, Ill.: NCTE, 1965.

Hakes, D. Psychological aspects of bilingualism. *Mod. lang. J.*, 1965, **49**, 220–227.

Haugen, E. Bilingualism and bidialectism. In R. W. Shuy (Ed.), *Social dialects and language learning*. Champaign, Ill.: NCTE, 1965. (a)

Haugen, E. Bilingualism as a goal of foreign language teaching. In V. F. Allen (Ed.), *On teaching English to speakers of other languages: Series I*. Champaign, Ill.: NCTE, 1965. (b)

Horn, T. D. *A study of the effects of intensive oral-aural English language instruction, oral-aural Spanish language instruction and non-oral-aural instruction on reading readiness in grade one*. Coop. Res. Project No. 2648. T. D. Horn, Austin: The Univ. of Texas, 1966.

Hovland, C. I. Human learning and retention. In S. S. Stevens (Ed.), *Handbook of Experimental Psychology*. New York: John Wiley & Sons, Inc., 1951.

Johnson, F. C. The use of visual stimuli to elicit controlled linguistic responses. In C. J. Kreidler (Ed.), *On teaching English to speakers of other languages: Series II*. Champaign, Ill.: NCTE, 1966.

Katona, G. *Organizing and memorizing*. New York: Columbia Univ. Press, 1940.

King, J. B. The most powerful educational weapon in our war on poverty: teaching English to environmentally handicapped pupils and to pupils of foreign language background. In B. W. Robinett (Ed.), *On teaching English to speakers of other languages: Series III*. Champaign, Ill.: NCTE, 1967.

Köhler, W. *The mentality of apes*. New York: Vintage Books, 1959.

Kreidler, C. W. Reading as skill, structure, and communication. In C. J. Kreidler (Ed.), *On teaching English to speakers of other languages: Series II*. Champaign, Ill.: NCTE, 1966.

Labov, W. Stages in the acquisition of standard English. In R. W. Shuy (Ed.), *Social dialects and language learning*. Champaign, Ill.: NCTE, 1965.

Lambert, W. E. A social psychology of bilingualism. *J. soc. Issues*, 1967, **23**, 91–109.

Lenneberg, E. H. Language disorders in childhood. *Harvard educ. Rev.*, 1964, **34**, 152–177.

Lenneberg, E. H. *Biological foundations of language*. New York: John Wiley & Sons, Inc., 1967.

Levine, J. M., & Murphy, G. The learning and forgetting of controversial material. *J. abnorm. soc. Psychol.*, 1943, **38**, 507–517.

Lin, S. C. *Pattern practice in the teaching of standard English to students with a non-standard dialect*. New York: Bur. of Publications, Teachers College, Columbia Univ., 1965.

Luria, A. R. *The role of speech in the regulation of normal and abnormal behavior:*

four papers. U.S. Dept. of Health, Education, and Welfare, Public Health Service, National Institutes of Health, Division of General Medical Sciences. Bethesda: Russian Scientific Translation Program, 1960.

Macnamara, J. *Bilingualism and primary education: a study of the Irish experience*. Edinburgh: Edinburgh Univ. Press, 1966.

McKinnon, K. R. *An experimental study of the learning of syntax in second language learning*. Unpublished dissertation, Harvard Univ., 1965.

McNeill, D. Developmental psycholinguistics. In F. Smith & G. A. Miller (Eds.), *The genesis of language*. Cambridge: M.I.T. Press, 1966.

Munn, N. L. Learning in children. In L. Carmichael (Ed.), *Manual of child psychology*. New York: John Wiley & Sons, 1964.

Officer, J. E. English in the education of Indian children. In V. F. Allen (Ed.), *On teaching English to speakers of other languages: Series I*. Champaign, Ill.: NCTE, 1965.

Osgood, C. E. *Method and theory in experimental psychology*. New York: Oxford, 1953.

Osgood, C. E. Psycholinguistics. In S. Koch (Ed.), *A study of a science, Volume 6*. New York: McGraw-Hill, 1963.

Ott, E. Organizing content for the bilingual child. In C. J. Kreidler (Ed.), *On teaching English to speakers of other languages: Series II*. Champaign, Ill.: NCTE, 1966.

Piaget, J. *Le langage et la pensee chez l'enfant*. Neuchatel-Paris: Delachaux & Niestle, 1923.

Politzer, R. L. *Teaching French: an introduction to applied linguistics*. Boston: Ginn, 1960.

Prator, C. H. Language policy in the primary schools of Kenya. In B. W. Robinett (Ed.), *On teaching English to speakers of other languages: Series III*. Champaign, Ill.: NCTE, 1967.

Rivers, W. M. *The psychologist and the foreign-language teacher*. Chicago: Univ. of Chicago Press, 1964.

Scherer, G. A. C., & Wertheimer, M. *A psycholinguistic experiment in foreign-language teaching*. New York: McGraw-Hill, 1964.

Slobin, D. I. New design in elementary second language teaching: field demonstration in the state of Israel and evaluation. Unpublished paper, 1961.

Stewart, W. A. Urban Negro speech: sociolinguistic factors affecting English teaching. In R. W. Shuy (Ed.), *Social dialects and language learning*. Champaign, Ill.: NCTE, 1965.

Thomas, O. *Transformational grammar and the teacher of English*. New York: Holt, Rinehart & Winston, 1965.

Thompson, H. Culture: the content of language. In C. J. Kreidler (Ed.), *On teaching English to speakers of other languages: Series II*. Champaign, Ill.: NCTE, 1966.

Tolman, E. C. *Purposive behavior in animals and men*. Berkeley: Univ. of California Press, 1949.

Torrey, J. W. *The learning of grammar: an experimental study*. N.I.M.H. Progress Report on Grant No. 07167, 1966.

Turgeon, F. K. *Cours pratique de Francais*. New York: Appleton-Century-Crofts, 1947.

Twaddell, W. F. Linguists and language teachers. In C. J. Kreidler (Ed.), *On teaching English to speakers of other languages: Series II*. Champaign, Ill.: NCTE, 1966.

Vildomec, V. *Multilingualism*. Leyden: Sythoff, 1963.

Vygotsky, L. S. *Thought and language*. Cambridge: M.I.T. Press, 1962.

Weir, R. H. *Language in the crib*. The Hague: Mouton, 1962.

Whorf, B. L. Science and linguistics. *Technol. Rev.*, 1940, **42**, 229–231, 247–248.

Woodworth, R. S., & Schlosberg, H. *Experimental psychology*. New York: Holt, Rinehart & Winston, 1955.

7

The Basis of Speech

WILLIAM S-Y. WANG
University of California, Berkeley

INTRODUCTION

As a person speaks, the movements of the various parts of his speech mechanism cause disturbances in the air around him. These disturbances are transmitted to the auditory mechanism of the hearer in the form of sound waves. The speaker communicates an idea by translating it *into* a train of sound waves; the hearer, in turn, receives the idea by translating it back *from* the sound waves. Two physical mechanisms are involved in this typical use of language: the speech production mechanism and the auditory mechanism. In this study, our attention will be primarily focused on the production mechanism, especially as it provides us with the conceptual framework within which the sounds of human speech are phonetically classified.

We will discuss the anatomy and physiology of respiration, phonation, and articulation. The physical properties of the sound waves produced by these processes have been studied by means of various instruments, especially the sound spectrograph; we will briefly review some of the results of such studies.

To limit our attention to the physical mechanisms, however, would be to miss the central point in the study of speech, which has to do with the ideas that are communicated. These ideas are translated into and from sound waves through systems of linguistic rules. The basic units of linguistic form, the morphemes, vary from language to language and are organized into sentences by syntactic rules which also vary from language to language. The

This study was supported in part by National Science Foundation Grant GS-1430. I am indebted to Betty Shefts Chang for her assistance in the preparation of the manuscript.

syntactic structure of a sentence, i.e., the particular way in which the morphemes are organized, has a direct bearing on how that sentence is pronounced.

In any effort to understand the relation between sound waves and the
ideas they carry, it is essential to investigate the basic form of morphemes
and their syntactic organization in sentences insofar as the latter affects the
physical aspects of speech. Without these more abstract linguistic considerations, which provide the underlying principles of organization, the study of
speech would be no more rewarding than the study of an arbitrary body of
noises. While our concern will be primarily with the processes of speech
production and perception, it should be a constant theme in our thinking
that these processes are to be considered the external manifestations of
various abstract linguistic structures which are ultimately formal representations of ideas.

Our discussion here is sufficiently general so that most of it applies to
all languages; to that extent, this is a study on phonological universals of
language.

SPEECH PRODUCTION

The process of speech production consists of three successive stages. First,
various abdominal and thoracic muscles work in such a way that air flows
alternately in and out of the body (i.e., respiration); it is on these streams of
air flow that speech is superimposed. Next, within the larynx, at the top of
the windpipe, the vocal folds act as valves to control the air flow. Working
together with the respiratory muscles, these folds provide voicing (i.e.,
phonation), control pitch, loudness, and voice quality, and participate, in
other ways, in the production of various types of glotalized consonants.
Finally, above the larynx, there is an array of chambers and valves which
constitute the vocal tract and the nasal tract. These determine in large part
the acoustical properties of the sounds produced (i.e., articulation).

The Pulmonic Air Source

When the volume of a chamber is decreased, the air in the chamber is compressed; the air pressure inside the chamber is greater than that outside it,
or positive. Conversely, when the volume is increased, the air within is
rarefied; the air pressure inside the chamber is then less than that outside it,
or negative. Since air flows from volumes of positive pressure into those of
negative pressure, changing the volume of a chamber controls the direction
of air flow. Movements of the thorax, the larynx, and the dorsum of the

tongue control the direction of the three major types of air flow relevant to the production of speech: pulmonic, glottalic, and velaric.

Pulmonic air is used as a fundamental source of acoustic energy in the speech production of all languages, because it can provide the greatest volume flow and because it can be easily integrated into the regular breathing process, i.e., respiration. During quiet respiration, the ratio of the duration of expiration to that of inspiration is approximately 1:1. During speech, however, the ratio is drastically changed, to 10:1 or even greater. Even though there are marginal exceptions (e.g., the prolonged ingressive sibilant in Japanese, which indicates "polite hesitation"), almost all speech sounds are produced with air going out of the thorax. The duration of a comfortable expiration is a physiological determinant of the average length of clauses.

There are languages in which the physical value of prosodic features is in part determined by the number of syllables in the clause. This is the case, for example, with tone in Mixtec or stress in English, where the value assigned by the phonological rules to a syllable is computed from the values assigned to other syllables in the same clause. For these instances, where the number of phonetic distinctions increases with clause length, we have a perceptual limitation on clause length, which has the same effect as the respiratory one mentioned in the preceding paragraph.

In line with the basic principle of air flow mentioned earlier, when the volume of the thorax is increased and negative pressure is created, air flows into it. This increase in volume is primarily achieved by (*a*) contracting the diaphragm, thereby lowering the floor of the thorax, and (*b*) lifting the ribs, thereby increasing the lateral as well as the front-back dimensions of the thorax. Both of these actions displace portions of the anatomy from their positions of rest.

When the diaphragm is relaxed, the viscera which it had pressed down (and outward) during contraction regain their original position by pushing the floor of the thorax back up. During the relaxation of the muscles which lifted the ribs, contraction of other costal muscles combines with the weight of the ribs themselves to decrease the volume of the thorax. Positive pressure results, and air flows out of the thorax, thus providing the pulmonic air stream upon which the majority of speech sounds are superimposed.

It has been proposed that during expiration the neural pulsation of the internal intercostal muscles regulates the production of phonetic units which correspond roughly to the syllable. This proposal has not been borne out by the results of recent research. Little temporal correlation has been found between units which linguists normally call syllables and either (*a*) the pattern of neural activity of the intercostal muscles (as this is measured in electromyograms) or (*b*) the pressure of the outgoing air, as measured just below the larynx.

Many aspects of speech production, such as the grouping of morphemes into temporal configurations (breath group, pause group, etc.) and syntactic units (phrases, clauses, etc.), or the control of voice loudness and laryngeal quality, require for their execution good coordination with the dynamics of the outgoing air. It appears, however, that our voluntary control over the manner of air flow is quite gross and that most of the adjustments and synchronization are made by the laryngeal and supralaryngeal mechanisms. In supplying the articulators with pulmonic air, we probably do little more than regulate the duration and average volume velocity of the breath stream in an approximate way. Indeed, a person speaking from a tank respirator does not have even that much control; yet such speech has been found to be not far from normal.

Laryngeal Mechanisms

The larynx is a box of cartilages that sits above the highest ring of the windpipe. Its base is formed by the cricoid cartilage, which is shaped like a signet ring with the plate in the back. The two small pyramid-shaped arytenoid cartilages, which ride on the back of the cricoid cartilage, are maneuvered by a delicate complex of muscles. The arytenoid cartilages can be moved in the lateral and front-back dimensions as well as rotated in planes which are roughly horizontal.

The vocal folds are made up of tissues and fat attached to and enclosing a pair of vocal ligaments. The front ends of the vocal folds come together in a fixed position just below the thyroid notch. The back ends are attached to the front points of the arytenoid cartilages. The behavior of the vocal folds is dependent on the position and movement of the arytenoid cartilages, as well as the air stream which acts upon the folds.

During respiration and the production of unvoiced consonants, the vocal folds are apart. The opening between the vocal folds and the central edges of the arytenoid cartilages, shaped roughly like an isosceles triangle, is called the glottis. The glottis measures approximately 20 mm at each side of the triangle and 8 mm at the base in the average male during conditions of rest. When the glottis is open and the vocal tract assumes the position of a vowel, a low-velocity air stream passing through the glottis produces a "whispered" or unvoiced vowel. If the rate of air flow is increased markedly, say doubled, friction at the glottis becomes prominent (if we continue to assume an open vocal tract). The sound produced in this way, the unvoiced glottal fricative [h], retains the acoustic resonances of its homorganic vowel. If the vocal folds are approximated, an air stream with sufficient velocity causes them to sustain a vibration, even when the front ends of the folds are in contact with each other. Depending on the amount of friction that is produced and the mode of vibration at the vocal folds, the sound is either a voiced glottal fricative [ɦ], or the corresponding vowel, with varying degrees of breathiness or laryngealization.

Though differences in the laryngeal quality which accompany vowel articulation have been said to be distinctive in some languages, little experimental information on this question is as yet available. The various laryngeal qualities (e.g., breathiness, trillization) are usually accompanied by a marked increase in the rate of air flow, up to several times that of the nonlaryngealized vowel; this drives the vocal folds into more complex modes of vibration. During the normal production of vowels, the range of the air flow is from 50 to 350 cc per second, varying according to voice effort and pitch. A typical wave form of the volume velocity of the glottal air is roughly triangular in shape; the peak value may be from two to four times that of the average. With increases in voice effort and pitch, the triangles become steeper, corresponding to a relative increase in the energy of the high-frequency components.

The difference between [h] and [ɦ] is probably not distinctive in the consonant system of any language: [h] occurs after unvoiced sounds (or pause), [ɦ] after voiced sounds. Both sounds occur word-initially in many Wu dialects of Chinese, but with different tone patterns. The presence or absence of glottal friction (i.e., aspiration) is an important feature in the manner of consonant production and is distinctive for fricatives, affricates, and stops. The use of aspiration as a phonetic feature is most frequent with stops and is more frequent with unvoiced consonants than with voiced.

The vocal folds can be firmly pressed against each other to create an abrupt onset or cutoff of the air stream, producing the glottal stop [ʔ]. Glottal closure or constriction can also be used as a phonetic feature in the production of stops and affricates; this feature is glottalization. When the vocal tract is blocked at some point and vocal folds are approximated, a volume of air is trapped in between these two points. If the larynx moves upward with the glottis closed, the volume decreases and the trapped air becomes compressed. Then, if first the oral closure, and next the glottal closure, is released, an ejective stop or affricate is produced. The friction which occurs between the two releases is driven by glottalic air; that which occurs after the glottal release is driven by pulmonic air, i.e., aspiration or [h].

If the larynx moves downward, the volume increases, and negative pressure results. The successive releases of the oral and glottal closures produce an imploded stop. In such cases, air first rushes into the pressure space in the mouth (as when a light bulb is shattered); then, as the glottis is opened, pulmonic air flows out. Because the subglottal pressure becomes increasingly greater than the supraglottal pressure as the larynx moves downward, air tends to escape through the glottis, causing the vocal folds to vibrate. The converse situation obtains in the production of ejectives. Thus, voicing is normally determined by the manner of glottalization: ejectives are unvoiced and implosives are voiced.

Due to the voicing of implosives, it is relatively difficult to create a strong negative pressure in the vocal tract. This presumably explains the absence of imploded affricates, since affricates require a stronger pressure for their production than the corresponding stops. Ejective affricates, however, are observed in a wide variety of languages. Further, there seems to be a tendency for compression to occur with smaller volumes of air, while rarefaction occurs with larger volumes. This may account for the fact that labial ejectives are comparatively rare and that velar implosives have not been reported.

Voicing is produced by the periodic approximation of the vocal folds, which interrupts the stream of air flowing through the glottis. Unlike the situation in the production of [ɦ] or breathy vowels, the closure made by the vocal folds during normal voicing is relatively complete. Under a constant driving pressure from the thorax, the subglottal pressure continues to build up when the glottis is closed, until it is sufficiently great to force the vocal folds apart; then a puff of air escapes into the supralaryngeal cavities, reducing the positive pressure below the glottis. The puff of air rushing between the vocal folds creates a force (the Bernouilli effect) which tends to suck the folds together. This force and the natural elasticity of the folds

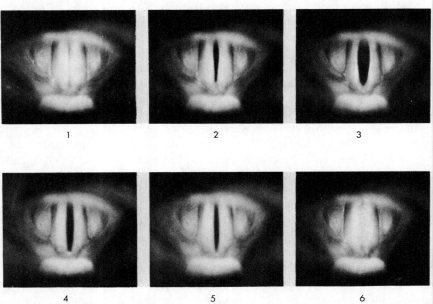

Figure 7-1. Six Successive Positions of the Vocal Folds in One Cycle

Successive positions of the vocal folds in one cycle of vibration. Top left frame shows the folds about to be blown apart. Top right frame shows the glottis at its widest. Bottom three frames show the glottis closing (after Farnsworth, Copyright © 1940, Bell Telephone Laboratories, Inc. Reprinted by permission of the Editor, Bell Laboratories Record).

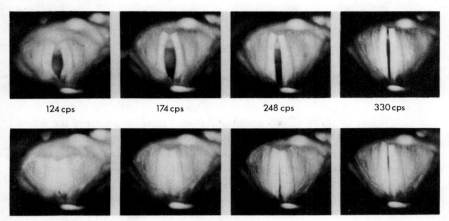

Figure 7-2. The Vocal Folds and Pitch Change

In the top row the leftmost frame shows the length and displacement of the vocal folds as they are vibrating at 124 cps. The next frames are at 174 cps., 248 cps., and 330 cps. The length of the vocal folds when the glottis is closed is shown in the corresponding photographs of the bottom row (after Farnsworth, Copyright © 1940, Bell Telephone Laboratories, Inc. Reprinted by permission of the Editor, Bell Laboratories Record).

combine to draw the folds together again, closing off the glottis until the next puff of air pushes through. This completes one cycle of laryngeal vibration.

In Figure 7-1, we see a series of photographs of the vocal folds which were taken by means of a mirror placed against the palate directly above the larynx. The photographs show six successive positions of the vocal folds in one cycle of vibration. In the lower part of the photographs, we can see the gross outline of the arytenoid cartilages.

The rate of vibration is increased when the vocal folds are made more tense. This can be achieved by moving the arytenoid cartilages backward, stretching and elongating the folds. Conversely, when the arytenoid cartilages move forward, the vocal folds shorten, become more lax, and vibrate more slowly. The vibratory process, including the control of the rate of vibration, depends upon a balance in the amount of tension in the vocal folds as against a relatively constant pressure of pulmonic air. The rapid changes in pressure around the glottis and the quick movements of the vocal folds constitute a local form of dynamic equilibrium that is created and maintained by the two forces: muscular tension and air pressure. The situation is very similar to the production of other types of vibration in speech, i.e., the vibration of the back of the velum in [R] and the tongue tip in [r]. Due to the greater mass of these organs, their rate of vibration seldom exceeds 30 cps. The vocal folds, on the other hand, vibrate at a rate ranging from some 60 cps for a bass to over 400 cps for a high soprano. (See Figure 7-2.)

Our understanding of the phonation process has been considerably increased in recent years through the use of high speed photography of the vocal folds. We are now able to observe more directly and accurately the various aspects of laryngeal vibration. We may, for example, measure from film the area of the glottis as it varies in time. Plotting the area against the ordinate and time against the abscissa, we observe that during the first half of a vibratory cycle the geometric configuration is that of a right triangle, and that the area of the glottis opening remains near zero during the second half. As the voice becomes louder, the hypotenuse of the triangle shortens and the wave form becomes more pulse-like. This indicates that the vocal folds come together more quickly as a result of increased tension. They remain together for a longer time within each cycle when producing a louder voice without changing the pitch. As expected, these observations correlate well with the remarks made above on the volume velocity of air flow.

Prosodic Parameters

Voice loudness and pitch are prosodic parameters which can, to a certain extent, be controlled independently of the supraglottal mechanisms (though obviously not altogether). There are two levels of linguistic function at which these parameters are relevant: the syntactic and the lexical.

At the syntactic level, loudness and pitch usually correlate quite well with duration. A greater degree of loudness is frequently accompanied by higher pitch and longer duration of the associated word. At this level, the scope of these parameters varies according to their function. Here we distinguish three types.

For the expression of such notions as declarative statement, interrogation, hesitancy, irony, etc., the scope extends over the entire sentence. That is, the same set of rules assigns phonetic values to these parameters for the entire sentence. The term *intonation* is sometimes applied to this use of the parameters. In this sense, intonation provides the speaker with another channel of communication by means of which he can express a more personal commentary on the sentence he is producing. This use of the prosodic parameters is probably universal in human language.

Another function of prosodic parameters at the syntactic level is to configurate speech into syntactic units of various sizes, e.g., words, phrases, clauses. Other phonetic parameters, usually laryngeal features such as glottal stop or aspiration, also correlate with the boundaries of syntactic units, especially words. As an example of phrase configurations of different types, consider the following pair of English sentences. The difference between an appositive and a restrictive clause, for instance, can be signaled by suitable modulations of pitch, loudness, and rhythm:

The student, who studied Swahili, went to Tanzania. (Appositive)
The student who studied Swahili went to Tanzania. (Restrictive)
(The one who didn't had to stay in Paris.)

The third function of prosodic parameters has a narrower scope: this relates to the derivational morphology of individual words. In English, there are nouns like *cóntract*, *pérmit*, *súbject*, etc., where the stress is on the first syllable. Phonetically, this means that the syllable is louder and has a higher pitch and greater duration. The verbs which correspond to these nouns bear the stress on the second syllable. In Mandarin Chinese, the verbs *shǔ* 'to count', *shān* 'to fan', *bēi* 'to carry on one's back', *liáng* 'to measure', *lián* 'to connect', etc., all have corresponding nouns with the falling tone, i.e., *shù* 'number', *shàn* 'fan', *bèi* 'back', *liàng* 'quantity', *liàn* 'chain'. The phonetic value of these stress and tone correspondences can be predicted from the morphology and therefore do not need to be specified for each lexical item.

Also functioning within the scope of the word is contrastive stress. It may perhaps be instructive to compare the workings of contrastive stress with those of emphatic stress, which has as its scope the sentence. Emphatic stress is used to distinguish the sentence from its negation. Its position of occurrence is not distinctive and is usually fixed. In English, it falls on the first word in the verb phrase of the declarative sentence. Contrastive stress, on the other hand, is used to distinguish a particular morpheme from other morphemes which may occur in the same position; it can fall on any syllable in the sentence. In either case, the pronunciation of the sentence is non-neutral, in that either it bears an extra stress, or the main stress of the sentence is displaced from the position it normally occupies in a neutral pronunciation. When an extra stress falls on the word which can bear emphatic stress, the sentence is ambiguous, in that the stress can be interpreted as being either emphatic or contrastive. Thus, the stress in a sentence like *he shóuld go there* distinguishes the sentence from either *he shouldn't go there* or a sentence like *he múst go there*.

At the lexical level, the prosodic parameters may constitute an accentual system. Here the phonetic values of these parameters cannot be predicted from the syntactic structure; rather, the features from which these values may be predicted must be specified for each morpheme, as is the case with other features of consonants and vowels which are not predictable by general rules. In contrast with the situation at the syntactic level, these parameters may vary independently of each other at the lexical level. Pitch, for example, may change in a way that is quite unrelated to the way loudness changes.

In tone languages, the accentual system is primarily based on the values of voice pitch on morphemes. A classic example of a tone language is Mandarin Chinese. The vowel [i], for example, pronounced with a high level pitch means 'clothes'; with a high rising pitch it means 'aunt'; with a low pitch it means 'chair'; and with a falling pitch it means 'intention'. Although tone languages are widespread in many parts of the world, the complexity of the accentual system seems to be greatest in the languages of southeast Asia; here there may be as many as nine distinct pitch patterns on mono-syllables.

Sometimes the tones of these more complex systems, especially the low tones, are accompanied by other glottal phenomena, such as breathy voice or [ʔ]; sometimes by differences in duration. Furthermore, both the distribution and the historical evolution of tones seem to be related to the feature of voicing in consonants in a large number of languages.

Tones can be differentiated into contour tones and noncontour tones. Contour tones can be divided into rising tones and falling tones, as well as into those which turn in the direction of pitch movement (i.e., rising-falling or falling-rising) and those which do not. In a recent survey of several hundred tone systems, it was found that very few languages have more than (a) four noncontour tones, (b) two rising tones, (c) two falling tones, or (d) two turning tones.

ARTICULATION

The movements of the supralaryngeal mechanisms in speech production may be referred to collectively as articulation. Basically, this comprises the widening and narrowing of the mouth at various points to produce alternating sequences of vowels and consonants. For most speech sounds, it is reasonable to assume that air is being pushed out of the thorax at a constant rate, so that interruptions of the air flow and local fluctuations in pressure are all consequences of the articulatory movements. The acoustic energy of speech and the prosodic parameters are primarily carried by the vowels; the consonants interspersed between the vowels add to the number of dimensions along which speech sounds may be discriminated. Let us now consider the approximate range of sounds which the articulatory movements can produce and how these sounds function in language.

The sagittal section of the speech tract in Figure 7-3 shows that there are two fixed walls, at about right angles to each other, which limit the articulatory possibilities: the back of the pharynx and the roof of the mouth. The moving parts are the velum, the lips, and the tongue, in conjunction with the lower jaw. Grossly speaking, speech is articulated by moving these parts against the two fixed walls. (See Figure 7-3.)

There is a set of muscles in the back of the mouth which can serve a sphincteric function by drawing the velum tightly against the pharyngeal wall, producing velic closure. This shuts off the nasal cavities from the rest of the speech mechanism. When these muscles are relaxed, as in normal breathing, the velum is down and the nasal cavities are coupled to the

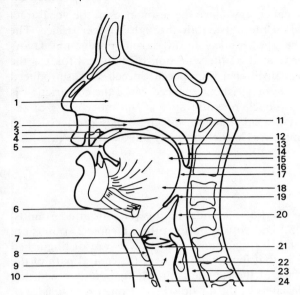

Figure 7-3. Mid-Sagittal View of the Speech Tract

1. Nasal cavity. 2. Hard palate. 3. Alveolar ridge. 4. Palate. 5. Tongue tip. 6. Hyoid bone.
7. Ventricular fold. 8. Thyroid cartilage. 9. Larynx cavity. 10. Cricoid cartilage (in front).
11. Nasal pharynx. 12. Tongue middle. 13. Velum. 14. Velic. 15. Tongue back. 16. Uvula.
17. Oral pharynx. 18. Tongue root. 19. Epiglottis. 20. Laryngeal pharynx. 21. Vocal fold.
22. Cricoid cartilage (behind). 23. Oesophagus. 24. Trachea.

pharynx and mouth. The position of the velum is thus crucial for an important feature in articulation: nasality. In the discussion of various sounds that
follows, we will assume velic closure unless stated to the contrary; that is,
as a rule we will be discussing nonnasal sounds.

The vocal tract between the glottis and the lips may be viewed, for the
sake of simplicity, as a pipe bent at a right angle. The vertical portion of the
pipe is the phraynx, the horizontal portion the mouth. Acoustically, the
basic function of articulation is to produce a sound source in the vocal tract,
which in turn causes the chambers of air in the vocal tract to resonate.

By positioning the lips and tongue in various ways, one can effect a
constriction or narrowing in the vocal tract; the narrowest region in the
vocal tract is the place of articulation. In referring to the cross-sectional area
at the place of articulation, let us distinguish among three degrees of opening:
(a) *degree 0:* a closure in the vocal tract stops air flow; that is, the construction
is complete; (b) *degree 1:* the opening is narrow enough so that fricative
noise is produced when air flows through it; and (c) *degree 2:* the opening is
wide enough so that the air flow does not produce friction.

Other things being equal, it is clear that a greater opening will produce a sound of greater acoustical energy, since the resonances in the vocal tract will be better transmitted to the outside air through a larger orifice. The characteristic state of the speech mechanism during production favors voicing, since the tone generated by the vibration of the vocal folds is the most important source of acoustic energy in speech. Speech sounds produced at a degree 2 opening are characteristically voiced, since the constriction is not sufficient to create any back pressure against the movements of the vibrating vocal folds. On the other hand, speech sounds produced with degree 0 or degree 1 opening are characteristically unvoiced.

Sonorants

At degree 2 there are two classes of sounds: liquids (laterals and r-sounds) and nasals on the one hand and vowels on the other. Degree 2 sounds are sometimes referred to collectively as sonorants. Vowels are distinguished from the other sonorants in that the air flow is over the central path of the vocal tract while the surface of the tongue is in minimal contact with the upper teeth and palate. In laterals, the air flow is over one or both sides of the tongue; in nasals, air flows out through the nostrils. In the production of laterals, while a closure is effected by holding the tongue tip against the alveolar ridge, the bulk of the tongue may assume different shapes to effect a secondary constriction, producing a variety of lateral sounds which share resonance characteristics with the corresponding vowels, especially [i] and [u]. The r-sounds are even more diverse, though most of them share the property of retroflexing the tongue tip upward and backward. Word-initial r in English is labialized, but the tongue tip does not cut off the air stream. If the tongue tip does briefly stop the air stream once, a flap [ɾ] is produced. If intermittent interruption is created, either by the tongue tip or by the velum, a trill is produced. As contrasted with the laterals, in which the closure is effected by controlled movements, the interruptions of the r-sounds are ballistic and partly effected by the force of the air stream.

Nasals usually have just one constriction which stops the air flow at some point in the mouth; the velum is down, and air is shunted out by way of the nasal cavities. There are languages, however, which are reported to have nasals formed with closure both at the lips and at either the alveolar ridge or the velum. In these compound stops, oral as well as nasal, it is natural to assume for perceptual reasons that the inner closure (the closure nearer to the glottis) would be initiated earlier and released later than the outer closure. Nasals and liquids are usually voiced and frictionless. There are a few instances, however, in which voicing is distinctive for liquids and nasals and instances in which friction is distinctive for liquids.

Vowels constitute a rich class of sounds, the members of which are distinguished along several dimensions. The major determinants of vowel quality are the position of the tongue and the shape of the lips. Although vowels may be devoiced in some contexts in some languages, it is very unlikely that voicing in vowels is distinctive at the lexical level.

In vowel production, the tip of the tongue typically stays down and the body of the tongue assumes a shape that may be viewed as part of a sphere posed against two fixed walls, the hard palate and the back of the pharynx. As the tongue moves front and up or back and down, its volume stays relatively constant. The volume of the pharynx and the volume of the mouth change according to the position of the tongue, each increasing or decreasing at the expense of the other. In the production of [i], the volume of the mouth is small as compared with that of the pharynx; the converse situation obtains in the production of [a].

Tongue position defined in terms of place of articulation has been traditionally quantized along two dimensions: tongue region and tongue height. Tongue region is traditionally divided into front : central : back. In terms of binary phonological features, these three terms correspond to (+palatal, −velar) : (−palatal, −velar) : (−palatal, +velar). The names of these features show the obvious relationship between the vowel regions and the places of articulation of consonants. For tongue height, where the traditional terms are (high) : (higher mid) : (lower mid) : (low), the feature specifications are (+high, −mid) : (+high, +mid) : (−high, +mid) : (−high, −mid). Languages with only two vowel heights utilize only the feature ± high.

The use of these features for the classification of vowels is illustrated in Table 7-1. The vowels [i e ɛ a ɑ ɔ o u] are the so-called cardinal vowels adopted by the International Phonetic Association which serve as reference points for the description of all vowel sounds. [i] was selected to represent the highest possible palatal vowel and [ɑ] the lowest possible velar vowel. Then [e ɛ a] represent vowels such that the perceptual distance between each of the pairs i-e, e-ɛ, ɛ-a, a-ɑ are approximately equal. [ɔ o u] represent velar vowels selected by a similar procedure. [æ] represents a vowel sound that typically occurs in such English words as 'hat', 'ram', 'lad', etc. It is pro-

Table 7-1. Vowels and Their Primary Features

	Tongue Region					
	−labialized			+labialized		
Tongue Height	+pal −vel	−pal −vel	−pal +vel	+pal −vel	−pal −vel	−pal +vel
+high, −mid	i	ɨ	ɯ	y	ʉ	u
+high, +mid	e	ə	ɤ	ɸ		o
−high, +mid	ɛ		ʌ	œ		ɔ
−high, −mid	a		ɑ			ɒ

nounced slightly higher and fronter than [a], with the lips perhaps a little more spread. [æ] and [a] do not contrast in any language.

Figure 7-4 shows an X-ray picture of the mid-sagittal section of the speech tract during the pronunciation of the Russian vowel [ɨ]. The tongue, the roof of the mouth, and the pharyngeal wall were coated with a barium mixture for improved visibility. In this picture, the hyoid bone and the upper part of the larynx are also clearly discernible. From such pictures, tracings can be made of the mid-sagittal section of the speech tract during the production of various sounds. Figure 7-5 shows oral tracings for the six Russian vowels.

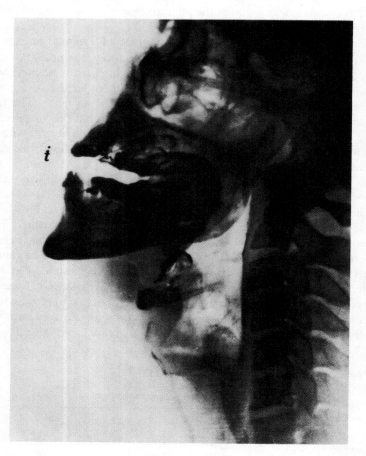

Figure 7-4. X-Ray Picture of the Mid-Sagittal Section of the Speech Tract

The tongue, the roof of the mouth, and the pharyngeal wall were coated with a barium mixture for improved visibility. The picture was taken while the subject was pronouncing the Russian vowel [ɨ] (after Fant 95).

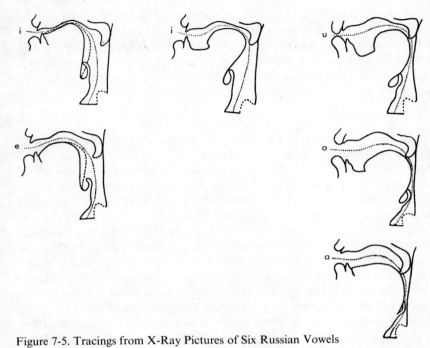

Figure 7-5. Tracings from X-Ray Pictures of Six Russian Vowels

Tracings of the median sections of the vocal tract from X-ray pictures of the Russian vowels [i], [ɨ], [u], [e], [o], and [ɑ]. The broken lines mark the rearmost contour of the larynx as well as some lateral contours of interest. The dotted line marks approximately the effective center line for the propagation of the acoustic wave within the vocal tract (after Fant 107).

Although it is difficult to find exact physiological correlates to these feature specifications, say on X-ray photographs, they nevertheless serve an important heuristic purpose in the study of speech. The third dimension of the traditional classification of vowels is in terms of lip rounding and is much more directly observable. It is usually quantized into a single opposition: rounded vs. unrounded, or +labial vs. −labial. The adequacy of this dichotomous classification has been questioned, in view of the claim that some languages have two distinct degrees of labialization in vowels, in addition to unrounded vowels. Before the present scale is revised, the counterevidence should, however, be examined carefully to determine if the extra vowel distinctions can be explained in terms of influence by phonological context or other dimensions of vowel articulation.

If we assume the $4 \times 3 \times 2$ scales of the preceding paragraph, there is a logical maximum of 24 distinct vowels, disregarding other factors such as nasality, duration, breathiness, laryngealization, frication, and retroflexion. Vowel systems are, however, considerably simpler in general. The five-vowel system of [i, e, a, o, u], for example, is widespread among the languages of the world. This fact is instructive on certain typical redundancies: the distinction of front-back usually correlates with that of rounded-unrounded; the high-low dimension is more exploited than the front-back dimension in that the central position is rarely used, especially for low vowels.

Obstruents

Consonants with degree 1 opening are fricatives (or spirants); those of degree 0 are plosives (or stops or occlusives). These two classes of sounds constitute the obstruents. We have already mentioned the features of glottalization, aspiration, and voicing as they apply to consonant articulation. For plosives, we must also consider the feature of affrication, which has to do with the manner in which the closure is released. If the opening changes from degree 0 to degree 2 gradually, noticeable friction is produced at or near the place of articulation before it reaches degree 2. In this case, the transient time during which the vocal tract assumes an opening of degree 1 is sufficiently long to produce a fricative. This sequence of a plosive followed closely by its homorganic fricative constitutes an affricate. If the change from degree 0 opening to degree 2 is abrupt, the plosive is not affricated.

Some combinations of the features of voicing, affrication, aspiration, and glottalization apply to all consonants. Thus, in the labial region affricates formed by occlusion followed by labiodental friction can be further distinguished vis-à-vis aspiration; [pf] and [pfʰ] are, in fact, distinct in some languages. Figure 7-6 illustrates the function of these features as they

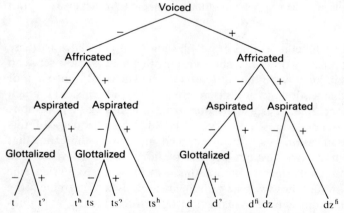

Figure 7-6. Classification of Some Alveolar Plosives According to Four Features

Branching to the right of a node indicates that the sound that branch dominates has a positive value for the feature which labels that node. Branching to the left indicates a negative value. Notice that the asymmetry in the diagram is due to the fact that glottalization is nondistinctive for aspirated plosives and for voiced affricates.

distinguish some plosives in the alveolar position. These features and their combinations do not, of course, exhaust the possible ways in which an alveolar plosive can be produced. In some languages, distinctions are made in the fricative part of the affricate, depending on the way in which the tongue tip leaves the alveolar ridge. The fricative may be of a lateral variety (i.e., [tɬ]), or it may be nonsibilant (i.e., [tθ]) rather than sibilant, as shown in Figure 7-6. There may be a constriction elsewhere in the vocal tract, nearly simultaneous with the alveolar closure. Thus, it is possible to produce compound stops which function as single segments, e.g., [pt] or [bd]. If the tongue is articulated against various portions of the roof of the mouth, a volume of air is trapped and rarefied, producing a special class of consonants. The velaric air stream thus produced underlies the so-called "clicks," found in some languages of South Africa. A detailed discussion of the sounds mentioned in this paragraph would take us beyond the scope of this essay, though there is considerable literature on the subject.

Many of the distinctions among plosives that can be made at the alveolar position can also be made at other places along the vocal tract. We now turn our attention to these places of articulation, which may be studied with reference to Figure 7-3 and Table 7-2. There are plosives which are made by the lips (bilabial) and by the lower lip against the upper teeth (labiodental).

Table 7-2. Consonants by Place and Manner of Articulation

Manner		Bilabial	Labiodental	Dental	Alveolar	Palatal	Velar	Uvular	Pharyngeal	Glottal
Ia	unvd	p		ʈ	t	c	k	q		ʔ
	vd	b		ɖ	d	ɟ	g	G		
Ib	unvd		pf	tθ	ts	tʃ	kx			
	vd		bv	dð	dz	dʒ	ɣ			
II	unvd	Φ	f	θ	s	ʃ	x	χ	ħ	h
	vd	β	v	ð	z	ʒ	ɣ	ʁ	ʕ	ɦ
III	nasals	m	ɱ		n	ɲ	ŋ	N		
	liquids				l	ʎ	ɫ			
					r			R		

NOTE: I = obstruents; Ia = plosives (stops); Ib = affricates; II = fricatives (spirants); III = sonorants.

The tongue tip may form a closure against the upper lip (labiolingual). Though this sound can be easily made by speakers of any language, it is known to occur functionally in only one language. On the other hand, the closure formed by the tongue tip in the dental-alveolar region yields a class of stops that is present in a majority of the languages of the world and has a very high frequency of usage. In some languages, the dental stop is distinct from the alveolar plosive. The raised tongue tip may also be drawn backwards to form a closure against the palate, thus producing a retroflex plosive. There are languages in which these three classes of plosives produced by the tongue tip are distinctive.

Closures formed by the middle of the tongue against the palate produce palatal plosives; those formed by the back of the tongue against the velum produce velar plosives. There are languages which distinguish two places of articulation against the velum; the one farther back is often called uvular or postvelar. At the end of the vocal tract, one can produce the glottal stop, which has been discussed earlier.

If the velic is open during the production of any of the oral plosives mentioned above, air escapes through the nasal cavities while the mouth is blocked. The articulation of nasal stops is, therefore, similar to that of oral stops, especially when the latter are voiced. There is, however, no language which distinguishes more than four nasal stops, though many languages have more than four oral stops. In no language do the nasals have more distinct places of articulation than the oral stops.

In connection with sounds produced with an opening of degree 2, the following places of articulation are relevant: bilabial, labiodental, dental, alveolar, palatal, velar, uvular, and glottal. Sounds produced at degree 1 (i.e., fricatives or spirants) may be classified by means of a similar scale, with the following differences. There are two fricatives, one voiced and one unvoiced, which are produced by pulling the body of the tongue far back so that it forms a constriction against the pharyngeal wall in the oral pharynx. Since it is not possible to effect a complete closure in that region of the vocal tract, there are pharyngeal fricatives but no pharyngeal plosives.

There is another difference between plosives and fricatives in the dental-alveolar region. The dental fricatives are formed with the surface of the tongue relatively flat and the tip at least as high as the upper edges of the lower incisors. These fricatives, [θ] and [ð], are sometimes called flat or slit fricatives, as opposed to those which are formed with a slight groove down the center front of the tongue. More important, the tongue tip is positioned behind the lower incisors in such a way that the air stream is forced over the upper edges of the lower incisors, producing a noise of greater intensity, especially in the high frequencies. The latter are sometimes called rilled or grooved fricatives; sounds whose production involves the forcing of the air stream over the incisors in this way are called sibilants.

Fricatives are sometimes paired with respect to voicing, although the unvoiced member is by far the more common, for reasons discussed earlier. The unvoiced ones, especially the alveolar [s], can be distinguished by some of the features of manner mentioned in the discussion of plosives. Glottalized unvoiced fricatives have been reported for many languages. Aspiration is rarer but attested; one Chinese dialect is reported to have distinct aspirated and unaspirated unvoiced fricatives of the labiodental, alveolar, retroflex, and palatal varieties: i.e., [fʰ] vs. [f], [sʰ] vs. [s], [çʰ] vs. [ç], and [ṣʰ] vs. [ṣ].

As we examine the literature which reports on the sound systems of a great diversity of languages, we find that certain principles may be extracted which relate to what classes of sounds tend to occur and how these sounds combine into sequences. That investigators of different training organize their materials in different ways and that these materials are not all equally reliable are inevitable difficulties we have to face in our attempt to interpret the literature and to integrate the results into a uniform framework. In spite of these difficulties, there is sufficient uniformity to permit some generalizations. Exceptions to generalizations based on the majority of cases are all the more interesting for phonetic theory, because counterexamples are the best clues to improvements in the theory.

A fundamental principle is that *the sounds of a language tend to maximize the phonetic distance from each other* within the articulatory range sketched above. This principle of maximum phonetic distance has been cited by some scholars as a central mechanism in the evolution of phonetic systems.

The implications of this principle seem to hold true at different levels. At the most general level, we notice that the features which partition sounds into major classes are distinctive in almost all languages. All languages have vowels and oral plosives; almost all languages have liquids, nasal stops, and fricatives. Within each class, the sounds continue to maximize their phonetic distance from each other. If a system has two vowels, for instance, one will be high and the other low. If it has three vowels, the tongue height dimension remains maximum, while the extreme values of the tongue region dimension (and, frequently, the lip-rounding dimension) are called into play, to yield [i], [a], and [u]. Similar observations may be made for the consonants. It is as though the sounds themselves are striving for maximum identity and distinctness in order to achieve the greatest intelligibility in deliberate speech and to counterbalance the damaging effects on intelligibility of a considerable loss of phonetic distance in casual and rapid speech.

The most stable characteristic of the way sounds combine is that a sequence containing only consonants or only vowels never gets very long, i.e., *short* sequences of consonants always alternate with *short* sequences of vowels. In speech perception, the vowels are important in supplying the acoustical power of speech; they are more audible than the consonants by a wide margin. A primary cue for the perception of certain obstruent articulations is their effect on the vowel; in fact, such a cue may override the one provided by the burst and/or friction of the obstruent itself. Consonants are important in that they add many more articulatory dimensions, to expand the inventory of phonetic units.

In many languages, the length of consonant sequences never exceeds one; i.e., there are no consonant clusters. Many other languages have sequences of length two. Sequences of length three or more are much less frequent, and these are usually the result of the joining together of several morphemes. If the cluster contains nasals and liquids, which are characteristically voiced, they tend to occupy positions contiguous to the vowel.

Voiced obstruents are not separated from their nuclear vowel by unvoiced sounds. Some sequences are frequent, e.g., homorganic nasals and obstruents, whereas others occur rarely, if at all, e.g., sequences of sibilants or liquids. The dental-alveolar region is favored, in that every set of initial or final sequences includes a sequence that contains a dental-alveolar obstruent.

SPEECH WAVES

The sound that radiates out from the mouth and/or nostrils may be represented as a wave form, with time along the abscissa and amplitude along the ordinate. All the properties of the sound wave are determined by the shape and movement of the speech mechanism. In the past quarter century, much effort has been made to further our understanding of how the sound waves are derived from the physiological aspects of speech production. Success in this area is attested by the construction of several electrical analogs of the vocal tract, which produce continuous speech with an impressive degree of naturalness. Advances in this area have made it possible for us to discuss the sounds of speech with greater clarity and precision.

In particular, the acoustical aspects of vowel production have been intensively studied. The fact that vowels are static sounds makes it possible for an investigator to make good use of X-ray techniques to yield precise measurements of the vocal tract.

Let us consider an idealized situation where the tongue is positioned in such a way that the cross-sectional area of the vocal tract is relatively uniform. From a physical point of view, the vocal tract is essentially a pipe, originating at the glottis and terminating at the lips. The facts that the pipe is "bent" and that its inner walls are soft tissue (rather than, say, hard wood or metal, as in the pipes of an organ) are of little consequence in the present context. The vibrating vocal folds form an imperfect closure at the lower end of the pipe, since puffs of air periodically push them apart. Let us, however, assume for the sake of easy conceptualization that the closure is complete. The situation is then simply that of a pipe that is open at one end and closed at the other. In the average male, the pipe is some 0.17 m long, i.e., the distance between the glottis and the lips. The characteristic resonances of the volume of air contained in the pipe can now be computed, once the velocity of sound is given. These resonances can be estimated from spectrograms, where they usually appear as dark bands. We will follow the usual practice of referring to these dark bands, and thereby also to the resonances, as formants. The one lowest in frequency is the first formant, F-1, the next to the lowest is the second formant, F-2, and so on. In a uniform pipe, the formants can be computed by means of the following formula:

$$F_i = (2i-1)\frac{\text{velocity of sound}}{4(\text{length of pipe})}$$

This formula simply asserts that the wave length of F-1 is four times the length of the pipe and that the formants are related to each other by the odd integers. Given that the velocity of sound in air is about 340 m per second, F-1 is 500 cps, F-2 is 1500 cps, F-3 is 2500 cps, and so on.

From this elementary formula, we can deduce several facts about vowel formants. It is clear that the frequency of the formants varies inversely with the length of the pipe. When the pipe is lengthened, as by rounding of the lips, the frequencies decrease and the formants fall closer together. Since women and children have shorter vocal tracts, their formants are higher in frequency and are farther apart. The vowel formants produced by the average male vocal tract are spaced some 1000 cps apart, as can be seen from the above computation.

It is important to note here that the frequency of formants is a function of the shape of the vocal tract; as such, it is not dependent on the frequency of the vibration of the vocal folds (i.e., voice pitch), which is controlled by the laryngeal mechanisms. The two sets of frequencies vary quite separately and independently as we speak. Indeed, the vocal folds do not vibrate when we whisper, even though we continue to make full use of the formants.

Values computed above for the uniform pipe rarely appear in natural speech. The reason is that vowels are produced with the tongue forming a constriction at various points of the vocal tract. This has the effect of displacing the formants in diverse ways, giving the vowels different acoustical properties. Extensive research on vowel formants in recent years has given us the following results.

While the vowels have quite a few formants of measurable intensity, perception of vowel quality is primarily determined by the first three formants. This can be easily demonstrated: if we remove all the frequencies above, say, 3500 cps, the intelligibility of the vowels is hardly impaired. Furthermore, F-3 is less variable in frequency than F-1 and F-2 and is therefore less important than the latter two. The typical frequencies of the formants for six common vowels produced by a male voice are shown in Table 7-3.

Table 7-3. Formant Frequencies of Selected Vowels

	[i]	[ɛ]	[æ]	[a]	[ɔ]	[u]
F-1	275	525	650	725	575	300
F-2	2300	1850	1725	1100	850	875
F-3	3000	2500	2400	2450	2400	2250

We can see from these values that a high F-1 is frequently associated with a narrow constriction of the back of the tongue against the pharyngeal wall and an unrounded, large mouth opening. On the other hand, a low F-1 is frequently associated with a small, round opening of the mouth, as in labialization, or with a narrow constriction within the mouth. F-2 covers a wider frequency range than F-1 or F-3. Table 7-3 shows a range of 275 cps to 725 cps for F-1, 850 cps to 2300 cps for F-2, and 2250 cps to 3000 cps for F-3, or a range of 450 cps, 1450 cps, and 750 cps, respectively. We can also see from Table 7-3 that a high F-2 is associated with front vowels and a low F-2 with back vowels.

Figure 7-7 shows a graph in which F-1 is plotted against F-2 to obtain a "vowel-formant loop." Note that in the graph, the ordinates intersect at the

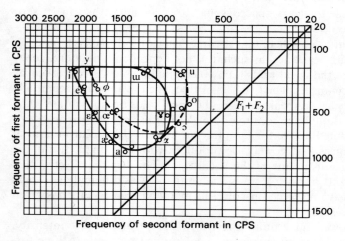

Figure 7-7. Formant Loops of Rounded and Unrounded Vowels

A plot of F-1 versus F-2 for sustained vowels pronounced by a native speaker of English. Each vowel was spoken twice. Positions connected by a solid line represent unrounded vowels; positions connected by a dashed line represent rounded vowels. Notice the considerable area of overlap of the two vowel loops (after Paterson, 1951).

upper right (rather than the lower left, as is customary). The formants are plotted in the *mel* scale, which assigns equal spacings to equal increments of pitch perception as these increments have been established by perceptual experiments with pure tones. It will be noted that such a vowel-formant loop bears a striking resemblance to widely used vowel diagrams, such as those proposed by the International Phonetic Association. These diagrams have been traditionally believed to bear a physical analogy to the "places" at which the various vowels are articulated. To the extent that vowel formants are the acoustic consequences of different physiological configurations, the resemblance of the vowel-formant loop to the traditional vowel diagram is, of course, not unexpected. Considering the fact that the physiology of vowel articulation was only properly understood quite recently (primarily by means of radiographic techniques), it is conceivable that the early user of the vowel diagram was significantly influenced by his perception of the vowels, as well as by his introspection on the position of his jaw and the shape of his tongue.

Figure 7-7 also makes it clear that F-1 and F-2 are not sufficient to distinguish vowel sounds. The solid loop encloses approximately the limits of the F-1 vs. F-2 values of unrounded vowels; all unrounded vowels would fall somewhere within the solid loop. The dashed loop, on the other hand, encloses rounded vowels. But notice the considerable area of overlap of these two loops. This means that within the area of overlap, a particular intersection of F-1 and F-2 is actually ambiguous, in that it represents two phonetically different vowels—one rounded, the other unrounded. Ambiguities of various sorts increase considerably when vowels produced by different speakers are grouped together. When F-3 is taken into account, so that the formants describe a three-dimensional rather than two-dimensional space, most of the ambiguities are resolved.

F-3 also plays a significant role in distinguishing the liquids [r] and [l]. Due to the retraction of the tongue in their production, [r] sounds are typically characterized by a very low (under 2000 cps) and relatively strong F-3. For the [l] sounds, on the other hand, F-3 is often canceled out altogether by an antiresonance in that frequency region which is created by the alveolar closure. What appears to be F-3 on spectrograms for [l] sounds is actually the fourth resonance of the vocal tract and is therefore more appropriately called F-4.

Given the frequencies of the formants, their amplitude relations are largely predictable. Roughly speaking, the amplitude of F-1 increases with frequency, and this increase raises the amplitude of the other formants as well. Consequently, the overall intensity of vowels increases with higher F-1, providing an analytic explanation for the observation that low vowels have the greatest acoustic intensity and high vowels have the least. This accords with the intuition that since the aperture of the mouth is greater in their production, the low vowels should be louder. Another predictable relation between formant frequencies and amplitudes is that when two formants are close to each other, the amplitudes of both are increased. Fant has computed that if the distance between two neighboring formants is divided by two, the peaks of these formants will rise by 6 decibels, and the valley between them will rise by 12 decibels. The decrease in amplitude of the higher formants is explained by the fact that these formants are primarily superimposed on the resonance curve of F-1, which decreases in amplitude at a rate of approximately 12 decibels per octave.

From these considerations, it is possible to predict that the F-1 of [ɑ] and [ɔ] would have high amplitudes, while the F-3 of [u] would have a very low amplitude; indeed, here the difference is sometimes over 40 decibels. Since F-3 is characteristically extremely weak in amplitude, it has a much less important effect on the perception of phonetic quality than F-1 and F-2, even though F-3 typically occurs in a frequency region to which the ear is especially sensitive, i.e., around 3000 cps.

It appears that some aspects of how languages select vowels may be explained in terms of formant frequencies. It has been widely observed that front nonlow vowels are generally unrounded, while back nonlow vowels are generally rounded. Systems which have front rounded vowels invariably also have front unrounded vowels but not conversely. Similarly, the presence of unrounded back vowels implies the presence of rounded back vowels but not conversely. When we look at the situation purely in physiological terms, it is difficult to explain why languages favor so overwhelmingly the combinations front-unrounded and back-rounded over the combinations front-rounded and back-unrounded, since the dimension of front-back is entirely independent of the dimension rounded-unrounded.

The situation is readily understandable if we take into account the formant frequencies involved. Intuitively expressed, the point is simply that the acoustical difference between, say, [i] and [u] is greater than that between either [i] and [ɯ] or [y] and [u], especially with respect to the frequencies of F-2. This can be seen clearly in Figure 7-7, where all four high

Table 7-4. Vowel Formant Frequencies in Estonian

High vowels in Estonian:		V_1			V_2	
	i	i/u	u		y/u	y
F-1	300	200	500		200	300
F-2	2300	1500	800		1200	2000
F-3	2800	150	2650		150	2500
		1850 cps			1550 cps	

Mid vowels in Estonian:		V_1			V_2	
	e	e/o	o		ø/o	ø
F-1	350	150	500		25	525
F-2	2275	1475	800		1000	1800
F-3	2750	1100	1650		1050	2700
		2725 cps			2300 cps	

NOTE: The figures for columns labeled V_1/V_2 represent the absolute difference in the respective formant frequencies of the two vowels. The difference is greatest between front-unrounded vowels and back-rounded vowels; see discussion in text.

SOURCE: From I. Lehiste, *Phonetica*, Supplementum *ad* Vol. 5: Accoustic-Phonetic Study of International Open Juncture, by Ilse Lehiste (S. Karger, Basel/New York).

vowels are plotted. Tongue-backing and lip-rounding have mutually reinforcing effects in the lowering of *F*-2. Therefore, [i] and [u] would be maximally different from each other since the two differ along both dimensions. This point is illustrated in Table 7-4, where the formant frequencies of some Estonian vowels are presented.

Since the middle 1940s, the sound spectrograph has been a key instrument in the study of speech signal. The spectrograph converts a short sample of the speech wave, usually 2.4 seconds, into a graphic record of the frequency characteristics of the speech wave. These records, called spectrograms, can then be visually inspected and measured with precision. Spectrograms have provided a wealth of reliable observations on the speech signal, on the basis of which we can make inferences about the nature of the mechanisms of both speech production and speech perception.

Most spectrograms are of two sorts: broad-band spectrograms and narrow-band spectrograms. An example of each type is given in Figure 7-8. The utterance from which the spectrograms are made is "speech production."

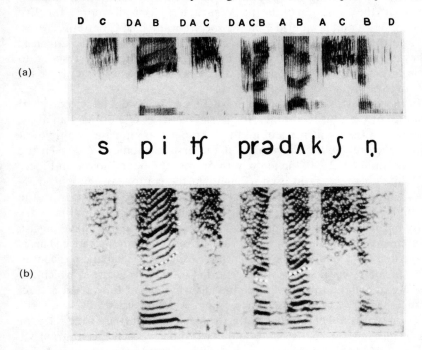

Figure 7-8. Major Spectrograph Patterns

The broad-band spectrogram shown in (*a*) illustrates the four major patterns: A = pulse; B = formant structure; C = noise structure; and D = gap. In the narrow-band spectrogram shown in (*b*), white dots are used to highlight the contour of the tenth harmonic of the voice.

In the broad-band spectrogram of Figure 7-8a, the four common types of patterns can be seen. The portions labeled A above indicate events in the speech signal marked by an abrupt opening of the vocal tract. These pulses correspond to the onset of the plosives [p d k] and the affricate [tʃ] in the utterance, the four sounds made with an opening of degree 0. Notice that of these four, only the pulse for [d] is preceded by low-frequency energy-markings near the bottom of the spectrogram which indicate that the vocal folds were vibrating before the onset of the obstruent.

The spectrogram of Figure 7-8a starts at about 0 cps and cuts off at a frequency somewhere above 3000 cps. The formant structures of the sonorants are displayed quite clearly in this frequency band. The portions labeled B above correspond to the sonorants [i ə ʌ] and syllabic [n]. We see that the formants move almost continuously in time, indicating that the articulators are virtually in constant motion. In [ə], the four lowest formants can be discerned. In the other three sonorants, F-4 is above the frequency cutoff. The [r] following the [p] appears to be entirely unvoiced and coterminous with the aspiration of the [p]. As such, it is physically more a fricative than a sonorant and is labeled C in the spectrogram. The C patterns correspond to turbulence or noise in the speech signal. In addition to the unvoiced [r], they are found for the [s] and [ʃ] sounds. The D patterns correspond to gaps in the speech wave. i.e., periods during which the vocal tract is closed off at some point.

In the narrow-band spectrograms of Figure 7-8b we see the individual harmonics of the four sonorants. From the methods of Fourier's analysis, we know that the frequencies of all the harmonics are integral multiples of the frequency of the first harmonic. If the first harmonic is F-0, then the second harmonic is $2 F$-0, the tenth harmonic is $10 F$-0, and so on. In Figure 7-8b, white dots have been used to highlight the contour of the tenth harmonic, which indicates the pitch of the voice. Thus, we see that in [i] the voice pitch is relatively high and rising and that in [n] it is low and falling.

By means of the sound spectrograph, we are also able to have precise measurements of the duration of the various sounds in an utterance. This is illustrated in the broad-band spectrograms of Figure 7-9. Japanese is chosen for this purpose, because it is often reported to be a language in which the moras are of equal duration. To examine to what extent this report is true, utterances with a constant sentence frame were recorded; five different four-mora words are embedded in this frame. The duration of the relevant moras is measured in centiseconds and marked below each spectrogram.

First, we should note that it is not always possible to determine from the speech wave the exact boundaries of the moras; the actual physical facts are often much more intricate than even the finest phonetic notation would reflect. Thus, while the /siñ/ is traditionally thought to be a sequence of two moras [ɕi] and syllabic [n], the spectrograms in 7-9b and 7-9c show that the nasal consonant has no independent time segment associated with it but

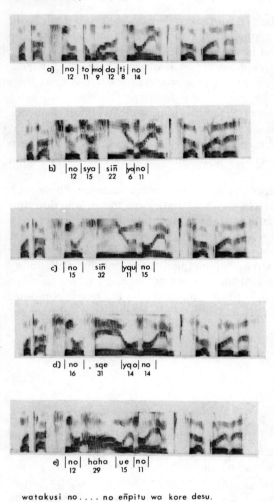

watakusi no.... no eñpitu wa kore desu.

Figure 7-9. Broad-Band Spectrograms of Five Japanese Utterances

Broad-band spectrograms illustrating some temporal characteristics of five Japanese utterances. The /q/ in (c) and (d) indicates that the following vowel is phonemically long. In each utterance, four moras are embedded in an identical sentence frame shown at the bottom. The units are in centiseconds. Notice that the ten instances of the mora /no/ range from 11 to 16 centiseconds in duration.

is manifested solely as nasalization on the preceding vowel; i.e., /siñ/ is [cĩ]. In physiological terms, this means that there was no alveolar closure, which would be necessary for the production of an independent [n]. Similarly, the /haha/ of 7-9e cannot be segmented into two equal moras, since its phonetic manifestation is [hfia]. And the two-mora sequences of 7-9c and 7-9d, /yqu/ and /yqo/, where the /q/ is a phonemic symbol which indicates that the following vowel is long, cannot be easily divided.

In spite of these difficulties, however, it is obvious that the Japanese mora varies a great deal in its duration. Thus, the /sya/ of 7-9b is more than twice as long as the /ya/ in the same word. Similarly, the first two-mora sequence, /siñ/, in 7-9c, is almost three times as long as the two-mora sequence which follows it. Clearly, then, as the spectrograms show, the assertion that Japanese moras are of equal duration needs to be modified to take into account differences in the segmental and accentual structure of the individual moras.

In addition to the sound spectrograph, many other techniques have been developed in the past quarter century for studies on the production and perception of speech. In particular, we should mention the development of a class of electronic instruments which can simulate speech sounds, i.e., speech synthesizers. The technology of speech synthesis has progressed to the stage where synthetic speech is of extremely high quality, not only in intelligibility but also in naturalness. Because of the complexity of the variables found in the speech signal, increasing use is being made of the electronic computer in controlling speech synthesizers and in providing mathematical analyses of the speech signal.

PERCEPTION AND ACQUISITION

It is clear that our discussion of the basis of speech in the preceding sections falls quite a bit short of covering the total speech situation. The focus of our attention has been primarily on the physiological configurations of the various types of speech sounds, and secondarily, on the acoustic consequences of these configurations. These areas are the best understood in the overall complex landscape of speech communication.

If we take the total chain of speech communication as beginning with a message in the nervous system of the speaker and ending with the same message arising in the nervous system of the listener, then obviously there are several important links that must be added before we can even begin to understand how it is possible for adults to use speech, and more ambitiously, how it is possible for children to develop this ability. To study this total speech chain effectively requires the combined expertise of several disciplines which have human behavior as their subject matter. Indeed, language is by far the most important key for unlocking the secrets of many aspects of human behavior. Over eighty years ago, when Fournier wrote that "Speech is the only window through which the physiologist can view the cerebral life," he could have well extended the remark to apply to all sciences which study man's behavior.

   To begin at the encoding end, we need to understand how the raw stuff of conscious thought can be associated with particular arrangements of linguistic units—the domain of semantics and syntax. We know that these arrangements are typically hierarchically structured and that some of the linguistic units have cognitive content, while others do not. Furthermore, we need to posit a level of linguistic arrangement that is more abstract than direct observations of spoken or written language would reveal, a level that has been called "deep structure." We may exemplify this with a pair of English sentences:

a. Ronald does not think that the earth is round.
b. Donald does not know that the earth is round.

Though the two sentences appear to be quite parallel in their linguistic arrangement, a moment's reflection will show that they are entirely different in their semantic structure. Whereas Donald may be said to be merely innocent, it is clear that Ronald holds an opinion on such matters and that he is wrong. The difference between the two sentences is reflected in the syntax. Whereas *a* is a paraphrase of *c*, *b* cannot be said to be a paraphrase of *d*.

c. Ronald thinks that the earth is not round.
d. Donald knows that the earth is not round.

   The deep structure representation of the speaker's message must be then converted to a level of representation that is more directly related to what he will ultimately say—a level that is called "surface structure." It is the surface structure representation that determines the basic form of the speech signal. A surface structure representation contains not only information on the sequence of sounds that make up the utterance but also such information as where the syntactic breaks are for pauses (e.g., in *the girl next door*, we can pause after the second or the fourth word but not after the third), or where to place the accent (e.g., if *permit* is a noun, accent the first syllable, if a verb accent the second), and so on.

   Given a surface representation that determines how a message is to be pronounced, it is by no means a simple task for the nervous system to cause the muscles to actually implement the pronunciation. There are literally hundreds of muscles involved in the pronunciation of almost any simple sentence, from the diaphragmatic contraction for the air intake to the coordinated movements of the complex of supralaryngeal muscles for articulation. When we recall that muscles differ greatly in their mass and that the neural paths which lead to them differ in distance and rate of conduction, we can begin to appreciate the intricacies of the problem in synchronizing all these activities. It is altogether remarkable that we are able to talk with such effortless ease, making as few mistakes as we do. Furthermore, the command of speech has no correlation with the degree of intelligence of the individual or the quality or quantity of his culture.

Once the sound waves leave the lips of the speaker, it becomes a problem of decoding for the hearer—how to recover the message behind the sound waves. The physical situation can be simply stated. These sound waves push on the ear drums of the hearer and cause them to vibrate. These vibrations are in turn converted into neural impulses which must then be assigned a surface structure representation, then a deep structure representation, and ultimately the message in cognitive terms. It should not be necessary to emphasize here again the importance of linguistic rules in this process. If the hearer does not share the bulk of the linguistic rules that the speaker used in encoding, then clearly the decoding cannot get even as far as the stage of the surface structure representation. This is in fact what happens, of course, when someone speaks to us in a language we do not understand.

The instrument that we have for speech reception is every bit as complex as that we use for speech production, and it is much less well understood. The extreme sensitivity of the ear is evidenced by the fact that at certain frequencies the vibrations of the ear drum are as small as one billionth of a centimeter —about one tenth of the diameter of the hydrogen atom! In frequency, it is sensitive to from about 20 cps to approximately 20,000 cps, a range of ten octaves.

We know considerably less about how speech is recognized than how speech is produced, though the past several decades of research in this area have led to some general conclusions that seem to be valid. It is certain that the way we process speech must be viewed as more than a completely passive activity, like pressing a template over a spectrogram to read off the phonemes. Rather, the process of speech recognition is an active interplay of guessing, approximation, expectation, and idealization that normally makes extensive use of all the redundancies found in a typical speech situation, phonological, morphological, syntactic, semantic, as well as many varieties of non-linguistic redundancies.

Evidence which leads to this conclusion comes in many forms. Detailed acoustic measurements show that the values of the speech sounds sometimes depart quite markedly from the values they would have in distinct and deliberate speech. The more casual the speech or the faster its tempo, the greater the departure from the "target" values. These deviant values would yield very different phonemic identifications for the template-matching recognizer than for the human recognizer.

Many parameters of speech sounds can only be recognized relative to each other. For instance, a low pitch level for a man with a high-pitched voice may be the same in absolute frequency as that of the high pitch level of another man. A similar situation obtains in the judgment of vowel sounds where the hearer needs to, in a sense, establish a reference vowel formant loop in his perceptual space that is particular to the characteristics of the speaker. For again, on an absolute scale the formant frequencies of one speaker's vowel X may correspond frequently to the formant of another speaker's vowel Y.

It is a commonplace observation, but nonetheless a striking fact, that the perceptual mechanism of the hearer will automatically correct or "edit" the utterances he hears, so effortlessly, in fact, that frequently the hearer will not even notice that the utterances contained mispronunciations, grammatical mistakes, false starts, etc. This observation is related directly to the difficulties that most of us have when we consciously try to catch mistakes, such as in proofreading a manuscript where the editing function of the perceptual mechanism is carried over to the visual modality.

No less striking is the observation that our perception of speech can be extremely selective. We are able to follow a conversation when the signal is embedded in a background of extreme noise, or even when the noise is quite similar to the signal itself, such as other conversations.

This variety of evidence conclusively points to the active role that nonphysical factors play in the recognition of speech. Early efforts to simulate speech recognition by electronic instruments produced very unsatisfying results primarily because of the neglect of these factors. In current theories of speech perception, there is an increasing concern to emphasize the communality between production and perception and to build knowledge of the former into the strategy of the latter.

If our understanding of the process of speech perception is meager at this time, then our understanding of the process of speech acquisition or learning can be said to be nonexistent. It is clear, however, that a distinction must be drawn between the acquisition of one's first language and the learning of other languages after the mastery of at least one language, since different factors are involved in the two tasks.

The evidence is overwhelming for the view that our genetic endowments play a crucial role in our acquisition of language. Man is unique in his possession of language; other animals do not acquire language, even when they are given learning opportunities equal to those of human children or intensive special training. The development of language appears to correlate very well in time with the development of general motor skills. Furthermore, when certain diseases affect the time schedule of growth and maturation, they do not disturb the intercalation of the milestones of speech development and motor development. In the words of Lenneberg, "The preservation of synchrony between motor and speech or language milestones in cases of general retardation is . . . the most cogent evidence that language acquisition is regulated by maturational phenomena."

The time schedule of the child's acquisition of language is remarkably uniform and is largely independent of the amount of exposure he has to the language, or the degree of his intelligence, or the particular structure of the language to be acquired, or the cultural setting within which the acquisition takes place. The understanding that the child achieves of his linguistic system is essentially perfect, though children differ in their virtuosity in using the linguistic system as a vehicle for expression, much as adults do in this respect. These differences are reflected in various ways, such as in a clever choice of words, the use of effective intonation and syntax, rate of articulation and rate of reading.

The distinction between understanding the abstract linguistic system and putting the system to effective use may be compared to that in arithmetic between knowing how to multiply and multiplying well. Language, of course, is a much more complex and intricate system than arithmetic and is correspondingly much more intimately interwoven into our mental processes. Of the information that flows incessantly between man and his external world as well as within his own consciousness, by far the greatest bulk flows via the channels of language. A deeper analysis of the nature of language and speech will surely improve our understanding of mental processes, and hopefully, will one day lead us to methods whereby we can raise the ceiling on our intellect.

REFERENCES

Abercrombie, D. *Studies in phonetics and linguistics*. London: Oxford Univ. Press, 1965.

Anderson, J. M. Repetition of phonetic change in Spanish. *Phonetica*, 1966, **14**, 16–19.

Aoki, H. *Toward a typology of vowel harmony*. POLA II.2. Univ. of California, Berkeley: Phonology Laboratory, 1967. Cited by *Internat. J. Amer. Ling.*, 1968, **34**, 142–145.

Beach, D. M. *The phonetics of the Hottentot language*. Cambridge: Heffer, 1938.

Biggs, B. Direct and indirect inheritance in Rotuman. *Lingua*, 1965, **14**, 383–415.

Boas, F., & Swanton, J. R. Siouan-Dakota (Teton and Santee dialects). In F. Boas (Ed.), *Handbook of American Indian languages*, Part I, 1911, 875–965.

Canonge, E. D. Voiceless vowels in Comanche. *Internat. J. Amer. Ling.*, 1957, **23**, 63–67.

Carnochan, J. Glottalization in Hausa. *Trans. Philol. Soc.*, 1952, 78–109.

Chang, K. Questions concerning the tones in Miao-Yao languages. *Bull. Inst. Hist. Philol. of Academia Sinica*, 1947, **16**, 93–110. (In Chinese). Shortened English version in *Language*, 1953, **29**, 374–378.

Chao, Y-R. A system of tone letters. *Le maître phonétique*, 1920, **45**, 24–27.

Chao, Y-R. Types of plosives in Chinese dialects. *Bull. Inst. Hist. Philol. of Academia Sinica*, 1935, **5**, 515–520. (In Chinese). English version in *Proc. 2nd Internat. Cong. Phonet. Sciences*, 106–110.

Chao, Y-R. Materials on the Tai-shan dialect. *Bull. Inst. Hist. Philol. of Academia Sinica*, 1951, **23**, 25–76. (In Chinese).

Chiba, T., & Kajiyama, M. *The vowel, its nature and structure*. Tokyo, 1941. Reprinted in 1958.

Chomsky, N. *Current issues in linguistic theory*. The Hague: Mouton, 1964. Reprinted in J. A. Fodor & J. J. Katz, 1964. Pp. 50–118.

Chomsky, N., & Halle, M. *The sound pattern of English*. New York: Harper & Row, 1968.

Cornyn, W. *Outline of Burmese grammar*. *Lang. disser*. 38. Baltimore: Waverly Press, 1944.

Delattre, P., Liberman, A. M., & Cooper, F. S. Acoustic loci and transitional cues for consonants. *J. acoust. Soc. Amer*., 1955, **27**, 769–773. Reprinted in I. Lehiste, 1967.

Ege, N. The Danish vowel system. *Gengo Kenkyu*, 1965, **47**, 21–35.

Emeneau, M. B. The vowels of the Badaga language. *Language*, 1939, **15**, 43–47.

Emeneau, M. B. India as a linguistic area. *Language*, 1956, **32**, 3–16.

Emeneau, M. B. Toda, a Dravidian language. *Trans. Philol. Soc*., 1957, 15–66.

Fairbanks, G. *Selected papers in experimental phonetics*. Urbana: Univ. of Illinois Press, 1967.

Fāng, Jìn. Fāng Cūn phonetics. *Zhōngguo yǔwén*, 1966, **141**, 137–146. (In Chinese). Peking.

Fant, G. *The acoustic theory of speech production*. The Hague: Mouton, 1960.

Farnsworth, D. W. High speed motion pictures of the human vocal cords. *Bell Telephone Laboratories Record*, 1940, **18**, 203.

Ferguson, C. A. Assumptions about nasals: a sample study in phonological universals. In J. H. Greenburg (Ed.), *Universals of language*. Cambridge: M.I.T. Press, 1963. Pp. 42–47.

Flanagan, J. L. Estimates of the maximum precision necessary in quantizing certain dimensions of vowel sounds. *J. acoust. Soc. Amer*., 1957, **29**, 53–54. Reprinted in I. Lehiste, 1967.

Flanagan, J. L. Some properties of the glottal sound source. *J. Speech Hear. Res*., 1958, **5**, 99–116.

Fodor, J. A., & Katz, J. J. (Eds.), *The structure of language*. Englewood Cliffs: Prentice-Hall, 1964.

Greenberg, J. H. (Ed.), *Universals of language*. Cambridge: M.I.T. Press, 1963.

Greenberg, J. H. (Ed.) Some generalizations concerning initial and final consonant sequences. *Voprosy jazykoznanija*, 1964, **13**, 41–66. (In Russian). English version in *Linguistics*, 1965, **18**, 5–34.

Greenberg, J. H. (Ed.) Synchronic and diachronic universals in phonology. *Language*, 1966, **42**, 508–517.

Halle, M. *The sound pattern of Russian*. The Hague: Mouton, 1959.

Halle, M. A descriptive convention for treating assimilation and dissimilation. *M.I.T. Quart. Progress Report*, 1962, **66**, 295–296. (a)

Halle, M. Phonology in generative grammar. *Word*, 1962, **18**, 54–72. Reprinted in J. A. Fodor & J. J. Katz, 1964. Pp. 334–352. (b)

Halle, M. Questions of linguistics. *Il nuovo cimento*, 1958, **13**, (Whole No. 10) 494–517. (Supplement). A revised version appears as *On the bases of phonology* in J. A. Fodor & J. J. Katz, 1964. Pp. 324–333.

Halle, M., & Stevens, K. N. Speech recognition: a model and a program for research. In J. A. Fodor & J. J. Katz, 1964. Pp. 604–612.

Harms, R. T. *The ABC's of generative phonology*. Englewood Cliffs: Prentice-Hall, 1968.

Hayes, K. J., & Hayes, C. A home-raised chimpanzee. In R. G. Kuhlen & G. G. Thompson (Eds.), *Psychological studies of human development*. New York: Appleton-Century-Crofts, 1952. Pp. 112–119.

Heffner, R-M. S. *General phonetics*. Madison: Univ. of Wisconsin Press, 1952.

Hockett, C. F. *A manual of phonology. Internat. J. Amer. Ling.*, Memoir 11. Baltimore: Waverly Press, 1955.

Hoenigswald, H. M. Declension and nasalization in Hindustani. *J. Amer. Oriental Soc.*, 1948, **68**, 2.

House, A. S., & Fairbanks, G. Influence of consonant environment upon the secondary acoustical characteristics of vowels. *J. acoust. Soc. Amer.*, 1953, **25**, 105–113.

Hudgins, C. V., & Stetson, R. H. Voicing of consonants by depression of the larynx. *Archives neerlándaises de phonetique experimentale*, 1935, **11**, 1–28.

Jakobson, R., Fant, G., & Halle, M. *Preliminaries to speech analysis. M.I.T. technical Report 13*. Cambridge: M.I.T. Press, 1952.

Jakobson, R. *Selected writings*. The Hague: Mouton, 1962.

Jones, D. *The pronunciation of English*. Cambridge: Cambridge Univ. Press, 1956.

Joos, M. The Trabresh dialect of Albanian. *Le maître phonétique*, Oct.-Dec., 1932, 76–78.

Joos, M. The medieval sibilants. *Language*, 1952, **28**, 222–231.

Kenyon, J. S., & Knott, T. A. *A pronouncing dictionary of American English*. Springfield: G. & C. Merriam, 1953.

Kim, C-W. *The linguistic specification of speech. U.C.L.A. Working Papers in Phonetics* 5, 1966.

Koenig, W., Dunn, H. K., & Lacy, L. Y. The sound spectrograph. *J. acoust. Soc. Amer.*, 1946, **17**, 19–49. Reprinted in I. Lehiste, 1967.

Kramsky, M. A quantitative typology of languages. *Lang. & Speech*, 1959, **2**, 72–85.

Kuipers, A. H. *Phoneme and morpheme in Kabardian*. The Hague: Mouton, 1960.

Ladefoged, P. *Elements of acoustic phonetics*. Chicago: Univ. of Chicago Press. 1962.

Ladefoged, P. *A phonetic study of West African languages*. Cambridge: Cambridge Univ. Press, 1964.

Ladefoged, P. *Linguistic phonetics. U.C.L.A. Working Papers in Phonetics* 6, 1967. (a)

Ladefoged, P. *Three aspects of experimental phonetics*. New York: Oxford Univ. Press, 1967. (b)

Ladefoged, P., & Broadbent, D. E. Information conveyed by vowels. *J. acoust. Soc. Amer.*, 1957, **29**, 98–104. Reprinted in I. Lehiste, 1967.

Lane, H. Motor theory of speech perception: a critical review. *Psychol. Rev.*, 1965, **72**, 275–309.

Lehiste, I. *An acoustic-phonetic study of internal juncture. Phonetica*. Basel: Karger, 1960. (Supplement) (a)

Lehiste, I. Segmental and syllabic quantity in Estonian. *American studies in Uralic linguistics: Ural and Altaic series*, 1960, **1**, 21–82. (b)

Lehiste, I. *Acoustical characteristics of selected English consonants*. Supplement to *Internat. J. Amer. Ling.*, 1964, **30** (3), Part 4.

Lehiste, I. (Ed.), *Readings in acoustic phonetics*. Cambridge: M.I.T. Press, 1967.

Lenneberg, E. H. Language, evolution, and purposive behavior. In S. Diamond (Ed.), *Culture in history: essays in honor of Paul Radin*. New York: Columbia Univ. Press, 1960. Pp. 869–893. An extended version appears in J. A. Fodor and J. J. Katz, 1964. Pp. 579–603.

Lenneberg, E. H. Understanding language without ability to speak: a case report. *J. abnorm. soc. Psychol.*, 1962, **65**, 419–425.

Lenneberg, E. H. *Biological foundations of language*. New York: John Wiley & Sons, 1967.

Li, F. K. Chipewyan consonants. *The Ts'ai Yuan P'ei Anniversary Volume. Bull. Inst. Hist. Philol. of Academia Sinica.* Vol. 1. Peking, 1933. (Supplement).

Li, R. *Handbook for research on Chinese dialects.* Peking, 1957. (In Chinese).

Liberman, A. M., Cooper, F. S., Harris, K. S., & MacNeilage, P. F. A motor theory of speech perception. *Proc. Speech Communic. Seminar, Royal Inst. Technol.*, **2**, Paper D3. Stockholm, 1963.

MacNeilage, P. F., & Sholes, G. N. An electromygraphic study of the tongue during vowel production. *J. Speech Hear. Res.*, 1964, **7**, 209–232.

MacNeilage, P. F., Rottes, T. P., & Chase, R. A. Speech production and perception in a patient with severe impairment of somesthetic perception and motor control. *J. Speech Hear. Res.*, 1967, **10**, 449–467.

Marlmberg, B. Distinctive features of Swedish vowels: some instrumental and structural data. In M. Halle (Ed.), *For Roman Jakobson.* The Hague: Mouton, 1960. Pp. 316–321.

Martinet, A. *Économie des changements phonétiques.* Bern: Francke, 1955.

Merrifield, W. R. Palantla Chinantec syllable types. *Anthropol. Ling.*, 1963, **5**, 1–16.

Mohr, B., & Wang, W. S-Y. *Perceptual distance and the specification of phonological features.* POLA II.1. Univ. of California, Berkeley: Phonology Laboratory, 1967. Also in *Phonetica*, 1967.

Newman, S. Bella Coola I: phonology. *Internat. J. Amer. Ling.*, 1947, **13**, 129–134.

O'Grady, G. N., Voegelin, C. F., & Voegelin, F. M. Languages of the world: Indo-Pacific fasc. 6. *Anthropol. Ling.*, 1966, **8** (2).

Öhman, S. Numerical model of co-articulation. *J. acoust. Soc. Amer.*, 1967, **41**, 310–320. (a)

Öhman, S. Word and sentence intonation: a quantitative model. *Speech Transmission Laboratory QPSR*, 1967, **2**, 20–54. Stockholm. (b)

Peterson, G. E. The phonetic value of vowels. *Language*, 1951, **27**, 541–553.

Peterson, G. E., & Barney, H. L. Control methods used in a study of the vowels. *J. acoust. Soc. Amer.*, 1952, **24**, 175–184. Reprinted in I. Lehiste, 1967.

Peterson, G. E., & Shoup, J. E. A physiological theory of phonetics, the elements of an acoustic phonetic theory, and glossary of terms from the physiological and acoustic phonetic theories. *J. Speech Hear. Res.*, 1966, **9**, 5–120.

A phonetic dictionary of Chinese dialects. Peking Univ., 1962. (In Chinese).

Pike, E. V., & Wistrand, K. Step-up terrace tone in Acatlán Mixtec. (Unpublished

Pike, K. L. *Phonetics.* Ann Arbor: Univ. of Michigan Press, 1943.

Pike, K. L. *The intonation of American English.* Ann Arbor: Univ. of Michigan Press, 1945.

Pike, K. L. *Tone languages.* Ann Arbor: Univ. of Michigan Press, 1948. manuscript.)

Posner, Rebecca. *The Romance language.* New York: Anchor Books, 1966.

Postal, P. M. *Aspects of phonological theory.* New York: Harper & Row, 1968.

Potter, R. K., Kopp, G. A., & Green, H. C. *Visible speech.* New York: Van Nostrand, 1947. Reprinted by Dover Publications, Inc., New York, 1966.

The Principles of the International Phonetic Association. London: International Phonetic Association, 1949.

Reeds, J. A., & Wang, W. S-Y. The perception of stops after *s. Phonetica*, 1961, **6**, 78–81.

Sapir, E. *Language.* New York: Harcourt, Brace & World, 1921.

Sapir, E. Notes on the Gweabo language of Liberia. *Language*, 1931, **7**, 30–41.

Sapir, E. *Selected writings of Edward Sapir in language, culture and personality*. Ed. by D. G. Mandelbaum. Berkeley: Univ. of California Press, 1958.

de Saussure, F. *Cours de linguistique générale*. Ed. by C. Bally & A. Sechehaye in collaboration with Albert Reidlinger. Paris, 1916. English translation by Wade Baskin. London: Peter Owen, Ltd., 1960.

Smalley, W. A. *Manual of articulatory phonetics*. (Rev. ed.) Ann Arbor, 1963.

Stanley, R. Redundancy rules in phonology. *Language*, 1967, **43**, 393-436.

Stetson, R. H. *Motor phonetics*. (2nd ed.) Amsterdam, 1951.

Stevens, K. N. The quantal nature of speech: evidence from articulatory-acoustic data. In E. G. David & P. B. Denes (Eds.), *Human communication: a unified view*, forthcoming.

Stevens, K. N., & Halle, M. Remarks on analysis by synthesis and distinctive features. In W. Wathen-Dunn (Ed.), *Models for the perception of speech and visual form*. Cambridge: M.I.T. Press, 1967. Pp. 88-102.

Stevens, K. N., & House, A. S. An acoustical theory of vowel production and some of its implications. *J. Speech Hear. Res.*, 1961, **4**, 303-320. Reprinted in I. Lehiste, 1967.

Stewart, J. M. The typology of the Twi tone system. *Bull. Inst. African Studies*, 1967, **1**.

Sweet, H. *A primer of phonetics*. Oxford: Clarendon Press, 1906.

Trubetzkoy, N. *Grundzüge der Phonologie*. Prague, 1939.

Turner, R. L. The Sindhi recursives or voiced stops preceded by glottal closure. *Bull. School of Oriental Studies*, 1923, **3**, 301.

Vihman, Marilyn May. *Palatalization in Russian and Estonian*. POLA II.1. Univ. of California, Berkeley: Phonology Laboratory, 1967.

Wang, W. S-Y. Transition and release as perceptual cues for final plosives. *J. Speech Hear. Res.,* 1959, **2**, 66-73. Reprinted in I. Lehiste, 1967.

Wang, W. S-Y. Stress in English. *Lang. Learn.*, 1962, **12**, 69-77.

Wang, W. S-Y. Phonological features of tone. *Internat. J. Amer. Ling.*, 1967, **33**, 93-105. (a)

Wang, W. S-Y. *Competing changes as a cause of residue*. POLA II.2. Univ. of California, Berkeley: Phonology Laboratory, 1967. Also in *Language* 1969, **45**, 9-25. (b)

Wang, W. S-Y., & Fillmore, C. J. Intrinsic cues and consonant perception. *J. Speech Hear. Res.*, 1961, **4**, 130-136.

Wang, W. S-Y., & Li, K-P. Tone 3 in Pekinese. *J. Speech Hear. Res.*, 1967, **10**, 629-636.

Wathen-Dunn, W. (Ed.), *Models for the perception of speech and visual form*. Cambridge: M.I.T. Press, 1967.

Westermann, D., & Ward, I. C. *Practical phonetics for students of African languages*. London: Oxford Univ. Press, 1933.

Yuáh, Ji ā-Huá. *Phonetic dictionary of Chinese dialects*. Peking, 1962. (In Chinese).

Zheng, Z. S-F. Wenchow phonetics. *Zhōnogguó yǔwén*, 1964, **128**, 28-60. Peking. (In Chinese).

APPENDIX I: ILLUSTRATIONS OF PHONETIC SYMBOLS

The English pronunciation indicated in the examples below is that reported in Kenyon and Knott (1953); the Spanish is that of the Castilian dialect. Brackets enclose pronunciations found in some dialect variants. The following examples do not exhaust the sound types of these four languages.

	English	German	French	Spanish
i	beat	bieten	qui	chico
I	bit	bitten		
e	bait	beten	des	queso
ε	bet	Betten	dette	regla
æ	bat			
a			patte	
ɑ	father	Name	pâte	
ə	above	eine	le	
ʌ	but			
y		grün	tu	
o		Höhle	deux	
œ		Hölle	peur	
u	pool	Mut	où	cura
ø	boat	Sohn	faux	adobe
ɔ	law	Sonne	fol	corro
β				cuba
f	fine	fahren	fable	facil
v	vine	wahren	vin	
θ	thin			cerca
ð	this			escudo
s	sink	lassen	sa	señora
z	zinc	sein	zèle	isla
ʃ	fission	Schuh		
ʒ	vision	Etage	agilité	
ç		ich		
x		ach		jarro
h	hat	Hut		
ɦ	ahead			
m	met	Mut	madame	madre
n	net	nein	nuit	neto
ɲ	sing	singen	montagne	pequeño
ŋ	sung	Hunger		banco
p	spin	spät	parle	
pʰ	pin	Pein		padre
b	bin	Bein	bon	buenos
t	sty	staat	ton	
tʰ	tie	Tank		tarde
d	die	Dank	dent	doble
cʰ	keel	kühn	qui	quince
ɟ	geese	giessen	guide	Guido
k		Skat	car	
kʰ	cool	Kasse		loco
g	goose	Gasse	gare	guerra
ʔ		Anlaut		
pf		Pferd		
ts	cats	Zug		
dz	adz			
tʃ	church	Deutsch		chico
dʒ	judge			

	English	German	French	Spanish
l	lip	Lippe	lapin	lado
ʎ				calle
ɫ	pill			
r		[rein]	[robe]	roca
R		rein	robe	
ɹ	red			color

APPENDIX II. EXAMPLES OF UNCOMMON CONTRASTS

Plosives and Affricates

ɓ : ɓʰ	àɓà	àɓʰà			Igbo
	power	jaw			(Ladefoged, 1964, p. 59)
ɟ : g	áɟà	àgá			Igbo
	pulling apart	walking			(Ladefoged, 1964, p. 59)
ɟʰ : gʰ	áɟʰà	àgʰá			Igbo
	earth	being useful			(Ladefoged, 1964, p. 59)
b : ɓ : g͡b	àbà	aɓa	àg͡bà		Kalabari
	a kind of fish	girl's name	offering		(Ladefoged, 1964, p. 60)
p : p : pʰ	pul	p*ul	pʰul		Korean
	tire	horn	grass		
t : t* : tʰ	tam	t*am	tʰam		Korean
	fence	sweat	envy		
k : k* : kʰ	koŋ	k*oŋ	kʰoŋ		Korean
	ball	frozen	bean		
tʃ : tʃ* : tʃʰ	tʃam	tʃ*am	tʃʰam		Korean
	sleeping	period of time	truth		
pf : pfʰ	pfu	pfu	pfʰu	pfʰu	Xīān
	pillar	boil	place	attend to	(Peking University, p. 86)

Sonorants

r : R	sɛːro	sɛːRo	gari	gaRi	Provençal
	evening	saw	to cure	oak	(Posner, 1966, p. 122)
ɲ : n	ɲi	ɲi	ni	ni	Chéngdū
	mud	you	plough	courtesy	(Peking University, p. 59)

Fricatives

f : fʰ	fu	fã	foʔ		
	wealth	merchant	fortune		
	fʰu	fʰã	fʰoʔ		Fāngcūn
	father	meal	dress		(Fāng, 1966, p. 138)

* p* t* k* tʃ* are tense obstruents.

Fricatives (continued)

s : sʰ	sei	si			
	shatter	diarrhea			
	sʰei	sʰi			Fāngcūn
	guilt	thank			(Fāng, 1966, p. 138)
	sa	sʰa			Korean
	wrap	buy			
ʂ : ʂʰ	ʂuei	ʂəŋ			
	tax	victory			
	ʂʰuei	ʂʰəŋ			Fāngcūn
	sleep	remainder			(Fāng, 1966, p. 138)
ɕ : ɕʰ	ɕiɔ	ɕyə?			
	filial	blood			
	ɕʰiɔ	ɕʰyə?			Fāngcūn
	school	excavate			(Fāng, 1966, p. 138)
i : e : ɛ : æ	milə	melə	mɛlə	mælə	Danish
	dune	sprinkle with flour	utter	paint	(Ege, 1965, p. 28)
	mi?l	me?l	mɛ?l	mæ?l	
	mile	flour	utter!	paint!	
i : y : ʉ : u	vi	ty	tʉ	ku	Swedish
	we	because	twosome	cow	
	pip	pys	ɕʉl	sup	
	spout	little boy	howl	rubbish	

tones on the syllable	+high +fall	−high +fall	+high +rise	Cantonese
/wei/	fierce	surround	destroy	
	−high +rise	+high −contour	−high −contour	
	great	fear	stomach	
/jʌm/	+high +fall	−high +fall	+high +rise	
	sound	lewd	drink	
	−high +rise	+high −contour	−high −contour	
	well-cooked	shade	rent	

u : v : w	ɛ́ʊɛ́	ɛ́vɛ́	ɛ́wɛ́	Isoko
	breath	how	hoe	(Ladefoged, 1964, p. 58)
ç : ɕ	çito	çjo	ɕito	ɕjo:	Japanese
	person	vote	disciple	general	

Duration contrasts

i : i· : i:	kire	ki·re	ki:re	Estonian
	passion (genitive)	ray (genitive)	fast	(Vihman, 1967)
p : p· : p:	hape	hap·e	hap:e	Estonian
	beard	acid	acid (genitive)	(Vihman, 1967)
l : l· : l:	kalas	kal·as	kal:as	Estonian
	in the fish	shore	he poured	(Vihman, 1967)

Nasalization contrasts

*e : ẽ : ę	ˀe	ˀẽ	ˀę	Palantla
	teach	count	chase	Chinantec
				(Merrifield, 1963,
				p. 14)

a : ã : ạ	ha	hã	hạ	
	such	he spreads	foam	
		open		

Vowel contrasts

i : y : ɯ : u	kil	kyl	kɯl	kul	Turkish
	fuller's earth	ash	hair	slave	

* ẽ is lightly or partly nasalized; ę is heavily or fully nasalized.

8

Speech Pathology

ROBERT WEST *

Emeritus, Brooklyn College of the City University of New York

Speech pathology is the study of abnormalities of speech—speech disorders. Not all defects of speech are disorders of speech. Some of them are deviations arising from the ready faculty of imitation. Some are deviations resting upon real abnormalities of structure and/or function. The nasalization of an English vowel, for example, may be designated as a disorder of speech if it rests upon paralysis of the ninth cranial nerve, but it is regarded simply as a speech defect if it results from the imitation of the nasalization of the speech of associates.

Allowances being made for children in the speech learning period, the speech of a given person may be regarded as defective under the following conditions: (*a*) when his voice is not loud enough to be easily heard in the practical situations of his vocational and social life; (*b*) when his speech is partially or wholly unintelligible because of inaccurate articulations; (*c*) when his speech is partially or wholly unintelligible by reason of serious lapses of grammar, syntax, or word use; (*d*) when, for any reason, his speech is intrinsically unpleasant to listen to; (*e*) when his utterance is so different in rate, rhythm, pitch, loudness, timbre, or individual sounds of speech from that of the average speaker of his age and sex that the differences serve to distract the hearer's attention from what is being said to how it is said; (*f*) when his speech is accompanied by extraneous mechanical or vocal sounds or by distracting grimaces, gestures, or postures. The *perception of speech—hearing—*is defective when it is inadequate for the individual's educational, vocational, and social needs. These deviations from the norm are not only *defects* but also *disorders* when they stem from the failures of basic functions of the muscles and nerves involved in speech.

*Deceased.

307

LANGUAGE FACILITY IN THE CHILD

There are five definite qualities, conditions, or tendencies that constitute speech (or language) facility. These five are statistical components that make up the complex of ontogeny of the child who, escaping demonstrable pathologies, becomes better than average in speech or language during the period of childhood or pubescence. These components are (Group I):

1. Better than average in constitutional growth and physical strength.
2. A member of the female sex.
3. Early and clear establishment of dextral preferences in an individual of dextral family stock.
4. Familial and personal inclination toward languages and arts (*L*-type of intelligence).
5. Personal and familial musicality.

LANGUAGE DISABILITY

There are five definite qualities, conditions, or tendencies that run counter to speech (or language) facility. These five are statistical components that make up the complex of ontogeny of the child who, escaping demonstrable pathologies, becomes poorer than average in speech or language during the period of childhood or pubescence. These components are (Group II):

1. Poorer than average in constitutional growth and physical strength.
2. A member of the male sex.
3. Delayed and disturbed establishment of laterality, especially with a similar family background.
4. Personal and familial inclination toward mathematics and sciences (*Q*-type intelligence).
5. Personal and familial lack of interest in music.

These contrasting parallel statements about the speech and language development of the child have been drawn from the monumental work of Luchsinger and Arnold (1965, p. 401), together with additions by this author. The statistical components are not equally balanced or weighted, and there is no way of stating what the predictive value is of any one component in comparison with the others.

The first and second components are more or less self-explanatory. The third component signifies the "handedness," either right or left, dextral or sinistral, in the preference for the use of hands in skilled acts. Left-handedness may often be interpreted as "delayed and disturbed" laterality. The fourth component, the two types of intelligence, *L* and *Q*, differ from each other not quantitively but qualitatively. In Arnold's section of *Voice-Speech-Language*, the *Q*-type of intelligence is described:

On one side of this graduated series from marked linguistic to quantitative types, we may place the extreme of the Q-type, with unilateral mathematical, scientific, and technical abilities as found in people who do scientific, statistical, or mathematical work. Rarely interested in the science and art of language, many members of these vocations demonstrate a tendency toward a concrete, precise, clipped, or even rigid formulation of thoughts [p. 409].

The L-type is described as follows:

At the other extreme of differential ability falls the *language facility* of the L-type, with humanistic, linguistic, and artistic talents. In this group belong the members of the teaching, philosophical, theological, and legal professions who usually excel in oral and graphic expression and find it easy to learn other languages [pp. 409-410].

The fifth component is musicality. This component is described in Arnold's section as follows:

As the next link in our reasoning, we find in many surveys that musical ability is in general more frequently present among members of the humanistic professions. . . . Hence we arrive at a close general *relationship between talent for language and music*. Although human abilities are distributed in most varied combinations, it is nevertheless a fact that musical inclination is found most frequently in the professions that rely on language skill. On the other hand, technical specialists often profess a marked lack of musical interest. At least, they are considerably less active in music than doctors and writers tend to be [p. 410].

By no means are all the language defectives in the second group, and neither does the first group contain no children with linguistic disorders. But the averages strongly point to the contrasting tendencies shown in Groups I and II. The Group II components are by no means factors of etiology, i.e., some children seem to be linguistic cripples without clearly recognizable symptoms of pathology which cause their language problems.

The first, second, and third components of speech (or language) disability (Group II) are interrelated, and they may be connected with pathology. Morbidity is generally higher in the male embryos, fetuses, and babies than in the females. This morbidity shows up in certain conditions that cause speech impairments. Male children are more frequently stutterers than the females, in a ratio of about 4 to 1. Cerebral palsy, which so frequently disturbs speech, is more common among males than females. Organic feeblemindedness, almost always causing speech and language disorders, is more common among boys than girls. Disturbed laterality often is connected etiologically with infantile aphasia and with reading and writing difficulties. It is also a factor in the production of stuttering.

THE ONSET OF SPEECH DISORDERS

There is great variation in the beginning of speech articulation in normal children. Many children have acquired all the phonemes at 30 months while some normal children may not acquire many of the consonants until later. The outside limit of normality for the establishment of the first phonemes is 42 months. If the phonemes [p, b, m, w] and [h] are used at 42 months, the girl child may be regarded as within normal limits, no matter what other sounds she lacks. The outside limits of normality for [t, d, n, k, g, ŋ] and [j] is 54 months; for [f] is 66 months; for [ʃ, ʒ] (if [ʒ] is used in the family), [ð, v], and [l] is 78 months; and for [z, s, r] and [θ] is 90 months. The limits here set for the onset of speech in the various phonemes may be thought of as applying to girls; allowance should be made for a later onset for boys.

Two careful studies have been made by Irene Poole (1934) and Florence Henderson (1938) on the development of speech of young children with particular reference to their articulation. Both attempted to determine the order and rate of development of the several English phonemes. A comparison of the two studies is interesting, since these workers made their researches quite independently, and their experimental groups of children came from greatly different social cultures.

BRAIN INJURIES CAUSING SPEECH DISORDERS

Some disorders of speech are due to damage of the peripheral nerves controlling the muscles of articulation. These nerves are cranial outlets from nuclei of the brain. The most important speech pathology of these nerves in children is bulbar polio.

One etiology which is sufficiently consistent to be definitely described is that of polio-encephalitis. The difference between this condition and the well-known and greatly feared poliomyelitis is largely in the level, or geographic locale, of the infection. If the lesions are located in the roots of the spinal nerves, the term *poliomyelitis* is used. If the lesion is in the extension of the spinal cord into the cranium, the condition is described as *polioencephalitis* or "bulbar polio." It begins with an acute episode characterized by fever, stiffness of the neck, muscular pain, and severe headache. The paralysis that remains to disturb speech does not usually show itself until the acute episode has run its course. The dysarthria caused by bulbar polio is chiefly of the peripheral type and as such is characterized by hypotonic muscular responses. The hypotonia manifests itself in nasality. Since a large proportion of the victims of this disease pass through the acute stage during the period of learning speech, bulbar polio is the cause not only of the disturbance of speech habits already formed but also of the arrest of the development of such habits [West, Ansberry, & Carr, pp. 104–105].

Most neuropathologies affecting the speech of children are central—that is, diseases of the brain itself.

1. Encephalitis. The term *encephalitis* signifies an inflammation of the brain sometimes referred to as brain fever. The most common of these fevers is epidemic encephalitis. This appears most often in the second, third, and fourth decades of life but also sometimes in childhood. It disturbs articulation as well as language.

2. Neurosyphilis. Syphilis in the blood stream frequently invades other tissues of the body, among which are the tissues of the central nervous system. These infections produce cranial nerve palsies, thus causing dysarthria, or generalized infections may occur, producing a condition called dementia paralytica, in which speech is disturbed not only by dysarthria but also by emotional, volitional, and aphasic disorders. This infection may occur in childhood and in youth. It is more common in males than in females.

3. Chronic subdural hematoma. Sometimes a cyst of blood tumor may occur under the outer covering of the brain. This presses down upon the brain itself and causes a paralysis and mental involvements that often disturb both articulation and language.

4. Intracranial aneurysm. An aneurysm is a swelling of an artery with attendant weakening of the walls. Sometimes, the swelling presses upon a nerve tissue, and thus, disturbs the functions of the surrounding tissue. Later, the stretched walls may burst, and a hematoma may develop in the region of the expanded aneurysm. So, in addition to the tumor at one part of the brain, other parts are weakened in function because of the lack of blood farther along the arterial channel.

5. Cerebral abscess. The abscess is an infection like a boil or a furuncle which cannot escape to the outside as it would if the infection were on the skin but remains within the brain so that the purulent material presses upon the tissues of the brain and also poisons them.

6. Glioma. A glioma is a tumor of the tissues of the structure that supports the rest of the nervous tissue as steel supports concrete in a building. One type of tumor, called the astrocytoma, is found in the cerebellums of children and produces articulatory incoordinations.

INFANTILE APHASIA

Linguistic impairments of childhood—congenital or infantile aphasias—overlap certain other infantile disorders. It is not universally agreed that infantile aphasia is a specific, identifiable, etiologic entity or is a condition secondary to other primary disorders. Those who think of infantile aphasias as secondary involvements call the primary disorders either high-frequency deafness, mental deficiency, cerebral palsy, or infantile schizophrenia. High-frequency deafness causes linguistic impairments in that the sounds of speech in the auditory ranges between 1000 and 4000 cps are those acoustic areas in which the discriminatory effects of speech are produced.

Muriel E. Morley, Speech Therapist-in-Charge, the United Newcastle-upon-Tyne Teaching Hospitals, reports in her chapter on the differential diagnosis of hearing loss for high tones that the general psychological development may be normal, apart from speech. The appreciation, however, "of inability to make contacts through speech produces lack of confidence which becomes increasingly apparent as the child gets older." There is often little delay in attempting speech, "but severe limitation in comprehension for speech, except through lip reading, and in the full use of language." The articulation is defective. The child "has no interest in radio speech, but may enjoy music . . . the speech developed is dependent on the degree and type of hearing loss [1957, p. 162]."

Most children who are of low-grade feeblemindedness are brain injured, and a larger proportion of them are boys. The mental retardation is aphasoid, i.e., characterized by paucity of vocabulary and defective syntax. In languages in which grammar is highly inflective, the mental retardates are thus even more linguistically impaired than in English, because in such languages the discriminatory meanings are carried by slight changes of word forms. Thus agrammatisms are more frequent.

The cerebral palsied children are aphasoid for two reasons. One, because the insult to the motor areas of the brain may also damage the association areas that are involved in symbolization and linguistic association. Two, because motor control of articulation is impaired, and the patient has difficulty in uttering what he would say if he could. Although his inner language may be valid, he is limited to phrases that he can utter or which his conversational partners can understand. So his speech seems aphasoid.

One of the chief characteristics of infantile schizophrenia is the autistic tendency of the patient to withdraw from social contacts. The child does not care to share experiences with his family or associates. The word *friend* is meaningless. Such a patient may understand what is said to him, but he has no desire to reply to what is spoken. Thus, a schizophrenic child may *seem*, if not *be* in reality, an aphasic. Consequently, many theorists think of infantile aphasia not as a disease sui generis but an involvement secondary to schizophrenia (Karlin, Karlin, & Gurren, 1965, Ch. 9).

Many authorities in the field of aphasia, however, maintain that there are, in addition to these secondary causes of aphasia, certain primary etiological factors that produce linguistic disorders. They assert that there are special language centers in the cerebrum and that if these centers are undeveloped or damaged, primary aphasia results. They hold that these primary speech areas are generally in the left cerebral hemisphere, even if the patient is a left-hander. This is counter to the previous a priori reasoning that, since the left brain of a right-hander controls the right motor system and the right brain of the left-hander controls the left motor system, one would expect that aphasia in the left-hander would result from underdevelopment or damage of the right hemisphere, the left hemisphere being unimpaired. Modern clinical and experimental evidence leads to the conclusion that unilateral impairment of the cerebrum generally does not produce aphasia unless the deficit is on the left hemisphere, whether the patient is right-handed or left-handed.

Many authorities divide the infantile aphasias into four groups: (*a*) aphasia proper, deficit of spoken language, motor aphasia; (*b*) auditory aphasia, deficit of the hearing of language; (*c*) alexia, deficiency of the reading of language; and (*d*) agraphia, deficiency of the writing of language. One must assume in naming these special types of aphasia that the direct motor and sensory equipment of speaking, hearing, seeing, and finger control are unimpaired. Paralysis of the tongue is not motor aphasia, though spoken language is blocked; peripheral deafness is not auditory aphasia, though the hearing of sounds is interfered with; blindness is not alexia, though the seeing of words is impaired; and paralysis of the fingers or impairment of vision is not agraphia, though the mechanical equipment for writing is defective. Though it is possible that in double handicaps both the brain and the tongue may be impaired, the use of the phrase *motor aphasia* implies only the central aspect of the impairment. So, similarly, with double handicaps of the brain and the ears, or of the brain and the eyes, or of the brain and the fingers, the words *auditory*, *alexia*, and *agraphia* imply only the linguistic aspects of the impairments, though other names for these deficiencies of communication may also be employed.

STUTTERING

The phenomena of stuttering are muscular spasms that interfere with speech. These spasms are clonic (repetitive) in type or tonic (continuous) in type. They result in interruptions of the smooth flow of speech.

a. The interruptions are of the phonation and articulation of speech, consisting of hesitations and repetitions.

b. The stutterer appears to struggle to overcome his spasms.

c. In this struggle, bodily and facial tensions appear when the patient is frustrated.

d. The spasms of stuttering and the associated facial and bodily tensions increase in various social situations. Sometimes these spasms and tensions disappear completely when communicative pressures are absent.

e. In an advanced case of stuttering, the spasms may spread from the muscles of phonation and articulation to other muscles, even to distant ones.

The syndrome of stuttering is characterized, in addition to the phenomena of stuttering, by the following:

1. Muscular hypertonicity. Stuttering takes on some aspects of spasticity as in cerebral palsy. Even when the child shows no real phonatory or articulatory spasms, he exhibits tension of lips, tongue, pharynx, and larynx. He exhibits vocal effort, often above normal in amount, and he produces changes of pitch and intensity from word to word or from syllable to syllable, but he reduces his inflections during the utterance of unit vowel sounds. He cannot shift relaxation from one muscle group to another. Even when he is not actually stuttering, his speech may take on the characteristics of spastic dysarthria—it may be clumsy, tense, and labored. Few stutterers, if any, have relaxed voices. The rate of articulation, in normal English at least, is often about that of maximum physiological speed. Many words severely tax the ability of the stutterer to follow the normal speed of utterance (Palmer & Gillet, 1938, pp. 3–12).

The stutterer is caught in a dilemma of whether to retard the rate of his speech to that of his own slow utterance or to adopt the rate of his conversational partners and compromise his articulation by the omission or assimilation of some of the sounds. Unless he takes one of these courses in the utterance of "fast" words, he will stutter badly. If he takes the first course, his speech becomes as conspicuous as though he were actually stuttering; if the second, his associates are likely to brand him a *clutterer*. Many a clutterer is a "cured" stutterer who has made the second compromise.

There are certain aspects of the syndrome of stuttering that are difficult to relate to the phenomena of stuttering.

2. The glycogen (animal sugar) is higher than normal in the stutterer's blood.

3. The pulse rhythms of nonstuttering children increase in irregularity. Palmer and Gillet conclude that "while increased irregularity of the heart beat is not the cause of stuttering, it is a part of the mechanism linked to stuttering and the sex metabolisms [p. 12]."

4. The incidence of stuttering is much higher in boys than in girls, and the chance of recovery from stuttering is greater among pubescent girls than boys.

5. The incidence is highest between 5 and 10 years of age, with rapid decrease of cases as puberty approaches.

West (1968) raises the problem of the distribution and incidence of stuttering:

The question now arises as to what faculty is so retarded as to involve the child in stuttering. The key to this puzzle is probably to be found in the lateness of development, or immaturity, of the speech skills of male, in comparison with that of female children. Stutterers as a class, largely males, are merely farther behind average females in developing speech skills than are average males. They hold their infantilisms of speech longer than do their brothers and are not ready to articulate skillfully until after social pressures and gregarious instincts have forced them to begin oral speech. Thus they compete in a game in which they are handicapped, and all children—boys or girls—so handicapped are potential stutterers. Boys constitute the vast majority of these articulatory cripples [p. 263].

6. Stuttering is inherited. Some cases can be explained on the basis of "social heredity" or "imitation," but these cases are difficult to justify if the stutterers have had no contact with their stuttering ancestors and in view of the fact that adopted children seldom take on the stuttering behavior of the families into which they have been adopted.

7. Multiple births tend to run in the families, and in such families, stuttering occurs more frequently than in others. But the stutterers in such families are not always the multiples.

8. Left-handedness often appears in family lines and is also related etiologically to stuttering, and again the stutterer may not always be the "lefty."

9. Kennedy and Williams (1938, p. 1306) report a linking of stuttering with allergies. Again, the correlation is not necessarily between the stutterer and the allergy victim but rather between the stutterer and the person who is a member of the allergic "family," even though all members of the family do not stutter.

10. Mildred Berry (1938, p. 200) finds that one of the stigmata of the stuttering syndrome is a vulnerability to respiratory infections, which she styles a "rheumatic diathesis." In families showing this diathesis, stuttering appears even before the respiratory infection. In hundreds of cases in her survey, stuttering usually antedated the infection.

11. Moral rigidity is another personality characteristic of the stutterer. He is possessed of an uncompromising conscience. He is a perfectionist. This moral rigidity is not unique with the stutterer, but few stutterers are without it (West, Ansberry, & Carr, pp. 265–266).

The fact that the stutterer has a conspicuous social blemish contributes to his anxiety about his standing among his associates. His perfectionism increases his stuttering. Were he indifferent to his speech blocks, there probably would be fewer such blocks; and the severity of stuttering between one social situation and another would be lessened.

Semantogenic Stuttering

The late Wendell Johnson emphasized semantogenesis as a cause of stuttering. By this he meant that the child acquires a pattern of anxiety about his articulatory clumsiness if his parents, relatives, friends, and teachers call his speech defect stuttering or any other name that signifies that his speech is peculiarly different from that of other children. So Johnson also called stuttering a diagnosogenic phenomenon. He declared that stuttering usually develops from the normal disfluencies of early childhood, which are seized upon by the parents and thought of as the development of the dreaded affliction, or "dis-ease," called stuttering. According to this widely accepted theory of the cause of stuttering, its greater prevalence among boys is due to the closer emotional identification between mother and son than between mother and daughter or between father and daughter. The mother, not the father, is the chief worrier about the speech disfluencies of the child, and she expends her worries chiefly upon her son rather than upon her daughter (Johnson, 1942, pp. 251–257).

Psychodynamic Stuttering

There are many theories of the psychologic etiologies of stuttering:

1. Stuttering may be an hysterical phenomenon to gain sympathy, attention, and freedom from responsibilities. The stutterer's protest that he wants to be "cured" of his affliction may be unconscious malingering (Luchsinger & Arnold, 1965, p. 781).

2. Stuttering may be a result of sexual permaturity or immaturity, or a form of oral eroticism or masturbation (Coriat, 1943, p. 167).

3. Stuttering may be a psychoanalytic resultant or compensation for fear, insecurity, or asocial attitudes (Bluemel, 1958, p. 263).

Organic Stuttering

Some specialists believe that stuttering is the result of conflicts of control between the right and left cerebral hemispheres, as though the two "speech centers" were in functional opposition to each other. This hypothesis is named the "cerebral dominance" theory (Luchsinger & Arnold, Ch. 6).

The Karlins (1965, p. 92) supported the "somato-psychic" hypothesis, suggesting that stuttering is due to the failure of, or delay in the development of, the myelin sheath of the central and peripheral nerves of the cerebrospinal system. The myelin covering develops during childhood and grows faster in girls than in boys. The assumption is that the nourishing and insulating functions of the sheath parallel its development. The Karlins thus account for the early development of speech in girls and the clumsiness of speech in boys.

CHOREIC SPEECH

Certain speech involvements appear in Saint Vitus' dance or Sydenham's chorea. Sydenham's is found in close association with rheumatic fever; hence, some call Sydenham's rheumatic chorea. Thus, some of the symptoms of Sydenham's chorea may appear to be those of rheumatic fever, such as chronic elevation of the blood temperature, heart lesions, and chronic pains in the limbs. The speech disorders of Sydenham's chorea may be confusingly similar to stuttering. A statement of the differential diagnosis is that each disorder is largely limited to a given sex—stuttering to boys and chorea to girls. Each is largely associated with childhood, stuttering *before* puberty and chorea *at* puberty. Stuttering is both tonic and clonic in its spasms; choreic speech is generally clonic. In stuttering, no personality and emotional changes take place during its onset; but with chorea, the child becomes irritable, quick tempered, and unreasonable.

If one mistakes the diagnosis of rheumatic fever by noting its speech symptoms, one may do the patient a serious disservice. To give stuttering therapy for the choreic patient is to delay dangerously the therapy he needs.

CLEFT PALATE AND ITS THERAPY

Cleft palate is a congenital deformity resulting from a partial or complete failure of union, in the first trimester of gestation, between the separate processes which are to form the lips, alveolar ridge, maxillary bone, and velum. The disunion at birth may take the form of (*a*) a hiatus along the central seam of the soft palate or (*b*) a gap on the alveolar border and the related structure of the lip. The first gap is usually called cleft palate proper and the second cleft lip. Cleft lip is practically never on the midline of the lip. It appears usually immediately below the opening of the nostril. Sometimes cleft lip is bilateral. These anomalies are found more often among members of the white race. The frequency is about one in 1000 births, definitely less frequently among blacks, with boys in the majority (Karlin, Karlin, & Gurren, p. 240).

Until some procedure has achieved such control of the opening into the nasal chambers that pressure can be built up in the mouth to produce the plosive, fricative, and sibilant sounds, very little effective therapy can be accomplished. Such a procedure is either a surgical repair of the cleft or the construction of a prosthetic device to fill the hiatus between the soft palate and the pharyngeal wall in order to provide for the mouth pressure necessary for the utterance of these sounds. The procedure of choice is usually plastic surgery, though with some patients surgery is impossible and the prosthesis is resorted to.

When the surgery or prosthetic dentistry has been accomplished, the effectiveness of the repair can be tested by asking the patient to swallow water, preferably leaning over a drinking fountain. If no water escapes through the nostrils, the surgery or prosthesis may be deemed successful. Then the therapy by the speech clinician begins. The goals of therapy are threefold: (*a*) to sharpen the consonants [p, b, t, d, k, g, f, v, θ, ð, s, z, ʃ, ʒ, tʃ] and [dʒ]; (*b*) to rid the patient of excessive nasality on all vowels and semivowels; and (*c*) to eliminate compensatory sounds and visible movements that the patient has developed as substitutions for his speech lapses.

NEGATIVE NASALITY: TREATMENT AND TRAINING

A large class of dyslalias is that caused by obstructions of the nasal passages, whose effects are quite the opposite of those produced by cleft palate or bulbar palsies. The obstructive deformities produce negative nasality. The conspicuous defects here are the substitutions of [b] for [m], [d] for [n], and [g] for [ŋ].

Perhaps, the most common cause of nasal obstruction is hypertrophy of the pharyngeal tonsil, usually called the adenoid. The adenoid is a benign tumor of the more or less compact mass of lymphoid nodules lying usually on the posterior wall of the nasopharynx. If the adenoid mass bulks large enough, it closes the nasopharynx and the Eustachian tubes as well, thus indirectly involving the middle ear and causing an impairment of the mechanism by which the patient monitors his speech. When the outlet through the nasal fossae is obstructed, air pressure can be built up in the mouth without employing the nasopharyngeal sphincter. Hence, the patient develops the habit of speaking with the velum relaxed and the port into the nasopharynx open. Thus, the vowels and semivowels are resonated not only through the proper mouth chambers but also through a cul-de-sac resonance chamber in the nasopharynx.

Other causes of stoppage of the nasal passages are legion. Swollen and irritated mucous membranes, hypertrophied turbinates, misshaped septum, elevated palatal arch, broken or deformed nose, and various growths such as nasal "tonsils," septal spurs, synechiae, polyps, syphilitic gummas, and neoplasms of many types are frequent causes of stoppage of the anterior nasal passageways. With either anterior or posterior stoppage the primary symptoms, other than voice and speech alterations, are disturbances of breathing. The patient tends to breathe through his mouth; when asked to breathe through his nose, he does so with difficulty, his nose breathing often being accompanied by fricative noises.

As with palatal and labial deformities, the first step in treating nasal obstruction is surgical or medical correction of the structural anomaly insofar as is possible and feasible in each case. The difficulty of such operations varies from the relatively simple adenoidectomies to complicated submucous resections of the septum. The decision as to surgery is often based upon a careful balancing of its benefits against cost and disadvantages. A speech advisor should be consulted, and he should be prepared to state to what extent the observed nasal obstruction is responsible for the speech defect and to predict the effect that removal of the obstruction will have upon speech. Many an operation to obviate nasal stenosis has been undertaken, not to improve the patient's general health but to eradicate articulatory defects that could not possibly be caused by the structural conditions against which the operation was directed. Only after a careful phonetic analysis can the speech advisor offer an opinion as to the need or benefit of an operation, if the surgeon considers it practical.

As with cleft palate and harelip, the operation may be only the first step in treatment. If the nasal obstruction occurs during adulthood and has been present only a short time, its removal is followed by a brief period of readjustment of speech habits, which the patient is always able to accomplish readily by himself. If, however, the obstruction appears during the learning of speech—or any part of the formative period, for that matter—its removal merely changes the rhinolalia from clausa to aperta, from negative to positive nasality. This is rather disconcerting to the parents who have been led to expect that the operation itself will improve the child's speech.

The reason for the appearance of rhinolalia aperta after the removal of adenoids is that the child has learned habits of speech in which the closing functions of the nasopharyngeal sphincter are quite unnecessary. If speech were innate, as is swallowing, the sphincter would function properly to open and close the passage into the nasopharynx whether or not any mechanical advantage was achieved; but because speech is a learned function, the sphincter plays no part that is not directly required for the articulation of a sound. With the nasopharynx quite occluded by pathological or hypertrophic structures, the mouth sounds are made practically as well with the nasopharyngeal port open as with it shut. If a child learns to speak when his nasopharynx or his nasal chambers are occluded, the sphincteric functions of the velum and Passavant's cushion are not built into his neuromuscular pattern for articulation.

The difference between such a child and the child whose nasopharynx, fossae, and nares are quite patent during the period of learning speech is more fundamental than appears from the speech symptoms. The child with a history of nasal or pharyngeal occlusion during the learning of speech has acquired a method of articulation in which the nasopharyngeal sphincter remains *open* during speech, and even after corrective surgery, he continues this method except with those sounds in which closure of the nasopharyngeal port is an absolute necessity—plosives, fricatives, and sibilants. The child with a history of normalcy during the learning of speech acquires a method of articulation in which the sphincter remains *closed* (or nearly so) during speech, except when its opening is an absolute necessity for the production of the nasal sounds. Thus, sphincteric activity takes place at different times and under different conditions in the speech of the two children. Because the habits developed by the child with a nasal or pharyngeal stoppage are abnormal, his speech reeducation is very difficult. If a child develops at two a stoppage which is not effectively removed until he is ten, his speech will present precisely the same problem after the operation as that of the patient who has undergone a successful operation for cleft palate. He has to be taught the use of the velum and Passavant's cushion.

DYSLALIAS CAUSED BY SUNDRY OTHER STRUCTURAL ANOMALIES

Many speech defects are wrongly blamed upon structural deviations of the oral and nasal cavities or of the muscles and organs of the mouth and nose. These errors of diagnosis are not limited to parents. Even professional advisors may overlook psychologic factors in etiology and seize upon these structural deviations that may have no connection with the defects that parents complain of. Here are some examples: (*a*) a bifid uvula; (*b*) uvula, completely wanting; (*c*) slightly scarred tonsil; (*d*) missing teeth, even to the number of four. There are few real cases of dyslalia caused by "tongue-tie," yet that condition is popularly believed to cause articulatory clumsiness.

Aside from cleft lip and palate, the structural anomalies that are blamable for speech defects are these:

1. Open bite. In this condition, the incisors of the upper arch do not meet or overlap the lowers. It may cause all fricative sounds to be defective.

2. Recessive jaw (short chin). This causes misarticulation of [p, b, m, s] and [z].

3. Prognathic mandible (the patient leads with his jaw). The chief problems here are the adjustments for [s, z, θ, ð, f] and [v].

4. High palatal arch (narrow and pointed roof of the mouth). This deformity is traceable to thumbsucking. It may cause the sibilants [s] and [z] to be defective.

DEFICIENCIES OF HEARING

Impairments of hearing often cause communicative disorders. Sometimes the disorders are failure to understand what persons say to the child, and sometimes they are speech disorders caused by failure in the monitoring of what the child himself speaks.

The *deaf* are those who have never been able to hear speech as such; i.e., their hearing loss dates either from birth or from so early in infancy that what speech they may have heard had no meaning for them and hence created no linguistic memories or habits of oral communication. The *deafened* are those who, though once able to hear speech normally, are now unable to do so; and the *hard-of-hearing* are those who hear speech but with some loss of efficiency as measured by normal standards. Though they can hear some modicum of speech under certain very favorable conditions, many people are *deaf* because they have always lacked usable hearing of speech. The line of distinction between the *deafened* and *hard-of-hearing* is often only a practical one. A person who once heard normally but is now gradually losing his auditory acuity is *hard-of-hearing* until he passes that point at which, for all practical purposes, he ceases to hear speech [West, Ansberry, & Carr, 1957, pp. 208-209].

The *deaf* child is impaired severely in speech reception as well as in speech production. The *deafened* child is impaired in both reception and production of speech to the degree to which he is deafened during the speech-learning period. The *hard-of-hearing* child is impaired in communication chiefly in the understanding of what he hears but rarely in the monitoring of his own speech.

The word *deaf* is used in two senses: first, to indicate the congenital impairment of hearing, and second, to signify the quality of impairment, such as high-frequency deaf, perception deaf, nerve deaf, etc. When the qualifier is used with the word *deaf*, it does not necessarily signify that the impairment is congenital.

From the point of view of etiology, deafnesses may be classified as of three sorts: (*a*) mechanical deafness, or conduction deafness, in which the impairment is in the sound receiving and transmitting apparatus, in the canal of the outer ear, in the ear drum, or middle ear; (*b*) cochlear deafness, impairment of the apparatus for transmiting the mechanical sounds into neural stimuli or of the sensory end-organs of the acoustic nerve; (*c*) nerve deafness, deficiency of the acoustic nerve or the various afferent nerves carrying signals from the cochleae to the auditory centers of the cerebrum. In addition to these three sorts of hearing pathologies, there are those called "nonorganic" deafnesses, referred to as psychogenic or hysterical deficiencies of hearing.

Perception (cochlear) deafness and conduction deafness show the same speech involvements, insofar as they are both forms of reduced acuity; but, in addition, each has its own peculiar speech symptoms. In conduction deafness, the patient's voice is subdued in volume, whereas in perception deafness, it may be increased, sometimes to an actual shout. In conduction deafness, there is a monotony of volume and pitch; but in perception deafness, though pitch inflections are lacking, the voice shows exaggerated modulations of volume. Conduction deafness is the less serious in its effect upon speech, because, although the patient cannot hear others well, he can often hear his own speech. In rare instances, the speech of such a patient, who is completely deaf for all practical purposes of hearing, may show no phonetic lapses at all.

Thus, in conduction deafness, the patient hears his own voice as louder than it really is, while others appear to him to be speaking very softly. Sudden increases in intensity of his own voice rumble in his head in a disagreeable manner; hence, he adopts the habit of speaking softly. But with perception deafness, the patient speaks very loud so he can hear his own voice as clearly as he thinks others should. Many a patient has a combination of both of these types of deafness, one ear having one form and the other ear the other, or both ears have both forms, with a consequent complication of speech symptoms.

VOICE DISORDERS

The normal speaking voice is characterized by the following conditions:
1. Adequate loudness.
2. Clearness of tone.
3. A pitch appropriate to the age and sex.
4. A slight vibrato.
5. A graceful and constant inflection of pitch and force which follows the meaning of what is spoken.

Any departure from these norms should be considered as a vocal defect —dysphonia or aphonia. (The difference between aphonia and dysphonia is one of degree. A vocal defect is a dysphonia unless it amounts to a complete loss of voice, when it becomes an aphonia). (a) Voices lacking adequate loudness may be described as weak, thin, or asthenic. (b) Those lacking clearness of tone may be hoarse, husky, or strident. (c) The terms high, shrill, eunuchoid, or treble usually refer to voices using pitch levels inappropriate to the age and sex of the possessors. (d) Voices that lack vibrato are said to be hard, metallic, or flat; those that exhibit too much or an irregular and uncontrolled vibrato are described as tremulous and palsied. (e) In terms of inflection or its lack, a voice may show exaggerated pitch changes or constantly recurring inflection patterns, such as a falling inflection, suggestive of fatigue, at the end of every phrase or again it may have very little change of pitch and force—it is monotonous. Rarely, indeed, can a defective voice be described in terms of only one of these categories; usually terms from two or more categories are needed to describe it adequately.

There is always a cause for any of these departures from the norm, but the cause is not always structural, i.e., not always due to structural defects of the larynx or of the resonators. Sometimes the dysphonia is rooted in neuropathology, sometimes in emotional disorders, sometimes in improper vocal habits.

The voice defects mentioned above are those most typical of structural anomalies, though any of them may be the result of other causes. These nonstructural causes—neuropathologies, emotional disturbances, and poor habits of vocalization—produce vocal effects considerably more diverse than those caused by structural conditions. Before any vocal training is undertaken, the cause of the dysphonia should be ascertained, and in the search for it, a laryngoscopic examination is the first step. The purpose of this examination is not so much a search for morbid conditions and their diagnosis as a study of the larynx as a producer of voice. The characteristics of the ideal glottis are as follows:

1. It must have two edges that can be brought into exactly parallel approximation.

2. This approximation must be so close as to prevent the escape of any air except when driven by considerable chest pressure.

3. The approximation must not be so close as to prevent the free movement of the bands when set in vibration by the air stream.

These three requisites of the normally functioning glottis should be kept in mind in the diagnosis. However, a fourth condition is also necessary for the production of the normal voice; the chambers of the throat and mouth should be open enough to permit the proper resonance of the tone and its proper delivery into the outer air.

DEFORMITIES OF THE GLOTTIS

It is obvious that irregularities on the vibrating edges of the vocal bands prevent the attainment of the four ideal conditions for voice production. Such irregularities allow streams of air to escape between the bands even when they should be in the closed phase of their cycle, giving to the voice a breathy, aspirate quality. These irregularities may take the form of growths upon the cords extending out into the glottal space or of depressions in the edges which leave small gaps even when the bands are closely approximated. Often these irregularities are not pathological but merely congenital or developmental variants from normal glottal structure. But they may be gravely pathological—tubercular, syphilitic, or tumorous. In many cases, the irregularities are scars of traumatizations of the vocal bands, such as those produced when a child inhales a solid object he has in his mouth. If it becomes lodged in the larynx, the reflex coughing that ensues is likely to lacerate the vocal bands. Intubation, or the forcing of an instrument between the bands when they are swollen shut or joined by a web in acute disease, may break their edges and cicatrize them. Sometimes misuse of the voice produces lesions of the edges of the cords called *contact ulcers*, which often upon healing form scars. In a large number of cases, the irregularity of the edge of the cord results from the presence of one or more nodules, called "singer's nodes." These are due primarily to a misuse of the voice, though they may have as contributing causes chronic laryngitis or lacunar tonsilitis.

Voice Training for Irregular Glottis

When it has been determined that dysphonia is caused by irregularity in the rima glottidis, the first step, before any therapeutic training is undertaken, is to rule on the possibility of progressive pathology. The patient is referred to the laryngologist for study. This specialist is also asked to suggest medical and surgical procedures to correct the laryngeal conditions that cause the dysphonia, even when there is no acute or active laryngeal pathology. When this study has been completed, the cases will fall into one of the three following classes:

1. Those whose bands show evidence of active pathology. Their salvation, if any, lies in the hands of the laryngologist, and voice training is positively contraindicated. Their only hope for vocal rehabilitation is in eradication of the pathology; hence, any attempt at voice training either is immediately dangerous or may serve to delay too long the steps that should be taken to combat the pathology.

2. Those whose bands show permanent and irremediable irregularities but no active pathology. Medicine and surgery have no help to offer these persons; most of them are also hopeless from the point of view of voice training. Their only possible hope for voice improvement lies in the development of sensory-motor control of the voice through careful ear-training drills. These patients may, by ear, learn to bring about adjustments of the larynx to compensate for the structural abnormalities.

3. Those whose bands show irregularities that are the result of misuse of the voice. This group consists of singers (both adults and children), auctioneers, newsboys, public speakers, and others who have used their voices rather vigorously for a comparatively long period of time. Irregularities in the vocal bands of such persons are caused by an improper pitching of the voice, necessitating the use of high pressure against the under surfaces of the bands. (No amount of vigorous vocalization can damage the edges of the vocal folds if the voice is properly used.) In their anxiety to reach all who hear them, public speakers "raise" their voices. This raising consists of an increase in volume, a heightening of the pitch, and a "tensing" of the quality. This raising of the voice is largely responsible for the appearance of irregularities upon the edges of the vocal cords. A singer who sings above his natural register also runs the danger of developing this condition. Singing or speaking outdoors tends to aggravate the condition, because more force is needed to "carry" the tone. An increased force of voice requires an increased pressure in the air beneath the glottis which can be brought about

only by a tighter contact between the bands. In their movements, the cords rub edges at least once in each cycle of vibration. Thus, at the pitch of middle C, a singer's bands make 250 contacts with each other during each second. If these rubbing contacts are made with a considerable head of pressure beneath the bands, corn-like beads or nodes are produced, consisting of stratified epithelium to protect the surfaces being rubbed.

Voice training in such cases must be an undoing of the damage resulting from improper use of the voice. Hence, the best treatment is a complete rest for the voice—no singing, no talking, not even laughing. Although relaxed whispering is harmless and may be indulged in freely, its prescription is usually rather too drastic for busy adults and out of the question for children. Some means must be employed, however, to reduce the friction between the two cords. If it is impossible for the patient to refrain from talking, relief must be afforded the rubbing edges by moving the point of greatest friction to some other portion of the glottic edge. As a rule, the voices of such patients should be lowered in pitch, because the vocal nodules generally come as a consequence of too high a pitch.

A more careful statement of the principles of therapy involves the following facts:

1. As the pitch of the voice rises, the point of greatest friction between the cords moves along the edge from back to front.

2. In the gamut of the pitch scale of each individual subject, there is one level at least (and in adult males usually two) at which the chambers of the mouth, throat, and chest have relatively high potential for the resonance of the laryngeal tone, i.e., there is a natural pitch at which the individual phonates most efficiently and makes the loudest tone for the least expenditure of energy—a pitch at which the greatest amount of the energy carried in the air column is transmuted into sound waves. Above and below this level of optimum resonance, the speaker requires greater air pressure to produce an intensity equal to that produced easily at the optimum level.

3. A reduction of the air pressure used in phonation lessens the friction between the bands.

The choice of voice "placement," therefore, should not be undertaken until after a careful study has been made of the patient's vocal habits and potentialities. A pitch must be selected that affords relief from friction at the points affected and permits the patient to phonate easily, i.e., with relatively low tracheal pressure; the adoption of such a pitch will reduce the friction. The first object of the study must be to determine what pitch the patient habitually uses in his speaking or singing. Next, the point on the cords at which the nodes appear should be considered; if it is near the front, i.e., near the thyroid attachment, the offending pitch has been a high one. Third, one should experiment with the patient's voice to determine his levels of optimum resonance, and if possible, one of these should be selected as the pitch for him to use during his period of voice training. However, if the nodes are near the front of the cords, high pitches should be avoided, no matter how great their resonating properties, for the farther the point of friction is removed from the nodes, the greater is the relief. The change from the habitual speaking or singing pitch should therefore be as radical as possible.

It sometimes happens that the pitch used by the patient in public speaking is quite different from his conversational pitch, and here the solution is the adoption, for public speaking purposes, of a conversational method. The patient should be advised to abandon his "public speaking voice," and instead, to increase the volume of his conversational voice, even though at first it may be something of a shock to his audiences, accustomed as they are to his higher pitch level.

One of the common vocal defects of the child at outdoor play is the use of a "pinched throat" in the attempt to make the voice more "carrying." This amounts virtually to screaming, with consequent development of vocal nodules.

Checking the Therapy

The nodules should show reduction in size within three months of training. Failure to do so is a sign that the treatment is not affording sufficient relief from the irritating friction, and relaxed whispering should then be the only form of speech allowed. This prescription is not usually feasible, because vocal nodules almost never occur except in people who use (or misuse) their voices in professional work. The patient should be cautioned even about his method of whispering, for a forced whisper, made through tightly approximated cords, should be avoided. Complete and prolonged vocal silence with no coughing and laughing is a reliable method for treating vocal nodules that have resulted from misuse of the voice. If the nodules have not disappeared after at least a month of the vocal-rest method, it is evident that they have been caused by conditions other than friction, and the case should again be referred to the laryngologist. Children who have undergone this extremely inconvenient therapy and have succeeded in ridding themselves of vocal nodules still need to be cautioned against returning to their former poor vocal habits. Every one of these patients should be warned that, unless he employs better vocal techniques, the nodules will return.

PHENOMENA OF THE CHANGE OF VOICE

One of the dysphonias occupying the borderline between structural and functional is the persistence into adolescence and adulthood of the prepubescent, high-pitched voice of the boy. Many psychic factors operate to cause the boy to rebel against the pubescent voice change; nevertheless, the new voice usually prevails, since the factors, both mental and physical, that favor the change are of great potency. In a significant number of cases, however, the factors favoring the change are overbalanced and the voice remains high-pitched. The following is the explanation of the conflict of these forces.

At puberty, the length of a boy's glottis nearly doubles in a few months. The human vocal tube has a principal resonating characteristic, varying widely from person to person, averaging about middle C. The pitch of this resonating characteristic is determined by many factors—the diameter of the vocal chambers, the textures of their linings, the cross sections of their apertures, and, probably chief of all, the total length of the vocal tube. Under the influence of these variables, the *band of principal resonance* ranges above and below 256 double vibrations per second. During the prepubescent period, the boy employs a vocal pitch within this band, because the frequency characteristic of the vocal tube and the vibratory rate of his relatively short rima glottidis are so matched that the resonance of the tube readily facilitates the vibrations of the vocal cords. When his vocal cords begin to lengthen, however, they no longer vibrate readily at a pitch within the band of principal resonance; hence, their movements are no longer facilitated. During this intermediate period, the voice is likely to be husky and lacking in clearness and loudness of tone.

As the cords continue to lengthen, their natural rate of vibration becomes slower and slower, until it has reached a point at which the rate is about one half the prepubescent frequency. Here, the boy has two pitches to choose from, either of which may be phonated with the support of facilitation by the resonance of the vocal tube. He may choose the higher pitch, at which his resonancy factor of facilitation is most efficient, but at which the vocal cords must vibrate at double their natural frequency; or he may select the lower pitch, at which the resonance factor is slightly less efficient, but where the cords vibrate at their natural and hence most efficient rate. With most boys, either pitch is produced with good volume and clarity. Hence, for a short time, the boy's voice may "break," i.e., alternate between these two choices. If he overtenses the vocal cords, they will vibrate with the support of the resonators at the highest pitch; if he phonates with relatively relaxed cords, they will vibrate at the lower pitch; with intermediate tension, they will fluctuate between the high and low pitches, though seldom vibrating at intermediate pitches. Finally, the more relaxed laryngeal adjustment becomes fixed by habit, and the low-pitched voice of adolescence prevails.

This is the pubescent vocal history of the average boy. With a significant number of boys, however, the shift of voice does not take place. When they are presented with the choice between two tones, either of which may be facilitated by the resonance chambers, they choose the upper one, for the facilitation of which their resonance chambers are the most efficient. The only sign of pubescent vocal change that they exhibit is a slight huskiness and weakness of tone during the interval when their vocal cords are in the intermediate state of pubescent growth. After this intermediate dysphonia has passed, the voice usually regains its clarity and loudness and becomes what may very properly be described as a *falsetto*.

The chief physical factors back of this falsetto are as follows:

1. Precocious Pubescence. If the larynx passes through its physical metamorphosis at an unusually early age, the boy's choice of pitch is pre-judiced by the fact that the other boys of his age have voices that would make him conspicuous if he chose the lower pitch. Hence, he adopts the falsetto to keep in style with his "gang." By the time the rest have come to puberty, his vocal habits have been fixed, and the change becomes difficult for him. If at that time, after his friends and acquaintances have become accustomed to his falsetto, he should, if he actually still could, change his vocal pitch, he would subject himself to a conspicuousness that would be even more disturbing than to continue to use the falsetto. Even if the lower voice were easily attainable, most boys in this dilemma of a choice between two evils choose the falsetto.

2. Length of the Vocal Cords. If at puberty the glottis lengthens greatly until its natural rate of vibrations is unusually low, i.e., below 100 double vibrations per second, the boy may choose to use his falsetto, first, because the lower pitch is too far from the resonance potential of his vocal tube, and second, because the adoption of an unusually low pitch on the part of a person who is still virtually a child is so startling as to bring upon him embarrassing attention from his amazed and amused associates. If on the other hand, the vocal cords lengthen very little at puberty, it may be im-possible for him to adjust them to the outrushing air stream so that they can vibrate at a sufficiently slow rate to receive the facilitation of resonance at the pitch of one octave below his band of principal resonance. He therefore employs an upper tone that is near enough to his facilitating resonance to make his voice efficient. If the pitch of the laryngeal tone is well within the band of principal resonance, his voice will be clear but will be a definite falsetto. If in order to avoid a conspicuous falsetto, he employs a pitch close to that of the average adolescent youth, his voice will be aspirate and lacking in volume.

One of the common causes of shortness of the vocal cords is glandular immaturity or imbalance. A failure of gonadal secretion or of pituitary activity or of both may arrest the metamorphosis of the larynx and hold the cords at their prepubescent length.

Vocal Abuse through Singing

One of the influences pulling the voice toward the falsetto is teaching the young boy to sing soprano and continuing the soprano during puberty. This training is likely either to produce a frank falsetto or to render the voice of the adolescent aspirate and lacking in vocal power. The singing of soprano during puberty, moreover, introduces a social problem that may profoundly condition his personality, in that it develops in him the habit of gaining his psychic income from his success in the more or less artificial type of expression of song pitched like that of women and children, rather than from his achievements in the natural means of expression through speech pitched like that of boys of his age. His singing tends to set him apart from others of his gang, with all the personality reverberations that this separation involves. The boy should not be asked to sing, except very softly, during his pubescent voice change, and certainly should not be expected to sing solos in public, with the long and arduous practicing that such solo work entails.

Vocal Training of the Falsetto

The first step to be taken in retraining the voice of the person with a falsetto dysphonia is psychotherapy aimed at bringing him to a real desire for a change of his voice and to a willingness to face the embarrassment that a change of voice will entail. This psychotherapy in some cases involves virtually a change of personality.

With an adolescent who is asked to make a radical change in his vocal pitch, it is often advisable to effect a change of social environment. Since he suffers so keenly under the scrutiny that a sudden change of voice always elicits from his associates, it is well, if possible, to remove him to an environment in which a lowered pitch will not seem conspicuous, or in other words, to an environment in which, to avoid appearing conspicuous, he will need to avoid his falsetto.

There are two alternate procedures for effecting the actual change of voice: (a) vocal tones are employed that gradually, week by week, are lower and lower until the optimum pitch is reached. This pitch is about one octave below his band of principal resonance and is a tone at which the voice is clear and free of aspirate quality. Only after this pitch has been reached are loud tones attempted. (b) Exercises are used that involve intonation at a vocal pitch exactly in the middle of the band of principal resonance, even though this may require an actual raising of the pitch above that used habitually. After this pitch has been developed until the tone is loud and clear, drops of one full octave are attempted. The boy is asked to phonate at the higher pitch and suddenly drop to the lower. At first, the upper note will be the stronger of the two, but he practices these drops until the higher note can be made softly and the lower note with a definite crescendo.

Usually the choice as to which of these methods will be employed depends upon whether the habitual pitch of the boy's voice is nearer the band of principal resonance or nearer the first octave below that band. If the habitual pitch is well below the band, the first method is employed; if the habitual pitch is near the band of principal resonance, or within it, the second method is employed. In some cases, changing the pitch of the voice is difficult because the boy has a poor ear for pitch—i.e., he is tone deaf. With such a person pitch changes can be made visible by means of a tonoscope, so that he can control by watching what he cannot control by hearing. A simple stroboscopic disk, mounted on a phonograph turntable and lighted by a neon flash from a microphone-amplifier circuit, may be used as the tonoscope. No intensive training of the falsetto voice is undertaken until puberty has been well passed and in fact, the pubescent boy should be encouraged to resist the temptation to sing or speak loudly and to yell and cheer.

CONCLUSION

In this chapter, we have considered the pathologies that interfere with oral communication. These disorders are sometimes as tragic as fatal diseases. Aphasia, stuttering, aphonia, and other disorders have served as the promptings to suicide. On the other hand, a cure, or even partial cure, of a severe disorder of speech offers a new life for the patient.

REFERENCES

Berry, M. The developmental history of stuttering children. *J. Pediatrics*, 1938, 209–217.

Bluemel, C. S. Stuttering: A psychiatric viewpoint. *J. Speech Hear. Dis.*, 1958, **23**, 263–267.

Coriat, I. H. *The nervous child*. 1943.

Henderson, Florence. Accuracy in testing the articulation of speech sounds. *J. educ. Res.*, 1938.

Johnson, W. A study of the onset and development of stuttering. *J. Speech Hear. Dis.*, 1942, **7**, 251–257.

Karlin, I., Karlin, D., & Gurren, L. *Development and disorders of speech in childhood*. Springfield: Charles Thomas, 1965.

Kennedy, A., & Williams, D. Association of stammering and the allergic diathesis. *Brit. med. J.*, 1938, 1306–1309.

Luchsinger, R., & Arnold, G. E. *Voice-speech-language*. Belmont: Wadsworth, 1965.

Morley, M. *The development and disorder of speech in childhood*. London: E. & S. Livingston, 1957.

Palmer, F., & Gillett, A. Sex differences in the cardiac rhythms of stutterers. *J. Speech Hear. Dis.*, 1938, **3**, 3–12.

Poole, Irene. *The genetic development of articulation of consonant sounds in children's speech*. Doctoral dissertation. University of Michigan, 1934, Abstracted in *Element. Eng.*, **11** 1934, 159–161.

West, R. W., & Ansberry, M. *Rehabilitation of speech*. (4th ed.) New York: Harper & Row, 1968.

9

The Ontogenesis of the Problem of Reference: A Review of Some Theories of Linguistic Symbols

JERRY A. FODOR
Massachusetts Institute of Technology

In diesen Worten erhalten wir, so scheint es mir, ein bestimmtes Bild von dem Wesen der menschlichen Sprache. Namlich dieses: Die Worten der Sprache benennen Gegenstande—In diesem Bild von der Sprache finden wir die Wurzeln der Idee: Jedes Wort hat eine Bedeutung. Diese Bedeutung ist dem Wort zugeordnet. Sie ist der Gegenstand, fur welchen das Wort steht.

L. Wittgenstein,
Philosophical Investigations

"The problem of language is the problem of meaning. The problem of meaning is the problem of reference. And the problem of reference is to explain how words name things." Until very recently, this equivalence has recommended itself to many philosophers of language and to practically all psycholinguists. Its acceptance as self-evident has had much to do with the form that philosophical and psychological accounts of language have taken since Locke. In this paper, we shall investigate several such accounts. But, before commencing, we will do well to consider the assumptions that have made this version of the problem of reference a matter of such obsessive concern to students of language; to cast doubt upon those assumptions is to question the view that naming is the central relation to be explained by theories in psycholinguistics.

Part of the work on this paper was done while I was a Fellow at the Center for Advanced Study in the Behavioral Sciences. I wish to thank the Center for its aid in the preparation of the manuscript. I should also like to thank Professor Sol Saporta for having read and commented on an early draft.

The view that calling someone by his name is the paradigm of reference is very nearly ubiquitous, both in traditional and in current accounts of the psychological processes underlying verbal behavior. Examples may be chosen almost at random. Thus Locke (1690), discussing the ontogenesis of language, traces the development of all general terms from prototypic proper nouns:

There is nothing more evident than that the *ideas* of the persons children converse with . . . are like the persons themselves, only particular. The names they first gave to them are confined to . . . individuals; and the names of *nurse* and *mama*, the child uses, determine themselves to those persons. Afterwards, when time and a large acquaintance has made them observe, that there are a great many other things in the world, that in some common agreements of shape, and several other qualities, resemble their father and mother, those persons they have been used to, they frame an idea, which they find those many particulars do partake in; and that they give, with others, the name *man* for example. And *thus they come to have a general name*, and a general idea. Wherein they make nothing new, but only leave out of the complex idea they had of *Peter* and *James*, *Mary* and *Jane*, that which is peculiar to each, and retain only what is common to all [Bk. III, Ch. 3].

Substantially identical approaches may be found throughout the current literature, where the assumption that naming is the paradigmatic speech act is widely taken for granted. Carroll (1964) remarks: "There comes a stage . . . when acquisition of vocabulary is extremely rapid; this seems to occur when in his cognitive development the child has reached the point of perceiving that things, events, and properties have 'names' [p. 32]." Again, in one of the central theoretical passages of *Learning Theory and the Symbolic Processes*, Mowrer argues that

As Fig. [1] shows, the word Tom acquired its meaning, presumably, by being associated with and occurring in the context of, Tom as a real person. Tom himself has elicited . . . a total reaction which we can label, R_T, of which r_T is a component. And as a result of the paired presentation or concurrence of "Tom"-the-word and Tom-the-person, the component or "detachable" reaction, r_T is shifted from the latter to the former. And similarly for the word "thief." As indicated in Fig. [2], this word is likewise presumed to have acquired its distinctive meaning by having been used in the presence of, or to have been, as we say, "associated with," actual thieves [p. 144].

The reader will notice that Mowrer's figures are isomorphic, i.e., that the theory provides precisely similar treatments for predicates and for proper names.

It is not difficult to understand why so many theorists have succumbed to the temptation to locate the nub of the reference relation in naming. In the first place, the one-to-one relation that holds between a name and its bearers suggests itself as sufficiently simple to be the aboriginal meaning relation from which all others differ in complexity but not in kind. One supposes that, if the relation between a proper noun and its bearer is taken as primitive, the relations that hold between other sorts of words and what *they* stand for are easily defined in terms of it. Indeed, it is characteristically maintained that the naming relation is everywhere the same, though it binds words to different sorts of entities in the case of each of the major syntactic word types. If a proper noun names the object that bears it, then a common noun is a word which can name more objects than one. Analogously, verbs are to be thought of as naming actions, prepositions as naming relations, adjectives and adverbs as naming properties of objects and actions respectively, and so on. This is presumably the semantic theory that Everyman carries in his head and teaches to every child in grammar school.

A second reason for supposing that the naming relation between proper nouns and their bearers is semantic bedrock is perhaps that the model comports well with an associationistic view of the psycholinguistic processes. This is a point we shall investigate in considerable detail later. But it is easy to see how it might be maintained that repeated co-occurrences of an object with utterances of its name set up, in a child learning a language, the habit of expecting the object when the name is uttered. Correspondingly, appropriate manipulation of patterns of reinforcement might be supposed to produce in the child an inclination to utter the name upon presentation of the object. If the existence of such habits and inclinations accounts for the fact that a name stands for what it names, and if naming is the fundamental semantic relation, then there is promise of a complete characterization of the psychological processes underlying verbal behavior in terms of the same, fairly simple principles of association psychologists often invoke to account for nonverbal learning.

Simplicity and compatability with widely accepted psychological theories are certainly more than can be claimed for most theories about language. Nevertheless, there is reason to treat the view that naming is the central function words perform with considerable skepticism. In the first place, there is a large class of words and phrases of which it is simply not reasonable to hold that they are kinds of names. Nor is this class of counterexamples homogeneous; the doctrine that all words are names admits of a number of different kinds of exceptions. Consider, for example, *for example*, *hello*, *and*, *whether*, *since*, *of*, *and so on*, and so on. Though desperation might suggest that *hello* is the name of a situation in which persons are greeting one another, this is a case in which the councils of desperation ought to be resisted. *What is the name of this situation?* is a bizarre question (cf., *What is the name of this dog?*), and *This situation is named 'hello'* is barely English (cf. *This dog is named 'Posh'*). If it is still insisted that all words are kinds of names, then it must be replied that there must be as many kinds of names as there are kinds of words; hence, there is no reason for supposing that the relation between names like *Posh* and their bearers provides a model for the relation between names like *hello* and *their* bearers.[1]

It is not a small matter that there should exist a sizeable number of kinds of cases for which the name-bearer model of meaning is not suitable. It means that, at very best, a theory of meaning based upon this model will need to be held jointly with theories rich enough to account for the exceptions. This, in turn, means that the argument that simplicity and psychological plausibility militate in favor of the naming model is not sound unless the theories that explain the exceptions are also simple and plausible. A theory that can handle *Mommy* but not *and* is clearly not good enough. And the presumptive fact that a theory that handles only the first is compatible with an associationistic psychology is no guarantee that a theory that handles both will be.

Another way to point out the implausibility of the view that a homogeneous relationship of naming is fundamental in semantics is to remark upon a striking difference between true names and all other sorts of words: proper nouns are uniquely undefinable. Hence, in the sense of "meaning," in which having a meaning is having a definition, proper nouns have no meaning. (Notice that while it makes sense to ask *What does 'polarization' mean?*, it makes no sense to ask *What does 'John Smith' mean?*, the only relevant question being *Who is John Smith?*) But if it is true that names have no meaning, it seems odd to maintain that what bestows meaning upon other sorts of words is the fact that they bear to their referents the same sort of relation that *John Smith* bears to John Smith. At very least if a theory says this, it will need to say more. If the naming relation is taken as primitive and homogeneous, some explanation will have to be given of the asymmetry we have just mentioned.

Third, it seems clear that the homogeneity of the naming relation can be maintained only at the expense of postulating metaphysical objects to stand in the sort of relation to common nouns, verbs, adjectives, prepositions, etc., that physical objects have to the proper nouns that name them. That is, the simplicity that is claimed for semantic theories based on naming is characteristically gained at the price of an extremely complicated (not to say extremely dubious) ontology. It is clear, for example, that adjectives cannot name the sorts of things that proper nouns do. For while the referent of a proper noun can be said to have a location, a date, an individual history, etc., not one of these things can be said about the referents of adjectives. Given that we nevertheless assume that adjectives *are* names we are ipso facto committed to the existence of a special kind of thing—a property or universal—that is tailor-made to be what adjectives are the names of.

---

[1] Lest it be supposed that no one could possibly hold the view here attacked, cf. Carroll (1964) where it is asserted that "Some signs, like *Hi* and *Thanks* bear referential relationship only to certain kinds of social situations (p. 6)." If *Hi* refers to the situation in which people say *Hi*, what does "the situation in which people say *Hi* refer to?" Cf. Fodor, 1965.

Similarly, *activity* becomes a technical word when it begins to be used as a cover term for the sort of thing a verb "names," and at least, one psychologist has supposed that "pastness" must be "a subtle property of events" in order that there should be something named by the *ed* in *violated* and the *t* in *lost*. One wonders, indeed, whether this project is not doomed to circularity. For example, it is uninformative to say that nouns all refer to objects if it turns out that all that "objects" have in common is that they are the referents of nouns; nor is it easy to see what else of interest is common to, say, short naps and tall stories.

The process of filling the universe with queer objects solely in order that there should be something for words other than proper nouns to name has sometimes been carried so far as to become transparently ludicrous. Thus, Bertrand Russell (Linsky, 1963) once held that "A phrase may denote ambiguously; e.g., 'a man' denotes not many men, but an ambiguous man [p. 75]." It is perhaps unnecessary to remark that, while there are bald men around, any one of whom may, on occasion, plausibly stand as referent for "a bald man," there are no ambiguous men to be named by "a man" tout court. As Linsky (1963) has pointed out, "It is senseless to ask 'To whom does "a man" refer?' [p. 75]" just as it is senseless to ask which one "this one" refers to. What is sensible is to ask to whom Smith was referring when he said he met a man of his acquaintance or to which one Mrs. Smith was referring when she said "This one is rotten." In these cases, however, referring is something that people—not words—are properly said to do.

It is important not just to see the senselessness of such questions about reference but also to understand why students of language have sometimes been inclined to take them seriously. In most such cases, part of the motivation is that a theory that equates meaning with naming has been assumed. It is not surprising that if one starts with the view that *a man* and *this one* are queer kinds of names, one arrives at the conclusion that what they name must be queer kinds of objects.

It is worth mentioning one more reason for taking a jaundiced view of the position that says that the naming relation is the fundamental one and that the primary task of semantics is to show how other kinds of meaning can be reduced to it. We have seen that one argument for taking naming seriously as the semantic primitive is that it appears to be a simple one to-one relation, the extension of which is specified by such rules as "*John Smith*" *refers to John Smith*, "*Snow*" *refers to snow*, "*White*" *refers to white*, etc. If, however, the extension of the naming relation is specified in this way, it turns out that the rules determining the referents of a word do not apply to every occurrence of the word. Moreover, it is by no means clear that the difficulty is not intrinsic; there is no obvious way to make the rules fully general. Consider, for example, the application of the rule "*lions*" *refers to lions* to the sentence *John is hunting lions*. The question is whether the rule holds for the occurrence of *lions* in this sentence. The answer appears to be that, on one way of understanding the sentence, it does, but on another way of understanding it, it does not. That is, if one understands *John is hunting lions* on the model of *John is hunting two lions, Leo and Lea*, it is clear that the rule holds. For, *lions* evidently refers to lions in the latter case; in particular, it refers to Leo and Lea. However, there is a way for understanding *John is hunting lions* on which the rule does not hold. Thus, consider *John is hunting lions but he won't find any*. It is clear that the question *To which lions does the "lions" of* this *sentence refer?* is a nonsense question, analogous to *Which man does "a man" refer to?* (cf. also, *To which unicorns does "unicorns" refer in There aren't any unicorns?*).

Hence, there is a way of understanding *John is hunting lions* on which the obvious reference rule fails to apply, an interpretation on which the occurrence of *lions* in that sentence is nonreferential. What's more, this phenomenon is not by any means local. Many examples may be constructed in which rules like *lions refers to lions* fail in the scope of such verbs as *want*, *desire*, *think of*, *believe*, *hope for*, *intend to*, etc.

The problem of what to do about so-called intensional contexts—contexts in which reference rules fail to hold—is very much an open one in philosophy. We do not intend to review the solutions that have been proposed. What is relevant for our purposes is the remark that the phenomenon of intensionality reveals unexpected complexities in the notion of reference. Such complexities serve to undercut the argument that a semantic theory based on reference can make do with one fundamental word-object relation articulated by a reasonably simple and intuitive set of rules. The reverse turns out to be the case. It appears that we must either say that the reference relation does not obtain in intensional contexts, or that, if it does, the reference rules for such contexts, far from being simple and intuitive, are so obscure as thus far to have defied unexceptionable formulation.

It may also be remarked that, even if a way could be found to make reference rules fully general, such rules would not, by themselves, amount to a theory of reference. At best, rules of the sort we have cited succeed in enumerating the pairs of items between which the reference relation holds. They do not, however, indicate what the character of this relation is. Thus, several philosophers who have held that an account of meaning should include a set of reference rules have also held that the nature of the reference relation is clarified by the assumption that speakers are somehow conditioned to respond with the linguistic items mentioned on the left-hand side of such rules to the presence of the objects, properties, or whatever is mentioned on the right-hand side. That is, the intended interpretation of the reference rules of a semantic theory is given by a hypothesized conditioning model of verbal behavior. It would not be a very gross exaggeration to say that the cash value of positivistic semantic theories has usually turned out to be a learning-theoretic account of meaning. (Cf. e.g., Morris [1949]; Quine [1960]; and Russell [1940].)

The arguments we have been examining suggest pretty strongly that our view of language becomes seriously distorted when we hold that referring is *the* characteristic function of words. It would seem, rather, that since referring is only one of a number of different functions words can perform, the problem of reference is only one of a family of problems about meaning.

Indeed, one way of summarizing the remarks we have made so far is to insist upon the necessity of distinguishing between problems about meaning and problems about reference. Thus, we have already seen that English proper names have referents but not meanings. It may now be remarked that the distinction between meaning and reference is implicated in the problem of intensional contexts. For synonyms and synonymous expressions can be interchanged in such contexts without altering truth value. But substitution of nonsynonyms that share their referents may produce such alterations. Thus, if *John believes that the Metro runs through the biggest city in France* is true, it must also be true that John believes that the Metro runs through the largest city in France. But it need not be true that John believes that the Metro runs through Paris, since John may be under the misapprehension that the biggest city in France is Rheims.

It is, moreover, obvious that while synonymous expressions—i.e., expressions that are identical in *meaning*—must have the same referents (if they have any), the converse need not hold. *The largest city in France* has the same referent as *The city the Metro runs through*, though it is clear that these expressions differ in meaning since Paris would remain France's largest city even if the Metro were moved to Rheims.

While the distinction between meaning and reference is important, it is also subtle. Thus, we know that *round square* has no referent *because* we know that it follows from the meaning of *round* and *square* that anything that is square is not round. Similarly, we know that the referents of *bachelor* are all male, because we know that *all bachelors are male* is analytically true (viz., true by virtue of the meanings of the constituent words), and we know that *the light box* may have two referents because we know that *light* has two meanings. Although a theory that treats seriously the *meaning* of words would presumably be concerned, in the first instance, to explain why expressions like *round square* are linguistically incoherent, why expressions like *male bachelor* are redundant, and why expressions like *light box* are linguistically ambiguous, such a theory would have the indirect effect of explaining certain complexities in the relations between words and their referents.

To say that the problem of reference is less general than it is sometimes supposed to be is not, therefore, to dismiss the problem. Still less is it to solve it. In short, at least one of the equivalences we mentioned at the start is false: the problem of meaning is by no means identical with the problem of reference. But there is no use denying that the two problems are intricately related, so that if we understood the mechanism of reference, we would probably understand a good deal about meaning as well.

An analogous point can be made about the relation of naming to reference. It must be obvious that the practice of viewing these relations as identical leads quickly to confusions since many expressions that have referents are not names (*the last rose of summer*) and many expressions that are strictly names have no referents (*Zeus*). But while the habit of confusing these relations is regrettable, it must be admitted that many names have referents and that many expressions characteristically used to refer are names. Presumably, we would know much more about reference than we know now if we had a clearer view of the way names work.

We do not propose to solve any of these puzzles. We do not know how. In fact, we shall present some reasons for supposing that the problem of reference is one of the last questions to raise about language; that reference is by no means a simple relationship and that an understanding of reference probably presupposes more information about language structure than anyone currently possesses. At present, however, we wish to indicate precisely what kind of problem reference is usually supposed to be and what kinds of solutions psychologists and philosophers have thought it amenable to. We shall try to show that it is not only the generality of the problem of reference that has been misconstrued. There is a certain sense in which the nature of the problem has not itself been correctly grasped, so that the models that have been proposed for reference have generally been somewhat irrelevant to the actual exigencies of the problem that reference poses.

One way of seeing what the problem of reference is supposed to be is to raise the question why reference has been thought to be problematic. Why is it that, while so many deep problems about language have been ignored, there has been practically universal agreement that there is a puzzle about reference? What is it precisely that people think needs to be explained?

We make a start towards answering this question when we notice that the doctrine that the problem of reference is the heart of the problem of language is almost invariably held in conjunction with the view that it is characteristic of human languages that they are systems of conventions. We shall presently try to make clear the exact relation between these two doctrines. For the moment, it is necessary to understand what is being claimed when the conventional aspect of human language is stressed.

It is commonplace among students of language to remark upon a certain arbitrariness that attaches to facts about human languages. By this is meant not only that it is a matter of historical accident that a given language is spoken in one place and not another but also that it is impossible to give any justification for persisting in particular linguistic usages other than the practical inconvenience of altering them. One (slightly misleading) way of putting this is to say that we could, in principle, alter any detail of our language simply by agreeing to do so, just as children do when they agree to converse in Pig Latin. This is meant to be analogous to saying, for example, that we could alter the conventions that determine what counts as correct evening dress simply by agreeing to do so, and to be *dis*analogous to saying that we could alter the way we walk simply by agreeing to limp. Precisely what is denied when the arbitrariness of facts about language is stressed is that something corresponds to a natural way of talking in the way that something clearly does correspond to a natural way of walking.

We say that this is a somewhat misleading way of making the point because it is evident that, for an adult speaker set in his linguistic ways, adopting a new set of speech habits would involve considerably more difficulty than adopting a new set of conventions for formal attire. To emphasize the arbitrary character of linguistic rules is not, of course, to deny this. It is rather to assert that, in principle, we could equally easily have learned a way of talking quite different from the way of talking we did learn; presumably, this is not true of alternative ways of walking.

That there must be something to the view when it is so stated is evident if only from the fact that human children born in different language communities all appear to be able to master their native tongues with approximately equal facility. What innate limits may be imposed upon this ability is not known, though there is some reason to suppose that there may exist specifiable language systems that a human could not learn as a first language (cf. Lenneberg, 1964). At any event, it seems evident that the natural languages that happen to exist are somewhat accidental choices from a presumably much larger set of possible human languages.

We could, to keep to quite trivial examples, institute the following changes in English. We could adopt the practice of henceforth using the phonemic sequence represented by the conventional spelling *boy* in just those cases in which the phonemic sequence represented by the conventional spelling *girl* has hitherto been used and vice versa. Or we could adopt the practice of pronouncing every other word in a sentence backwards, or of replacing it by its translation in French, etc. Such considerations have led theorists to argue that, since we could alter the facts about language by adopting the relevant *explicit* conventions, it is useful to think of such facts as obtaining by virtue of *tacit* conventions. In short, then, what lies behind the notion that facts about language are arbitrary is the view that, within whatever broad restrictions are placed upon the structure of languages by innate preferences for one or another kind of linguistic system, linguistic facts obtain by virtue of a social rather than a logical or an empirical constraint.

It will be noticed that though the examples we have been discussing were drawn from conventions concerning the representation of a word as a series of shapes on paper or as a sequence of sounds in speech, the principle of conventionality is usually held to be a general truth about facts about language and is thus intended to cover facts about the meaning and reference of words as well as facts about their spelling or pronunciation. Indeed, to say that we could use the sound sequence *boy* in place of the sound sequence *girl* and vice versa, is, inter alia, to say that we could use *boy* to refer to girls and *girl* to refer to boys. To say that this is guaranteed by the principle of conventionality is to say that the possibility in principle of such inversions is an intrinsic feature of human languages.

The same point is sometimes made by saying of human languages that they are systems of *symbols* rather than systems of *signs* and that it is this that makes them essentially different from animal "languages." A symbol, on this understanding, is precisely a linguistic element, the meaning of which is conventional in the sense discussed above. A sign, on the other hand, is a linguistic element the meaning of which is determined by some nonconventional relation it bears to some object or situation. Thus, the warning rattle of the jackdaw is a sign and not a symbol because the occasions on which it is uttered, its acoustic shape, and the behavior characteristic of its hearers are all fixed by causal laws (cf. Lorenz quoted by Brown, 1968, p. 166).

One of the ways in which a sign may be related to what it signifies then is as effect to cause. The jackdaw's rattle presumably signifies the presence of its releaser (a black, dangling or fluttering object) in very much the same way and in very much the same sense that clouds signal rain and smoke signals fire. In all these cases, the relation between the sign and its significate is directly or indirectly causal, though in the case of animal signs, the causal contingencies are presumably the local and specialized effect of the evolutionary process.

Cause and effect is not usually held to be the only relation capable of relating sign to significate. Another such "natural" (i.e., nonconventional, i.e., nonsymbolic) relation which may provide a source of signs is resemblance. Thus, it is widely maintained that while a word like *face* cannot conceivably be related to its referent by anything stronger than a convention, there is clearly some nonarbitrary element in the relation between that referent and the referent of Figure 9-1.

(a)   (b)

Figure 9-1. Representational (*a*) and Nonrepresentational (*b*) Sketch of "Face"

Doubtless such figures are enormously stylized so the ability to recognize what they are intended to portray must be to some extent the result of socialization. But it seems equally undeniable that though Figure 9-1a is a conventional representation in the sense that simplifications of a drastic sort are tolerated by anyone who recognizes it as a face, this conventionality is different in kind from the sort that would be operative if we decided to adopt Figure 9-1b as a symbol of faces. There is surely at least this much point to distinguishing between "conventional" and "natural" relations: it points to the distinction between the distortions that subjects will accept as representations of objects and those they will not.

It is notable that the problem of reference is always raised as a problem about symbols and never as a problem about signs. This is far from accidental. On the contrary, it provides a very clear insight into what the problem of reference has generally been taken to be. We have seen that there is presumably a straightforward causal answer to the question what relates the jackdaw's rattle to its "referent." It is also possible to argue that there must be a relatively simple answer to the question what relates Figure 9-1 to the objects it is capable of representing. But, now, what is to be said about the relation of the word *face* to its referent? To say that that relation is conventional is not to *explain* the relation but only to say that any acceptable explanation must account for its alterability in principle. Even to claim that the relation is *literally* the consequence of a tacit convention among speakers would be unhelpful since it tells us neither what the conventions are, nor how they are learned, nor what psychological mechanisms are employed when a speaker behaves in conformity with them. Indeed, the very caution that the relevant conventions are *tacit* is, in effect, an admission that neither the kinds of rules involved nor the way they are learned nor the psychological mechanisms involved in applying the rules are of the sort that would obtain in the case of explicit conventions. The notion that conventional reference relations literally rest upon conventions thus accounts for their alterability but for nothing else.[2]

To put the matter in the crudest possible terms, it is obvious what sticks signs to their significates: the glue is provided either by causation or by resemblance. That is why—barring problems about the nature of resemblance—no one has ever thought there was a problem of reference for signs. There *is* a problem of reference for symbols, however, precisely because while the conventional nature of the relation between a symbol and its referent apparently precludes directly attributing it either to a natural law or to resemblance, it is unclear what other sorts of relations could, in principle, account for the fact that words can refer to objects. The problem thus has the form of a dilemma: the reference relations we can reasonably claim to understand depend upon causation or resemblance. Hence, they cannot hold between arbitrarily selected objects. But the defining property of a symbol is that it is an arbitrarily selected object which, nevertheless, succeeds in referring.

Not only does the comparison between signs and symbols illuminate the very close relation between the classical formulation of the problem of reference and the traditional allegiance to the doctrine of conventionality, it also points to the form of the traditional solutions of the problems of

---

[2] Though, probably, the social contract theory of language is no more intended to be taken literally than is the social contract theory of government. Indeed, so taken, the two theories suffer from analogous flaws.

reference. Almost without exception, traditional attempts to deal with reference have involved trying to break the dilemma by showing that the conventional relation between words and their referents can in fact be reduced to one or the other or both of the natural relations holding between signs and their significates. That is, it has been almost universally assumed that the proper solution of the problem of reference must consist in showing how the relation between a word and its reference must consist in showing how the relation between a word and its referent can, after all, be explained in terms of cause and effect or of resemblance. The tantalizing analogy between signs and symbols has had so powerful an effect on students of language that it has only been very recently recognized that the analogy may, in fact, be thoroughly misleading. Indeed, one still searches through the psychological literature almost in vain for an acknowledgment that the relation between a word and its referent may be different *in kind* from the causal relation between an innate response and its releaser or from the causal relation between an operant response and its conditioned stimulus.

The terms of the problem admit of only three ways in which one might try to reduce conventional relations to natural ones. One might say (*a*) that the symbol-referent relation can be explained by an appeal to causation and resemblance operating jointly, or (*b*) by an appeal to resemblance operating alone, or (*c*) by an appeal to causation operating alone. Not surprisingly, all three positions have been occupied at one time or another. We shall review the first two briefly and the third in some detail.

The view that the relation of a word to its referent can be accounted for by a simultaneous appeal to the notions of causation and resemblance is characteristic of the philosophy of language shared by the British empiricists and by the psychologists they directly influenced. To correctly understand what empiricists say about reference, it is necessary to bear in mind the following complicating fact: for the empiricist, the referent of a word is characteristically a mental content. In particular, what a word refers to is either a "simple idea" (such as *red, moist, bitter* or some other sensation or "qualia"); or a "complex idea" (such as the idea of a particular material object or of a particular person) which is in turn presumed to be reducible in principle to some concatenation of simple ideas; or an abstract idea (such as the idea of color, triangularity, etc.) which is supposed to be the idea of a common property of a set of simple or complex ideas.

Though it must be borne in mind in reading the empiricists that everything they say is, so to speak, at one degree of remove from the world—so that what *box* refers to is not a box but the mental idea or representation of a box—it should also be mentioned that this feature of the empiricists' mentalism is not intrinsic to their view of language. It is rather a carryover from their doctrines about epistemology according to which our knowledge of objects is indirect via "Our senses, conversant about particular sensible objects, do convey into the mind several distinct ideas or images, according to those various ways wherein those objects do affect them . . . neither can external objects furnish the understanding with any ideas but of sensible qualities, because they operate on the senses no other way. And so we can have no other notice of them . . . [Locke, 1690, Bk. II, Ch. 1]."

Upon the distinction mentioned above between three sorts of ideas or mental contents, empiricists superimposed a distinction between sensory impressions and perceptions on the one hand and memories, thoughts, reflections, etc., on the other.[3] It is extremely characteristic of the movement that this was held to be a distinction of degree rather than of kind. A recollection of an object agrees with a perception of the object in being a mental image. It differs only in the force, vivacity, liveliness, etc., with which the image presents itself. Thus Hume (1735):

All the perceptions of the human mind resolve themselves into two distinct kinds which I shall call IMPRESSIONS and Ideas. The difference betwixt these consists in the degrees of force and liveliness with which they strike upon the mind, and make their way into our thought or consciousness. Those perceptions, which enter with most force and violence, we may name *impressions*; and under this name I comprehend all our sensations, passions, and emotions as they make their first appearance in the soul. By *ideas* I mean the faint images of these in thinking and reasoning; such as, for instance, are all the perceptions excited by the present discourse excepting only those which arise from the sight and touch and excepting the immediate pleasure or uneasiness it may occasion [Bk. I, Pt. 1, Sect. 1].

and again:

The first circumstance that strikes my eye is the great resemblance betwixt our impressions and ideas in every other particular, excepting their degree of force and vivacity. The one seems to be in a manner the reflexion of the other; so that all the perceptions of the mind are double, and appear both as impressions and ideas [Bk. I, Pt. 1, Sect. 1].

Hume proceeds to qualify this remark by noting that some *complex* ideas may exist as objects of imagination or reflection though they never existed as impressions. But though my complex idea of a unicorn has no sensory *doppelganger*, it is to be supposed that the simple ideas (white, having a horn, having four legs, etc.) of which that complex is constructed must each have its appropriate counterpart in sensation. The "empiricist principle,"

---

[3]Certain unavoidable confusion enters into any exposition of the empiricists as a result of their failure to agree upon a uniform terminology. We have followed Locke in using *idea* as a cover word for any mental content. It is thus possible to save *impression* as a synonym for *sensation* or *perception* where these latter words have something like their current psychological meaning. Hume, on the other hand, uses *perception* where we have *idea*, *idea* where we have *memory*, *thought*, or *reflection*, and *impression* for "any sensation, passion, (or) emotion." The modern notion of a percept has no very important role in Hume, largely because the only sort of organization of sensory input Hume envisages is a simple summation of atomic "simple ideas" into molecular "complex ideas." Insofar as anything in Hume corresponds to having a percept, it is perhaps having a complex impression.

correctly stated, is not that there is no idea that does not originate in sensation but rather that there is no *simple* idea that does not do so.

After the most accurate examination, of which I am capable, I venture to affirm that the rule here holds without any exception and that every simple idea has a simple impression which resembles it, and every simple impression a correspondent idea[4] [Bk. I, Pt. 1, Sect. 1].

Such passages form the groundwork for the empiricist theory of reference: the edifice is completed with the assumption of the usual associationistic principles of psychological causation, in particular the principle that ". . . two objects are connected together in the imagination when the one is immediately . . . contiguous to . . . the other [in experience] [Hume, Bk. I, Pt. 1, Sect. 1]." Granted this principle, the empiricist may now argue as follows. The utterance of a word (i.e., the occurrence of an acoustic sensory image of a word) causes in the hearer memory images of whatever perceptions have previously been frequently associated with utterances of that word. ". . . such . . . for instance are all the [ideas] excited by the present discourse excepting only those which arise from the sight and touch and excepting the immediate pleasure or uneasiness it may occasion [Hume, Bk. I, Pt. 1, Sect. 4]." Such also would be the image of a bed which presumably arises in the mind of anyone who has very often heard the word *bed* uttered simultaneously with perceiving a bed, or the image of a car which presumably arises in the mind of anyone who has very often heard the word *car* uttered simultaneously with perceiving a car . . . and so on through the entire vocabulary.

It will be remembered that, according to our analysis, the classical problem of reference arises from the supposition that the relation holding between a word and its referent is conventional. Classical solutions of the problem have the form of attempts to reduce this conventional relation to "natural" relations of resemblance and/or causation. We can now see how closely this analysis fits the empiricist approach to language. For while, on the empiricist's view, the relation between a word and its referent is conventional, the relation between a word and the memory image it evokes is presumably not. This latter relation is supposed to be the consequence of the operation of psychological laws of association and has thus as much claim to be rooted in a law of nature as the relation between smoke and fire. Moreover, just as the relation between a word and a memory image is a "natural" relation in the sense in which we have been using that term, so also is the relation between a memory image and its corresponding sensory image. For this relation is explicitly one of resemblance: what makes a memory a memory is its relative lack of force and vivacity. But what makes it a memory

---

[4]We are leaving out of consideration as irrelevant to our discussion the so-called "ideas of reflection" which were supposedly derived not from sensations but from the mind's introspective examination of its own processes.

of one impression rather than another is precisely the resemblance it bears that impression.

It is thus the empiricist's view that though the reference relation is not itself a natural relation, it may nevertheless be explained solely in terms of natural relations. Though words do not resemble their referents and are not directly causally connected to them, each word *is* causally connected with a memory image and that image *does* resemble the referent of the word.

Yet the empiricist's theory accounts in a fairly plausible way for the alterability in principle of the word-referent relation. Since the principle of association purports to hold for arbitrarily selected pairs of ideas (since, i.e., it states that *any* two ideas that are sufficiently frequently conjoined will eventually tend to evoke one another), it follows that no restrictions are placed upon the acoustic shape of a word by any feature of its referent. Hence, given the appropriate training of speakers, any sequence of sounds could, in principle, be used in place of any other. But this is precisely what is meant when it is claimed that the reference relation is arbitrary or conventional.

The empiricist theory of language thus manages to resolve the dilemma that we saw was at the heart of the traditional puzzle about reference. On the one hand, it accounts for the fact that words can stand for things without resorting to any relation not already required to account for the bond between signs and their significates. On the other hand, it achieves this without prejudice to the conventional character of the word-referent relation. In short, it shows how the meaning of a word might be accounted for by causation and resemblance without denying that it is an historical accident that a word means what it does.

Moreover, it is clear that we must credit the empiricists with having devised the first "two-stage" or "mediational" account of meaning. A memory image is properly described as a mediator between a word—to which it is related as effect to cause—and the referent of the word which, presumably, it resembles. In effect, the empiricist is arguing that it is not words but the memory images associated with words that, in the first instance, have referents. It is the employment of such images to mediate the word-referent relation that is the characteristic feature of the empiricist's approach to language. Given that the relation between a memory image and the sensory image it "refers" to is one of resemblance, there is presumably no more of a problem about how the former can stand for the latter than there is about how a portrait can represent its subject. Given that each word is causally associated with such a mediating image, the problem of reference is reduced to the problem of representation.

We have seen that it is essential to the empiricist account that words evoke images and that images resemble the referents of the words that evoke them. That the latter postulate has undesirable consequences was recognized rather early in the empiricist movement in connection with the problem of abstract or general ideas. It was Berkeley who first pointed out that if abstract ideas are supposed to represent common features of classes of objects, images are uniquely unsuited to be the vehicle of such representations, for images are unalterably particular. Thus, it is clear how an image could represent, say, a particular triangle (i.e., by resembling that triangle more than it resembles any other). But it is unclear how an image could represent triangularity in general since this would require it to resemble all triangles equally and simultaneously. To do this, the image would need to possess incompatible properties: e.g., it would have to be both scaline and obtuse in order to resemble both scaline and obtuse triangles, and this is clearly impossible in principle.

Hume's solution to this difficulty was typical of the empiricists who followed Berkeley. In the case of an abstract idea, the vehicle of representation is indeed an image, but as Hume (1735) wrote: "The image in the mind is only that of a particular object, tho' the application of it in our reasoning be the same as if it were universal [Bk. I, Pt. 1, Sect. 4]." Our image of triangularity is the image of a particular triangle, but we ignore its irrelevant details when we use it in reasoning about (or, presumably, in mediating references to) triangularity in general.

It seems unlikely that any of the empiricists recognized how enormous a concession was involved in this proposal. In effect, it meant acknowledging that, if the reference of general terms is to be accounted for, the mediator in reference must be not only an image but a set of rules for applying the image. To put it slightly differently, it meant holding that when an image mediates the reference of an abstract word, its relation to what it images cannot be accounted for solely on the basis of resemblance, for an image cannot resemble an abstract object. But if an appeal to rules for applying the image is essential to explaining how the image associated with utterances of "triangularity" represents the property of triangularity, then the program of reducing all cases of reference to natural relations has been tacitly abandoned.[5]

Moreover, it appears that, at least in some cases, the suggestion that the vehicle of reference is an image *with rules for its application* is otiose, since if rules are allowed, the need for the image drops out. Consider, for example, the set of rules that would be required to specify the features of an image of a triangle that are relevant when the image is to be taken as a representation of triangularity in general. The rules would have to distinguish such relevant features as having three sides, being a closed figure, etc., from such irrelevant features as the length of the sides and the size of the

---

[5] On this point, the psychologists were occasionally more faithful to the unadulterated image theory than were the philosophers. "Titchener is one of the few men who has ever claimed to see an image of Locke's abstract triangle . . . a flashy thing, come and gone from moment to moment: it hints 2 or 3 red angles with the red lines deepening into black, seen on a dark green ground. It is not there long enough for me to say whether the angles join to form the complete figure or even whether all 3 of the necessary angles are given." (Titchener quoted by Brown, 1958)

angles. But, to supply rules adequate to specify the set of features that an image must possess if it is to represent abstract triangularity is equivalent to providing a general definition of "triangularity." And it is very unclear that a speaker who had associated such a definition with the word *triangle* would also need an image in order to use the word correctly to refer to triangles. Presumably, the word refers to all and only those things that satisfy the definition, so that, given the definition, appeals to the image would be redundant.

Not only are images inadequate as the vehicles of reference in cases involving the referent of abstract words, it is also notorious that they are highly unreliable. The content of the images associated with particular words seems to vary considerably from person to person; many subjects report no imagery whatever in the course of normal conversations, and some report none even when introspection is encouraged. Yet it will hardly do to say that this intersubjective variation indicates that speakers who belong to the same speech community and manage to communicate without difficulty nevertheless do not mean the same things by the words they use. It is a condition upon whatever state, object, psychological content, or mechanism we choose to identify with the meaning of a word that all speakers who communicate successfully by employing that word must have that state, object, content, or mechanism in common. Hence, interpersonal variation in the imagery associated with words is an argument for the semantic irrelevance of such imagery.

The incidental character of the imagery associated with words is brought out most strikingly by the fact that subjects occasionally report such images even in the case of words which cannot possibly be supposed to have referents. Thus, "Titchener's image of 'but' was of the back of the head of a speaker who often used this word while Titchener sat behind him on a platform [Brown, 1958, p. 91]." Such an association is doubly irrelevant: first, in that it is idiosyncratic and thus could have nothing to do with the linguistic meaning of *but*—a meaning that is presumably known by all speakers of English—and second, because the knowledge speakers of English have of the meaning of *but* could not conceivably take the form of an image of its referent, since *but* does not have a referent and does not mean anything that can be imaged.

The image theory thus shares with other associationistic accounts of meaning an intrinsic inability to provide a plausible answer to the question how speakers arrive at a consensus about the meaning of words despite what must be very considerable interpersonal differences in their linguistic experience. That such a consensus must be achieved is evident, since it is a precondition of communication. That it is unlikely to be accounted for by an associationistic model is evidenced by the prevalence of such idiosyn-cratic associations as those Titchener reports. Since, according to such theories, what gets associated with a word by a given speaker is very much dependent upon what co-occurrences between utterances of that word and states of affairs happen to have been frequent in that speaker's experience, associationistic models automatically predict that the meanings of words ought to vary approximately as much as the personal histories of speakers do. Such theories are, so to speak, especially sensitive to features of personal history in formulating their predictions about the meaning a speaker will associate with a word. But this feature of associationistic models unfits them for explaining the existence of communication within speech communities. A theory of language learning must account for our extraordinary achievement in speaking the same language despite considerable variation in the conditions under which we learn the language.[6]

What led to the abandonment of the empiricist approach to language was not, however, the sorts of arguments we have been discussing here. Rather, philosophers and psychologists arrived at a general methodological agreement to forego explanations that invoke mental contents like ideas and images in favor of explanations couched in terms of entities whose observation does not depend upon introspection. That the basis for the abandonment of the empiricist *solution* to the problem of reference was essentially methodological was important since it meant that the integrity of the empiricist's *analysis* of the problem was never seriously challenged. Though psychologists no longer believe that the conventional relation between words and their referents can be reduced to the natural relations of causation and resemblance operating together, they have by no means surrendered the view that the problem of reference is that of providing *some* sort of reduction of conventional to natural relations. In fact, the failure to provide a theory that can account for reference in terms of causation and resemblance operating together has, somewhat paradoxically, been interpreted as showing that reference must be accounted for as the result of one or the other operating alone. Thus, the history of the problem of reference in Gestalt psychology has been that of an attempt to treat reference in terms of resemblance, and the history of the problem in learning theory has been that of an attempt to treat reference in terms of causation.

To attempt to account for reference in terms of causation alone may be compatible with holding that the relation is essentially a conventional one. For, associative learning provides for the possibility of establishing causal connections between events not previously so connected. The essence of conditioning resides in its availability as a mechanism for permitting

---

[6] It may be argued that the impressive fact is the degree to which subjects concur in their associations to a particular stimulus word, and that the sort of idiosyncratic associations we have mentioned are in fact rather rare. Our point, however, is not that there is not considerable consensus in the associations subjects have for given words, but rather that the principles usually invoked to explain the development of associative links are ill-equipped to account for such homogeneity. These principles are extremely sensitive to features of the personal history of the subject, and the characteristic feature of language learning is that speakers with very different histories end by speaking the same language.

certain broad ranges of stimulations to cause responses to which they were previously neutral. Hence, if the reference relation in some way depends upon the conditioning of behavior, it is in a reasonable sense a conventional relationship. If *boy* refers to boys solely as the result of some feature of the conditioning of the behavior of English speakers, then a different pattern of conditioning would presumably have led, with equal facility, to *boy* referring to girls. The essence of the principle of conventionality—that reference relations are alterable in principle—is thus preserved on this kind of a causal view of reference.

On the other hand, adopting the view that reference is to be accounted for by an appeal to resemblance operating alone is tantamount to denying the conventionality of reference. If a word needs to resemble what it refers to, then it is not in principle possible that any word could refer to anything. It is perhaps because holding that reference depends directly upon resemblance is not compatible with holding a version of the principle of conventionality, that relatively few philosophers or psychologists have seriously defended this view.

There are, nevertheless, some arguments for it, and these have often been stressed by psychologists in the Gestalt tradition. The most striking of such arguments comes from the apparently universal occurrence of onomatopoeia. It appears that every language contains at least a few words the sound of which, though consonant with the phonemic rules of the language, clearly imitates nonverbal sounds: *cuckoo*, *splash*, and so on. It is interesting too that such words appear to resist phonetic alteration more persistently than most words do.[7]

Direct onomatopoeia is presumably too rarely a property of words to be of more than anecdotal interest from the point of view of a general theory of reference. While it need not be denied that onomatopoetic words provide a counterexample to the claim that reference is *universally* a purely conventional relation, they scarcely argue against the claim that reference is *characteristically* a conventional relation. Moreover, it must be stressed that onomatopoetic words do not violate the phonemic rules of the language in which they occur. If their relation to their referents is not fully conventional, it is at least conventionalized. Finally, what is striking about the sound systems of languages is that they are chosen from among an extremely limited subset of the vocalizations physiologically possible to a human being. This is precisely what one would *not* expect if imitation played any essential role in reference.

But though the gross acoustic properties of words appear to be largely irrelevant to their semantic behavior, it is sometimes claimed that their

[7] This can scarcely be used as an argument for the view that resemblance provides a general key to reference, since it shows that words that are strikingly similar to their referents are *a*typical in their behavior relative to the laws of sound change.

more subtle "physiognomic" properties are not. Thus, Werner and Kaplan (1963) have claimed that:

. . . at genetically early levels of representation, the vehicle is produced or taken as a mimetic facsimile of the referent: for example, there are the onomatopoetic vehicles that represent referents by phonemically imitating noises characteristic of the referents. A developmentally more advanced representation is indicated by a relation between vehicles and referents still formed by a bond of external "similarity" where, however, the similarity is carried by DIFFERENT modalities: thus, phonic properties may "synaesthetically" represent shapes, sizes, or colors of figures (for example, "zig-zag"). Still more advanced genetically are representations by conventionalized patterns; here the external forms of vehicle and referent have lost most, if not all, of their surface similarity. Thus, there is a progressive distancing—a decrease in tangible "likeness"— between the external forms of vehicle and referent [pp. 47–48].

Werner and Kaplan also refer to Köhler's demonstration of the fact that subjects spontaneously recognize a relation between drawings of sharp objects and nonsense words like *takete*. This is taken to point up the dynamic similarity of phenomena in different sensory modes in terms of which the resemblance between words and their referents is supposed to be explicated.

Two things need to be proved if this sort of view is to be taken seriously as an account of the nature of reference. First, that words and their referents do in fact characteristically share some underlying "dynamic similarity" despite the contrary surface appearances, and second, that this similarity plays some part in establishing linguistic reference relations. The difficulty in demonstrating the first is, of course, that there is often no way of precluding the possibility that cases in which words are treated as if they resembled objects may be the result of the speaker's having formed a learned associative bond between the word and the object rather than of his having perceived an inherent dynamic similarity between them. That is, what must be shown if the resemblance theory is to be maintained is that word-object similarity is a *condition* rather than a *consequence* of the existence of a reference relation. To take one example, Werner and Kaplan have demonstrated that there is a characteristic error of judgments of the height of a visual image of the word *mountain* and that this error is opposite in direction from that which infects judgments of the height of images of the word *valley*. They argue that this ought to be construed as a demonstration of inherent dynamic similarity between a word and its referent. "The measurement pertains to a peculiar effect of directional dynamics inherent in the perception of certain objects on the apparent location of these objects in space; that is, the spatial locale at which such objects appear to the subjects are seen relatively higher or lower depending on whether their dynamics are directly upwards or downwards, etc." Yet, it is unclear why the experiment must be interpreted this way. It seems we might equally hold that what has been demonstrated is some sort of response transference from an object to the word referring to it, a transference which, presumably, might be predicted on the usual associationistic principle that responses characteristically elicited by an object will, under appropriate circumstances, transfer to objects paired with it. On this interpretation, what Werner and Kaplan's experiment shows is simply a case of "semantic generalization," viz., of the generalization of responses from a word to its synonyms or from an object to a word referring to it.

The example quoted from Köhler cannot, however, be plausibly treated as a case of response generalization, since it concerns a response to a novel stimulus word. Rather, we appear to be dealing with a spontaneous tendency to see cross-modal correspondences between acoustic and visual nonsense patterns. It might be argued that such tendencies represent the consequence of generalizations based upon repeated pairings of words which share certain phonemic features with objects sharing certain non-linguistic properties. That is, it might be maintained that *takete* suggests angularity to English speakers because tacks, tools, tips, and trowels are all often sharp. But, first, there is no very good empirical support for the claim that for speakers to pair *maluma* and *takete* with the appropriate drawings it must be the case that their language contains many words that commence with *m* and refer to smooth objects and many words which commence with *t* and refer to sharp ones. Second, even if this could be shown, it would at best serve to replace the question how cross-modal correspondences are to be accounted for with the question why, if reference is an arbitrary relation, do we find so many cases where classes of words which partially correspond phonemically refer to partially similar objects.[8]

However, the question that has to be raised in the case of such examples as those cited by Köhler is not only whether they in fact show a spontaneous recognition of the "inherent similarity" of perceptual objects in different modes, but whether such correspondences are of more than marginal significance in determining reference relations. Here, it is worth noticing, for example, that there is no particular tendency for full synonyms to exhibit phonemic features in common (*perhaps* and *maybe*, *bachelor* and *unmarried man*), while, conversely, words that are literally phonemically identical (*box* as a verb and as a noun, *bank* when it refers to the institution or when it refers to the side of a river) need exhibit no similarity of referent. While such cases do not show that the sort of similarity mentioned by Köhler and by Werner and Kaplan plays *no* role in the establishment of reference relations, they do show that the presence of such similarities is neither necessary nor sufficient to determine identity of reference.[9]

Of the three possible treatments of reference in terms of the "natural" relations of causation and resemblance, the one that has most characterized

---

[8] The problem is, of course, that there is no independent syntactic motivation for postulation in English morpheme (t) meaning *sharp*.
[9] For an extensive discussion of Werner and Kaplan's views, cf. Fodor, 1964.

recent psycholinguistics in America has been the attempt to account for reference in terms of causation. In particular, reference is to be accounted for in terms of certain features of the conditioning of the behavior of speakers. Roughly, and with some variations, the current view is that a word refers to an object in case, first, speakers have been conditioned to respond to the presence of the object with utterances of the word, and second, speakers have been conditioned to respond to utterances of the word with behavior that would be appropriate to the object.

So widespread among American psychologists is the view that some such learning-theoretic explanation of reference is possible, it must be discussed in some detail by even the most cursory survey of psychological theories of reference.

It is overwhelmingly the consensus of psycholinguists that the stickle-back which responds to an aggressive male by raising his spines, the rat which responds to an intense light by pressing a bar, and the human who tells the dentist to stop when the drilling begins to hurt are all exhibiting essentially the same sort of behavior. In each case, either as the result of innate endowment or as the result of a history of conditioning, the organism is able to produce some quite specific response which may usually be relied upon to terminate aversive stimulation. Conversely, it is equally the consensus of psycholinguists that the stickle-back which produces a fighting response when exposed to a schematic fish, the rat which learns to choose the door marked with a triangle, the human who learns to bring his umbrella when the morning is cloudy and the human who learns to bring his umbrella when the weather forecaster says "rain today" are also exhibiting behaviors that differ in degree of complexity but not in kind. In each case, the organism has either learned or developed the capacity to respond differentially to a stimulus on the basis of "natural" relations between that stimulus and some other object. The stickle-back responds to the schematic fish because, to its wayward eyes, the schematic fish resembles the male stickle-back to which its fighting response is innately associated. The rat chooses the door with the triangle because the experimenter has so arranged the causal contingencies that going through that door has regularly been followed by food. The human brings his umbrella in the first instance because it has previously been his experience that clouds are regularly followed by rain. He brings his umbrella in the second instance because it has previously been his experience that utterances of the acoustic shape "rain today" are also regularly followed by rain and discomfort.

In short, the central point about psycholinguistics is that there is no central point about psycholinguistics. Osgood (1963) has said ". . . I believe that we wish nor require *no special theory of language behavior*. Just because language behavior is intimately associated with abstract thinking and symbolizing does not necessarily imply that it is different in kind from ordinary behavior." And Mowrer (1960) has argued that, given the certainty of the essential homogeneity of verbal and nonverbal learning, the fact that humans and no other animals have achieved speech can only be attributed to the relatively advanced development of motor control of the vocal system in man. ". . . it can hardly be doubted that the greatest single 'mutation' which separates man from other anthropoids consists precisely of this: new and more abundant neural connections between the speech center in the brain and the speech organs [p. 111]."

The question we must thus investigate is whether a causal theory of reference is tenable. In particular, we must ask whether it can be convincingly maintained that the relation between a word and its referent is that of a conditioned response to its discriminative stimulus. To begin with, while there can be no objection to considering the verbalizations of fluent speakers to be "linguistic responses," one must not suppose that, in this context, "response" means what it usually means: "A stimulus-occasioned act. An (act) correlated with stimuli, whether the correlation is untrained or the result of training."[10] On the contrary, a striking feature of linguistic behavior is its freedom from the control of specifiable local stimuli or independently identifiable drives states. In typical situations, what is said may have no obvious correlation whatever with conditions in the immediate locality of the speaker or with his recent history of deprivation or reward. Conversely, the situation in which such correlations *do* obtain (e.g., the man dying of thirst who predictably gasps "Water!") are intuitively highly atypical.

Indeed, the evidence for the claim that linguistic responses are responses *in the strict sense* would appear to be nonexistent. There is no more reason to believe that the probability of an utterance of *book* is a function of the number of books in the immediate locale than there is to believe that the probability of an utterance of the word *person* or *thing* is a function of the number of persons or things on view. Lacking such evidence, what prompts one to these beliefs is, first, a confusion of the strict sense of "response" ("a stimulus-correlated act") with the loose sense in which the term applies to *any* bit of behavior, stimulus correlated or otherwise, and second, a philosophy of science which erroneously supposes that unless all behavior is held to consist of responses in the strict sense some fundamental canon of scientific method is violated. But the claim that behavior consists solely of responses cannot be established on methodological grounds alone. On the contrary, such a claim constitutes an extremely general and prima facie quite implausible empirical hypothesis about the degree to which behavior is under the control of specifiable local stimulation.

The second inadequacy of simple *S-R* models of language is also a consequence of the identification of verbalizations with responses. In laboratory situations, an organism is said to have mastered a response when it can be shown that it produces any of an indefinite number of functionally

---

[10] This is the definition given in standard texts like Hilgard and Marquis, 1940.

equivalent acts under the appropriate stimulus conditions. That some reasonable notion of functional equivalence can be specified is essential, since we cannot, in general, require of two actions that they be identical either in observable properties or in their physiological basis in order to be manifestations of the same response. Thus, a rat has "got" the bar press response if and only if it habitually presses the bar upon food deprivation. Whether it presses with its left or right front paw or with three or six grams of pressure is, or may be, irrelevant. Training is to some previously determined criterion of homogeneity of performance, which is another way of saying that what we are primarily concerned with are functional aspects of the organism's behavior. We permit variation among the actions belonging to a response so long as each of the variants is functionally equivalent to each of the others. In short, a response is so characterized as to establish an equivalence relation among the actions which can belong to it. Any response for which such a relation has *not* been established is ipso facto inadequately described.

We have just suggested that it is not in general possible to determine that there exist stimuli with which verbal responses are reliably correlated. It may now be remarked that it is not in general possible to determine when two utterances are functionally equivalent, i.e., when they are instances of the same verbal response. This point is easily overlooked, since it is natural to suppose that functional equivalence of verbal responses can be established on the basis of phonetic or phonemic identity. This is, however, untrue. Just as two physiologically distinct actions may both be instances of a bar press response, so two phonemically distinct utterances may be functionally equivalent for a given speaker or in a given language. Examples include such synonymous expressions as *bachelor* and *unmarried man, perhaps* and *maybe,* etc. Conversely, just as an action is not an instance of a bar press response (however much it may resemble actions that are) unless it bears the correct functional relation to the bar, so two phonemically identical utterances (as, e.g., *bank* in *The bank is around the corner* and *The plane banked at forty-five degrees*) may, when syntactic and semantic considerations are taken into account, prove to be instances of quite different verbal responses.

It appears, then, that the claim that verbal behavior is to be accounted for in terms of *S-R* connections has been made good at neither the stimulus nor the response end. Not only are we generally unable to identify the stimuli which elicit verbal responses, but we are also unable to say when two bits of behavior are manifestations of the same response and when they are not. That this is no small difficulty is evident when we notice that the problem of characterizing functional equivalence for verbal responses is closely related to the problem of characterizing such semantic relations as synonymy, a problem for which no solution is at present known.

Again, the identification of verbalizations with responses suffers from the difficulty that verbalizations do not normally admit of such indices of response strength as frequency, intensity, and resistance to extinction. It is obvious, but nevertheless pertinent, that "meaningfulness" in the technical associationist sense has nothing to do with meaningfulness tout court; that verbal responses which are equally part of the speaker's repertoire may differ vastly in their relative frequency of occurrence (*heliotrope* and *and* are examples in the case of the idiolect of this writer); that intensity and frequency do not covary (the morpheme in an utterance receiving emphatic stress is not particularly likely to be a conjunction, article, preposition, etc., yet these "grammatical" morphemes are easily the most frequently occurring ones); and that extinction of verbal responses is extremely rare except in such pathologies as aphasia. What is perhaps true is that one can vary the frequency of intensity of a verbal response by the usual techniques of selective reinforcement (cf. Kasner, 1961). This shows that verbal behavior can be conditioned but lends no support to the hypothesis that conditioning is essential to verbal behavior.

There would thus appear to be very little or no basis for the view that the referent of a word is a discriminative stimulus prone to raise the probability of utterances of the word. There would seem to be still less basis for the view that understanding a word is being prone to produce a characteristic form of behavior when the word is uttered, i.e., that understanding a word is responding to it in ways that would be appropriate to its referent. It is literally the case that no one has ever provided a plausible candidate for the relevant "characteristic" behavior for any word in any language. And, everyone knows that, in the vast majority of cases, the answer to the question *What do we do when people speak?* is *Listen.*

Is there, then, at least some evidence for the view that conditioning plays an essential role in the *learning* of language? In fact, there is none. Practically nothing is known about the special character (if any) of the environment in which children learn languages beyond the obvious fact that children manage to learn under what would appear, prima facie, extremely adverse conditions. Excepting differences in *size* of vocabulary, no one has demonstrated that the learning of a first language is in any degree sensitive to such "reinforcing" factors as extent of explicit tuition, degree of encouragement from parents, emotional attitudes of the parents, or of the children themselves, etc. So far, the implications for pedagogy that are often drawn from reinforcement theories of verbal learning have no empirical basis whatever.

Faced with such criticisms, there has been some inclination for psychological theories of reference to go full circle. In particular, recent interest in "mediational" theories of meaning are more than a little suggestive of a return to classical empiricism. Thus, Carroll (1964) explains that while *S-R* accounts of reference are *essentially* correct in supposing that "the learning paradigm that seems to fit (reference) most directly is that of *classical conditioning*, where a conditioned stimulus (such as the sound of the word *dog*) presented simultaneously with . . . a real dog or a picture of one . . . comes independently to evoke a conditioned response similar to the unconditioned response evoked by the unconditioned stimulus." Nevertheless, such accounts seem to have certain prima facie difficulties.

What, exactly, is the unconditioned response to the sight of a dog [that transfers to utterances of "dog"]? . . . Some writers on this subject have tried to identify such a response with *overt* responses, such as patting, withdrawal, signs of emotion, but this line of reasoning is unnecessary and probably incorrect. It seems sufficient to say that before a child starts to learn the meanings of linguistic signs, he learns to make pure perceptual responses to objects and events in the world around him. . . . This long digression was necessary to establish what kind of responses function as the unconditioned responses when an infant is conditioned to respond to a linguistic sign by classical conditioning . . . it is a fractional representation of the identifying response to whatever perceptual invariant is involved in the linguistic sign [Carroll, 1964, p. 35–36].

The reader will no doubt have remarked that there is nothing in this passage that could not have been written by Locke. Theoretical advance in this area appears to have been limited to the substitution of "conditioning" for "association" and of "pure perceptual response" for "image." It may be further remarked that Berkeley's objection—that, as a matter of fact, perceptual invariants cannot be identified in the case of the referents of words like *triangle* and *dog*—is ignored here and elsewhere in Carroll's discussion.[11]

We have now considered three sorts of attempts to show that the relation of a word to its referent can be accounted for either by an appeal to resemblance or by an appeal to causation or by both. We have seen that such attempts are motivated by a certain analysis of the problem of reference: the problem is to show that the relations that confer meaning upon signs also confer meaning upon symbols.

This analysis may, after all, prove to be correct. But the failure of three sorts of theories which accept it to provide an adequate account of reference surely argues against that possibility. We might, therefore, tentatively raise the question: what options would remain if we were to abandon the analysis, if, that is, we were to give up the view that a correct theory of meaning must demonstrate either that a relation of resemblance connects a word to its referent or that a relation of causation does.

Consider playing tag. Children who learn to play that game also learn when it is appropriate to designate someone as "it." Learning this would appear to be a perfectly legitimate case of learning how to apply a noun to its referent: being "it" is, from a semantic point of view, comparable to being President: like *President*, *it* is a title for which practically anyone of a

---

[11]For further discussion of Carroll's and related views, cf. Fodor, 1965b; for an excellent general discussion of learning theoretic models of language and their shortcomings, cf. Chomsky 1959.

certain age may qualify, though only one person may hold it at a time.

What is interesting about this undoubtedly frivolous example is that it is clearly misdescribed by any of the kinds of theory of reference we have been dicussing. Thus, it is simply irrelevant to whether or not a child has learned to use the word *it* that he has or has not got images when he hears *it* uttered. It is, of course, relevant to deciding whether he has learned the word that he respond correctly to utterances of *it*. But this does not mean that he must respond to utterances of *it* the way he responds to the player who is "it," or that he must respond to the player who is "it" by uttering *it*. On the contrary, the appropriate responses to the player who is "it" is not to say *it* but to run. Conversely, the occasions upon which it *is* appropriate to say *it* are, in large part, fixed by the rules of the game. Since alteration of such rules would presumably alter the occasions on which *it* gets uttered, it seems implausible to argue that any pattern of conditioning could be prerequisite to mastering the use of the word. Finally, it is not only irrelevant but downright absurd to ask whether, or in what way, the word *it* and the child who happens to *be* "it" resemble one another. To be the referent of *it*, pro tem, all you need to be is in the game and slow on your feet. There is clearly no place here for an appeal to even the most refined sort of onomatopeia.

We can see that the theories of reference we have been discussing are irrelevant to explaining what the child learns when he learns how to us *it*, because we know how to describe what he does in fact learn. What he learns is that a player is "it" just in case he is in the game and

1. He was chosen "it" at the beginning of the game and has touched no one in play since he was chosen, or

2. He was touched by someone who was "it" and has touched no one since.

Granted that a child refers to a player as "it" only when one or other of these conditions is satisfied, no further question about the child's imagery or about his verbal or nonverbal reponses need be raised. Learning that it is correct to refer to a player as "it" only when one or other of these conditions is satisfied is just learning to determine the referent of *it* under the specialized conditions imposed by tag.

It is an open question to what extent this example offers a paradigm for learning the referent of words in less artificial cases. However, a number of interesting points arise upon the assumption that this example is not atypical. In the first place, the question *What is the nature of the bond that ties a word to its referent?* seems much less pressing once we maintain that reference, when a feature of symbols, is a different *kind* of property than reference when a feature of signs. If what makes an object the referent of a word is only that it satisfies conditions articulated by rules for using the word referentially, then there is no theoretical motivation for trying to find some reduction of reference to causation or resemblance. Involved in the notion that reference is essentially a relation determined by rules is the abandonment of the analogy between signs and symbols, an analogy which, as we have seen, has dominated much of the psycholinguistic literature.

Second, if learning the referent of a word involves learning rules that determine when the word is correctly applied, there is reason to abandon the supposition that verbal behavior differs from paradigmatic conditioned behavior only in relative complexity. Conditioning models are notoriously unsuited for explaining the learning and application of rules. This is roughly because the occasion for rule governed behavior need not be identifiable in terms of any observable feature of the "stimulus" object toward which the behavior is directed. What makes a child "it" is his role in the game, and that is not a "stimulus property" in the sense that height or hair color are. Similarly, what makes a response conformable to a rule need not be identifiable in terms of the topology of the response. What distinguishes a pawn move in chess from a rook move is not some special feature of the gesture of the player's hand, it is the way the move is related to the rules of chess and to the state of the game.

Third, implicating the notion of a linguistic rule in the explanation of reference is incompatible with the view that reference is a simple, primitive, and homogeneous relation. It is evident at once that three such different sorts of words as *John*, *thief*, and *today*, though they may perhaps all be properly said to have referents, must be controlled by quite different sorts of reference rules. There is thus very little temptation to suppose that the relations that obtain between these words and their referents are in any sense homogeneous.

Finally, on the view that reference is a rule governed relation (or family of relations), it becomes relevant to ask how much information about the reference rules for a word can be elicited from an examination of, e.g., the syntactic rules governing the word, and what interconnections may obtain between the reference rules and the rules that determine such other semantic features as synonymy, autonymy, copredictability, and so on. Seen in this light, it is plausible to argue that reference may be determined by complicated interrelations between different sorts of linguistic rules and thus can be profitably studied only after those other rules are fairly clearly understood. Thus, it must be at least in part a consequence of the operation of syntactic rules that the Pope is referred to in *I want to meet the Pope* but not in *I want to be the Pope*. A theory of reference adequate to deal with the asymmetry between such sentences will thus need to have information about their syntactic differences available to it.

There is a moral to these reflections, fragmentary and unsatisfactory though they surely are. It is that the problem of reference is probably more like other problems about language than has traditionally been supposed. That is, it is likely that problems about reference, like problems about syntax and phonology, are essentially problems about how rules are learned and applied. But while this conclusion is agreeable in that it holds out the ultimate promise of an integrated treatment of the psychology of language, it must also be admitted that the part of cognitive psychology that is currently least well understood is precisely that part which concerns the assimilation and manipulation of rules. If, as I have been trying to suggest, there is very little in contemporary psychological theories of reference that was not proposed by Locke and refuted by Berkeley, that is perhaps because psychologists have supposed that reference is the one part of linguistic competence that can be forced to fit familiar learning paradigms. But, as the analogies and interdependencies between reference and other linguistic relations become clearer, one is increasingly impressed both with the coherence of language structure and with the inadequacy of current psychological models to cope with it.

REFERENCES

Brown, R. W. *Words and things.* New York: Free Press (Macmillan), 1958.

Carroll, J. B. *Language and thought.* Englewood Cliffs: Prentice-Hall, 1964.

Caton, C. *Philosophy and ordinary language.* Urbana: Univ. of Illinois Press, 1963.

Chomsky, N. A review of *Verbal behavior.* In J. A. Fodor & J. J. Katz (Eds.), *The structure of language.* Englewood Cliffs: Prentice-Hall, 1964.

Feigl, H., & Sellers, W. (Eds.), *Readings in philosophical analysis.* New York: Appleton-Century-Crofts, 1949.

Fodor, J. A. Review of Werner and Kaplan's *Symbol formation. Language,* 1964, **40,** 566–578.

Fodor, J. A. Could meaning be an r_m? *J. verb. Learn. verb. Behav.,* 1965, **4,** 73–81. (a)

Fodor, J. A. Review of Carroll's *Language and thought. Mod. Lang. J.,* 1965, **59,** 384–386. (b)

Fodor, J. A., & Katz, J. J. *The structure of language.* Englewood Cliffs: Prentice-Hall, 1964.

Hilgard, E. R., & Marquis, D. G. *Conditioning and learning.* New York: Appleton-Century-Crofts, 1940.

Hume, D. *A treatise of human nature.* 1735.

Krasner, L. Studies in the conditioning of verbal behavior. In S. Saporta (Ed.), *Readings in psycholinguistics.* New York: Holt, Rinehart & Winston, 1961.

Lenneberg, E. H. The capacity for language acquisition. In J. A. Fodor & J. J. Katz (Eds.), *The structure of language.* Englewood Cliffs: Prentice-Hall, 1964.

Linsky, L. Reference and referents. In C. Caton (Ed.), *Philosophy and ordinary language.* Urbana: Univ. of Illinois Press, 1963.

Locke, J. *An enquiry concerning human understanding.* 1690.

Morris, C. W. *Signs, language and behavior.* Englewood Cliffs: Prentice-Hall, 1949.

Mowrer, O. H. *Learning theory and the symbolic processes.* New York: John Wiley & Sons, 1963.

Osgood, C. E. On understanding and creating sentences. *Amer. Psychol.*, 1963, **18**, 735–751.

Quine, W. V. O. *Word and object*. Cambridge: M.I.T. Press, 1960.

Russell, B. *An inquiry into meaning and truth*. New York: W. W. Norton & Co., 1940.

Saporta, S. *Readings in psycholinguistics*. New York: Holt, Rinehart & Winston, 1961.

Werner, H., & Kaplan, B. *Symbol formation*. New York: John Wiley & Sons, 1963.

10

Lexicography

YAKOV MALKIEL
University of California, Berkeley

Over the years, the dictionary—to the extent that it represents a genuine lexical compilation, not merely some guide, alphabetically arranged, to a branch of knowledge—has developed into a powerful tool of either information or instruction. The border line between these two disparate purposes appears, it is true, occasionally blurred; but even where, fundamentally, the two purposes are to be served at once, the one must, at the very least, be clearly subordinated to the other.

Lexicography in its narrowest sense is a subdivision of applied linguistics concerned with the techniques of gathering lexical data and of presenting them most cogently in reference works and textbooks. Conversely, the rival label *lexicology* is best reserved for such analytic inquiries as deal, in synchronic or diachronic perspective, with the total lexicon of a given language (also, on the genetic level, of a close-knit language family) or with its separate ingredients, ranging from molecules (groups of words meaningfully arranged) via atoms (individual words) to subatomic units (suffixes and other "bound" forms). If the attention of the investigator is focused on the origin of a word and on the initial segment of its trajectory, the resulting approach may be described as etymological.

In harmony with the general scope and character of this book, the bulk of the present chapter is slanted in the direction of lexicography proper, and it places throughout much heavier stress on the didactic or "mixed" than on the purely informational services of the dictionaries. Thus, to cite just three otherwise prestigious "genres" here deliberately shunted off— historical dictionaries, which inventory the successive forms and meanings of a given word; concordances, which either briefly identify or extensively quote all the passages in which the word at issue appears in a certain text or in the writings of a chosen author; and etymological dictionaries, which examine in varying detail the conjectures launched in a search for the ancestry, incubation, and itinerary of a lexical item—will here be relegated to the background, to give continued prominence to the dictionary as an instrument of language learning.

However intricate the classificatory schema that the typologist may devise for a scientific taxonomy of dictionaries, the average layman, at this midtwentieth-century juncture, unhesitatingly associates the consultation of a dictionary with two sharply distinguishable real-life situations. Under one set of circumstances, that layman is in doubt as to the (social or aesthetic) propriety or the exact denotation or a striking connotation of some word—dimly remembered or never before encountered—of his own mother tongue, in which case he turns for help to a monolingual dictionary. Alternatively, he may require assistance in deciphering or savoring a specimen of some foreign language, dead or living, standard or dialectal, general or specialized, or else in translating some oral or written message of his own into that medium (which in the process becomes the target language). The obvious answer to his need is a bilingual dictionary. In the past, especially throughout the Renaissance and immediately thereafter, the tri-, quadri-, and plurilingual dictionary (say, English-Latin-Greek) held sway, but the domain of this variety has lately shrunk to a few dwindling and highly technical uses. Because of the neat polarization that the "monolingual" and the "bilingual" species of the genus dictionary afford, they lend themselves effectively to contrastive treatment. Though at present monolingual dictionaries are far more widespread (a *Webster*, a *Duden*, a *Larousse* are household words in their respective countries or cultural alliances of countries), they rank in the historical perspective, compared with their bilingual counterparts, as relative newcomers.

The monolingual dictionary most likely to reach the layman's desk frequently embodies the reduction to handy format of a bulky, monolingual encyclopedia; this is certainly true of such popular ventures as the *Larousse universel*, the *Nouveau Larousse classique*, the *Nouveau* and *Petit nouveau Larousse illustré*, etc., all of them derivatives and epitomes of P. Larousse's monumental *Grand dictionnaire universel du XIXe siècle* (*ca.* 1869–90). Or else such a manageable reference work may involve successive expansions— layer by layer, accompanied by suitable distillations, of an initially less comprehensive undertaking; such are the consecutive transformations of Noah Webster's original *American Dictionary of the English Language* (1828) through the author's own revision (1840), his immediate successors' enlargements (1847, 1859), the so-called "unabridged" version (1864; with supplement, 1884), the "international version" (1890; with supplement, 1900) down to its "new international" garb, which made its initial appearance in 1909. It also happens that a radical paring in format and in volume of documentation goes hand in hand with gradual enrichment, from one editor to another, in sheer numbers of short entries. This is precisely the fate that befell the Spanish Academy Dictionary on the long itinerary from its inception (1726–39) to its currently influential 18th edition (1956). The fact that either an encyclopedia-style compilation (or exhaustive thesaurus) or else an academy-inspired venture, necessarily puristic, typically underlies the modern desk and pocket dictionary explains that the learning conveyed is, on balance, of two orders. The dictionary rooted in an encyclopedia stresses technical terms, the vocabulary of sciences, crafts, and arts, defining each item as objectively as possible. Its counterpart traceable to an academy tends to be preceptive and arbitrarily selective, concentrating on nontechnical ingredients of the lexicon and aimed at weeding out solecisms, at enhancing elegance and amenity, etc. Theoretically, then, the two types, viewed in isolation, cater to different types of learners. In practice most modern dictionaries show an amalgamation of the two categories, and in this process of merger—a symptom of our technological age—the authoritative, normative function tends to recede in favor of the impartial, unpedantic observation of actual usage. In this respect, the transition from the second (1934) to the third (1961) edition of Merriam-Webster's *New International Dictionary* was particularly dramatic and aroused much bitter controversy (chronicled and digested by Sledd, 1962).

The kind of information a monolingual dictionary is called upon to furnish is, from the linguist's vantage point, basically twofold. A large share of that information bears on matters not intimately related to the realm of language proper, e.g., on features of the "tangible" outside world, on past events, or on elements of man-made systems extraneous to the system of language. Characteristically, this sort of encyclopedic enlightenment is concentrated in the definitions of nouns, spilling over, in standard average European at least, into comments on secondary (and tertiary) or "learned" adjectives, adverbs, and verbs. Thus, even though our dictionaries, unlike their eighteenth-century predecessors, no longer offer any prolix digressions on flora, fauna, etc., the careful reader can glean from them a few slivers of information on matters pertaining to such diversified disciplines as zoology (*vertebrate*, n. 'animal having an internal skeleton with a backbone'), geometry (*equilateral*, adj. 'having all sides equal'), psychology (*introspectively*, adv. 'in a manner involving self-examination'), and logic (*to subsume*, v. 'to place any one cognition under another as belonging to it'). Significantly, for the selection of this so-called "technical" vocabulary and for the periodic refurbishing of the relevant definitions, the more ambitious publishers of leading American dictionaries retain the services of specialists and go so far as to list their names under "Acknowledgments," crediting to each his expertise.

Where the dictionary impinges on actual language learning, and by that token, trespasses on the territory of the linguist rather than of his fellow scholars is in coping with the residue of the lexical material, i.e., with "general" terms. The hard core of these includes (*a*) functional items (which, by definition, are also of heightened interest to the syntactician), e.g., pronouns, prepositions, conjunctions; (*b*) the overwhelming majority of primary verbs; (*c*) in the ranks of nouns and adjectives those of extra broad scope, which derivationally happen for the most part to constitute primitives and stratigraphically more often than not pertain to the older, truly vernacular layers of the lexicon.

The prime difficulty encountered in grappling with these troublesome words—ironically, the highest ranking of all on the scale of usefulness—relates to their selection, and given the broad semantic spectrum most of them display, to the most cogent classification of meanings. The prevalent criteria of selection, to start with the first intricacy, are four: (*a*) frequency (which is measurable, though rigorous computations do not yet exist for all languages); (*b*) confinement to regional dialects (in most instances objectively ascertainable and even inviting cartographic representation); (*c*) restriction to social dialects (teasingly elusive in a fluid society predominantly urban); and (*d*) obsolescence. The last mentioned criterion is least easily applied since the active use of a word and its mere intelligibility need not coincide in a literate society such as ours which teaches its children to appreciate Shakespeare and adopts a reverential attitude toward the King James version of the Bible. The muddled state of affairs is further complicated by the fact that some writers, with or without the aid of dictionaries, have deliberately blurred the dividing lines between successive stages of the same language, its lexicon included (as when Rabelais, France's outstanding Renaissance figure, irresponsibly tampered with Old French, or Pérez Galdós, the dean of Spain's late nineteenth-century novelists, incrusted his chastened prose with words extracted from Cervantes), just as other writers, prompted by a different cultural climate and unusual proclivities, have stooped to the use of dialect dictionaries in an effort to flavor their prose with colorful regionalisms (this is true, as D. Isella has recently demonstrated, of C. Dossi, a Lombard near-contemporary of Napoleon).

The classification of meaning is a major problem still in abeyance, as regards both theory and practice. It is indeed a rare monolingual dictionary of recent vintage that would, for economy's sake, consistently lump together obvious homonyms, such as bay_1, adj. 'reddish brown', bay_2, n. 'inlet of the sea, inward bend of the shore', bay_3, n. 'space between columns', bay_4, n. 'laurel tree', bay_5, v. 'to bark'—though some respectable bilingual dictionaries otherwise quite up-to-date and workmanlike do just this as a matter of policy (cf. E. B. Williams's *"Holt" Dictionary for Spanish and English*). But it is easier to adopt theoretically than to implement in daily practice the decision to keep homonyms apart, because words of like appearance, even if historically unrelated, may tend to coalesce, while others, clearly traceable to a single prototype but afflicted with a critical excess of polysemy, may conversely tend to disintegrate into clusters of "autonomous" homonyms.

Yet quite aside from the pitfalls of fission and collision, the semantic structure of numerous words raises well-nigh insoluble problems if authors and readers of dictionaries were to insist on uncompromising rigor. Here is a relatively simple "first step": in organizing an entry, lexicographers incline to segregate the congealed stereotyped phrases whose meaning cannot easily be predicted from any previous familiarity with their individual constituents. These fossilized sequences, popularly known as "idioms," are customarily assembled at the end of an entry or as a supplement to it; since it is virtually impossible to order them in any cogent array, the listing is ordinarily alphabetic—that is, in the last analysis, conventional if not random; cf. in English *to make after* 'to follow or pursue', *to make away with* 'to squander', *to make believe* 'to pretend', *to make bold* 'to take the liberty', etc. There will always be a residue of borderline cases such as *to make a figure* 'to be conspicuous' or *to make amends* 'to render compensation', where opinions are split on the degree of ossification; also lexicographers are divided on the wisdom of listing just once or twice a binuclear idiom such as *to make sure* 'to be certain of', and if the single listing is preferred, there will be those advocating the choice of the core word (*sure*) as against those favoring the selection of the element that comes first either in the actual utterance (*make*) or in the alphabetic concatenation (in this particular sequence, coincidentally also *make*).

Teacher and student and layman alike, to the extent that they are thoughtful and sensitive rather than casual and indifferent consulters of a dictionary, are for the most part eager, first to ascertain the referential kernel of a given word, then to identify the pattern of that word's semantic ramification, and in the process, to select the one meaning that best fits the problematic context. The superior desk dictionary may be geared to satisfying some facets of the typical user's diffracted curiosity; but if it does, the picture presented threatens to grow all the less coherent. For conventional reasons (in response to a demand in many quarters almost extinct), the more elaborate standard dictionaries still list—as a rule, in parentheses or square brackets, immediately after the head-word—the remote origin of the word, and if conservatively slanted, they may even record a few of its congeners; but this information is clearly incidental, not to say obtrusive, in any context other than that of an etymological dictionary expressly so labeled. If one disregards this entertaining "flashback," the relevant semantic nucleus might be best represented by the word's oldest meaning still in living use. But what about the rather numerous cases in which that meaning has become so critically obsolescent as to be restricted to a few set phrases or compounds, as is true of E. *meat* 'food'? If so, should the meaning currently commonest, so identified through statistic devices, be placed, regardless of its genetic rank, at the head of the procession? Even if this side issue of determining the "leader-meaning" could be quickly settled, the lexicographer would still be plagued with the task of persuasively arranging the remainder of the given lexical unit's semantic nuances. This assignment is formidable; for while the analyst is at liberty to operate with "sememes" (or "semantemes") as against "allosemes," the job of delimiting each hue as neatly as possible—typically through permutation—is most often still performed by rule of thumb, in the absence of simple, sharp-edged minimal-pair contrasts so helpful in phonology. Assuming further, in an optimistic vein, that the individual shades have been objectively circumscribed, and by the same token, all embarrassing overlaps eliminated, the lexicographer faces the new obligation of arraying these shades in some close-knit scheme. By electing the conventional linear sequence for the complex definition of a word which he credits with, say, five meanings, he runs the risk of creating the erroneous impression that Meaning 2 issues forth from Meaning 1, that Meaning 3 flows from Meaning 2, etc., whereas in reality Meanings 2–5 may almost simultaneously have rayed out in different directions from a single semantic kernel and thus seem to invite some miniature diagrammatic projection, typographically costly and cumbersome. Then again, the argument that a linear succession may defensibly be made to suggest the historical order of events could be countered with the remark that the chronological hierarchy in which derivative meanings demonstrably appear in datable texts need not faithfully reflect the (conjectural) chain of their gradual crystallizations in actual speech. Finally, if some magic wand could help us remove all these irksome complications, we should still be confined to a semantic edifice historically structured—a structure in many instances utterly unwelcome to the average user under the present circumstances. While current front-line research in semantics, on the two levels of denotation and connotation, is briskly advancing the frontier of knowledge, some time will doubtless be required before the filtered results of these experiments can be injected into the daily practice and habits of lexicographers.

It is a commonplace of linguistics that grammar (sound structure included) and lexicon form the two major domains of every known language's inalienable property. It is equally true that a ruthlessly strict separation of these two provinces, though theoretically conceivable and for certain operations even desirable, is seldom if ever in the best long-term interest of smooth language learning. In other words, experience shows that the most propitious climate for the painless acquisition of language skills is one which allows a few drops of lexical information to ooze into grammar and vice versa. What kind and what amount of grammatical information can a middle-of-the-road dictionary be legitimately expected to offer?

The structure of clauses and sentences clearly transcends the responsibility of a lexicographer: the reader will be grateful to him for being told that in Latin *timeō* requires *nē* and *nōn dubitō* calls forth *quīn*, but any hint of just what happens inside the *nē* and *quīn* clauses, as regards tense, mood, etc., must be elicited from other sources of information. Limiting our horizon to Indo-European languages, we may expect the dictionary to provide, as the first of its two major grammatical services, the barest minimum of insight into the paradigm of an inflected word, beyond those forms one can readily predict from the base form heading the entry; hence, the need for such formulaic statements familiar to Latinists (and, in turn, presupposing the reader's acquaintance with the rudiments of Latin grammar) as *miles, -itis* 'warrior' beside *castra, -orum* 'military camp', or *faciō* (*fēcī, factus,* 3) 'to do, make', or *ācer, ācris, ācre* 'sour'. The other service relates to such information as enables the user to link the word with its immediate environment. From reading *mōns,* m., *nūrus* beside *arbōs,* f., and *mare,* n., we brace ourselves for such sequences of varying degrees of normality as *mōns altus* 'high mountain', *nūrus pulchra* 'beautiful daughter-in-law', *arbōs sicca* 'dry tree', and *mare nostrum* 'our sea'. Government, by means of either preposition or case ending, is perhaps the single most important grammatical cue conveyed by a dictionary, but even the best-architectured among them are selective in this respect; also, the monolingual dictionary ideally focuses the reader's attention on matters of scaffolding different from those highlighted by its bilingual counterpart. Thus, a monolingual dictionary may state whether a given verb is self-sufficient or requires, to communicate a complete message, some "goal"; it may indicate the declensional case favored by a verb if the choice of that particular case is semantically, syntactically, or stylistically relevant to the native speaker (e.g., genitive vs. accusative with Lat. *oblīvīscor* 'I forget' and *meminī* 'I remember').

We have imperceptibly entered the domain of bilingual dictionaries, a category raising the greatest variety of disparate problems. To begin with, a layman normally expects such a dictionary to be bidirectional (say, German-Italian and Italian-German), and most of them actually are, but one can cite important qualifications and downright exceptions. Where dead languages are involved, especially those associated with classical antiquity, the reference work will usually be unidirectional, since—unlike the leading spokesmen for humanism and the pioneering scientists of the seventeenth century—few persons today have occasion to translate modern thought into Latin or Greek. At most, a slender, unnuanced English-Latin dictionary, cut to the needs of collegiate exercises, will accompany a far more massive and elaborate Latin-English compilation. Where a dead language has been resuscitated, as has Hebrew in our lifetime, the situation is bound to change abruptly, since persons originally immersed in a Slavic-, German-, Yiddish-, or Arabic-speaking environment have suddenly had to adjust themselves to a nascent culture using Hebrew as a vehicle of communication and channel of thought. Strictly "academic" dictionaries of such medieval languages as Old and Middle English, Old and Middle High German, Old Provençal, and Old Church Slavic are with rare exceptions unidirectional, a state of affairs satisfying philological and literary curiosity but severely detrimental to advanced linguistic research. The author of a distinguished etymological dictionary may settle on a compromise, appending to his reference work, in index-like fashion, a mere guide in reverse direction (cf. Meyer-Lübke's long tone-setting *Romanisches etymologisches Wörterbuch*, 1930–1935). An analogous situation prevails in the ranks of dialect vocabularies. Thus, the average Hispanist is eager to understand words collected in some colorful corner of the Iberian peninsula—say, Andalusia, Asturias, or Navarre—or overseas, in some section of Colombia, some nook of the Philippine Islands, or some district of Tangier or Istanbul, and consequently welcomes books, articles, and pamphlets listing such regionalisms with standard Spanish glosses; but only a bizarre sense of heroism could prompt an eccentric local patriot to prepare a volume slanted in the opposite direction or to engage in a bidirectional venture. Only where a dialect is struggling for recognition as a full-blown literary language does such an endeavor (welcome, of course, to the professional linguist) make any sense; cf., against the background here suggested, Crespo Pozo's recent Castilian-Galician dictionary, 1963.

Occasionally, the two parts of a single bidirectional bilingual dictionary project will be assigned to two experts using slightly different techniques and criteria and endowed with different supplies of talent, perseverance, and factual information. The results may then be as discrepant as they were in the case of Slaby's Spanish-German (original edition, 1932) as against Grossmann's complementary German-Spanish dictionary (original edition, 1937), both sponsored by Teubner in Leipzig and forming a closely integrated set.

The average user of a bilingual dictionary, particularly a language learner, expects of his tool a number of services, which can be provided at sharply varying cost. There is, first, the matter of pronunciation. It takes a language like English, with its lack of consistency in item-to-item correspondences between sounds and letters, to prompt a native speaker to consult a monolingual dictionary of his own language for this sole purpose; a Russian would glean from his authoritative *Dal'* the pattern of word-stress so difficult of prediction, and a German would, at long intervals, let a lexicographer-orthoepist guide him in selecting, from rival variants, the most desirable pronunciation (Should *Chemie* 'chemistry' be pronounced with a [k], a [š], or a [ç]?). When it comes to exploring a foreign language, however, nearly every student is in need of some phonetic guidance.

On the recommendable amount of such guidance, there exists no actual consensus. Where the correlation of pronunciation and spelling is highly aberrant, or worse, unique, and the foreign learner may slip up on several phonemes, as is true of E. *boatswain* or of Fr. *monsieur*, the phonetic transcription of the entire word is, of course, the obvious solution. But in most instances a single feature of the lexical units is doubtful; thus, the outsider confronted with the English word *lead* seeks no enlightenment, at least not in his dictionary, on the finer contours of the *l* or the *d*, but simply faces a choice between two vowel phonemes. It would be most economical, and at the same time, didactically most effective to reduce the phonetic information here to the problem directly involved; to instruct the German reader, say, that *lead* /ɛ/ is a noun and matches his 'Blei', while *lead* /i/ is a verb corresponding to his 'führen'. If the standard spelling uses no accent marks and the word stress bids fair to puzzle the user, an extra gentle stroke (preferably in a font or in a color setting it off from the remainder of the word) may provide a priceless clue: the learner, on seeing E. *consént* (n., v.) flanked by no variations as against *súbject* (n., adj.) accompanied by *subjéct* (v.), will immediately grasp the difference between the two situations. Where curved or slanted marks do appear in official spelling, a small vertical bar unmistakably distinct from them or some other auxiliary device may be cautiously introduced. Diacritic marks added with a measure of discretion can likewise prove helpful; they will tell, for instance, the foreign student of Italian the difference between *cọlto* 'cultured' and *cọlto* 'caught', between *mẹzzo* 'overripe, sickly, flabby' and *mẹẓẓo* 'half', between the voiceless *s* of *casa* 'house' and the /z/—its voiced counterpart—of *caṣacca* 'cloak'. (These examples, incidentally, show that to obviate confusion, only one of two sounds inadequately distinguished in conventional spelling need be marked: unmarked *s* and *z* are then understood to denote the voiceless, *ṣ* and *ẓ*, the voiced sibilant and affricate, respectively. By applying a minimal use of distinguishing marks, the British Italianist Barbara Reynolds has learned to contrast *ẹ* with *e*, *ọ* with *o*, discarding *ę* and *ǫ* altogether.) In Semitic languages, the explicit use of any vowels is something of a phonetic clue; as the foreign adult learner (or the native child) strengthens and refines his "Sprachgefühl," these crutches, little by little, can in most instances be safely removed—least easily in borrowings.

One highly controversial point is the exact amount of grammatical information that a lexicographer can or should properly convey. The border line between "structure" (i.e., grammar) and lexicon has been traced with varying results by several outstanding theorists of linguistic science, but their analyses, for all their sophistication, do not abolish one fundamental, embarrassingly trivial fact: that the raw lexical data lend themselves incomparably better to itemized alphabetization than do the data of grammar, all analytical indexes available notwithstanding. The majority of language learners, who of course share neither the enthusiasm nor the scholarly leisure of professional linguists, are easily irritated by the need to interrupt their readings and go back to the handbook of grammar, not only on account of the moral humiliation (everybody has graduated from a grammar, yet nobody ever fully graduates from a dictionary and is ashamed to admit gaps in lexical knowledge), but because this operation is time-consuming. The levelheaded user's secret wish is to find, at a glance, all the requisite grammatical and lexical assistance wrapped into a single package.

This wish is not easy to fulfill. To be sure, the lexicographer can report with formulaic laconism which of two competing past participles is the commoner (e.g., F. *résous* or *résolu*, from *résoudre*) or how they are differentiated; he can remind his customers that Russ. *mužčina* 'man' and *gorodiško* 'small town' are masculine despite their endings, which happen to point in entirely different directions; he is free to record the genitive of Lat. *iter* 'way' (*itineris*) and of Lat. *iecur* 'liver' (*iecineris*), which no tyro would have conjectured on his own; he is welcome to identify the virtually unpredictable broken plural of a noun in classical Arabic. But if most elements of inflection can thus be capsulized, only a meager portion of syntax lends itself to such treatment.

To begin with, a policy of selectivity ordinarily presides over the side glance at syntax (as against inflection) provided by even the best-balanced bilingual dictionaries. The absolute number of observable constructions being exceedingly high, those features in which the two languages at issue— and sometimes they alone—happen to disagree are chosen for preferential or exclusive listing. Thus, the construction of Lat. *meminī* 'to remember' and *oblīviscor* 'to forget' are so manifold, and on balance, so sharply divergent from what English usage leads a learner to expect (with genitive, with accusative, with *dē*, with infinitive, with indirect question, in absolute use) that lexicographers will be tempted to record the details punctiliously, but where the constructions in the two languages contrasted happen to coincide, they may not be accorded any mention, let alone comment. This bias is, as has been often observed, detrimental to stringent scientific description; it rarely harms the language student for whom the dictionary has been compiled in the first place, but impairs that dictionary's usefulness for any third party (e.g., any less than a versatile Russian who may be forced to use an English-Thai dictionary).

More serious for the average learner's workaday life is the reluctance of most lexicographers to impart knowledge on matters of word order and clause construction, in large part because relevant instructions, and especially, illustrations might require excessive space. Except for a few overworked examples, such as *nuevo sombrero* 'newly acquired hat' vs. *sombrero nuevo* 'new-style hat', the English-speaking student of Spanish will receive on this score severely limited help from his bilingual dictionary. Also, he may glean such stray bits of information as that clause openers like *antes* (*de*) *que* 'before' and *sin que* 'without' govern the subjunctive (a firm rule) but he is unlikely to learn much about those modal constructions which either allow free choice or demand far narrower rigid rules, as is true of Sp. *después que* 'after', *hasta que* 'until', *mientras* (*que*) 'while', etc.

It is, however, by definition in the lexical field, specifically anent the art of stringing words together, that layman and learner expect an extra generous dosage of help from their dictionary, and in this legitimate expectation, they are usually to some extent disappointed. For centuries—ever since the Renaissance—authors of good dictionaries have striven not only to provide bare lists of word correspondences but to endow these equations with life by citing characteristic phrases and idiomatic combinations. In fact, some old-time lexicographers have spiced their brainchildren with hundreds upon hundreds of proverbs, thus unwittingly—and, from our viewpoint, indefensibly—amalgamating a lexical and a paroemiological reference work. The modern lexicographer keeps vocabulary and folklore strictly apart, just as, unlike his eighteenth-century predecessors, he steers clear of any confusion of dictionary and encyclopedia (once interwoven, as were also biography and bibliography). He limits the "frills" to deeply entrenched idiomatic sayings; the omission of this optional feature distinguishes the pocket dictionary from its middle-sized and full-sized counterparts. Thus, in consulting a collegiate dictionary, one expects to find some clue to such "idioms" as irreversible binomials: *in this day and age, lo and behold, by hook or by crook*, etc. How else, save by explicit listing, can the foreigner guess that it is mandatory in English to say *up and down, back and forth*, rather than—as is equally conceivable on logical grounds—*down and up, forth and back*? Colorful comparisons congealed into fixed sequences likewise qualify for inclusion in an elaborate dictionary; e.g., French *sage comme une image, bête comme un chou, sotte comme une linotte*, which convey a message not too distant from such German compounds as *himmelblau, Tageshelle*, etc. Also, one is pleased to find between the same two covers such miscellaneous fossils as *wie ein Häuflein Unglück aussehen, über den Haufen werfen*, which the Spaniard will not spontaneously associate with his own *estar hecho una desgracia* and *echar abajo* (=*atropellar*).

But between the countable number of these hardened stereotypes, at one extreme, and at the other, combinations arrived at through the exercise of maximum freedom and even deliberate unconventionality (as demanded by, say, modernistic poetry, markedly subjective), there extends an intermediate zone of habitual combinations, which the professional writer identifies as clichés and trains himself to shun. Through a cruel irony, the degree of language mastery which a highbrow native speaker and especially a writer can afford to despise and to reject within his own medium is, under ordinary circumstances, the highest level of accomplishment to which a very versatile adult learner of a foreign language may, with a measure of luck, realistically aspire.

The following examples may illustrate the point. The German present participle *eingehend*, used adjectivally, is an equivalent of 'detailed, circumstantial', and this is the slim volume of accurate information that a dictionary will convey. But the sequence *nach eingehender Prüfung*—a stereotyped expression, a cliché, a recurrent formula, if you wish, but not yet a fossilized "idiom"—corresponds to 'after searching examination'. The departure is too slight to warrant listing, if the allowance for space is not to be exceeded.

Russ. *bojkij*, adj., *bojko*, adv., lit. 'hitting', is tantamount to 'spunky', 'pugnacious', 'aggressive'. The qualifier has achieved a certain prominence with respect to oral delivery and written verbalization: *govorit' bojko* is 'to talk smoothly, with assurance, aplomb', *pisat' bojko* is 'to write with vigor, energy, and ease'. The three semantic ingredients, then, are the combined displays of strength, effortlessness, and marksmanship, especially in conversation. This use alone is truly idiomatic; yet how many dictionaries specifically pair off verb and qualifying adverb?

Aside from the elusive linkage of word to word, there exist special contextual matrixes for words and phrases—matrixes shielded from open view even in the best dictionaries. The highly racy exclamation *Erst können vor Lachen!* is not simply an equivalent in German of E. *Impossible!* or Sp. *¡Imposible!*, as the best available dictionaries intimate. It denotes the explosive refusal to do something that one's interlocutor has just suggested (*Your idea causes me such fits of irrepressible laughter that I just can't muster the strength to do it*). Outside this narrowly defined situational matrix, the substitution of the German phrase for any such interjected remark as *Impossible!* would be not even understandable, let alone appropriate.

The main psychological problem that the tyro in language learning has to cope with is the gradual realization that, despite all appearances to the contrary, the vaunted lexical item-to-item correspondences by and large do not represent a piece of linguistic reality. To put it differently, the paradox consists in that the standard bilingual dictionary, by its very organization of entries in the target language and of glosses in the tool language, conjures up a false image of valid substitutions. The confusion is compounded by the fact that in certain restricted sections of the total vocabulary, a system of item-to-item equations does prevail, thus arousing in the student hopes and expectations which in the majority of the sections cannot be fulfilled. This element of inequality in the lexical situation is fundamentally the same as in phonetics and in grammar: because English and French, *grosso modo*, share numerous consonants, the member of either speech community is doubly frustrated on discovering that the vowel systems of the two languages are so irreconcilably opposed. The many obvious—and historically understandable—grammatical resemblances between English and German make certain incompatibilities (the formation of the plural, the use of tenses, word order) even more exasperating. Out-and-out permutability is best observed in technical narrow-gauged nomenclature: E. *lynx*, G. *Luchs*, R. *lys'*, Sp. *lince*, etc., have exactly the same ambit and are, moreover, transparent congeners. E. *otter*, G. *(Fisch)otter*, It. *lontra*, Sp. *nutria*, Fr. *loutre* show greater diversification of form but are equally exchangeable as regards their frame of reference. In the case of certain exotic (or extinct) animals and the less common minerals, there obtains such a degree of near identity that all the reader can expect to gather from a bilingual dictionary is an incidental detail of spelling and pronunciation, and possibly, information as to gender: cf. such truly international words as *jaguar*, *puma*, *quartz* (= Sp. *cuarzo*, Russ. *kvarc*), on whose semantic content encyclopedias and monolingual dictionaries ("Websters") are more enlightening than are bilingual reference works.

At the other extreme of the spectrum are the key verbs and certain prepositions and conjunctions (e.g., E. *yet*, Sp. *ya*, R. *a*) on which capsulized information cannot be provided. The ambit of Sp. *dar* is incomparably wider than that of Fr. *donner*; E. *do* and G. *tun* are far from identical in scope, so that one is tempted to speak of "deceptive equivalents" in much the same vein as one refers to "deceptive cognates" (*les faux amis*). Even in the use of broader, generic words descriptive of the outer world overlaps between individual languages are notorious; the borderline between *trees* and *bushes* (or, for that matter, the frontier separating *fruits*, *berries*, and *nuts*) varies from one cluster of speech communities to another.

Despite all these handicaps and limitations—some of them inherent in the genre, others due to ineradicable traditions—there has been a steady progress in the manufacturing of bilingual dictionaries ever since their inception, on a modest scale, as Greco-Latin glosses in late antiquity. Just because bilingual compilations, as a rule, lack that normative authority vested in some monolingual ventures which has made the brainchildren of Dr. Johnson, N. Webster, É. Littré, and the Darmesteter-Hatzfeld-Thomas team (*Dictionnaire Général*) real classics and potent sources of influence on contemporary literature and standards of taste, the bilingual species need not represent intrinsically inferior accomplishments, and some of the latest must be acclaimed as veritable gems of craftsmanship. To ensure further progress, the lexicographer must strive not only after completeness—a goal relatively easy to achieve given the requisite time and pool of human resources—but also after tidiness, specificness (indication of speech level, territorial range, phrasal environment), economy (ruthless elimination of the obsolete, judicious marking of the obsolescent, scrupulous extirpation of the spurious, i.e., of "ghost-words"), and above all, the most effective structuring of information. The learner, conversely, must reconcile himself to the fact that the handiest dictionary can, at best, dole out stray bits of useful direction without ever qualifying as a replacement for a phonetic guide, a handbook of grammar, a stylistic mentor, a repository of folkloristic bric-à-brac, or a compact encyclopedia.

Whether mono- or bilingual, the dictionary arranged in a single alphabetic sequence is, of course, representative of the species, so much that, informally, the book trade tends to dub any explicative presentation of itemized knowledge a "dictionary," just as any set of fixed rules, outside the realm of language, may, under exceptional circumstances, be called a "grammar." (Directories, gazetteers, and all manner of indexes and inventories are excluded from the category of dictionaries because, by definition, they are not explicative.) But the straight alphabetic succession of entries is not a mandatory prerequisite for inclusion. In the late Middle Ages, it was by no means unusual for the glossarist to break down his total supply of items into word-classes: nouns, verbs, participles, particles, etc.; this procedure was favored, shortly after 1500, by the Granadan convert Pedro de Alcalá in his pioneering Arabic-Spanish vocabulary, while an anonymous medieval Portuguese-Latin verb dictionary may, in the course of transmission, have split off from just such a venture. Within each subcategory so delimited, the array continued to be alphabetical.

Instead of grammatical form, the province of life (that is to say, meaning) could act as a prime classifier. The idea of devising some such philosophical scheme as would enable a lexicographer to fit all words into a single tightly structured semantic edifice was too farfetched for the pacesetters of lexicography, who were not, as a rule, trained philosophers, encyclopedists, or polygraphers. What seemed within reach was the compilation of short lists (sometimes alphabetically arranged) for such lexical items as formed easily identifiable "clusters": numerals, time units as codified by the calendar (seasons, months, weekdays, etc.), kinship terms, designations of animals, plants, and minerals (according to vernacular taxonomy), etc. Such lists were frequently appended as an ancillary extra feature to the more pretentious of older dictionaries, along with specimens of conversation, grammatical compendiums, prosodic guides, rhyming vocabularies, and other auxiliary instruments of training and entertainment. It is from the coalescence of such partial lists, at the outset concomitant, highly selective, and noncommittal to the point of randomness, that the modern semantic dictionary has crystallized.

The full-blown semantic dictionary—a genre exemplified by such classics as Roget's *Thesaurus*, Boissière's *Dictionnaire analogique*, and Casares' *Diccionario ideológico*—purports to fragment the "world of words" into discrete provinces of meaning, an experiment particularly risky where adjectives, verbs, and elements predominantly relational or functional are involved. The major difficulty lies not in devising some appropriate schema reconciling a bold cosmic view with continued attention to minute (often trivial) lexical detail, but in training busy users to accustom themselves to such an unorthodox arrangement of otherwise familiar data. Fortunately, most semantic dictionaries are equipped with alphabetic indexes ensuring smooth and instantaneous orientation in the jungles of lexical meaning. Since the practical usefulness of this approach is confined to avoiding confusion of words deceptively similar but not quite identical in meaning, there has arisen, for pedagogical and clinical purposes, a special by-form, the dictionary of synonyms (which, ironically, is predicated on the assumption that no language really tolerates complete synonymy).

We have so far concerned ourselves with lexicographic ventures operating with definitions; whether mono- or plurilingual, a dictionary so conceived comprises a succession of *entries*, each of which elicits a *gloss*, i.e., a translation or a circumlocution. An occasional companion feature of the gloss, distinctly less austere in tone, is the *illustration*, which, in turn, may be either *verbal* or *graphic*.

Verbal illustrations show a word in action, i.e., in characteristic, revealing context. On this point, there exist two schools of thought in modern lexicography: the one, traceable to the seventeenth and eighteenth centuries, insists on collecting illustrative examples from the classics and from leading contemporary, or near contemporary, writers of high prestige. The other school rejects this canon of taste, stressing the artificiality and sheer caprice of the more exquisite specimens of artistic prose, and particularly, of pretentious hermetic poetry. The follower of this sect is encouraged to coin all illustrative examples himself or to try to overhear and unobtrusively record them as they emerge in casual, spontaneous conversation.

Graphic illustrations—which may be mono- or polychromatic, involve drawings, maps, or photographs and appear on separate plates, on foldout sheets, in pockets or portfolios, or alongside the printed text—represent, in many ways, a concession to modern taste: the older dictionaries were squarely based on straight verbalization. Even today, the visual aids amount to an optional feature, cherished as a timesaving device and as a bright spot, allowing those readers who are so inclined to skip tediously circumstantial descriptions, characterizations, and definitions of tools, containers, plants, animals, and the like. Strictly speaking, this material befits an encyclopedia rather than a dictionary and has so far been particularly infrequent in bi- and multilingual dictionaries, except those accompanying textbooks keyed to the direct method. Inevitably, in any sample of graphic illustrations, the nouns are heavily favored; typically, they alone are accorded this distinction of dual representation. In language learning, however, diagrams outlining the functions of prepositions and prefixes are also very helpful and have often been tried out informally under classroom conditions, in reference to such languages as classical Greek and Russian; one sees no reason for permanently excluding such schematic delineations from formal lexicographic ventures. Then again, the exact semantic nuances of certain verbs—notably those involving violent, sudden action, like *to hit*, *whack*, *tumble*, *jump*, *bounce*— might be quite effectively evoked by apposite cartoons; and at least those adjectives—and participles used adjectivally—which refer to size and shape (*jagged*, *curved*, *angular*, *obtuse*, *protruding*, *thick*, *thin*, *obese*, *gaunt*, etc.) lend themselves to visual projection within the bounds of academic seriousness and decorum.

The size and coverage of a dictionary codetermine, of course, its price, but a greater deterrent than high cost may be the inferior service that an over-bulky compilation sometimes provides. The thicker the dictionary, the more urgent the need for a superb inner organization, through skillful use of fonts and running heads, a denser network of cross-references, the insertion of a handy thumb index, and the like. Aside from such externals, the entire architecture of the content demands reinforced underpining and periodical cleanings.

It is not enough to add words to an older inventory from current literature and from direct aural observation of fluid present-day usage. Every existing vocabulary that serves as a starting point for a new project is likely to contain "ghost-words" (a residue of old misprints, carried over from one reference work to another, of unsuccessful nonces and facetious ad hoc coinages hardly worthy of a permanent record, and the like). This unwelcome excess baggage must, at intervals, be ruthlessly discarded. Then again, words and constructions which enjoyed a vogue only a century ago may now be on their wane, understandable marginally (from hearsay or readings) or not at all and definitely not recommended for active use. In language learning, it is important that every purchaser of a dictionary give priority to a work calibrating and qualifying each entry as meticulously as possible in regard to still unrestricted vitality, limited applicability, bare intelligibility, avowed unconventionality or stridency through an overdose of archaism, provincialism, or modernity, downright impropriety by the standards locally enforced, etc. A small dictionary highly selective and deftly arranged will, on balance, furnish better guidance than a massive but untidy accumulation of data in alphabetic sequence.

Aside from standard dictionaries of changeable perspective and varying degrees of comprehensiveness, there exist other categories of lexicographic compilations which do not aim at offering a selection or cross section, still less a full inventory, of the given language's motley vocabulary. Frequency counts, initiated forty years ago, are today facilitated by computers that efficiently perform on a scale then unforeseen and allow the analyst to skim just the cream of the lexicon, in terms of recurrence. The items selected can be ranked in a single consecutive list, which of course overrides any alphabetic or semantic considerations. The alternative is to break down the roster in multiples of, say, five hundred ("most common items," "unusually common items," "very common items," and so forth) and then to organize the material so obtained within each sublist according to some principle other than sheer frequency: alphabetic, referential, grammatical, etc. The availability of frequency lists has strongly—and by no means adversely— influenced the manufacturing of textbooks in recent years.

Another self-imposed limitation arises from the compiler's desire to concentrate of the preferences and requirements of certain particular age groups. The average dictionary purports to serve the needs of the adult and to cater to his tastes; this has at all times been understood by implication. The study of child languages, initiated by psychologists, educators, and linguists alike, and the concurrent development of a book trade seeking to capture the child's, the adolescent's, and the college student's attention have jointly produced the need for broader and more precise information on the gradual expansion of a growing person's lexical resources. To cite but one example: within an American upper-class family, the same boy or girl will, at different age levels, become familiar with *maybe* alone and with *maybe* besides *perhaps*, an equipment to which academic environment will in due time add *possibly* and study in a graduate school, *conceivably*. By introducing the element of age (and level of social background and training), experts break down the rigidly monolithic structure of the lexicon into an elastic succession of layers. On the American commercial book market, commendably progressive in this particular respect, one finds dictionaries cut to the specific demands of the 6-, 8-, 10-year-old child, either "average" or "gifted," etc., and further refinement as to stage and ability is to be expected.

A fairly unusual type is the syntactically oriented dictionary, as exemplified by the torso of R. J. Cuervo's masterly *Diccionario de construcción y régimen*. In this bold late eighteenth-century experiment, the great Colombian scholar decided to shed light only on such lexical elements as raised problems of phrasal construction, deliberately confining his horizon, by and large, to verbs, pronouns, prepositions, and articles, and pouring out, by way of compensation, an inordinate amount of fine-meshed information, preceptive and historical, on each of the none too numerous items that qualified for inclusion.

Still more remote from the standard dictionary are such vocabularies as focus on a single strain (or streak, or stock) within the motley lexicon of a representative language. Strictly speaking, unless the learner has developed an almost morbid curiosity about language history, he need no more worry about the provenience of words than does a child in first committing such items to memory. In fact, a lay person untrained in the intricacies of historical grammar cannot ordinarily tell either an Anglo-Saxon from a Norse word in English, or, for that matter, a Latin from (*a*) a Germanic word in French (e.g., *rouge* 'red' vs. *gris* 'gray'), or (*b*) from a Basque word in Spanish (e.g., *derecho* 'right' vs. *izquierdo* 'left'), or (*c*) from a Greek word in Italian (e.g., *cugino* 'cousin' vs. *zio* 'uncle'). It thus stands to reason that vocabularies of Gallicisms in Spanish and Italian, of Batavisms in French, of Lusisms in Castilian (and vice versa), of Germanisms and Polonisms in Russian, of Slavisms and Hungarisms in Rumanian, etc., while useful as part of the technical apparatus of an advanced linguistic scientist, are of little or no concern to the language learner.

And yet, the tyro has no right to brush such compilations aside without further thought. To begin with, in certain situations a perceptive layman can dimly recognize an adventitious strain ("admixture") in his own language or in a foreign language he is striving to master. The ancient Arabisms stand out quite sharply in Spanish and Portuguese; a person rooted in Mexican Spanish identifies with little difficulty the sprinkling of local Aztec or Maya components; a semisophisticated speaker of German, with a flair for phonic and prosodic features, can rather neatly slice off at least the younger layer of Gallicisms, quite possibly obnoxious to him; on the American scene, the exoticism of such geographic names as *Dakota, Wyoming, Tamalpais, Shasta* will be readily apparent to all but the most obtuse observer; and, more important, native users of English on both sides of the Atlantic immediately recognize by their perplexing syllabico-accentual structure

such erudite words, to which they were not exposed in nursery or kindergarten, as *obstreperous, preposterous, supererogatory, diaphanous, prevaricate,
impediment*, and *obfuscation*, though most of them may be in doubt as to
whether Hellenisms or Latinisms or something else, not readily identifiable,
are involved. Most of these words were absorbed by the upper classes at a
time when, at least in their own social environment, thorough training in
the two prestige languages of antiquity was taken for granted. To the original
borrowers, then, and to a few generations of their disciples and followers,
the cumbersome structure of these involute polysyllabic words was entirely
transparent; they had the skill not only to peel off, from, say, *preponderant*,
the prefix *pre-* and the suffix *-ant* (this elementary operation most moderns can
still perform with relative ease), but also to endow with meaning or imagery
the nuclear element *-pond-*, opaque or obscure to the typical midtwentieth-
century learner. Also, it would hardly have occurred to any native speaker of
English steeped in the humanistic tradition to toy with divorcing, in actual
pronunciation, *inherent* from *coherent*. Because the modern student needs so
much more orthoepic, orthographic, and semantic guidance on this particularly slippery ground, special dictionaries of "classical roots," Greek and
Latin words, etc., have quite legitimately made their appearance in the
English-speaking countries and generally throughout the humanistically
impoverished Western world.

There exists, in every major culture, a medley of auxiliary and supplementary dictionaries which bid fair to become increasingly useful past the
stage of elementary apprenticeship, when routine training gives way to
sustained and discriminating reading practice, to responsible translation
work, or to high-level teaching activities (including the preparation of
teaching materials by the erstwhile student). The learner-turned-scholar
must attune himself, within the language specialty of his own choice, to these
additional sources of information—not all of them, as a rule, readily accessible. For some of the best-known languages, whose exponents and exegetes
may boast a tradition of centuries of uninterrupted lexicographic activities,
there have frequently accumulated the following concomitant sources of
information (separate book ventures or articles of monographic size):
addenda and corrections to (by way of exception, even subtractions from) the
latest authoritative academy dictionary; lists of regionalisms, which may
involve territories ranging from a characteristic district or borough of a
metropolis (e.g., New York's East Side, Harlem, or Brooklyn) via medium-
sized areas (e.g., the English of southern Colorado, the Spanish of Santo
Domingo, the Russian of Kamchatka) to quasi-continental expanses (e.g.,
the English of North America, Asiatic Russian, Brazilian Portuguese); items
culled from conspicuous social dialects, jargons, and the like within clearly
delimited "subsocieties"; words of broad denotation favored by high school
students, athletes and circus gymnasts, sailors, chimney sweeps, gamblers,
card dealers, pickpockets, counterfeiters, pimps and prostitutes; racy,

opprobrious, or obscene words omitted from standard dictionaries out of—proper or misguided—regard for socially enforced decorum; highly technical terms understood and used within narrowly confined quarters: designations of parts of a horse's harness or of an old-fashioned carriage (or of a modern automobile, as viewed by an articulate repair mechanic), names of masts and other parts of a traditional seafaring vessel, labels of tools used in an old-style smithy, tags attached to fashion after fashion of women's garments, messages and observations (not a few of them foreign-sounding) that make sense only at a race track, in a printing shop, in an armory, in or around a gymnasium or bullfighting arena, and throughout each country's (or the entire West's) hospitals, ballet studios, and conservatories, not to mention restaurants appealing strictly to gourmets. The amusing list of available printed collections of such lexical "frills" and technical niceties (that is what these semi-intelligible words amount to when examined from the angle of the general native practitioner of the given language, and a fortiori, of a levelheaded outsider) can be prolonged almost indefinitely, at least in the case of such powerful vehicles serving highly literate, and at the same time, socially stratified speech communities as are English, German, French, and Italian.

On the side of distinctively literary usage, even more capricious and no less kaleidoscopically motley, the learner may tap, for generous amounts of optional information, concordances permitting minute inspection of a tone-setting author's lexical preferences; dictionaries spanning a single work of great distinction, or the entire works of an influential writer, or even the total production of an artistic movement; short glossaries appended traditionally to the better editions of classics and almost obligatorily to academic editions of recalcitrant medieval texts, and to all manner of chrestomathies and anthologies bristling with difficulties. These aids have become so numerous and so hopelessly scattered that there have lately sprung into existence special bibliographic guides to them, also, whenever possible, master lists consolidating the myriad molecules of explanatory bric-à-brac. Typically, all these exegetic activities are carried on by philologists, textual critics, and pedagogues; but lately some creative writers, anticipating their readers' perplexities, have agreed to equip with glossaries their own fiction too heavily larded with piquant provincialisms.

Up to this point, we have been operating on the tacit assumption that the function of dictionaries is and always has been to provide information as objective, detached from partisanship, and aimed at the user's rational faculty as possible, a triple qualification which justifies the commonsense classing of dictionaries, glossaries, and the like as reference works par excellence. This assumption is correct in the overwhelming majority of instances, wide as may be the margin of inequality in actual performance. At the periphery of lexicographic activities, however, there linger on certain varieties of dictionaries which fail to live up to our list of minimum standards, and in fact, are not even primarily intended to provide enlightenment.

One such exceptional category comprises dictionaries meant to champion a certain cause—very often the linguistic facet of a broader cultural or specifically political issue. In many European and a few cis-Atlantic countries there has occurred, at some point in recent history, a violent reaction to the infiltration of Gallicisms, a revulsion against successful intruders rationalized as a return to the pristine, unadulterated purity of the language threatened with Frenchification. Under these circumstances, we can expect purists to issue a preceptive (or rather prohibitive) dictionary, cautioning patriotic users to beware of certain pitfalls or lures of current usage. (Such politically inspired clarion calls must be sharply distinguished from the innocuous lists of deceptive cognates, or as the French call them, *faux amis*—lists which impartially and commendably include such potentially confusing items as Sp. *sustituir*: not 'to substitute', but, counter to an English-speaking person's expectation, 'to replace', or Fr. *ignorer*: usually 'to be unaware, ignorant of' rather than 'to ignore'.) Another example: throughout the past century, the intellectual élites of Spanish America were in the grip of the apprehension that their countries were culturally drifting apart and that the unifying thread of the common language might eventually snap; hence, the touching zeal with which fear-ridden experts and amateurs would collect local words and phrases diverging from Castilian usage (as allegedly codified by the Madrid Academy) and would in strident tones excoriate all those who indulged such illicit deviations. Witness the scores of books, pamphlets, tracts, and articles denouncing such behavior and offering immediate remedy. Being severely at odds with the puristic motivation of such schoolmasterish interferences and condemning the framework in which most bits of supporting information along this line have been doled out, many linguistic scientists have run riot against these (to them, irresponsible) pamphleteers. A more coolheaded approach and one which would greatly benefit the experienced sophisticated learner is to use with maximum restraint and circumspection any dictionary so tinged, extracting from it stray data of information without for one moment abandoning a persistent attitude of sharply honed alertness.

The other unusual kind of dictionary—by American standards not only exotic but downright eccentric—need not detain us long, given its scant relevance to language learning; it is the dictionary aimed not at satisfying curiosity but at providing light entertainment. Several cultures geared to verbal exhilaration favor such facetious dictionaries, in which the entries, jocosely phrased, are selected for their anecdotal flavor, their titillating power (through double entendre), etc. In the hands of the mature experienced scholar, such samplers of piquancies may yield useful information on taboo, irksome homonymy, verbal prurience, and other by no means negligible forces in language, but books of this sort should not clutter up the shelf of the beginner.

It may not be amiss to append to this survey a few remarks on the rapport a learner would be well advised to establish with his dictionary. To begin with, it is impractical to rely, at all stages of one's apprenticeship, on the services of a single dictionary. An inordinately comprehensive or excessively nuanced reference work, which may be the delight and the salvation of the expert, can actually block the progress of a tyro through inopportune diffraction of attention. Second, as the student advances from pocket-sized through intermediate to the more extensive repositories of the lexical stock, he must reserve more and more time for the task of mastering the increasingly complex machinery of his successive tools. Very few users of even the most expensive dictionaries take the trouble to peruse the front matter with any degree of concentration. Yet close acquaintance with the compilers' design, sources, criteria of selection, abbreviations, arsenal of symbols, interplay of fonts, etc., is a prerequisite for the fullest possible benefit that a learner can expect to reap from consulting a polished, richly orchestrated dictionary. Ironically, as a rule only unhurried fellow lexicographers bother to examine under a microscope and can thus truly appreciate such a piece of precision engineering.

For his own welfare, the learner must train himself not to expect miracles of even the most up-to-date and rigorously edited dictionary; neither should he adopt an attitude of bland passivity vis-à-vis his trusted lexical guide. While grammatical rules, at least, give the superficial impression of being fixed and finite in number at any given moment, the ceaseless fluctuation of lexical usage and the limitless size of the lexical inventory are no secrets even to the uninitiated layman. Moreover, in many cultures imaginative speakers and writers are encouraged, by their whole milieu, to coin new words, most of them doomed to remain ephemeral. The ingenious politician in search of a fresh formula or slogan, the experimental poet bent on eschewing the trite and stale and on shocking his admirers by his daredeviltry, the witty columnist eager to shake the readers of the morning paper out of their somnolence by pricking them verbally through all sorts of jocular distortions and contaminations, the gifted *raconteur* in the neighborhood coffeehouse and the professional comedian in the night club or on the radio program, the serious scientist who—perhaps naïvely—believes that only a set of new terms will do justice to the turns and twists of his uniquely original thinking, the enterprising group of teenagers groping for words not readily understood by their elders—all these, however varied their motivations and dissimilar their talents and however divergent their chances of ultimate success, are, in the last analysis, equally ambitious coiners of words. The language learner who prefers not to condemn himself to a strictly bookish attitude must develop an eagerness for tapping the live supply of new words in any truly dynamic culture, and along with that eagerness, he must cultivate a keen understanding of the social and psychological contexts in which absolute innovations and inadvertent or deliberate departures from established usage are to be expected. He must further develop a special knack—germane to a "light touch" in contact with fellowmen—for inquiring about the meaning of words and phrases not readily intelligible to him and nowhere recorded, without giving the impression either of heavy-handed condemnation of the unfamiliar and uncodified, or possibly worse, of coolly detached observation by a blasé social scientist. The correct stance is one of zestful, but not uncritical, participation in the vital experience.

This broadly based attitude of alertness and self-reliance in matters lexical can be translated into far more precise terms. It is vitally important for the learner to become acquainted not only with the existing minute facts but also with the latent broad-gauged possibilities of word formation, as embedded in the productive models of derivation and composition. To some extent, gaps inevitably found even in the most inclusive dictionaries will prepare him for this more active role. Thus, it is quite customary for English and Romance lexicographers not to clog their volumes with such low-frequency compounds as familiar, easily detachable and readily analyzable prefixes like *ex-* 'out', *extra-* 'outside, supremely', *inter-* 'between, among, reciprocally', *intra-* 'inside', *pre-* and *pro-* 'before', *re-* 'back' or 'again', *sub-* 'below', *super-* 'above', *trans-* 'beyond'—provided, first, that the ingredient conjoined with them is transparent (this condition holds for *subtropical*, but not for *rehearse* or for *subsume*), and second, that the composite meaning of the compound flows smoothly from the amalgam of the separate meanings of its constituents (as is true of *remit*, *return*, and *revolve*, but not of *resign*). By the same token, the economy-minded author of a German dictionary may take liberties with words containing sharply silhouetted *auseinander-*, *entgegen-*, *wider-* (also *wieder-*), or *zurück-*, once he has unequivocally identified these grammatical morphemes under separate entries, but he would be ill advised to extend this liberalization to such semantically amorphous units as *er-* and *ge-*. Another classic example of legitimate shortcut, particularly in Romance and Slavic languages, is the omission of such diminutive, augmentative, meliorative (or hypocoristic), and pejorative "satellites" as pose no special problems of form or meaning for the inexperienced user. It is not absolutely necessary for the learner to commit to memory, or to have expressly identified for him by his lexicographic cicerone, such equivalents of 'little house, cottage, lodge' as Fr. *maisonnette* (besides *maison*), Sp. *casita* and Ptg. *cas-inha* (besides *casa*), G. *Häus-chen*, *-lein* (besides *Haus*), or R. *dóm-ik* (besides *dom*), while change of gender does militate in favor of including It. *cas-ino*, m. (alongside *casa*, f.), or for that matter, *tavol-ino* 'little table' (alongside *tavola*). On the other hand, G. *Frau-chen* and *Fräu-lein* (from *Frau* 'woman, wife'), and R. *dév-ka* ('loose woman'), *dévuška* ('young woman'), and *dévočka* ('little girl'), all three from *deva* 'Virgin', show such referential, and above all, connotative discrepancies as to make the separate listing of each item unavoidable, by way of precautionary measure.

Germans use composition so freely that it is both materially impossible and methodologically unwise to stuff between two covers every example culled from reading and recorded conversation. *Regenbogen* 'rainbow' may be essential, particularly for those whose native language lacks any imagerial equivalent (R. *ráduga*, It. *arcobaleno*, and Sp. *arco iris* take us farther afield in this respect than does Fr. *arc-en-ciel*); but the meaning of *Regen-mantel, -messer, -rinne, -tag, -tonne, -tropfen, -wasser, -wetter, -wind, -wolke, -zeit* can be conjectured with a modicum or minimum of effort. Displaying these and other comparable words individually would involve the same amount of luxury and downright pampering as might reserving separate pigeonholes for, say, *rainy day, rainy season, rainy weather*, etc., in English. What the user of a German dictionary may rightly demand under any circumstances is a hint of the "bound form" in which the first recurrent element of such a family of compounds is likely to appear, because at this point any prediction from the "free (absolute) form" would be hazardous: *Spiel-* from *Spiel* is simple enough, but what about *real-* from *reell, Rechts-* from *Recht, Schiffs-* from *Schiff-, Staats-* from *Staat-, Standes-* from *Stand*; *Sprach-* besides *Sprachen-* from *Sprache, Stell-* beside *Stellen-* from *Stelle*?

However, the learner's flair for ever-present potentialities should go much farther, and above all, encompass situations where no alphabetic listing of compositional and derivational devices could possibly be within easy reach. Take colloquial modern (in part, ultramodern) English: without too heavily depending on his dictionary, the foreign learner must sharpen the fine edge of his sensitivity to the point where humorous formations—for which only algebraic skeletons can be provided—like *go-go, pooh-pooh, hush-hush, helter-skelter, roly-poly, namby-pamby, razzle-dazzle, chit-chat, flim-flam, flip-flap, ping-pong, tick-tock*, and the even racier suffixal and interfixal neologisms of more recent vintage, in *-o-rama, -o-matic, -nik, -cade, -kini*, etc. (extracted, through "false separation," from *panorama, automatic, sputnik, cavalcade*, and *Bikini*) can be immediately grasped both in their amusing denotations and in their teasing overtones and associative bonds.

The practical study of vocabulary is, then, best pursued through an imaginative combination of judicious recourse to dictionaries and intensive direct observation of one's environment. The more demanding the users' attitude toward existing compilations, the better the chances for steady improvement, in the future, both of diversified reference works and of the art of lexicography as a whole. But the learner's dependence on dictionaries must not be allowed to blunt his own active inquisitiveness or stifle his initiative. Just as the forceful writer who recently "generated" the daring abstract *adamancy* from *adamant* required no stamp of approval from any recognized authority, so the vigorous student, sensitized by earlier experience to the interplay of *-ant* (*-ent*) and *-ancy* (*-ency*) in etymologically less startling contexts, need not control his response to a lexical challenge by consulting some trustworthy tome.

The acquisition of lexical knowledge in one's own and in a foreign language (dead or living) can and must be zestful. It is radically different from the mastery of pronunciation and of basic grammar, representing a more conscious and drawn-out process appealing to the maturer mind, and being far more closely integrated with the realities of life, in fact, leaving open no avenue of retreat to any ivory tower. Despite or rather by virtue of these peculiarities, lexical curiosity discloses, speaking with the Provençal troubadours, a world of mirthful knowledge, of *gai saber*.

REFERENCES

Académie Française. *Dictionnaire, dédié au roy*. 2 Vols. Paris, 1964; facs. reprod. Lille, 1901; (new ed.) Lyon, 1776; (5th ed.) Paris and London, 1814; (8th ed.) Paris, 1931–1935; *Compléments* N. Landois & L. Barré (Eds.). Paris, 1842; *Abrégé*, M. P. Lorain (Ed.). Paris, 1862.

Accademia della Crusca, Florence. *Vocabolario degli accademici*. Venice, 1623, 1680, 1697. Later editions: Florence, 1729–1738; Venice, 1741; Verona, 1804–1806; Florence, 1833–1840 and 1863–1914 (Letters *A–O*).

Alcalá, P. de *Vocabulista arávigo*. Granada, 1505; included in facs. reprod. of *Arte para ligeramente saber la lengua aráviga*. New York: Hispanic Society, 1928.

Barnart, C. L. (Ed.), *The American college dictionary*. New York: Random House, 1960.

Boissière, P. *Dictionnaire analogique de la langue française: répertoire complet des mots par les idées et des idées par les mots*. (6th ed.) Paris, ca. 1890. Revised for Larousse by Charles Maquet. Paris, 1936.

Casares, J. *Diccionario ideológico de la lengua española. Desde la idea a la palabra; desde la palabra a la idea*. Barcelona: Gustavo Gili, 1942.

Crespo Pozo, J. S. *Contribución a un vocabulario castellano-gallego*. Madrid, 1963.

Cuervo, R. J. *Diccionario de construcción y régimen de la lengua castellana*. Paris, 1886–1893 (Letters *A–D*). Fragments of the section on *E-* have appeared in *Thesaurus; Boletin del Instituto Caro y Cuervo*. Bogotá, 1945.

Dal, V. I. *Tolkovyj slovar živogo velikorusskogo jazyka*. 4 Vols. (2nd ed.) 1880–1882. facs. reprod. Moscow, 1935; (3rd ed.) I. A. Baudouin-de-Courtenay (Ed.). St. Petersburg, 1903–1909.

Darmesteter, A., Hatzfeld, A., & Thomas, A. *Dictionnaire général de la langue française*. Paris, 1890–1900. (6th ed.) 1920.

Devoto, G. *Dizionari di ieri e di domani*. Biblioteca di "Lingua Nostra," VI. Florence, 1946.

Duden, K. *Der grosse Duden*. Mannheim: P. Grebe, forthcoming. See *Rechtschreibung der deutschen Sprache und der Fremdworter*. Vol. 1. 1961; *Stilworterbuch der deutschen Sprache*. Vol. 2. 1956; *Fremdworterbuch*, Vol. 5. 1960; *Etymologie: Herkunftsworterbuch der deutschen Sprache*. Vol. 7. 1963 (based on Duden's *Etymologie der neuhochdeutschen Sprache*). Cf. *The Duden pictorial encyclopedia in five languages*. New York, 1943; *The English Duden: A pictorial dictionary with English and German indexes*. Mannheim: Duden, 1960.

Grossmann, R. *Wörterbuch der deutschen und spanischen Sprache: Deutsch-spanisch.* Leipzig: B. Tauchnitz, 1932–1937. Cf. R. J. Slabý, 1932.

Littré, E. *Dictionnaire de la langue française.* 4 Vols. Paris 1863–1872; (new ed.) 1873–1877, etc.; *Supplément, suivi d'un dictionnaire étymologique de tous les mots d'origine orientale.* M. Devic (Ed.). Paris, 1877, 1892. Reprinted: 7 Vols. 1959–1961, 1962–1963. *Abrégé,* A. Beaujean (Ed.). 1960, 1964.

Malkiel, Y. Distinctive features in lexicography: a typological approach to dictionaries exemplified with Spanish. *Romance Philol.,* 1958–1959, **12**, 366–399; 1959–1960, **13**, 111–155. See also, A typological classification of dictionaries on the basis of distinctive features, included in F. W. Householder and S. Saporta (Eds.), *Internat. J. Amer. Ling.,* 1962, **4** (2, Whole No. 38), 3–24.

Meyer-Lübke, *Romanisches etymologisches wörterbuch (REW).* Heidelberg: C. Winter, 1911–1920; (rev. ed.). 1930–1935.

Migliorini, B. *Che cos'è un vocabolario?* (2nd ed.) Florence: Monnier, 1951.

Panzini, A. *Dizionario moderno delle parole che non si trovano nei dizionari comuni.* (8th ed.) rev. by A. Schiaffini & B. Migliorini. Milan: Hoepli, 1942.

Reynolds, Barbara (Ed.), *The Cambridge Italian dictionary.* Vol. I: *Italian-English.* Cambridge: Cambridge Univ. Press, 1962.

Roget, P. M. *Thesaurus of English words and phrases arranged so as to facilitate the expression of ideas* . . . (2nd ed.) London, 1853; (25th ed.) 1868; enlarged and indexed by J. L. Roget, New York, 1879; (new ed.) enlarged and revised by S. R. Roget, 1925, 1940; see also, e.g., *Everyman's thesaurus of English words and phrases,* rev. by D. C. Browning, London: Dent; New York: Dutton 1952.

Slabý, R. J. *Wörterbuch der spanischen und deutschen Sprache: Spanisch-deutsch.* Leipzig: Tauchnitz, 1932. Cf. R. Grossmann, 1932–1937.

Sledd, J. H., & Ebbitt, W. R. *Dictionaries and that dictionary: a casebook on the aims of lexicographers and the targets of reviewers.* Chicago: Scott, Foresman, 1962.

Sledd, J. H., & Kolb, Gwin J. *Dr. Johnson's dictionary: essays in the biography of a book.* Chicago: Univ. of Chicago Press, 1955.

Thorndike, E. L. *Thorndike century senior dictionary.* Chicago: Scott, Foresman, 1941.

Webster, N. *A dictionary for primary schools.* New York: Huntington, 1833.

Williams, E. B. *"Holt" Spanish and English dictionary.* New York: Holt, Rinehart & Winston, 1955.

11

Language in the Schools

RUTH G. STRICKLAND
Emeritus, Indiana University

Every child comes to school with a language. It is a complex of verbal and nonverbal signs, meaningful and acceptable in his speech community and indicative of his life experience and the person he has become. If he followed the normal pattern of 98 percent of the world's children, he learned the pronunciation system of his language by the age of 4 and will close the books on its grammatical system by about the age of 8. Vocabulary, the third aspect of his language acquisition, began while these other stages were in progress and will probably taper off, as it does for many people, by the age of 20.

Children in the elementary schools of the United States speak a wide variety of kinds and qualities of English. At no point in our national life does the multiplicity of regional and social dialects show more clearly than in the speech of these children, since every child has absorbed the dialect of his home and neighborhood. The child was fortunate if this chanced to be a standard or prestige dialect, unfortunate and perhaps forever handicapped if it was not. Regardless of what it was, he follows its grammatical rules unswervingly. Any elementary teacher who views her experience realistically recognizes that her teaching of school grammar has little or no effect on the grammar of many of her pupils; it has come too late. The child's own grammar has become habitual, and to him, it presents no obstacle, because it is identical with community custom and meets all of his recognized needs. Consequently, since it is the nature of human beings to change their comfortable, habitual behavior only when it becomes an obstacle in the path to a desired end, it is not easy to find ways to motivate a child to add to or modify his language in the direction of a school-held goal. To the child, *real* life is outside the school, not in it.

If the school is to succeed in helping children expand and improve their language, teachers need to know as much as possible about language in general and about the language of the children in their classes. Until recently, very little has been available to help teachers understand the language of children and little more to help them know what to do about it. To fill a long existing gap, two major studies of the language of elementary school children have been undertaken in recent years, one a horizontal study and the other a longitudinal study.

The first of these (Strickland, 1962), a study of the informal oral language of 575 elementary school children recorded in a relatively unstructured situation, indicates quite clearly the extent of their mastery of language. Regardless of the dialect they spoke and its relationship to standard usage, these elementary school children utilized all of the basic sentence patterns of English and showed considerable flexibility in their expansions and elaborations of these patterns. In this study of the oral language of approximately 100 children at each grade level from 1 through 6, the most frequently used pattern throughout the age range was the subject-transitive verb-object pattern, used both simply and in many types of expansion, as in the following examples:

I have a bicycle.
A hunter came in and shot the wolf.
A girl that is fourteen reads it.
They planned that, since they didn't want to go away and be separated, they'd run away.
I remember looking over the forest and wondering about it.

Sentences built about intransitive verbs appeared less frequently but took several forms:

I may go to summer school.
He works in the School of Business.
I don't care much about that.
Peter Pan's shadow started running ahead of him so he went after it.

Linking verbs were used in a variety of sentences such as the following:

That book is real good.
The rug feels funny under your feet when you walk on it.
It tasted so good I went back for seconds.
The trial wasn't fair and the king was just awful.
These aren't children, they are everybody.

The language patterns which children used with great frequency at all grade levels appear as the basic building blocks of their sentences. The fact that these basic patterns were the same at all age levels, 6 through 12 years of age, tends to validate the statement that children master the basic grammatical patterns of their language by the time they are 6 to 8 years old. They combined these basic patterns with other patterns in phonological units in a great number of ways. The fillers they used in the various slots in their sentences differed considerably in shape but did not vary greatly with the age of the child. Children at all grade levels in this study could expand and elaborate their sentences through the use of movable elements expressing time, place, manner, cause, and through the use of types of subordination.

A final step in this study was a comparison of the oral language used informally by the 575 children with the language in selected widely used reading textbooks. It was found that the language used by these children was far more advanced than the language of the books in which they were taught to read. Perhaps this is as it should be, but evidence is needed as to whether children would be aided or hindered by the use in their early textbooks of sentences more like those they use in their speech.

A study by Ruddell (1963) in which he tested the reading skill of fourth grade children with reading material built to utilize the high frequency patterns found in the oral language of children at this grade level indicated significantly greater comprehension with this material than material using the lower frequency patterns of oral language. Not only the Indiana University study but also the one accomplished by Loban at the University of California at Berkley indicate that the best measure of the maturity of a child's language appears to be his ability to expand and elaborate basic sentence patterns and to use them with a high degree of flexibility.

Loban's (1963) longitudinal study of children's language followed a group of 338 children over a seven-year period, kindergarten through sixth grade, recording a sample of speech in an interview situation each of the seven years. This was part of a thirteen-year study which followed 220 of these children from kindergarten through the twelfth grade. Loban's stratified sample of children was drawn from a population in Oakland which represented a wide ethnic range as well as the usual wide socio-economic range.

In analyzing his annual recordings of the 338 children, Loban found expansion each year in the number of words children used and in the number and length of their communication units. Most important of his findings was that it was not the patterns a child used but what he did to achieve flexibility within the patterns that proved the best measure of the child's effectiveness and control of language for his level of development. Significant also was the discovery that the children high in general language ability were also high in reading ability and the conclusion that competence in spoken language appears to be basic to competence in reading and writing.

In line with this latter conclusion by Loban was the finding of a study of the language of sixth grade children by Evertts (1962). She concluded that there was clear relationship between the structure of children's oral language and their oral reading interpretation and silent reading comprehension. Listening comprehension was also related to the kind and quality of a child's use of oral language.

In addition to his report which charted in numerous ways the variations in the language proficiency of the children in his total sample and their sensitivity to the conventions of language, Loban (1965) has called attention to examples of nonstandard oral usage among his High Caucasian, Low Caucasian, and Negro groups. In enumerating children's problems with oral usage, he found that the difficulties of subjects speaking standard English tended to be matters of sensitivity to clarity and precision of communication rather than errors of usage. Among subjects speaking a lower social class dialect, the most troublesome problems related to the use of verbs, particularly the verb *to be*, although these children also needed help with coherence.

Verb problems in Loban's groups were most evident in lack of agreement of subject and verb, omission of the verb *to be* or of auxilliary verbs together with nonstandard use of verb forms and inconsistency in the use of tense. These were not disputed items such as *It's me* but clear deviations from standard English such as:

The calf don't want no milk.
He has ate.
They was here yesterday.
She bes my best friend.

Pronoun problems were next in order with examples such as:

Her went to town.
He go he house.

Clearly, the great need of elementary school children whose usage and syntax are nonstandard is opportunity to hear and use standard forms until they sound right when the child hears them and feel right when he says them. These children have well-developed language learning skills which they have demonstrably put to use. People who emphasize the value of teaching a foreign language to children beginning at the age of 8 or 9, earlier where school conditions permit, use as their major justification for starting at this age the fact that children learn easily by ear and that their speech is still flexible, so that they can learn proper sound sequences and intonation. Yet all too often these very people want to improve children's nonstandard English in a classroom in which the children are rarely permitted to talk by teaching the formal grammar of the scholar, more often still the old borrowed Latinate grammar but increasingly now a formal, highly systematic approach to the structural or transformational grammar as recently devised by certain linguistic scholars. Good though some of this systematic study may be, it is not the major need of the children whose usage is nonstandard. They need oral experience in quantity and all of it of the practical sort which they can learn to apply in the actual situations of life.

Martin Joos (1964) has said of children's grammatical errors:

When a child is said to speak "ungrammatically" the fact is always that he is obeying a vast number of grammatical rules, a very small fraction of which happen to be different grammar rules from the ones that the critic subscribes to. The critic does not notice, for the reason already given, that the child is obeying any rules at all. For that vast majority in which there is identity between the child's grammar and the critic's grammar, the critic notices no rules because there is no conflict; in that small minority of all the rules for which there is conflict instead of identity, the critic notices only the conflict and does not recognize that the child's pattern has its own logic and is part of a different grammar just as rigid as the critic's own. Hence the critic says that the child has no grammar at all, when in fact he has just as much grammar as anybody, very little of it non-standard [p. 206].

The "errors" of the child whose language faults are at the level of *Who do you want?* and *He gave it to John and I* frequently yield readily to ear-tuning experience, as do the problems of the little child who is striving for more verb consistency than English permits him when he says, "Look what I brang you! I runned and runned so I wouldn't be late." The grammatical and usage problems of the more handicapped child who uses the *Me and him ain't got none* level of English will yield less readily to mere listening and imitation techniques but those will be necessary if he is to change his speech patterns. Some of the direct pattern practice of foreign language teaching is often most helpful until the child's ear and speech accept and reproduce patterns easily. The Negro child who says "He go he house" knows nothing of verb inflections and pronouns for the third person singular. His need is for comfortable freedom to use the language he knows, even encouragement to use it in every possible way, while he is given quantities of experience in listening to better usage and practice with the intonation and flow of oral English in choral reading of poetry and in dramatic play and role playing.

Many of the language problems Loban has isolated in his study are problems of social class dialect, not regional dialect, and are a special concern of the school because they tend to be of a kind which can handicap even the brightest and most capable people as they strive toward social and economic opportunity and acceptance. Actually, dialect problems may have both social and regional aspects, e.g., in Appalachian, Louisiana Cajun, and Hawaiian pidgin, or may involve people who must learn English as a second language—the American Indians, Spanish, and Oriental groups. Closed societies have tended to use language as a means of social control and have set up their schools accordingly. In this country, school systems seek to diminish this element of social control by helping disadvantaged children learn to use a prestige dialect alongside their own.

Both Loban (1963) in his study of substandard dialects used by children of varying social and ethnic backgrounds in Oakland and Bernstein (1960), in his study of London Cockney speech, have come to believe that a basic difference between these dialects and standard or prestige dialects is the failure of the former to use the potential of the language. These researchers found the basic grammatical structure of sentences to be the same at all levels. Speakers from lower socioeconomic groups, however, made no use of devices for expressing clear thinking about cause and effect, subjective reactions of feeling and emotion, and the nuances of ideas. They lacked the repertoire, possessed by more effective users of language, which would enable them to extend and amplify basic sentence patterns. Their limitations stem from the fact that language in disadvantaged homes tends to be used only in objective concrete situations and kept at the barest minimum for communication. Compensatory education, therefore, calls for a great deal of oral language and stimulation of every possible sort to encourage children to expand their use of language and to employ it in new ways. Since this development will have to take place in the child's own language, Loban strongly recommends that teachers ignore usage problems for a time while they work to help children explore the possibilities of language and find satisfaction in new uses of it.

On the basis of his intensive study of children's language, Loban (1963) concludes that what must be done in schools, beginning in preschool and kindergarten, is to persuade disadvantaged pupils to talk as much as possible. The teachers' questions can encourage these children to grapple with ideas and thus to amplify and embroider these ideas, foresee consequences, and learn to follow through with thinking "If this—then what?" or "Why?" Older children in later grades who speak a nonstandard dialect will not be ready to give attention to grammar and to study the structure of sentences until they can use language freely for a wide variety of purposes.

Increasingly, teachers have come to realize that to criticize the language a child learned in his home is to cut off all motivation for learning something better. The first requisite for helping a pupil of any age to improve his language is respect for the language he uses. This does not mean that teachers fail to recognize their obligation to raise the level of the pupil's language. It means that they put first things first. Attention can be called to the fact that people do not all speak in the same way and that the same individual may speak differently at different times and for different purposes. The mass media as well as the subjects pursued in school can be drawn upon for examples.

Through the literature program children can be led to see that differences in the dialects of other times and places add interest to English and do not, of themselves, present problems of communication or handicap their users. Young children are introduced to older forms of expression and obsolete words through Mother Goose and the old folktales. They meet British expressions in the poems of Robert Louis Stevenson, A. A. Milne, and Walter de la Mare. They encounter regional dialects in the United States through the tall tales of the westward movement, the stories of Uncle Remus, and the poems of James Whitcomb Riley. Older children are made aware of earlier forms of English expression through the stories of Robin Hood and

King Arthur and of regional dialects in America through *Johnny Tremain* and *Tom Sawyer*. They come to recognize the regional flavor in the dialects of Presidents Roosevelt, Truman, Eisenhower, Kennedy, and Johnson through recordings as well as television and radio broadcasts.

The social studies program offers innumerable opportunities to give attention to the relationship of language to life in the United States. All too often, however, children study the history of their community or region with no attention to the language backgrounds of the early settlers and builders who established the community and left their imprint through the place names and customs they brought to it. A study of American history is incomplete without attention to the language of Captain John Smith's Virginians, the Puritans of New England, the Dutch of New Amsterdam, the Quakers of Pennsylvania, the Germans who came to the Midwest, the Scandinavians of Minnesota, and the residue of language left by the French explorers of the Mississippi Valley, the French settlers of Louisiana, and the Spanish explorers of the Southwest.

Through attention to current happenings in the United States and the world, both younger children and older students are made aware of the significance of language in the world today. Almost any issue of the newspaper tells of the efforts of statesmen to solve major world problems through face-to-face talk. The work of the Congress and the courts as well as civic, fraternal, and social organizations is conducted through oral language and presented to the American people through newscasts over television and radio as well as through leaflets, newspapers, and magazines. By the time children have reached the fifth or sixth grade they can be made aware of the quality and kind of language in which this work is done and begin to recognize the need to add this dialect to their own language stock. They can understand increasingly as they grow older that home and local dialects which may be adequate there can close the doors to social and economic opportunity in a wider setting.

It is at this point that the school's persistent efforts to surround the child with standard English begin to bear fruit. If the child has grown in the meantime in power to express in his own dialect a wide range of reactions and interests and has had experience in speaking better English in situations which called for it, he can now begin to work intensively to attain the universally acceptable dialect, because he understands the need for it and the personal advantages it offers him.

Adults to not consciously change their language as they move into new and wider speech communities but almost invariably time and prolonged contact with a new regional speech bring some modification of the original speech in the direction of that of the new community. It is said that another decade of television and radio listening may cause the speech of the average American to resemble more closely what has come to be called "network English," the required standard broadcasting dialect with no strong regional characteristics. If it is true that adults are influenced by the language they hear, it is even more true of children. Thus, if the teacher is a person whom children respect and admire, perhaps even love, and if the atmosphere of the classroom is one of mutual respect, children absorb quite effortlessly some of the language of the school. Consequently, when the time comes that children can recognize their need for standard English, increasing emphasis can be placed on the need for practice in using this language, and this only, at school.

Obviously, not all children come to school with nonstandard English. Some have known throughout their lives only the kind of English the school is responsible for teaching. American public interest has a way of concentrating on one cause at a time and swinging from it to a new concern as national or local happenings point the way. The impact of Russia's sputnik caused a wave of interest in gifted children and nationwide emphasis on recognizing them and providing educational programs to challenge their potentialities. Concern for the culturally disadvantaged and integration of the races occupy stage center at the moment. But the schools have not laid aside their interest in the children whose background and ability make possible a superior program of language development. Nor have they forgotten all the children in between—the mythical average.

Oral language is the first essential for every individual. Unfortunately, teachers, curriculum makers, and textbook authors forget this all too often. The writer's visits to classrooms in several states reveal that many teachers are quite unaware of how little opportunity they allow for children to talk. In many schools, the language program is completely textbook- and workbook-centered and deals in material some of which is of little consequence for language learning. The starting point for any good language program must, of necessity, be the language of the pupils in the class.

It is also clear that much more needs to be done to link language with thinking. Teachers who are aware of the importance of inductive thinking, the usefulness of categories, the power of analogies, and what it means to generalize will be teachers who are more likely to elicit language for such purposes. Not only *what* and *when* but also *suppose that . . . what if? . . . why? . . .* will be the approach of teachers in all areas of the curriculum, not just in language arts or English (Loban, 1966, p. 72).

Inasmuch as language is essentially oral, schools need to give more attention to oral language—not, of course, encouraging mere talk and chatter but rather emphasizing what might be called thinking on one's feet —learning to organize ideas in group discussion, to cleave to the heart of a topic, to make progress with ideas, and to generalize when enough illustrations have been given. Pupils in such situations will learn how to retreat gracefully from untenable positions, to be tentative but forceful in presenting ideas, to welcome differences of opinion, and to realize that one should have the courage to present minority opinion so that the group may have access to all sides of an issue. Loban found all pupils in need of experience which would help them develop sensitivity to clarity and precision in their use of language. This should receive major emphasis in a program for children who speak standard English.

Class work in social studies, science, and mathematics abounds in opportunities for such concentration. Problems and explanations of processes in mathematics call for economy of words and clear, precise statement. Science experiments must be explained accurately. Social studies content must be presented with care and precision lest it be distorted or misinterpreted. However, it is through the study of literature that young people of all ages come to appreciate the richness and power of their language. They learn how words can be used to create moods, paint pictures, develop empathy, incite action, and trace human growth and development. The language of the home, community, even the school and the textbooks serves practical, workaday purposes, while in literature language is used with artistry. The more children hear of good literature in the elementary grades and the more deeply they study it in later years, the more respect they have for the possibilities of their language.

Study of language as a human phenomenon, what it is, how it operates, and how it grows and changes, warrants increasing attention from kindergarten through graduate school. A good language program in the elementary school should put children well on the way to understanding language through the gradual development of concepts such as these:

1. Language is a system of sounds.
2. The sounds convey meaning only when put together in patterns of words and sentences.
3. The patterns of sound convey meaning to people who know the language.
4. Pitch, stress, and juncture are a part of the sound system of the language and help to convey meaning.
5. The sounds and their connection with the things they represent are purely arbitrary.
6. The sounds of a language are put together in characteristic designs; these designs can be composed of a great variety of fillers.
7. A language changes as people have new experiences; old words may be given new meanings and new uses.
8. Likewise, old words are dropped and new words are coined of old parts to represent new meanings and modifications of old ones [Strickland, 1965, pp. 7–8].

Classroom work at all age levels abounds in opportunities to introduce and to reinforce these concepts, but to recognize the opportunities and to capitalize on them, teachers must have a clear understanding of language and of the concepts to be developed.

The first five concepts can be developed simultaneously in a variety of situations. Young children are intrigued to learn that the dog they are talking about would be called 'le chien' in French, 'der Hund' in German, or 'el perro' in Spanish or that the *thank you* they are reminded to say would be 'danke schön', 'merci', or 'arigato' in German, French, or Japanese. Even elementary knowledge of another language can be put to use at many points if the teacher sees value in doing so. Opportunities arise in social studies, science, and particularly in spelling to call attention to the fact that English is an inveterate borrower of words from other languages. An increasing number of schools offer a systematic program of foreign languages from fourth or sixth grade, occasionally from kindergarten through high school. These reinforce basic concepts regarding language.

The ways in which the suprasegmentals of pitch, stress, and juncture function as part of the sound system of the language intrigues even young children. A simple question such as *What are you doing?* can carry at least five different meanings depending on the use of pitch and stress and the silent language of facial expression, gesture, and bodily stance. The pitch of a speaker's voice signals a question or a statement. *When are you going home?* ends with a rising intonation, while the answer, *In a few minutes*, ends with a falling intonation. The exclamation *Now!* might be either a statement or a question, depending on the pitch employed. The sentence *While we were eating, Mother told us a story* can be ridiculous if the pause after eating is omitted. Even high school students may read orally very poorly unless they recognize which words in a sentence must be kept clotted together and which separated by pauses of varying degree. Clearly, recognition of the function of pitch, stress, and juncture as conveyors of meaning is important to spoken English as well as to oral reading and its interpretation. Also, the better the reader understands the function of the suprasegmentals, the greater is his comprehension in silent reading.

In their report on "The Basic Issues in the Teaching of English" (1959), representatives of four scholarly organizations stated:

A knowledge of traditional English grammar is sometimes considered an intellectual discipline and a social necessity. Accordingly, over the past century, grammar has been taught in thousands of classrooms, but with little apparent effect upon the written or spoken language of many pupils. Perhaps it was naive to expect it, in terms of what we know today about the language learning process; but in any event, new approaches to this problem may be worth considering.

The descriptive linguists offer one such possibility. In place of the schoolbook grammar of past generations, quite adequate for describing Latin and Greek but not so adaptable to an analysis of English, they provide a descriptive technique which attempts to achieve scientific rigor and precision by concentrating upon the contrastive patterns of form and arrangement characteristic of the structure of the language.

. . . we must ask whether this new method offers a clue to a better correlation of the knowledge of language structure with writing ability [p. 9].

Some of the structural and transformational approaches to grammar recently proposed by linguists are being taught in junior and senior high schools and appear to result in clearer understanding of the structure of

English sentences. Little has been done with these approaches in the elementary school and almost no practical help is yet available to elementary teachers. There is reason to believe that some of what Chomsky and his followers, as well as the structuralists, are offering may be of considerably more value to younger children than what is now being given them in the elementary school. Inherent in children and young people are two types of motivation on which a program can be built: they enjoy manipulating language, and they like to know concretely how forces in their environment, including language, operate though they do not respond well to technical abstractions.

The grammar children know when they enter school has been learned intuitively. They are not aware of knowing it, but they are thoroughly attuned to the sentence patterns that are typical of their language. A sequence of words such as *The boy told his mother about the accident* will be accepted as a proper statement whereas a sequence such as *His mother the boy the accident about told* would be considered amusing and unacceptable. In this sense, they can distinguish sentences from nonsentences, though they would not consider such a response as *All by himself* a nonsentence even though it is structurally incomplete.

Study of some of the language textbooks in wide use in elementary schools reveals that definitions of sentence and parts of speech appear early. Typical are definitions which state that "a sentence expresses a complete thought" and "a verb is an action word." Some textbooks series offer children simplified or interim terms, such as "naming word" and "action word" instead of noun and verb. Children who talk glibly about space capsules, auxilliary rockets, and supersonic speeds prefer correct names for things and have little need for juvenile aids. Increasing amounts of time are spent in succeeding grades on the teaching of formal grammar, yet all of it is repeated in the junior high school.

Children's concepts of the things and ideas they encounter develop without benefit to definitions. All who have been talked and read to at home know what a word is. They develop their first concept of "sentence" in kindergarten or first grade when the teacher says, as she writes the children's stories from their dictation, "Let me write this sentence first, and then I'll be ready for your next sentence." Their concept of sentence is nebulous and incomplete, but it meets the need at the time without encumbering the children with explanations they cannot understand. The concept will be expanded through further experience and can be defined inductively in later years when the children have the background and are ready for abstractions.

Chomsky's (1957) concept of kernel sentences appears a logical one with which to begin the study of the structure of English sentences. Research reveals that children use the three basic sentence structures at an early age. Sentences with transitive verbs appear to predominate in their talk, though intransitive and linking verbs are used freely. As early as third grade, teachers can call the attention of native speakers of standard English to a sentence kernel and guide them in putting other words into each of its basic slots. Sentences taken fresh from the lips of children are more interesting to work with than sentences in a textbook or workbook. By fifth grade, attention can be called to subject and predicate positions and the kinds of words which fit each position.

Some teachers are experimenting with the expansion of sentences through encouraging children to add elements expressing *what*, *when*, *where*, *why*, or *how* to the basic pattern and noticing at what points each can be used. Children are interested to discover which elements are movable and whether placing them in different positions affects emphasis or meaning. During the course of this, the traditional names are given to the various parts of speech as attention is called to certain words in the sentences. Children may test different verbs, adjectives, or adverbs in a sentence in an effort to present meaning clearly, accurately, and vividly. The grammatical terminology is incidental, but increased experience with it deepens understanding of the function of each category. Concepts of determiners, qualifiers, form words, and structure words can be introduced as they are useful.

All of the work with grammar must be done orally if it is to take root and function, since power in oral language is basic to the development of power in reading and writing. Poor reading is all too frequently caused by inability to comprehend and to interpret sentences, and no child writes better sentences than he can speak. The extent to which work with grammar profits a child or a group depends on their individual language needs and on the skill of the teacher in meeting those needs.

Transformational grammar is still new to elementary teachers and untried in many schools. No research evidence regarding its value is yet available and cannot be until teachers themselves learn more about modern concepts of grammar and devise a variety of ways of teaching them. Unfortunately, a few scholars having only recently caught onto transformational grammar themselves, rushed into print with textbooks for the elementary school. It seems reasonable to assume that no linguistics scholar is ready to give Zeusian birth to a full-fledged program until his ideas have been tried out in many schools with many types of children. The teaching of traditional grammar has been of small value. The possibilities of transformational grammar appear promising, but there is no clear evidence at the present time that it will do more for speech and writing than traditional grammar has done. The questions of what grammar, how much, when, and for whom all remain to be answered. Scholars in linguistics, specialists in elementary English, and classroom teachers will have to work together to find the answers. No one of them can do it alone.

The available textbooks designed to teach modern grammar in the junior and senior high schools are being used in an increasing number of schools. In practically every instance, this grammar is being superimposed on the beginnings in traditional grammar made in the elementary school. There is no record of a modern program which has been used consistently through the three school levels, nor is the evidence clear on values in the high school as they affect the speaking and writing of students. Action research by teachers in many classrooms is badly needed. One may wisely hope that enough of this can be done before systematic, controlled research comparisons are made to prevent the death of good possibilities before they have a chance to develop.

While children are giving attention to the characteristic designs in which words are arranged to express meaning in English, they can also be made aware of the changing nature of language. This is most easily done through attention to vocabulary. Each new unit of subject matter which is taught in any of the basic subjects introduces pupils to new vocabulary which they learn to understand and use in the context that requires it. To the basic vocabulary of 2500 or more words of a typical 6-year-old, at least a thousand more words are added each year. The accretion may in many instances be far greater than that because of contact with mass media and the wider experience which many modern parents provide for their children to supplement the work of the school.

Both children and teenagers can become interested, even excited, over watching for newly coined words which are created to meet new needs. A profusion of examples results from space exploration as well as from the rapid development of new concepts, processes, and products in many of the sciences. A list of words new since the last world war would fill many pages. Older students would be interested in the structure of such words as *astronaut*, *cosmonaut*, and its latest companion, *aquanaut*. Even fourth-graders could understand the coining of *telstar* through noting other words they know beginning with the syllable *tel*.

Dictionary study includes attention to changes in word meaning over periods of time and to sources of borrowed words. Any group would be interested in listing new words which do not yet appear in dictionaries and considering which are necessary because no existing words serve the same purpose, which, though not absolutely necessary are truly useful because they express a concept economically, as is true of *baby sitter* or *rambunctious*, and which are modern "hip" talk which will almost certainly change rapidly and which sets its users apart from the cultural mainstream.

Junior and senior high school English programs are giving increasing attention to introducing students to the history of English and the relationship of language and languages in the lives of countries and people. The more students know about language and its relationship to life, the more interest many of them take in refining their own language and expanding its usefulness. Interest in language and people leads them into interest in foreign languages and the cultures of the people who use them.

The last of the language skills which children achieve is, of course, writing. This is probably the point at which the teaching of the schools is most vulnerable to criticism. Members of the National Council of Teachers of English are giving attention to the problem at all levels. Both controlled and action research are going on in various places to determine not only what and how pupils write but what kind of help they need to improve writing. Some of the Project English studies financed by the U.S. Office of Education are designed to teach writing as an outgrowth of the study of literature. The programs centered in the Universities of Wisconsin and Nebraska are examples of this.

A recent study by Hunt (1965) at Florida State University of the grammatical structures used by pupils of grades 4, 8, and 12 provides significant information about structures used by a restricted population in 1000 words each of school writing. His unit of study, the *T*-unit, is exactly equivalent to the phonological unit used by Loban in his study of oral language. Hunt found that lengthening of sentence units was closely tied to level of maturity. Younger students produced short separate units because their span of grammatical concern or attention was narrow. As the students matured, there was consolidation which discarded needless words, lessened redundancy, and added succinctness. Growth, as Hunt (1965, p. 144) sees it, may move through the stages he illustrates in the example which follows. A fourth grade child might write

The sailor finally came on deck. He was tall. He was rather ugly. He had a limp. He had offered them the prize.

A more mature writer might have reduced the five units, averaging 5.4 words each, to three units by coordinating two of them with *and*:

He was tall and rather ugly and had a limp.

A still more mature version, such as might be written by an able older student, might combine the five original sentences into one, such as:

The tall, rather ugly sailor with a limp, who had offered them the prize, finally came on deck.

One wonders whether extended contact with the short, abnormal sentences of the typical early reading textbooks has caused younger children to write sentences which they would never speak. Research is needed here also, to determine whether the sentence units written by younger children are the result of the difficulty of the writing task or the result of the early conditioning to "primerese" as writing model. Further study of sequences of growth in the acquisition of writing skill are badly needed. The present interest in such studies has long been overdue.

Whether a program is one of secondary school English which is said to have three components—language, literature, and composition—or one of elementary school English, commonly called the language arts, whose components are listening, speaking, reading, and writing, with spelling, hand-writing, grammar, and children's literature as parts of the constellation, language is both the subject and the medium of operation. The current nationwide interest in what the schools can do to teach the significance of language, what it is, how it operates, and in what forms and styles it can best serve the individual and collective good augurs well for the future.

REFERENCES

Bernstein, B. Language and social class. *Brit. J. Sociol.*, 1960, **11**, 271–276.

The basic issues in the teaching of English. Definitions and clarifications from a series of conferences sponsored by American Studies Association, College English Association, Modern Language Association, and National Council of Teachers of English. Supplement to *Element. Eng.*, 1959, **36**, No. 6; and *Eng. J.*, 1959, **48**, No. 6.

Chomsky, N. *Syntactic structures*. New York: Gregory Lunz, 1957.

Evertts, E. *An investigation of the structure of children's oral language compared with silent reading, oral reading and listening comprehension*. Unpublished doctoral dissertation, Indiana University, 1962.

Hunt, K. W. *Grammatical structures written at three grade levels. NCTE Res. Report No. 3*. Champaign, Ill.: NCTE, 1965.

Joos, M. Language and the school child. *Harvard educ. Rev.*, 1964, **34**, No. 2.

Loban, W. *The language of elementary school children. NCTE Res. Report No. 1*. Champaign, Ill.: NCTE, 1963.

Loban, W. *Problems in oral English. NCTE Res. Report No. 5*. Champaign, Ill.: NCTE, 1965. (a)

Loban, W. A sustained program of language learning. *Language programs for the disadvantaged*. Report of the NCTE Task Force on Teaching English to the Disadvantaged. Champaign, Ill.: NCTE, 1965. Pp. 221–231. (b)

Loban, W. What language reveals. In *Language and meaning*. Washington: Association for Supervision and Curriculum Development, National Education Association, 1966.

Ruddell, R. B. *An investigation of the effect of the similarity of oral and written patterns of language structure on reading comprehension*. Unpublished doctoral dissertation, Indiana University, 1963.

Strickland, R. G. The language of elementary school children: its relationship to the language of reading textbooks and the quality of reading of selected children. *School Educ. Bull.*, Indiana Univ., 1962, **38**, 1–131.

Strickland, R. G. The contribution of structural linguistics to the teaching of reading, writing, and grammar in the elementary school. *School Educ. Bull.*, Indiana Univ., 1965, **40**, 7–8.

12

Second-Language Teaching

ROBERT LADO
Georgetown University

While retaining some of its pre-World War II grammar-translation features, second-language teaching today consists largely of the wartime and postwar linguistic practices, refined and expanded since the enactment of the NDEA (National Defense Education Act) in 1958, along with the first applications of transformational linguistics. The dominant views of earlier periods have left their imprint on the present and point to future developments that merit close study.

The pre-war scene of grammar translation and reading objectives that produced the Coleman report (1929) was shattered by a revolutionary change brought on by the challenge of World War II and by the then new structural linguistics. This change was put into practice in the intensive language-and-area courses of the ASTP (Army Specialized Training Program) and CATS (Army's Civil Affairs Training Schools). The application of linguistics to English as a foreign language was also effected at this time under Fries (1945) and his associates at the English Language Institute of the University of Michigan.

The change was not simply a different method of teaching but a new view of language, its structure and role. The prewar view was a mixture of the grammar-translation concept described in the *Report of the Committee of Twelve* (Thomas, 1901) and the reading proposals of the Coleman study. The Committee of Twelve was appointed by the Modern Language Association of America in 1892 to advise the National Education Association on curriculum and methods. It gave as its objectives "the higher ends of linguistic scholarship and literary culture" and rejected the ability to converse as an important aim. Linguistic scholarship was actually philological knowledge of the kind that might eventually result in editing and annotating some older literary text. Literary culture meant translating for comprehension some of the classics. This objective gave rise to the possibility of reading the classics in translation, thus largely eliminating the need for foreign language study, but the suggestion was countered by pointing out the values of reading the classics in the original and of studying the grammar of a literary language in order to develop the ability to think straight. The advantages of going to the original might be questioned on grounds of the poor understanding that accompanies imperfect knowledge of the language, but the straight thought argument was not questioned. Good language form was found in the style of written masterpieces; conversational forms were considered inferior or not worthy of study.

The grammatical tradition of the grammar-translation method required the conjugation of verbs, declension of nouns, and memorization of grammar rules. "He knows Latin who can conjugate and decline well," went the saying, and conjugating and declining meant reciting by heart in fixed order the various forms of tenses and cases. Whether or not the student could use these forms habitually in connected discourse was of no apparent interest. In the modern languages, any student who came to class with a speaking knowledge acquired abroad or at home was quickly disabused of any thought that he knew the language; he had to recite the tenses and cases by technical name.

This view reflected the broader social fact that education was the mark and privilege of a select few, and after all, anybody could converse, but only a select few could translate a classic or recite the tenses and cases. There is nothing trivial about experiencing the classics in the original—restricted as this objective appears, now that we aim to use the language for communication—but it was not being accomplished. Deciphering Caesar or Cervantes word for word by thumbing the dictionary to form precarious, malformed translations a few lines a day is hardly reading or experiencing the classics.

With the advent of mass education, a general dissatisfaction with the methods and objectives of modern language teaching led to the Modern Foreign Language Study, a series of investigations on methods, tests, word counts, syntax, and idiom lists, conducted from 1923 to 1927. The Coleman report was the most vigorously discussed volume of the eighteen published as a result of the study, and it advocated a limited reading knowledge as the only attainable goal. This resulted in a reading method, which shifted emphasis from translation of good literature to partial comprehension of simplified texts. Although widely discussed, in practice it merely resulted in the addition of simplified readers which were often translated for comprehension as before. Where grammar was studied, the grammar part of the grammar-translation method remained intact.

This then was the grammar-translation scene before the challenge of World War II and the linguistic revolution it introduced.

World War II brought together (*a*) the need for large numbers of people who could speak and understand foreign languages and (b) the new theory of linguistics which had been developed by Edward Sapir, Leonard Bloomfield, and their associates for the analysis of American Indian languages which had no written tradition.

The need was plain: oral competence for the deployment of the Armed Forces in geographic areas where knowledge of the spoken local language was vital. Needed were Japanese, Turkish, Thai, Russian, Burmese, and other languages for which there were no pedagogical materials or teaching experience in the United States. The Armed Forces turned to the ACLS (American Council of Learned Societies) which, through one of its constituent associations, the LSA (Linguistic Society of America), was able to guide them in their search for linguists.

A small group of American linguists had been working with American Indian informants, transcribing their utterances in phonetic and phonemic writing, to determine the phonology, morphology, and syntax of a variety of indigenous languages spoken on this continent. They were writing and discussing not only descriptions of the languages themselves, but more importantly, their theories of language analysis, and they were consciously bringing their theories together to form a science of linguistics.

When the call came to teach foreign languages intensively to the armed services, they were ready for the task. With their new knowledge and experience, they sought native-speaking informants who could be drill masters and whose utterances the linguists then analyzed as they taught the language.

This linguistic approach to second-language teaching was in sharp contrast with the grammar-translation-reading methods of the prewar period with respect to objectives, languages taught, methods and materials, as well as the intensity and theory of language learning. The new objectives were to speak and understand colloquial conversational speech used by native speakers. Therefore, the students were required to speak and listen at normal conversational speed with all its contractions and reductions. To these linguists, language was speech, and writing, a partial, conventional representation of speech. Where the two differed, speech was the norm. This contrasted sharply with the older view, which considered the written classics as the norm.

To the linguists, any language was as good as any other, and the teaching of literary languages such as French, German, and Spanish was undertaken on the same basis as the so-called primitive or nonliterary languages. To them, all languages have grammar, their own grammar, whether it be heavily inflected as in Latin and Russian or lightly inflected as in Chinese. The older view could not accept all languages as equal. The literary languages had to be taught for their literature, and primitive languages, alas, had no written literature.

To the linguists, a language was a set of habits internalized in the nervous system of its native speakers. Consequently, to learn a second language the student had to internalize through overlearning the set of habits of the second language. He did this by memorizing basic sentences and reciting them by heart. Bloomfield (1942) put it this way in his *Outline Guide for the Practical Study of Foreign Languages*: "The command of a language is not a matter of knowledge: the speakers are quite unable to describe the habits which make up their language. The command of a language is a matter of practice [p. 12]." This too was in sharp disagreement with the grammar-translation view. The student's role was to analyze the classics and make commentaries on them, to talk *about* their language.

The materials were drastically different also. The linguistic ones had dialogues and basic sentences for memorization (overlearning), notes on pronunciation and aids to listening, grammatical descriptions clarifying the structure of the material overlearned, and exercises for the manipulation of the basic sentences through various changes. The grammar-translation materials had vocabulary lists for study, grammar rules, conjugations and declensions for memorization, and excerpts for translation.

The linguistic breakthrough, in which the idea of language as speech, as a set of habits to be internalized through overlearning of dialogues and basic sentences, as a structure system with its own grammar to be mastered in use rather than talked about, was coupled with the intensity and length of the armed forces courses (servicemen studied nothing but language all day with native informants under the direction of a linguist for nine to eighteen months)—all this, sparked by the fever pitch of wartime motivation, produced dramatic results. Americans, who traditionally had been considered deaf to languages, spoke them fluently in record time. The materials developed by linguists for the ASTP were later published by the Henry Holt Co. as the *Spoken Language Series*.

During this same time, Charles Fries was able to apply the new linguistics to the teaching of English to foreign professionals and students at the University of Michigan. In his *Teaching and Learning English as a Foreign Language* (1945), he formulated clearly the structural treatment of the sound system of a second language, including its intonation, against the background of the learner's native language habits. He defined the learning of a second language linguistically as mastering the use of the sound system and the grammatical patterns in speaking and listening within a limited vocabulary, a definition which is still useful today. And he explored the areas of cultural difference that needed to be learned with the language. This attention to the native language background of the learner was coupled with minimal use of the native language itself in the classroom and the rejection of translation as an exercise.

In line with this linguistic rationale, *The Intensive Course in English for Latin American Students* was prepared, which has had a profound influence on all the teaching of English as a foreign language to this day. Kenneth L. Pike contributed the pronunciation-intonation lessons and published separately (1945) *The Intonation of American English*, his structural analysis of the suprasegmental features of English.

The postwar experience in second-language teaching is summarized by Moulton (1961) in "Linguistics and Language Teaching in the U.S. 1940–1960." A strong core of the linguists who had devised the wartime courses moved to Cornell University and continued the linguistic tradition under a less intensive college program. Later, Henry Lee Smith, Jr., and G. L. Trager established this same linguistic tradition at the Foreign Service Institute of the Department of State. The English Language Institute at Michigan continued implementing and extending its theory of pattern practice, sentence patterns, and language testing.

The controversy between the linguistic view and the grammar-translation tradition continued unabated, with the latter rejecting the validity of the wartime experience in the regular academic programs of high schools and colleges. In an attempt to settle the controversy objectively, an investigation of second-language teaching was conducted at Chicago, in which the achievements of oral and traditional classes in different types of schools were compared. The results, published by Agard and Dunkel (1948) and Dunkel (1948), were inconclusive, partly because of the inherent weakness of experimental control in these large-scale experiments and partly because of difficulties in testing the oral skills. The essential differences, that is, in the new view of linguistic structure—emphasis on the contrastive features of native and foreign languages, the internalization of a new set of linguistic habits through pattern practice, etc.—were not sufficiently taken into account when the groups were divided into experimental-oral and control-traditional for the investigation, as was soon pointed out by Fries (1949).

A major nonlinguistic development of the postwar period was the appearance and commercial production of tape recorders and their integration into language laboratories, a development most successfully pursued at the Georgetown University Institute of Languages and Linguistics. Although phonographs and courses on records had been available earlier, it was now the versatile tape recorder in the hands of the linguist that became a major tool in second-language teaching. The tool was so obviously useful and so easily accessible to the nonprofessional that it was often grossly oversold and indiscriminately employed without the essential linguistic control that made it useful and effective. The controversy over proper use of the ever more elaborate electronic laboratory still rages today, with technology running rampant, without effective control on the part of linguists and language teachers. Constructive statements on proper uses and standards for language laboratories are available, however, in Hutchinson (1961), Hayes (1963), and Stack (1966) among others.

Two linguistic publications of the early fifties had a strong influence on applied English linguistics of the postwar period: *An Outline of English*

Structure by George L. Trager and Henry Lee Smith, Jr. (1951), and *The Structure of English: An Introduction to the Construction of English Sentences* by Charles C. Fries (1952). The publication of the *Outline* caused a major flurry of discussion and activity. Trager and Smith added an analysis of juncture, accepted Pike's structural analysis of intonation, restated the morphological outline of English, and suggested how English syntax might be analyzed in similar terms.

The *Outline* was soon followed by a series of ten English textbooks adapted to speakers of Burmese, Mandarin Chinese, Greek, Indonesian, Korean, Persian, Serbo-Croation, Thai, Turkish, and Vietnamese, with Martin Joos as publication editor. A pamphlet by William E. Welmers (1953) gave general suggestions for the use of the textbooks by teachers. These books used the phonemic analysis and transcription of the *Outline* and other elements from a "General Form" compiled by several linguists for the purpose and published as *Structural Notes and Corpus: A Basis for the Preparation of Materials to Teach English as a Foreign Language* (1952).

Almost simultaneous with the *Outline*'s appearance was the publication of *The Structure of English* by Fries, which marked a significant advance in the description and explanation of English sentences. It described English syntax as patterns of function words and form classes into which speakers cast the lexical items of the language to form their statements, questions, requests, and calls. These patterns were represented by strings of symbols which brought out the critical differences between questions and statements, requests and calls, etc. Thus, greater generality was provided for the general patterns and a more differentiating structure for the subpatterns. The contrastive study of English and other languages for pedagogical purposes was now made possible at a more effective level.

The impact of *The Structure of English* by Fries and *An Outline of English Structure* by Trager and Smith was shown by the subsequent appearance of a series of English grammars by Roberts (1956), Lloyd and Warfel (1956), Francis (1958), and others whose syntax followed almost entirely that of Fries and whose phonology was that of Trager and Smith.

It was the syntax that formed the basis for the revised edition of *The Intensive Course in English* edited by Fries and Lado under the separate titles of *English Sentence Patterns* and *English Pattern Practices*. Here the concept of pattern practice was fully developed as a manipulation of the patterns with shift of attention away from its mechanics by means of substitution, transformation, expansion, and other variations. It was these works and the *Outline* by Trager and Smith that have especially influenced the foreign language materials of the NDEA period. Lado's *Linguistics Across Cultures* (1957) also helped many teachers of English and foreign languages to understand the value and importance of this approach to linguistics by showing in nontechnical style how to contrast the target and native languages for pedagogical purposes.

The conviction that postwar linguistic experience was not finding its way into the mainstream of texts and classroom practices and that rather a wide split remained between the linguistic movement (except for English as a foreign language) and the teaching of foreign languages, led to the Foreign Language Program of the MLA. Initiated in 1952, it brought together foreign language teachers and linguists and resulted in highly positive accomplishments, two of which in particular had far-reaching effects culminating in a statement on "Qualifications for Secondary School Teachers of Modern Foreign Languages" (1955) and the "Conference on Criteria for a College Textbook in Beginning Spanish" (1956), both of which contributed, in large measure, to the publication of *Modern Spanish* (1960).

The "Qualifications" included, in addition to competence in the four skills (understanding, speaking, reading, and writing) and cultural, as well as professional preparation, what was referred to as "language analysis" and described at the superior level as "ability to apply knowledge of descriptive, comparative and historical linguistics to the language teaching situation." Since these qualifications were endorsed by the executive boards or councils of eighteen foreign language associations, they had the effect of establishing linguistics as one of the seven requirements of a professionally trained foreign language teacher. As a result, applied linguistics was included in the foreign language teacher institutes sponsored by the NDEA (National Defense Education Act) and in the MLA Foreign Language Proficiency Tests for Teachers and Advanced Students, which are used as part of the teacher certification procedure in a number of states.

Modern Spanish was designed by linguists and language teachers in order to persuade publishers and college faculties that a new type of college text was possible and practical. It combined successfully the Trager-Smith type of phonology, applied to Spanish by Bowen and Stockwell (1960), with the syntax and pattern practice mode of the revised Michigan English materials, along with readings and cultural notes of a contemporary tone. The text was immediately accepted on a wide scale, and it established a new standard in publication and teaching that continues in a slightly modified form to this day. As predicted, other books began to appear in the new key, and publishers began to welcome manuscripts written in this newly established tradition.

The publication of *The National Interest and Foreign Languages* by William R. Parker (1954), secretary of the MLA, was a ringing call to action by linguists, language teachers, and citizen groups; in it, the terms of the NDEA were anticipated and undoubtedly also predicated.

When the successful launching of the first Russian sputnik dramatically brought home our apparent lag in scientific training *and* foreign languages, Congress passed (1958) the National Defense Education Act (NDEA). Suddenly, there was unprecedented support of all phases of foreign language teaching and study. The MLA Materials Center was created, institutes for foreign language teachers were staffed to provide practice in the spoken language, applied linguistics, language laboratory experience, increased understanding of the target culture, the new methodology, and demonstration classes. The MLA Materials Center produced audiolingual texts and tapes for high school, boldly adopting mimicry-memorization, pattern practice, and grammatical comments of the pattern type. The materials were produced for French, German, Italian, Russian, and Spanish. The teacher institutes increased from twelve during the summer of 1959 to more than ninety a few summers later, and they reached deep into the rank and file of foreign language teachers in elementary and high schools.

Publishers sought manuscripts with an oral-linguistic approach, and as foreign language enrollments increased, a variety of texts and supplementary materials became available. They naturally showed individual variation, but a more or less standard format prevailed. At present, materials are expected to have conversational dialogues for memorization, pattern-practice exercises usually with a sentence-pattern type of grammatical explanation, pronunciation and intonation notes or lessons, as well as vocabulary and reading material.

One of the most significant contributions of the NDEA was the unprecedented support of research in foreign language teaching and related disciplines. From this effort came the audiolingual materials of the MLA Materials Center. The MLA Cooperative Foreign Language Tests (1964) and the MLA Proficiency Tests for Teachers and Advanced Students (1962) in French, German, Italian, Russian, and Spanish also resulted from this research effort. They represented a full advance to the new oral-linguistic objectives.

Since second-language teaching and testing are highly complex activities, it cannot be expected that any single set of materials or tests will be equally effective for all purposes and under all conditions. Furthermore, the materials can only be as good as the knowledge available, and much of the knowledge about second-language teaching is still incomplete even where it seems theoretically well based. Take, for example, the use of contrastive studies between the target language and the native language of the student. This notion was generally accepted at the time of the research on materials and tests, but detailed comparisons between the foreign languages and English were not available. They were undertaken with NDEA research support, by the Center for Applied Linguistics, under the general editorship of Charles A. Ferguson and are now in published form. These contrastive studies provide a wealth of linguistic information for the textbook writer and teacher.

A significant part of the NDEA research effort went into the preparation of materials for teaching the so-called neglected or critical languages. Often, the chief problem in such research was the linguistic description of the target language, which had to be undertaken in connection with the preparation of the materials themselves. Basic texts and/or other materials were thus written for more than 25 languages, including Arabic, Hindi-Urdu, Bengali, Burmese, Japanese, Chinese, Hausa, Modern Dutch, Portuguese, Polish, Russian, and Serbo-Croatian. These were prepared by linguists under U.S. Office of Education contracts.[1]

Another activity receiving partial support from NDEA research funds was the attempt to produce or evaluate television materials for the teaching of foreign languages. Considerable interest developed, particularly at the level of FLES (Foreign Languages in Elementary Schools), where expansion called for solutions that might bypass the need for large numbers of trained teachers. TV programs in foreign languages were used in school systems with and without the participation of trained teachers. Experimental research gradually showed that without the full participation of a trained teacher, preferably a specialist, results were always weaker and sometimes clearly disappointing (Reid, 1961; Carroll, 1966). TV programs as additional motivation and enrichment and as a supplement to a teacher-directed course have much to offer, but TV programs that attempt to take over the whole business of foreign-language teaching are bound to fail. The reasons for this may not only be the linguistic sophistication, or lack of it, in the TV programs or the inflexibility of absentee grading and scheduling, but the very nature of teaching and learning as a social activity along with the broader role of the teacher as the motivating personality and the reason for learning.

The excited interest in teaching machines of a few years ago has subsided and given way to a more sober exploration of programmed instruction. Carroll (1966), who has been active in the field of foreign-language programming, states: "It is evident that self-instructional programs in foreign languages are not only perfectly feasible but also highly effective—more effective, in general, than conventional teacher taught courses." He goes on to say that sufficiently motivated students can learn all four skills through self-instructional programs, although "most successful programs do, however, utilize the teacher to some extent, but only for instruction that the teacher is best qualified to give." Programmed self-instruction still faces problems, which according to Carroll are (a) how best to present the content of instruction, (b) adaptation to individual differences, (c) complication rather than simplification of the role of the teacher, (d) motivation, (e) exacerbation of the problem of the enormous amount of time needed to learn a language, and (f) difficulty of applying programmed instruction to lower age levels.

Research is greatly needed in the partial supplementary uses of technological advances which center on the foreign-language teacher rather than

[1] An up-to-date list with status of these materials is available in Completed Research, Studies, and Instructional Materials, List No. 5, published by the USOE (OE–12016–65).

bypassing him. The research designs should be specific rather than general (cf. Carroll, 1966, p. 15). Comparisons of total methods, be they audio-lingual, grammar-translation, programmed, machine based, or mass media, are doomed to inconclusive results because of the many factors involved and the near impossibility of controlling all of them.

As we review second-language teaching today, a number of overall impressions emerge. Linguistics, particularly applied linguistics, has earned an important role in the training of teachers. There is some confusion as to what the applied linguistics course should be. A few teachers make it an introduction to theoretical linguistics, others concentrate on contrastive linguistics, and perhaps the majority combine the more elementary notions of structure and linguistic analysis with various types of oral drills and pedagogical devices.

A number of books and pamphlets have been used for this aspect of the training: *Manual and Anthology of Applied Linguistics*, edited by Belasco (1960) with German, Spanish, and French sections later published separately as *Applied Linguistics: German* by Marchand (1961), *Applied Linguistics: Spanish* by Cárdenas (1961), and *Applied Linguistics: French* by Valdman (1961); *Teaching French: An Introduction to Applied Linguistics*, Politzer (1960); *Teaching Spanish: A Linguistic Orientation*, Politzer and Staubach (1961); *Linguistics Across Cultures*, Lado (1957); *Language and Language Learning, Theory and Practice*, Brooks (1960); *Language Teaching, A Scientific Approach*, Lado (1964); *The Sounds of English and German*, Moulton (1962); *The Grammatical Structures of English and German*, Kufner (1962); *The Sounds of English and Spanish*, Stockwell and Bowen (1965); *The Grammatical Structures of English and Spanish*, Stockwell, Bowen and Martin (1965); *The Sounds of English and Italian*, Agard and DiPietro (1966); *The Grammatical Structures of English and Italian*, Agard and DiPietro (1966).

Language laboratories have become part and parcel of second-language teaching in college and high school, and there are language laboratories in use at the elementary school level. This innovation has permeated second-language teaching in record time and has been adopted throughout the world. Yet everywhere, there is still the same dissatisfaction with the use being made of this electronic aid.

Probably some of the best second-language teaching in the U.S. is now to be found in the high schools, where improved materials, better command of the language, and linguistically trained teachers are the order of the day. Foreign language in the elementary school is spotty in standards and performance, with much wasted motion and doubtful activity to be observed along with occasional superior attempts. Some conservatism without justification is still to be found at the college level, and the complaint is heard among high school graduates (and their teachers) that they waste time when they enter college.

The unfounded hopes for easy miracles in teaching foreign languages at the turn of a dial are not being realized, as witness the fact that Berlitz and the other commercial language schools are doing a booming business with native informants and fairly primitive techniques at expensive rates. There is a faint sound of computers in the background of second-language teaching, but it may remain only that for a variety of reasons, not the least of which is the cost of such equipment and its programming.

There is also a rumble of transformational grammar which thus far is noticeable in some reviews and in Chomsky's (1966) comments at the 1966 Northeast Conference on the Teaching of Foreign Languages. This rumble, however, is an echo of the very vigorous and vital revolution fully underway in linguistics, representing already a great amount of work on the analysis of English and some foreign languages. Teachers of second languages will have to understand the new linguistic statements even if there are no deeper implications for the whole field, and there seem to be deeper implications not only in the strictly linguistic elements of second-language teaching but in the equally vital field of learning theory as well.

While applied structural linguistics and the audiolingual pattern-practice approach were being expanded and refined in the NDEA period to an unprecedented degree, a new theory of linguistics was being developed by Chomsky (1957) and others. It had a strong rationalist base which was to throw off those extreme empiricist, behavioristic constraints that had restricted linguistics to description rather than explanation.

Transformational grammar commanded wide attention immediately, and in the short span of ten years largely took over the center of the stage from neo-Bloomfieldian linguistics, to the point where a majority of the papers presented at recent meetings of the Linguistic Society of America have been on transformational grammar. It seems quite likely then that grammatical studies of the major foreign languages taught in the United States will be increasingly based on transformational linguistics.

With this revolutionary change of direction in linguistics, the language teacher and the applied linguist face a difficult problem. One of the major accomplishments since World War II, as we have seen, was the acceptance of the relevance of structural linguistics for both the training of the language teacher and the materials and methods used with students. In fact, the very progress made during these historic years was largely due to the stimulation of structural linguistics. The use of linguistics in second-language teaching was, as a matter of fact, far in advance of the use of linguistics in psychological research on verbal learning, which had advanced with almost total disregard for grammar or linguistics of any sort until the advent of transformational grammar.

Today, as teachers of foreign languages with high professional motivation approach the study of linguistics, the linguistic description of the language they teach, or its contrastive study with the native speech of their pupils, they will increasingly face this newer phase of linguistics, which either attacks what they glimpsed in their applied linguistic contacts as the basis for audiolingual pattern-practice approach or claims no pedagogical application, implication, or interest.

Regardless of the way transformational grammar is first introduced, the decision to use it should not be in doubt, for obviously good reasons:

1. Linguistic studies of English and the major foreign languages taught in the United States will be increasingly written in transformational terms. No applied linguist, foreign-language textbook writer, or teacher of linguistics to language teachers can afford to overlook Lees' *The Grammar of English Nominalizations* (1960), Owen Thomas' *Transformational Grammar and the Teacher of English* (1965), and other recent publications of a similar nature that are beginning to appear on French, Spanish, German, Russian, and Italian.

Teachers and writers of materials for less widely taught languages will still find the descriptive studies their main source for some time to come. This includes the large number of descriptive studies written in tagmemic linguistics of the Pike school (Pike, 1954–1960).

2. There can be little doubt that transformational grammar provides a fuller, more explicit, more complete basis for the systematic explanation of grammar than previous models. This claim of the transformationalists seems well founded.

The possibility of "deriving" a complex sentence from a matrix sentence and embedded constituent sentences through explicitly stated transformational rules, for example, permits fuller explanation at a higher level of linguistic use than phrase structure patterning alone, and the added power is even greater in deriving phrase modification structures from matrix and constituent sentences. This brings grammatical explanation to the semantic level, which had previously been neglected, and does it with a rigor and explicitness that have not been possible in general semantics.

3. Transformational grammar has faced up to the problems of semantics, which are vital to the language teacher and which had been neglected by descriptive linguistics. Compare Chomsky's (1965) illustrative fragment of the base component that includes the lexical entry *sincerity*: (*sincerity* [+N, +Det——, −Count, +Abstract, ˙ ˙ ˙]) (p. 107) where *N* represents the feature noun; *Det*——, in the environment, "preceded by a determiner"; −*Count*, not a count noun; +*Abstract*, an abstract noun; ˙ ˙ ˙, and other factors. These represent semantic features that are relevant to the syntactic distribution of *sincerity* and are part of what the student of a foreign language must learn.

4. Psycholinguistic research, whose findings are relevant to second-language teaching research, has been tremendously stimulated by transformational grammar to face linguistic problems that are of much greater interest than the overly simple paired associate and serial learning tasks of

verbal learning research (cf. Rosenberg, 1965).

One familiar with applied structural linguistics will not find the transition to transformational grammar entirely foreign. He will find kernel sentences, or strings that underlie kernel sentences in the deep structure, where he had become familiar with basic sentence patterns and sentence frames. The number of kernel sentences will be smaller than that of basic sentences.

He will learn to derive questions, requests, negative sentences, etc., by transformations from the kernel sentences. He may wonder whether speakers actually go through these transformation rules in using the language, but he should not wonder, since transformational grammar makes no such claim but merely indicates that this is an explicit way to explain the transformed sentence—which is obviously related to the kernel one. This is somewhat like, though not the same as, his applied linguistic technique of contrasting a question pattern with its minimally different parallel statement. Transformational grammar carries a reduction of the variety of actual sentences one step further by admitting as basic kernel sentences only simple affirmative statements. Where he had learned to identify the critical contrasts between statements and questions, statements and requests, simple statements and compound statements, etc., he will derive the statement from a kernel sentence and transform it into the sentence string he is attempting to explain.

He will learn to use such abstract symbols as *NP* and *VP* where he previously expected the symbols for function words and form classes, e.g., *D, Adj., N, Adj. N, DN,* or simply *N*. This too is clearly a gain for him, since he previously used such diverse fillers in the frames but could not symbolize them as a group without listing them separately or without referring to them as subject, thus mixing their function and their composition, with obvious loss of generality for the *NP* concept.

If he had become attached to the epistemological elegance of considering the formal evidence for the form classes and function words as in Fries (1957), he may be temporarily disturbed at the lack of concern for the basis on which something is called an *NP*. Yet here is precisely where the new formulations are most useful to him by breaking away from excessive concern for discovery procedures that characterized empirical descriptive grammar, while achieving instead greater power to explain more of the grammar at a higher rational level, which undoubtedly agrees better with the level of abstraction normally involved in human language. He will do well to leave the problems of epistemological elegance to theoretical linguists and accept the greater usefulness of the new symbolization and system of explanation.

He may be temporarily irked by the apparent clumsiness of symbolizing rewrite rules for each single change of a symbol, but eventually he will become familiar with the usual rules and will again be able to think his way through a derivation or a tree with satisfying speed. And he will appreciate the explicitness of the rules, even though he may not wish to go through them step by step in his teaching.

He will readily appreciate the elegance of the auxiliary transformation for English, for example, though if he knew this from his previous linguistic sophistication, he may be irked by the implication that it is all a discovery of transformational grammar. It would be more palatable to read that here is a more efficient or more elegant way of stating or symbolizing these facts which are undoubtedly well known to the reader.

Above all, he must not let the manner of presentation, which in some instances may be typical of youthful vigor, becloud the power and value of the system being presented. While not all structural, descriptive grammars were exclusively taxonomic and nongenerative, it is to the credit of transformational grammar that it aims deliberately at explanatory rules even when relying on the available findings of descriptive and traditional grammars.

To order this information into a rational system of maximum explanatory power from a minimum base of kernel sentence strings would be a major accomplishment indeed. The testing of such a system against a representative corpus of actual sentences would be additionally satisfying. Meanwhile, we should encourage efforts to solve the yet unclear problems faced by transformational grammar, since their solution would greatly help the teacher of a second language. A teacher will certainly delight in the effort to include lexico-semantic rules and symbolization, for here he has not received much help from linguistics in the past.

How much transformational grammar he can or should use in second-language teaching is not at all clear. Surely he must not make the old mistake of teaching transformational grammar as a substitute for the target language, for in so doing he would not give competence in the target language but only in the system of transformational grammar. The issue of how much linguistics to include in the teaching of the language is not a new one: it had to be faced earlier in the application of structural linguistics. Some favored no linguistic or grammatical statements at all, inductive or deductive, that is, no explicit verbalizations of the rules of grammar. This extreme stimulus-response behaviorism has been challenged by cognitive learning theorists whose findings (Spielberger, 1965) would seem to support the view of others, including the writer, who favor simple linguistic statements based on examples actually manipulated by the student. Still others would depend heavily on rules illustrated by examples. This is the kind of issue that might presumably admit of solution by controlled experiments. Judging from the strong rationalist base of transformational grammar and the reservations about the role of habit in language acquisition expressed by Chomsky (1966), we might easily assume that the increased use of transformational grammar would encourage an emphasis on rules rather than on practice. Thomas (1966) nevertheless still favors inductive presentation of the rules to native speakers of the language. Resolution of the issue, therefore, obviously awaits the outcome of further experimentation.

REFERENCES

Agard, F. B., & Di Pietro, R. The sounds of English and Italian. In C. A. Ferguson (Ed.), *Contrastive structure series.* Chicago: Univ. of Chicago Press, 1966.

Agard, F. B., & Dunkel, H. B. *An investigation of second-language teaching.* Boston: Ginn, 1948. Cf. also Fries, 1949.

Bloomfield, L. *Language.* New York: Holt, Rinehart & Winston, 1933.

Bloomfield, L. *Outline guide for the practical study of foreign languages.* Baltimore: Ling. Soc. Amer., 1942.

Bowen, J. D., & Stockwell, R. P. *Patterns of Spanish pronunciation: a drillbook.* Chicago: Univ. of Chicago Press, 1960.

Brooks, N. *Language and language learning, theory and practice.* New York: Harcourt, Brace & World, 1960. (Rev. ed.) 1964.

Carroll, J. B. Research on teaching foreign languages. In N. L. Gage (Ed.), *Handbook of research on teaching.* Chicago: Rand McNally, 1963. Pp. 1060–1100.

Carroll, J. B. Research in foreign language teaching: the last five years. *Language teaching: broader concepts, 1966.* Reports of the working committees of the Northeast Conference on the Teaching of Foreign Languages.

Chomsky, N. *Syntactic structures.* The Hague: Mouton, 1957.

Chomsky, N. A review of *Verbal behavior* by B. F. Skinner. *Language,* 1959, **35**, 26–59. Reprinted in J. A. Fodor and J. J. Katz, 1964.

Chomsky, N. Linguistic theory. *Language teaching: broader concepts, 1966.* Reports of the working committees of the Northeast Conference on the Teaching of Foreign Languages.

Coleman, A. *The teaching of modern foreign languages in the United States. Publ. of Amer. & Canad. Committees on Mod. Languages,* Vol. 12, 1929.

Dunkel, H. B. *Second-language learning.* Boston: Ginn, 1948.

Educational Testing Service. *A description of the MLA foreign language proficiency tests for teachers and advanced students.* Princeton: Educational Testing Service, 1964.

Ferguson, C. A. Applied linguistics. *Language teaching: broader concepts, 1966.* Reports of the working committees of the Northeast Conference on the Teaching of Foreign Languages.

Fife, R. H. *A summary of reports on the modern foreign languages with an index to the reports.* New York: Macmillan, 1931.

Fodor, J. A., & Katz, J. J. (Eds.), *The structure of language: readings in the philosophy of language.* Englewood Cliffs: Prentice-Hall, 1964.

Francis, W. N. *The structure of American English.* New York: Ronald Press, 1958.

Fries, C. C. *Teaching and learning English as a foreign language.* Ann Arbor: Univ. of Michigan Press, 1945.

Fries, C. C. The Chicago investigation. *Lang. Learn.,* 1949, **2**, 88–99.

Fries, C. C. *The structure of English. An introduction to the construction of English sentences.* New York: Harcourt, Brace & World, 1952.

Gleason, H. A. *Introduction to descriptive linguistics.* (2nd ed.) New York: Holt, Rinehart & Winston, 1961.

Hayes, A. S. *Technical guide for the selection, purchase, use, and maintenance of language laboratory facilities. U.S. Office of Education Bulletin No.* 37, 1963.

Hill, A. A. *Introduction to linguistic structures: from sound to sentence in English.* New York: Harcourt, Brace & World, 1958.

Hockett, C. F. *A course in modern linguistics.* New York: Macmillan, 1958.

Hutchinson, J. C. *Modern foreign languages in high school: the language laboratory. U.S. Office of Education Bulletin No.* 23, 1961.

Katz, J. J., & Postal, P. M. *An integrated theory of linguistic descriptions.* Cambridge: M.I.T. Press, 1964.

Kufner, H. L. *The grammatical structures of English and German: a contrastive sketch.* In C. A. Ferguson (Ed.), *Contrastive structure series.* Chicago: Univ. of Chicago Press, 1962.

Lado, R. *Linguistics across cultures, applied linguistics for language teachers.* Ann Arbor: Univ. of Michigan Press, 1957.

Lado, R. *Language teaching, a scientific approach.* New York: McGraw-Hill, 1964.

Lees, R. B. *The grammar of English nominalizations.* Bloomington, Ind.: Research Center in Anthropology, Folklore, and Linguistics, 1960.

Lloyd, D. J., & Warfel, H. R. *American English in its cultural setting.* New York: Alfred Knopf, 1956.

Lumsdaine, A. A., & Glaser, R. *Teaching machines and programmed learning: a source book.* Washington: Department of Audio-Visual Instruction, National Education Association, 1960.

Marchand, J. W. *Applied linguistics: German, a guide for teachers.* Boston: D. C. Heath, 1961.

Mead, R. G. (Ed.) Language teaching: broader contexts. *Reports of the working committees of the Northeast Conference on the Teaching of Foreign Languages,* 1966. Available through MLA Materials Center, 62 Fifth Avenue, New York, N.Y. 10011.

MLA foreign language proficiency tests for teachers and advanced students: French, German, Italian, Russian, Spanish. Princeton: Educational Testing Service, 1962.

MLA cooperative foreign language tests: French, German, Italian, Russian, Spanish. Princeton: Educational Testing Service, 1964.

Modern Spanish. A Project of the Modern Language Association. (Working committee: D. L. Bolinger, J. D. Bowen, A. M. Brady, E. F. Haden, L. Poston, Jr., N. P. Sacks.) New York: Harcourt, Brace & World, 1960.

Moulton, W. G. Linguistics and language teaching in the United States 1940–1960. In C. Mohrmann, et al. (Ed.), *Trends in European and American linguistics 1930–1960.* Utrecht: Spectrum Publishers, 1961.

Moulton, W. G. Pattern drills and grammatical theory. In *Wert und Wort. Festschrift Else M. Fleissner.* Aurora, N.Y., 1965.

Parker, W. R. *The National interest and foreign languages.* U.S. National Commission for UNESCO, Department of State. (Prelim. ed.), 1954; (Rev. ed.), 1957.

Pike, K. L. *The intonation of American English.* Ann Arbor: Univ. of Michigan Press, 1945.

Pike, K. L. *Language in relation to a unified theory of the structure of human behavior.* Glendale: Summer Institute of Linguistics, I, 1954; II, 1955; III, 1960.

Politzer, R. L. *Teaching French: an introduction to applied linguistics.* Boston: Ginn, 1960.

Pressey, S. L. A simple apparatus which gives tests and scores—and teaches. *School & Society*, 1926, **23**, No. 586. Reprinted in A. A. Lumsdaine and R. Glasser, 1960.

Pressey, S. L. A machine for automatic teaching of drill material. *School & Society*, 1927, **25**, No. 645. Reprinted in A. A. Lumsdaine and R. Glasser, 1960.

Qualifications for secondary school teachers of modern foreign languages. *PMLA*, 1955, **70**, 46–49. (Sept. supplement)

Reid, J. An exploratory survey of foreign language teaching by television in the United States. In *Reports of surveys and studies in the teaching of modern foreign languages.* New York: Modern Language Association of America, 1961.

Roberts, P. *Patterns of English.* New York: Harcourt, Brace & World, 1956.

Rosenberg, S. (Ed.), *Directions in psycholinguistics.* New York: Macmillan, 1965.

Sapir, E. *Language, an introduction to the study of speech.* New York: Harcourt, Brace & World, 1921.

Skinner, B. F. The science of learning and the art of teaching. *Harvard educ. Rev.*, 1954, **24**, No. 2. Reprinted in A. A. Lumsdaine and R. Glasser, 1960.

Skinner, B. F. *Verbal behavior.* New York: Appleton-Century-Crofts, 1957.

Spielberger, C. D. Theoretical and epistemological issues in verbal conditioning. In S. Rosenberg, 1965.

Stack, W. E. *The language laboratory and modern language teaching.* (Rev. ed.) New York: Oxford Univ. Press, 1966.

Stockwell, R. P. The place of intonation in a transformational grammar of English. *Language*, 1960, **36**, 360–367.

Stockwell, R. P., & Bowen, J. D. *The sounds of English and Spanish.* In C. A. Ferguson (Ed.), *Contrastive structure series.* Chicago: Univ. of Chicago Press, 1965.

Stockwell, R. P., Bowen, J. D., & Martin, J. W. *The grammatical structures of English and Spanish.* In C. A. Ferguson (Ed.), *Contrastive structure series.* Chicago: Univ. of Chicago Press, 1965.

Thomas, C. (Ed.), *Report of the committee of twelve of the Modern Language Association of America.* Boston: D. C. Heath, 1901.

Thomas, O. *Transformational grammar and the teacher of English.* New York: Holt, Rinehart & Winston, 1966.

Trager, G. L., & Smith, H. L. *Outline of English structure. Studies in Linguistics, Occasional Papers, No.* 3, 1951. Reprinted, Washington: American Council of Learned Societies, 1957.

Twaddell, W. F., & O'Connor, P. Intensive training for an oral approach in language teaching. *Mod. Lang. J.*, 1960, **44**, No. 2, Part 2, vi, 42.

Valdman, A. *Applied linguistics: French.* Boston: D. C. Heath, 1961.

Welmers, W. E. *Spoken English as a foreign language: instructor's manual.* Washington: American Council of Learned Societies, 1953.

Index